D1243536

A REPUBLIC OF MIND AND SPIRIT

The Library
St. Mary's College of Maryland
St. Mary's City, Maryland 20686

A REPUBLIC OF MIND AND SPIRIT

A Cultural History of American Metaphysical Religion

Catherine L. Albanese

Yale University Press
New Haven & London

Published with assistance from the foundation established in memory of
Philip Hamilton McMillan of the Class of 1894, Yale College.

Copyright © 2007 by Yale University. All rights reserved. This book may not be
reproduced, in whole or in part, including illustrations, in any form (beyond that
copying permitted by Sections 107 and 108 of the U.S. Copyright Law and except by
reviewers for the public press), without written permission from the publishers.

Set in Electra by Tseng Information Systems, Inc. Printed in the
United States of America.

Library of Congress Cataloging-in-Publication Data
Albanese, Catherine L.
A republic of mind and spirit : a cultural history of American metaphysical
religion / Catherine L. Albanese.
p.   cm.
Includes bibliographical references and index.
ISBN-13: 978-0-300-11089-0 (cloth : alk. paper)
ISBN-10: 0-300-11089-8 (cloth : alk. paper)
1. United States—Religion. I. Title.
BL2525.A435 2006
299'.93—dc22   2006013968

A catalogue record for this book is available from the British Library.

The paper in this book meets the guidelines for permanence and durability
of the Committee on Production Guidelines for Book Longevity of the
Council on Library Resources.

10 9 8 7 6 5 4 3 2 1

For my loved ones in the spiritland—
Louis and Theresa Albanese,
Samantha, Selene, and Leah

When I watch that flowing river, which, out of regions I see not, pours for a season its streams into me, I see that I am a pensioner; not a cause, but a surprised spectator of this ethereal water; that I desire and look up, and put myself in the attitude of reception, but from some alien energy the visions come.
—RALPH WALDO EMERSON, "The Over-Soul"

Man is a god in ruins. When men are innocent, life shall be longer, and shall pass into the immortal as gently as we awake from dreams. . . .
. . . The kingdom of man over nature, which cometh not with observation,—a dominion such as now is beyond his dream of God,—he shall enter without more wonder than the blind man feels who is gradually restored to perfect sight.
—RALPH WALDO EMERSON, *Nature*

The *Western* new United States of America convert intelligent observers to the belief that there is a REPUBLIC OF SPIRIT embosomed and gestating in the dominant political organism.

The only true America is the coming spiritual Republic.
—ANDREW JACKSON DAVIS, *Beyond the Valley*

CONTENTS

Part Three. Arrivals

ACKNOWLEDGMENTS

Writing this book has brought back former moments in my career and riveted me simultaneously to the present. Feeling very much like Ralph Waldo Emerson's "pensioner," I have watched the texts of earlier times open out to tell their story, in the process delving into long-forgotten materials collected during my academic journey and seeing them and their connections in new ways. Whatever paths things took to come together, I spent long hours glued to my computer, forgetting time and transfixed by a virtual world that kept me in it sometimes into the wee hours. And I kept noticing how much the work of other scholars and their insights help me to shape my narrative—how much the serendipities of the moment leaned heavily on the grace and generosity of others.

Librarians as long ago as the 1980s at the American Antiquarian Society, the Unity School of Christianity, and the Palmer School of Chiropractic provided materials that eventually made their way into my narrative. Later, librarians at the University of California, Santa Barbara, and at Krotona (Theosophical) Library in Ojai, California—where Lakshmi Narayan warmly welcomed me—helped enormously. A one-quarter sabbatical leave from the College of Letters and Science at UCSB in the fall of 2000 launched the project. Then—after the project had been mostly on hold for the next two or more years—a full year's sabbatical in 2003–2004 opened the way to a year of writing as intense as any I have done. Supported by a John Simon Guggenheim Memorial Foundation Fellowship and a University of California Presidential Fellowship in the Humanities, as well as by Dean David Marshall's generous leave policy in the College of Letters and Science, the free year enabled me to complete a draft of what turned out to be an exceedingly long manuscript. Yale University Press and its editors demonstrated impressive patience and support with that length and, also, afterwards with a year-long process of revision. Meanwhile, part of one section of chapter 6

("Metaphysical Asia") has appeared in a different form as "Sacred (and Secular) Self-Fashioning: Esalen and the American Transformation of Yoga," in Jeffrey J. Kripal and Glenn W. Shuck, eds., *On the Edge of the Future: Esalen and the Evolution of American Culture* (Bloomington: Indiana University Press, 2005).

Well before that, former and present students helped with various aspects of the project. Martha Finch supplied me with materials on the logic of Petrus Ramus, Michael Cox with the same on Swami Ramacharaka and other arcane matters, Taylor Hines with facts and insights on New Thought, and Sarah Whedon with bibliographical assistance on a variety of fronts. Dissertations by former students Gary Ward Materra and Elijah Siegler demonstrated for me clearly how much learning is the gift the student gives the professor, not just the other way round. On another front, my colleagues in South and East Asian (religious) studies — Barbara Holdrege, William Powell, Vesna Wallace, and David G. White — proved friendly avatars, helping me in rough places as I puzzled through the relationship between the Asia of their studies and the American Asia of the metaphysicians. From his quarter J. Gordon Melton made himself thoroughly available as a generous ally in lending books and insights.

Wouter J. Hanegraaff helped immeasurably with his close reading of chapter 1, with its Renaissance-forward European story. I owe him a debt of gratitude for his detailed suggestions for its improvement and his generous bibliographical assistance. Later, in the section of chapter 3 on Joseph Smith and Mormonism, D. Michael Quinn commented in especially helpful ways. Paul G. Hackett steered me clear of a host of falsehoods concerning the metaphysical yogis Pierre and Theos Bernard and provided important new material on the two. For the project as a whole, Ann Taves, then at Claremont Graduate University and Claremont School of Theology and now at UCSB, read the manuscript critically for me in draft form; my narrative is better because I had to make the distinctions she demanded in order to answer her questions. Stephen Prothero likewise gave assistance in important ways with his own careful reading and critique, which I kept before me as I revised. I, of course, am responsible for outcomes and errors that others may hereafter discover.

About a decade ago, I tried to persuade Bret E. Carroll, now at California State University, Stanislaus, to name a book of his "A Republic of Spirit." I am very glad that instead he chose otherwise, since I have now almost taken my own advice. My special thanks go to him for acquainting me with Andrew Jackson Davis's pungent phrase. Outside the academy, Reverend Linda Morrow Spencer of Unity Church of Santa Barbara opened a wealth of sources to me and helped me to understand Unity's editing practices in ways it would have been more difficult for me to discover on my own. Meanwhile, colleagues and students supported me awesomely throughout my sabbatical year, respecting my need to not be involved—even though physically I was attached to a computer only three or four miles away from the university.

More personally, over the writing of this narrative have hovered the decline and death of both of my parents. After more than a year of slippage, my mother died in June 2001. Two years and two weeks later, in June 2003, my father's passing came—just as I was beginning the sabbatical year in which I produced most of this book. As I wrote my way out of his and my mother's death, I remembered how proud they had been of all that I accomplished. During the last weeks of his life, my father carried around in his walker the Guggenheim announcement in the *New York Times* that listed me among fellowship winners—my tireless publicity agent to the end. Three months later, when my beloved feline Leah died suddenly, she joined Samantha and Selene—likewise of the feline persuasion—in the special spaces of my heart reserved for the missing. So it is appropriate that I dedicate a book about metaphysicians, minds, and spirits to all of them, whom I fondly envision as somewhere in that shadowy spiritland of metaphysical report.

INTRODUCTION

Living in the first decade of the twenty-first century invites, for an American religious historian, a backward glance at the centuries before. There we can observe something like an American ethnicity—a set of traits or cultural turns characterizing those born, or born again, in the United States. This American ethnicity (although not always named as such) has invited scholarly scrutiny at least since the middle-to-late decades of the twentieth century, when a nascent American studies movement became enchanted with "American exceptionalism." It also received less admiring attention from the time that some observers began to brand Americans abroad as "ugly Americans." In religion, American ethnicity became linked to an Anglo-Protestant evangelicalism that, whatever its early connections with Britain and later ones with the former British colonies, has evolved in distinct ways.[1] For many historians—both in general American history and within the discipline of religious studies—the key to understanding what is *American* about American religion has, in fact, been its strong leaning toward evangelical forms and expressions.

Consider, for example, William McLoughlin's now-classic interpretation in *Revivals, Awakenings, and Reform*. In the study of American religious history probably no single survey was more influential throughout the 1980s and 1990s than McLoughlin's small book, written without notes and with only a short bibliographic essay appended. This widely used work by the then-senior and respected historian of American revivalism argued the case for four "great awakenings" or "periods of ideological transformation" in the United States, periods that —although independent from Protestantism by the late nineteenth century— had been indelibly imprinted by their beginnings in, and long entwinement with, Protestant revivals. The ideology that arose was, McLoughlin declared, "indi-

1

vidualistic, pietistic, perfectionist, millenarian." American history itself was "best understood as a millenarian movement." [2]

McLoughlin, in many senses, had put his finger on the pulse of the culture, and he had surely made a strenuous case for what has come to be called the "evangelical thesis" concerning American religious history. Conventional first images of religion in America evoke the revival tradition from Jonathan Edwards and George Whitefield through Charles Grandison Finney, Dwight Moody, Billy Sunday, and Billy Graham. Or less favorably, they point to the Elmer Gantrys among the revival preachers and brethren. But not everyone doing American religious history agreed. By 1992, Yale historian Jon Butler was arguing strongly against the evangelical thesis, an interpretive tool, as he said, used by American historians to make sense of the role of religion in the history of the United States. "During the past two decades," Butler reported, "evangelicalism has emerged as the academic historians' single most common tool with which to describe and explain the unfolding of American society." He complained that the evangelical thesis was replacing more conflict-driven accounts of American religion that historians had been writing and that as an interpretive tool the thesis was partial, limiting, and falsifying. Indeed, it had reintroduced a misinformed consensus model for understanding past and present American religion. "The evangelical thesis obscures history as it dominates our historiography," Butler reproved. [3]

Jon Butler had already done more than his share to sabotage the evangelical thesis before 1992. In 1990, Harvard University Press had published his groundbreaking book *Awash in a Sea of Faith*. Subtitled *Christianizing the American People*, the work retold the story of American religion to the time of the Civil War. The narrative was constructed around a plot line that told of only gradual Christianization in a land that from the first had played host to a multitude of spiritual forces, many of them what Butler termed "occult." In the America he wrote about, evangelicals shared space with occultists and Christ took turns with magic. Nor were evangelicals recognized as pivotal forces for Christianization. In fact, the evangelical Great Awakening, a fond and favored cultural marker for historians of the eighteenth century, became for Butler only an "interpretive fiction." The role of evangelicalism was minimal in the American Revolution, which he called a "profoundly secular event." And significantly, when (evangelical) Methodists appeared on his historiographical stage in the nineteenth century, they were noticed not for their organizing genius, as in standard historical accounts, but instead for their celibacy (which made them seem akin to Catholics) and shamanic dreams (which hinted vaguely of their secret sympathies with occultists).

Over all, Butler's revision of American religious history stressed the role of the European state churches before the Revolutionary War and the mainstream denominations that succeeded them thereafter. The state-church/denominational tradition, he argued, had proved *the* coercive force for Christianization. In effect, Butler had radically revised the standard historical narrative concerning American religiosity. He had substituted for evangelicalism and its consensus a different explanation of how religious unity and symmetry came to be, insofar as there was such unity and symmetry at all. The emergent national religious regulator was one that had triumphed, in Butler's account, over a pervasive popular occultism, and it was modeled on — of all things — Roman Catholicism. In this reading, the inherited state-church tradition of Anglo-Protestant America, transformed through the alchemy of the American Revolution into mainline denominations, became the new American version of what some European nations had ordained in their official Catholic religious establishments. In fact, in an essay published just a year later, Butler argued forthrightly for the utility of a "catholic" reading of United States religious history.[4] *Awash in a Sea of Faith* had been the narrative historiographical demonstration of what he later, more theoretically, would unfold.

As both the wide acclaim for McLoughlin's book and the pervasive popular images of religion in the United States suggest, Butler was certainly right in his argument that the evangelical thesis had won out in American historical studies about religion. Moreover, his triangulation of religious forces — Protestant evangelical, mainstream Christian denominational, and occult — for the first time introduced a narrative complexity that earlier historians had overlooked and/or undervalued. Former-day "church historians" had surely paid attention to the history of American denominations, especially Protestant denominations, but they had overall embedded these accounts into larger narratives of a characteristic evangelical ethos, and they had for the most part emphasized a national Protestant consensus. Moreover, some, like the widely acknowledged Sydney Ahlstrom, had cast an eye toward an "occult" dimension in American religious history in cursory treatments of spiritualism, "harmonial" religion, and what for these historians were other exotica.[5] But Butler did more and went further. His work deserves credit not only for questioning tales of blanket evangelical triumph but also for lifting occultism from fringe to center, so that what emerges in his account is a complex of distinct and formidable forces operating often at cross-purposes and ends. Still, in the Butler historiography the center to which occultism made its way was one that did not hold — a center that became a theater of conflict in which Christianity, through its "catholic" denominational forms, gradually prevailed.

This book, however, tells another story. It is a story that, with Butler, agrees that evangelicalism must be reckoned as only one factor in the complex that came together to form an American religiosity (although, more than Butler, it continues to acknowledge evangelicalism's importance). The point of the story here, though, is different. This book is suspicious about the fringe status of what Butler termed occultism and is suspicious as well about the defeat of the "occult" player in the American religious drama. It argues, to the contrary, that what is mostly overlooked in a McLoughlin-like evangelical thesis and its Butler or Butler-like antithesis is the shaping role of what I will call metaphysics or metaphysical religion, especially from the nineteenth century. Whereas Butler read the path of occultism to end, with the eighteenth century, in its "folklorization," my tale is instead an account of its vigorous growth in the nineteenth century as metaphysics, achieving its mature form after the Civil War.[6] This is a growth that continued into and through the twentieth century and that, as I write in the early twenty-first century, shows no sign of abating and every sign of flourishing into any future that can be foreseen.

Still more, both the evangelical thesis and the denominational-establishment antithesis omit the role of metaphysics as a *major* player in the evolution of the national religiosity. Thus my reading, with Butler's, sees the evangelical thesis as false because it is partial—but, departing from his, it sees the thesis as partial because it tells only one piece, however important, of a larger story. That story has been seriously skewed by perspectives and data deployed to protect and promote the role of Christianity in the nation's history. The evangelical thesis leaves out the state-church/mainstream-denominational tradition, true enough. But also, and as significantly, the evangelical thesis leaves out the metaphysical religious substrate that Butler read as a large segment of the spiritual chaos that the state-church/mainstream-denominational tradition began to order. If Butler's triangulation of religious forces provides a better account of American religious history, and if McLoughlin and other historians of evangelicalism give us one third of the story and Butler a second third (at least for the pre–Civil War period), there remains a large and missing third. Hence, in what follows I argue a metaphysical thesis about American religious history, understanding metaphysical religion, both in Christian and non-Christian forms, as key to making sense of the nation's religiosity. Metaphysical religion, I hope to show, is at least as important as evangelicalism in fathoming the shape and scope of American religious history and in identifying what makes it distinctive—the sign, in religious terms, of an emergent American ethnicity. Metaphysics, also, is surely as important as the state-church/mainstream-denominational tradition to which Butler paid attention because of its organizing ability and, so, its impact on public culture.

What is at stake in the historiographical reconstruction I propose is, from a religious studies perspective, the recognition of three major forms of religiosity whose interplay and, in many cases, amalgamations have worked their way through the nation's history. In the first, or evangelical, form, religion favors the cultivation of strong emotional experience that is felt as life-transforming. Religious change is sudden, and the individual is emphasized. But so is the community, as in the collective Protestant cultural forms that became revivalism—forms that, as Donald Mathews has argued for the Second Great Awakening, together constitute a process of social control.[7] The mentality underlying evangelicalism is built on a sense of separation from the source of spiritual power (historically, in Christian America, God or his son and emissary Jesus) that needs to be overcome. The convert, helpless as an individual, tells of feeling overpowered by the intruding grace of God, and then the convert—become missionary—intrudes, in some sense, on the space of others, hoping to bridge the separation (from God, Jesus, community) with help divinely come. What does such intimate experience and expression mean for history? The evangelical thesis answers by turning the private drama into collective explanation, chronicling what happens when converts and continuing believers make their impact on public culture. Sheer numbers become important, and so do the organizations that arise to channel and employ evangelical commitment for social transformation. Thus public culture and American history are read in light of the shaping and controlling force that is evangelical passion. The secret of American individualism becomes the secret of the evangelical heart. The direct and personal experiences of the revivals, in this history, have indelibly imprinted something that we can call the American character.

By contrast, in a second, or liturgical, form of religiosity—the one that predominates in the state-church / mainstream-denominational tradition that Butler emphasized—religion turns, in the broadest sense, on communally organized ceremonial action. Formal symbolic practice in designated sacred spaces and times functions to make the world safe and intelligible. Such practice carries the authority of tradition and enacts its authoritative knowledge through the socially and ritually educated body. In forms that favor the importance of social nurture for learning religion and, so, that favor gradualism, the individual body is always understood with reference to the body of the community. The sacred world is circumscribed by a benevolent institution, with its hegemony protecting more than stirring up, containing more than pushing outward. Instead of being thrust strongly toward missionary work, adherents are encouraged to function as established social contributors. Mainstream denominationalists acknowledge the same separation from God (in the Christian tradition the doctrine of sin) that, for evangelicalism, God overcomes, but these "catholic" believers give more to the inner correspondences that they acknowledge between themselves and the divine. Grace here is more important than sin, and grace is present, too, in some sense, in the natural world and human community. To invoke William James's well-known categories regarding religious experience, the evangelical—who is "born again"—can be counted clearly among the twice-born and inhabits a two-story religious dwelling, with the natural first floor requiring a supernatural second one to make it complete.[8] But the mainstream denominationalist resides in a religious house that is probably only a floor and a half—not just once-born but not fully twice-born either—in the same way and with the same seriousness as the evangelical.

In historiographical terms, accounts like Butler's that stress a catholic (that is, mainstream-dominant) reading instead of an evangelical one are less invested in single and dramatic explanations of the nation's religious history stressing departures from the past. They are also less interested in recurring historical leitmotifs (as, for example, McLoughlin's millenarian explanation of American religious history). The catholic narrative plays instead within a more complex and varied arena, with gradual changes and multiple factors written into the script. But always, the catholic narrative acknowledges the role of public power, of hierarchy, of organization. This narrative, if anything, suppresses individualism and discloses that the body that counts is the social body with its authoritarian head.

Finally, the third, or metaphysical, form of religiosity is different from either the evangelical or the mainstream-denominational. For metaphysics, as the term itself vaguely suggests (more on that below), religion turns on an individual's experience of "mind" (instead of "heart," as in evangelicalism). In this context, metaphysical forms of religion have privileged the mind in forms that include reason but move beyond it to intuition, clairvoyance, and its relatives such as "revelation" and "higher guidance." Here versions of a theory of correspondence between worlds prevail. The human world and mind replicate—either ideally, formerly, or actually—a larger, often more whole and integrated universe, so that the material world is organically linked to a spiritual one. In this vision of "as above, so below," metaphysicians find a stream of energy flowing from above to below—so powerful and constitutive of their reality that they discover themselves to be, in some sense, made of the same "stuff." If there are differences, they are of degree and not of kind. Moreover, the influx of energy (let us now call it "divine") that enlivens their world is a healing salve for all its ills and—in the strongest statement of their view—renders them divine and limitless. For metaphysicians, religious change may happen either suddenly or gradually, and practice arises organically out of these beliefs about correspondence, resemblance, and connection. Ritual thus involves enacted metaphors. To put this another way, metaphysical practice is about what may be called magic, and magic—

defined in the way that I will do here—lies at the heart of American metaphysics. Thus, noticeably more than the denominationalist who also does ritual, the metaphysician brings its willed instrumental quality to the fore. Still further, for the magical believer the trained and controlled human imagination brings one part of the world—one symbolic form, if you will—to operate or act on other "pieces." In the eyes of the believer, such activity is an effective way to bring desired and seemingly miraculous change.

Seen from this perspective, for American metaphysical believers and practitioners ritual means—in the terms I employ for this narrative—"material," or more usually, "mental" magic. In material magic, symbolic behavior involves the use of artifacts and stylized accoutrements, in ritual, or ceremonial, magic. Here imagination and will join forces with the body and the material "field" in which it dwells. In mental magic, the field is internalized, and the central ritual becomes some form of meditation or guided visualization—so that the mental powers of imagination and will can affect and change the material order, abolishing apparent flaws by realizing its unity with a cosmic Source. In both cases, the sought-for result leans toward the attainment of states of contentment, self-possession, and mastery, with the successful religionist an exemplar of the "spiritual" instead of either a missionary or established social contributor. Individualism, therefore, is privileged (as in evangelicalism); the community, at first glance, seems less important (perhaps a difference from evangelicalism). In even more of a contrast from evangelicalism, here are William James's "once-born," dwelling in their one-story houses, be they California ranch or Texas sprawl. Religious naturalism, in effect, is often the message in the metaphysical world, and the supernatural "second floor," like the "second birth," is generally absent. Mind and world are the givens with which one must work in the here and now: all of reality is made of the same cosmic material, and therefore all is "natural." Still, the cosmology of the once-born can mislead. There is clearly more pain and misery in the single metaphysical story than James's metaphor was designed to acknowledge. As we shall see, even in one-floor houses, evil did not go away without the saving work of religion. Even illusory realms required correction, and they especially needed illumination and the dissolving of difference. This was the point of the magic.

In contrast to metaphysical goals of dissolving difference, historiographically speaking, the metaphysical world provides abundant materials that emphasize, especially clearly, its pluralism and, more, its fractiousness. Metaphysicians joined communities, as American religious history demonstrates, but they joined somewhat warily and tended to be so strongly led by inner voices that their communities often fragmented easily. Thus community among them has tended to be ad hoc and flexible, and authoritarian voices and concerns have not gotten very far. A historiographical account that seeks to make sense of this form of religion, therefore, pays particular attention to religious manyness and highlights religious difference. It begins to ask questions about new and distinctive forms of community—less organized from the top down, more fluid and egalitarian. This historiography is led toward religious democracy and "people's" history, and it finds itself drawn particularly toward networks. This is not to say that networks have not been noticed in the other religious camps—indeed, evangelicals probably invented them, and historians have paid attention. But historians of the metaphysical must take account of networks that appear especially temporary, self-erasing, self-transforming.

With the community emphasis more to the foreground in the first and second forms of religiosity, it is no surprise that their prominence in American religious history is easy to spot. Evangelicals *did* organize, as I have already suggested, and they did so exceedingly well. Meanwhile, it goes almost without saying that denominationalists were masters of the art of institutionalizing. For historians, then, both groups are relatively easy to follow. There are central headquarters and archives, public buildings and structures with observable rituals, written personal testimonials, letters, and journals aplenty, and numerous press accounts of religious presence, to cite only the most obvious and accessible sources. To write the metaphysicians' tendencies into history, however, often requires harder work. Lack of unity in practice means lack of unity in record keeping; values of privacy and intimacy foster less public acknowledgment and demonstration; emphasis on practice and presentism many times tends toward ahistoricism. Hence excavating the history of American metaphysical religiosity is a daunting task and one that will probably be only partially successful. It will require poking around in less studied and less formally documented places, and it will require a "creative" reading of evidence—the kind of reading that surely invites some anxiety for a historian. Yet we will never know if the risks are worth the chance unless we give the project a try, something that the chapters that follow aim to do.

Beyond the problem of what counts as historiographical evidence, however, lies the epistemological problem of what counts as *religion* and how we count it. Without rehearsing an extended theoretical critique of definitional problems in religious studies, it should be clear that studying American religious history from the perspective of its metaphysical component takes a historian squarely into issues regarding what often has been called "popular" religion, even though the term itself is problematic. In order to uncover a metaphysical story, a historian needs to back away from understandings of religion that stress its official, organized character but also to do so carefully, avoiding a conceptual split (often found in conceptualizations of "popular" religion) between official elites and unchurched or semi-churched ordinary people. Consider, for the purpose, Leonard Norman Primiano's notion of "vernacular religion," a form of religion that, he tells us, is neither official nor popular but is simply "religion as it is lived," religion "as human beings encounter, understand, interpret, and practice it." Instead of the popular religion of the many and the elite religion of an official or intellectual few, Primiano would have the religious vernacular in which *everybody* glosses a tradition in one or another way to put life's pieces together. In the religious vernacular, *everybody* creates; *everybody* picks and chooses from what is available to constitute changing religious forms.[9] Building on this assessment, I suggest that just as the "vernacular" is a description of language and just as language is the shared property of a community, vernacular religion is most properly understood as the appropriated beliefs—and lifeways—of a group of people who "speak" the same religious language. Hence I see my task in this book as one of providing a historical account of the groups of people who speak, in the United States, the religious language called metaphysics and who order their lives in terms of it.

By now readers have probably begun to question the easy use of the term *metaphysics*, and it is time to be clear on what counts, in this narrative, as metaphysical. Some, like Charles Braden over forty years ago, have closely identified metaphysical religion with the American New Thought, or mind-cure, tradition, and also with Christian Science (despite the denominationally driven objections of the official Christian Science establishment). Still, as Braden made clear in his own history of New Thought, the tradition is but one major American expression of a much larger religious orientation that includes domestic as well as Asian and European elements. Briefly and successively, he pointed to Mormonism, spiritualism, Oriental thought, Christian idealism, Theosophy, and likewise mesmerism, even as he linked metaphysics to Phineas P. Quimby and Mary Baker Eddy, to New Thought and Christian Science. "This broad complex of religions," he wrote, "is sometimes described by the rather general term 'metaphysical,' because its major reliance is not on the physical, but on that which is beyond the physical."[10]

A few years after Braden wrote, J. Stillson Judah—while nodding to the origins of the term *metaphysical movement* in New Thought—used it to study the broader strand in American religion and culture that Braden himself had at least partially acknowledged. For Judah, this strand included New England Transcendentalism as well as occultism and spiritualism, and it encompassed Theosophy (with offshoots such as the Arcane School of Alice Bailey and the Astara Foundation of Robert and Earlyne Chaney) as much as it did the mental-healing traditions of New Thought and Christian Science. Judah provocatively called the metaphysical movements "the mirror of American culture," and he distinguished their metaphysics from traditional philosophical usage, seeing the American version of metaphysics instead as a "practical type of philosophy," one to be considered "both scientific and religious." "In the words of one of its exponents," Judah explained, "it 'stands for the deeper realities of the universe, the things which . . . stand above and beyond the outer phenomenal realm.'" He went on to quote his American metaphysical source, declaring that "'it [metaphysics] especially concerns itself with the practical application of that absolute Truth of Being in all the affairs of our daily and hourly living.'"[11] Of course, were Braden and Judah writing in or after the 1980s, they would acknowledge the New Age movement as a late-twentieth-century reconfiguration of the metaphysical. Both the lineages and ideas of the major New Age leaders and teachers make the identification easy and uncontested. And so, this book will be able, as they could not, to explore this latter-day metaphysical history. Moving more widely, it will also be able to examine cultural forms in which metaphysics has strongly colored American religious life through a pervasive "new spirituality"—a movement much broader than the self-conscious New Age movement.

As Braden noticed, metaphysics does etymologically point to realities that are acknowledged beyond the physical world. And as Judah hinted with his reference to philosophical thought, metaphysics—as the term was traditionally used—had its roots in Western philosophy. Historically, the term referred to that portion of the scholastic philosophy of the European Middle Ages that concerned questions of existence or being. Also known as ontology, metaphysics was the study of being as being, and it built on a series of Aristotelian categories to ponder what it meant, in a physical, material, and human world, to have being. Within this discourse, issues of essence and existence, nature and purpose, and functionality and teleology were all intertwined.[12] There, too, Roman Catholic monks and priests presided over discourse and knowledge, and metaphysics became inseparably linked to the official Catholic establishment as the foundation for its theology and, especially, the language of that theology's articulation. Since, within it, Greek discursive categories had more and more superseded biblical Hebraic ones, by the sixteenth century this Grecophile Catholicism became an easy target for Protestant Reformers and, later, their descendants. Thus, when metaphysics emerged in the discourse of Anglo-Protestant America, it had long since acquired negative connotations in both elite and popular parlance. Perhaps no clearer example exists than in the pervasive Baconianism of the nineteenth century.

Americans with middle- or high-brow education after 1810 increasingly invoked Francis Bacon and his *Novum Organum* of 1620 and thought in terms of categories they attributed to him.[13] In their homage to the Englishman and his classic work, Americans were signaling their enthusiasm for the inductive method of modern science as well as their disdain for a classical and medieval Aristotelianism that reasoned axiomatically and deductively from unquestioned propositions. In so doing, Americans believed that they were putting their premium on "facts" that could be supported by evidence, that they were discarding forever the "hypotheses" and fanciful speculations of "metaphysics" within the scholastic baggage of Catholicism. Instead of the vilified "mysticism" of the Catholic Middle Ages, an enlightened American citizenry, formed and shaped in the Protestant mold, could rely on empirical method and, with it, an antitheoretical ideology that could support its increasingly self-conscious pragmatic leaning. Francis Bacon became the symbol par excellence of the American preference for direct experience—a preference that found expression both in evangelicalism and in the new national metaphysics that replaced the medieval European version.

Linking the Baconian antimetaphysical ideology and the birth of the new American metaphysics, however, was the unraveling, in the nineteenth-century United States, of Protestant orthodoxy. In the shadow of the "village Enlightenment" in New England and elsewhere, free inquiry brought a new egalitarianism to religion. Indeed, what Nathan Hatch has called the "democratization of American Christianity" had more-than-Christian effects, rippling out into religious culture and helping it to create and re-create itself. Here new religious entrepreneurs took their cue from an Enlightenment ideology that American patriots had popularly endorsed in the late eighteenth century and transmuted that ideology into an emerging declaration of religious independence. Elitist authority became compromised. Meanwhile, technology drove a revolution in the print media, as (mass production) stereotype printing brought information to people far more quickly and cheaply than ever before. With more effective ways of processing and disseminating information, nonspecialists increasingly felt capable of acquiring the knowledge that could make them persuasive conversation partners in public religious discourse. Knowledge equaled ownership, and ownership transmitted power—both social and spiritual—to ordinary people.[14]

With ironies abounding, mysticism—which for Anglo-American Protestants was code for Catholicism, for abstract, impractical reasoning, and specifically for dogmatism with trappings of cultural naiveté and lack of proper criticism —this mysticism crept back into culture. Now, however, it came in an altered guise, bringing with it the glowing admiration for science that pervaded the Baconian universe. Far from the "folklorization" of the occult (as Butler would have it), a new urban and semi-urban American public, largely middle class and lower middle class, became invested in complex patterns of religious thought and practice, partially inherited from the past and partially created in the moment. This emergent religious thought and practice exploded occultism into a new and larger category. The work of the new American proponents of metaphysics was one of religious imagination, and they had been prepared for it not only by Catholic "superstition" and Enlightenment democracy, by scientific and popular Baconianism and a new print technology. The new metaphysicians had been prepared, too, by the seventeenth-century English Puritan culture broadly disseminated throughout the United States through the textbook preferences of growing numbers of common schools and through the vast network of informal contacts among Anglo-Protestants and cultural "others," chief among them Indians and blacks.[15] By the end of the nineteenth century, for its distinctive American following "metaphysics" meant all that was good in religion, all that concerned Truth and its practical feats of saving power in everyday life. By this time as well, it meant a catholicity of mind and spirit signified, especially, by an openness to Asia and an embrace of South and East Asian religious ideas and practices. And by the end of the twentieth century, metaphysics continued to point to some of these same concerns even as the term became a self-styled name for Americans who understood themselves as seekers on a "spiritual" path.

Unlike many of the cultural products explored under the rubric of "esotericism" by religious and cultural historians, American metaphysicians could not by and large be noticed for either their countercultural proclivities or their broad-scale inaccessibility.[16] By contrast, even with its share of darkened séance rooms and similar phenomena, the American metaphysical project operated under a religious sunshine law. Secrets were open and public; books and newspapers were accessible and ubiquitous; advocates were unabashed in their appeal to the vernacular and their democratic celebration of the same. Hence, this book adopts American usage—as well as the earlier usage of Braden and Judah—in its preference for the language of metaphysics. To invoke "esotericism," or—in related moves—the "occultism" of Butler and others, or—the alternative of some scholars—American "gnosticism" seems more problematic than simply to talk, as advocates do (and as the subject headings in Borders bookstores now do, too), of metaphysics. Culturally, we have moved away from the nineteenth-century Baconian vilification of "metaphysics" as well as from an identification with the medieval scholastic category. For our time, metaphysics more easily and clearly signals what its etymology suggests—those preoccupied in some sense with what lies beyond the physical plane. Meanwhile, esotericism, occultism, and gnosticism—all three—bring connotations that are narrower or more negative or both. Even as esotericism is linked to elite speculation, most frequently with European credentials and heavily symbolist, occultism hints of ritual practice connected with negative witchcraft practice, and gnosticism offends an Anglo-Protestant theology that privileges the public order and suspects too deep an inward turning.

In this book, therefore, metaphysics will stand for an American religious mentality (thought, belief, emotional commitment, symbolic and moral behavior) organized in terms of an identifiable set of themes. As an early advance forecast, I single out four. First and most obvious is a preoccupation with mind and its powers. Metaphysical mind, however, must be understood in a way that is broad and inclusive. It is surely not confined to the brain, nor to pure and abstract thinking, nor to the rational faculty as it has been understood in the Grecized classical philosophy of the West. In fact, the "mind" of metaphysics blends the European Enlightenment with Romanticism, even as it expresses the pragmatic philosophy and techno-scientific orientation that mark it as made in America. Mind encompasses poetry and intuition; it also includes cognitive capacities such as clairvoyance and telepathy that in our time have been called "psychic"; it dwells comfortably with altered states of attention such as trance and meditation; it includes visionary, auditory, tactile, kinesthetic, gustatory, and even olfactory manifestations; it translates to action and material transformation. Mind, in short, is about consciousness and all that derives from and returns to it—with emphasis ever on the mental awareness by which humans interact creatively with their environments.

Second, American metaphysics signals a predisposition toward the ancient cosmological theory of correspondence between worlds as that theory was carried forward in the esoteric tradition of the West, in its Renaissance neoclassical form, and in its Elizabethan English version. In alignment with this high cultural theory, American metaphysics has likewise embraced ideas of the correspondence between worlds implicit in vernacular traditions about human interaction with nature and the environment. These were also advanced in the English country tradition, and they appeared as profusely in American Indian and African American cultures, which mixed often with each other and with the English legacy. In time, as European and other immigrations brought new and different peoples, ideas of correspondence in old-country traditions combined and folded into the earlier American substrate. Meanwhile, in a different fashion a culture of books and reading from the nineteenth century gradually introduced religious and philosophical classics from Europe and Asia to a self-conscious audience of American seekers.

While a number of variants to the theory of correspondence exist, the most prevalent high-culture version in the West (and the one that had major impact on the American metaphysical tradition) posits a macrocosmic-microcosmic equivalence that is, in theoretical terms, mystical. Here metaphysicians have acknowledged the prior (in some sense) existence of a macrocosm—a larger (than our world) world of divinity, Nature, or the metaphysically favored eternal or collective Mind (alternatively, Truth, the Idea, the Ideas, and the like). On this macrocosmic world, the microcosm—the smaller human (and sometimes natural) world and/or mind—was modeled, so that the microcosm could be described as made of the same stuff, or "material," as the macrocosm, like it in all things except in scale. Thus the "as above, so below" adage has explained the nature of earthly existence and the (mystical) rules for interaction between the spheres. Meanwhile, a series of folk traditions have brought their own implicit cosmology of correspondences existing in nature and in the human world, correspondences that can be found between one piece of the world and another, between one material—often symbolic—entity and another related to it by structural symmetries, parallel functions, contiguity, content, or the like. In these traditions, the human mind—often acting out its imaginative grasp of the world through the body and thus through ritual—has operated as the transformative agent, taking advantage of the secret symmetries and connections for its own purposes. Religion thus is above all a work of the practical imagination.

Third, far from understanding mind and its correspondences in fixed and static ways, American metaphysicians have thought in terms of movement and energy. Indeed, by the early twentieth century, their preference for the energetic shifted into high gear, with energy, its existence, and its dynamic thrust and flow seemingly everywhere for the metaphysically inclined—a point that I will emphasize when my narrative reaches this era. But the logic of their preoccupation was present from the beginnings of American metaphysics. If metaphysical religion is a work of practical imagination and will, this is because the prior perception of worlds in motion has run through metaphysical thinking. To trace that logic is to come squarely to terms with the implications of the inherited doctrine of correspondence. When every piece of the world is related to other pieces, when macrocosm and microcosm are made of the same stuff, when secret mystical sympathies and likenesses abound and wait just below the surface to be discovered, action must move through all the spheres or the apparent fact of motion in the present world can be neither explained nor intuited. The search to perceive the motion of the spheres is on. Close behind that search, too, come notions of proper and correct motion. To translate this in more specific cultural terms, along with celebration of our basic connections to grandeur, a sense of sin and loss has haunted metaphysicians in Anglo-Protestant and Calvinistically inclined America. For them, there are obstacles to be overcome, wrongs to be righted, reconciliation with the true nature of things to be found through a kind of cosmological forgiveness, with the dwellers in the microcosm—the human piece of the larger whole—reunited to their parent and/or true being. In this vision of ever-increasing energy, the practical imagination joins forces with will. We enter the realm of what properly may be described as magic, but—and this is important—magic read in a healing mode.

Hence, and fourth, American metaphysics formed in the midst of a yearning for salvation understood as solace, comfort, therapy, and healing. In the context of metaphysical naturalism in the materialistically oriented United States, sin and loss were graphically reordered and re-understood in social, cultural, and somatic terms. Sin meant the absence of loved ones that spiritualist séances sought to ease. It signified the body in pain instead of pleasure, and it implied, too, the absence of the material good(s) that would enhance the body's (and the spirit's) pursuit of freedom and immortality. It told of wounded relationships and the pain of emotional separateness that needed overcoming. Thus the pragmatism that attended the mind of American metaphysics was directed toward a felt and physical salvation for individuals and communities. Metaphysics might be about what lay beyond the physical, but it was never totally abstract or theoretical. It always had a point and purpose on earth, always spent its attentiveness on salving wounds and making wounded people whole. For American metaphysicians— their once-born credentials defying the Jamesian category—being aligned with spirit (the goal) meant standing in the free flow of spirit energy. This energy would heal and restore, bring correspondence with the macrocosm back again, and end the sin of separation that had been inscribed on bodies, minds, and the physical terrain.

To sum up, if—as I have already suggested—magical practice may be read as a logical corollary of an "energetically" based theory of correspondence (with material magic stressing symbolist practice and mental magic emphasizing the work of consciousness), all American magic comes down to salvation, and salvation means healing and therapy. Who in America needed such salvation and healing through mystical and magical means? The answer is practically everyone. It is, of course, tempting to link material magic (spells, charms, talismans, and so forth) to country traditions and middling-to-lower classes, and to associate mental magic—mesmerism, mind cure, positive thinking, meditation, and the like— with urban locales and the middling (and higher) classes. But in fact, the division is too pat and simple. Material magic, especially in its European-inspired forms, could be "high magic" with its corresponding high-culture clientele, and this in urban settings. And as we will see, mental magic could be found in country as much as city and likewise (and often enthusiastically) among the poor. Meanwhile and through it all, a historian needs to be especially alert for narratives that, as I have argued elsewhere, form "dissident histories."[17] These are histories created from and predicated on the theory of correspondence, with attention to the dynamic flow of energy entering our world from the macrocosm to transform the lives of individuals. They are stories of past lives in preexisting worlds and times, with "karmic" predispositions and agendas for present earthly existence incorporated. Such accounts are explanatory narratives for making sense of the magic, for understanding its profoundly serious religious underpinnings for proponents, and for glimpsing what, for them, are its teleological implications. They are stories that come from Western, and, by the end of the nineteenth century, Eastern sources, but they are stories that carry a distinctly American tone in their emphasis on pragmatism and progress.

Narrating the complex connections of these themes represents a fairly large — indeed enormous — project. When to this we add the pluriform, ever-fragmenting, and continually transforming demography of metaphysical communities, we engage a subject that is, once again, surely elusive. My study of American religion and culture, however, convinces me that metaphysics is a normal, recurring, and pervasive feature of the American spiritual landscape. In order to organize the data on which the case rests narratively, therefore, the seven chapters that follow are grouped in three chronologically controlled sections. Part One, "Beginnings," traces a pre-seventeenth-century Hermetic and vernacular magical background for American metaphysical religion ("European Legacies") on the Continent and in England in both elite and vernacular culture. Then (in "Atlantic Journeys, Native Grounds") it turns its attention to similar materials (elite and vernacular) through American colonial times and into the Revolutionary War era, adding Native American and African American forms as well. The intent here is to show that there was material aplenty in this new American world to construct a proto-metaphysics (to impose the later and Anglo-American-derived term).

Part Two, "Transitions," follows nineteenth-century developments to the time of the Civil War. One chapter ("Revolutions and Enlightenments") tracks metaphysical themes in a series of cultural revolutions intertwined with "village" and elite "enlightenments" that include Freemasonry, Mormonism, Universalism, and Transcendentalism. A second ("Communion of Spirits") explores mid-century spiritualism from the Shakers, to mesmerism, harmonialism (Andrew Jackson Davis and his sympathizers), and the séance spiritualism that united mesmerism and harmonialism with mediumistic phenomena. This chapter attempts, too, to identify the ways that African Americans and Indians (especially) were woven in and out of the mass-market spiritualism of the era.

Part Three, "Arrivals," examines mature forms of metaphysical religion from the postbellum era to the present. "Spirits Reformed and Reconstituted" underlines how much postbellum developments—the Theosophical Society (so small but so large in cultural impact), Christian Science, and New Thought—were related to earlier American involvement with spiritualism. "Metaphysical Asia" constructs the processes and results as Americans reinvented South and East Asia according to their Americanized metaphysical categories. It does not aim to cover all Asian religion in the United States—certainly not that of the Asian immigrants themselves nor that of Asian traditions, like forms of Buddhism, that acculturated to their new locale without being absorbed under the metaphysical rubric. The last chapter, "New Ages for All," follows the diffusion of metaphysical religion into the present in a series of different cultural practices and sites. Finally, "Coda: The New New Age" charts the early and later New Age movement and suggests what befell it.

At least part of this narrative's concern, however, is historiographical in more general terms. Constructing a cultural history of American metaphysical religion is an essential historical act of recovery. The triangulation of religious forces—evangelical, mainstream-denominational, and metaphysical—requires a careful inquiry into metaphysics in order to tell the story of all of the major directions in which religious people in the nation moved. But such an inquiry is also necessary in order to tell the story of what began to render them, in religious terms, into something like an ethnic group (in process of forming) with an identifiable religious orientation. This is because the three forces that Jon Butler identified have not existed on these shores as isolates. Indeed, religious people at the same times and in the same places have embraced more than one of them. Evangelicals could also be mainstreamers; mainstreamers could have their metaphysical side; and so, too, could evangelicals. There were seemingly endless connections to be made and exploited. As Ann Taves has pointedly shown, religious experience in the evangelical revivals (the "enthusiasm" and "fits" decried by more rationalizing Protestant opponents) slid easily into the alternative religious experiences of spiritualists and other metaphysicians (the "trances" of clairvoyant and mesmeric subjects).[18] In the midst of all of this, in their own terms metaphysicians assiduously combined whatever was at hand to construct their religious forms, doing blatantly what others, outside the self-conscious metaphysical camp, were doing perhaps more subtly.

Thus, beyond gaining a purchase on metaphysical projects and acts, recovering the narrative of American metaphysical religions sets the stage for a new revisionary account of all of American religious history that privileges the study of contacts and combinations. Neither the story of consensus (Anglo-Protestant or other) nor the story of conflict purely and solely (although it surely includes conflict in certain sites and situations), nor of "tolerance," this story features, especially, the religious worlds that people made together and often, without consciously taking note of it, with each other's cultural property. Writing metaphysical America becomes a way to chronicle a profusely rich and hybrid series of contacts among religious peoples, ideas, and practices. These spendthrift products of human religious activity tell of the spiritual work of both elites and ordinary people. They express contexts and constituencies that overlapped groups, classes, and commitments. And they provide a model for tracing the history of other overlaps, religiously and more generally. They help us get the story right in political and social terms as well as in religious ones.

Part One

BEGINNINGS

European Legacies

American metaphysics is a combinative venture with beginnings in numerous places and times. Some of its sources were products of the nineteenth century and—for twentieth-century and later versions—thereafter, but others arrived earlier. The oldest legacies were culturally available in certain forms on American shores in the seventeenth century, and it is these sources that had the first say on what became the tradition. The classical and Hellenistic Greco-Roman world (which included northern Egypt), behind and beside it the Near East, later medieval Christian, Jewish, and synthetic lores and practices, Renaissance and continuing religious scholarship and experiment, a series of European folk traditions, their English equivalents, an English Elizabethan high cultural inheritance, Native American narratological traditions and ceremonial work, African American versions of the same—all came together in the British North Atlantic colonies that later became the United States. Later, West Coast, southwestern, and Mississippi Gulf inhabitants, and even Sandwich-Islanders-become-Hawaiians would add their materials. So, of course, would Asians, and so would a series of others whose "influences" became so many and various that a kaleidoscope of sources emerged. Indeed, its tangled contents defy isolation and separate identification.

Earlier sources, however—though challenging to name and identify—leave more marks. This chapter follows some of the oldest of them to acknowledge the major western European (including English) cultural resources up to the seventeenth century for the creation of American metaphysical religion. Major themes that would surface later in the mature American metaphysical tradition were here already apparent—the power of mind, the worldview of correspondence and connection, the preoccupation with summoning energy from on high to "save" the human situation, and thus the healing of what was humanly amiss. The material in this chapter is divided into three sections. The first surveys the elite literature and practice (insofar as that is recoverable) of the Continental metaphysical tradition (with major sources coming from North Africa and the Near East). It focuses especially on the tradition as it passed through the lens of the European Renaissance and continued thereafter on into the seventeenth century. The second follows this learned tradition as it got refracted further through English materials. Finally, the third pays particular attention to Continental and English vernacular culture, moving beyond high culture to tease out a commonality of metaphysical belief and practice shared broadly through different strata of culture.

LITERATURE AND PRACTICE ON THE CONTINENT

HERMES OF THE SOUTH

In 1460 or thereabouts, the story goes, one Leonardo da Pistoia, a monk employed to collect manuscripts for Cosimo de' Medici—that scion of the wealthy banking family who was effective ruler of Florence—arrived in the city from Macedonia with a Greek manuscript. He presented Cosimo with a not-quite-complete copy of what has come to be known as the *Corpus Hermeticum.* Close to the end of 1462 or the start of the new year, Cosimo, who was also a renowned patron of learning and art, turned to Marsilio Ficino (1433–1499), at the time poised to produce what would become the first complete translation of Plato's writings into Latin. So important did the new manuscript seem to Cosimo—who, as Frances A. Yates observed, probably wanted to read it before he died—that, at Cosimo's behest, Ficino dropped Plato temporarily and instead began to translate the Hermetic document into Latin. The text, thought to be the work of the mysterious Hermes Trismegistus, an Egyptian of great antiquity, was made up of fourteen treatises containing variations on a mystical philosophy. (Modern versions include seventeen—the last three tractates translated in 1481 or 1482 by Lodovico Lazzarelli [1447–1500] and published initially as *Diffinitiones Asclepii* by Symphorien Champier in 1507.)[1] Renaissance contemporaries believed that this new-old material would illuminate the religious aspects of Platonism and, especially, Neoplatonism. Ficino finished his translation by April 1463; it was published in 1471; and before the sixteenth century ended it had gone through at least sixteen editions, not counting printings that were only partial.[2]

Ficino's translation of the Greek manuscript was officially titled *Liber de Potestate et Sapientia Dei*, but it was familiarly called the *Pimander*, after its first discourse, which claimed to be the work of a speaker today known as "Poimander" or "Poimandres" (most probably an epithet for the Egyptian God Thoth, the personified creative "intelligence" of the supreme Egyptian God Re, and—in a pun in the Greek—the "shepherd of men").[3] Before the Latin translation appeared, Renaissance and earlier Europeans had heard of Hermes Trismegistus, with the oldest references being from the Christian church fathers Lactantius and Augustine. They were also acquainted with a Latin text called the *Asclepius*, believed to contain the Hermetic wisdom of ancient Egypt and (falsely) considered the work of Apuleius of Madaura. Later scholarship, beginning with the work of Isaac Casaubon in 1614, would expose the linguistic evidence for a much later date and more combinative milieu for the *Corpus Hermeticum* and related Hermetic literature. By this time, though, Hermes Trismegistus had already acquired a reputation as a contemporary of Moses, and many admirers of the Hermetic literature ignored or sloughed off the new critical knowledge. The "Thrice-Greatest Hermes," as his name is usually translated and as the title "Poimandres" already suggests, had been linked in various ways to the Egyptian God Thoth as a Greek adaptation. Brian Copenhaver has called Trismegistus "the name that would signify a new way of sanctifying the heathen past for Christian scholars of the Renaissance" and "a name that still charms the learned in our own time."[4]

Professional scholars of the Hermetic tradition underline the abiding importance of Hermes and Hermetic literature for western European culture and its offshoots. That the Hermetic texts were "translated prior to those of Plato" testified to the "interest they aroused and to the importance attributed to them even before they could be read," according to Antoine Faivre. Many years earlier, Frances A. Yates said the same. The translation of Trismegistus before Plato was a testimony "to the mysterious reputation of the Thrice Greatest One." "Egypt was before Greece; Hermes was earlier than Plato. Renaissance respect for the old, the primary, the far-away, as nearest to divine truth, demanded that the *Corpus Hermeticum* should be translated before Plato's *Republic* or *Symposium*."[5]

In the centuries that ensued, Hermes and his lore would continue to inspire a small army of devotees and, as we will see, the Hermetic writings made their way out of the closed world of high cultural texts and into the vernacular culture of the West. What was it that Hermetic followers so admired about Hermes other than his purported age and mystery? What was it about his teaching that caught attention as a way to explain and enhance their lives? What spiritual treasures did they believe Hermes offered that were not available, or were not available so profoundly and powerfully, elsewhere? To answer these questions is to enter an expansive world of cosmological speculation that also had clear pragmatic ramifications. It is to enter a world in which the philosophical high-mindedness of the *Corpus* (and the Latin *Asclepius*) mediated a clear existential concern, with a search for salvation as the engine driving it. Thus religious and cultural practice of some sort were implied as corollaries. Indeed, alongside the *Corpus* and the *Asclepius* there existed a series of popular Hermetic texts that offered "how-to" advice of a generally (material) magical kind.[6] These technical Hermetica, akin to other magical texts in the ancient world but attributed to the authority of the mysterious and mystical Hermes, included writings such as the texts and fragments to be found in the *Anthology* of Stobaeus as well as various other texts and literary fragments. "Salvation in the largest sense," writes Copenhaver, was a "common concern of theoretical and technical *Hermetica* alike, though the latter texts generally advertised a quotidian deliverance from banal misfortunes of disease, poverty and social strife, while the former offered a grander view of salvation through the knowledge of God, the other and the self."[7]

So we have religious or spiritualized philosophy on the one side and magic on the other, and we have the contemporary scholarly suggestion that both in some sense belong together. Such a conjunction of theory and practice, whatever its strength in the ancient world, would become the high sign of American metaphysics and the mark of its success in the nation. The connection, of course, would be American-made and more conscious of itself as "discovery" than as legacy, but the connection would be there nevertheless. Meanwhile, the *Corpus Hermeticum* that reached the Renaissance, even if it did not in itself announce its relationship to a larger world of magical practice, was already in other ways a conjunctive document. The scholarly commentary on the *Corpus* through the years has argued on its provenance—whether it is Egyptian or Greek, whether strong Jewish and Christian influences may be found, and what links there are to other Near Eastern, especially Gnostic, traditions. Composed as a series of Greek texts in Alexandria, Egypt, between the first and third centuries, the *Corpus* and related Hermetica, scholars conclude, reflect the combinative culture of the Hellenistic world in which these writings achieved the form in which they were transmitted to western Europeans.[8]

The earlier scholarship of A.-J. Festugière in the 1950s announced a major fault line between treatises in the *Corpus* that present "incompatible doctrines" and "opposed attitudes." At its strongest, this meant that in some of the treatises "the world is penetrated by divinity, therefore beautiful and good." In others, "the world is essentially evil, not the work of God or, in any case, the First God." Festugière went on to conclude that "notions so diverse" could not "lead to the same mode of action but must result in two antagonistic moralities" and that therefore they could not be attributed "simultaneously to the same religious sect." Frances Yates, in her well-known study of Hermeticism in the world of Giordano Bruno, followed the Festugière division between pessimistic and optimistic gnosis in an essentially astrological cosmological framework:

> For the pessimist (or dualist) gnostic, the material world heavily impregnated with the fatal influence of the stars is in itself evil; it must be escaped from by an ascetic way of life which avoids as much as possible all contact with matter, until the lightened soul rises up through the spheres of the planets, casting off their evil influences as it ascends, to its true home in the immaterial divine world. For the optimist gnostic, matter is impregnated with the divine, the earth lives, moves, with a divine life, the stars are living divine animals, the sun burns with a divine power, there is no part of Nature which is not good for all are parts of God.[9]

More recent scholarship, however, minimizes the significance of this distinction, with Garth Fowden seeing the differences as sequential instead of contradictory. For Fowden, by understanding the philosophical treatises of the *Corpus* within the technical world of related magical writings, the distinctions between pessimistic and optimistic cosmologies can be read as reflections of stages in an initiate's spiritual journey. With magical practice being the tangible sign of cosmological thinking, early and later moments in a spiritual seeker's journey become expressions of profoundly different "takes" on the world. More recently, Roelof van den Broek, while pointing to a borderline world in which Gnostic and non-Gnostic texts are difficult to distinguish, has argued for strong differences between Hermetism and classical Gnosticism regarding theology, anthropology, and—to the point here—cosmology. Acknowledging that some Hermetic texts did "come close to the negative worldview of the Gnostics," he goes on to emphasize that "nowhere in the Hermetic texts do we find the idea that the cosmos is bad, or that it had been created by an evil demiurge." Nor, he argues, was the human body "the soul's prison devised by the bad demiurge"; it was instead the epitome of "God's creative power."[10] Again, this interpretive solution points the way toward the ambivalences within an American metaphysics, in which positive readings of the natural world yield a "nature religion" of the metaphysical at the same time as others in the tradition deny or negate the concrete world, but ultimately—and perhaps paradoxically—in order to serve life-enhancing and world-affirming ends. But this is to get ahead of the story.

If we return to the fifteenth-century text of the *Corpus Hermeticum* at least briefly, we can outline the set of ideas and concerns that acted as a lens to carry the theosophy of the ancient world through the prism of the Renaissance and into modern and American times. Within the ideas and concerns of the text—and its concealed subtext—we can begin to find the answers to the questions about what drove the burning interest that Hermes and Hermetic literature seemed to awaken. Ficino's dedication of his translation, or *argumentum* as he called it, points to the aspects of what he read that inspired him. The "Pimander"—the Teacher and Guide—was for him the Divine Mind, the Intelligence that could flow into the human mind—if humans learned, as the text taught, how to rise above sense deceptions and turn in contemplation to God, just as the moon turned to the sun.[11] Even if the discourses of the *Corpus* did not march lock-step to this message, the contemporary scholar Jean-Pierre Mahé has seen them as united and their unity a function of literary form based on the gnomic sentences of ancient Egyptian wisdom literature. Meanwhile, Peter Kingsley has read them as apparently originating "in the Egyptian temple practice of consulting dream oracles."[12] Rather than be a near-passive receptor of the divine Intelligence, set against the backdrop of a vast cosmology based on astrological laws through which the earth as we know it is ruled by the stars and the seven planets, the Hermetic discourses present the individual religious seeker as agonist. Longing for illumination, for the intuitive wisdom-knowledge of the divine, the Hermetic seeker searches out salvation—but this without the personal God or redeemer of Christian teaching. Instead, even granting a distant oracular background, salvation comes from the seeker's own work, from the effort that yields the wisdom-knowledge itself.

Against this recent scholarly backdrop, a reading that looks for resemblance more than difference yields, for the contemporary reader, persuasive evidence of a family of concerns and answers that run through the Hermetic discourses. Cast as formal dialogues, these texts function more properly as monologues, with the Teacher—in most cases, Hermes Trismegistus—authoritatively revealing religious truth to the existentially engaged seeker and student. In so doing, the Hermetic discourses offer a limited set of answers to an equally limited range of questions. To be sure, the answers in some cases are in tension with one another, and in Discourse VI ("That the good is in god alone and nowhere else"), for example, the tension is exceeding. Still, it is fair to say that the discourses are pervaded by the theory of correspondence between a greater world (the macrocosm?) and our (microcosmic) human one, and by preoccupations regarding energy, its states, its sources, and its moral qualities (the problem of evil and the meaning of death). The discourses consistently revere the divine quality of Mind, and within this context the God and power they understand is male and masculinizing (the "Father," never the "Mother"), even as this divinity creates in the mode of craftsman (that is, according to the directions of a mental template). Here it is significant that the Egyptian Thoth, the primal referent for Trismegistus, was considered not only God of the moon but also of messages and writing. The Greek Hermes, of course, was intimately identified with communication, and in Discourse IV it is no accident that Trismegistus instructs, "The craftsman made the whole cosmos by reasoned speech."[13] Likewise, the presence of Asclepius, whose name evokes the Greek God of healing, seems suggestive: it is knowledge that not only creates but also repairs.

What can be said of the ultimate deity in all of this? In a qualified sense, the God of these dialogues is not alone but inhabits a pluriform universe in which other, clearly lower gods reside. Moreover, in keeping with the overarching theory of correspondence, the discourses generally regard the divine being, the cosmos (alternately "nature"), and humanity in mimetic relationships and even as identical. ("For there is nothing in all the cosmos that he is not. . . . There is nothing that he is not, for he also is all that is.") Likewise, for the most part they affirm a noetic mysticism that ends with humans as gods, even as they ponder the riddled and dual nature of human life (immortal/mortal; godlike/subject to corruption). Some of the discourses do provide glimpses besides of a mystical sexuality in which Nature figures prominently: in Discourse I, for example, we read that "man saw in the water the form like himself as it was in nature, he loved it and wished to inhabit it; . . . Nature took hold of her beloved, hugged him all about and embraced him, for they were lovers." There are other references to "cosmic fecundity" in the *Corpus* later. There are glimpses as well of the mystical materialism that, centuries later, would run through the American metaphysical tradition (as in Discourse V, in which "the matter composed of the finest particles is air, but air is soul, soul is mind, and mind is god").[14]

Always though, the human path is one that is linked to the kind of knowledge that may be characterized as illumination. "Your mind is god the father," says Poimandres in Discourse I, and "they are not divided from one another for their union is life." "The greatest evil in mankind is *ignorance* concerning god," announces Discourse VII in its title, while "forgetting" is called "vice" in Discourse X. Significantly, being born again is being "born in mind" in Discourse XIII, in which Tat says rapturously to Hermes, "Father, I see the universe and I see myself in mind," and Hermes responds, "This, my child, is rebirth." And, in a climactic assessment, with remarkable explicitness Discourse XI instructs that the reason a human should aspire to become a god is in order to know what God knows and so to know God: "Unless you make yourself equal to god, you cannot understand god; like is understood by like. . . . Go higher than every height and lower than every depth. Collect in yourself all the sensations of what has been made, of fire and water, dry and wet; be everywhere at once, on land, in the sea, in heaven; be not yet born, be in the womb, be young, old, dead, beyond death. And when you have understood all these at once—times, places, things, qualities, quantities—then you can understand god."[15]

As this last suggests obliquely, what generally lurks beneath the surface of these Hermetic discourses is a search for the technical knowledge—the metaphysical "know-how"—that can lead to mystical attainment. How does one banish ignorance and forgetting? By what means can one be "born again" into knowledge? What tools does a person need to become God in order to know him? The best way to answer these questions is to leave the *Corpus* momentarily and turn instead to the pages of the Latin *Asclepius*—because it is here that a Hermetic document reveals both text and subtext bluntly and explicitly. In so doing, it becomes immediately clear to a reader of the *Corpus* that the *Asclepius*, which western Europeans knew first, is preoccupied with a similar set of concerns and issues. Even a familiar Hermetic cast of characters is present—Hermes Trismegistus himself, Asclepius, Tat, Hammon/Ammon. Question-and-answer dialogue runs back and forth between Asclepius as interlocutor/spiritual seeker and Trismegistus as wisdom teacher, who—with traditional mystical caution—warns that "the mind is irreverent that would make public, by the awareness of the many, a treatise so very full of the majesty of divinity." Against a vast cosmological frame, topics of the discourse include human nature understood as a blend of mortality and immortality, death and judgment, the possibilities of human divinization ("one who has joined himself to the gods in divine reverence, using the mind that joins him to the gods, almost attains divinity"), the composition of matter, and the existence of spirit within it. Discourse answers treat as well the nature of true (that is, spiritual) understanding, the relationship of consciousness to the gods, the masculine and simultaneously androgynous nature of the deity ("father" and yet "completely full of the fertility of both sexes and ever pregnant with his own will"), and the pervasiveness of the divine presence ("god is everything; everything comes from him").[16]

As this discussion already suggests, continuity with the themes of the *Corpus* is obvious. But that is only one side of a story that, manifestly, has two. Juxtaposed to this text of resemblance stands another text of difference. There is one topic that Ficino's *Corpus* did not treat—a series of observations and somewhat cryptic instructions regarding the statues of the gods and the nature of their "life" in the public temples of the land. The discussion begins innocently enough, given the recurring themes. "It exceeds the wonder of all wonders," Hermes of the *Asclepius* explains, "that humans have been able to discover the divine nature and how to make it." This seems far from remarkable, since the Hermetic literature in general wears its mystical preoccupations with human divinization as a kind of heavenly arm badge, and the reader can recall earlier remarks that the *Asclepian*

Trismegistus has made about the possibilities of human divinization. Matters get murkier, however, when Hermes begins to instruct that the ancestors "discovered the art of making gods." Even though they "could not make souls," he says, they "called up the souls of demons or angels and implanted them in likenesses through holy and divine mysteries, whence the idols could have the power to do good and evil." Imitating the power and fecundity of the ultimate progenitor God, humans—on the way to being gods themselves—fashioned the objects of ritual and cultus with the materials they had at hand, and so these statue divinities were morally ambiguous. They were the "earthly gods," and their existence was the spiritual sign of a human creativity that was itself godlike. The quality of these human-made gods, recounts Hermes, "comes from a mixture of plants, stones and spices . . . that have in them a natural power of divinity. And this is why those gods are entertained with constant sacrifices, with hymns, praises and sweet sounds in tune with heaven's harmony: so that the heavenly ingredient enticed into the idol by constant communications with heaven may gladly endure its long stay among humankind. Thus does man fashion his gods."[17]

So there are heavenly gods, and there are earthly ones; and it is humans who have created the earthly ones—a daunting but not impossible task, even if the animation of a statue is a profoundly lesser endeavor than the mystical divinization of the self.[18] Moreover, the animation of statues is itself suggested rather cryptically in the *Corpus Hermeticum*. Indeed, if one returns to its later discourses (the ones unknown to Ficino and Cosimo but in print from 1507) with the *Asclepius* on the horizon of memory, certain passages gain a measure of clarity that they did not have before. In the fragment that is Discourse XVII, for example, the Hermetic utterance takes on new meaning: "There are reflections of the incorporeals in corporeals and of corporeals in incorporeals—from the sensible to the intelligible cosmos, that is from the intelligible to the sensible. Therefore, my king, adore the statues, because they, too, possess forms from the intelligible cosmos." And in Discourse XVI, we learn more about the demons whose energies humans might implant in the statues. The demons, we are told with astrological erudition, "follow the orders of a particular star, and they are good and evil according to their natures—their energies, that is. For energy is the essence of a demon," and "some of them . . . are mixtures of good and evil." "The demons on duty at the exact moment of birth, arrayed under each of the stars, take possession of each of us as we come into being and receive a soul. From moment to moment they change places, not staying in position but moving by rotation. Those that enter through the body into the two parts of the soul twist the soul about, each toward its own energy. But the rational part of the soul stands unmastered by the demons, suitable as a receptacle for god."[19]

In her memorable study of Giordano Bruno, Frances Yates pointed to connections for Ficino and other Renaissance figures between the "religion of the mind"
and the practice of (material) magic. Although, as newer scholarship suggests,
she probably overstated her case, her reading is instructive in coming to terms
with resemblance. The *Asclepius,* for all its focus on mystical teaching, does incorporate a cultus that befits the life of a philosopher. "Sympathetic astral magic"
became a way to draw down the energies and blessings of heaven, even if Renaissance magi expressed continuing concern about remaining faithful Christians as
they did so. What all of this suggests, then, is not so much the religion-magic distinction so cherished by a major tradition of scholarship but something more like
what Stephen Wilson has identified for "popular" religion as "a magico-religious
spectrum or a single field embracing religion, magic, and much else, including
proto-science" (more on this last later).[20]   •

Yates herself went on to trace the inclusion of the Kabbalah in a combinative mystical practice promoted especially by Giovanni Pico della Mirandola
(1463–1494), associated with Ficino in Cosimo's Platonic Academy. Blending
Neoplatonism and Hermeticism with Hebrew studies, Pico and others saw a
symmetry between the Hebrew Moses and the Egyptian one the Renaissance
had discovered. Using the power of Hebrew names and numbers, the Kabbalah
seized on the word—on language itself—to produce material realities, as it were,
magically. In its Christianized form shaped by Pico and others (it continued to
be elaborated into the seventeenth century), the Kabbalah emerged as a fit ac-
companiment to the natural magic of the stars taught in the Hermetic literature.
It was Pico, observes Joseph Dan, who promoted an "orientation towards the
Hebrew language and the works of Jewish esoterics and kabbalists, as well as a
romantic glow," linking the attestation of Christian truth to Kabbalah and magic.
The highest names became Christian names, but the intellectualized series of
correspondences featured in the Hebrew Kabbalah endured. "Practical Cabala,"
wrote Yates, "invokes angels, archangels, the ten sephiroth which are names or
powers of God, God himself, by means some of which are similar to other magical procedures but more particularly through the power of the sacred Hebrew
language." She went on to explain that there was "a relationship between the
Sephiroth [the emanations that are associated with the Godhead] and the ten
spheres of the cosmos, composed of the spheres of the seven planets, the sphere
of fixed stars, and the higher spheres beyond these."[21]

We can see these patterns displayed, for example, in the work of the Francis-
can friar Francesco Giorgi (1466–1540) of Venice. In his *De harmonia mundi*
(1525) and *In Scripturam Sacram Problemata* (1536), Giorgi brought together
the Florentine Neoplatonic movement, Venetian Hebraic studies (Venice was

renowned for its Jewish presence), and the Kabbalah as mediated by Pico della Mirandola. Convinced that the Kabbalah proved the truth of Christian teaching, Giorgi developed a correlation between Hebraic and Christian angelic systems more thoroughgoing than Pico's, and he believed that he had found in the concept of number the secret of the universe's existence. In ways that, as we will find, paralleled the northern European work of Cornelius Agrippa, Giorgi argued for the numerical relationships between three worlds: a supercelestial dwelling of the intelligences or angels; a celestial canopy of the stars (the planets and signs of the zodiac) through which the higher influences poured; and an elemental world in which humans resided and through which the influences from the higher world flowed down.[22]

But the Kabbalah, for its Renaissance enthusiasts, went beyond the stars to the spiritual realm of God himself. The Renaissance magician became a "divine man," buttressed by the illuminated teaching of Hermes Trismegistus that had been wedded to the Platonic and Neoplatonic tradition and, now, the Christian Kabbalah. Nor did the urge to synthesize in the quest for godliness stop with these sources. A medieval tradition of magic did not go away, and new sources of illuminative spirituality continued to appear both alongside and within the Christian tradition. If so, here was a template upon which later Europeans and, in turn, Americans could manufacture their own versions of the spiritual quest and determine how, metaphysically, they could advance it. Here was warrant for the linkage of religiophilosophical views collected under the rubric of correspondence and religiocultural practices enacting ideas as works of the material imagination; in other words, as magic.[23] In this context, the Hermetic tradition itself came with all sorts of accompaniments trailing. It became a catch-all for an evolving metaphysical brand of spirituality, which as time passed included a series of ancient and more modern theoretical components with, as their corollaries, programs of imaginative action. Indeed, to return to explicit Hermetism, the "technical" Hermetic writings, which had experienced a different textual history from the *Corpus Hermeticum* and the *Asclepius* (as Copenhaver says, "perhaps for no better reason than the accidents of textual transmission or the prejudices of Byzantine compilers") were all about such matters as "astrology, alchemy, magic and other beliefs and practices called 'occult' in modern English speech." Going even further, Peter Kingsley has argued regarding the Hermetica in their entirety that "there can be no doubting that originally the Hermetica were not written as mere philosophical or intellectual exercises. On the contrary, they were clearly the products of specific circles of people belonging to a living tradition; and they rose out of, and served as pointers towards, a way of life based on mystical practice and realisation."[24]

In the company of Renaissance angels and their stars, metaphysical practice led to an astrological milieu. Hidden behind the Hermetic-Egyptian cultus of the stars and star energies lay the legacy of Babylonian astrological lore from as far in the past as the third millennium B.C.E. Behind it, too, lay concern for later Greek and Roman astrological prognostication (as, for example, in the Greco-Egyptian Claudius Ptolemy's astrological textbook of the second century C.E., the *Tetrabiblos*). Akin to the Gnostics in the high place it accorded to *gnosis*, the Hermetic doctrine of salvation through knowledge revealed its secret only to seekers, to would-be initiates who understood that the divine and saving spark of sacred wisdom/intuition was already planted within and who knew that they needed to take active steps to connect interior worlds with the cosmos.[25]

Nor did Christians eschew the Hermetic legacy. In the fertile mix centered on the Alexandrian culture of Hellenistic Egypt, Gnostic elements that taught salvation through revealed knowledge blended into a version of Christianity, mingling together Jewish with Greek and Iranian cultural forms only after the fact labeled as heresy. Meanwhile, the resemblance between, on the one hand, the Hermetic "Father" whose creation was "intelligence" or "Mind" (a cosmology that for its own part resembles Neoplatonism), and the Father and Son/Word of a Grecized Christian Trinity, on the other, deserves more notice than it usually receives. The early church father Lactantius (240?–320?) championed the Hermetic writings among Christians because he saw them as pointing, from their pagan obscurity, toward Christian revelation, even if, later, Augustine (354–430) in his *City of God* attacked the *Asclepius* for its god-making in and through statues. Learned medieval Christians, in general, had known the *Asclepius*, as we have seen. Moreover, after the fall of Toledo in 1085, Arabic translations of broadly Hermetic materials (although not necessarily ascribed to Hermes Trismegistus) became available to the Latin West in new translations. Meanwhile, as I have already begun to suggest, a European medieval tradition of ritual magic independent of the Hermetica helped to create a climate in which some priests practiced magic, astrology, astrological medicine, and alchemy.[26]

Often understood as the ancestor of modern chemistry, this last—along with astrological medicine—became widely linked to a developing Hermeticism, suggesting already the combinative ambience and enthusiasm for "science" that would characterize the metaphysical tradition in Europe and America. For the proponents of what became the "Hermetic art," the Hermetic legacy, in fact, *was* science, but science of a higher sort, in which illumination was key. Faivre has noted that the earliest alchemical text we know—attributed to Robert of Chester as his Latin translation (*Liber compositione alchemiae quem edidit Morienus Ro-*

manus) of an Arabic work in 1144 (but probably later)—credited Hermes with inventing the arts and sciences. A spate of alchemical texts thereafter refer to Hermes so that, as Faivre says, "on the eve of the Renaissance, it is still hard to distinguish between the Hermes of alchemy and the Hermes of the Hermetica, which is not surprising since they represent almost identical attitudes of mind." To this one could add that alchemy, Hermeticism, and the spiritual longing displayed in the mystical tradition of the late medieval and early modern Christian church could—and did—come together in synthetic ways for faithful Christians in search of God and the marks of divine presence in the world. Ficino of the Italian Renaissance had been ordained a priest, and Pico della Mirandola contemplated entering a monastery toward the end of his life. The gold of alchemy was not "common gold," averred the sixteenth-century *Rosary of Philosophers*. Beyond the work of "sooty empiricks" and "puffers," alchemy became for many in the profession a spiritual discipline, and as Petrus Bonus wrote in *The New Pearl of Great Price*, it was God's revelation for spiritual well-being, and it imposed moral requirements on the alchemical seeker. Writing of Renaissance (and later) alchemy, Allison Coudert observed that, for spiritual alchemists, "all the ingredients mentioned in alchemical recipes—the minerals, metals, acids, compounds, and mixtures—were in truth only one, the alchemist himself. He was the base matter in need of purification by the fire; and the acid needed to accomplish this transformation came from his own spiritual malaise and longing for wholeness and peace. The various alchemical processes . . . were steps in the mysterious process of spiritual regeneration."[27]

HERMES OF THE NORTH

So far I have been arguing that Hermeticism and its attendant arts such as alchemy acquired a distinctive, if broad and complex, shape as they passed into and out of the European Renaissance. I have hinted, too, that these acquisitions as well as the inherent combinativeness of Hermeticism—alongside its themes of correspondence, mind, energy, and salvation (healing)—had much to do with what took form in the nineteenth-century United States as metaphysical religion. However, as the Renaissance waned and a later era dawned, there were other important carriers for the Hermetic cultural cargo that traveled to England and its North American colonies. Significantly, these carriers came from northern Europe—in a Protestantizing culture that would have important ties to a transatlantic Anglophile world and, in turn, produce a major cultural complex to interact with other sources. Among these Renaissance–post-Renaissance carriers were Cornelius Agrippa and his legacy; Paracelsus and, more important, the Paracelsian tradition; Rosicrucianism; and a general efflorescence that is best described as Christian theosophy and that was shaped in major ways by Jacob Boehme.

Heinrich Cornelius Agrippa von Nettesheim (1486–1535), in a life that moved from preoccupation with magic, alchemy, and the Kabbalah to exaltation of the authority of the Bible, consistently sought, as Andrew Weeks has argued, "'illumination' as the source of truth." With a presumed background as a student of law and medicine in Cologne, Agrippa served as a soldier and later spent much of his life, like the slightly later Paracelsus, as a wanderer. He was drawn early to Johannes Reuchlin's *De Verbo Mirifico* (1494), a Christian Kabbalistic work of classic proportions that had significant influence on the eve of the Reformation, positing the harmony of Jewish, Christian, and Pythagorean beliefs, using Hebrew texts, and employing Kabbalistic numerology to proclaim a mystically inflected Christian Word. So important was Agrippa's reading of Reuchlin that, according to Joseph Dan, "the Christian kabbalah became part of European magical and scientific traditions when it was integrated with the wide realm of the 'occult' in the work of Cornelius Agrippa of Nettesheim."[28]

Later, Agrippa turned to the English Christian humanism of John Colet (1467?–1519), who became dean of St. Paul's Cathedral in London and whose lectures on the Apostle Paul were attended by Agrippa. This apparently marked a turn for Agrippa toward emphasis on biblical themes and concern for the imitation of Christ. But it was Agrippa's *De occulta philosophia* (initially completed in 1510 and published in revised form in 1533) that made its mark on evolving Hermeticist and metaphysicalizing culture. Moreover, its publication two years before his death and after a period in which Agrippa exalted scripture and its teaching suggests that, for Agrippa, the magus could be a pious Christian. Although his *Declamatio de Incertitudine et Vanitate Scientiarum and Artium atque Excellentia verbi Dei* (written probably in early 1526) found certitude only in scripture, his *De occulta philosophia* demonstrated that Hermeticism and Christianity were not incompatible. As G. Mallory Masters observes, Agrippa thought that all of the sciences needed to be set "in proper perspective." By themselves they did not possess validity, but collectively they were valuable "as partial expressions of truth," with "Truth as such . . . only revealed by God in Christian faith."[29]

Placed against this background, *De occulta philosophia* seems misread as the work of an unsavory magician who mastered the arts of darkness—a guide for Mary Shelley's Victor von Frankenstein or, much earlier, Christopher Marlowe's alchemical Doctor Faustus. By contrast, Agrippa's classic work brought together, within a generally Neoplatonic frame, the natural magic of Ficino and the Christian Kabbalism of Pico in what Frances Yates called "the indispensable handbook of Renaissance 'Magia' and 'Cabala.'" Agrippa had argued, in his compendium, that the universe was divided into three worlds—the natural or elemental, the heavenly or celestial, and the intellectual or angelic—with each successive world being influenced by the one above it. Agrippa's own work had devoted its first book to natural magic in the elemental world; its second to celestial magic or, as he called it, "mathematical magic," involving number in the attraction and use of the influences of the stars (recall the Hermetic literature and Kabbalistic speculation at which we glanced); and its third to ceremonial magic, intended for the supercelestial world inhabited by angelic spirits. He had taken his three-tiered world from Neoplatonism, and he understood it to be held together by God, the "sovereign Archetype."[30]

Put more explicitly, the influence pervading all the worlds and the divine Archetype holding them together meant that all things existed in all things. Significantly, the human role was thereby enhanced, as Andrew Weeks has noted: "The motif of *omnes in omnibus* [all in all] is complemented by the motif of hierarchy. The higher world communicates itself to the lower by means of the 'virtues' that operate in things. These are forces, hidden properties, and astral influences in nature. Containing all three worlds within itself, the human microcosm, through knowledge, exerts a magic influence on external nature. . . . For the Humanist Agrippa, this trichotomous anthropology also gives rise to a doctrine of free will and to an exalted estimation of the human capacity for knowledge and the power that goes with it." In this reading, the evocation of the magus became an encoded referent for the perfected human being, and the realization of all of the possibilities of mind became a task encompassed by the Christian message. As Agrippa himself understood the magus, he was, in the paraphrase of Marc van der Poel, a person who possessed "profound and divine wisdom." The "occult philosophy" was the "'absoluta consummatio philosophiae' ['the absolute consummation of philosophy'] that opens the way to the knowledge of God."[31]

This kind of combinative spirituality, with its exaltation of the human project in a Hermetic context, continued in the work of Agrippa's younger contemporary Paracelsus. Theophrastus Bombastus (Philippus Aureolus) von Hohenheim (1493?–1541), to give the German-Swiss physician, surgeon, and alchemist his actual name, may—like Agrippa—be seen as a transitional figure and read in Renaissance or non-Renaissance ways. His recent intellectual biographer Andrew Weeks regards him as "an idiosyncratic creature of the early Reformation, whose notion of experience was tangential to the beginnings of empirical science even in his own time." Still more, scholars have compared him to Martin Luther in his

inward and individualistic construction of religious experience and in his rebel-
lious stance toward conventional and accepted authority. A medical theorist and
philosopher of nature who was not notably successful in his career throughout
his life, Paracelsus elaborated a mystical theosophy with Neoplatonic overtones,
holding that humans know nature to the extent that they are nature and that
they know God to the extent that they become wholly identified with him. At
the foundation of these understandings was the familiar doctrine of correspondence between macrocosm and microcosm, the abiding epistemological stance
that led, seemingly inevitably, toward a mystical construction of reality. As Allison Coudert has summarized the Paracelsian view, "Because man is the microcosm he contains within himself all the elements of the greater world, or macrocosm. Knowledge therefore consists in an intuitive act of recognition, in which
the knower and the known become one."[32]

With a related agenda, Weeks has argued strongly that the medical thought
of Paracelsus was decidedly more religious than scientific, that it was intimately
related to the crisis of authority occasioned by the early Reformation, and that in
that context it employed imagistic thinking to extend "the articulation of divine
authority from Scripture to created nature." Meanwhile, Faivre states categorically that Paracelsus, along with most representatives of early German *Naturphilosophie*, "owed practically nothing to Hermetism" (here meaning the specific
collection of Hermetic writings and the literature that they generated in medieval, Renaissance, and later eras rather than a more broadly based Yatesian-style
Hermeticism). Faivre has also pointed to the limits of reading Paracelsus as an
unreconstructed Neoplatonist, since the itinerant sixteenth-century physician
and thinker found no place in his system for the stages that the Neoplatonic tradition had posited between the divine principle and the natural world but instead saw nature itself as "epiphany." More important, for Faivre — and significant
here — Paracelsus became the "turning point" for Western alchemy, with an "all-
encompassing vision" in which chemistry itself was linked to astrology so that
the stars became representations of the "interdependencies of the universe" and
"as much 'within' Man as they are outside of him." "Just as our physical bodies
draw nourishment from the elements," writes Faivre summarizing Paracelsus,
"so do our invisible sidereal bodies nourish themselves by allowing the '*Gestirn*'
(the spirit of the stars) to work within and act upon them."[33] Thus Paracelsian
alchemy was, as alchemy in general has sometimes been called, the "science of
Hermes." The star-shaping of humans had its paler shadow, perhaps, in the divinizing statue-making of the *Asclepius*, but more important were the Hermetic
concerns with religiocultural practice that were signaled. A Hermetic and related
magic was at work here, and one that, with historical hindsight, pointed toward

the magic of mind and imagination that would characterize the American meta-physical tradition. Thus it was combinatively that a later tradition would read and understand Paracelsus.

Nor is this circumstance surprising. It is clear from the first that the Paracelsian tradition employed the name of the master as a catchword for a series of evolving metaphysical views that reached well beyond the actual work of Paracelsus. In fact, medical historian Heinrich Schipperges in a revisionist vein has complained strenuously of a "distortion of Paracelsus in the sixteenth and seventeenth centuries," marking strong disparities between the concrete and nature-based spirituality of the *Corpus Paracelsicum* and that of later disciples of the renowned physician. Schipperges especially notes Paracelsus's apparent concept of the *arcana* (Latin, literally, for "secrets") present in nature — in Paracelsus's own words, "the mysteries from which the physician is to grow," with the physician understood as one who has "spent his days with the *arcana* and has lived in God and in nature as a powerful master of the earthly light." By contrast, argues Schipperges, a series of deutero-Paracelsian writings and followers spiritualized the concrete *arcana* away. By the second part of the sixteenth century, forgeries were being produced that "merely made use of Paracelsus as a symbol; the language and content no longer had anything in common with the spirit of Hohenheim." Reading between the lines of the Schipperges complaint, what emerges clearly is that the Paracelsists carried the thought of their master into a patently Hermetic and magical world in which healing concerns became increasingly metaphysicalized. In this new "Paracelsian" world, the body of matter became so impregnated by spirit that it reproduced not a direct contact with almighty Nature but instead the mediations that led on an upward path to mind and illuminated knowing . "The concrete *arcana* turned into the *mysterium magnum* of the *arcanum*, which could be interpreted only in spiritual terms and finally became an *arcanum sanctum*."[34]

If this was the case, as I think it was, then the changes in the Paracelsian world lead us to a new cultural manifestation bringing the Hermetic synthesis into further combinations and on into England and America. This was Rosicrucianism. With its troubled historiography in the wake of contemporary disavowal of Frances Yates's argument for a "Rosicrucian Enlightenment" as the intermediary phase between the Renaissance and the seventeenth-century scientific "revolution," it is easy to miss the point of Rosicrucianism for a cultural history of American metaphysics.[35] The noetic reading of Rosicrucianism — as "enlightened" — already points to the now-familiar epistemological concerns that characterized later narratives concerning the existence of the so-called Rosicrucian "movement," both in and out of the Yatesian framework. Rosicrucianism, Yates had declared, "is a phase in which the Renaissance Hermetic-Cabalist tradition has received the influx of another Hermetic tradition, that of alchemy." More recently, Roland Edighoffer has pointed to the Christian Kabbalistic strain and the influence of Paracelsus within a Rosicrucian context, noting the connections between Hermeticism, alchemy, and early Rosicrucian themes, a characterization with which Antoine Faivre concurs. At the same time, Edighoffer has argued that "the end of the sixteenth century and the beginning of the seventeenth were in fact the golden age of religious Hermeticism."[36]

Here, though, as in the cases of Agrippa and Paracelsus, we are in northern lands, in a cultural landscape marked by a Reformation, and especially Lutheran, ambience. According to the early-seventeenth-century Rosicrucian myth, Rosicrucians were members of a secret society, a mysterious sect that originated at least a century or more earlier. Leadership and membership in the group, however, were notoriously difficult to establish at the time, and contemporary scholarship has concluded that the Rosicrucian appearance was literary—the product of three well-publicized early-seventeenth-century texts—and any secret society was nonexistent.[37] Ironically, though, in the Rosicrucian case, fictive texts fostered real appearances. As Faivre has observed, "the belief that a Rosicrucian society actually did lie behind these manifestoes caused real societies to spring up. The explosion of initiatory societies in the Western world from the seventeenth century onward was a direct result of this."[38]

If so, they took their cue from the initiatory context mediated by the three documents that appeared mysteriously in early-seventeenth-century Bohemia to tell the story of one Christian Rosencreutz. These were the *Fama Fraternitatis* (1614), the *Confession Fraternitatis* (1615), and the *Chymische Hochzeit Christiani Rosencreutz* (Chemical Wedding—an initiatory novel published in 1616). The earliest, the *Fama*, narrated an account of a German scholar who was born in 1378, traveled widely in the Holy Land and in North Africa and Spain, established with three others in 1418 the Society of the Rose Cross (whence the name *Rosicrucian*) to care for the sick, and himself lived to be 106 years old. According to the narrative, over a century after Rosencreutz's death, when followers opened his tomb as he had instructed, they found along with his intact corpse a number of artifacts and a series of teaching texts. What the texts expounded was a version of the religious synthesis that had come to characterize metaphysical spirituality in the Hermetic tradition—a blend of the Hermetic legacy and its inbuilt quest for illumined knowing, alongside Kabbalism, alchemy, and Paracelsism. The three texts are now generally considered the work of Johann Valentin Andreae (1586–1654), a Lutheran pastor and theologian.[39] The Rose Cross (in German "Rosencreutz") was associated already with the coat of arms of Martin Luther, with its white rose, red heart, and black cross. For the mysterious Rosicrucian order it became the symbol—the cross and rose inscribed together (and note the simultaneous historicized and natural readings that the rose occasions) —of the death and resurrection of Christ. Thus Rosicrucianism presented itself as a Protestant Christian wisdom tradition, a version of the metaphysical inheritance that brought it consciously into conversation with Reformation Christian categories and concerns, pointing toward a northern European *Naturphilosophie* and a more general, yet distinctive, Christian theosophy. Indeed, as Roland Edighoffer has observed, the Rosicrucian manifestos "intend to persuade us that the religious, moral, and cultural evils of the age could not be rooted out by the conversations of eminent scholars but only by a new Reformation that would combine Hermetic philosophy with Christian theology."[40]

Already the preface to the first Rosicrucian document that appeared, the *Fama*, contains an anti-Jesuit reference and, as Yates argued, "suggests that the Rosicrucian manifesto is setting forth an alternative to the Jesuit Order, a brotherhood more truly based on the teaching of Jesus."[41] The narrative itself tells more. Whereas the *Corpus Hermeticum* of Renaissance celebrity was cast in dialogue form on the ancient philosophical model of a school—where students sought wisdom through the question-answer modality in a community of inquiry and action, Rosencreutz emerged as a solitary pilgrim, performing in geographical space the inner journey that the spiritual seeker took. Even with the Rosicrucian "brotherhood" in the background, there was something strikingly individualizing about Rosencreutz and his journey. That the brotherhood could never be found by seekers of the period suggests, too, how evanescent was its function to the entire enterprise. In encountering Rosencreutz and his story, we enter a world more akin to that of John Bunyan and his fabled *Pilgrim's Progress* than that of the Platonic or Neoplatonic academy or, by medieval and Renaissance times, the monastic mysticism that was still so strongly predicated on community. In sum, in Christian Rosencreutz the Hermetic legacy, become a metaphysical spirituality, was taking a turn that would shape it for an American Protestant world.

Still more, it was taking a turn that would shape it for an American Enlightenment world in the age of the American Revolution and its aftermath. As Arthur Versluis has emphasized, the Rosicrucian vision moved beyond an explicitly Christian framework to espouse a nonsectarian and universalist spiritual culture, one that he has described by employing the seventeenth-century European term *pansophy*. Elaborating the Rosicrucian "dream" in words that point toward an American future, he notices Rosicrucian dedication to "the language of nature, written in the microcosm and in the macrocosm." Rosicrucian culture, he declares, was "founded on Kabbala and alchemy, that is, on a pansophic mysticism." As important for that American future, the pansophy that accompanied

Rosicrucian culture contained a strong sociopolitical program encompassing so-cial transformation and utopian expectation.[42] That it would flourish in America alongside and intermingling with an explicitly Christian theosophy—and a far more generalized evangelical Christianity—was testimony to the essential com-binativeness of Rosicrucian dreams and instantiations.

This is the place to turn to that more explicitly Christian theosophy in a north-ern European context, with an eye once again to its American future. Such Christian theosophy, as distinguished from Christian *theology* with its pursuit of rational and discursive knowledge of the divine, sought a knowledge of God that was direct and experiential, characterized by an intellectual luminescence that located it within the general wisdom culture of northern Europe. If we seek an individual as the major exponent of this version of Christianity, the voice that must be heard is that of Jacob Boehme (1575–1624), the near legendary shoemaker of Görlitz, Germany, whose work represents a striking and specu-lative synthesis of the mystical currents he encountered in his northern Euro-pean Protestant context. Boehme had read Paracelsus with attention to his al-chemy, and since Boehme did not know Latin, it was most probably through Paracelsus as well as through discussions with learned acquaintants that he absorbed elements of Hermeticism. He had also read Sebastian Franck (1499–1542), an Anabaptist spiritualizer who saw the true church as entirely spiritual; Caspar Schwenkfeld (1489–1561), a spiritualist who advocated withdrawal from sacramental participation in the churches; and Valentine Weigel (1533–1588), a Lutheran nature mystic who combined pantheism and Platonism. Boehme, however, was a man of direct experience. Awakened in the Lutheran Pietist movement that came to Görlitz with Martin Moller—a follower of Johann Arndt (1555–1621) whose *True Christianity* became a major impetus for the new seven-teenth-century devotionalism—Boehme himself was a visionary. With his own experience to guide him, he took the language of relationships and correspon-dences between things visible and invisible from mystics and astrologers, func-tioning as a conduit for Hermetic-Kabbalist themes into a Protestant world.[43]

Boehme's early work *Aurora* (1612) was sufficiently dubious from an orthodox Lutheran standpoint that it was banned by the local minister, even as Boehme was forbidden to engage in further writing. But Boehme's concern with the prob-lem of theodicy continued to pursue him. Seven years later—after a powerful illuminative experience—he began to write again, and before the end of his life he published twenty more treatises. There was *On the Three Principles of the Divine*, a work filled with alchemical speculation, and then, in 1620, *On the Three-Fold Life of Man*, *On the Incarnation*, *Six Theosophical Points*, and *Six Mystical Points*. Works continued to flow from his pen in quick succession, among them *Concerning the Birth and Designation of All Being, On Election to Grace*, and *Mysterium Magnum*, this last an extensive commentary on the biblical book of Genesis that Arthur Versluis has called "a kind of kabbalistic exegesis . . . in Christian theosophic terms." And there was a series of tracts collectively titled *The Way to Christosophia* that mixed speculation, devotion, and edifying discourse in ways that Peter Erb has read in the context of Lutheran theology. With their expansive and revelatory qualities, Boehme's writings continued to be deemed problematic, and the controversial shoemaker was for a brief period exiled. The contest and controversy, however, did not dampen his lasting influence, and his work, as we will see, carried weight in England and later in North America. "After Böhme," Arthur Versluis argues, "Christian theosophy takes on its most historically aware form, and far from being a forgotten province suitable only for scholars, in fact represents . . . an essential spiritual alternative within Christianity."[44]

Boehme's intricate exposition of the Christian trinity yielded a dialectical and progressive triad that modeled the path of the soul through its own transmutation and illumination. Here, as Ingrid Merkel has noted with special attention to the *Aurora*, the driving force for Boehme's work was a sense of "radical alienation," a preoccupation with the presence of fundamental conflict in the world. In the theological cosmology that Boehme constructed, there was literally no beginning—for nothing could not generate something. Instead, a radically transcendental Godhead called the *Ungrund*, or Abyss, in order to manifest itself brought itself "into a will," the familiar Father of the Christian Trinity, and its contrary or opposing principle—the desire that was the Son. Here were a fire-world and a light-world, respectively, a "wrath-spirit" and a "love-source," and their interrelationships produced a third Principle, the Holy Spirit. The dialectic continued in the divine production that was creation, with the Father's will conceiving in the mind (the Son) the new element of Wisdom—the heavenly Virgin Sophia who would in Christian theosophical circles become a personified mystical symbol and object of cultus. It was in the mirror of his Sophia, which stood before him, that God contemplated the seven "fountain-spirits" or qualities from which came the structure of the created world. Together these qualities, or at least the lowest ones among them, formed Eternal Nature, and together, too, they recapitulated the divine Triad, with the first four qualities as the First Principle (wrath), the next two the Second (love), and the last the Holy Spirit, the "magia" of the Godhead that manifested the Abyss in creation.[45]

Into the created world of pristine and delicately balanced energies, evil came through a rupture, or broken harmony, that was a by-product of the freedom of all beings of the Third Principle. It was the self-will, whether of the well-known

Lucifer of Christian theodicy or Boehme's androgynous Adam before the Fall, that wrought havoc in the original scheme. Adam, the ancestor of humanity, had possessed a perfect balance of fire and light and of male and female. After the Fall, these four elements were "awakened," and male and female parted ways. "Thereafter," Peter Erb has summarized, "human beings have chosen the fiery origin that, untempered by light, love, or the spiritual water of the new life, would destroy each individual human Being." But the outlines of the traditional Christian story, told in a new key, emerged to save and heal. "In his mercy, however, God fully revealed the light element in the New Man, Christ, in whose perfect balance each human being can once more live in harmony with the divine contemplation, the virgin Sophia." Here, at its highest (mystical) realization, was what Boehme often called the marriage of Sophia with the soul.[46]

The emanation cosmology of Boehme's writings came bearing echoes of earlier Neoplatonic, Gnostic, and Kabbalistic schemas and, of course, of clear elements culled from the generally Hermetic world. (Merkel, in fact, has located him in "Hermes' extended Renaissance family.") However, as in that world, the complex theodicy of the Boehmian synthesis, for all its intellectual elements, existed to advance a deeply practical program of spirituality. The progressive dynamic of the original dialectic, ending in the tragic-hopeful reading of the human situation, emphasized what for many became a vernacular and nonelite "path of the heart." It conveyed a radical pietism that disdained the orthodox scholasticism into which the Lutheran Reformation settled, and it concerned itself above all with what Versluis has called the "soul's nature, transmutation, and illumination"—its inward transformation by a new birth in Christ and its dialogue with Sophia, the accessible glory and presence of God.[47] It was practice, above all, that would commend Christian theosophy—as other sources of metaphysics—to its North American future.

ENGLISH ELITE TRANSFORMATIONS

LEARNING AND LITERATURE

If significant aspects of European Continental Hermeticism as well as pansophic (universalistic) and more explicitly Christian theosophy would make their way directly to early America, they would be carried by northern European immigrants who brought them along with their Protestant ways. But another, perhaps more obvious, route to North America passed through England, for the British North Atlantic colonies inherited the literature and practice of old England in things metaphysical alongside everything else. Hermeticism crossed the

English Channel, together with its early modern accoutrements of Paracelsian and, later, Rosicrucian lore, and the amalgam kept company in elite circles and even among royal courtiers in the Elizabethan age. In an England in which the Puritan movement was growing, Frances Yates could still argue that the "dominant philosophy of the Elizabethan age was precisely the occult philosophy, with its magic, its melancholy, its aim of penetrating into profound spheres of knowledge and experience, scientific and spiritual, its fear of the dangers of such a quest, and of the fierce opposition which it encountered."[48] Indeed, at a time when on the Continent the Counter-Reformation was generating suspicion and hostility toward the Renaissance with its Neoplatonic and Hermetic tendencies, England looked strikingly different. There a flourishing Elizabethan Renaissance brought mystical and metaphysical themes, for a time, into prominence and even fashion, although, to be sure, they were always an elite undercurrent in essentially Protestantizing times. For these themes, we look especially to John Dee (1527–1608/9) and his younger contemporary Robert Fludd (1574–1637).

The mathematician John Dee was also a Paracelsian, and he earned a reputation in his own time and thereafter as a practitioner of the occult arts. Son of an official at the court of Henry VIII, he received a Cambridge education but later found himself accused of using sorcery against Queen Mary I—a charge from which he was acquitted to become a court favorite of Mary's half-sister Elizabeth I. We are told that he also prepared geographical and hydrographical data for her on the new territories that were being discovered across the seas and that he helped to ready England for the Gregorian calendar. Both the literary sources from which he drew and the mystical leanings of his mathematics are signaled in the preface that Dee wrote for Henry Billingsley's English translation, in 1570, of the work of Euclid. Here Dee managed to invoke the "Divine Plato" and to emphasize the significance of number in ways that evoked the German Cornelius Agrippa, in fact building his preface to the Euclid translation squarely on Agrippa's three worlds.

Dee understood mathematics in ways that were at once both practical and mystical, and his Hermeticism, in a familiar pattern, incorporated Kabbalistic themes. It also flowed naturally into astrology (he advised Queen Elizabeth and courtiers on these matters, and in 1558 he was consulted on the best date for her coronation). More than that, his Hermeticism was related to alchemical theory and practice. Attached to the Dee library, which William Sherman calls "his country's largest collection of books and manuscripts," were three laboratories for alchemy, even as the alchemy books in the library were the "most consistently annotated collection."[49] Dee's interest in alchemy had drawn him into close relationship with one Edward Kelley, who was rumored to have discovered the secret of transmuting baser metals into gold. Kelley likewise worked with Dee to call or conjure angels in a Kabbalistic vein. From 1583 to 1589, the two men practiced a Christianized angel magic together on the Continent—in Bohemia, in Cracow, and later in Prague, where Rudolf II reigned as emperor and strongly favored the occult arts at his court. Dee used the work of Cornelius Agrippa—with its elaborate instructions for angel-summoning—in his attempts, and Kelley, his medium, was also well read in Agrippa. Dee himself reportedly spent over thirty years trying to converse with angels, perhaps because, as György Szönyi has argued, he lost faith in the ability of the human sciences to answer ultimate questions about the universe. Dee thus needed to learn the language of the angels. According to Szönyi, this was "Dee's goal," and it led him "to conjure up celestial beings daily in the endless sessions of his so-called 'Enochian magic.'"[50]

By a half century after Dee's death, the angel-summoning began to erode his reputation when Meric Casaubon in 1659 published portions of Dee's spiritual diaries with a long premonitory preface declaring the text to be "deemed and termed *A Work of Darkness.*" Dee's stature waxed and waned in the context of religious conflict in the era of Britain's seventeenth-century civil wars and its Puritan interlude. As important, the "wise doctor," as he was called by contemporaries, has continued to intrigue scholars into our own time. Frances Yates in the 1960s read him as a Renaissance magus, and she saw his cultural tracks in high places, in literary circles, and in Continental Rosicrucianism—in ways that gave him a formative role in the mystical "brotherhood." Peter French, who worked with Yates, in his book-length biography of Dee understood him in similar terms.[51]

More recent scholarship has seriously questioned this reading, pointing instead to a Dee who was a far more complex figure. Nicholas Clulee, for example, has historicized the stylized portrait of Dee that emerged from the Yatesians. He has pointed to the changing nature of Dee's ideas, seeing the early Dee as more a medievalist and an Aristotelian and the later one as more drawn to Neoplatonism and Renaissance magic. Emphasizing medieval sources throughout, Clulee has located Dee's natural philosophy in a complex middle place in which magic, religion, and angels are linked seamlessly with a desire for knowledge of the natural world. William Sherman, in turn, has called Yates's story of Dee as a magus a "myth"—"an interpretive strategy imposed on Dee"—even as he has declared that neglected sources "cast serious doubts on the packaging of Dee as—exclusively or even primarily—a Hermetic, Neoplatonic magus." Sherman has gone on to argue that, in the case of Dee, humanism and Hermeticism were far from being the polar opposites that the Yatesian school had made them. "While Dee's activities were delimited by his socio-economic possibilities," he says, "the two motives—courtly or commercial service and the knowledge of nature—were far from exclusive." Later work has continued to emphasize the complexity of Dee's character and activity as well as the confluence of science, philosophy, and religion in the Elizabethan world in which Dee flourished.[52]

The Dee of recent scholarship is a convincing figure, and his nuanced relationship to Hermeticism in the context of the science and philosophy of his day calls attention to a combinativeness that looks thoroughly familiar in later American terms. Theory and practice mingled consistently in Dee's life and work, even as the urge to synthesize followed him throughout his long career. And although the evidence for any personal connection with Rosicrucianism is flimsy—Sherman calls it "tenuous (at best)"—Dee's work provided, in Sherman's words, "a significant textual impetus" to would-be Rosicrucians.[53] By contrast to the purely textual nature of Dee's Rosicrucianism, however, there was nothing tenuous about the Rosicrucian interest of Robert Fludd, born nearly a half century later than Dee. Fludd's first printed works, published on the Continent in 1616 and 1617 respectively, came as a defense of the Rosicrucians in the wake of the appearance of their manifestos.[54] Produced at a time when the Rosicrucian excitement was beginning to die down in Germany itself in the context of the Thirty Years' War (1618–1648), his writings reflect his personal interest as well as a continuing English interest in Rosicrucian themes. Indeed, a series of works that Fludd produced until 1633 kept on valorizing Rosicrucians. It is evident that he admired the Rosicrucian literature, but with no actual brotherhood to join, as William H. Huffman has argued, it is problematic to call him a Rosicrucian. Perturbed by Rosicrucian nonappearance (even though he himself believed that the fraternity was real), Fludd chose to call his work "Fluddean" and then—signaling his allegiance to Christianity—the "Mosaicall Philosophy."[55] In fact, what these labels suggest is that the strongest reason for Fludd's defense of Rosicrucians lay in the ideas in Rosicrucian literature that were already his own.[56]

Fludd was decidedly a cultural and social "insider." Huffman has conspicuously noted Fludd's status as "an establishment member of conventional society; a man of noble descent, wealthy son of a knight, Oxford-educated, member of the College of Physicians of London and successful physician, with English kings as his patrons, sometime tutor to and friend of high nobility and clergy as well as contemporary physicians, patentee to make steel, from his own invention, in England." Yet the "Mosaicall Philosophy," as I have already suggested, was hardly divorced from the Hermetic themes that the Rosicrucian label signaled in its mystical Christian context. If Fludd was a physician, he was also a Paracelsian physician who, before he finally passed his examinations from the College of

Physicians, failed several times over because of his non-Galenic beliefs. If he had been educated at Oxford, he had also learned on the Continent. He wanted to put his worlds together, and as a mystical philosopher and alchemist, he sought to reconcile his Paracelsian learning with the new science that was percolating through elite circles in seventeenth-century England. He was also and not surprisingly influenced by the Christian Kabbalah.[57] His huge volumes *Utriusque cosmi historia* (History of the Two Worlds)—published on the Continent beginning in 1617 to probe the theme of universal harmony—concerned, as part of the translated title indicates, the "Great World of the Macrocosm and the Little World of Man, the Microcosm." The language, of course, immediately evokes Paracelsian categories.

Like Paracelsus, too, in his early work Fludd sought to show the connections between physical and spiritual truth, arguing for God as a pervading presence, or form, in humans and the world. He wanted chemistry and theology kept together, believing that alchemy was, in the words of Christopher McIntosh, "a deep well of divine truth," and his famous debate with the French scientist and theologian Marin Mersenne argued on the side of a mystical alchemy in touch with both worlds. Indeed, as G. J. Gibbons has maintained regarding Fludd, "The transmutation of souls rather than metals was the philosopher's true goal, but the alchemical process was nevertheless a metallurgical reality."[58]

Fludd was a friend of William Harvey—renowned in medical history for his discovery of the circulation of the blood—and Harvey's work corroborated the macrocosmic and microcosmic parallels so important to Paracelsian learning. Thus the "sun" and the "heart" were central for both Harvey and Fludd, and Gibbons declares that for Fludd the linkage of the terms was "no mere figure of speech." The human body, with its heart in the center, reflected the universe, with the sun in the center—in a solar mysticism that achieved noticeable seventeenth-century popularity. But Fludd also stood in the shadow of John Dee and the general combinative metaphysical learning that had come to England from the Continent. The conflictual themes that could be found in the work of Jacob Boehme, roughly Fludd's contemporary, for example, could also be discovered in Fludd's own cosmology, and similar echoes of Kabbalism characterized him. In the case of Fludd, God existed as a divine "Nolunty" and "Volunty." Here, as Huffman explains, "the first of these is defined as remaining in potentiality, or not willing (nilling), reserving itself within itself, and is expressed by darkness and privation (Dark Aleph); and the second is the willing, or acting of God, represented by the outpouring of life-giving, and sustaining, light (Light Aleph)." The Hebrew letter *aleph* pointed to the Kabbalah and to the wisdom of Moses at once, in a Fluddean grand synthesis in which the creation contained elements of darkness and light and in which evil and good were in conflict until their resolution in time was complete.[59]

For Fludd as for the tradition of Renaissance Neoplatonic Hermeticism in which he stood, cosmology, following the law of correspondences, established a *practical* anthropology. In a formulation that echoed Francesco Giorgi and Cornelius Agrippa, he understood creation in terms of three worlds, here comprised of different mixes of light and darkness. The highest world, with light that exceeded darkness, was the empyrean or heaven; the middle world, or ethereal world, contained equal parts of light and dark compounded into what was known as the ether; the third, or elemental, world held more darkness than light, and from it came the familiar four states of matter—fire, gas, liquid, and solid substance. Thus from the vast expanses of the starry skies Fludd returned to the human project, which he envisioned as a return to the divine source of the self. Shrinking from the high magic of the Renaissance Hermeticists (he was content with simpler alchemical experiments), he proposed a similar path of interiority, counseling a return "unto thy self," a "diving into thy inward treasure" in order to be made one spirit with God "by which thou shalt be glorified and exalted." There, in the interior regions, one would discover all the others: "Thus, I say, wilt thou know, that each man is thy brother, and that thy brother is a part of thy self."[60]

We have here a series of revolving doors leading from the Continent to England to the Continent and back to England. And we have in Robert Fludd an important voice for the transmission, in elite form, of the ideational complex that would ground American metaphysical religion with its themes of interiority and yet human and universal connection. Indeed, Fludd's volumes, with their elaborate copper-plate engravings that summarized highly complex formulations in succinct diagrams, provided a relatively accessible form by which to convey his grand synthesis of the Christian Hermeticism of an earlier era.[61] When Frances Yates concluded that Fludd, and before him Dee, were "entitled to be called Renaissance philosophers, representing a delayed infiltration into England of the Hermetic tradition in particularly potent forms," she clarified major lines of discourse that, through key literary translations, would deeply affect the American inheritance. There is not space here to enter into the specifics of Yates's argument regarding the cultural trail of English Hermeticism or what she herself often termed Rosicrucianism—this in what Huffman calls "a historically cultural sense, to stand for the Renaissance Christian Hermetic-Cabalist-Alchemical school of thought which ended in the seventeenth century." Yet it would be hard to imagine that writings such as those of Dee, Fludd, and their fellow travelers would leave no imprint on the literary life of their nation. Figures like Edmund Spencer, Christopher Marlowe, William Shakespeare, and the Puritan John Milton wrote in neither an intellectual nor cultural nor social vacuum, and it would be difficult to argue that themes in the Hermetic air found no echoes in their work.[62]

We need not accept all of the intricacies in Yates's complex reading of the presence of Hermeticism in Elizabethan and seventeenth-century England to understand the message of combination between Hermetic and, especially, Puritan categories in ways that are evocative for American metaphysical religion. If we look for resemblances and connections, the metaphysical sympathies of New England Puritans and even of Continental European immigrants to the other British North Atlantic colonies become less curious and more historically grounded. Surely not every New Englander had heard of John Dee or Robert Fludd, and—even with New England's high literacy rate—most Anglo-Americans had probably not delved deeply into English literary classics. But elite discourse never could be hermetically (if readers will pardon the pun) sealed from vernacular culture. Ideas succeed and continue by attaching to other ideas, they are made manifest in odd sites and unexpected places, and so the process of cultural conversation continues.

COSMOLOGICAL SPECULATIONS

Still another elite route carried the metaphysical inheritance of Europe to Anglo-America from Elizabethan England. Based on familiar ideas of macrocosm and microcosm, a general cosmological consensus among the learned applied its model to the planet, to the universe as a whole, and, at the other end of the scale, in humoral theory to the human body. According to the basic terrestrial scheme taught by ancient Greek philosophy and science, the material composition of the earth could be understood in terms of the complex relationships between four elements—earth, water, air, and fire—and four qualities—cold, hot, dry, and moist. In this view, the elements combined with the qualities in every part of the material world. Thus earth was cold and dry, while water was cold and moist. Air was hot and moist, and fire was hot and dry. What differentiated terrestrial substances from one another was the proportional representation of the elements and qualities. Earth was the lowest and grossest element, and fire the purest and highest—judgments that would not be lost on evolving metaphysical symbol systems. On terrestrial ground, the material substance of the earth existed, for learned Elizabethans, in the context of these four elements and related qualities.

For the universe beyond our planet, however, in an understanding that was essentially Ptolemaic, there was an unchanging fifth element or "quintessence."

Here the earth was still a fixed body at the center of a universe in which the planets of our solar system, along with the sun and the moon, revolved around earth, each in a crystalline sphere of its own. These spheres were encased within one another, like the complex mechanism of a clock, and as they moved they played the memorable "music of the spheres." Beyond these came the sphere of the fixed stars and finally that of the *primum mobile*—literally, the "first moving thing"—which carried all of the other spheres and imparted motion to them. The quintessence, the highest of the elements, permeated all nature, and it was of this substance that the heavenly bodies were composed. Within this orderly universe with its crystalline music and its mysteries of number and proportion, astrology provided a guide to the course of the heavens and the relations of humans to the stars.

Meanwhile, within the microcosm of the human body, the four terrestrial elements became the four humors inherited from the Greeks, with again a related set of four qualities. So there was the sanguine humor of the blood, which was hot and moist like air, and the choleric humor, or yellow bile, which was hot and dry like fire. There was the melancholic humor (black bile), cold and dry like earth, even as the phlegmatic humor was cold and moist like water. Moreover, just as other earthly substances were composed of different proportions of the elements, so were humans. Hence the differences among basic human "constitutions" could be explained to Elizabethan satisfaction, and so could the body's disorders and diseases—situations occasioned when harmonial proportions were disturbed and one element became too overbearing or deficient. Likewise, different character types and personalities could be read in terms of the humors: the cheerful, or sanguine, person boasted a predominance of the blood, while the melancholic individual was ruled by black bile. A lazy person was one in whom the phlegmatic humor dominated, and someone who could be called a "hothead" had been generously bestowed with yellow bile—he or she was "choleric."[63]

In a cosmology of resonances and replications, even though the heavenly bodies were formed of the quintessence, astrology could understand them in terms of "signs" that connected them to the four terrestrial elements, to earth, air, water, and fire. Some stars were earth signs and some air signs; some were identified with water and some with fire. Similarly, there were mysterious connections between the stars and the humors that governed individual human bodies, with different stars ruling each of the humors. The stars were the arbiters, too, of time. With a universe in which nothing was without significance and in which spheres resided compactly within other spheres, correspondences were key. So each moment in time possessed its correspondences. Time, in effect, had been spatialized with the crystalline spheres. Each different instant possessed a quality that it shared with the momentary configuration and disposition of bodies in space, resonating with the kind and condition of energy that was pulsing through.

For astrologers, then, the stars became cosmic clues, and in the Elizabethan world their science was still divided into the two branches called natural and judicial astrology. Natural astrology studied the relationship between the stars and events in the natural world, most notably issues like the weather and health matters. There were, literally, "signs of the times," and there were good and bad days for different agrarian activities like planting and harvesting—in a society that was predominately agricultural and counted on the cooperation of the weather. There were also good and bad days for certain forms of bodily activity, be it conceiving a child or healing a disease. More problematic from a Christian theological perspective, judicial astrology explored the relationships between the stars and the destiny of individuals. With its challenge to the doctrine of free will, this form of astrology also implicitly undercut the providence of God. Still, in the Elizabethan and seventeenth-century English world, astrologers were kept busy with predictions and prognostications, as they later would be in the British North Atlantic colonies. Among them, Ptolemy's *Tetrabiblos* still was recognizable as the master text and template. But English astrological publications abounded, with a peak near the end of the sixteenth century, a lull in the twenty years preceding the Civil War, and then, according to Keith Thomas, an "unprecedented torrent" until the seventeenth century wound down. With John Dee at the English court as a visible model, astrology held its own among intellectuals as a topic of "consuming interest," as Thomas noted. "A random list of sympathisers could include such celebrated names as those of Sir Walter Raleigh, Robert Burton, the Anatomist, Lord Herbert of Cherbury, Sir Kenelm Digby and Sir Thomas Browne."[64]

Regarding the earth itself, Elizabethan learning had inherited ideas from the ancient Greeks about three kinds of souls—a vegetative soul for plants connected with fertility and growth, a sensitive soul for animals that added to these qualities those of sensation and motion, and a rational soul for humans that capped the powers of the former two with intellect, or reason. The space between the humorally based body and the immaterial soul was bridged by what the Elizabethans called the spirits—"substances" that existed in a half-world between matter and nonmatter and that were variously identified according to their respective functions. Herbert Leventhal succinctly summarized them: "The natural spirits, which were generated in the liver from the blood, flowed through the veins carrying out the vegetative functions of life and growth. In the heart, some of these were transformed into the vital spirits which traveled in the arteries and maintained the body's heat. In the head, some of these in turn were themselves transformed into animal spirits. These linked body to soul, and traveling through the nerves carried the impulses of the rational soul to the material body." As the English metaphysical poet and cleric John Donne (1572–1631) related, "As our blood labours to beget / Spirits, as like soules as it can, / Because such fingers need to knit / That subtile knot, which makes us man."[65]

INSTITUTIONAL MANIFESTATIONS

The various spirits inhabiting this metaphysical underworld already suggest one leitmotiv that would achieve a noticeable prominence in American meta-physical religion—a fascination with the mechanisms of connection between matter and what was conceived to lie beyond it. This fascination was articulated, of course, in what became the conventional terms of, for example, Cartesian phi-losophy. But for metaphysicians other ideas and sources offered more potent ex-planations—at various times in terms of received Gnostic and Kabbalistic specu-lation about emanations from a Godhead or an epistemology of the ether or a later epistemology of the quantum. If such speculations tease, there was also an-other, institutional story to be told about the Hermetic-Kabbalistic synthesis in Elizabethan, and here especially, seventeenth-century England. Beyond litera-ture and cosmology, by the first half of the seventeenth century there were clear references to a secret society that embodied the metaphysical program. That was Freemasonry.

The speculative Freemasonry that characterized the English—and later American—Masonic lodges had its roots in the guilds of medieval craft masons, "operative" masons who represented a different social class from the "gentlemen" who inhabited the Anglophile lodges. These operative masons had laid the stone to build the great European cathedrals and had already thereby achieved a cer-tain social status. It is true, too, as Antoine Faivre has noted, that certain elements of their fellowship pointed in the direction of later speculative Masonry. Already in the Middle Ages the masons accepted nonpractitioners into their brother-hood; and guild apprentices likewise had to follow a set of spiritual and moral directives beyond their technological knowledge. The two Saint Johns, who fig-ured at the center of later Freemasonic ritual, were their patrons. More than that, as Faivre also reminds readers, the cathedrals that the masons built trans-mitted "a system of symbolic and cosmic values," and they followed "the law of numbers and signs" as the "concrete expression of God's thought." Still, these masons worked with their hands and could not be described as members of an elite, unlike the English lodge brothers who would later reconstitute the guilds into something other. More than that, English "speculation" consisted in an elaborated set of mystical and ethical meanings that took the encoded Hermetic-Kabbalistic legacy of medieval masons in transforming and, especially, Protestantizing directions. The English lodges, as *speculative* societies, constructed symbolic meanings based on the building trade into moral and mystical edifices of their own. They elaborated the ritual dimension of the guilds of the past in ever-aggrandizing ways, and at the same time they promoted the advancement of a nascent science. Above all, as Frances Yates argued, they were *secret* societies, and the model she suggested for their secrecy was the (legendary) Rosicrucian order.[66]

Indeed, the first known reference in an English context hints of the same. In a poem that was published in 1638 in Edinburgh, we read: "For what we do presage is not in grosse, / For we be brethren of the Rosie Crosse: / We have the *Mason word* and second sight, / Things for to come we can foretell aright."[67] These prognosticators of the future word had apparently formally organized themselves in Edinburgh at least by 1641. In that year Robert Moray, who later played a prominent role in the establishment by Charles II of the Royal Society of London (Britain's earliest scientific organization), joined an Edinburgh Masonic lodge. Five years later, in 1646, Elias Ashmole (1617–1692), who would figure significantly in Freemasonry, joined an already existing lodge at Warrington in Lancashire. Ashmole, like Moray, would become a charter member of the Royal Society. Moreover, Ashmole, who revered John Dee as magus and teacher, could be clearly identified with Rosicrucianism. He was, in fact, so intensely interested that he copied out by hand English translations of the *Fama* and *Confessio*, adding to these a letter of petition to the "most illuminated Brothers of the Rose Cross" asking to join their society.[68] We need not follow Frances Yates down a long path of speculation regarding Freemasonry as a kind of anglicized Rosicrucianism to notice that Elias Ashmole and the other gentlemen of the Royal Society were also often alchemists and astrologers and that within Freemasonic lodges Hermetic learning, under new guises, was still followed and revered.

Nor did such understandings—unified, coherent, part of a grand religiophilosophical synthesis among the learned—remain segregated from the rest of society. As the general cosmological speculations of Elizabethans and seventeenth-century English people already suggest, metaphysical understandings fanned out from elite culture to what may be called the vernacular. Here, as in this book's introduction, I refer to a common culture shared by elites and ordinary people, a kind of cultural lingua franca that everyone in a given societal matrix knew and used. And if we can separate out from this vernacular that which some historians and social commentators call (somewhat problematically) popular culture—as the culture specifically of the nonelite, the "ordinary," the "folk"—then these understandings percolated into this cultural world as well. One historiographical story that can be told regarding the inherited synthesis and its practical ramifications is that of change and disjuncture between elite and "popular." Leventhal's work, for example, has emphasized the pulling apart of these worlds in the eighteenth century, especially in America, and it has underscored the continuance of ideas that became discredited among elites in a distinctly "underculture" register. In this reading, the vernacular—as a kind of in-between world—responded ambiguously, demonstrating a tolerance for carrying some of the old synthesis but also a decline in its authority and influence. Meanwhile, Leventhal's narrative resonates, too, with Jon Butler's reading of the "folklorization" of the occult in eighteenth-century America.[69] For American metaphysical religion, however, as I will show, the transformation was more complex. Not quite a "folklorized" religion and, moreover, a congeries of speculation and practice amply expressed by rising middle classes and elites, American metaphysical religion would develop a vernacular of its own, distinct from the public Christian language of the times. The English heritage—both literary and vernacular—would be enormously important to the emergent metaphysical synthesis in America. So would a Continental vernacular. For these reasons, we look briefly at vernacular culture on the Continent and in England.

VERNACULAR CULTURE ON THE CONTINENT AND IN ENGLAND

We gain a tantalizing glimpse of how pervasive Hermetic knowledge was in Continental vernacular culture in the fifteenth-century figure of Giovanni ("Mercurio" by at least 1482) da Correggio, whom Wouter J. Hanegraaff has called a "hermetic Christ." Correggio first came to public notice as an enigmatic apocalyptic prophet when he appeared at the steps of the papal palace in Rome in 1481 with a huge symbolically inscribed Bible and a call to repentance for all who entered. Three years later on Palm Sunday, Correggio rode ceremoniously through the streets of Rome with two servants walking ahead of him and two behind. Then, leaving the city, he removed the rich garments he had been wearing and draped himself instead with a linen mantle stained with blood. He placed on his head a crown of thorns, on top of which was an inscribed silver crescent moon declaring, as part of a longer Hermetic-Christian message, "This is my Servant Pimander, whom I have chosen." Correggio, we are told, accoutred himself again with mystically symbolic paraphernalia and climbed on the back of a white ass, wherefrom he delivered a speech in which he claimed to be the "Angel of Wisdom, Pimander, in the highest and greatest ecstasy of the

Spirit of Jesus Christ." Eventually he progressed to St. Peter's, where, as one account reported, he made his way to the high altar and left his mystical apparel as an offering, though this is uncertain. Later, in 1486, Correggio appeared in Florence and afterward in Lyons and other cities, blending Hermetic and Christic prophecies and messages and, as time passed, stressing more and more his prowess as a master of alchemy and natural magic.[70]

"Mercurio is of interest to the historian," Antoine Faivre notes, as providing "evidence for the vogue of Hermetism among the common people." Is this too affirmative a statement? Correggio himself could surely read and write: he distributed excerpts from his sermons in at least some instances, and he also printed longer texts.[71] Moreover, his performance assumed a widespread acquaintance with Hermetic texts — texts that were seen as thoroughly compatible with Christianity and, indeed, blended seamlessly with it. But texts have oral as well as written lives, and Correggio's performance drew on symbolic elements that appealed visually and assumed a vernacular resonance. Otherwise, the drama would have carried little, if any, weight as a call to religious transformation, and Correggio's performance — as a performance — would have failed. In this context, the snapshot provided by Correggio's story suggests a world in which symbols and texts were shared and, though better known by some than others, were available to a broad enough audience to be labeled vernacular.

The Hermetic synthesis influenced vernacular culture less spectacularly but surely more pervasively through art and architecture incorporating and inscribing Hermetic themes. Faivre, for example, has pointed to the "explicitly Hermetic art" of the Renaissance, embodied in the Florentine painter Sandro Botticelli's *Primavera*, a work that he painted in 1478, just seven years after the Latin translation of the *Corpus Hermeticum* appeared. By the following decade, an unidentified artist was putting in place the striking tiles on the floor of the cathedral in Siena. There Hermes Trismegistus was portrayed as an old and bearded sage, adorned in robe, cape, and miter. Surrounded by other personages, evidently admiring, Hermes was also accompanied by an inscription that Faivre calls "very typical": it announced in Latin, "Hermes Trismegistus, contemporary of Moses." Later Alexander VI, the Borgia (family) pope who was himself intensely interested in magic and astrology, had a huge fresco painted in the Vatican's Borgia apartments by the Umbrian artist Pinturicchio (Bernardino di Betto). The work was saturated with Hermetic symbols and astrological signs, and in it Hermes Trismegistus was depicted alongside Moses and Isis.[72]

Numbers of medieval cathedrals were filled with Hermetic signs. The floor of the great cathedral of Palermo, which was once a Muslim mosque, for one example, still contains — on a diagonal vector — a series of astrological signs said to be placed on the earth's "ley lines." A modern-day tour of France or Italy incorporates visits to any number of other cathedrals with the Hermetic mystical emblems inscribed on choir chairs or carved into stonework or frozen into stained glass. As these so tellingly show, the mystical metaphysical complex that would eventually make its way to America was hardly news in vernacular culture. Medieval cathedrals, with material representations that were connected to Hermetic lore, already incorporated these themes and taught them. Later, during the Renaissance and its aftermath, the Hermetic symbology of the sacred continued to be displayed, and the teaching endured. Set alongside traditional Christian symbols, the Hermetic signs presented a theological and devotional challenge. But if a few recognized the points of disjuncture and conflict, mostly—in these public places of piety and sacred learning—the two worlds stood in quiet combination. Cognitively dissonant they might have been for official church teaching; practically consonant they were.

We can measure the pervasiveness of the Hermetic-Kabbalistic complex and its privileging of natural and pagan themes in still another way. We can examine, however briefly, the hostility and anger it provoked, glancing at the measures that the official church and state authorities of the times took to quash it. Frances Yates, of course, devoted an entire work to the world of Giordano Bruno (1548–1600) and emphasized the inescapably religious character of his philosophy and its implications for theology and discipline.[73] The spectacle of his Roman execution by being burned to death after imprisonment was surely meant to teach a counter-lesson about the mystical metaphysics of Hermes and fellow travelers to both elites and ordinary people. Other and similar trials leap from the historical record as reminders that negative learning was readily employed to halt and dampen a positive belief system deemed by authorities to be already too widespread. Consider, for example, the earlier fourteenth-century "heretics" memorialized by Emmanuel Le Roy Ladurie in his classic *Montaillou*. There Pierre Maury, a shepherd, and Pierre Clerge, the village priest, languished in prison after their respective interrogations by the Inquisition in the small village in the Pyrenees of southern France. Followers of Albigensianism or Catharism, a form of Gnostic belief and practice, they and other assenting villagers provided culturally embedded evidence for an alternate spirituality unendorsed by the official church.[74]

Meanwhile, Inquisitorial depositions, in general, have supplied enough material to support a small cottage industry among historians of "popular" culture who seek to discover the common tenor of life and belief by determining what the Inquisition wanted to stamp out. Roughly two centuries after the Albigensian Pierres, for instance, there was Domenico Scandella, more commonly known as Menocchio, who would be remembered in our time because of the historical excavations of Carlo Ginzburg in the archives of the Inquisition. A sixteenth-century miller from the hill town of Montereale in the Friuli, Menocchio was hauled before local representatives of the Roman Inquisition in 1584 because of his theological ruminations. An apparent autodidact, Menocchio had shared with too many others his cosmological conclusions. "In my opinion," he told his interrogators, "all was chaos, that is, earth, air, water, and fire were mixed together; and out of that bulk a mass formed—just as cheese is made out of milk—and worms appeared in it, and these were the angels." Combining the ancient Greek elements with simple agrarian experience, he went on to incorporate what seemed an oblique Gnostic allusion. "Among that number of angels," he added to his testimony, "there was also God, he too having been created out of that mass at the same time, and he was made lord, with four captains, Lucifer, Michael, Gabriel, and Raphael." Menocchio, not exactly a nobody (he had been mayor of his town and likewise administrator of the local parish church), had expressed his own version of the vernacular. He went to prison for two years for his candor with Inquisitors, and then, after he successfully obtained a release, again grew careless with his tongue. When he was rearrested in 1599, he told the Inquisitors that he was "a philosopher, astrologer, and prophet." Menocchio was burned at the stake the same year, even as Giordano Bruno was en route to Rome and his own public and fiery end.[75]

If Ginzburg's work provides a window into a vernacular culture in which ideas that resonated with the Hermetic legacy were alive and well, he and other historians have led us into a mostly rural world in which less self-consciously and philosophically inflected forms of metaphysics flourished as practical enterprises. Stephen Wilson, for example, in his compendious *Magical Universe*, has immersed readers in a premodern European culture of "sympathies" that linked occult and metaphysical meanings to a seemingly endless catalog of practices—concerning land, livestock, and work; calendar and weather; fertility, marriage, and family; health and healing; and life and death. Ostensibly everywhere throughout this European landscape there were divinatory signs, even as spirits and occultly significant animals abounded and words and gestures possessed power to help or harm. Magical practices borrowed from church rituals and sometimes became part of them. They pointed to a domain of protection in an unpredictable and often hostile and dangerous society.[76] They also pointed toward an implicit vernacular theory of connection and correspondence between micro and macro aspects of natural and social worlds.

If we return to Carlo Ginzburg, we can enter the Friulian world again, this time of the seventeenth as well as the sixteenth century—a meeting place for

German, Italian, and Slavic culture and a place that still kept touch with the fertility cultus of an earlier Europe. Here the *benandanti* or "good walkers," members of a ritual organization who had all been born with a caul, practiced their trance sleep on designated nights of the year. In what religious studies scholars might call shamanic endeavors, their souls departed temporarily from their bodies, sometimes in animal form. Thereupon the good walkers used stalks of fennel to engage in what many agreed were night battles with evil witches, also male, in order to safeguard the harvest. The good walkers likewise had reputations for healing the sick, and they engaged in other practices of magical benevolence. When the Inquisition began to question their activities from the 1570s to 1640s, the judicial representatives of the official church categorized them as witches and demanded their confessions of participation in diabolical sabbath rituals. The *benandanti*, in other words, got reclassified as witches (and actually came to be transformed in that direction under Inquisitorial pressures); for the Inquisition, they became perpetrators of evil in a dualistic universe in which God and Satan warred and God finally triumphed.[77]

Ginzburg's good walkers, transmogrified into demonic witches, received Inquisitorial notice in the continuing context of a European "witchcraft" epidemic. Indeed, official persecution of witchcraft constituted probably the strongest evidence of a widespread metaphysical overlay in vernacular culture. Here much of the official venom was directed not at male "witches" like the *benandanti* but at women. The classic text that underwrote the misogynist venom was the notorious *Malleus Maleficarum* (in English, *The Witch's Hammer*), the work, apparently, of two Dominican monks, Johann Sprenger and Heinrich Kraemer, who were Inquisitors in the service of Pope Innocent VIII in northern Germany and in Rhineland territories. Published between 1487 and 1489, with an academic endorsement from the faculty of theology at the University of Cologne (obtained with some pressure), the text was printed ten times before 1669. Before another century was out, it appeared in nine further editions. In three sections, it respectively endeavored to prove that witchcraft existed, to categorize different kinds of witches and establish the marks by which they could be identified, and to explain the legalities of examining and sentencing them. Yet as Gregory Zilboorg observed, the text was hardly cold and legalistic but rather "polemical, argumentative, scornful or threatening in tone, and uncompromising."[78]

Such a literary presentation, the success of its publishing history, and the related and sustained waves of witchcraft persecution, of course, argue for widespread agreement with the authors of the *Malleus* about the witchcraft threat. Witches must have seemed, to churchly contemporaries, to be practically everywhere. And perhaps they were. The perception, of course, hinged on who or what got defined, respectively, as witch or witchcraft. But that exercise itself suggests the combinative habit of medieval and early modern churchmen and laity, and it points the way to remote sources for an American metaphysics. For one thing, because witchcraft was widely perceived as a female enterprise—in a strongly authoritarian and patriarchal culture—it was doubly suspect. Indeed, in the philological understanding that controlled the authors of the *Malleus*, the word *femina* (Latin for "woman") originated from the root words *fe* and *minus*, inscribing in language the deficiency—the minus status—of women. "It should be noted," declared the *Malleus*, "that there was a defect in the formation of the first woman, since she was formed from a bent rib, that is, a rib of the breast, which is bent as it were in a contrary direction to a man. And since through this defect she is an imperfect animal, she always deceives." Even more, women represented the epitome of sexual threat and transgressive lure: "What else is woman but a foe to friendship, an unescapable punishment, a necessary evil, a natural temptation, a desirable calamity, a domestic danger, a delectable detriment, an evil of nature, painted with fair colours!" Women, for the authors of the *Malleus*, as Zilboorg summarized, were "inferior by nature, lying, vicious, and hopelessly impure," and they were "naturally the most serviceable and most willing tool of the devil."[79]

If we pursue this last (the "hopelessly impure" character of women), we come up against the obsessive antieroticism of the *Malleus*, an antieroticism found nearly everywhere in the document. Moreover, if the antieroticism is followed down its imagistic and metaphorical trail, it leads to considerations of the sexuality of nature in general—in other words, to themes of fertility. Women and the devil were already apparently in league; but beneath their alliance lay the natural powers of land and agriculture, a different image of women, and a connection to the religion of the land, to the paganism of early and tribal Europe, and to the high paganism of the Greco-Roman world. If Carlo Ginzburg's *benandanti* were any clue, the discredited anthropological thesis of Margaret Murray from the 1920s, linking witchcraft to ancient fertility cultuses, contains an element that, many have thought, requires more historical consideration. In the present historical climate, in which feminist concerns rank high, new studies of medieval and early modern witchcraft in western Europe are making links and connections that earlier works eschewed.[80]

Without attempting to enter into the substance of this research in any detail, suffice it to say that in the cultural linkages—witch, woman, devil, sex, fertility, nature, supernature, death—we have, in some ways, readings of witchcraft that illuminate its resonances with the Hermetica, the strongest difference being that the cosmic message of human capacity for godhood is muted or missing. Still, vernacular culture had its own independent sources of a wisdom that was suspect and transgressive. Within these sources, as we have already to some extent seen, the old theory of correspondence reigned supreme—inflected in a new key with woman ensconced beside nature, sex, and the devil. In terms of cultural practice, what the literature shows—as Wilson's *Magical Universe* has suggested—is that myriads of local worlds dotted the European landscape.[81] These were worlds in which women often functioned as suppliers for social need. Here women (and, less frequently, men) worked for a large part in ways that were considered beneficent, as in healing and helpful magic to counter disease, look into the future, control bad weather, or find lost items and buried treasure. They also worked in ways that were more ambivalent, in spells and counter-spells meant to manipulate others in social situations in order to attract love, repel harm, or protect against the harm of other, more malevolent witches by returning evil for evil. And they worked, finally, in ways that contemporaries saw as maleficent—to curse and to wreak personal as well as social harm through charms and poisons that could dry the milk of a dairy cow or end a human life, often in reputed league with the devil.

In terms of cultural practice, the linkages between women, nature, supernature, and effective force in society told of a metaphysics on the ground, if you will, a habit of mind and life that would continue through the centuries into rural, and later urban, American times. It was there, across the Atlantic from old Europe, that—under the banner of democracy—the separate traditions of the rural or village wizard and the intellectual magician, of the pragmatic operator and speculating scientist, would come together in new and noticeable combinations.

However, the European path across the Atlantic takes us first, for a good part of the story, to England. There a purported witchcraft enjoyed its own efflorescence and suffered its own persecution, although, for all its severity not so severe as on the Continent. We gain an early glimpse of that witchcraft in John Bale's *Comedy concernynge Three Lawes, of Nature, Moses, and Christ* (1538), in his depiction of the character "Idolatry." George Kittredge has summarized the portrayal memorably:

The old witch Idolatry can tell fortunes; by saying Ave Mary and "by other charmes of sorcerye" she can ease men of the toothache, can cure the ague and the pox, can recover lost property, can fetch the devil from hell, can milk cows and draw drink out of a post. She is a good midwife and can charm children so that spirits cannot hurt them. She can work wiles in war, can keep corn and cattle from thriving, can make the ale in the vat lose its head and strength. No man can brew or bake successfully if she opposes. She can dry up wells and

cause trees and plants to wither. She can kill poultry by her arts. If she is favorably disposed, her charms speed the plough and make the cows give plenty
of milk; the mill, the cradle, and the mustard-quern shall "go apace" if she is
pleased. She can play tricks akin to table-tipping—can cause phenomena like
those which we read of in many narratives of *poltergeister* and haunted houses:
merely by throwing her glove she makes stools dance and earthen pots prance.
She knows spells to protect chickens from foxes and other vermin as well as to
cure sick ducks and geese; so likewise to cure colts of "lampes" and of the bots.
She has drinks for coughs and for "hyckock" and the "chycok," and charms for
the pip. Headache she can prevent, and insomnia vanishes if you will follow
her directions.[82]

Clearly Bale's "old witch Idolatry" had many talents, and she was, at best, an
ambiguous presence. Scholars who have studied English witchcraft, however,
have pointed—in a distinction that is helpful here—to the role of the cunning
folk. These were women and men in rural and village England with magical
knowledge, or "cunning," and with a reputation for using it in ways generally
regarded as beneficent and popularly distinguished from the activities of other,
maleficent, witches. "A great many of us," wrote Bishop Hugh Latimer in 1552,
"when we be in trouble or sickness, or lose anything, we run hither and thither
to witches or sorcerers, whom we call wise men . . . seeking aid and cure at their
hands." It is significant that the good bishop said "we," for the first person plural
pronoun suggests the mutuality that was part of vernacular culture. Like the linguistic vernacular, it was constituted by practice that was generally shared, even
though the context of Latimer's sermon and the ellipsed words made it clear that
he was condemning resort to the "wise." (He warned that there was "no man so
foolish and blind as they be: for the devil leadeth them according unto his will
and pleasure.") The cunning folk, apparently, were consulted so pervasively that,
perhaps unawares, Latimer could identify with his congregation. Nor probably,
as Hildred Geertz has argued, did most ordinary Elizabethans separate religion
from magical practice.[83]

Summarizing the textual evidence for pervasiveness, Keith Thomas noted that
at the end of the sixteenth century "well-informed contemporaries" considered
the "wizards" to be "roughly comparable in numbers to the parochial clergy."
Since their consultations were "more or less furtive affairs" with ecclesiastical
and parliamentary penalties attached, he added, assessments were hard to cor-
roborate; authorities, however, probably were "more lenient" with the "cunning"
form of magic. In Alan Macfarlane's earlier study of Essex County, England,
during the latter half of the sixteenth century and all of the seventeenth (a pros-

perous county that was also, significantly, a radical hotbed for Puritanism), he observed the same ubiquity for the cunning folk. "One sorcerer asserted in 1549," he reported, "that there were over 500, and some seventy years later Robert Burton argued that 'Sorcerers are too common, Cunning men, Wisards and white-witches . . . in every village.'" Macfarlane himself expressed a fair certainty that from 1560 to 1680 forty-one of the cunning lived in Essex and practiced there. They were mostly consulted regarding matters of health and lost property, and this with apparent ease. "Nowhere in Essex was there a village more than ten miles from a known cunning man," Macfarlane wrote. "The county was covered by a network of practitioners, sometimes several in a town."[84]

In an England in which the theory of correspondence between macrocosm and microcosm was still widely held, Thomas found the procedures of the cunning to be "debased reflections of Neoplatonic or hermetic theories," although he acknowledged little that suggested awareness of these intellectual sources among them. "Healing, counter-witchcraft and thief-magic were almost totally unaffected by the speculations of contemporary intellectuals," he assessed, even if intellectuals themselves were stimulated by cunning activity because they sought explanation for folk success. The only exception to this pattern that Thomas saw lay in the practice of conjuring spirits, an activity for which books of magic were essential and in which contemporary intellectual influences were visible. Moreover, new evidence has clarified the late medieval legacy for these magical texts, as Frank Klaasen's survey of manuscripts from 1300 to 1500 has shown. Still, Thomas could point to the "obvious parallel" between village wizards and intellectual magicians, a parallel that is important if we cast an eye toward an American future.[85] For it was in America, in what many Europeans called the "new world," that the old worlds came together in combination to produce a new form of metaphysical religion.

Indeed, as Macfarlane's work suggests, the cunning folk, like Renaissance and later magicians in the Hermetic tradition, believed in the benignity of the powers that aided them, and they employed language that resonated with the Hermetic world. Contemporaries reported that the cunning thought their powers descended to them from angels or from "'the soules of excellent men, as of Moses, Samuel, David, and others.'" "All agreed," Macfarlane wrote, "that their power was supernatural, that they learnt to control spirits, or to say spells of great force. They were believed to use powers already at work in the universe, channelled by their special rituals." Here he made an important distinction: "In this we can distinguish them from their enemy, the witch, whose power lay primarily within her, in an evil essence rather than in the acquisition of a set of magical techniques." Not only that, but they must have regarded themselves as quasi professionals, since they generally charged or accepted modest fees for service. That their profile was distinct from that of the maleficent witch was clear yet again in the ambivalent attitude, apparently, of local clergy toward the cunning. Despite official church censure, said Macfarlane, "it is possible that some of the country clergy more than tolerated them; they may even have been seen as godly parishioners." In one instance, he quoted the contemporary George Gifford: "'The Communion cup was stollen: the Churchwardens rode to a wise man, he gave them direction . . . and certainly they had it again.'" In fact, one churchwarden was himself a cunning man, and another visited a cunning man to gain some information regarding his landlord's lost horse.[86]

What of the maleficent witch or the witch regarded as a bringer of harm by neighbors and a conscious ally of the devil by church authorities? What did this witch have to do with a metaphysical narrative viewed from an Americanist perspective? Only a short answer can be given here, and it is that the metaphysical religion flourishing by the mid-nineteenth century in the United States took its lineage from sources that were surely and abundantly multiple but in which the Satanic witch mostly did not figure. Robert Fuller has pointed to the reconfiguration of the American "unconscious," suppressing Freudian shadows and darker linkages in favor of themes of harmony, restoration, and revitalization.[87] The report for metaphysical religion was similar. Lineages of benignity were in favor; lineages of darkness were usually out.

Meanwhile, back in old England, other versions of the metaphysical world flourished, too, in vernacular culture. Keith Thomas made it a point to notice the democratization of the elite magical tradition during the English Civil Wars and Interregnum, observing that "there was a spate of translations into English of the major Continental works on magic, hitherto couched in the learned obscurity of Latin or a foreign language." "They included," he added, "the writings of Agrippa, [Giovanni Battista] della Porta, 'Hermes,' [Gabriel] Naudé and Paracelsus; and they coincided with the publication or republication of the native compositions of Roger Bacon, John Dee, Elias Ashmole and Thomas Vaughan," all of them, in our terms, metaphysicians. Nor did the more conventionally Christian side of the aisle look very much different. Vernacular notions of divine providence came trailing ideas about chance or coincidence, about remarkable prodigies and signs in the natural world that spoke of the supernatural, about portents and judgments in which God entered the world through such uncanny events as galloping horses or dragons in the sky or sometimes armies in battle. Here, in keeping with a vernacular theory of correspondence, "physical disorders in the heavens were believed to presage or reflect moral and social disorders upon earth." Leaders among the Protestant devout sometimes thought the prodigies and signs were linked to the Reformation. More personally, even so august a personality as Archbishop William Laud was unnerved in 1640 when he discovered one day that a portrait of himself had dropped to the floor. Significantly, Thomas reported that the Puritans had been readiest of all to see God's hand in the course of events, made — by their dramatic and "unnatural" mode of presentation in disasters, accidents, and the like — into extraordinary signs.[88]

More than that, as John Brooke has succinctly noted, by the seventeenth century England was demonstrating a Christian-Hermetic fusion through the presence of radical sectarians who stood "both as the culmination of the Radical Reformation and as the immediate precursor of critical themes in popular religion of the early American colonies." Arguing for an efflorescence of Hermetic-Rosicrucian ideas and attitudes in a millenarian vernacular culture that looked to a restored Paradise, Brooke points to the spate of utopian schemes that characterized the times. Jan Comenius (1592–1670), Samuel Hartlib (1600–1662), and others, for example, in their "Spiritual Brotherhood" and "Invisible College" promoted Hermetic educational reform on the "pansophic" ideal. These visions of Paradise institutionalized through schools were, he adds, available in print for all to read at a time when royal censorship and licensing had lapsed. After 1645, excerpts from the writings of the German Lutheran mystic and theosopher Jacob Boehme began to appear in English translation; by 1661, a complete translation of Boehme's writings was available. Meanwhile, amid the tide of esoteric writings that were flooding England, intellectuals increasingly kept to themselves in the universities. In this context, John Brooke tells us that "these intellectuals left the field to two familiar groups, the inheritors of the Calvinist Magisterial Reformation, the Presbyterians and Independents, and the inheritors of the Spiritualist and Anabaptist Reformation, the Seekers and a proliferation of sectarian movements."[89] Acknowledging the roots of sectarianism in English Lollardy, he underlines the importance of Continental groups like the Family of Love as their belief and practice made its way to England.

Associated with the charismatic Hendrick Niclaes (Henry Nicholas; 1502?–1580?), the Familists, as they were called, appeared in the Netherlands in the 1540s, from whence they came to England, becoming numerous and influencing the Quaker movement there. The Familist vision was one of communitarian and experiential holiness, orchestrated by a hierarchy of elders understood as "begodded" individuals who ought to be obeyed. Believers considered themselves to be tabernacles of God, ready and prepared for an imminent millennium, since the Trinity, and especially the Holy Spirit, dwelled within them. Worship was Spirit-filled, if disciplined, so that inspired speech was encouraged and promoted, while in their ordinary lives members of the group were expected to offer an authentic "service of love" to one another. Significantly, in England Familism spread among the mercantile classes and then among humbler folk, a good many of them illiterate and transient. Adamic divinization—the Hermetic inheritance with all its centuries of elaboration—had now become "begoddedness" and, as such, could be the aspiration of everybody's people.

Astrological lore and prediction, as well, constituted a thoroughly vernacular enterprise, domesticated into homes through what Keith Thomas called "the most widespread form of fugitive literature in early modern England," the almanac. With the invention of printing to support dissemination, six hundred different almanacs were in print in 1600 and perhaps two thousand in the seventeenth century. And they were apparently printed in large runs, with no legal limits by stationers on the size of a printing. William Lilly's *Merlinus Anglicus,* for example, sold probably thirty thousand copies a year by 1659. Almanacs entered the worlds of ordinary and elite people packed with information of all sorts, from medical formulas, to gardening hints, to lists of fairs and markets, to road guides.[90]

Especially, the almanacs were sources of astrological knowledge. The better ones, as Thomas explained,

> included Ephemerides, or tables showing the daily position of the heavenly bodies throughout the year. With their aid the reader could predict the movement of the planets through the signs of the zodiac, and foresee the various conjunctions and oppositions. Thus armed, he was in a position to set about casting his own horoscopes. In addition he could consult the almanac's diagram of the Anatomical Man indicating the dominion of the different signs of the zodiac over the different parts of the human body. From this he could work out the appropriate time for taking medicine or medical treatment. Above all, there was the prognostication, in which the author of the almanac demonstrated his virtuosity by detailed forecasts of politics, the weather, the state of the crops, and the health of the population in the year to come.[91]

What did the church do in the face of this culture of the almanac? From what we know, ecclesial bodies hardly presented a unified front to counter vernacular convention. Puritans strongly opposed astrology, and so did Presbyterians; but Independents as well as radical sectarians were frequently enthusiasts, since astrology resonated with their often-illuminist teachings. Even orthodox clergy were known sometimes to turn to astrology, and likewise the "godly laity."[92]

Elizabethan and seventeenth-century England, then, flourished in a metaphysical milieu in which, in some way or other, virtually everyone participated. As late as the seventeenth century, for vernacular culture learning and scholarship still signified material magic, with learning widely seen as the practical means that could enable successful dealing with spirits. Reportedly, in 1600 one could not be judged a scholar by the populace without being able to "tell men's horoscopes, cast out devils," or possess "some skill in soothsaying."[93] And if the learned often practiced magic or read about it, the parallel tradition of the cunning folk stirred the minds of those who did not open the Hermetic books, appealing to the imagination of clients who sought healing or help with life's vicissitudes. Guidance came to them, too, from the stars and from the configurations of the visible heavens as well as from the strange signs and portents they produced. From cradle to grave, English communities of the era were surrounded by a metaphysical world in which they participated, often without self-consciousness or special notice. It was this metaphysical world, with its practiced beliefs about powers of mind and imagination, about cosmic correspondences and their energies for earthly healing, that they would carry to America as a significant part of their cultural baggage. A sizable number of Continental immigrants to the British North Atlantic colonies would bring cultural baggage that was similar.

2

ATLANTIC JOURNEYS, NATIVE GROUNDS

Europeans made their way across the Atlantic in an era without steam or advanced technology, when each journey took months and could easily end in disaster. But European journeys across the Atlantic Ocean were not the only ones. In a seeming land of volunteers, captives arrived after Atlantic journeys from Africa and then from the West Indies. Meanwhile, others came from South and Central America, mostly Indians or Africans or Afro-Indians. In the land of their birth, indigenous peoples changed their habitation patterns to accommodate foreign invaders become settlers. But beneath the master-servant model that—at least for Europeans—dominated British North Atlantic meetings, more varied forms of exchange began to be manifested. Cultural borrowings were inevitable by-products of social encounters with different peoples. Cultural amalgamations and fusions were bound to happen, and they did.

This chapter sorts out strands of difference and combination in the British North Atlantic colonies that later became the United States. It suggests how complex and multifaceted the cultural meetings and borrowings were—not only between different ethnic and national groups but also to some extent within them. The chapter addresses English and Continental European themes as well as Native American, African American, and Afro-Caribbean ones. More explicitly, this is a narrative about what would later emerge as metaphysical religion in a dominant American culture that was not what at first it seemed (English) nor what it liked to believe it was (Anglo-American). This is also a narrative about resemblance in the midst of difference, about cultural correspondences that ironically replicated implicit and sometimes explicit ideas regarding cosmic symmetries. And this is a narrative about perceived powers of mind and imagination thought to affect the material world, marshaling more-than-normal energies to heal and help.

ATLANTIC JOURNEYS

In his monumental study *Albion's Seed*, historian David Hackett Fischer has traced the cultural belief and practice of four different waves of British immigrants who, between 1629 and 1775, made their way to the North Atlantic colonies.[1] The first was an eastern English Puritan immigration to Massachusetts from 1629 to 1640, and the second, the passage to Virginia from about 1649 to 1675 of a Royalist elite from southern England, together with large numbers of indentured servants. A third wave of immigrants departed from the North Midlands region of England and Wales to settle in the Delaware Valley from 1657 to 1725. Finally, a fourth wave of people came from the north of Britain and northern Ireland, mostly from 1718 to 1775, making their American homes in the Appalachian backcountry. Although Fischer duly notes the many common characteristics the four groups shared, his work especially points to their differences. In his words, "they spoke distinctive dialects of English, built their houses in diverse ways, and had different methods of doing much of the ordinary business of life. ... They also had four different conceptions of order, power and freedom which became the cornerstones of a voluntary society in British America."[2] Important here, they brought to their new homes different conceptions and practices from the magico-religious repertory that helped to shape American metaphysics.

The cultural differences that Albion's people carried in their baggage did not remain the private domain of each ethnic British subgroup. Rather, Fischer argues, "in a cultural sense most Americans are Albion's seed, no matter who their own forebears may have been. Strong echoes of four British folkways may still be heard in the major dialects of American speech, in the regional patterns of American life, in the complex dynamics of American politics, and in the continuing conflict between four different ideas of freedom in the United States."[3] Also, we may add, in four different mentalities—habits of life and action— regarding religion and, within it especially, metaphysics. Accordingly, we can track these different mentalities not only in the early decades when their initial bearers first made landfall but also, as appropriate, throughout the seventeenth and eighteenth centuries (Fischer's last migration is at its initiation an eighteenth-century story). We can search for snapshots of the materials that were combined and transformed in the making of American metaphysical religion.

Fischer's work is richly suggestive in documenting metaphysical practice in what became the United States. Among the Puritans, to begin, no event was random or arbitrary; God's providence was ubiquitous and intrusive, and material magical practice was as enveloping. Significantly, most of the founders of the Massachusetts Bay colony came from a tri-county area in eastern England that included Suffolk, Essex, and Cambridge, while 60 percent of settlers came from a more inclusive area of nine eastern counties, with the three largest groups from Suffolk, Essex, and Norfolk. When we recall that Alan Macfarlane's study of English witchcraft focused on Essex County, we have a clue to the preoccupations of American Puritans, and one that is surely borne out by Fischer's study. Witchcraft, for Puritans, was a category that signaled danger, interwoven with Christian beliefs about demonic alliances and the like. Even so-called "white" witchcraft (the cunning folk) loomed ominously in this universe of Protestant sectarian faith. In 1637 one Jane Hawkins got in trouble with authorities because she was selling oil of mandrakes as a magical potion in Boston.[4] And twenty-two years before Dorcas Hoar of Beverly, near Salem, was tried for witchcraft, she was rumored to be a fortune teller and had confessed to her minister John Hale that she owned a book of palmistry. These were ominous signs that pointed to her later Salem witchcraft trial.[5]

For our purposes here, though, more important than overt and official Puritan attitudes toward what we call magic, is the virtual certainty, given the geographical sources of immigration to New England, that cunning folk, witches, and wizards were disembarking from English ships in Massachusetts Bay along with everyone else. In fact, historian John Demos has noticed the connection. Writing in his well-known *Entertaining Satan*, Demos in part cited Macfarlane's data on witchcraft trials and executions in England, adding that "Essex was beyond doubt a center of witch-hunting within the mother country; and Essex supplied a disproportionately large complement of settlers for the new colonies across the sea. The linkage is suggestive, to say the least." Over a century earlier, in 1869, Samuel G. Drake was even surer. Explaining why New England witchcraft cases were "so similar to those which took place in England," he thought the similarity "easily accounted for." "Witchcraft," he declared flatly, "was itself imported by those who first practised it here, and was perpetuated by the Importers and their immediate Descendants." More than that, even though scarcity and high prices kept books from being "common," still, "books on Magick, Sorcery and Witchcraft were brought to this Country by the early Settlers. These were studied, and their Contents enlarged upon according to the Powers of the Imagination of those who were ambitious to appear wiser than their Neighbours."[6]

In the specific matter of the cunning, it is fair to add that John Demos was less certain about their presence in New England, finding "little sign that individual persons achieved (or wanted) a public reputation of this sort, as was plainly the case in the mother country." He notes, too, that in New England the terminology of the cunning was not much used, "and then only as a form of name-calling."

To be called a "cunning woman" in New England was, clearly, not to be complimented. Yet Demos goes on to acknowledge evidence for the healing practices of some women—practices that looked suspiciously "cunning," even as they were elided by contemporaries in legal proceedings with (demonically inspired) witchcraft. And Jon Butler has also noticed the presence of the cunning people as late as the eighteenth century in New England. Meanwhile, it bears remembering that most of the settlers in New England were not actually Puritans. The fact remains that—whether they were liked or disliked by an official Puritan culture, and whether they were public practitioners or secret workers—it would be hard to make the case that none of the cunning (or, read in negative Christian theological terms, the witches and wizards) came to American shores. As Samuel Drake argued for witchcraft—and in a judgment that here encompasses the practice of the cunning—"it was a Part of the social Life of the People, and to them of the greatest Importance through all the earlier Periods of their History."[7]

If the rural and village metaphysics of the cunning arrived unobtrusively in New England, so did a learned practice of the occult arts. Certainly, prestigious ministers among the Puritans believed that this was the case. Increase Mather, for example, inveighed against those who held "a correspondence with hell," making it evident in the process that he knew the literature of an erudite Hermeticism. "Trimethius['s] . . . book *de Septem Intelligentiis*, and Cornelius Agrippa's books of occult philosophy, wherein too much of these nefandous abominations is [*sic*] described, are frequently in the hands of men. Several other books there are extant which do professedly teach the way of familiarity with daemons; the titles whereof, as also the names of the authors that have published them, I designedly forbear to mention, lest haply any one into whose hands this discourse may come, should out of wicked curiosity seek after them to the ruine of his soul. There are famous histories of several who had their *paredri* or familiar spirits, some in one likeness, some in another, constantly attending them."[8]

There were, however, more positive opinions of the presence of the occult arts among Mather's contemporaries. Jon Butler, in fact, found marks of high regard among scientifically oriented Puritans, and he has commented on their preoccupation with alchemy even as they investigated the natural world. The most egregious example is none other than John Winthrop Jr., the oldest son of the governor of Massachusetts Bay and himself the first governor of Connecticut. The younger Winthrop transported his huge alchemical library to the colony, including many books that had once belonged to the renowned John Dee. Known as a "spagyric" physician—a practitioner of herbal alchemy—he was called after his death "Hermes Christianus" by Cotton Mather. Yet Winthrop was only one among a series of prominent individuals who engaged in alchemical practice.

Robert Childe and George Sirk, both familiar to English alchemists, conducted alchemical experiments in New, and later in old, England in the seventeenth century. Meanwhile, Jonathan Brewster, the oldest son of William Brewster who had helped to found the Plymouth colony, was also an alchemist, borrowing books from Winthrop to support his work. Gershom Bulkeley—son-in-law of the well-known liberal Christian and president of Harvard Charles Chauncy, and himself a Harvardian, minister, and surgeon—also corresponded with Winthrop on alchemical themes. More Harvard matriculants who practiced alchemy included George Starkey, John Allin, John Alcocke, and others. Starkey, later an alchemist of considerable repute, claimed that in 1644 he was "first invited to this study by Mr. Palgrave, physician of New England, while I was living at Harvard College under the tutorship and presidency of Henry Dunster."[9]

One mysterious and pseudonymous American adept, Eirenaeus Philalethes (perhaps Starkey himself or even John Winthrop Jr.), published his alchemical writings in England in the 1670s and was read in America. Indeed, even at the end of the century at Harvard College, Charles Morton's *Compendium Physicae* (1687), a textbook in the natural sciences, commended the use of a learned version of astrological lore in the practice of medicine even as it castigated more vulgar application. "Complexions are Cheifly handled in Medicine with their proper signs and Inclinations to deseases," Morton—a Harvard tutor —wrote. At Yale, Ezra Stiles, who was its president a century later, from 1778– 1795, indicated his own interest in alchemy and his acquaintance with practicing alchemists. Noting the widespread nature of such evidence, Arthur Versluis has estimated that the alchemical worldview "permeated the New England consciousness much more than has been generally recognized." Versluis acknowledges the essential difference of this stance from the rationalist mindset that, at least overtly, would come to characterize modernity, and so he has identified alchemy with a strong belief that the universe is alive and that humans are not separated from it. Versluis has been quick to point to the pragmatism of Americans in practicing laboratory, as distinct from spiritual, alchemy, but he has also argued that—with a mystical view of nonseparation between subject and object inherent in both forms of alchemy—there was a logic that led from one to the other. "Given this profoundly different view of subject and object," Versluis writes, "one can see how the various aims of alchemy flow from it, including the possibility of turning lead into gold, or of creating an elixir that can prolong physical life indefinitely or bring about immortality." For a frontier people separated by an ocean from old England, this spiritual nonseparation must have looked exceedingly attractive. Beyond that, the Puritan predilection for reading "God's signs in nature and events" was "a religious expression of an impulse similar to what we find in alchemy."[10]

In addition to the learned practice of the occult arts and its intersection with strong interest in the natural sciences, Puritan elites trod another path that led in the direction of later American metaphysical religion. The universities that taught them had thrown out the traditional Aristotelian logic grounding medieval philosophy in favor of a newer, more Protestant version. It is arguable that this new, Ramean, logic predisposed American Puritans and their heirs to look kindly on imaginative universes that could, with the passage of time, turn identifiably metaphysical. Petrus Ramus, or Pierre de La Ramée (1515–1572), was a French philosopher and humanist who challenged the Aristotelian logic as taught by medieval scholastics in a bold revisionism. With a master of arts thesis in 1536 that argued "Whatever Aristotle Has Said Is a Fabrication," he created controversy and consternation among contemporary scholars, especially at the University of Paris; he was prosecuted before a civil magistrate and later his books were banned. In what Perry Miller called a "revolution in intellectual history," he produced the highly influential *Dialectica* (French edition, 1555, and Latin, 1556), later known as the *Logica*, a work that was published in almost 250 editions or adaptations, most of them Latin. Ramus himself eventually received a chair of rhetoric and philosophy at the Collège de France, sided with the Reformers in the religious strife of the era, and died in the St. Bartholomew's Day massacre in Paris.[11]

The Ramean logic sought to unify the rules of discourse that governed both science and "opinion," so that both the logician and the rhetorician used the same system. No longer, therefore, should certainties and necessities govern a scientific argument while dialectic reigned in oratory and art. In order to achieve this unification, Ramus and his followers transformed the linearity and the temporal quality of Aristotelian argument—that is, the fact that it aimed to govern spoken words sequentially presented and leading incontrovertibly to certain conclusions—to a more spatialized and aesthetically contemplative form of presentation. In a cultural world in which the new technology of typography made it possible to behold an argument as an entire spatial construct, the Ramean logic ordered argument through its schemes of classification that were based on dichotomies and divisions. Major divisions were each subdivided to produce other, smaller divisions. Argument, in its logical terms, resembled a megagraph in which every mental construct held its oppositional place in relation to another. In this spatialized dialectic, logic was classed as either "invention" or "judgment." "Invention" could be "artificial" or "inartificial"; and "artificial" and "inartificial" were divided and subdivided into smaller and smaller units in clusters that organized previously empty pages.

There was, indeed, a Platonic "feel" to the world of the Ramean logic, even if Walter Ong has seriously questioned its essential Platonism.[12] Ramus had methodized the spoken word, making it available to the educated gaze as symmetry in space. In so doing, he had imposed an order on the world in which his followers delighted. When "man," Ramus wrote, "shall have before his eyes the art of invention by its universal kinds, as a sort of mirror reflecting for him the universal images and the generals of all things, it will be much easier for him by means of these images to recognize each single species, and therefore to invent that which he is seeking; but it is necessary by very many examples, by great practice, by long use, to burnish and polish this mirror before it can shine and render up these images."[13] To practice, one gazed; to gaze, one assumed order; and to assume order, one brought precognitions about nature and the naturalness of order.

Ramus had propounded a "natural method," and in that context he had immersed himself in the writings of the famed Roman orator Cicero, whose understanding of natural law informed his own. English and New England Puritans were already predisposed toward a Ciceronian concept of the law of nature, and they found ease and comfort in the new Protestant logic that made its way among them with its assumption of a "natural moral order" reflected in rationality. The earliest translation of the *Dialectica* in England had come in 1574, the work of one Roland MacIlmaine (his name is spelled variously). This MacIlmaine rendition emphasized Ramus's use of natural method more than did Ramus himself, so that links and connections to natural law could be amplified in Puritan minds and hearts. Thus the Ramus of this translation told readers that "the methode is a disposition by the which amonge many propositions of one sorte, and by their disposition knowen, that thing which is absolutely most cleare is first placed, and secondly that which is next: and therfore it contynually procedethe from the most generall to the speciall and singuler."[14]

In old England, the university at Cambridge became a center of Rameanism, and there Richard Mather, the father of Increase, who was the father of Cotton, read his Ramus. Other Puritans, like the famed William Perkins whose writings figured in witchcraft cases, became Ramist scholars.[15] New Englanders were shaped in their knowledge of Ramus not only by the MacIlmaine translation but also by the commentaries of George Downame and Alexander Richardson. This last was probably first printed in 1629, and a copy appeared under the title *The Logicians School-Master*, the production of Samuel Thomson, in 1657. One of two copies of this work, now in Harvard's Houghton Library, belonged to Jonathan Russell, a student at Harvard in the late seventeenth or early eighteenth century. "Remember the purpose of Logick is to direct man to see the wisdom of God . . . first by taking at simples, then by laying them together," instructed the text.[16]

To see the wisdom of God meant to gaze aesthetically, to place the contemplation of beauty, in a kind of mystical rapport, at the fountainhead of being. As Perry Miller observed, for New England's Puritan Ramists, God "framed a pattern of ideas which was marvelously wise and flawlessly just," a pattern that he "actualized . . . out of sheer love for its beauty." And yet for all the poetry and aestheticism of this divine order, the path of the Ramean logic led as well to an unflappable pragmatism. Ong wrote surgically that "the Ramist account-book interpretation of knowledge and actuality appealed strongly to the bourgeois mind," and Miller himself before Ong was noticing the pragmatic cast that coexisted with Ramean logic in Puritan circles. "Since nature was seen as the revelation of God's will in action," he declared, "then whatever necessity dictated or opportunity offered could be justified on the grounds that it had been decreed by God, and whatever would work could be held to that extent ordained from on high."[17] Gazing at the spatialized logic of dichotomies told the story that the world was ordered and under control—the control of the gazer. Under control, it could be maneuvered and manipulated in accord with one's interests, whatever they were or might become.[18] Mysticism and pragmatism, apparently, could be partners, and contemplation could merge with agency. The partnership would be fully realized when nineteenth-century America discovered metaphysics.

New Englanders, however, were hardly the sum and total of American metaphysical beginnings. There were other English immigrations to North America, and they, too, provided significant sources for what was to come. In Virginia, well before the settlement of the Massachusetts Bay colony and the even earlier Plymouth colony, the Jamestown settlement had dug in. But Fischer's model takes us past those early years to the time from about 1642, when the advent of a small Royalist elite along with their servant supporters was noticeable. On different North American terrain, and with different cultural roots, Royalist English settlers yielded a version of proto-metaphysics distinct from that of New England. Here we learn not so much about the presence of cunning folk, who represented a different social class from the planter gentry, nor about dread of demonic witchcraft (there was surely witchcraft, but there were never any Virginia executions for witchcraft offenses, and the courts actually punished those who falsely accused their neighbors of witchcraft activity). Rather, in Virginia, we learn more about an educated Hermetic inheritance that accompanied those with southern English gentry-class status. Here, for example, certain forms of naming contained allusively Kabbalistic resonances, and certain times and seasons evoked a complex astrological rendering of their significance. Fischer has cited the particular ambience that surrounded the naming of children in Virginia, with names consciously selected for their magical valences. "Astrologers were consulted in an attempt to find a fortunate name," he writes. "The 'fortune books' of the first gentlemen of England and Virginia were full of astrological lore on this question." In fact, the "search for a lucky name tempered the use of necronyms in this culture. The Virginians, like the New Englanders, tended to repeat forenames whenever children died. But they did so with some reluctance, for when children died young, their fathers feared to use names which had seemed unlucky."[19]

Nor did preoccupations with astrology in the context of personal fortune end there. The same fortune books that helped to name the children of Virginia's gentlemen were packed with material to help ensure luck in all aspects of life from cradle to grave—good health, safe travel, love, marriage, and sexuality all were covered in these treatments of personal fate and promise. As Fischer observes, "the gentlemen of Virginia were deeply absorbed in the study of stars, planets, spheres, and portents—not as signs of God's purpose [as was the case for portents in New England] but as clues to their own fate. They believed that every man possessed a certain fixed quality called fortune, which could be understood by knowledge of these things."[20]

Virginians carried over old-country practices from the southern and western parts of England, carving ancient signs on their houses to bring good fortune, in what Fischer calls "a sort of liturgy" and a "ritual" of propitiation to fortune's powers. Fortune, indeed, functioned as a pervasive metaphysical absolute among the Virginia gentry, in an understanding in which life possessed mysterious game-like qualities impersonally established in the universe and requiring to be read by the astute. In this context, a practice so seemingly secular as gambling acquired meanings that went beyond mere recreation for idle Virginia planters. Instead of being banned, as in Massachusetts Bay, gaming in Virginia was protected and regulated by law. "The cabalistic patterns that the dice made as they tumbled out of the box," assesses Fischer, "represented something more than merely an idle amusement, and something other than a form of status-striving. A gentleman's dice were like the soothsayer's bones from which they had descended—a clue to the cosmos, and a token of each individual's place within it. If the Puritans searched desperately for signs of God's redeeming providence in the world, the Virginians sought another sort of assurance about *fortuna* in their incessant gambling."[21]

Cultural practice included books and libraries. As Jon Butler has detailed, metaphysical titles graced private Virginia library collections "with some frequency." Among favored works were those by Nicholas Culpeper and William

Salmon (both astrologer-physicians) along with a series of other titles in astrology and alchemy. As a case in point, the Reverend Thomas Teackle's estate inventory in 1697 contained copious literary evidence for the Hermetic, Paracelsian, and Christian synthesis that must have attracted the Virginia pastor, in what Butler calls "an amazing collection of occult books that rivaled his Puritan works." Within the collection, for example, was William Salmon's huge *Medicina Practica* of 1692, which presented a synopsis of the teachings of Hermes Trismegistus even as it offered practical astrological help and handed down some four hundred pages of alchemical works from medieval and early modern Europe. Still more, Teackle possessed a collection of Rosicrucian works that suggested in sheer number "far more than an accidental or peripheral interest."[22]

William Byrd, master from 1704 of a vast Virginia estate at Westover and a member of the Council of State, is a case study in the everyday metaphysics of a Virginia gentleman of the period. He believed in dreams and omens, counting them important as prophecies of the future—especially so in the instance of death both in his own family and among plantation blacks. In one example, his diary told of his worry at seeing in the sky a sword in flames and a cloud shining and shaped like a dart. Afterwards, several of his slaves died, and he clearly connected their demise to the portents he had witnessed. Byrd visited fortune tellers and employed witches to bring favorable winds. He experienced ritual as containing magical power, and as Mechal Sobel summarizes, "he was very much a believer in magic and conjur [*sic*] along with God, and it is likely he 'talked to his people' about matters of this sort as well."[23]

The North Midlands immigration to the Delaware Valley from 1657 yielded still another metaphysical pattern that would eventually be strongly assimilated into an emerging American metaphysical religion. Folk magic came to Pennsylvania and West Jersey along with its immigrants, even if the Quaker leadership discouraged it in favor of the doctrine of the inner light. Witchcraft beliefs were ubiquitous, and witches did not always fare well in a colonial setting in which the populace generally feared and hated them. Pennsylvania courts, for example, never ordered a witch to be executed, but there were mob scenes and hangings and even one stoning (to death) after the Revolution. Quakers frowned at popular practices such as prophecy, divination, geomancy, chiromancy (that is, palmistry), and astrology, yet ironically—through their own "magic" of the inner light—members of the Society of Friends brought the metaphysical into their everyday world.[24] Quakers, after all, were heirs to the radical sectarian vision of the England of their time. Hence the Quaker inner light shone in ways that suggest other and earlier doctrines of divinization: Familist teachings and the writings of Jacob Boehme have been acknowledged by historians for their influence both on Quaker founder George Fox and on the receptivity of those who heard his message. In fact, among Pennsylvania Quakers the Keithian schism of 1692 — well known in Quaker history for its challenge to Pennsylvania founder William Penn and its putative role in his temporary loss of the colony's proprietorship (1691–1694) — had ties to the Hermetic Kabbalah. George Keith (1638–1716), who after Fox's death led public attacks deploring what he deemed lax discipline and doctrinal heresy, had himself departed from the Quaker identification of Christ with the inner light after considerable study of the Hermetic Kabbalah under the influence of Francis M. Van Helmont. Although Keith eventually returned to Anglicanism and was ordained a priest, his Kabbalistic connection — including a brief alliance, in the Delaware Valley, with German Kabbalist and preacher Henry Bernard Koster — was telling.[25]

Meanwhile, in Chester County, southwest of the city of Philadelphia, occult practice must have been, according to Jon Butler, "particularly widespread." Here, near the end of the seventeenth century, two members of the Quaker Meeting got into trouble with authorities for their practices involving astrology and divination as well as geomancy and chiromancy; and it was clear from the books that one of them owned that he was familiar with the teachings of Cornelius Agrippa. At the same time, there were Chester County allusions to a "wise [that is, cunning] man."[26] On the other side of the Delaware River, in West Jersey, the surveyor general Daniel Leeds (who may have been practicing the esoteric and divinatory version of his art in geomancy) was also a Quaker who left the tradition — here because of his publication of astrological almanacs from 1687. Indeed, the next year, when his second almanac appeared, the Philadelphia Friends suppressed it, a circumstance that led him on a public print offensive against his former coreligionists, encouraged by George Keith. The same year — 1688 — saw the publication of the first book in the city of Philadelphia: Leeds's mostly Boehmian compendium of Christian theosophy, *The Temple of Wisdom for the Little World; in Two Parts.*[27]

Accounts such as these, of course, point to the contact zone in which Pennsylvania — and earlier English — Quakers lived. On both the English and the American side of the Atlantic, there was ready access to German sources of Continental Hermeticism, particularly as mediated through the works of Jacob Boehme. Especially in the Pennsylvania and New Jersey settlements, contact was as ready with Germans who lived and practiced Boehmian theosophy. Even among those who remained Quakers and who displayed fewer overt signs of German influence, metaphysical belief and practice flourished. Fischer, for example, has noted Quaker beliefs in the Holy Spirit's healing power, in reincarnation, and — following the historian G. F. Nuttal — in Hermetic ideas regarding human fall from and restoration to unity with all of nature. Already here, the metaphysical realm was personal and communicative in ways that differ sharply from the Virginia gentry's impersonal notions of fortune.[28] Still more, communication with spirit assumed its largest proportions when the Quakers bequeathed to the later United States a species of spiritualism. Fischer has recounted how seventeenth-century English Quakers made repeated attempts to interact with the dead, going so far as to try to raise them from their graves. "In Worcestershire, for example," he writes, "one English Quaker dug up the body of another, and 'commanded him in the name of the living God to arise and walk.' There were many similar events in which Quakers attempted to resurrect the dead."[29] Spirit could speak to spirit, inner light reach out to other light beyond the grave. It would be significant, by the late eighteenth and the early nineteenth century, that it was among the Shakers, with partial roots in English Quakerism, that spiritualism emerged as a noticeable cultural practice. It could be an easy glide from such practice, too, to expanded concepts of revelation.

Finally, in the eighteenth-century Appalachian backcountry settled by British borderlanders, a rural metaphysical culture prevailed that was different from practice in New England, Virginia, or the Middle Colonies, a culture that can be read through its traces into the twentieth century and beyond. In the rough-and-tumble terrain of what to the English were borderlands, the signs that came to ordinary folk came from nature—a nature linked to the cosmos in impersonal and unfailing ways and a source of wisdom, guidance, and, especially, warning in everyday life. Correspondences were seemingly everywhere, and they were imaginatively deployed. The signs of the zodiac governed the planting of crops, and there were good and bad days to execute the various tasks that were connected with agrarian life. Here the role of the moon was ever-controlling. In the twentieth century, if mountaineers killed a pig in its light, the project would come to grief. Mountain people were required to make their soap at the right time of the moon and to nail down their roofs, likewise, at the designated time. Moontimes spun out into general considerations of the weather, so that mountaineers counted fogs in August to predict it—or examined the color of woolly caterpillars carefully, or looked closely at how the ground hornets were making their nests. Likewise certain character traits (human *nature*) made agricultural and related tasks easier or harder. People needed to curse well if they wanted to raise healthy gourds and to be bad-tempered to produce healthy peppers. From the very beginning of life, signs greeted and accompanied a newborn who entered this Appalachian backcountry world. A woman placed a necklace of corn beads around a baby's neck to help it with teething, and a bullet or coin was used to keep away nosebleeds. Mountain folk killed the first wood tick found on the tiny body of a child with an ax so that the child would grow up to be a good worker. In an addendum, if parents wanted the child to have a good singing voice, one of them killed the tick on a banjo or bell. Still further, they scrutinized the body of the child itself for clues to future births in the family. If the baby had the same number of creases in both of its legs, the next child born would be a girl.[30]

Throughout the colonies, the pervasive presence of almanacs alongside Bibles (recall the enterprise of Daniel Leeds) spelled out a combinative astrological Hermeticism that had survived the British Atlantic passage and continued to be a familiar feature of vernacular culture in the eighteenth century and after. Herbert Leventhal has documented the astrological content of colonial almanacs, preoccupied as they were with medicine, farming, and weather predicting—all issues of considerable importance to rural agricultural communities. As in England, the American almanacs featured the "anatomy" prominently, a stylized graphic depicting a "cosmic" man, the various parts of his body correlated with the signs of the zodiac and thus pointing to the correspondence between the heavenly bodies and human health that was the leitmotiv of astrological medicine. In fact, Leventhal's research indicates that, by the eighteenth century, although astrology was declining in American quarters especially among educated elites, it still survived; and its "primary vehicle" of dissemination was the "lowly almanac, the literature of the semiliterate."[31] As for the Hermeticism, aside from Leeds, Pennsylvania's Jacob Taylor provides a useful indication of how ordinary almanac makers could be clearly versed in Hermeticism and even "adepts." In 1710, we are told, Taylor was quoting Hermes Trismegistus and Cornelius Agrippa in the almanacs he constructed. As for Leeds himself—who not only published the works of Jacob Boehme but also those of the English mystic George Wither—Jon Butler has characterized him memorably: "He complained about Christianity's absurd heresies and defended what he felt were true religious principles against corrupt sects and denominations. He equated astrology with theology, quoted Hermes Trismegistus, summarized seventeenth-century astrological predictions of William Lilly and John Partridge, trumpeted Hermetic and Paracelsian medicine, quoted the book of Psalms to prove that the 'first Cause' used stars as 'second causes of Effects upon Mankind' much as angels were used as agents, and told readers to gather herbs only 'when the Planets that governed them are dignified and friendly aspected.'"[32]

What this short tour of the four British immigrations and their relationship to metaphysical practice suggests, then, is both the pervasiveness and diversity of a proto-metaphysical religion of correspondence and its recruitment of imaginal thinking in the service of what could broadly be termed health and well-being. It points as well to its ability to meld with a combination of different cultural patterns and its endurance in the British North Atlantic colonies that became the United States. What, though, of the non-English European immigrants? Aside from their occasional influences on the Quakers, what of those Continental comers who would have been heir, at least partially, to a vernacular culture tinged with Hermetic beliefs and behaviors broadly understood? Did they bring a significant and enduring mystical presence to American shores? Can we find evidence of Atlantic journeys that brought a substantial Continental metaphysics to America?

Writing in the context of establishing the Hermetic roots of early Mormonism —a theme to which I will return in the next chapter—John Brooke has charted the course of Continental Hermeticism in early America. Brooke argues that he and his readers might "reasonably assume a transfer of occult practices and hermetic perfectionism to the New World from the Old, a transfer carried both on the streams of migration that peopled early America and on the tides of print culture that washed across the Atlantic." Looking past the migration of Puritans to New England in the 1630s (for whom he saw the "hermetic occult" as "a minor, muted undercurrent"), Brooke turned instead to the heirs of the Radical Reformation who settled the mid-Atlantic colonies. "In the migrations of Quakers, Baptists, Pietists, and perfectionists, coming primarily to the new provinces of Pennsylvania and the Jerseys, and swelling to greater and greater numbers between the 1650s and 1730s," he assesses, "the Radical traditions of Adamic restoration and hermetic divinization were definitively brought to the New World."[33]

We have already met some of these Hermetic devotees among the English Quakers in the Pennsylvania colony. Here, however, it is important to note the sizable Germanic immigration that also brought a Protestantized Hermeticism to the mid-Atlantic region. Consider, for example, the Pennsylvania German community of Johannes Kelpius (1673–1708) along the Wissahickon Creek in Germantown (now within the city of Philadelphia). From 1697, the Society of the Woman in the Wilderness—so named by others because of its millennialist perspective that looked to the New Testament book of Revelation—drew together a brotherhood that taught and practiced an esoteric version of Christianity and combined it with a stylized religion of nature. The brothers self-consciously inaugurated their settlement with rituals to honor the summer solstice, building bonfires from native trees and bushes, chanting, and invoking the sacral powers that could bless their enterprise. They blended pagan, Christian, and Jewish elements in a totalizing religious world that made magical practice an everyday affair. With their forty-foot-square log tabernacle with telescope on top (to read the celestial signs of the impending millennium), their astrological amulets, their incantatory healing rites, their alchemical paraphernalia, and the learned texts that grounded their practice, they brought Hermeticism, Rosicrucianism, Kabbalism, Lutheran Pietism, and Boehmian mysticism together.

The millennialism of the brothers deserves further scrutiny. It took its inspiration from the twelfth-century millennial vision of history associated with Joachim of Fiore (1132?–1202), and in keeping with this vision, the brothers held to a three-stage unfolding of time. But the Joachimite ages of Father, Son, and Spirit became, in their rendering, the ages of the "barren wilderness," the "fruitful wilderness," and, coming imminently, the "wilderness of the elect of God." At the dawn of the eighteenth century and well outside the Anglo-American political orbit, the Kelpius community was already sacralizing the American landscape, drawing it into a message of imminent hope and expectation that stressed the metaphysical possibilities of the land, its correspondences now extending into the future. It was a combinatory vision—Christian, Boehmian and Hermetic, naturalistic and neopagan at once—that augured a different religious history for the soon-to-be United States. Moreover, even as they were engaged in their culture of grand millennial vision and practice, the community of expectant hermits was not particularly isolated from outsiders. Kelpius, we are told, obligingly cast horoscopes for visitors. He also tried to help educate children in the area, offered herbal medicine to takers, and divined for water and metals. His correspondence included letters to Philadelphians in Europe as well as to colonists as far removed as Long Island, Rhode Island, and Virginia, reflecting what Butler has called "an occult Christian network that spanned considerable distances."[34]

Among Kelpius's followers was the same Henry Bernard Koster with whom the erstwhile Quaker George Keith had formed a connection. Koster, the German preacher and mystic who was learned in the Kabbalah, had attracted Delaware Valley Quakers into the earliest Baptist groups in the area and formed the "True Church of Philadelphia or Brotherly Love" (1697). He may perhaps be considered emblematic for what Brooke has called "a continuing fascination with universal restoration, the occult, and hermeticism among the Pennsylvania Germans," even as they established new sects and engaged in religious experiment.[35]

Most notable among the experiments was the Ephrata Community, formed in Pennsylvania near Lancaster in 1732 by Johann Conrad Beissel (1691–1768), who had come to America to join the Kelpius community only to find it disbanded. He had already, in Germany, joined a number of esoteric groups, absorbing, as Brooke notes, "Pietist, Boehmist, Rosicrucian, hermetic, and millenarian traditions and espousing a monastic celibacy." Ephrata itself emerged in part as a German Seventh Day Baptist community. Committed to what Arthur Versluis has called an "esoteric millennialism," in which—as Beissel himself wrote—"the whole Restauration of all Things doth depend upon the Seventh Time," Ephratans saw the "Seventh-Day Sabbath," in a temporal version of the theory of correspondence, as "a Type of the Eternal Sabbath."[36] With its distinctive version of Boehmian mysticism, the utopian community practiced community of goods and celibacy, along with a series of rituals inherited from the German Dunkers. The German immigrants who shared the Ephrata lifestyle believed that their worship of the Virgin Sophia would bring them to a gnostic union with God. "With antecedents running through Boehme to the 'Pimander,'" Brooke observes significantly, "Beissel's theology revolved around an alchemical construction of a sexually androgynous God, composed of tinctures of male fire and female wisdom. Divided with the Fall of Adam into male and female, humanity could be restored to its original whole, as in alchemical marriage, or *coniunctio*."[37] In effect, we have here—despite the celibacy—one path to the production of healing energy through erotic mysticism, a feature that would continue to infuse later American metaphysical religion.

Yet this mysticism, like so much of the mysticism that would flourish in the United States, turned not only esoterically inward but also outward to a public world. Beissel's successor at Ephrata, Peter Müller (1710–1796), was acquainted with Benjamin Franklin, George Washington, and other prominent politicians. Indeed, Müller was especially strong in arguing the case for conscientious objectors in the Revolutionary War era, writing letters to well-known patriots in support of religious freedom. It is significant that when Washington's army was defeated at Brandywine in 1777, some five hundred wounded soldiers were treated at Ephrata. At the same time, the Ephrata group, though singular like the Society of the Woman in the Wilderness, was also surprisingly well-connected to other lay Germans. Brooke noted that so-called Ephrata "Householders" affiliated to the monastic Solitaries "provided a conduit to the sects and to the church people." The esoteric Ephrata message apparently was dispersed freely among the Pennsylvania Germans, who brought with them, too, their own remembered traditions of vernacular magic. One alchemical preparation imported from Germany and called the "Gold Tincture" or the "Elixir Dulcis," according to Brooke, "was widely used before the Revolution and remained in use down to the 1850s."[38]

Beyond the Pennsylvania Germans, John Brooke has further documented the mingling of Hermetic strands into Radical Reformation heritages, especially among sectarians in southeastern New England. "With their own connections running back to the radical experience of the English Revolution," Brooke writes, "the New England sectarians were receptive to the systematic hermetic perfection of the German sectarians; certainly they were themselves the reservoir of a great proportion of the fragments of occult belief and practice floating around seventeenth- and eighteenth-century New England." Citing evidence collected by Peter Benes on New England "conjurers" from 1700 to 1775, Brooke argues that the cunning folk and their kin were making their homes more in Rhode Island than elsewhere, thriving on the combinative mystical brew that they could there imbibe. Meanwhile, in the matter of treasure hunting—a theme important to Brooke because of the Mormon focus of his work—he found that mid-Atlantic and Germanic sources were noticeable, with the esoteric lore of Agrippa and Paracelsus continuing in German metallurgical tradition. In the course of their mining enthusiasms, he notes, "non-Germans among the colonial populations began to reeducate themselves in the rudiments of the hermetic system, presenting themselves as miners and smelters, and providing an important channel of dissemination of Renaissance traditions in eighteenth-century America. Similarly, the unprecedented wartime intermingling of peoples during the Revolution may have brought fragments of hermetic knowledge into New England from the Mid-Atlantic."[39]

These Revolutionary War notes and themes, however, get ahead of the story. The point thus far has been that the combinative Hermeticism of the European past and its vernacular equivalent in the cultures of the Continent and especially England had successfully executed Atlantic passages. Not seriously damaged by their separate Atlantic journeys but now open to new causes and connections in the blending of peoples and ideas, the metaphysical religion of the European world was ready to be a major ingredient in an American efflorescence. That efflorescence would proceed slowly, to be sure, coming into its own as a distinct and identifiable creation only by the nineteenth century. Yet it would proceed. Among the first encounters that bent it into new shapes and sizes were those between Europeans and other Atlantic travelers—the travelers who made forced journeys from Africa.

AFRICANS

The Africans who crossed the Atlantic in the seventeenth and eighteenth centuries had felt the heavy hand of Europe from at least the fifteenth century. In 1441, Portuguese crusaders who had sailed down the West African coast attacked villages they considered Islamic, enslaving captives in what they understood as a "just war." Later, they gave up raiding and began instead to trade with Africans for gold and spices but also for slaves. So the African slave trade began, as the Portuguese used the slaves on island sugar plantations and then across the Atlantic. Other European nations eventually got involved—Spain in 1502 on the Caribbean island of Hispaniola, and then Holland, France, and England. From the fifteenth to the nineteenth century, in a period of some four hundred years, the

Atlantic slave trade flourished. By the mid-seventeenth century, ten thousand African slaves were carried from their homes into what Michael A. Gomez has called a "culture of coercion," and the numbers of Africans captured and sold did not fall below this number until around 1840. Indeed, until the decade before that, more Africans than Europeans made the transatlantic journey. Between 1700 and 1810—the height of the slaver economy—about 6.5 million Africans found themselves unwilling targets of the export trade.[40]

Compared to Portugal and Spain, the English had started rather late in the trade, and they did not reach West Africa until after 1550. Here until the seventeenth century they were more intent on trading with the natives than in capturing and trading the natives themselves. In British North America, blacks came first to Virginia in 1619, and we have the almost casual reference by John Rolfe to the event: "About the last of August came in a dutch man of warre that sold us twenty Negars." The record thereafter suggests that the slave presence was not large for the next half century or so. One report from 1649 states that there were perhaps three hundred in a Virginia population of fifteen thousand, and it was only after 1660 that provisions regarding slavery were legally enacted. That picture changed, however, at the end of the seventeenth century when large numbers of slaves began to arrive, a situation no doubt accelerated by the 1672 charter given to the Royal African Company. A similar pattern unfolded in the neighboring colony of Maryland, where slavery appeared after 1634 and where, in 1671, the Maryland legislature decided that conversion to Christianity would not affect the legal status of a slave. In South Carolina, the story was different, since slaves had arrived there a century earlier, in 1526, as part of a Spanish expedition that proved unsuccessful. Black settlement thus preceded the British presence and the formation of the colony. The new masters of South Carolina only encouraged the slave economy, offering land in exchange for the importation of slaves. The process was so successful that in 1715 there were more blacks than whites—10,500 to 6,250. Five years later the black population was nearly double the white, and in 1724 it was triple the white population.[41]

In New England, where slavery never became economically central, the picture was more muted. As early as 1679, however, the governor of Connecticut, William Leete, noted that blacks came "sometimes three or four in a year from Barbados." In neighboring Rhode Island, by 1708 Governor Samuel Cranston was reporting "between twenty and thirty Negroes" annually, also from Barbados. And in Rhode Island's Providence, one James Brown told his brother Obadiah to bring some of the slaves he was selling home to the colony if he could not sell them elsewhere. "I believe they will sell well," he encouraged. As William D. Piersen has observed, many of the slave arrivals were considered "refuse slaves,"

Africans in poor condition who would not stand up under southern plantation labor. Whatever their backgrounds, there were some 400 blacks in Massachusetts by 1690, some 200 in Connecticut, and 250 in Rhode Island. Fifty years later, the numbers had grown: there were over 3,000 in Massachusetts, over 2,500 in Connecticut, and nearly the same number in Rhode Island, and the black population was 2 percent of the Massachusetts total, 3 percent of the Connecticut colony, and a larger 10 percent of Rhode Island's total population.[42]

Elsewhere in the colonies, slaves were arriving, too, and—as is clear from what we saw for Virginia, Maryland, and South Carolina—in much greater numbers in the South. In the colonies as a whole, from 1650 to 1670 the black population doubled each decade, and the doubling repeated from 1680 to 1700. After that the number of blacks continued to double every twenty years until 1780 with, a decade later, a black population as large as 757,000.[43] Michael Gomez's careful study has worked hard to distinguish the ethnic origins of these African arrivals and their American-born children, to discern their "country marks" in the years before the language of race obliterated the distinctions among blacks. Meanwhile, scholars in general agree that most of the Africans came originally from West and West Central Africa, many of them through the West Indies— more the case for blacks in certain colonies and at certain times. The two largest sources of slaves in British North America were West Central Africa (which included Congo—the former Zaire—and Angola) and the Bight of Biafra (which encompassed present-day southeastern Nigeria, Cameroon, and Gabon). Together these two regions accounted for over 50 percent of slave imports. Other major sources were Sierra Leone, Senegambia, and the Gold Coast—each of the three hovering close to 15 percent of the total of slave imports. Among these three, Senegambia was an early and substantial player, whereas Sierra Leone started slowly and increased its role as time passed. Meanwhile the Gold Coast supplied a steady stream of slaves from 1673 until the end of the slave trade. For this reason, Gomez cites the Gold Coast alongside the Bight of Biafra and West Central Africa for standing out as the regions "from which Africans were initially and consistently recruited into British North America."[44]

It is important here that in the earliest period of the North American slave trade, significant numbers of Africans were entering the colonies through the West Indies. This was certainly true for South Carolina, where Peter H. Wood estimated that before 1700 most of the slaves came from the Indies, usually through Barbados but also from St. Kitts, Nevis, Jamaica, the Bahamas, Bermuda, Antigua, Montserrat, and the Leeward Islands. Similarly, in New England— and especially in Massachusetts, Connecticut, and Rhode Island—from the beginning of the trade through the eighteenth century what William Piersen calls the "West Indian connection" continued to play a major role, with the British islands, particularly Barbados, but also Jamaica, St. Kitts, and Montserrat, the chief sources from which the African-born slaves arrived. Indeed, until after 1750, the largest single source for New England's slaves was the West Indies.[45]

The Africans who came spoke diverse languages, represented different ethnic and culture groups, lived under distinct governance units in their homelands, and practiced separate and different religions. Yet the West and West Central African ethos was manifestly dominant, and it provides an important clue to a spiritual universe that would generate an African and African American contribution to American metaphysics. Some African comers were Muslims, but most practiced the traditional religions of their particular region and society. We know, for example, that Islam was not a factor in West Central Africa and that the number of Muslims who arrived on the west coast of Africa for export from the Bight of Biafra was small. Reviewing the evidence of the Muslim presence, Gomez has concluded that among the 481,000 Africans who entered British North America "Muslims may have come to America by the thousands, if not tens of thousands."[46] We are left, then, with an overall black population that leaned strongly toward traditional African religions.

What can be said as a whole about this traditional West and West Central African religiosity? With its practitioners coming from numerous distinct social units and cultures, were there enough elements of commonality to make it worthwhile for scholars to generalize? Or were differences so striking and profound that a discourse of resemblance would emerge as superficial and slighting? In either case, could the Atlantic journeys from Africa in any way supply material for the construction of a polycultural American metaphysical religion? One way to answer this set of questions—and indeed, the more familiar way—is to look past distinctive deities and practices and to focus instead on overarching worldviews or cosmologies from Atlantic Africa or an up-and-coming African American world. A key example of this approach has been the "creed" that Leonard E. Barrett hypothetically composed in his book *Soul-Force* to summarize the beliefs of West Africans: "I believe in a supreme being who creates all things, and in lesser deities, spirits and powers who guard and protect their descendants. I believe in the efficacy of sacrifice and the power of magic, good and evil; and I believe in the fullness of life here and now."[47] With some differences but still with common threads, Maulana Karenga more recently has synopsized traditional African religious beliefs with an eye toward black religion in the United States. He cites the affirmation of "one Supreme God," who was "both immanent and transcendent, near and far," emphasis on "ancestor veneration," emphasis likewise on "the necessary balance between one's collective identity and responsibility as a member of society and one's personal identity and responsibility," a "profound respect for nature," and a strong preoccupation with issues regarding "death and immortality."[48] Barrett and Karenga overlap in clear ways—themes of one high God, of ancestors, and of quality of life stand out. Moreover, from the vantage point of concern regarding an emerging American metaphysics, the invocation of "spirits," "magic," and "profound respect for nature" surely attracts attention. But there are also clear differences in the short lists, and they, of course, raise questions regarding data, evidence, and interpretation.

Be that as it may, certainly the most sophisticated example of the cosmological approach to black resemblance has been the work of Mechal Sobel, who not only writes with nuance and detail about a West African "sacred cosmos" but also argues for an "enslaved African/American sacred cosmos" and eventually a new "Afro-Baptist" one. Sobel has constructed her model of the West African sacred cosmos by combining African epistemological categories—a high God, other divinities, humans, pervasive preoccupations with spirit or power—with contemporary ones she gleans from Thomas Luckman's work in the sociology of knowledge—time, space, causality, and purpose. She knows the work of Leonard Barrett, and her own short list is not dissimilar to his. But Sobel goes on to make claims for a transforming and then, in Afro-Baptism, a transformed new vision. It is the first and earlier of these—the enslaved African American cosmos—that concerns the account here: "The vast majority of the Africans brought to America found themselves in the South Atlantic section of the country where, in proximity to the Anglican church, a unified quasi-African world view was created. This initial culture contact was a crucial one. In rejecting Anglicanism and in being allowed to reject it, blacks found the psychological space to continue to shape their own world view."[49]

Juxtaposed to the rejected Anglicanism, Sobel argues for an African cosmos in the American South in which matter was for the most part "permeated or penetrated by the holy" and in which, as in traditional Catholicism, there was more space for (material) magic and the "religious control of the arational." However, without the ability to re-create the social institutions that supported the African cosmos in Africa, American black slaves, under continual attack by Anglo-Christian social and epistemological culture, incorporated inconsistencies, believing at once that spirit had fled and yet, in voodoo, that spirit was operating again. Conflicts grew and abounded and, with them, the "ontological confusions" that meant that American slaves more and more lost touch with life's "wider meaning."[50] Sobel had set the stage for the later emergence of Afro-Baptism to rescue, for many, the religious situation. That time of Afro-Baptist salvation, however, falls outside the early American narrative. What is important here is that Sobel has gone beyond previous accounts of more or less static West African "creeds" to argue for an interactive situation in which social events and outcomes were impacting previous thought forms and changing them—not into pale replicas of white cosmologies but into new and original creations.

Relative to Barrett and Karenga, therefore, there is a social historical sensitivity and diachronicity to Sobel's account. But is it enough? Is the Sobel African American sacred cosmos the best way to articulate issues around black presence in American metaphysical religion? Are there other intellectual places to go, other ways to frame the situation? What if, instead of taking the predominately stable view that comes with concerns over cosmology, we look at how African and African American religiosity *worked*? What if we study its functionality and what John Thornton has called its "dynamic" aspects?[51] What kinds of issues emerge, and how can they serve to throw light on the larger picture of American metaphysical religion?

Thornton himself does this with impressive results in his study of African religions and Christianity in the Atlantic world. Arguing for what might be termed a "revelation epistemology," he begins with the experience of communication with nonworldly beings common both to traditional African religions and Christianity, an experience in which information, ideas, images, and the like come as received and subsequently generate the need to interpret their message. In these acts of interpretation, Thornton thinks, religious philosophies were born and, alongside them, religions and cosmologies. What could be called revelations thus became the working sources for the construction of "a general understanding of the nature of the other world and its inhabitants (a philosophy), a clear perception of its desires and intentions for people to obey (a religion), and a larger picture of the workings and history of both worlds (a cosmology)." But the revelations came first—were primary. The special people who received them, as well as the ways in which they did so, occupied central positions in an economy of interaction and relationship in which the intercourse of heaven and earth, the exchanges between worldly and otherworldly intelligences, functioned at the center of spirituality. To push this even further, perhaps, than Thornton himself does, and in the direction of the work of Robert Orsi, the discourse of "meaning" in religion gave way here before another discourse of relationship and its effects.[52]

For traditional African religions, this discourse of relationship came directly through persons who possessed a kind of "sixth sense," a keenness and ability to hear voices and to see visions that others did not hear or see. Often (but certainly not always) these gifted individuals found themselves part of traditional priesthoods. However, the discourse of relationship was not merely the province of the gifted few (or some). African revelations came indirectly as well—through augury and divination or through dreams and their interpretation. In the more dramatic sixth-sense cases, spirit mediums or possessed humans, animals, or material objects became conduits to a world that upended the one in which ordinary people lived, turning it into a contact zone where fixed realities were unglued and everything could be changed. Central Africa was "the land of the spirit medium par excellence," observes Thornton, citing detailed seventeenth-century descriptions of Angolan and Kongolese mediums who were possessed. According to the Italian Luca da Caltanisetta who watched them, people consulted mediums to discern the cause of death or sickness, or else to find a lost item or another item that they sought. Forming a circle around the medium and singing and praying "for the Devil to enter the head of that priest," indigenous African seekers asked their questions and raised their concerns in a conversation with spirit that became two-way. For Giovanni Antonio Cavazzi in Angola, the descriptions were similar.[53]

These encounters with spirit, of course, worked in ways that were not far from the Christian mark. Throughout the European centuries, Christians, too, had operated under an epistemology of revelation in which experience was the ultimate arbiter of religion. Christian revelation was, in the main, what Thornton calls "discontinuous," because—with a strong, institutionalized clergy and the power of the state to buttress it—the canon of revelation was set in the Bible. Yet, even in the Christian world, there were ways that revelation could function continuously. Thornton cites the writings of the Fathers and Doctors of the church, which were understood by believing Christians to be inspired by the Holy Spirit. Significantly, he goes on to comment, too, on the vernacular world of sixteenth-century Europeans, in which "a variety of auguries, divinations, and apparitions of otherworldly beings took place constantly, and they regularly consulted astrologers, geomancers, and other diviners and healers."[54] In this description, we are entering the discourse community of the Hermetic world, a place where the revelations of spirit managed to manifest themselves, apparently not seriously hampered by canonical strictures or cultures of churchly constraint. In this loose community of believers and practitioners, spirit often agreed with spirit but could also contradict. Relations between heaven and earth possessed symmetry and connection (correspondence again), but they also came apart in surprising ways and the ruptures between flesh and spirit always needed spirit energy for mending and healing.

For Africans still in traditional Africa and for Africans who were making or had made Atlantic journeys to the Americas, the merger of African and Christian traditions was inserted into this overarching European spirituality. As Thornton writes, the process was relational, "not simply a meshing of cosmologies," nor an "intellectual enterprise," but instead a "complex examination of revelations conducted by both Africans and Christians."[55] A major result of this complex examination was the variety of forms of African and African American Christianity, the shapes and circumstances of which Thornton details. However, if we shift our gaze to the metaphysical framework that an enlarged version of European and Euro-American spirituality already encompassed, we can notice the symmetries between the heaven-and-earth vectors of traditional Atlantic Africa and European North America.

For Africa, Thornton has emphasized the absence of orthodoxy because of the weakness of priestly structures and institutions, an absence that fostered a presence—the continuous and enthusiastically received presence of revelations.[56] For North America, which is the concern here, the earliest sources from which a developing metaphysics arose also functioned free of internal institutional constraints, in a vernacular world in which what may be termed continuous revelations flourished. For European North America, the vernacular—and, in the broad sense, Hermetic—world was a world of illumination and illuminism, as otherworldly spirit communicated with human spirit and light metamorphosed into relationship, bringing power and comfort for ordinary mortals. For transplanted Africans, conversations with spirit illumined the harsh features of the slave landscape and the servile life, transfiguring them, too, with the power and comfort of otherworldly relationships. For both Africans and Europeans—and here especially for Africans—spirit functioned pragmatically. Conversations with God, with godly beings, or with the devil enhanced one's ability to operate on a terrain in which the ground was decidedly unequal and opportunities for disaster loomed seemingly everywhere. As Leonard Barrett declared, the African "does not conceive of the world as a place in which to *contemplate* life. He sees his world as an arena for activity. Life for him is a *pragmatic reality*. Gods and Spirits are the sources of his being and all things below him are the agencies of his life. To live strongly then is his most engaging concern."[57]

Barrett went on to find the greatest expression of black spiritual pragmatism in African folktales, oral literature in which the theme of the weak overcoming the strong appears repeatedly (recall the well-known Br'er Rabbit stories) and in which the little people triumph in conditions of adversity and scorn through their craftiness, cunning, and speed. Barrett found the pragmatism equally in African proverbs that affirm in America a spiritual legacy from the old world in which practical instruction for the preservation of life is uppermost so that categories of morality, caution, respect, gratitude, temperance, and the like provide clear direction.[58] The spiritual pragmatism, however, was reflected not simply in oral literature but also and especially in the ritual conduct of life. Rather than looking to the overarching moral and religious protection afforded by society, as in official white Christianity, a number of African religions taught that individual ritual action could manipulate the presence and power of evil by contacting the spirits who mediated between the high God and humans.[59] We can glimpse this world of black cultural practice first, and especially richly, in the West Indies, where sources are more detailed than those for the North American continent.

There, in the Indies, witchcraft became, in Barrett's words, "the most important ritual force in the New World." In a culture rife with anxiety and oppression, for both blacks and whites such belief and practice were shot through with fear of the sorcerer and with the need for ritual means to overcome the sorcery. For example, in Jamaica, where the Asante (Akan) African presence was strong, obeahism (witchcraft) flourished, and so did myalism, the possession state in which an obeah could be identified and, it was hoped, stopped. As early as 1696, the legislature of Jamaica was concerned enough to forbid slave meetings and, especially, to target drumming, connecting the practice with witchcraft and the like. Writing in the early twentieth century, Herbert G. DeLisser, a Jamaican native, recorded that "both witches and wizards, priests and priestesses, were brought to Jamaica in the days of the slave trade, and the slaves recognized the distinction between the former and the latter. Even the masters saw that the two classes were not identical, and so they called the latter 'myal-men and myal-women.'" DeLisser went on to note the healing work of the myal-men and women, undoing the damage that an obeahman might have done, but he also added that many African priests became obeahmen in Jamaica "for the very simple reason that they could not openly practice their legitimate profession."[60]

The eighteenth-century English planter Bryan Edwards told a largely similar tale in his late-eighteenth-century history of the British West Indies. The "professors of *Obi*," he noted, were always "natives of Africa," and their "science" was "so universally practiced" in Jamaica that he thought there were "few of the larger estates possessing native Africans, which have not one or more of them [obeahmen]." He had also noticed some of the refinements of the practice and its cultural power. The "oldest and most crafty" obeahmen were the ones who usually attracted the "greatest devotion and confidence." Age, together with a "forbidding" physical demeanor and "skill in plants of the medicinal and poisonous species," qualified practitioners. "The negroes in general," he explained, "whether Africans or Creoles, revere, consult, and fear them; to these oracles they resort, and with the most implicit faith, upon all occasions, whether for the cure of disorders, the obtaining revenge for injuries or insults, the conciliating of favor, the discovery and punishment of the thief or the adulterer, and the prediction of future events." In the context of Jamaican slave rebellion in 1760, one law—to which Edwards referred—specifically named the practices and ritual accoutrements of the obeahmen and women. The law was drastic, with its threat of death or exile, and never received royal approval. But its catalog of the ways that could be employed to "pretend" to "Supernatural power" was instructive: "making use of blood, feathers, parrot's beak, dog's teeth, alligator's teeth, broken bottles, egg shells or any materials related to the practice of witchcraft." The point of the ritual use of these or similar objects was attempted communication with spirits ("the devil and other spirits," according to the law itself), and the reason that the Jamaican legislature was so concerned was fear of the power of African witchcraft against whites.[61]

Africans, however, had their own extralegal sources of protection. As an African counter to the witchcraft, myalism functioned in Jamaica in what eventually became known as Cumina societies, in which devotees sought possession by ancestors through ritual dance. Edwards had pointed to the existence of myalism and subsumed the myal-men under the obeah rubric, linking the myal-men, too, to the use of a "narcotic potion, made with the juice of an herb." In the trance state that the herb induced, he wrote, the myal-men tried to "convince the spectators of their power to re-animate dead bodies." Even earlier, in the 1770s, historian Edward Long was referring to the introduction of what blacks called the "myal-dance" and their establishment of "a kind of society, in which they invited all they could."[62]

The Jamaican evidence may be viewed as paradigmatic for most of the English Caribbean islands, since Akan slaves arrived early and in large numbers in all of the islands. Familiarity with obeah was pervasive. Indeed, in his history Edwards remarked that the Jamaican obeah practices he had described were not "peculiar to that island only." He believed that "similar examples" could be found "in other West India colonies," noting especially that "*Pere* Labat, in his history of Martinico, has mentioned some which are very remarkable."[63] In Barbados, as early as the 1660s the Swiss medical doctor Felix Christian Sporri castigated slave behavior because of the "idolatrous" rituals the slaves performed to honor "their God who is mainly the devil." With an account of all-night dance and spirit possession to the sound of drumming accompanied by shrieking and graphic physical movement, Sporri clearly signaled white disdain for a nonrational form of spirituality that he found appalling. Similarly, in the early eighteenth century Thomas Walduck, an officer in the military who was serving in Barbados, invoked the "diabolical Magic" of the slaves, specifically noting the leadership role in ceremonies of the "obia." Walduck recognized, too, the healing work of obeahmen. He was also astute enough to notice what may be described as image magic, in which both blacks and Indians constructed images of clay, wax, dust, and the like and used them in attempts to inflict pain on subjects whom the images were meant to represent.[64]

While these early descriptions seem crude and less than discerning, they still make clear that blacks were engaging in forms of spiritual practice that white Christians alternately scorned and regarded as inimical to their own religion and even material well-being and that they generally understood in terms of magic. Moreover, we can trace this West Indian presence—and fear of its spiritual agency—especially in New England, where a large number of African-born slaves had been imported from the Indies. In 1706, for instance, Cotton Mather could plead his case for the Christianization of "Negro-servants" by warning his readers that "very many of them do with Devillish Rites actually worship *Devils*, or maintain a magical conversation with *Devils*. And all of them are more *Slaves* to *Satan* than they are to You."[65] Mather's contemporaries took note of the African penchant for "fetish" worship, even when blacks converted to Christianity. Earlier, during the notorious Salem witchcraft trials of 1692, at least three, and possibly four, blacks stood among the accused (depending on whether we include the well-known Tituba from Barbados, who—if Elaine Breslaw was right—was Indian).[66] Among them, the Barbados slave Candy was probably a practitioner. Although at her trial she insisted that she had learned witchcraft from her white mistress, she produced for the court material evidence that strongly suggested otherwise. A knotted handkerchief, some rags, cheese, and a piece of grass all pointed toward African and African American cultural practice.[67]

Meanwhile, blacks themselves were at least as fearful of witchcraft as other Massachusetts inhabitants and believed as certainly that they could be its victims. In Narragansett, the collected reminiscences of Alice Morse Earle throw light on a society in which blacks were steeped in a culture of magical practice. Her portrait of "old Cuddymonk" is instructive: "Cuddymonk was a typical Narragansett negro—sharp, shrewd, and in the main thrifty. He was deeply and consistently superstitious, and knew a thousand tales of ghosts and spirits and witches and Manitous, old traditions of African Voodooism and Indian pow-wows. He was profoundly learned in the meaning of dreams and omens and predictions, and he did not hesitate to practise—or attempt to practise—all kinds of witch-charms and 'conjures' and 'projects,' though he was a member in good standing, as he proudly stated of 'de Pistikle Church.'"[68] The conflation of Indian (manitous, powwows) and Anglo-Christian (Episcopalian church) cultural markers with the black practice she called conjure is important here—a point to which I shall return later because it already directs us toward the combinative cultural project that American metaphysical religion would be. Significantly, this was a confluence not lost on Earle herself, who remarked in her foreword that Narragansett was "a community of many superstitions, to which the folk-customs of the feast-days of the English Church, the evil communications of witch-seeking Puritan neighbors, the voodooism of the negro slaves, the pow wows of the native red men, all added a share and infinite variety."[69]

Elsewhere in the colonies, the "conjure" flourished as well and, as in New England, in a cultural world in which black and white beliefs overlapped and interacted. The West Indian connection fanned out into general West and West Central African practice in North America—with its power to provide a pragmatic framework in which desire itself could be conjured and, by the labor of human imagination, made concrete. Heaven acceded to earthly black demands, not on the macro scale of history but on the more intimate level of personal relationship. This material magic (for it was surely that in the terms of this narrative) was about making change in the lived world of human interactions with one another. Under the banner of "voodoo"—which we have already met in New England with Earle—or "hoodoo," magical practice was a pervasive and important part of American slave life. "No slave area was without spirit-workers," writes Mechal Sobel, "and virtually no slave was without contact with spirits. . . . Innumerable priests, mediums, witch doctors, herb doctors, and diviners functioned from the outset of slavery through its close, as well as afterwards." Sylvia R. Frey and Betty Wood have argued similarly. "The reputation of priests, prophets, herbalists, rain-makers, witch doctors, and witches and the reverence and fear in which they were held by African peoples survived the Middle Passage largely intact," they declare.[70] And Michael Gomez reads the evidence in the same way: "Throughout the colonial period, the vast majority of African-born slaves and their progeny continued to practice various African religions."[71]

By the early 1680s, the Anglican ecclesiastic Morgan Godwyn was noticing black incantatory practices in Virginia as well as in Barbados, trying to get the London Anglican hierarchy to send missionaries. Blacks engaged in "*Idolatrous Dances, and Revels*," he wrote, and they danced "*as a means to procure Rain.*" A half century later in the colony, one slave was granted freedom and a pension for life for finding a way to cure "all Distempers arising from an inveterate Scurvy, such as the Yawes, Lame Distemper, Pox, Dropsy etc." At the same time, a South Carolina slave enjoyed similar treatment for passing on a cure for rattle-snake bite.[72] Frey and Wood found divination practiced along with the "root doctoring" and healing, and they cite the presence of a "rudimentary version of Obeah" as well as ritual leadership reflecting traditional African models for men and women.[73]

The obeah work of the West Indies mingled in places like South Carolina and Virginia with the spiritual traditions of peoples such as the Igbo and other West and West Central Africans. Archaeological digs have uncovered evidence suggesting that in South Carolina Congo-Angolan slaves used magical bowls made of clay to "cook" the "medicine" that constituted protecting charms. They inscribed the underneath of many of the bowls with a symbolic figure in the shape of a cross, probably to signal the power inherent in the Bakongo cosmos, before they cast them into the river waters nearby—in an association that may have expressed the pervasive West African concern for water spirits. Meanwhile, in Virginia, archaeology has confirmed the presence of conjure (understood as the "formalization" of the knowledge and use of charms) from as early as 1702. And in Maryland, at Annapolis, excavations in the kitchens and laundry rooms of the large houses of wealthy whites (Charles Carroll was one of them) have revealed Kongo-style minkisi. These were spirit caches or bundles (charms) containing materials (clay, grave dirt, funerary objects, crystals, pebbles, roots, metal, rings, crab claws, cloth, and the like) to evoke the spirits, to instruct them on a task to be done, and to direct their action toward a specific person. Hearths, doorsills, and northeast corners of rooms were all favored locations—places from which the spirits came and went—and the minkisi were used to direct them and also to protect, to divine the future, and to diagnose disease. Often called "hands," "mojos," or "tobys," these spirit bundles were the work of the African and African American specialists who knew how to use them.[74]

Under the aegis of Christianity, as this account has already suggested, the African spiritual universe became darker. Obeah work and minkisi bundles had always been ambiguously marked, and the new-world story was that increasingly conjurers were recognized and feared by blacks and often whites. They were both exploited and condemned, and in Christian terms witchcraft figured flatly as consorting with the devil. It was a dangerous activity, understood in clearly negative terms. For the colonies as a whole, William Piersen has declared that African American fears of antisocial magic increased over the years. "Both Christian and non-Christian blacks came to emphasize the negative role of haunts, witches, wizards, and Voodoo in general," observes Mechal Sobel.[75] In one example, an African belief in dual souls continued in the American South, but different from in Africa—where neither soul was marked as totally good or evil—a Christian culture taught blacks to think in ghostly terms of a "Holy Ghost," a spirit from the "insides," and another, evil ghost linked to the body. Throughout the American South, in general, by the first half of the nineteenth century, conjure and witchcraft were functioning as large and intrinsic parts of black culture. Indeed, the power of conjure often served as a counterweight to the power of slave owners and masters. A Kentucky conjurer named William Webb, for example, after prayer in the slave quarters on one plantation got the slaves to collect and bag roots, ceremonially march around their cabins, and point the bags each morning toward their owner's house. When, around the same time, the master dreamed that his slaves were taking revenge on him, he reformed his ways of dealing with them. Whatever the cause-effect calculus from any outside perspective, for the slaves the meaning was clear, and it added up to the power of the conjurer's ways. Meanwhile, black nurses and playmates fed the fear of conjure to privileged white children growing up on plantations, and conjurers sometimes earned the fear and regard of whites as well as blacks.[76]

We gain another glimpse of how conjure worked in the autobiography of Henry Bibb, the escaped slave who became a celebrated antislavery lecturer. With some condescension at his former self, Bibb recalled his unsuccessful attempts to avoid flogging from his planter master by enlisting the aid of a conjurer. By paying a "small sum," Bibb procured a powder of alum, salt, and other materials to sprinkle around his master and a bitter root to chew and spit toward him. His first try seemed successful, and so he got bolder; but to his chagrin—after an overnight stay off the plantation without permission—he was severely punished. Not to be deterred, Bibb tried another conjurer in the neighborhood, and this time he received, for "a certain amount in cash," instructions on visiting the cow pen at night, obtaining manure, mixing it with red pepper and the hair of white people, and cooking it in a pot "until it could be ground into snuff." He was told to sprinkle the highly irritating blend in his master's boots, hat, and bedroom, the "smallest pinch . . . enough to make a horse sneeze," and he kept at it with the intention of avoiding beatings, the theory being that the concoction would act as a "kind of love powder" to change the heart of his master. To no avail. One night Bibb tried harder and sprinkled "a very heavy charge," so that master and mistress coughed and sneezed pronouncedly. The only thing Bibb got for his efforts was the worry that he might be discovered, and so he concluded that he would be better off running away from slavery.[77]

Bibb was clearly a nonbeliever when he looked back on his conjuring days, and he was convinced that he had been seduced by "superstition." The evidence, though, makes him much in the minority, and it also suggests that there are other ways to regard and value the conjuring legacy. Looking back on the American slave experience at the beginning of the twentieth century, W. E. B. Du Bois offered the different assessment that, coming from the African past, "the chief remaining institution was the priest or medicine man. He early appeared on the plantation and found his function as the healer of the sick, the interpreter of the unknown, the comforter of the sorrowing, the supernatural avenger of wrong and the one who rudely, but picturesquely, expressed the longing, disappointment and resentment of a stolen and oppressed people."[78]

African and African American magical practice continued to flourish—both to heal and to hurt—in the antebellum South and on after the Civil War into the twentieth and twenty-first centuries. As it did so, it kept on functioning as a conduit for what can be called revelation. Such revelation came channeled through material-spiritual correspondences, the power of human imagining, and the energy it generated to alter life situations, often in healing ways. This, therefore, was revelation that consistently aimed to work pragmatically—for needs at hand. The Atlantic journeys of Africans had been made, in large measure, without ritual artifacts, but the greatest artifact of all was memory. Memory served to create an African American spiritual world that would contribute an important share to U.S. metaphysical religion, with its own ambiguous attempts to gain pragmatic power and at the same time efface it. There have been cues already about the overlap of black spirituality with that of whites and, especially, with that of Native Americans. This is the place to look more closely at what Native American religion and spirituality would bring to a later American metaphysics.

NATIVE GROUNDS

ENDOWMENTS

The indigenous inhabitants of North America listened to their own continuing sources of revelation, not unlike the African Americans who became their unwitting partners in challenging the official revelation of Anglo-Protestantism. Organized in small-scale societies with orality as the chief means of communicating and remembering, Native Americans in North America at the time of contact with Europeans spoke numerous different languages (some 550 were eventually identified) and were divided into five major cultural and linguistic groups. North of the Rio Grande River, at the time of the contact a conservatively estimated eleven million people dwelled, between five and ten million of them in the present-day United States. By 1800, according to Colin G. Calloway, their numbers had diminished to about 600,000, whereas by that time in North America the population stood at a little less than five million whites and about one million blacks.[79] Decimated by European diseases like smallpox, Native American cultures encountered crises unlike any their people could recall. Indeed, scholars have called the ravages of diseases like the smallpox, bubonic plague, measles, and hepatitis among Indian populations—who possessed no immunological resistance—not epidemics but *pan*demics. "From the moment Europeans set foot in America, hundreds of thousands of Indian people were doomed to die in one of the greatest biological catastrophes in human history," writes Calloway. "Established and well-traveled trade routes helped spread disease. Indians who came into contact with Europeans and their germs often contaminated peoples farther inland who had not yet seen a European; they in turn passed the disease on to more distant neighbors." The biological assault—alongside declining birth rates, increasing warfare, and general social calamity—transformed Indian America into what Calloway calls a "graveyard."[80]

What spiritual resources for coping with disaster of this magnitude did the indigenous population possess? What revelatory voices were they hearing, and how might the onslaughts of evil have changed the messages of the voices they heard? If, in particular, we pursue the fortunes of Native Americans in the areas in which they encountered Anglo-Protestants and their spiritual forces, what can we determine about Indian spirituality? Which among indigenous revelations could help to shape a combinative American metaphysical religiosity? In order to answer these questions and others like them, we are led largely to the eastern seaboard from New England to the Carolinas and Georgia. Here the earliest certain encounters between Indians and English came in the southern portions of the territory.

Even in the first quarter of the sixteenth century, local Indians in the Chesapeake Bay area may have seen Europeans directly when Giovanni da Verrazano and Estevan Gomez reconnoitered in the Chesapeake Bay area.[81] The English came toward the century's end, at Roanoke Island off what is now the North Carolina coast, where colonists arrived in 1584 and again in 1587. The first expedition returned to England quickly because things went badly; the second stayed under John White. After White returned to England for supplies and came back again in 1591, he discovered few traces of the former group of some 118 settlers, although there were some grounds for believing that the stranded English colonists had been adopted by the local Indians. Others, however, have argued that the colonists died from disease and Indian attacks, while some of them moved to the interior. Whatever the explanation, the colony itself was "lost." Even so, the religion of the Indians at Roanoke had its chronicler in Thomas Hariot, an English scientist and mathematician with strong magical and metaphysical connections of his own. (Indeed, we are told that he was briefly jailed in England under James I because the king heard rumors that Hariot had cast horoscopes for the king himself and his children, an operation that James apparently believed could lead to his and their bewitchment.)[82]

The Algonquian religion that Hariot met in the Carolina Outer Banks reflected the agricultural lifestyle of its practitioners, with dancing, clapping, the use of tobacco, and the presence of rattles in what may have been an early version of the Green Corn Ceremony of later Southeastern Indians. Hariot's *A Brief and True Report of the New Found Land of Virginia,* in its first edition by 1588, provided an advance report on Native American religiosity by a highly attentive observer. Among the coastal Algonquians, he reported, there flourished belief in "many Gods which they call *Montóac,* but of different sortes and degrees; one onely chiefe and great God, which hath bene from all eternitie." The sun, moon, and stars were "pettie gods," and it was out of the "waters" that the gods "made all diuersitie of creatures that are visible or inuisible." The gods were conceived in human shape, they were represented in images, and their images were placed in "houses appropriate or temples," where they became sites for ritual. Especially prominent in the cultus of the gods was tobacco. "Being in a storme vppon the waters, to pacifie their gods, they cast some vp into the aire and into the water: so a weare [weir] for fish being newly set vp, they cast some therein and into the aire: also after an escape of danger, they cast some into the aire likewise: but all done with strange gestures, stamping, sometime dauncing, clapping of hands, holding vp of hands, & staring vp into the heauens, vttering therewithal and chattering strange words & noises."[83]

Hariot's freeze frame of ritual invocation among Carolina Algonquians seems, at first glance, religiously unremarkable, except for the degree of cultic organization it suggests among the Indians. However, closer scrutiny ferrets out elements that pointed to trance ("staring vp into the heavens") and what scholars today might call shamanic activity ("strange gestures, stamping, sometime dauncing . . . chattering strange words & noises"), basic elements that can be linked to active spiritual practice. The picture becomes clearer—literally—when we turn to the Theodor de Bry edition of Hariot's manuscript (1590), which was illustrated by the drawings of John White in the copper engravings of De Bry. Decidedly better as artist than as governor, White depicted aspects of Indian life to accompany the Hariot text. Significantly, one of his plates portrayed a "conjurer" and explained his calling: "They haue comonly coniurers or iuglers which vse strange gestures, and often co[n]trarie to nature in their enchantments: For they be verye familiar with deuils, of whome they enquier what their enemys doe, or other suche thinges. . . . The Inhabitants giue great credit vnto their speeche, which oftentymes they finde to bee true." Another plate illustrated native people seated around a fire by the seashore praying with rattles, and still another showed what might be an antecedent to a Green Corn Ceremony.[84]

Conjurers spoke to spirit powers, and they spoke, with authority, to humans. They were conduits of what we can consider revelation, living links to nonordinary sources of knowledge and healing to enable indigenous Carolinians to cope with their lot. By the early seventeenth century, the fabled Captain John Smith of the Jamestown colony more or less confirmed, if more negatively, earlier descriptions of their work and the religiosity from which it sprang. In his 1608 account of the colony, Smith remarked on the "religion and Ceremonie" he observed among the Indians when he was their prisoner. "Three or foure dayes after my taking, seuen of them in the house where I lay, each with a rattle began at ten a clocke in the morning to sing about the fire, which they inuironed with a Circle of meale, and after a foote or two from that, at the end of each song, layde downe two or three graines of wheate: continuing this order till they haue included sixe or seuen hundred in a halfe Circle; and after that, two or three more Circles in like maner, a hand bredth from other. That done, at each song, they put betwixt euerie three, two, or fiue graines, a little sticke; so counting as an old woman her *Pater noster.*"[85]

At the end of each song a leader clad in animal skins made "many signes and demonstrations, with strange and vehement actions," throwing large cakes of deer suet, deer, and tobacco into the flames. In his 1612 account, Smith shed further light on what the Indians were about. The long and elaborate ceremony was a divination rite to determine what Smith intended and whether he was alone or other Englishmen would also appear. In this version, the divination work continued for eight to twelve hours at a time and for three to four days before the Indians were satisfied. The ritual numbered among their "diuers coniurations," about which he could report other instances—divination before hunting, work to calm turbulent seas, the casting of the first portion of food into fire before a meal. Smith was sure that "their chiefe God they worship is the Diuell," and he in some detail recorded the ritual activity of "Priests," who painted their faces, employed rattles, and devoted themselves, with their people, to ardent and expressive songs. "The manner of their devotion is sometimes to make a great fire in the house or fields, and all to sing and dance about it, with rattles and shouts togither, 4 or 5 houres." Earlier, in 1608, he had noticed the protracted labor of the ritual leader: "To cure the sick, a man, with a Rattle, and extreame howling, showting, singing, and such violent gestures and Anticke actions ouer the patient, will sucke out blood and flegme from the patient, out of their vnable stomacke, or any diseased place, as no labour will more tire them."[86] The catalog is a forecast: it hints of the divinatory activity, magical ritual, and shamanic healing work that would come to prominence, if often less dramatically, in the metaphysical religiosity of a later, multicultural United States.

In New England, where Algonquians dwelled, Englishmen were as uncomprehending as colonists in Carolina and Virginia regarding Native American beliefs and practices. In the large area bounded to the north by the Saco River (flowing southeast from present eastern New Hampshire and southwestern Maine into the Atlantic), encompassing the colony of Massachusetts Bay, and including

to the south the present southeastern Rhode Island and Connecticut, an estimated 50,000 to 144,000 American Indians could be counted at earliest European contact. By the time permanent English settlements came, their numbers
had been reduced by as much as 80 percent or, for the Ninnimissinuok of northern and central Massachusetts Bay, perhaps 90 percent—in the familiar narrative of drastic decline we have already encountered. Population estimates by the
contemporary Puritan Daniel Gookin, which were careful, controlled, and specific to each separate Indian group, suggested the extent of the devastation. Indeed, in all of New England after the epidemic of 1616–1617, writes Alden T.
Vaughan, perhaps only 15,000 to 18,000 Indian people remained; and the Massachusett Indians, for whom the colony was named, may have dropped from
3,000 to 500 people.[87] In an eyewitness account of what was happening, John
Winthrop described the effects of the later epidemic of 1633–1634, in which "for
three hundred miles' space, the greatest part of them are swept away by the smallpox, which still continues among them." Not even fifty Indians still lived, a sure
sign for Winthrop of the presence of God's hand, clearing the land for himself
and his Anglo-American tribe. The Indians had put themselves under "our protection," and things were thereby going well for the English.[88]

Hence English accounts of Indian spiritual vision and action reflected, even
more strongly than in the Virginia colony and its predecessor at Roanoke Island,
cultures in crisis. Nor did New England's observers and settlers understand Native American spirituality in theological terms different from their Virginia coun-
trymen. Indians worshiped the devil, even if—in some accounts—New Englanders recorded a pronounced spiritual dualism. The Reverend Francis Higginson,
for example, writing to his friends in Leicester, England, in 1629, explained that
the Indians worshiped "two gods, a good god and an evil god. The good god
they call *Tantum*, and their evil god, whom they fear will do them hurt, they call
Squantum." William Wood, in 1634, thought similarly, pointing to "Ketan, who
is their good god" and to whom the Indians prayed for their crops, for fair weather
or for rain as needed, and for healing—but also reporting that, if they got no
answer, they betook themselves to the more sinister power of the devil through
their powwows. And in 1674, Daniel Gookin was likewise reporting a dualism:
the New England Indians generally acknowledged "one great supreme doer of
good; and him they call Woonand, or Mannitt; another that is the great doer of
evil or mischief; and him they call Mattand, which is the devil; and him they
dread and fear, more than they love and honour the former chief good which is
God."[89]

English observers told of other names for the two opposing forces—Kiehtan
or Cautantowwit for the God of the good, and—as principal deity—Hobbamock

(Abbomacho) or Cheepi/Chepi (Chepian), the God of evil.[90] The cultural limitations of contemporary English sources are especially handicapping in trying to make religious sense of this God of "evil," this "devil" in English eyes, but it is in this deity's presence that we must search for the spiritual strands that would be woven into later American metaphysics. New England powwows, like their Virginia contemporaries, were not unlike shamans, and the ardent work in which they engaged in the midst of cultural catastrophe and collapse was akin to material magical practice. Indians were attempting the focused work of the mind and imagination that would enable them to cope, survive, and take back power in a time of disaster. Cheepi represented, as William S. Simmons says, "spirits of the dead," and it was to the spirit power of their ancestors that the Indians repaired.[91]

Meanwhile, even among uncomprehending English observers, there was an alternate report regarding Native American religiosity. Gookin, for example, had prefaced his account of "Woonand, or Mannitt" and "Mattand" with the notice that, like "other gentiles," some Indian peoples "for their God, adore the sun; others the moon; some the earth; others, the fire; and like vanities." Even earlier, in 1643, Roger Williams explained that Indians believed that God existed, that he rewarded "all them that diligently seek him," and that he "made all." He went on to identify what he considered the particular Native American "misery": Indians branched "their God-head into many Gods" and identified divinity with "Creatures." He confided that the natives had given him the names of thirty-seven or thirty-eight of these deities, some linked to geographical directions (southwest, east, west, and the like), some to social groupings (women, children), some to heavenly bodies (sun, moon), and some to other natural forces (sea, fire). In a recognition that was significant for the future coalescence of metaphysical religion, the Native Americans whom Williams met went so far as to connect godliness (Manittóo) to certain exceptional human beings and other creatures. "Besides there is a generall Custome amongst them, at the apprehension of any Excellency in Men, Women, Birds, Beasts, Fish, &c., to cry out *Manittóo*, that is, it is a God, as thus if they see one man excell others in Wisdome, Valour, strength, Activity &c. they cry out *Manittóo* A God." The designation even extended to the products of English technology—ships, large buildings, field plowings, books, and letters. Williams's own theological gloss on this conceptual practice was not negative. Native Americans, he thought, were displaying "a strong Conviction naturall in the soule of man, that God is; filling all things, and places, and that all Excellencies dwell in God, and proceed from him, and that they only are blessed who have that Jehovah their portion."[92]

Williams's reading of almost-panentheism did not lead him to connect belief to behavior. But it is, of course, possible to do so, and from this interpretive perspective the ritual practice of the powwows reveals a structure of intelligibility that before was occluded. There were reports aplenty on the activity of the powwows, the priest-"shamans" of the New England Algonquians, and some of the earliest English reports are the most instructive. William Wood, for instance, described a healing ceremony in which the powwow, in the presence of assembled Indians, bellowed and groaned, stopped and waited for a congregational response, and then proceeded, "sometimes roaring like a bear, other times groaning like a dying horse, foaming at the mouth like a chased boar, smiting on his naked breast and thighs with such violence as if he were mad." The work would continue "sometimes half a day," to Wood's all-too-apparent distaste, and he thought it thoroughly diabolical. Williams likewise took note of the "laborious bodily service, unto sweating" of the powwow and his people, and of the powwow's "strange Antick Gestures, and Actions even unto fainting." Like Wood, he especially noticed contexts of curing, in which the powwow would "threaten" and conjure out the "sicknesse." "They conceive that there are many Gods or divine Powers with the body of a man," he added significantly. "In his pulse, his heart, his Lungs, &c."[93]

"Their Physicians are the *Powaws* or *Indian* Priests who cure sometimes by charms and medicine," wrote the English traveler and naturalist John Josselyn, who also thought them "little better than Witches" for their "familiar conference" with the devil, who made them "shot-free and stick-free."[94] But as in Virginia, in New England Indian conjure extended beyond healing. Medicine was needed for all of life and its exigencies, so that, as William Bradford reported for the Plymouth colony, before the people native to the region, in March 1621, made overtures of friendship toward the English they "got all the Powachs of the country, for three days together in a horrid and devilish manner, to curse and execrate them with their conjurations." One account from the time of King Philip's War reported that when a violent wind and rain storm arrived in August 1675 "the Indians afterwards reported that they had caused it by their *Pawwaw*, (i.e. worshipping the Devil)."[95] Daniel Gookin provided perhaps the most complete, if somewhat negative, seventeenth-century description of the identity and work of the New England powwows:

> There are among them certain men and women, whom they call powows. These are partly wizards and witches, holding familiarity with Satan, that evil one; and partly are physicians, and make use, at least in show, of herbs and roots, for curing the sick and diseased. These are sent for by the sick and wounded; and by their diabolical spells, mutterings, exorcisms, they seem to do wonders. They use extraordinary strange motions of their bodies, insomuch that they will sweat until they foam; and thus continue for some hours together,

stroking and hovering over the sick. Sometimes broken bones have been set, wounds healed, sick recovered; but together therewith they sometimes use external applications of herbs, roots, splintering and binding up the wounds.[96]

Powwows were apparently numerous enough to be noticed, and they serviced an Indian population that wanted and needed them. As late as 1761, for example, the Niantic Indians confided to Ezra Stiles that among three or four hundred people as many as ten or twelve powwows could be present. Summarizing their spiritual functions, Kathleen Bragdon linked them, in a broader North American context, to activities involving divination and prophecy, healing (including hunting and fertility magic), and the preservation of religiocultural tradition.[97] Significantly, divination, prophecy, and healing all would become leading motifs in the metaphysical religion that coalesced in the United States by the middle of the nineteenth century, and to this complex spiritual product Native Americans had much to contribute. A closer look at divining and prophesying can conduct us into the culture of immediate and continuous revelation that the powwows and other New England Indian people shared with African Americans and Anglo-American country folk in seventeenth- and eighteenth-century America.

In this regard, it is especially important that Hobbamock (Abbomacho) typically manifested himself to the Algonquians through visions and dreams. With a name associated with the color black, Hobbamock was often glimpsed at night, according to Edward Johnson, who in 1654 told of how the deity came "in the most hideous woods and swamps" and in the guise of the English or Indians, animals or objects, or even mythical creatures. Fearsome though Hobbamock was, Edward Winslow pointed to the high status a vision of the fierce God conferred, for he appeared only to "the chiefest and most judicious amongst them," even though "all of them strive to attain to that hellish height of honour." Powwows became powwows in a ceremony that began with a recitation of an initiatory dream experience and then continued for two days of celebration. More rigorously, among the Massachusett and Wampanoag Indians, the strongest and most promising male children underwent an exhaustive and debilitating ritual ordeal involving sleep deprivation, fasting, and the heavy use of emetics in order to obtain a special vision of Hobbamock. If successful, the initiate became a *pniese*. With that status, he became counselor to the sachem, or leader, of his society; he commanded tribute; and he helped shape decisions regarding war making. For powwows, in general—like the pnieses—the path to the profession was through visions or dreams of Hobbamock. With a name related, as Simmons writes, to "death, the deceased, and the cold northeast wind," Hobbamock's spiritual message was clear. Only those who had looked death in the face could grasp hold of the mysterious engine that catapulted ordinary mortals into radically different states of awareness. Only thus, through an uncanny form of spiritual initiation, could the power be obtained to do what in the terms of this narrative could be called material magic.[98]

For the disconcerted English and their Christian form of discourse, of course, death meant the devil and all of his allies. Visionary testimonials of strange animal guides and powers translated as alien and sinister forces. One powwow who renounced his former ways and turned Christian at Martha's Vineyard, for instance, told Thomas Mayhew Jr. that "Diabolical Dreams" had led him to his calling. He elaborated on his initiatory vision in language that suggested its richness as he recalled "the Devill in the likenesse of four living Creatures." One of them was "like a man which he saw in the Ayre, and this told him that he did know all things upon the Island, and what was to be done; and this he said had its residence over his whole body. Another was like a Crow, and did look out sharply to discover mischiefs coming towards him, and had its residence in his head. The third was like to a Pidgeon, and had its place in his breast, and was very cunning about any businesse. The fourth was like a Serpent, very subtile to doe mischiefe, and also to doe great cures, and these he said were meer Devills, and such as he had trusted to for safety."[99]

To the exceeding discomfort of English ministers, Narragansett and Mohegan converts to Christianity credited their new faith to the dreams and visions they had received rather than, as the English wanted, to the Bible. In their dream epistemology, the Indians were assisted by an Algonquian cosmology in which there were three realms—the upper one of the sky, the middle of the earth, and the lower under the waters. In dream-soul form, humans could regularly cross the worlds, and likewise traffic came from the other side when the souls of the dead and other-than-human entities aimed to enter the world of human society. The trail of this commerce between the worlds could light the night sky. John Josselyn recalled in the 1670s that the New England Indians had "a remarkable observation of a flame that appears before the death of an *Indian* or *English* upon their *Wigwams* in the dead of the night: The first time that I did see it, I was call'd out by some of them about twelve of the clock, it being a very dark night, I perceived it plainly mounting into the Air over our Church, which was built upon a plain little more than half a quarter mile from our dwelling house."[100] Juxtaposed to the church was the world of lights and dreams—a fitting synecdoche for the traffic not merely between living and dead but between cultures in contact and their eventual yield in American metaphysical religion.

Algonquians, however, were hardly the only dreamers among the indigenous peoples of North America whom the English met. Indeed, dreams and dreamers, visions and visionaries were ubiquitous. Among the Iroquois in what became the New York colony and in outlying regions, too, the dream culture of the Indians stood in strong relief. In 1609, the Iroquois Confederacy included the Five Nations of the Mohawk, Oneida, Onondaga, Cayuga, and Seneca, and they claimed a territory from the Hudson River to Lake Erie. Here they encountered European venturers and colonists, first the French and then especially the Dutch, who established New Amsterdam in 1623, and the English, who forced the Dutch to surrender and renamed the territory New York in 1664. By 1722, the Five Nations were joined by the Tuscaroras of the Carolinas to form the Six Nations. Throughout the seventeenth century and into the eighteenth, the Iroquois functioned as a formidable political presence in North America, acknowledged in a far wider domain than their home territory. Moreover, Iroquoian peoples outside the Confederacy, like the Hurons, shared the broad outlines of Iroquois cultural practice, so that Iroquois dream culture was extensively spread. Colin Calloway has recounted, for example, how the Jesuit Jacques Frémin characterized the Seneca as having "only one single divinity . . . the dream," and he has also cited the more well-known Jesuit missionary Jean de Brébeuf for his declaration that dreams were "the principal God of the Hurons."[101]

The Jesuits had begun to preach to the Seneca in 1668, and they tracked a culture of the dream among them that was rigorous and authoritative. For the Seneca, as Anthony F. C. Wallace has so well detailed, dreams provided guidance for daytime matters in ways that went far beyond what Europeans had before encountered. The missionary Frémin provided an elaborate, if disdainful, account of how the Seneca people observed their dreams:

> The people think only of that, they talk about nothing else, and all their cabins are filled with their dreams. They spare no pains, no industry, to show their attachment thereto, and their folly in this particular goes to such an excess as would be hard to imagine. He who has dreamed during the night that he was bathing, runs immediately, as soon as he rises, all naked, to several cabins, in each of which he has a kettleful of water thrown over his body, however cold the weather may be. Another who has dreamed that he was taken prisoner and burned alive, has himself bound and burned like a captive on the next day, being persuaded that by thus satisfying his dream, this fidelity will avert from him the pain and infamy of captivity and death, which, according to what he has learned from his Divinity, he is otherwise bound to suffer among his enemies.[102]

As early as 1648, Jesuit observance of the Huron in their dream logic suggested, for the European mind, the psychospiritual ambience of Iroquoian dream practice. The Huron moved beyond overt desires to contact in their dreams "inborn

and concealed" desires "from the depths of the soul," declared the Jesuit missionary Paul Ragueneau. Dreams, however, might be difficult to discern, and so the
Hurons turned for assistance to the medicine persons whose "sight" penetrated to
"natural and hidden desires . . . though the soul has declared nothing by dreams,
or though he who may have had the dreams has completely forgotten them."[103]
Dreams held the key to healing through the revelation of suppressed desires, the
gratification of which could cure and save. Indeed, in an affirmation that suggests how old in North America New Thought ideas may have been, the human
mind—alongside physical injury and witchcraft—was one of the three causes of
disease in Iroquoian etiology. And Iroquoian dream logic endured. Well over a
century later, at the end of the eighteenth century, the Quaker Halliday Jackson
told of how, during the winter of 1799, when one of the Friends was teaching
Seneca children, other Senecas from a confederacy eighty miles away sent a message. A female child among the distant Senecas had dreamed that "the devil was
in all white people alike, and that they ought not to receive instruction from the
Quakers, neither was it right for their children to learn to read and write." The
dream posed a serious challenge to the Quaker enterprise, since a local Seneca
council was called to confer and many Indians subsequently removed their children from the school for some time.[104]

Wallace argued that the Iroquoian dreams of early America were of two types.
Some, like the ones considered above, were symptomatic, manifesting the desires of the dreamer's soul. Others, which Wallace called visitation dreams,
brought "powerful supernatural beings," who "usually spoke personally to the
dreamer, giving him a message of importance for himself and often also for the
whole community." Such dreams could be transformative, resolving doubts and
indecisions and inaugurating a new level of personality integration and "a new
feeling of health and well-being." They could be linked to male initiatory experience at puberty, when the young went out alone into the forest, fasting and
meditating in a vision quest that brought, if successful, a guardian spirit to supply
help and protection. Wallace's list of the gifts that the guardian spirits could bestow is at least partially instructive from the perspective of later metaphysical
religion. "Some gave clairvoyant powers, some gave unusual hunting luck and
skill, some gave luck, courage, strength, and skill in war. Clairvoyants possessed
particularly potent guardian spirits that enabled the shaman, simply by breathing on a sick man's body, to render it transparent. Prominent shamans claimed
the power to foretell coming events, such as approaching epidemics, and other
great public calamities."[105]

To the south of the Iroquois, in the Middle Colonies, the Delaware, or Lenni
Lenape (the "real people," as they called themselves), prevailed. According to

their own account, in the region that stretched from the north and the St. Lawrence River and Great Lakes, to the west and the Mississippi River, to the east and the "Great Salt-water Lake" (the Atlantic), and to the south and the country of the Creek, Cherokee, and Florida Indians, there were only two nations—themselves and the Iroquois, whom they called the Mengwe. The Lenape were Algonquian in linguistic stock, and their traditional lore told of an origin far away to the northwest. At the time of their early contacts with Europeans, however, they were dwelling in lands that formed the basin of the Delaware River in present-day Pennsylvania, New Jersey, and New York, and there they had met, among others, the Dutch, Swedes, and English. In 1681, in what would become an important part of this vast territory, the Quaker William Penn, son of the late Admiral Sir William Penn to whom the English King Charles II owed a significant debt, secured proprietary rights to nearly the entire present state of Pennsylvania in payment. By a year later, he had designed a government that offered religious liberty to colonists, laid out the city of Philadelphia (the "city of brotherly love"), and executed a treaty of friendship with the Delaware.

More positive in his estimation of the Indians than most of the New England English, Penn in 1683 published an open letter to the Committee of the Free Society of Traders in London in order to promote his colony. Like everything else in "Pennsilvania," the Indians mostly glowed. Penn, though, was not unobservant of what he considered aboriginal flaws, and in the matter of religion, Penn's Delawares were surely flawed. "These poor people are under a dark night in things relating to religion," he wrote. Yet he was quick to acknowledge that "they believe a God and immortality," even if—in an ironic statement in light of later American religious history—"without the help of metaphysics." He went on to describe their worship. It consisted, first, of "sacrifice" of the "first-fruits" of the hunt, in which the ritual leader engaged in trancelike behavior, singing a "mournful ditty" accompanied by "such marvellous fervency, and labour of body, that he will even sweat to a foam." Second, Delaware worship meant "cantico," performances that were accomplished "by round dances, sometimes words, sometimes songs, then shouts, two being in the middle that begin, and by singing and drumming on a board, direct the chorus." Penn confided, too, that "postures" throughout the dance were "very antic, and differing, but all keep measure."[106] Important here, Penn made no mention of the devil as he detailed the proceedings.

Penn's report did not dwell, either, on conjuring activity, although the entranced behavior of his worshipers surely suggests the ritual work of the imagination that could open easily in the direction of conjure. A century and more later, the Delaware endured defeat by the Iroquois in 1720, and they were gradually pressured to move westward into Ohio. In the years after 1748, smallpox swept many of their villages, and meanwhile they fought the British in Pontiac's rebellion in 1763 but supported them in the Revolutionary War. In light of the trauma of Delaware eighteenth-century history, it is not surprising that a report on conjure made up a good portion of the work of John Heckewelder, a Moravian missionary who in the late eighteenth century worked among the Indians in Pennsylvania and Ohio. Unlike Penn, Heckewelder was decidedly contemptuous of what he saw.

Distinguishing those he called "doctors"—in keeping with Indian custom— or "jugglers" from Indian physicians, whom he admired ("good and honest" and generally "perhaps more free from fanciful theories than those of any other nation upon earth"), Heckewelder flatly declared the "doctors" to be "professional impostors." They "pretend to be skilled in a certain occult science, by means of which they are able not only to cure natural diseases, but to counteract or destroy the enchantments of wizards or witches, and expel evil spirits," he wrote dismissively. They were knowledgeable about the "properties and virtues of plants, barks, roots, and other remedies," like good physicians, but they went on from there, embellishing their practice in ways that the Moravian found unacceptable. The doctor demanded a large fee, proclaimed himself the only practitioner capable of relieving the effects of witchcraft, and attired himself and performed in dramatic fashion with "all the antic tricks that his imagination can suggest."[107]

Heckewelder's reference to imagination was surely germane, for in the terms supplied by European discourse—which this narrative also reflects—he was acknowledging the active imagination of a practitioner engaged in magical work. "He breathes on him [the client/patient], blows in his mouth, and squirts some medicines which he has prepared in his face, mouth and nose; he rattles his gourd filled with dry beans or pebbles, pulls out and handles about a variety of sticks and bundles in which he appears to be seeking for the proper remedy, all which is accompanied with the most horrid gesticulations, by which he endeavours, as he says, to frighten the spirit or the disorder away, and continues in this manner until he is quite exhausted and out of breath, when he retires to wait the issue."[108] Heckewelder's "jugglers" counted as shamans in the scholarly discourse that would become standard, and they possessed a full repertoire of thaumaturgical interventions. Some claimed to bring rain; others, good luck; still others to "make philters or love potions for such married persons as either do not, or think they cannot love each other." In one incident that the missionary himself witnessed, he told of meeting an old man who said he had been hired "to do a very hard day's work" of bringing rain. The old man staked out the territory ritually, muttering his prayers, and warning that Indians on the river should be sent home instead of trying to fish (because of the impending rain). Heckewelder was honest enough to record the positive result—although, to be sure, he had a rational explanation, based on the keen observational skills of the old man, to explain them. "About four o'clock . . . all at once the horizon became overcast, and without any thunder or wind it began to rain, and continued so for several hours together, until the ground became thoroughly soaked."[109]

Heckewelder portrayed the impostures he read into acts of conjure in dark and sinister tones. He told of Indians ascribing the powers of the "sorcerer" to "a 'deadening substance,' which he [the sorcerer] discharges and conveys to the person that he means to '*strike*,' through the air, by means of the wind or of his own breath, or throws at him in a manner which they can neither understand nor describe." Yet for all the dark force of Indian sorcery as portrayed by Heckewelder, he acknowledged in the Lenape a connection to the earth that could not be gainsaid. The "American savage," though entangled in "superstition," understood something more. "The Indians consider the earth as their universal mother. They believe that they were created within its bosom, where for a long time they had their abode, before they came to live on its surface. They say that the great, good, and all powerful Spirit, when he created them, undoubtedly meant at a proper time to put them in the enjoyment of all the good things which he had prepared for them upon the earth, but he wisely ordained that their first stage of existence should be within it, as the infant is formed and takes its first growth in the womb of its natural mother."[110]

Then, as if to underline the seriousness of the acknowledgment of the earth mother among the Indians, Heckewelder cited a Mohawk (Iroquoian) source, extracting a paragraph from the "manuscript notes of the late Reverend Christopher Pyrlaeus." For Heckewelder, the words "taken down . . . in January 1743, from the mouth of a respectable Mohawk chief named *Sganarady*, who resided on the Mohawk river," supported Heckewelder's own contention that "these notions must be very far extended among the Indians of North America generally." Thus, despite the large shadow of conjure, he admired and praised the Indians at least for their "ingenuity." Pyrlaeus, whom the notes explained had been "instructed in the Mohawk dialect by the celebrated interpreter Conrad Weiser" and who was "well acquainted" with the Iroquois language, recounted the Indian tradition that the people had dwelled in the earth until one among them found a hole to climb out, walked about and found a deer, brought it back below, and shared the meat. And so, the people "both on account of the meat tasting so very good, and the favourable description he had given them of the country above and on the earth, their mother, concluded it best for them all to come out." There was, in short, a "curious connexion," which seemed to "subsist in the mind of an Indian between man and the brute creation." In relation to the animals, Indians were "the first among equals," and they inserted themselves thoroughly into the natural world. "All animated nature, in whatever degree, is in their eyes a great whole, from which they have not yet ventured to separate themselves. They do not exclude other animals from their world of spirits, the place to which they expect to go after death."[111]

Heckewelder worried that he was not narrating Indian belief accurately because, as he confided to readers, the Indians "have no metaphysicians among them" (he meant something like intellectual systematizers).[112] As for Penn, so for the Moravian missionary; in a consummate irony (if unintended), the file report on American Indian metaphysics was empty. It would remain for nineteenth-century and later American seekers to use Native American metaphysics to construct their own spiritual worlds. The correspondence that Heckewelder never saw between the conjurer who could lay a man flat or, alternately, help and heal and an Indian connection to earth, great mother of all, would be exploited later in the new-old world of American metaphysics.

MEETINGS

"New worlds for all," Colin Calloway announces in the title of his nuanced study of Indians and Europeans in the shaping of early America. To Calloway's new worlds we can add another—from Africa directly or by way of the Caribbean. Despite the models constructed by earlier historiographers, it was not just Europeans who left an "old world" to find a new one. In the spaces of meeting, challenge, confrontation, and exchange, new circumstances, relationships, and meanings were wrought for everybody. The land under Indian feet was reentered by native peoples made over by their encounters with Europeans and Africans, just as the Europeans and Africans walked on unaccustomed terrain. Much of this history of interaction has been occluded, the exchanges being read mostly in terms of European influence on the "lesser" and "simpler" peoples from Africa and North America—or simply not seen at all, since much of the cultural trade occurred without benefit of archives. Certainly, hardly anyone celebrated the possibility of cultural change and amalgamation in which Europeans learned from blacks or Indians. The "white Indians" who were captured or ran away to the Indians, in some cases refusing ransom and never coming home to Puritan settlements in New England, were, in Euro-American terms, a shameful secret to be tightly locked in cultural closets.[113]

In colonial times, probably the Englishman Thomas Morton of the fabled Mare-Mount (Merrymount)—the settlement he founded at what is now Quincy, Massachusetts—had the most to say in behalf of cross-fertilization (and that, literally). Morton had come as a trader and adventurer, probably in 1622 or the next year, and aimed to attract a fur trade with the Indians in return for rum and guns. Not a Puritan Separatist from the Church of England, like Miles Standish and the colonists at Plymouth, which was the nearest colony, Morton slept with Indian women and instituted the British country practice of May games and a Maypole at his settlement. For his efforts, he was arrested and tried by the Plymouth government and returned to England. In *New English Canaan,* the book he wrote (and published in Holland) in rhetorical rebuke, Morton achieved lasting notoriety, substituting a biblical new Canaan (pagan land become promised land) for a new Israel, and thus signaling that the native inhabitants of the land were strong partners in the new creation that ought to come.[114] But Morton saw the new creation in racialist terms, in which the healthy stock of Indian people would invigorate a depleted European stock, infusing the genuine and wholesome character traits of natural Indians into the tired blood of England. Significantly, what England could bring to the mixture was Christianity, for the Indian religion was not really religion or worship at all; and the Indians were primitive and innocent children who evoked the early childhood of humankind. Thus Morton at once glorified and effaced Indians, wiping away the spiritual moorings of their culture even as he sought to proclaim native virtue and fruitfulness.

Yet there *was* evidence to tell a different tale, and—especially from the perspective of American metaphysical religion and its inauguration—we can find a trail of vernacular meetings and exchanges that are at least suggestive of a spiritual future. The trail requires close attention, since most of the work of the past few decades that situates red, white, and black partners on common North American ground has not kept religion clearly in mind. Indeed, religion enters this work, if at all, as a minor theme.[115] Yet the parallel tracks on which Indian and black spiritual practice and English "superstition" were traveling were not lost on some observers. Beyond that, we can also glimpse some of the learning that Anglo-Americans and other European settlers acquired from non-European cohorts in the land.

Among present-day scholars, for example, Karen Kupperman has noticed that the descriptions of the Carolina Algonquians put forward by Hariot and White would have seemed familiar to late-sixteenth-century English readers. After all, "virtually every parish had a magical practitioner, a 'cunning man' or 'wise woman' who used a combination of herbal medicine and charms to effect cures, just as the Indian shamans did. Moreover, the combination of religious and magical functions was also seen in England; often the parish priest doubled as the 'cunning man.'" Kupperman went on to point to the common worlds of English and Indians that were populated by supernatural beings and to notice, too, the sense in both cultures that some individuals had special talents for using the spirit world to enhance or impede human plans and projects.[116] William Simmons echoes this assessment from another perspective, emphasizing that both New England Puritans and their Native American contemporaries "attributed larger, if different, symbolic meanings to natural calamities such as storms, earthquakes, and epidemics, and both groups believed in witchcraft and in divine intervention in personal and national affairs." And Colin Calloway remarks of Huron views of disease that they resonated with English ones of the period, since in both cultures witchcraft could cause sickness, and since sin, for the English, could explain disease and signal the need for prayer or pilgrimage for its assuagement.[117] Meanwhile, parallels between blacks and Indians are easy enough to draw. For both, revelation was a continuous process, spirit powers were near and malleable, animal beings with preternatural wisdom and (in European terms) magical skill abounded, and pragmatic results could be obtained after trance encounters with the metaphysical world.

Nor were these parallels, especially in the case of Indians, lost on earlier observers. In his notes to his *Old Indian Chronicle*, for example, Samuel G. Drake in 1867 referred readers to Cotton Mather's *Wonders of the Invisible* (1693), telling them that the Indians' belief that they could influence the weather through their powwows was really not so unusual. "It is not strange that the Indians were thus superstitious, at a Time when the most of their English Neighbors were equally so. The Indians could never have been under greater Delusions than those Neighbors were almost twenty Years later."[118] Among seventeenth- and eighteenth-century Europeans in North America, perceptions were similar. Thus Karen Kupperman has noted that as the English confronted Indian priests and medicine persons their most frequent comparison was to "our English witches," with Thomas Morton himself calling the powwows "weak witches."[119] And we already have glanced, however briefly, at English commentary on devil worship among the Indians and their powwows.

Even on the eve of the American Revolution, the Anglo-American surmise was little different, if the observations of Ezra Stiles are any indication. The liberal Stiles, a minister for twenty-two years in Rhode Island and New Hampshire and later president of Yale, recorded in his *Literary Diary* his estimate of the connection between Indian powwows and the magical world of English-inspired society. "The Powaws of the American Indians," he thought, were a "Relict" of an "antient System of seeking to an evil invisible Power." He went on to reflect on the similarity to a cultural world closer to home: "Something of it subsists among some Almanack Makers and Fortune Tellers, as Mr. Stafford of Tiverton lately dead who was wont to tell where lost things might be found and what day, hour and minute was fortunate for vessels to sail &c. Some old Women (Midwives) affect it, as old Granny Morgan aet. 70 now living in Newport accustoms herself on occasion to a hocus pocus, & making Cakes of flour and her own Urine and sticking them full of pins and divining by them." Stiles was relieved that "in general the System" was "broken up," and he felt confident that no powwow then existed in New England.[120]

Earlier, however, the system seemed strong and real enough to encourage a Stiles to worry more. Besides, although the English in North America mostly constructed the likeness they perceived negatively, once they noticed connections they could not entirely wish them away. Indeed, on occasion and from a distance, some even approved the spirituality they saw among the Indians. In an example already partially noticed, Roger Williams explained that in his "converse" with the indigenous inhabitants, he had received "many Confirmations of those two great points . . . That God is" and "That hee is a rewarder of all them that diligently seek him." With his own championship of the rights of conscience, it was not lost on Williams that the Indians had "a modest Religious perswasion not to disturb any man, either themselves *English*, *Dutch*, or any in their Conscience, and worship." He identified among the natives "an exact forme of King, Priest, and Prophet, as was in Israel typicall of old in that holy Land of *Canaan*, and as the Lord *Iesus* ordained in his spirituall Land of *Canaan* his Church throughout the whole World."[121] Later, as we have already noticed, too, William Penn acknowledged that the Lenni Lenape believed in God and immortality.[122]

Beyond the observed parallelisms, though, there were interactions, and a considerable body of evidence survives to suggest the spiritual intimacies that developed among Euro-American, Indian, and African American worlds. Spiritual intimacies began, in some cases with physical intimacies, and the record has supplied only tantalizing glimpses of what these may have been. We already know, for example, about the white Indians of New England—people who were captured by the Indians and chose to stay when the opportunity for ransom was at hand, or people who simply ran away to the Indians because they preferred their way of life. We have likewise seen the cultivation of intimacy at Thomas Morton's Ma-re-Mount.

Moreover, white Indians were not confined to New England. As we earlier briefly saw, existing belief had long held that the settlers at the abandoned Carolina colony at Roanoke had gone to live with the Croatoan Indians, a belief supported by two carvings at Roanoke, the signs of orderly departure, and later sightings of light-complexioned Indians. Ralph Hamor, who published a work on Virginia in 1615, told of encountering an Englishman who had lived three years among the Indians and who resembled them "in complexion and habite." And in fact, runaways were an issue for the Jamestown colony, in general. The Virginia House of Burgesses, like Massachusetts Bay legislators, acknowledged the magnitude of the problem by passing laws to enforce white residency. "Virginia and Massachusetts Bay both legislated against being absent from the plantation without permission," recounts Kupperman. "People who did run away to the Indians might expect very extreme punishments, even up to the death penalty." Despite the legal frown and, more, stern punitiveness, however, a class of men in Virginia—who as boys had lived with the Indians during Jamestown's early years—functioned as valued go-betweens for English-Indian communication. They translated and advised, and they often acted as guides who assisted in the location of settlements and needed commodities.[123]

A century and more later, Hector St. John Crèvecoeur, writing of the plight of farmers in the Susquehanna Valley in the Revolutionary War era, mused philosophically on the white Indians who had been encouraged by the social upheaval of the times. Stripped of property, the settlers fled to the Indians for refuge. "Where else could they go?" Crèvecoeur asked rhetorically. He also noted that others, who had a choice, were simply tired of conflict and more freely "took the same course." "I am told," he confessed, "that great numbers from the extended frontiers of the middle provinces have taken the same steps." Crèvecoeur went on to reflect: "What a strange idea this joining with the savages seems to convey to the imagination; this uniting with a people which Nature has distinguished by so many national marks! Yet this is what the Europeans have often done through choice and inclination, whereas we never hear of any Indians becoming civilized Europeans." "You cannot possibly conceive," he added, "the singular charm, the indescribable propensity which Europeans are apt to conceive and imbibe in a very short time for this vagrant life; a life which we civilized people are apt to represent to ourselves as the most ignoble, the most irksome of any. Upon a nearer inspection 'tis far from being so disgusting." Indeed, the Indian life was so far from being disgusting that Crèvecoeur had pondered and planned flight to a native village for himself and his family in the midst of Revolutionary War politics and social turmoil. His preoccupation with the flight of others was an extension of a preoccupation that came close to home, even though in his own case the plan never materialized.[124]

Not so for others of the era. At Oswego, on Lake Ontario in northern New York, whites in the (French and Indian) war-torn area taken by the Indians refused to go back home when the chance at last came. Meanwhile, blacks, too, joined in the confluence of lives and cultures. The Moravian missionary Bishop August Gottlieb Spangenberg chronicled his journey to Onondaga in 1745 in which he encountered an Iroquois sachem known to all as the Black Prince, a name he acquired because of his color—in one popular explanation because one of his parents was black. At Mashpee, Massachusetts, by 1802 there were 380 people of African as well as Indian and European descent, who according to William Simmons "lived in wigwams or small cottages and who farmed, whaled, fished, and made woolens, cheese, brooms, and baskets for a living."[125]

Amid this seventeenth- and eighteenth-century world of cultural mixture, it is no surprise that spiritual practices were exchanged and adopted by people outside the original group that possessed them. Often, the reason was manifest physical need. Thus we can especially find evidence for the use by whites of Indian healers and medicines in various contexts in early America. To be sure, much of white interest was directed toward indigenous herbalism. Colin Calloway has recounted the clear eighteenth-century record of recourse to Indian medicines from the writings of Crèvecoeur and a number of others. In one instance, Crèvecoeur, while visiting Oquaga, an Indian settlement along the Susquehanna River, discovered Pennsylvania colonists there who were looking for help from Indian healers. He went so far as to try to intoxicate one native healer in order to pry out her secrets. Likewise, in a general essay on the "manners of the Americans," Crèvecoeur alluded generically to "a skilful grandmother . . . who formerly learned of the Indians of her neighbourhood how to cure simple diseases by means of simple medicines."[126]

For the late eighteenth century, too, John Heckewelder (whose esteem for Indian physicians we have already briefly seen) amply supplied anecdotes and generalizations regarding white use of Indian physicians, even for surgical needs. "I have myself been benefited and cured by taking their emetics and their medicines in fevers, and by being sweated after their manner while labouring under a stubborn rheumatism," he confessed. "I have also known many, both whites and Indians, who have with the same success resorted to Indian physicians while labouring under diseases." He thought the Indians particularly excelled in "the cure of external wounds," and he extolled the virtues of Indian "surgeons" in doing so—there was "no wound, unless it should be absolutely mortal," that the best of Indian physicians could not heal. At least by the nineteenth century, it became an advertisement for a remedy to be called Indian. The publishing record speaks for itself: there was, in 1813, *The Indian Doctor's Dispensatory*; in 1836, *The Indian Guide to Health*; and in 1838, *The North American Indian Doctor; or, Nature's Method of Curing and Preventing Disease according to the Indians*. As Virgil J. Vogel has detailed, the white "Indian doctor" flourished as a staple of the American frontier, and among the Pennsylvania Germans the practices of folk healing that included magical conjurations were subsumed under the title "powwowing." Meanwhile, the *United States Pharmacopeia*, with its first appearance in 1820, listed more than two hundred items of Native American provenance, the large majority of them from North America.[127]

Itinerant Indian physicians became a fact of colonial life, ministering to all three races—Indians, whites, and blacks. The fabled Molly Ockett, for example, traveled through western Maine addressing the needs of her own Abenaki people and white settlers alike. Such indigenous physicians brought Indian spirituality with them, and they elided herbals and spirits as a cultural precondition of their trade. In fact, according to Karen Kupperman, "descriptions of Indian medicine rarely mention the use of herbal medicine," with the colonists instead mostly describing "incantations and magical charms," even as sick Englishmen "submitted to treatment by Indian medicine men." Calloway echoes the Kupperman assessment, declaring that "settlers not only used Indian remedies but sometimes did so in accordance with Indian customs and rituals." The negative evidence from ministers is telling: they tried to prevent recourse to Indian healers by warning their fellow colonists that the sources of Indian healing powers were demonic.[128]

Apparently, though, some colonists were not afraid of the devil. The evidence suggests that a number may have turned to Indians for help in matters beyond disease and illness and were quite ready to enter the world of Indian magic. In the same decade as the Salem witch trials, for example, Matthew Mayhew told of an Englishman who consulted a powwow as if he were a cunning man, seeking help to determine who had stolen goods from him. "This Powaw being by an English-man, worthy of Credit (who lately informed me of the same) desired to advise him, who had Stolen certain Goods which he had lost, having formerly been an eye witness of his ability." [129] However, many were plainly terrified by the alien power they felt to be present in the Indian spirit world. Popular beliefs surrounding the notorious Salem witchcraft trials of the late seventeenth century already suggest the same, with judges, victims, and onlookers readily accepting allusions to Indian or African witchcraft on the part of the slaves Tituba, Candy, and others, as we have already seen.

But there was earlier evidence to support the existence of white fears. Samuel Drake, for example, in chronicling the events leading up to the outbreak of 1692–1693, confided that for the year 1675 the "Practice of Witchcraft among the Indians gave the English a good deal of Trouble." In Connecticut, the trouble was felt to be so oppressive that the General Court of the colony in that year enacted a law ostensibly directed toward the Pequot Indians: "Whosoever shall Powau or use Witchcraft, or any Worship of the Devill, or any fals Gods, shall be convented and punished." It needs to be asked here to whom the "whosoever" referred. Were whites resorting to Pequot powwows? If not, Anglo-American legislators were surely admitting belief in the power of Pequot incantations by forbidding them. And belief, of course, functioned as, once again, a negative testimony to the perceived efficacy of Indian practice. Certainly in the case of the governor of New York in the early 1690s this must have been so. As the mass anxiety generated in the witchcraft epidemic in New England spilled over into the formerly Dutch colony, according to at least one history of the era its governor expressed the fear "that the Indian medicine-men were directing their incantations against himself."[130]

In the case of African belief and practice, appropriations were apparently more casual and less fraught with anxiety. Unlike the Indians, blacks were seldom objects of white accusations of sorcery, even though, as we have seen, they sometimes directed their efforts toward their white masters in order to alleviate their own conditions in slavery and there was some knowledge and fear of conjure among whites. William Piersen has noted that fortune-telling and divination —practices of African provenance—were accepted in the American colonies by whites precisely because they so much resembled the folk beliefs of Euro-Americans themselves. In one example of cultural combination, the West African toss of cowrie shells—a form of divination—became the new American game of gambling that was known as "paw paw" (from the name of a West African slaving station). In seaport towns in early America, both blacks and whites played the game. More than that, whites resorted to blacks for quasi-magical help when they thought they needed it. "During the colonial era," says Piersen, "many African Americans became well-known practitioners of the magical arts, working for both black and white clients."[131]

Even as this world of vernacular practice points toward the combinative metaphysical activity of a future America, the more speculative practice of metaphysics to come was signaled in the poetry of one former American slave, the well-known Phillis Wheatley. Kidnapped from Africa as a child and sold to John Wheatley in Boston in 1761, she was thoroughly encouraged by him. By the time she was twelve she was reading and translating Ovid, and she was writing her own poetry by the time she was fifteen, publishing her *Poems on Various Subjects Religious and Moral* in 1773, when she was twenty.[132] On the eve of the American Revolution, Wheatley broke the confines of circumstance in a statement of universalism and connection that, conceptually, prefigured the language of metaphysics:

> Soaring through air to find the bright abode
> Th'empyreal palace of the thund'ring God,
> We on thy pinions can surpass the wind,

And leave the rolling universe behind:
From star to star the mental optics rove,
Measure the skies, and range the realms above,
There in one view we grasp the mighty whole,
Or with new worlds amaze th'unbounded soul.[133]

There were echoes of Africa in the God of thunder and in the winged flight of the imagination, evoking the flight to an unknown realm of an old-world spirit adventurer, be the seeker devotee or shaman. Yet here was a language that looked toward a later time when Americans with far different histories would embrace the flight of spirit into higher realms. Phillis Wheatley's expectations of the "mighty whole" would blend with those of countless other Americans.

Part Two

TRANSITIONS

3

REVOLUTIONS AND ENLIGHTENMENTS

In 1847, on the eve of the spiritualist excitement that would sweep across mid-century America, poet and Quaker John Greenleaf Whittier published a small but revealing work of prose. Based in part on materials that had appeared in print as early as 1833 and again in 1843, Whittier's *The Supernaturalism of New England* told in its claims and caveats a story about how the times had changed.[1] His essay stood as one emblem of the new culture of expectation that, after the American political revolution, subsumed the past into a simultaneously Enlightened and Romantic vision for the present and future. It pointed to a culture's re-memberings and forgettings, to its pretensions and promises for the time to come.

As his book unfolded, Whittier planted himself squarely on rationalist ground that he, at least, had failed to find among his seventeenth-century forebears. Expressing gentle disdain at their credulity, he also let himself admit that there were mysterious aspects to life that he—in case after case—could not satisfactorily explain. Significantly, he headed his first chapter with an epithet drawn from John Josselyn's *New England's Rarities* of 1672: "There be no beggars in this country, but witches too many."[2] At first the condition of having too many witches seemed not all bad. "Beneath the outward mask and habitude of the New England character," Whittier confided, "there is a spiritual activity—an undercurrent of intense, earnest thought—an infinity of Belief—a capacity for Faith in its most transcendental possibilities."[3] Spirit, though, in contact with the Indian inheritance that pervaded the land and certain aspects of English history, could lead to fearful presences. Here one could discover "no infrequent traces of the Old Superstition—that dark theory of the Invisible World, in which our Puritan ancestors had united the wild extravagance of Indian tradition with the familiar and common fantasies of their native land, and that gloomy, indefinite awe of an agency of Evil which their peculiar interpretations of the Sacred Volume had inspired." In one telling sentence, Whittier had perceived links between Native American powwows, English cunning folk, and a biblical devil—and he had made it clear how little he liked what he saw. From the post-Enlightenment place where he stood, he could only feel dismay for a fusion that mystified "the plainest passages of the great laws of the universe" and was responsible for "poisoning the fountains of education."[4]

For Whittier, the results were easy to spot. Wild enthusiasms stalked New England. There was Millerism—with "thronging thousands" expecting the Apocalypse at Boston's "Temple of the Second Advent." There was also Transcendentalism—with "nightly gatherings of 'Disciples of the Newness'" awaiting their own millennium. And there was animal magnetism (mesmerism)—with its "marvels" that threw "far into shadow the simple witchcraft of our ancestors." Searching for signs of the present in the inherited past, Whittier was drawn again to its Indian ghosts. He wanted to know how much New England's "superstitions" had been "modified," indeed *acclimated*, by commingling with those of the original inhabitants." Moreover, he could at least begin to answer. "The Indian peopled Nature with good and evil intelligences," he wrote. "The waterfall, the lake, the mist, the rock, and tree, had each its spirit. Every species of animal in the woods, and of bird in the air, had its spiritual archetype. The Powah was, in almost all cases, a conjuror, employing magical rites and grotesque incantations to drive away disease or avert misfortune; and it is certain that many of his charms and remedies are still practised among us." He could also point to the continuing presence of Africa in the spirit work of the New England present. "There is still living, within a few miles of my residence," he told readers, "an old colored woman, who during the last twenty years, has been consulted by hundreds of anxious inquirers into the future."[5]

Even as he named the combinative character of New England's spiritual culture, Whittier disclosed his own learning in a European tradition of magic. He quoted Cornelius Agrippa at least four times in his essay and cited Agrippa's German disciple Johann Wierus (Weiher or Weyer). In the midst of invoking the well-known doctor Robert Child, who had immigrated to Puritan New England and who was to be counted among "learned and scientific wizards," Whittier identified a 1651 work that in English translation compared Child's "'sublime hermeticall and theomagicall lore' . . . to that of Hermes and Agrippa." His sixth chapter began with a quotation attributed to Sir Walter Raleigh: "It is confessed of all that a magician is none other than *Divinorum cultor et interpres*, a studious observer and expounder of divine things."[6]

Whittier's work evolved as a survey of instances of "supernaturalism" in the New England of the poet's present, and he reported, somewhat standoffishly, a series of anecdotes in which various unexplained healings and other magical acts occurred. In the midst of it all, he managed to find his own intellectual and confessional voice in what might be described as a metaphysicalized rationalism. He had heard the accounts and read of the contemporary witches and the animal magnetism used to spot them. He knew his Agrippa and his learned wizard lore. But he also knew the Enlightenment; he knew the Romanticism that succeeded it; and he remembered the moralism of the Puritan past and his own Quaker present: "This mysterious Universe, through which, half veiled in its own shadow, our dim little planet is wheeling, with its star-worlds and thought-wearying spaces, remains. Nature's mighty miracle is still over and around us; and hence awe, wonder and reverence remain to be the inheritance of humanity; still are there beautiful repentances and holy deathbeds, and still over the soul's darkness and confusion rises star-like the great idea of duty. By higher and better influences than the poor spectres of superstition man must henceforth be taught to reverence the Invisible, and in the consciousness of his own weakness and sin and sorrow, to lean with childlike trust on the wisdom and mercy of an overruling Providence."[7]

The "phantasms" that captivated Whittier's naive fellow New Englanders were "but the hieroglyphic representation of spiritual and moral phenomena." By contrast, "in the undefinable power of mind over mind" he could find a solution to his ancestors' witchcraft.[8] Whittier, thus, by 1847 stood poised at the edge of a new metaphysical America that would open out beyond him. Themes of correspondence and the power of mind would continue to be linked to further themes of securing energy to heal body and spirit and to enhance living. Bringing in its train the inherited worlds of English and Continental Europeans, of Indians, and of Africans, the new metaphysics would carry along, too, the cultural events that constituted the Enlightenment and Romanticism, even as it reinvented them under the impress of contemporary excitements like the Transcendentalism and mesmerism that Whittier cited. Nor would the metaphysical America that evolved be devoid of explicitly Protestant roots, for it would be the open-ended future for a Calvinism that had first turned Arminian and then liberalized even more. Metaphysical America would function, literally, in a borderlands at the edge of liberal Protestantism—and with, sometimes, even bits and pieces of more conservative and evangelical Protestantism added. This chapter surveys the culture of a series of revolutions and enlightenments that sprang up in the aftermath of political revolution and in the broad cultural climate of the Enlightenment and an emerging Romanticism. The revolutions meant turnings—revolvings—of the world as it was known and lived, so that new times—new ages of millennial expectation—came into being. The agents of the revolutions were numerous and varied, and it would be impossible to tell the stories of all of them here. Still, we can gain some purchase on their agency by exploring the metaphysicalizing work of major movements and movers in the new order. To do so, we look at the end-century, new-century time from the era of the American Revolution through the early national period. We notice especially the presences and performances of Freemasons, Mormons, Universalists, and Unitarians-turned-Transcendentalists in a new and combinative republic of the spirit.

FREEMASONRY AND THE ENLIGHTENMENT
OF THE VILLAGE

The Scottish Masonry of Robert Moray (1641) and the English version (1646) into which Elias Ashmole, celebrated founder of Oxford's Ashmolean Museum, had been inducted (see chapter 1) both reflected an earlier seventeenth-century Masonry that became significantly altered in Britain's North American colonies. Already, as we have seen, operative Masonry was undergoing the crucial renovation that would transform Freemasonry into the speculative performances of well-born gentlemen. Indeed, by 1717, members of the so-called four "old lodges" of London came together to create the Premier Grand Lodge of England. Among their number were a group of individuals who had worked to create the Royal Society of London, dedicated to the new sciences, and at the emerging lodge's head members installed a nonoperative or "accepted" Mason. The story of colonial, and then early national, American Masonry, however, moved well beyond that change. At first it became a tale of attenuation for Hermetic strands (both Moray and Ashmole had practiced magic as well as science), whatever their earlier strength may have been. It also became a story about the reinscription of the Masonic "secret" in moralistic terms that at once continued the inscription of the past and simultaneously made it new by dipping it into the ink of American Protestant evangelical culture and circumstance. Finally, it became a tale of democratization that seized on divisions between "modern" and "antient" lodges to promote a "village enlightenment"—to borrow a term from David Jaffee—bringing Enlightenment discourse into the lived worlds of numerous late-eighteenth- and early-nineteenth-century American men.[9]

Freemasonry came to Britain's North American colonies by the 1730s. In Philadelphia, St. John's Lodge began meeting around 1730 and by the following year had formed itself into a grand lodge, with Benjamin Franklin a member and then, in 1734, grand master. A lodge flourished in Boston in 1730 as well, and by 1733 the Grand Lodge of London had appointed Henry Price of Boston as "Provincial Grand master of New England and Dominions and Territories thereunto belonging." Masonic groups began to spring up in other colonial cities and towns—in Savannah in 1733 and 1734; in Virginia (with Scottish affiliation) in 1741; in Newport, Rhode Island, in 1749; in Maryland the same year; and in New Haven in 1750. By 1800, we are told, there were eighteen thousand Masons in the new United States, with forty-five lodges in Connecticut alone. A quarter century later, New York state—which counted roughly five hundred Masons before the Revolution—was by itself home to twenty thousand.[10]

Franklin's enthusiasm for both Masonry and the printing trade led to the American publication, in 1734, of the definitive work attributed to James Anderson. *The Constitutions of the Free-Masons: Containing the History, Charges, Regulations, &c. of That Most Ancient and Right Worshipful Fraternity* transformed the Grand Lodge into a central governing agency and, in the words of Dorothy Ann Lipson, changed the organization "from a general assembly of members into an association of lodge Masters and other officers." In the process of doing so, the document compiled old legendary lore from a variety of sources to construct a putative history of Masonry, and it also announced the Freemasonic stance toward God and divine things. Important here, Anderson—a genealogist and also a Presbyterian minister—produced the 1723 work with the help of others, including especially the Anglican priest John Desaguliers, who was a well-known London scientist and educator. When Franklin, just over a decade later, printed the Anderson *Constitutions* on the other side of the Atlantic, he provided a charter for a particular way of seeing and understanding the American Freemasonic venture.[11]

In fact, even as the *Constitutions* spun its fanciful history of the Masons extending back to the foundations of the universe and certainly to biblical times, it functioned as a representative document in the spread of Enlightenment ideas and values—in their vernacularization. The legendary history that included generous allusions to Hermes Trismegistus and that styled Abraham as a Kabbalist had been reconstituted without overt Hermeticism. Commenting on the gradual process that brought the change, Margaret C. Jacob notes that as late as the decade of the 1690s Masonic manuscripts evoked a "secret mathematical wisdom descended from Hermes." But the new world of Masonry would resonate differently, and "gradually," Jacob writes, "the Hermetic lore would be replaced by the 'magic' of Newtonian science." Yet the Hermeticism would be encoded, still, "in a mysticism that could easily lend itself to the worship of nature," and—along with the vanished artisans and builders of cathedrals—"in a dedication to the study of mathematics, and of course in ceremonies and rituals for the installation of grand masters and the initiation of apprentices, in aprons and emblems such as the square and the compass."[12]

We gain a glimpse of the new vision of what a Mason should be in the words of the Anderson *Constitutions,* which eighteenth-century American Masons were reading to tell them who they were:

> A *Mason* is oblig'd, by his Tenure, to obey the moral Law; and if he rightly understands the Art, he will never be a stupid *Atheist,* nor an irreligious *Libertian.* But though in ancient Times Masons were charg'd in every Country to be of the Religion of that Country or Nation, whatever it was, yet 'tis now thought more expedient only to oblige them to that Religion in which all Men agree, leaving their particular Opinions to themselves; that is, to be *good Men and true,* or Men of Honour and Honesty, by whatever Denominations or Persuasions they may be distinguish'd; whereby Masonry becomes the *Center* of *Union,* and the Means of conciliating true Friendship among Persons that must else have remain'd at a perpetual Distance.[13]

In this rendition it seems almost that the secret had disappeared from the secret society. The dark, mysterious, and theosophized universe of Hermeticism had dissolved in the clarified presence of Enlightenment-style deism. Bright sun shone into mystical cobwebs to clear away confusion; and without this sort of conceptual debris, one did not need to protest futilely as a "stupid atheist." Instead, one turned confidently toward a just deity who functioned as a kind of upper-end counting-house manager, rewarding virtue and punishing vice after death and encouraging benevolence and good works before that. Put differently, the secret had been turned inside out to support—not the esotericism of the Hermetic path—but the exotericism of an upright Protestant moralism that countenanced being "square" and "on the square." In the American context, the Mason would belong to a good Protestant denomination that would be neither too contentious nor too opinionated, and—in the era of revolutionary expectations— Masonic aspirations toward union would work as an important social force.

Dorothy Ann Lipson has pointed to the enterprise of social architecture in the London production of the Premier Grand Lodge. In America, the social vision of the Masonic brothers would register significant agreement along the eastern Atlantic seaboard as the American Revolution progressed. Brother Benjamin Franklin had prestigious company among the founding fathers of the new nation, and George Washington freely gave the Masonic sign as he traveled through the colonies. The Sons of Liberty, who perpetrated the Boston Tea Party in 1773 dressed as Mohawk Indians, the story went, had earlier in the evening been meeting as Masonic brothers. Nine of the fifty-six signers of the Declaration of Independence were clearly Masons, and about two dozen more have been claimed for Masonic affiliation.[14] More explicitly, at least two Freemasonic authors have attributed the growth of the notion of union among the colonists to the brotherhood.[15]

Yet, as demonstrated in the rise of African American Prince Hall Masonry (1774)—and the white Masonic protests it generated concerning its legitimacy—Masonic brotherhood was only for some. Moreover, even in its Prince Hall version, black Freemasonry replayed white practice, for not all blacks were candidates for lodge membership. As Lipson has so well detailed for the London scene, the Masonic brothers were distinctly clubby. In fact, when "acceptance" grew among Masons it did so in a milieu in which old guild members stood for moral purpose but did so as *clubmen*.[16] They were an exclusionary society, and exclusivism was essential to their union, for lodge members were keepers of privileged knowledge. At the center of their selective union was the reinvested secret, the new old story of former and mystified Builders and the ritual that supported it, teaching the moral meanings that lodge members were to embody in their lives.

Even as brother Masons reveled in their secret, however, it had ironically already been revealed. In the wake of the American Revolution and in the midst of their new democracy, Americans who were not Masons could read an exposé that purported to tell all. As early as the 1760s, in London, *Hiram; or, The Grand Master-Key to the Door of Both Antient and Modern Free-Masonry* was available to instruct voyeurs in the details of how the initiations were accomplished. The frontispiece to the second edition of 1766, in fact, portrayed a grand master seated on a raised platform before a large table, while around it a group of well-clad gentlemen stood and a blindfolded candidate for initiation faced them, a mason's square on the floor at his feet. More important on the American side of the waters, the 1762 exposé *Jachin and Boaz*—which in its very title revealed the secret initiatory words for the Entered Apprentice and Fellow Craft degrees—had gone through sixteen English editions by 1825 and, in the midst of these, appeared in an American edition in Boston in 1794. Thereafter the small book, or pamphlet, went through a series of other American editions and printings. The on-line catalog of the University of California by itself lists some seventeen by 1818, and they appeared not only in Boston and New York City but also in places like Windsor (Vermont), Suffield (Connecticut), Poughkeepsie and Albany (New York), Lancaster (Pennsylvania), and Wilmington (Delaware).[17]

Reading *Jachin and Boaz*, men in small-town America could learn the solemn, secret history of the building of Solomon's Temple in biblical times and of the murder and then raising up of its master builder Hiram Abif, the first Masonic grand master. Hiram had stalwartly refused to give the Master's Word to workers not authorized to receive it. The secret and carefully guarded word carried practical implications for labor assignments and pay but also intimations of mystical worlds beyond, and workers who wanted the word conspired to use force. Rushing to the various doors of the temple to escape his accosters, Hiram met with violence at each one, until, at the west door, "he received a terrible Fracture upon his head with a Gavel or Setting Maul, which occasioned his Death."[18] He was buried the next night at midnight by his assassins, and King Solomon, noticing his absence, sent out a search party—to no avail. Then twelve of the "Fellow-Crafts" who had been accomplices, "their Consciences pricking them," confessed what they knew to Solomon, located the three actual assassins, and brought them to Solomon for execution. Thereafter, at the king's bidding, the Fellow Crafts sought to disinter the body of Hiram to be buried again solemnly, and—since they could not find a "Key-Word" about the "mangled" corpse— took the first "Word and Sign" uttered in the body's presence to Solomon, who adopted it as "the grand Sign of a Master Mason." (In the ritual it became "Mahabone" or "Macbenach," its very inscrutability hinting of a mystical past.) There were difficulties in raising the body out of its makeshift grave, and the workers needed to use a special grip—the "Master's Grip" or the "Five Points of Fellowship" ("Hand in Hand," "Foot to Foot," "Knee to Knee," "Breast to Breast," "The Left Hand supporting the Back").[19] Communication of this secret word and grip provided the heart and center of initiation to the third degree as Master Mason, the degree specifically created by speculative Masons as they transformed the formerly operative guilds.[20]

American men did not learn from *Jachin and Boaz* what, specifically, the accepted Masons had done to revise and expand the ritual. If the book's disclosures are to be believed, they did, however, find out the content of the initiation ritual not only for the Master's degree but also the two older ones that preceded it— the degrees of Entered Apprentice and Fellow Craft. They discovered that the Entered Apprentice's grip was given by pinching "with your Right Thumb Nail upon the first Joint of your Brother's Right Hand," and they learned that the word was "Jachin." They learned, too, that, for the degree of Fellow Craft, the grip involved putting the thumb nail on the *second* joint of the right hand and the word was "Boaz."[21] Readers likewise were told of "two fine Brass Pillars" on the porch of the temple of Solomon. Depending upon their familiarity with scripture, they might have known that Jachin and Boaz were explicitly named both in 1 Kings 7:21 and 2 Chronicles 3:17 (not 3:15, as the exposé stated) as the right and left pillars respectively on the porch or the front of the temple.[22]

Still more, in the midst of this apparently thoroughly biblicized Masonic world, readers encountered lodge prayers that skillfully combined the Bible of the past with the deism of the eighteenth-century Masonic present. "O Lord God, thou great and universal Mason of the World, and first Builder of Man, as it were a Temple," one began, and then it continued: "Be with us, O Lord, as thou hast promised, when two or three are gathered together in thy Name, thou wilt be in the midst of them."[23] The Bible stood beside square and compass, and together, in their combinative symbolism, they drew the initiated into a new religious world. Here, first, was the God of nature; second, surrounded as he was by the implements of the builder's trade, here was a secret that enticed men not into a heart of Hermetic darkness and magical power but—for all the exploits associated with Hiram Abif's ghoulish "resurrection"—into a moral correspondence and a moral life.

That famed celebrator of reason and rights Thomas Paine—in a now discredited argument that Freemasonry had descended from the Druids—was still astute enough to read the signs that suggested in Freemasonry something akin to sun worship. In his "Origin of Freemasonry," written originally in New York City in 1805 and published only posthumously, Paine trotted out evidence for his Druidic theory, which, read differently, supported a more general theory about the presence of natural religion in the lodges. "The roof of their temples or lodges is ornamented with a sun," Paine noted, "and the floor is a representation of the variegated face of the earth either by carpeting or mosaic work." Heavily buttressed by George Smith's *The Use and Abuse of Free-Masonry* (1783), which declared for the centrality of the sun ("the emblematical sun is the center of real Masonry"), Paine noticed the east-west orientation of the lodges (toward the rising sun) and the designated place for the lodge master (the east), to open the lodge as the sun opened the day. Paine did not mention that, for both Americans and western Europeans, Jerusalem was also in the east. He did, however, point to further sun-oriented specifics in the lodges, and then he read the "high festival of the Masons"—the feast of St. John the Baptist on June 24—as a celebration of the summer solstice ("every enlightened Mason must know that holding their festival on this day has no reference to the person called St. John").[24] Paine was silent about the other major Masonic festival in the annual cycle—that of St. John the Evangelist on December 27, close to the time of the winter solstice—but he had made his point.

Anderson's *Constitutions* had already made the winter feast of St. John clear, and, of course, the nature symbolism of the sun ruled over the midwinter festival when the sun conquered darkness and the days grew longer.[25] Nor did men have to be Masons to know about the feasts of both of the Johns. Cities and towns of the period regularly witnessed public Masonic parades on these occasions, and homilies and sermons to mark them were public events. External nature and its God, though, always led to the social world and to the passions and commitments that governed how society worked and operated. The new exoteric esotericism—the revealed secret—of the Masons concerned the interior depths of the heart and the upright *human* nature that operated out from the heart and into a moral community. The "Gentleman" of the Jerusalem Lodge who claimed authorship of *Jachin and Boaz*, at the beginning of his revelatory narrative, told readers straightaway that he was "inclined to think, that the chief Design of the Establishment" was "to rectify the Heart, inform the Mind, and promote the Moral and Social Virtues of Humanity, Decency, and good Order, as much as possible in the World." "Some of the Emblems of Free-Masons," he added, "confirm this Opinion, such as the Compass, Rule, Square, &c."[26]

What had "raised" Hiram Abif was neither a biblical miracle nor the magic of an Elias Ashmole or John Dee, despite the resonances in the secret Master's Word of Hiram with an ancient magical tradition. Instead, what had raised Hiram was the willed effort—the strength or virtue—of a community of caring brothers who stood hand in hand, toe to toe, knee to knee, breast to breast, and with hands supporting the back in order to enable a dead man, whose flesh was rotting away, to stand up. To leave no reader in the dark on the point, *Jachin and Boaz* had moralized its way quite thoroughly through its textual description: "Hand in Hand signifies that I will always put forth my Hand to serve a Brother as far as in my Power lies.—Foot to Foot, that I never will be afraid to go a Foot out of my way to serve a Brother.—Knee to Knee, that when I pray, I should never forget my Brother's Welfare. Breast to Breast, to shew I will keep my Brother's Secrets as my own.—The Left Hand supporting the Back, that I will always support a Brother, as far as I can, without being detrimental to my own Family."[27] The secret words for the Entered Apprentice and Fellow Craft degrees—Jachin and Boaz—expressed the "pillar" quality of upright brothers in constructing the holy temple of a moral society, and they told of, behind it, the "pillar" quality each man must acquire to construct the moral temple of the self. The inside-out secret still carried mystical weight, but it had transformed the mysticism into moralism and social vision.

In the new United States, the social vision took concrete form under the banner of democracy. Gradually, the elitism of the founding generation of the Republic began to erode, as emerging social forces were unleashed and as the very language that had provided an ideological ballast for revolutionary behavior began to be taken seriously by large groups of people. Nature and the rights of "man" became the family values of self-conscious citizens of the new-made Republic, and the village enlightenment spread its light seemingly everywhere. Although Freemasonry would always remain clubby, the club got broader. Steven Bullock has chronicled the divisions between "ancients" and "moderns" in the American Freemasonic community in the Revolutionary War era and beyond, the divisions reflecting an earlier English division among the lodges but also the growing class awareness and particular interests of Americans. In England, Irish weavers and other workers were turned away from London lodges, even though they had apparently been initiated as Masons by the Grand Lodge of Ireland. When the rejected brothers formed themselves into their own lodges, harking back to a right of "immemorial usage," the Grand Lodge of London before 1738 made changes to the ritual, "to prevent," as Sidney Morse wrote, "the visitation of these brethren in the regular lodges." Irish lodges claimed a propaganda victory out of the London action, styling themselves "Antient York Masons." The Londoners, of course, were disreputable "moderns."[28]

By the time of the American Revolution, the division between ancients and moderns had encouraged the formation of new and rival lodges in England, and the ancients were continuing to enjoy a broad appeal. They simply looked good in any public relations schema: they were democratic and reached out to different social classes, and they were liberal in their overall policies. The moderns, by contrast, behaved more traditionally. In America, even before the Revolutionary War, social changes were afoot that put pressure on the Craft brothers to honor and admit new members—new not only as individuals but also in terms of the social classes they represented. Artisans in East Coast cities turned to Masonry for status confirmation, while in the interior the elites, caught up in the westward expansion of the era, also became Masons as they, too, sought a stabilizing social institution in the midst of rapid change. The welcoming lodges for both groups were "antient." As Bullock writes, "Ancient lodges offered a way to assert a new importance—and a concrete example of Revolutionary equality and participation. Masonic affiliation also provided a means of redefining social position and claiming the honor previously reserved for gentlemen of wealth, education, and family. The same upheaval that shaped the new political geography of post-Revolutionary America also created Ancient Masonry."[29]

If, as Bullock argues, "the rise of Ancient Masonry formed part of the American redefinition of honor and social status," the statistical record in unambiguous terms supports the tale. Yet the new artisans in eastern seaboard ancient lodges were hardly card-carrying members of the great unwashed. They emerged, instead, from "the upper ranges of men outside the elite." Their country cousins who joined ancient Masonic lodges did so for other reasons, in a kind of supply-side model of new social availability. "Beginning slowly before the Revolution but then picking up rapidly," Bullock recounts, "Ancient Masons spread their fraternity into the interior. By the beginning of the next century, more American lodges met in inland villages than on the urban seaboard."[30] A new gentility was being symbolized in the ancient lodges of the interior, and older social ar-

rangements were forced to yield. With the combined energies of the new arti-
san members in the east and the rising gentlemen of the interior, a Masonic social revolution had been perpetrated. "By 1795," Bullock summarizes, "Ancient
masonry dominated the American fraternity."[31]

If so, so did democratic values. The enlightenment of artisans and villagers
broadened the reach of the rationalist doctrine that had made late-eighteenth-
and early-nineteenth-century Masonry, for all its biblicism, a propaganda vehicle
for the spread of notions of republican virtue and citizen spirituality. Moreover,
in some places, ancient-modern tensions may have been less important than
other factors in Freemasonry's democratizing role. Sometimes the lines of class
distinction were blurred because the real line of distinction lay between city and
country, and the new Enlightenment-style democracy of the urban center flourished in the discourse communities of the lodges, where, significantly, Jews as
well as Christians found brotherhood.[32] Nor did immediate Revolutionary War
problems—with loyalists to the British cause in Masonic ranks—in any lasting
way disrupt the emerging pattern. As Bullock notes, despite the challenges and
the traditional British source of status for the lodges American Masonry came
out of the war with new authority and acquired a strong republican reputation.
Civilian lodges had been able to control the loyalist sentiment in their midst because of a strong patriot presence. Masonry had successfully aligned itself with
the Revolution and the new order that the Enlightenment endorsed. Democratization of the old elite establishment continued.[33]

Freemasonry itself—standing tall after the Revolution as a beacon of republican light—came crashing down in 1826, when the notorious William Morgan
affair unleashed an epidemic of Antimasonry throughout the nation. Morgan
had disappeared, never to be seen again, after his just-being-printed book *Illustrations of Masonry* claimed to reveal the secrets of his lodge in western New
York. With public hysteria being fueled by politicians, Masons were accused of
murdering him and hostility escalated, so that, in the first third-party movement
in the United States, a national Antimasonic party became, until the election
of 1832, part of the American political scene.[34] It took until the 1840s and after
for Masonry to recover. For the men who, as late as 1818, had read *Jachin and
Boaz* in a series of American towns and cities, the planned revelation of Masonic secrets that led to the rise of Antimasonry must have raised some eyebrows
and occasioned some comment. But that is a matter to visit later. In its heyday
in the era of the Revolution, Freemasonry had functioned as a significant social vehicle to spread Enlightenment values, to link them with the specifically
American politics of a new republican order, and to democratize an emerging

liberal religiosity. In so doing, it had transformed an old Hermetic secret into a new moralistic one that was not really secret any longer.

What, then, can be said about the relationship of this late-eighteenth-, early-nineteenth-century Freemasonry to the formation of American metaphysical religion? Alongside the general public propaganda that came through news-papers and other ephemeral literature and language, Freemasonry provided powerful tools—cultural squares and compasses, if you will—for enlarging the pragmatism of the metaphysical secret. Men engaged in clandestine, almost adolescent-style, rituals of initiation in order to foster community. They fostered community in order to shore up their public moral selves so that they might do good. They did good to cement the bonds of fellowship with one another—in a circular exchange of cultural energy that led from and to themselves. Their concerns were this-worldly and not of a place beyond; they sought not the oblit-eration of self in the absolute, but its enhancement in the well-lived life in so-ciety. By moving from mysticism and angel-summoning to public performance and the feeding of orphans and widows, they also made an intellectual move that would later help to lift metaphysics, for many, out of its magical past and into a more rationalized future.

Here the esoteric became exoteric, and revelation aspired, at least in theory, to encompass all. It was perhaps a poetic clue to the role of Freemasonry in the metaphysical future of the United States that some linked its lodges to the sym-bolism of the sun. Masonry, literally, let the sun shine into the occluded secret of the Hermetic past. The "Mohawk Indians" who had poured tea into Boston harbor were expressing their *public* concerns for their American tribe. For all its clubbiness, Masonry aligned itself with the democratic many, at least the many of the middling sort. Indeed, not only were there—despite white Masonic pro-tests—African American Prince Hall Masons, but there were Masonic accounts of American Indians who had become Craft brothers, too.[35] Cunning folk, now, were not the only quasi-democratic bearers of secrets. And in the growing urban centers, inhabitants who pursued the commercial interests of their class were also enjoying the society of the lodges. In the wake of the declassified secret, the new culture of expectation that came with the Revolution brought anticipations of light for all—for better living in the here and now.

The story, however, did not end here, and its sequel proved that the Enlighten-ment narrative of progress to greater light was not the only plotline that could be invoked. Enter—into this pragmatic and thoroughly Protestant Masonry of the revealed moral secret—the Royal Arch. And enter, behind the Arch, a series of contrived elaborations on ritual that brought a remysticized almost-Hermeticism to more and more Masonic lodges. The earliest known American record of the conferring of the Royal Arch degree (a degree that emerged in British Masonry in the 1740s among the schismatic ancients) dates from 1753 at the Lodge of Fredericksburg, Virginia, the lodge to which George Washington belonged.[36] The first Royal Arch chapter came later, at Boston's St. Andrew's Lodge in 1769, and the higher degrees—Mark-Master Mason, Past-Master Mason, Most Excellent Master-Mason, and Royal Arch Mason—were adopted in new ancient lodges during the war period. But the mystique of the Royal Arch was to take hold rapidly well past the time of the American Revolution, especially after Thomas Smith Webb published his *Freemason's Monitor* in 1797, a work reprinted widely in the Northeast for the next twenty years and more.[37] By 1827 (in the wake of the Morgan furor), according to Steven Bullock, New York could claim 125 Royal Arch chapters, and in the frontier interior of Tennessee half of the nearly forty lodges were Royal Arch. More than that, the four degrees that culminated in the exotic and mystical Royal Arch initiation were only part of the story. Degrees proliferated, and increasingly elaborate ceremonies accompanied them, so that by 1802 in Charleston, to cite one example, the supreme council had oversight over some thirty-three.[38]

In the Webb account of the new degrees, we gain a sense of the mystification that the initiations were designed to provide. In a text that, he freely acknowledged, drew heavily in its earlier sections on William Preston's *Illustrations of Masonry*, Webb began in accord with Enlightenment convention, extolling the God of Nature, praising the "symmetry, good order, and proportion, which appear in all the works of creation," and noticing especially the "universal harmony and affection which subsists among the different species of beings, of every rank and denomination."[39] The broadcast light of Nature, however, soon gave way to the dimmer, more mysterious world of secrets. "The usages and customs of masons have ever corresponded with those of the Egyptian philosophers, to which they bear a near affinity," wrote Webb. "Unwilling to expose their mysteries to vulgar eyes, they concealed their particular tenets, and principles of polity, under hieroglyphical figures; and expressed their notions of government by signs and symbols which they communicated to their Magi alone, who were bound by oath not to reveal them." Webb disclosed no grips, secret signs, or passwords in his exposition, but he told enough—and especially told enough Masonic "history" that accompanied the conferring of each degree—so that readers would surely be enticed to the lodges to learn more. While the seventh, or Royal Arch degree, was "the summit and perfection of ancient masonry," now there were more to come. Beyond the summit, there lay the "Ineffable Degrees," and Webb insisted on their "total difference" from what went before.[40]

Webb carefully detailed the histories and charges for these degrees, and then—in a long and elaborate myth/legend that each initiate would live out and through—took his readers into the secret chambers of the penultimate degree. Here, in the account of the Degree of Knights of the Ninth, or Royal, Arch, readers learned the mysterious saga of Enoch the Prophet. For those who had read or heard of the fabled Christian Rosencreutz of the Rosicrucian manifestos and knew of his opened tomb with its intact corpse and mystical texts, the narrative evoked a wisdom world they had encountered before. Webb instructed readers that the lodge should be held in a "most secret place," with "a vault under ground . . . in the centre of the top of which there must be a trap door, for the admission of candidates." He told them of Enoch's transfigurative vision on a mountaintop, where "he beheld a triangular plate of gold, most brilliantly enlightened, and upon which were some characters which he received a strict injunction never to pronounce." To commemorate the vision, Enoch built an underground temple with "nine arches, one above another," and in the ninth and "deepest" arch he deposited a triangular golden plate, like the one he had seen, having "engraved upon it the same ineffable characters which God had shewn to him" and "placed it on a triangular pedestal of white marble." He also erected two pillars, one of marble and one of brass, with hieroglyphics engraved on both—on the marble one a record of the treasure hidden in the arches underground, and on the brass one "the principles of the liberal arts, particularly of Masonry."[41]

Thousands of years passed, and the time came when the foundation was being dug for King Solomon's legendary temple. In the process, workers by happenstance discovered "the ruins of an ancient edifice" and its treasures. Directed by the king, one of his three "Grand Master Architects" descended ever more deeply through what were the arched vaults of the structure until he arrived at the ninth. Here a fortuitous accident put out his light, and he was "immediately struck with the sight of a triangular plate of gold, richly adorned with precious stones; the brilliancy of which struck him with admiration and astonishment." Later the Solomonic seeker and his companions discovered the characters engraved upon the plate. They also announced their discovery to King Solomon, who was with the King of Tyre and who made them Knights of the Ninth or Royal Arch. The two kings apparently knew all about the mysterious engraving on the plate—the unspeakable sacred name of the deity. Now that his knights were "in possession of the true characters, King Solomon would soon give them the true pronunciation." Instead of the "corruption" of the name in false Gods, such as "Juba of the Moors" and "Jupiter of the Romans," they would possess the "true name"—and so the gnostic (and Kabbalistic) truth.[42]

All, however, did not remain in light and splendor. Some who desired to behold the mysteries of the arches were refused by Solomon. They attempted to descend to the vault anyway, but in a "dreadful accident" that befell them "the nine arches fell in upon them," and "no remains of the arches" were "to be seen." There remained only "a few pieces of marble, upon which were engraved certain hieroglyphics." These King Solomon had deciphered and was "fully assured" that they were part of the "marble pillar that had been erected by Enoch" (along with the brass one). Hence Solomon had them deposited in a "Sacred vault."[43]

In the underground darkness of the vault, reached by descent after descent, metaphysical Truth was the ultimate treasure. It was found by arduous labor, and its possession meant ownership of secret and privileged revelation. The bright sun of Revolutionary-era Masonry had given way to shadow, and Masonic initiates had entered a romanticized Hermetic world, even as they carried along with it the enlightenment of the Age of Reason. It was this combination of the clear light of reason and the dark shadow of secrecy out of which American metaphysical religion was poised to emerge, even as it transformed darkness into light. The first major formation to advance this new combinative metaphysical project was the work of a poor and seemingly unremarkable inhabitant of rural upstate New York.

MORMONISM AND THE ENLIGHTENMENT OF MAGIC

The Hermetic world disclosed in the elaborations of Masonic degrees was freshly encountered by a young Joseph Smith (1805–1844) in the social matrix that nurtured him from his early years. Beyond that, the Mormonism that was his enduring foundation brought together, in this first remarkable metaphysical synthesis of the nineteenth century, the enlightenments of a series of spiritual movements and cultural worlds. Joseph Smith would be fascinated by Freemasonry until he joined a lodge himself at last in 1842. He would clearly be acquainted with the story of Enoch's plates of gold and their found-and-lost-again history in the age of Solomon. He would likewise know something of the mystical revelations of the celebrated Swedish author and visionary of the period, Emanuel Swedenborg (1688–1772), who, in Smith's nineteenth-century upstate New York environment, had become something of a Hermetic household magus. But he would also be a cunning man and a lover of Indian lore. And, in the midst of all of this, he would anguish as a religious seeker struggling with the discordant messages of Christian evangelical preachers around the era's revival fires.

Smith's exposure to Freemasonry began with his family's familiarity with it from the 1790s in Vermont, where his parents then lived. The senior Joseph Smith, after he moved his family to New York, may have joined the Ontario Lodge in Canandaigua in 1817 (there was a "Joseph Smith" recorded on its membership lists), and his second son, Hyrum, joined the Mount Moriah Lodge in Palmyra, where the family lived, in the 1820s. Nor was the family as a whole unfamiliar with Masonic symbols and significations. Lucy Smith, for example, in a preliminary draft from the 1840s of her later history of her son, indicated a thorough immersion in a magical world (more on this later) that was also a Masonic one. Protesting that the family kept its workaday focus, she insisted that they did not try to "win the faculty of Abrac, drawing magic circles, or sooth saying, to the neglect of all kinds of business." This faculty of Abrac, associated with magical amulets and their powers, was part of the ambience of eighteenth-century Masons, and Craft manuals reflected the familiarity—in a culture in which the Webb text and other Freemasonic writings were readily available.[44] A tangled network of relationships also existed among early Mormon converts with Freemasonic backgrounds. Meanwhile, a series of commentators on Smith's "translated" *Book of Mormon* point to its Antimasonic themes, reflecting the post-Morgan epidemic of Antimasonry in upstate New York during the later 1820s and thereafter. Morgan, after all, was kidnapped outside the Canandaigua jail, a bare twelve miles from the Smith family household.[45]

Joseph Smith's early condemnation of secret societies, however, harbored a fascination for them. In Illinois, he joined the Nauvoo Masonic Lodge, which Mormons—with his permission—had petitioned the Grand Master of Illinois to begin. By March of 1842, he later wrote, he "rose to the sublime degree." Illinois Masons discontinued the controversial Nauvoo Lodge. But just before Smith's murder in 1844 by a mob at the Carthage, Illinois, jail, he was said to have given a Masonic distress signal that should have brought Craft brothers to his aid.[46]

Whatever his official relationship to Masonry, more important was the access that Smith gained to Masonic secret initiations and their role in shaping Mormon temple ceremonies. As early as 1832, Smith had declared that he was Enoch the Prophet. In so doing he paved the way for an association between himself and the secret and buried (Masonic) knowledge thought to descend from Adam to Enoch to Solomon. When, like Solomon, he was linked to the discovery of golden plates in the depths of the earth, he added a link, too, to the chain of associations he was forging. When he also claimed the "Urim" and "Thummim" by means of which to translate the inscriptions on the plates, he echoed a biblical language—the name of the jewels or stones that formed the center of Aaron's "breastplate of judgment"—made familiar in public Masonic discourse.[47] When, likewise in the early 1830s, he proclaimed a restored biblical priesthood of Melchizedek, his revelation followed a formula central to Royal Arch Masonry (both the Canandaigua and Palmyra lodges were Royal Arch) in acknowledging the passage of the priesthood from Adam to Enoch to Solomon. But the culmination came in Mormon temple foundations, and in its full form it came later. As Smith's emerging theological and ritual creations took concrete shape, his restored priesthoods found in newly built temples appropriate spaces in which to exercise function and authority. Solomon's temple rose again in each Mormon foundation, and from one point of view what Smith was doing was bringing a renewed and purified Masonry—a "true Masonry"—to his followers. It was only a matter of months after Smith himself had become a Mason that his elaborate endowment rituals were initiated. Indeed, writing in the Mormon journal *Dialogue,* Michael W. Homer cites the "candor of Smith and others" regarding the "close connection between Freemasonry and Mormonism." Early Mormon leaders, Homer argues, "recognized this connection and did not consider it too sacred or controversial to discuss." "In the eyes of his family and his closest followers," John Brooke in his turn writes, "Smith's endowment rituals of 1842–3, the foundation of a new Mormonism promising a progression into godhood for the faithful, signaled the restoration of the hermetic promise of a pure Gnostic Freemasonry." Even if Brooke's study on the whole may obscure the biblical and Christian legacy (beyond the Radical Reformation) that Smith's Mormonism also incorporated, his work is telling and important here.[48]

In a comprehensive rehearsal of Mormon temple borrowings from Royal Arch Masonry, Brooke points to elements as varied as the pulpit veils in the Kirtland, Ohio, temple of 1836 and the temple endowment ritual that, by the early 1850s, Brigham Young was said to have called "Celestial Masonry." The ceremony was complex, intricate, dramatic, and richly combinative, and it would be too simple to attribute its creation to a single source, as significant as Masonry was for Smith and a good number of his followers. Still, the lengthy rite featured grips, signs, passwords, the prevalent form of the Masonic five points of fellowship, and other clues to provenance. Brooke notes in the rituals the "striking similarities with Masonic symbolism," especially the symbols used in "the York Rite, which was established at the Nauvoo Lodge." He cites also the "temple garments, very similar to Masonic ceremonial garb" with "an apron with Masonic compass and square," a motif repeated on the temple veil. "The language of the tokens and penalties of the Mormon priesthoods had exact parallels in Freemasonry," Brooke summarizes, "progressing from parallels with the first three degrees of Entered Apprentice, Fellow Craft, and Master Mason to parallels with the Royal Arch and the higher degrees." Besides the near-simultaneous work of Homer, Brooke has other, earlier company in the connections he notices. "The observant Craftsman cannot be long among the Mormon people without noting the frequent use made of certain emblems and symbols which have come to be associated in the public mind with the Masonic fraternity," S. H. Goodwin wrote by 1924. He went on to supply a clear bill of supporting evidence in the temple ritual and its accoutrements. Moreover, it is hard to discount the "twenty-seven parallels between the ritual of the Masons and the Mormon Temple ceremony" that Jerald and Sandra Tanner have cited, along with the observations of a series of church insiders before the appearance of Homer's lengthy essay.⁴⁹

To connect the dots between Smith and Freemasonry, as I have been doing here, is well enough. But the task of historical recovery involves a deeper archaeology of Mormon foundations. In the vaults of Smith's memory and attachment were links that identify the Mormon founder with a broad Hermeticism that he and many of the people who joined him inherited from the received vernacular world of his culture and time. The order of Melchizedek was not the ritual ground of Masons only. Nearly a century before the dedication of the Kirtland temple, Ephratans were celebrating the restored order of Melchizedek, and in Smith's own time so were the communitarian societies of the Shakers and the Rappites, all with demonstrable ties to Hermeticism.

No early-nineteenth-century schoolmaster ever handed Smith a copy of the *Corpus Hermeticum,* so far as the historical record can reconstruct. But, as Brooke has succinctly argued, "Smith arrived at an approximation of many of its fundamental points by a process of reassembling scattered doctrines available in dissenting and hermetic sources." Brooke is ready to acknowledge the role of "what Mormons would call revelation" in the process, although he notes that others would regard the work as one of ("powerful") human imagination.⁵⁰ Indeed, in an ironic echo of the central myth of the sixteenth-century Lurianic Kabbalah with its narrative of a cosmic "breaking of the vessels" and scattering of light, Smith, as it were, picked up the scattered pieces of light in his world in order to repair and reconstruct a Hermetic whole.⁵¹ In so doing Smith addressed what Brooke calls a "prepared people," as his own reconstructions of the Atlantic journeys of the survivors of the Radical Reformation demonstrate. As the previous chapter noted, Brooke reads a German-style Hermetic inscription on the culture of the mid-Atlantic colonies. He also points, in telling terms, to southeastern New England sectarians as important conduits for this Hermetic teaching. "With their own connections running back to the radical experience of the English Revolution," he notices, "the New England sectarians were receptive to the systematic hermetic perfection of the German sectarians; certainly they were themselves the reservoir of a great proportion of the fragments of occult belief and practice floating around seventeenth- and eighteenth-century New England." Among them could be counted the "ancestors of Joseph Smith and Brigham Young, as well as quite a number of other Mormon forebears."⁵²

Out of the complex cultural amalgam available to Joseph Smith, he shaped a theology that resonated clearly with a Hermetic past. "Mormon concepts of the coequality of matter and spirit, of the covenant of celestial marriage, and of an ultimate goal of human godhood," says Brooke, displayed "striking parallels" with "the philosophical traditions of alchemy and hermeticism, drawn from the ancient world and fused with Christianity in the Italian Renaissance." And if a prepared people were conduits to bring Smith to his new creation and in turn to receive it, so, too, was the print culture of upstate New York. With newsprint and even bookstores surprisingly accessible, the "enduring, revitalized texts" sat ready for popular consumption by Joseph Smith and his contemporaries.[53] Thus text disclosures of Freemasonic secrets fanned out into a world of other and further disclosures. Read from a metaphysical perspective, perhaps none was so significant for the Hermetic content of Mormon theology as the texts that revealed the teachings of Emanuel Swedenborg.

Swedenborg was born in 1688 into a Lutheran family with a mining background in Stockholm, Sweden. His father would become a bishop in the church at Skara by 1718, and as part of the appointment the family—then Swedberg—was ennobled and its name changed to the familiar form. By that time, the future mystic and seer (who had completed studies at Uppsala University in 1709) had been serving for about two years as Extraordinary Assessor in the Royal College of Mines, and he would continue to do so until 1747. He also spent some fifty years in the House of Nobles—one of four "estates" in the Swedish legislature. A significant technological and scientific resource in his time, Swedenborg made discoveries in fields as varied as metallurgy and the biology of the cerebral cortex and the nervous system. More than that, he achieved renown as an original and precocious thinker who seemed a veritable Leonardo da Vinci of the north. And if human consciousness and metals dug from the earth formed the poles of Swedenborg's professional interest, they prefigured what was to come. Beginning in 1743 and 1744, he began to experience a series of voice-visions that led him in trance to other worlds both celestial and infernal. He would become a master and adept of altered states and an archaeologist of the deep recesses of the human mind. By this time, too, he had already been steadily and intensively writing on philosophical themes, understanding them in the tangible, material terms that would yield books with titles like *Principles of Chemistry* (1720), the three-volume *Philosophical and Mineralogical Works* (1729–1734), and the two-volume *The Economy of the Animal Kingdom* (1740–1741)—this last what Sig Synnestvedt calls Swedenborg's "search for the soul."[54]

Echoing the received Hermeticism of northern Europe, in the alchemy of his own mind Swedenborg transmuted philosophy into theology. The decade and more from 1747 to 1758 saw the composition and publication of his twelve-volume *Arcana Coelestia*, his earliest major work of theology. With its title signifying the "heavenly secrets" that he, as Christian initiate, would reveal concerning the biblical books of Genesis and Exodus, the work extended over seven thousand pages. Here and in later writing, Swedenborg promulgated the age-old theory of correspondence, the coincidence of worlds in which the "as above" was replicated in the "so below." In formulations that echoed one another in a series of heavenly and earthly registers, he conflated heaven and earth, spirit and matter, and energy and form. Worlds merged into other worlds, and connecting them was a spirit influx from above, which permeated all that was below as its source and sustenance. "Communication by correspondences is what is called influx," Swedenborg wrote, and the term became well-nigh ubiquitous in his works. "The life of every one, whether man, spirit or angel," he testified, "flows in solely from the Lord," a Lord who "diffuse[d] himself through the universal heaven, and even through hell."[55]

Thus the Christian Trinity was subsumed into a God who manifested himself in Jesus Christ as the principles of inexhaustible love (the Father), divine wisdom (the Son), and divine and sanctifying energy (the Holy Spirit). This Christ himself summarized and subsumed all of humanity. The spirit world that Swedenborg visited many times and recorded for readers in his *Heaven and Its Wonders and Hell* (1758) was populated by angels who were "wholly men in form, having faces, eyes, ears, bodies, arms, hands, and feet." Meanwhile, "heaven in its whole complex" reflected a "single man"—an "arcanum hitherto unknown in the world." This Hermetic divine man, or Christ-man, summarized the existence of the angel-men of the heavenly sphere, where they dwelled in two kingdoms, the "celestial"—a higher kingdom of those who received "the Divine of the Lord more interiorly"—and the lower, and less interior, spiritual kingdom. Still more, Swedenborg identified three heavens—the celestial, the spiritual, and the natural—and he detailed the heavenly life in various societies in which mansions, table settings, clothing, and flower gardens all took concrete form and color for the benefit of readers. A cryptic script common to the life of heaven employed secret Hebraic characters, in which "every letter involved arcana of wisdom," its secret writing strikingly reminiscent of Christian Kabbalistic themes.[56]

Strikingly, there was sex in Swedenborgian heaven, as his later *Conjugial Love* (1768) would carefully explain. The "love of the sex" was a love that "especially remains," wrote Swedenborg, "because a man is a man after death and a woman is a woman, and because there is nothing in soul, in mind, and in body, that is not masculine in the male and feminine in the female."[57] This sexual love was raised and transmuted in its spiritualized form as "conjugial" love, and the distinctions between the two formed at least part of the burden of Swedenborg's work. Finally, in "conjugial" love as in all else, heaven existed as a progressive place in which "every society" would "daily" become "more perfect," as would "heaven in general." The angels in Swedenborg's heaven were thus continually "perfected in wisdom," a process that went on into eternity. Here no requirement for redemption existed in the traditional Christian sense. In a theological universalism that would surely have vernacular echoes in America, Swedenborg announced that "the Lord casts no one into hell; the spirit casts himself down."[58]

Swedenborg, in effect, had articulated in one form or another a number of the major tenets of Mormon theology as Joseph Smith put it forward through his revelations. D. Michael Quinn has detailed the presence in the Palmyra library of a popular reference work on religion, with editions from 1784 through 1817, which recounted Swedenborg's personal testimony of a spirit calling. As early as 1808, the Swedenborgian confession of spirit calling and angelic communication had appeared at Canandaigua, where the notorious Mason William Morgan was later jailed, on the front page of the *Western Repository*.[59] Meanwhile, Swedenborgians published their own pamphlets and tracts to spread their message to a rural audience in early-nineteenth-century America. Thus it would be harder to argue *against* a familiarity with Swedenborgian teaching on the part of Smith than to argue for it. Indeed, he himself in the late 1830s was said to have admitted to a Mormon convert his acquaintance with the Swedish seer: "Emanuel Swedenborg had a view of things to come, but for daily food he perished."[60]

Whatever Swedenborg's daily spiritual ration, he spoke a theological language that reappeared in the new Smith teaching. Swedenborg's anti-Trinitarianism, to be sure, was replaced in Mormon theology by a tritheism in which the Father, Son, and Holy Spirit continued to be distinct and separate.[61] However, Swedenborg's cryptic heavenly writing—with its echoes of hieroglyphics, secrets, Kabbalism, and Hermetic lore—found echoes in the "Reformed Egyptian" text that Smith's golden plates announced to the world. Moreover, the careful correspondences of the Swedenborgian cosmos were refracted in a Mormon light in which heaven was, indeed, an earthlike place and earth itself shone with the borrowed light of the heavenly world. "There is no such thing as immaterial matter," declared Joseph Smith in a revelation in 1843. "All spirit is matter, but it is more fine or pure, and can only be discerned by purer eyes." Still further, the heavenly realm was inhabited by a God suspiciously similar to Swedenborg's Divine Human and to the Hermetic vision in general. In a funeral oration for his friend King Follett in 1844, Smith announced to fellow-Mormon mourners: "I will tell you & hear it O Earth! God who sits in yonder heavens is a *man like yourselves*." "That God if you were to see him to day," he continued, "you would see him like a man in form, like yourselves." And if God was a man, humans were themselves potentially divine. Adam had been formed in God's "image and talked with him & walkd with him," and so humans needed to learn to make themselves "God, king and priest," going from "a small capacity to a large capacity" until they arrived "at the station of a God." Almost a year earlier, in the context of a revelation on the eternity of marriage, Smith had already affirmed the same of the future state of glory: "Then shall they be Gods, because they have no end. . . . Then shall they be Gods, because they have all power, and the angels are subject unto them."[62]

Beyond that, the Mormon cosmos existed as three worlds that refracted differing degrees of glory and also reflected a Swedenborgian and generally magical, perhaps Agrippan, ambience. As early as 1832, the "natural" heaven of the Swedish seer was paralleled by Smith's "telestial" one, a place of severely limited beatitude where those whom contemporary evangelicals would clearly call sinners could safely dwell. Swedenborg's "spiritual" heaven found a correlate in Smith's "terrestrial" realm, for the virtuous who were Gentiles; that is, non-Mormons. And Swedenborg's "celestial" and highest heaven was echoed in Smith's version of the same, a paradise where Mormons ruled as Gods, where they eternally progressed and grew ever more perfect, and where, as Smith's revelation would later unfold, the "conjugial love" that Swedenborg had averred for the heavenly order brought bliss to the eternally wedded just.[63]

Both the Swedenborgian vision and the Smith revelation point back toward a larger Hermetic universe, in which the Father-Mother God prevailed. The *coniunctio*, or conjoining, of the metaphorically male and female elements in alchemical vessels produced the pure gold of the philosopher's stone. Kabbalistic speculation, in its turn, presented a divine "En Sof" who had revealed himself as two—the male element, the seed of wisdom, and the female, its womb. In the writings of the revered Jacob Boehme the dual deity likewise ruled. The androgynous Adam, as a primordial being, had been shaped in the image and likeness of God because he contained originally within himself both seed ("limbus") and womb ("matrix").[64] Here in America, Conrad Beissel's eighteenth-century community at Ephrata, Pennsylvania, had been heir to Boehmian beliefs about the androgyny of God and, originally, of Adam. There were still, in the 1820s, German-language productions of Boehme's writings at Ephrata, probably by descendants of the founding members of the group or their associates.[65] Meanwhile, other utopian groups in the early nineteenth century—the Rappites, or Harmonists, and the Shakers—were also teaching their version of the Father-Mother God.

As early as 1839, Smith apparently had caught the outlines of this "conjugial" vision, since he was reported to have invoked an "eternal Mother, the wife of your Father in Heaven." Smith's "theology of the conjunction," however, encompassed polygamous marriages and plural wives. His thirty-two marriages, eighteen of them likely accomplished under astrologically auspicious signs, bore witness to what Brooke has called an "institutionalized antinomianism" in the Hermetic tradition. If the mystical *coincidentia oppositorum* was necessary for divinization and if, as in Smith's revealed secret, godliness was progressive—with the God of scriptures still limited and humans in a process of heavenly becoming—then more sex meant more divinity.[66] Indeed, the progress of Smith's theology wrote large the progress already present in Swedenborgianism and Hermeticism in general—a quest for increasing perfection that could be successful *on earth* as above. Here the Swedenborgian formulation of divine influx appeared in the Mormon revelation in a new key. Meanwhile, Smith's teaching of the eternity of matter and the preexistence of souls articulated a version of Hermeticism only vaguely suggested, if at all, in the Swedenborgian teaching of a pre-Adamite humanity. The teaching stretched the road of progress from a murky past into a never-ending future.[67]

In the distinctly American *coniunctio* of Joseph Smith and Mormon revelation, there were whispers of the sexual magic that some future metaphysicians would later explore. The message was clear: heaven was a place of bliss, and a place of bliss was a place of bodies. Spiritual marriages had something to do with flesh. Here, in a higher, better materialism, the old Calvinist God who avenged the blight of sinners was effaced in favor of a milder, more lenient—and more limited—deity. As Fawn Brodie declared, Smith "had taken a long step toward Universalism, for even the 'liars, sorcerers, adulterers, and whoremongers' were guaranteed telestial glory, and only a handful of unregenerates called the Sons of Perdition were to be eternally damned."[68] But here, too, the bodies of bliss were enlightened bodies, and the enlightenment came—not through the rationalism of the eighteenth-century European and American philosophers but through the reformation of magic. Joseph Smith had conjoined a folk magic of dowsing and treasure-seeking to the high Hermetic tradition of magic that Masonry, Swedenborgianism, and other and related sources had mediated to him.

Smith grew up in a family with a long tradition of magical belief and practice. Vermont was what D. Michael Quinn has called a "treasure-digging mecca" when Joseph Smith Sr. lived there, and in the western New York to which he eventually relocated, he found a congenial environment for magical practice, as Palmyra's local newspaper in the 1820s revealed. Even some clergy apparently carried dowsing rods in this nineteenth-century world, and Christianity blended seamlessly into the magic of the folk. The "magical milieu of the Smith family," Quinn summarizes, "included seer stones, astrology, talismans, a dagger for drawing magic circles of treasure digging and spirit invocation, and magic parchments for purification, protection and conjuring a spirit." There were, indeed, sophisticated magical artifacts in the Smith family, and it was clear that the family practiced ritual magic. Joseph Smith's Masonic brother Hyrum—with whom he was later to be assassinated in Carthage—possessed at the time of his death a magic dagger and three parchments, or lamens, used for ceremonial magic work.[69]

Joseph Smith himself was, by any standard, a cunning man. What was new, however, was that Smith (and others like him) was a cunning man not simply in a rural countryside but in a rapidly urbanizing and industrializing environment. By 1822, a section of the Erie Canal linking Rochester to Utica, New York, had been completed, and the canal ran through one end of the village of Palmyra. As the economy of exchange boomed in commercial venues, so it did in goods of the spirit. With books, newspapers, and people with metaphysical knowledge readily available, a would-be magus could quickly absorb a varied portfolio in the magical trade.

By the time the Book of Mormon appeared, Smith had already acquired a reputation as a local money-digger and treasure-hunter, employing the familiar divinatory techniques of English country magic. To accomplish his work he used a stone to "see" what needed revealing, and he was sought out for his skills. At one time, in fact, he was part of a company of money-diggers who traveled around to various places in New York and Pennsylvania seeking old Spanish and Indian treasure in the earth. By 1826, these activities had gotten him in trouble with the law, when the nephew of a treasure-seeking client thought that his uncle was being swindled and swore out a warrant for Smith's arrest. Tried at South Bainbridge, New York, as a "disorderly person," Smith was as a result convicted, but as a first offender he walked away. What is especially interesting about the case, however, is how much it revealed about his magical practice, its connection with old lore about the simultaneous obstinacy and slipperiness of buried treasure, and the level and degree of its magical sophistication. Smith, who worked for Josiah Stowell along with others, claimed that he found treasure but could not extract it, and this for magical reasons. He needed to wrest the bounty from its guardian spirit, and so he engaged, albeit unsuccessfully, in a repertoire of magical actions that reportedly included magic circles, zodiacal consultation, and even animal sacrifice.[70]

Smith could also use a forked divining rod, and he did so apparently with his early convert Oliver Cowdery in the 1820s. There was, in fact, an earlier history to their relationship and use of the rod. In Middletown, Vermont, the fathers of the two had been friends and members together of Nathaniel Wood's New Israelites, a group that came under the influence of a charismatic diviner who urged them to seek secret prophecy and miracle-working root medicines with the help of the rod.[71] The move of the Smiths and the Cowderys to New York did nothing noticeable to dampen their faith in dowsing. Indeed, a revelation from 1829 addressed by Joseph Smith Jr. to Oliver Cowdery alluded to his "gift." "Doubt not," Smith assured his friend, "for it is the gift of God, and you shall hold it in your hands, and do marvelous works."[72]

For the period nearly a decade earlier, Quinn has invoked the "apparent magical context for Smith's first vision" in 1820. Read a certain way, the vision's heavenly pronouncement to Smith that all of the sects were wrong was an endorsement of magical practice as a replacement. This line of inquiry points to the spiritual territory that Jan Shipps has trodden in her well-known reconstruction of the discovery and translation of the Book of Mormon.[73] The puzzle of the prophet can be solved with convincing ease if one follows Smith in the elision of material and spiritual treasure. One should dig for gold, yes, but—for a New World alchemist of the earth—the gold should be the philosopher's stone of a new religion.

When Smith sought the plates of the Book of Mormon on the Hill Cumorah for the first time in 1823, they proved as hard to get as the treasure of magical lore that exonerated his later failure in the Josiah Stowell project. In fact, the juxtaposition of the two "treasures" illumines the combinative magical project to which Smith committed himself in pursuit of the plates. Quinn has documented the earliest accounts of uncanny events leading to their discovery—newspaper reports that spoke of Smith's thrice visitation "by the spirit of the Almighty in a dream" who informed him of a "golden Bible" in the earth. In an elaborate reconstruction of "favorable" astrological progressions and ritual magic instructions for spirit invocation in a generally Agrippan framework, Quinn has also argued that Smith was actively engaged in necromancy or psychomancy. The hours during which Smith communicated with the spirit "corresponded exactly with instructions for the successful magic invocation of spirits." Hence the claimed appearance of a spirit later identified as the angel Moroni represented "the dramatically successful result of ritual magic."[74]

In this reading, the English country magic of the cunning folk, represented in seer stones and dowsing rods, has gone decidedly high and has come trailing Hermetic nuances. Still further, Smith's inability to carry away the treasure year after year until 1827 evokes folkloric motifs regarding treasure guardians who prevented its acquisition. It evokes, too, a tradition of enchantments that made the treasure forever elusive, slipping away as it was almost within grasp. The inability, however, also suggests an initiatory period during which the adept must undergo testing and be purified before treasure can be possessed. Thus, as Quinn has observed, Smith "dramatically expanded the religious dimensions inherent in folk magic."[75]

After the treasure was at last claimed, the conflation of religion and magic continued in the translating practice of Smith. Officially, the Urim and Thummim —with their biblical and also culturally Masonic associations—provided the source of vision to enable Smith's task. More intimate accounts, though, point to a Smith who typically worked in a different fashion with a seer stone he especially favored. For example, David Whitmer reported that Smith "would put the seer stone into a hat, and put his face in the hat, drawing it closely around his face to exclude the light; and in the darkness the spiritual light would shine."[76] Even more, the declaration that the material to be translated was written in hieroglyphics, in "Reformed Egyptian," hints of the ancient home place of Hermes Trismegistus and, as well, the preoccupations with secret language in the Kabbalah, in Masonry, and even in Swedenborg. So the Book of Mormon echoed a magical tongue with—contained in that formula—the power of the revealed secret to aid and assist nineteenth-century Americans. As Quinn has suggested, the presence and subtlety of these magical allusions "may explain why religious seekers from folk religion were attracted to Mormonism from 1830 on, and why these seekers, for what may have been the first time, seemed to feel at home in an organized religion."[77]

Smith himself did not stop employing seer stones after 1829, and Brigham Young, too, endorsed their use. Moreover, Smith habitually wore or carried as a pocket piece a magical silver Jupiter talisman (in Smith's astrological chart, Jupiter was his ruling planet) to bring wealth and good fortune.[78] But the Smith who used seer stones and possessed an auspicious magical talisman was also a young man who had woven into his magical and religious practice the haunting memory of the indigenous dwellers in the land. Joseph Smith could not forget the Indians, and their ghosts trod in his mind and in the countryside around him in New York. Even the heavily edited, official version of Lucy Mack Smith's story of his life recounted: "During our evening conversations, Joseph would occasionally give us some of the most amusing recitals that could be imagined. He would describe the ancient inhabitants of this continent, their dress, mode of traveling, and the animals upon which they rode; their cities, their buildings, with every particular; their mode of warfare; and also their religious worship. This he would do with as much ease, seemingly, as if he had spent his whole life among them."[79] The Book of Mormon, we recall, claimed to reveal the true beginnings and the history of the Indian peoples on this and the South American continent. Indeed, the "spirit" who had come to Joseph Smith three times in 1823 had come with the message that a record of ancient Indian history was contained in the golden plates. Such an announcement was congruent with what Dan Vogel has called the "persistent legend of a lost Indian book" abroad in the region during the early national period.[80]

Smith's ventures into money-digging, as I have noted, often involved digging for Indian treasure, and thus Indian mounds were often the sites of his and his associates' labors. Nor did he and his friends have a hard time finding locations. Both the New England that Smith's father left and the New York State in which he himself lived possessed landscapes dotted with mounds and memorials of Indian provenance.[81] Americans of Smith's time and earlier had speculated as well on Indian origins. Were the indigenous inhabitants of the land pre-Adamites and, so, outside a biblical framework? Paracelsus had argued this, and in mid-seventeenth-century France the Calvinist Isaac de la Peyrère had produced the first book-length endorsement of the theory; Carolina explorer Thomas Hariot apparently shared the view, and so did Britisher Bernard Romans, whose natural history of Florida appeared in 1775. Were the Indians instead among the descendants of Noah? Early American notables such as Cotton Mather, Jedidiah Morse, and Timothy Dwight were convinced that this was the case. More explicitly, were the native people of America of Hebrew descent and perhaps from the lost tribes of Israel? The renowned Puritan Indian missionary John Eliot thought so, and likewise Roger Williams and William Penn shared the view. By 1775, James Adair had written a thoroughgoing defense of the Hebraic origin of the Indians in his *History of the American Indians*, and in the early nineteenth century, former congressman Elias Boudinot popularized the Israelite theory, using Adair's work to do so. Still more, were the mound builders really Indians, or did their massive and superior constructions suggest a race different from the natives encountered in the sixteenth and seventeenth centuries by Europeans? Jeremy Belknap, for whom Harvard University's prestigious Belknap Press is named, favored the two-migration theory, and so did Governor DeWitt Clinton of New York in 1811. The same Solomon Spalding who, before Fawn Brodie demolished the theory, was rumored to have authored the Book of Mormon also held to the two-group theory. Questions and answers such as these about the Indians spilled over into print in vernacular media like commonplace books and newspapers, with descriptions of the mounds readily available to readers in various places, including the area in which Smith was raised.[82]

Thus Smith and the Book of Mormon were preoccupied with the memories encrypted into the land—in its earthworks and arrowheads, in its variously answered questions and untold histories. The very title page of the Book of Mormon announced its intention "to show unto the remnant of the House of Israel what great things the Lord had done for their fathers; and that they may know the covenants of the Lord, that they are not cast off forever." Moreover, by 1831 Smith was enjoining Mormon missionaries to marry Indian wives. But there was more. The Book of Mormon had been delivered on golden plates and its content connected the mounds to the use of metal, so that, as Vogel writes, the "Book of Mormon's righteous Jaredites and Nephites" were presented as "advanced metallurgists." From whence did this high metallurgical ascription come? If we look to the historical and archaeological record, metallurgy was not the particular forte of mound builders.[83] In the received esotericism of Europe, however, things were different. Enoch had found a triangular plate of gold, and the Hermetic tradition had produced its hieroglyphics, even as the Urim and Thummim and the ubiquitous seer stones of the cunning could enable one to read them.

What I am suggesting, then, is that in the mind and cultural practice of Joseph Smith we have, at firsthand, a dazzling display of the kind of combinativeness that would be the preeminent feature of American metaphysical religion. In him we see, coming together in an early representation, the ingredients that would conjoin in the mature tradition. From this perspective, literary and cultural critic Harold Bloom is decidedly close to target when he points to the Mormonism of Smith's early production as a prototype for an American religion with "Gnostic, Enthusiast, and Orphic" qualities. It was, for Bloom, a "post-Christian" religion. Even if—recognizing the inherited Christianity of the Mormon theological venture—we do not accept the post-Christian label, we can acknowledge the light his general analysis sheds. What held the principles of Mormonism together, Bloom thinks, is the "American persuasion, however muted or obscured, that we are mortal gods, destined to find ourselves again in worlds as yet undiscovered."[84] He could have added, destined to find ourselves by combining the pieces of many cultures in a new and distinctly American synthesis.

Beyond this, what is so interesting about the metaphysical synthesis that Smith achieved is its corporate quality. Smith's religion had begun as a family affair, had speedily become a family-and-friends affair, and then—as it grew—had emerged as a distinctly communal production. In fact, the communalism of early Mormons provided a strong reason for the fear and hatred they seemed to generate wherever they settled. Americans read Mormon separateness in political terms, and Mormons themselves did little to discourage that estimate. Smith, after all, aimed to run for president of the United States in 1844.[85] As the institutional cement for communalism was developed by Smith in his elaborate organization-building, it became clear that Mormon metaphysics was not something that one did alone. The mysticism of Hermetic solitudes gave way to the larger familiarism of polygamous social practice and corporate ritual practice in secret temple ceremonies. Like the Freemasons, whom in part they emulated, Mormons did religion in community. Nonetheless, the theological path that led Joseph Smith to announce American Mormon divinity had been cleared—and was being cleared—by votaries of the decidedly individualistic doctrine of universalism and by the denominational organizations that would bring this new gospel to waiting and receptive Americans.

UNIVERSALISM AND THE
ENLIGHTENMENT OF RELIGION

In the last month of 1797, Joseph Smith Sr.—the father of the Mormon prophet—along with his elder brother Jesse, their father Asael Smith, and over a dozen others signed a formal declaration in Tunbridge, Vermont, where they were living. The declaration made them members of the newly forming Tunbridge Universalist society. Later, a Universalist convention meeting in New Hampshire in 1803 announced the essential doctrine of the faith—belief in a God of love "revealed in one Jesus Christ, by one Holy Spirit of Grace," who would "finally restore the whole family of mankind to holiness and happiness." What Fawn Brodie called Joseph Smith Jr.'s "long step toward Universalism" thus had already been a longtime family affair.[86] The combination of a Radical Reformation universalist heritage with vernacular Hermeticism—the stuff of the now well-rehearsed Brooke thesis—surely made Vermont hill towns like Tunbridge fertile ground for new American universalist pronouncements. Not surprisingly, from the 1790s preachers from Massachusetts and New Hampshire moved into the neighboring state, and universalism, as a belief and a denomination, came to flourish there. By 1830, we are told, Universalists could be found in over eighty towns.[87]

Writing in the late nineteenth century, Universalist denominational historian Richard Eddy declared that universalism, as a doctrine or belief, held "that it is the purpose of God, through the grace revealed in our Lord Jesus Christ, to save every member of the human race from sin." Eddy went on to argue that no implications regarding founder, location, particular ecclesiastical polity and ritual, or christology—of equality or subordination of Jesus with God the Father—were contained in universalist belief. He also proceeded to discover universalism in the early ages of Christianity in phenomena as varied as the pseudepigraphal Sibylline Oracles, forms of Gnosticism, and the writings of Clement of Alexandria and of Origen. As Peter W. Williams has observed, this claimed lineage provides an important clue to the "character of American liberal movements." Their self-understanding has been "based on a sense of mission to spread the message that true religion consists of a pattern of attitudes and actions that may be fostered by specific ideas, movements, and institutions but cannot and should not be confined to them."[88] This, of course, could be construed as a recipe for institutional weakness and fractiousness — for a promotion of individualism that looked away from community. As a historical tool, however, the distinction between belief and its institutionalization helps to make sense of American metaphysical religion.

Universalism as a belief can be found even in seventeenth-century New England. There Samuel Gorton, arriving by 1637 from England, went from Boston to Plymouth and, banished from both, to Rhode Island, troubling the esteemed Cotton Mather with his antinomian and antitrinitarian views. Gorton held conspicuously to the opinion that eternity existed already in the soul's life in the present and — like American metaphysicians of the future — that heaven and hell were states of mind. He thought that the soul functioned independently of place and, likewise in mystical vein, that past and future were contained in an eternal now. Prolific in his writing, he was fond of allegory and hidden meaning, but as Richard Eddy noted, he was clearly a universalist. So, too, was Sir Henry Vane, who was elected governor of Massachusetts in 1636. Supporting the mystical and antinomian Anne Hutchinson, who was forced into exile in Rhode Island for her views, Vane himself was, as Eddy declared, a mystic and a proponent of Origenist ideas of universal salvation.[89] Nearly two centuries later, by the early nineteenth century, New England had become a hotbed of universalist belief, and the good news of the benevolent deity who wanted the salvation of all humankind spread into the fabled "burned-over district" of New York and flourished, too, in New Jersey and Pennsylvania. It served as an abiding foil to doomsday evangelicals. At the same time, it intersected in complex ways with both Calvinist and Arminian free-will beliefs. And although John Murray (1741–1815) and Elhanan Winchester (1751–1797) are usually credited as founders of the denomination and Hosea Ballou (1771–1852) as its later leading light, this American universalist belief had many starting points. From a religiocultural perspective it is more to the mark to point to multiple sites where the new and benevolent God reigned.

Murray, born in England, had been reared in Ireland and joined the Methodists there. A Calvinist in conviction, he moved to London to be with George Whitefield and his congregation, but contact with the universalist preaching of James Relly, which Murray meant to oppose, changed his thinking radically. He was won for universalism. In 1770, after the death of his wife and child and a time in debtor's prison, Murray made his way to the British Atlantic colonies, where he landed in New Jersey and met one Thomas Potter. The elderly Potter had already come by universalist beliefs because of his contacts with Conrad Beissel's German Dunkers from Ephrata (see chapter 2). Their gloss on the Radical tradition of the Reformation became a shaping element in the christology that

Murray had already learned from Relly, with its teaching that the atonement of Jesus on the cross united all of humanity to him.

With his belief in Jesus as Second Adam and its mystical recapitulation and reversal of the life of humankind summarized in the first Adam, a transformed Murray began to itinerate in New Jersey and the middle colonies generally. Moving further north, he evangelized in New England and then settled in Massachusetts and ministered to a congregation in Gloucester, which became the first covenanted Universalist church (the denomination) in the country. Murray continued, too, to itinerate, and he also wrote. In 1788, he remarried. His second wife, Julia Sargent Stevens—suggesting the general reform ambience that would characterize Universalists in their denomination—was an early advocate for women's rights. Meanwhile, by 1793 Murray served a church in Boston, where he continued until his death. Nor did Murray relinquish his Calvinism in subscribing to universalist belief; he continued to embrace such traditional doctrines as the fall of humankind, the divinity of Jesus Christ, and the trinity of God, even as he Arminianized by championing a human capacity to believe. "The universalism of Murray," wrote George Huntston Williams, "*looked back* to the definitive and decisive recapitulation of the human race by Christ as the Second Adam and affirmed that mankind was already saved for eternity and had but to be apprised of this in preaching and seized of this faith to enjoy this redemptive security already *in this present life.*"[90]

By contrast, Williams told readers, the universalism of Elhanan Winchester "*looked forward* to an eschatological restoration of all creatures, not however without some painful purgation *in the afterlife* for the sinful." The theological difference reflected the difference in sources and sites from which Winchester's version of universalism had come. Massachusetts-born and mostly an autodidact, Winchester experienced a conversion in 1769 that drew him to the Separate Congregational church in Brookline, where he lived. But before the year was out, he had been immersed and joined a Baptist church in Connecticut instead. Like Murray, his theological views changed, becoming increasingly Calvinist and linking him to what was called the "hyper-Calvinism" of the theology of John Gill. Dismissed from his Baptist ministry because of his views, Winchester itinerated until 1774, when he settled in South Carolina, working as a revivalist and growing in antislavery convictions. In 1778, however, Winchester read the book that would change his thinking one more time and radically change his life. *The Everlasting Gospel* (1710), by German mystic Paul Siegvolck (George Klein-Nicolai of Freissdorf), published already in five editions before 1750, had been produced in English in 1753 by the also mystically inclined physician George De Benneville. Then a resident of Germantown near Philadelphia, De Benneville had formerly been an associate of Jacob Boehme's disciples in the German states of northern Europe.[91] Siegvolck's book taught a theology that closely resembled that of the heterodox early-church Origen (c. 185–c. 254), in which the atonement of Jesus was meant to encompass all of humankind and there would be a universal restoration to come. But its universalism also echoed Boehme's teaching that—after the destruction of sin and human evil by fire—there would be a universal reconciliation with the divine, so that good would be the end result and "perfection" would come from "imperfection."[92] Like Murray in his initial response to Relly, Winchester resisted. But the universalism of Siegvolck's work would not go away, and its restorationism—in a future after purgation and pain—became the new gospel that Winchester owned. His conversion process was greatly enhanced by the move that Winchester made in 1780—to the largest Baptist congregation in America, at Philadelphia, as its pastor.

There Winchester's personal friendship grew with De Benneville, who was close to German pietists and had been preacher to Indians as well as to whites. De Benneville's former encounters with death had surely shaped him, and derivatively they shaped Winchester, too. (De Benneville had nearly been executed in French Normandy for his preaching, and in Germany the report was that he had taken sick, was believed dead, and placed in a coffin before he revived with a message of universal restoration.)[93] Winchester also felt the liberalizing presence of famed Philadelphia physician Benjamin Rush and Anglican minister Jacob Duché, who had been first chaplain to the American Congress. But his prestigious Philadelphia church heard rumors of his evolving beliefs about universal restoration, and a time of reckoning came. Winchester and some one hundred others were forced out, forming a separate society of Baptists dedicated to universalist teaching. Like Murray, too, Winchester was prolific in writing—numerous books, including *Dialogues on Universal Restoration* (1788) and several collections of hymns.[94]

Commenting on the connections and disconnections between Murray and Winchester, Stephen Marini observes that "each man took a similar trajectory through Radical Evangelicalism, yet they had irreconcilable theological differences. Murray was Calvinistic, Rellyan, doctrinaire, and imperious; Winchester was Arminian, restorationist, rationalistic, and irenic."[95] What is clear about the two of them, however, is that each came by his universalism in a way that included German influence emanating from the mystical fringe of the Radical Reformation. Indeed, in the case of De Benneville, whose influence on Winchester was so far-reaching, as we have seen, he came by his universalist convictions after a claimed experience in which, in the context of a grave illness, he left his body and engaged in a species of soul travel. It was in this altered state that

De Benneville beheld the stages of an afterlife in which souls suffered to attain purification until they were ready for the divine presence.[96] With the Ephratans and Jacob Boehme hovering on the horizon of influence, we are not far from a Hermeticism of northern European provenance. The theological word of early universalism turned on the initial and ultimate benevolence of God, but it also pointed the way toward a humankind that shared a secret identity, through the work of Christ, with the divine. Moreover, the theology had its social register. It became a noticeable fact that among the nineteenth-century Universalists could be counted a series of religious experimenters who moved in the direction of what, by midcentury, could be described as metaphysical religion. But this is to move forward too quickly. There were other currents and creeds as the denomination began to evolve.

Among them, Marini has noticed especially the theological ground-breakers in post-Revolutionary rural New England in a hinterland of the spirit that was also a hinterland of hills and interior regions. The physician Isaac Davis, for instance, brought a universalism that denied the reality of hell or devils to the Connecticut Valley and towns like Oxford, Douglas, and Milford, Massachusetts. In central New England, Adams Streeter, who had converted from the Baptist faith—possibly under the influence of Davis—continued Davis's work, organizing Universalists denominationally at Oxford, Massachusetts, and providing what Marini has called "much-needed social cohesion." But the man whom Marini identifies as "the most important native New England Universalist leader" was Caleb Rich (1750–1821).[97] A Baptist evangelical like Winchester, Rich grew increasingly restive about the doctrine of hell and its use as a threat to induce salvation. Fear, he thought, was a tainted and selfish reason for converting. Then, in 1772, in a troubled state of mind after a conversation with his brother challenging his beliefs, Rich claimed a series of voice visions confirming the slavish nature of the fear of hell, warning against the path of the Baptists, and encouraging the scriptural study that led him to teach the total annihilation of sinners after their death. According to his own account, by 1778 a further series of visions turned him toward Christ as Second Adam. Then, after an experience in which he "felt as it were a shock of electricity," he came face to face with a Christ who instructed him to "feed my sheep and lambs." He was convinced that he had received the gospel "by the revelation of Jesus Christ, through the medium of the Holy Spirit in opening my understanding to understand the scriptures."[98]

As early as 1773, Rich founded a Universalist society in Warwick, Massachusetts. He later established similar congregations in Richmond and Jaffrey, New Hampshire, in 1780. Distinct in his views from John Murray, despite some resemblances, Rich based his beliefs not on authority but on the conviction brought by his own experience. Moreover, beyond his importance as the man whom Stephen Marini calls the universalist movement's "principal early leader," he gave universalism its most celebrated convert in Hosea Ballou (1771–1852).[99] Son of a New Hampshire Baptist minister and student in Quaker academies there, Ballou by 1791 embraced the universalist gospel. He taught school in Rhode Island thereafter, itinerating, assuming pastorates in Portsmouth, New Hampshire, and Salem, Massachusetts, and then moving to Boston, where for thirty-five years he served as minister to the Second Universalist Society. Ballou was active in denominational politics and periodical publishing, and he came to epitomize the denominational Universalism of his generation. Indeed, his *Treatise on Atonement* (1805) carved a new path in universalist doctrine and added theological leadership to his already visible role in the growing denomination. In a tract that bore the rationalist imprint of the day, Ballou revealed his familiarity with the work of Ethan Allen and Charles Chauncy, the former the well-known deist author of *Reason the Only Oracle of Man* (1784) and the latter the liberal Boston minister and author of the influential *Salvation of All Men* (1784). Ballou also drew on the work of Ferdinand Olivier Petitpierre in his *Thoughts on the Divine Goodness* (1786), which emphasized what David Robinson has called a "quietist determinism."[100] Moving from a trinitarian to a unitarian position and championing the use of reason in religion, Ballou saw Christ as a divine agent. He also rejected the orthodox teaching that Christ died as a substitute for humankind before a God whose justice needed vindicating.

Instead, Ballou's work—in a position that came to be called ultra-universalism—taught that the results of human sinfulness were limited to earthly life alone. God's love assumed primary proportions as Ballou argued that God would use the redeeming love of Christ—not his incarnation or sacrifice on the cross—to bring all people to himself, whatever their belief and behavior. Ballou's position, in the language of Richard Eddy, made the atonement a "moral and not a legal work." It reconciled humans to God, not God to humans. "The reconciling, the at-one-ing work of Christ," wrote Eddy of Ballou's treatise, "is the bringing of man into harmony with God, a moral and spiritual result produced in the sinner, who needs changing, not a scheme or effort for changing the unchangeable God, nor for turning aside any penalty of his perfect law."[101] Still more, as Stephen Marini summarizes, for Ballou "complete sanctification was not attainable in the finite state, but progressive perfection and gradual recovery of the Adamic powers were necessary concomitants of 'the Abrahamic faith.'"[102] The Ballou of this portrait thus encompassed the seemingly contrary impulses that were moving through the universalist belief of the period and through the larger early- and mid-nineteenth-century spiritual world in which it flourished. On the one hand, the universalist gospel seemed an appropriate Christian step toward deism, instructed by its rationalism and its human-centered God but also keeping faith with biblical teaching. On the other, universalist teaching evoked the mystical boundary where Christianity touched Hermeticism and where, in its nineteenth-century embodiment, a progressivist Romantic vision came to dominate numbers of American spiritual quests. The God who loved humans and sought to "happify" them was also the God who beckoned along a road to ever-increasing perfection and, so, ever greater spiritual power. At the same time, divine "necessity" authored sin, used it, and, in the divine mystery of love, saved all, regardless of their condition.[103]

Absorbing cultural currents of the day into its own theological center, the universalism of the Ballou era expanded and grew. In the fabled "burned-over district" of western New York, Whitney Cross claimed, by 1845 the Universalist denomination could boast nearly as many congregations as the Episcopalians. In the nation as a whole, Universalists counted some 700 societies and more than 300 preachers, while a decade later the numbers doubled and individual adherents were said to number 800,000.[104] Moreover, while it is appropriate to point, with John Coleman Adams, to the theology of Ballou as a "forerunner" to that of Horace Bushnell, Henry Ward Beecher, and Phillips Brooks (in other words, the liberalizing tradition in American Protestantism),[105] here it is important to notice another sort of connection. Universalism, both in the substance of its thinking and in the disciples who followed its doctrines, extended outward—as the narrative of its origins already suggests—into a metaphysical borderland already being marked with identifying forms.

"Students of American culture and church historians alike have quite neglected the Universalists," wrote Whitney Cross, "and the oversight seems to be a serious one." He went on to observe that by the late 1830s and early 1840s Universalism (both the belief and the denomination) could be linked to the spread of such movements and ideas as "phrenology, mesmerism, land reform, Fourierist communism, and Swedenborgianism." In the cultural milieu in which mesmerism and Swedenborgianism fed into one another and led on to spiritualism, for example, Universalist ministers or ex-ministers were key players. Men like John Murray Spear, Adin Ballou, Charles Hammond, Thomas Lake Harris, William Fishbough, and S. B. Brittan come immediately to mind—immersed in a world in which mediumship and spirit facilitation were prominently part of the game and in which the reform impulse worked compatibly alongside it. John Murray Spear, a medium who would construct a perpetual-motion machine called the New Motive Power under what he was sure was spirit direction, for instance, was active with his brother Charles in penology and prison reform.[106] In the combinativeness that brought the Enlightenment together with the romantically read mysticism of the Hermetic tradition, the cultural pursuits Cross noticed—like phrenology and mesmerism—supported universalist belief. Both also suggested, in Cross's words, "that natural laws rather than whimsical miracles embodied God's purposes for humanity." Thus they pushed toward scrutiny of human mental capacity in a context in which the law of correspondence joined humans to the universe and its inexorable laws. Concomitantly, they pushed toward the corporate project of human society in ways that searched for its secret laws and sought to make them conscious and useful in grand schemes of land reform and communism.[107]

Perhaps the most visible example of this corporate project was Universalist minister Adin Ballou's community at Hopedale, an experimental association that John Humphrey Noyes—himself the founder of a controversial religious and socialist community at Oneida, New York—called the "blossom of Universalism."[108] With a compact from 1841, the community's real beginning at Hopedale, near Milford, Massachusetts, came in 1842. Hopedale lasted until 1856, and during that period Adin Ballou (a distant and younger relative of Hosea Ballou, a restorationist, and an opponent of the older Ballou's ultra-universalism) argued the group's vision and rationale. We gain some sense of the moral universalism that such a vision could generate in a tract that the Hopedale founder published in 1851.

Hopedale was, Ballou told readers, "a universal religious, moral, philanthropic, and social reform Association." Besides being a "Missionary Society" with worldwide ambitions, it was a "moral suasion Temperance Society on the teetotal basis," "a moral power Anti-Slavery Society, radical and without compromise," and a "Peace Society." It existed as a "sound theoretical and practical Woman's Rights Association," a "Charitable Society for the relief of suffering humanity," and an "Educational Society, preparing to act an important part in the training of the young." Finally, the list ended, Hopedale was a "socialistic Community, successfully actualizing, as well as promulgating, practical Christian Socialism —the only kind of Socialism likely to establish a true social state on earth." In a society that harmonized "just individual freedom with social co-operation," it looked to "a world ultimately regenerated and Edenized."[109] Here the forward-backward expectation of a regenerated nature told of a primal innocence to be reconstituted, a secret restored and made actual in the process of living. It could be added that part of the Edenized life of Hopedale was spirit communication, and Ballou opened that particular secret to others when he published a book on spiritualist theory and phenomena in 1852.[110] All the while, however, the association functioned according to rationalized market principles of stock ownership,

and, in fact, the community ended when two members who had assumed ownership of three-fourths of the stock decided to liquidate.

To evoke nature, natural laws, and reform in the same context as rationalized market principles is, of course, to signal a world in which Enlightenment
thought could function comfortably and enable a transformed Hermeticism to
become the cutting edge of a new order. Yet contrary to the declarations of Cross
on whimsical miracles versus natural law, universalism could lead back into the
world of miracle and magic. We gain an early sense of how these thought processes worked in the autobiography of John Murray himself. After his catalog
of English woes, Murray had embarked for America and the port of New York,
only to be subject to a series of seemingly random events that "astonished" him
with what he believed were the power and presence of God. As Murray's ship
sailed from Philadelphia in 1770 (where the captain had decided to go first because of concerns about New York's enforcement of the nonimportation agreement), a dense fog came up, and through a series of circumstances, their boat
was grounded after it struck a bar and then passed into a place called Cranberry Inlet (Good Luck, New Jersey). The next morning the wind had shifted,
and there was no chance of proceeding to New York. Murray and the boatmen
went ashore to procure food, and then Murray, leaving the others and agitated
in mind, "pursued a solitary walk through the woods."[111]

It was thus that John Murray encountered the man who was to change his life.
Directed to a house beyond a meeting house that, startlingly, stood in the wilds
of Good Luck, he found plenty of fresh fish but also a man who refused to sell
them to him. Thomas Potter would only give them away; and he pressed Murray
to stay at a room he had prepared for him. "'Come,' said he [Potter], 'my friend, I
am glad you have returned, I have longed to see you, I have been expecting you
a long time.' I was perfectly amazed." Potter added to Murray's amazement by
supplying an account of his religious conviction. Unlettered though he was, he
testified to a "great and good Being, to whom we are indebted for all we enjoy,"
one who had "preserved, and protected" him through "innumerable dangers."
Through the years he had invited passing ministers to preach but never found
the right one. "They pronounced me an odd mortal, declaring themselves at a
loss what to make of me: while I continued to affirm, that I had but one hope;
I believed that Jesus Christ suffered death for my transgressions, and this alone
was sufficient for me." Still waiting for a heaven-sent minister, Potter eventually
built a meeting house.[112]

Now Potter was sure that in Murray he had met the minister God was sending
him. "The moment I beheld your vessel on shore," he declared, "it seemed as if
a voice had audibly sounded in my ears, There, Potter, in that vessel, cast away

on that shore, is the preacher you have been so long expecting." Murray himself confessed in the pages of his autobiography that he was "astonished, immeasurably astonished." It was—Potter said regarding Murray—"'what I *feel*, which produces in my mind a full conviction.'" Murray's remembered account continued with a send-not-me narrative in which the English universalist, Isaiah-like, resisted what he perceived as the "hand of God." He prayed and wept "through the greater part of the night; dreading more than death . . . the thought of engaging as a public character." Potter, however, was certain that the wind would not change until Murray had addressed the people. And Murray in turn felt compelled to acknowledge an "uncommon coincidence of circumstances" and "an over-ruling Power" that "seemed to operate, in an unusual and remarkable manner."[113]

What followed was a classic testimony to the particular providence of God, couched in terms that pushed miracles of meaningful coincidence toward an emerging language of metaphysical magic.

> I could not forbear looking back upon the mistakes, made during our passage, even to the coming in to this particular inlet, where no vessel, of the size of the brig 'Hand-in-Hand,' had ever before entered; every circumstance contributed to bring me to this house. Mr. Potter's address on seeing me; his assurance, that he knew I was on board the vessel, when he saw her at a distance; all these considerations pressed with powerful conviction on my mind, and I was ready to say, If God Almighty has, in his providence, so ordered events, as to bring me into this country for the purpose of making manifest the saviour of his name, and of bringing many to the knowledge of the truth . . . am I not bound to submit to the dispensations of providence?[114]

Absorbed into the narrative structure of miracle and magic, Murray decided that the changing of the wind would be a high sign from God. If the wind blew against a voyage, God wanted him in Good Luck and he would stay. God, of course, obliged the narrative structure; Murray remained, and the rest—as some would say—was glory. He preached, and then the wind changed. He left for New York, only to return later, as he promised Potter, to Cranberry Inlet and Good Luck. He was, as he wrote again "astonished," and he saw "that the good hand of God was in all these things."[115] And if the unchanging wind of Murray's memory had been the divine high sign, God would continue to grace Universalist ministries, according to the preachers and their fellow travelers, with miracles as signs of blessing. Even as the universalist message announced an enlightened deity who had lost his vindictive ways and temperamental concerns for personal justice, it pointed the way to a new kind of enlightenment—at least in the Anglo-American context.

It is perhaps indicative that Murray reported in his autobiography at one point that, in Providence, he was introduced to a certain Mr. Williams, who was "strongly attached to the writings of Jacob Behmen." It was likewise indicative that his widow, completing the biographical narrative that Murray did not live to finish, could conclude with a statement of beliefs that announced the mystical import of the Second-Adam faith: "Adam the first was a figure of Adam the second. Adam the first, the prototype; Adam the second the substance of the prototype, the Creator of all Worlds, the Lord from heaven. The sacred scriptures abound with figures of this mysterious, this ennobling, this soul-satisfying UNION; among which, perhaps, none is more expressive than that of the *Head* and *Members* constituting one body, of which Jesus Christ was the immaculate Head." [116] The enlightenment that universalism preached pushed toward a mystical republic of the spirit. It only remained for new-made Christian mystics to follow the lead of Mormon Joseph Smith and become convinced of the divine nature of their inner selves. They, too, would be "as gods," or they would come to operate out of the living Christ presence within. They would be metaphysicians.

TRANSCENDENTALISM AND THE ENLIGHTENMENT OF THE SPIRIT

The Universalists who rode through the New England hills to announce the benevolent deity had their city cousins, and nowhere more than in the familiarly called "neighborhood" of Boston. In a quip attributed both to Thomas Gold Appleton (brother-in-law of Henry Wadsworth Longfellow) and Thomas Starr King (Unitarian missionary and prominent California public figure), the difference between Universalists and their Unitarian spiritual kin spelled resemblance. Universalists "believed that God was too good to damn them forever," while free-enterprise Unitarians held that people like themselves "were too good to be damned." [117] American Unitarianism, as distinct from its Continental relative in the Radical Reformation, grew out of the liberal, Arminianized preaching that increasingly came to characterize the Boston pulpits of the late eighteenth and early nineteenth centuries. [118] Congregationalist ministers like Jonathan Mayhew and Charles Chauncy were its forerunners, as they shifted pulpit language from preoccupation with hellfire to plain talk on Christian virtue for those whose free will, in keeping with Arminianism, could enable them to embrace a life of increasing good. If Jacob Harmensen (James Arminius), with pastoral concerns uppermost, had become a Calvinist heretic in the Netherlands, his American sympathizers managed to keep their pulpits and promote a free-will gospel all the same. American liberals were also linked by contemporaries to ideas about the nature of Jesus that sounded, for many, suspiciously close to the early church "heresies" of Arius—that Jesus was subservient, and not equal, to his heavenly Father, a divine messenger to humans but not eternally subsisting as the Father had been. The new ideas came, however, not without conflict and contestation.

The so-called "Unitarian controversy" dominated Massachusetts Congregationalism from 1805 to 1825 and, in the end, split it, leading to the formation of the American Unitarian Association in 1825. Already, in 1805, the election of Henry Ware Sr. as Hollis Professor of Divinity at Harvard sounded the guns for war. Ware, a well-known liberal, signaled the beginning of a new era at the university, and concerned Calvinists, by 1808, had founded Andover Seminary to maintain the purity of orthodox teaching. With Jedidiah Morse leading a pamphlet battle against Arminianism and Arianism through the publication, in 1815, of *American Unitarianism*, liberals responded more forcefully. By 1819, William Ellery Channing (1780–1842), already a leading liberal, was thrust further into the limelight with his ordination sermon in Baltimore for Jared Sparks and its subsequent publication as *Unitarian Christianity*. The Channing manifesto accepted the Unitarian name for the emerging movement and marked its self-consciousness as a separate religious party. Rejecting a literal reading of the Bible, Channing championed the use of human reason in religious matters. At the same time, he held to the unity of God, the single human nature of Jesus, and the significance of the moral life for Christians who followed an ethical deity— a divine parent rather than a temperamental judge. In the Channing and Unitarian reading, Jesus saved humans from their sins not through a substitutionary atonement but through moral example. Humans were free in their will, and revivalists were suspect. Channing's published sermons continued to argue for the innate spiritual potential in humans and to foster a religious life devoted to self-cultivation.[119] In effect, a Unitarian reform movement was perpetrating a revolution, overturning the traditional Calvinism of the Congregational faith and inaugurating a new form of liberal religion.

"Self-culture" became the *bon mot* within Unitarian ranks, following a spiritual logic from outer to inner. With the banishment of hellfire from pastoral pulpits, with the new emphasis on human freedom and the moral life, as Daniel Walker Howe showed definitively, moral philosophy came to dominate the Harvard curriculum and the theological reflection of Unitarian divines.[120] Moreover, liberal Christians had bequeathed to the emergent Unitarian movement a conviction that one could embrace rational religion without also embracing deism.[121] Put another way, Unitarians believed that they could uphold the banner of reason in religion *and* keep faith with biblical revelation. The path to this combinative project lay through the tangled landscape of human conscience, and the task at hand came to be clearing out the brush and shining, above all, rational light on human projects and plans. So the clear light of reason began to undergo its own kind of transformation: to search the conscience and clarify it meant to turn, inexorably, within.

Clarification, in short, became cultivation. As David Robinson has noted, organicism pervaded the Unitarian language of the moral life. The sun of reason shown relentlessly on a seed ground where virtue needed to germinate and vice to be weeded out. The term *culture* in Unitarian usage, Robinson observes, "still carried most of the horticultural associations originally connected with the word." Hence Unitarian "sermon and devotional literature" revealed "a conception of the soul based upon the organic analogy of germination, development, and fruition." In this reading, "just as a plant needed direct and careful culture in order to grow and be productive, the human soul required a constant attention to bring it to its full capacity. Moreover, the development of both the living plant and the soul seemed to be directed by an inner potential, a force which, if it were not hindered or altered, would assure a well-proportioned and continuing process of growth."[122] William Ellery Channing embodied this notion in *Self-Culture* (1838), and so did a series of other articulate early Unitarians. Still, the organic metaphor limped—and that was because, in the mysterious process of agriculture, the *farmer* tended the seed. By contrast, within the "agricultural" domain of the human mind, no outside farmer engaged the task. The seeds of human virtue needed to grow of themselves. What Robinson has called the "emphasis on the discipline of life in the formation of character" turned attention to the quest for perfection.[123] Humans needed to search their deep interiors in forays of self-examination to weed out the unwanted and to engage in fertile projects of self-construction. In so doing, they felt their own vital energies and their waxing powers. They were pursuing a growing project that, taken far enough, could grow them into gods.

This is precisely where New England Transcendentalism—itself growing out of Unitarian soil as a still newer reform movement—made crucial turns and connections that advanced the project of American self-divinization. When the later New Thought tradition of the end of the nineteenth century looked back to Ralph Waldo Emerson (1803–1882) and other Transcendentalists as founding spirits and guides, they knew their mentors. If, as Robinson notes, the teleology of culture meant that cultivation—"a means to an end"—became "an end in itself," then the Transcendentalists, in effect, were orienting Americans toward early metaphysical religion.[124]

Transcendental possibility thinking revealed itself first to a Unitarian public in 1836 in a controversial debate over the New Testament miracles of Jesus. When

James Martineau published his *Rationale of Religious Enquiry* in London, on the American side of the waters Unitarian divine George Ripley (1802–1880) took note.[125] Attached to what were being called the "new views," Ripley stood among the Transcendentalists within the denomination who were beginning to make their voices heard. As he reviewed Martineau's book in the official Unitarian *Christian Examiner*, Ripley used the occasion to transpose issues of evidence and proof from external verification to the production of internal states. The New Testament Jesus converted the crowds who came to hear him because he touched the deep places in their souls rather than because of the sensational quality of his deeds. The manifest character of Jesus demonstrated the divine far more convincingly than the thunder and flames of Mount Sinai (a reference to the biblical Moses receiving the Ten Commandments). The miracles of Jesus expressed his character rather than functioning to support his mission formally.[126] Unitarian "pope" Andrews Norton, whose conserving rationalism saw the miracles of Jesus as external proof of his teaching, was not well pleased, and the conflict spilled into print. Two years later, Norton would return with a vengeance—after Emerson, invited by a committee of Harvard's graduating class to address them, told them that the "very word Miracle, as pronounced by the Christian churches" was "Monster."[127]

In 1836, when Ripley wrote the Martineau review, he was not alone in his move away from Enlightenment philosophy. Other Unitarian clergy with new views were also challenging rationalism. William H. Furness, for example, published *Remarks on the Four Gospels* with its argument for the natural world as the container of the supernatural and its challenge to the resurrection of Jesus as a miraculous event. Orestes Brownson, an erstwhile Universalist preacher and now a Unitarian, brought out his *New Views of Christianity, Society, and the Church*, in which he argued that Unitarianism represented a victory for materialism in the warfare between the material and the spiritual. Convers Francis published *Christianity as a Purely Internal Principle*, a tract the title of which suggests its contents. The aim of Christianity was, in fact, "to purify and sweeten the fountains in the deep places of the soul, that refreshing influences may thence go forth."[128] Meanwhile, Amos Bronson Alcott (1799–1888), not from Boston and not a Unitarian but very much Emerson's friend and a missionary for the new views, published the first volume of his *Conversations with Children on the Gospels*, a record of his educational experiments.[129] At the Temple School, which he had founded, Alcott—in Platonic fashion and deeply influenced by Swiss educational reformer Johann Heinrich Pestalozzi (1746–1827)—aimed to draw from his young charges the knowledge they already possessed, including knowledge on sexual themes. His attempt brought heat and controversy to the

Temple School, but it fully reflected the intuitional theory of consciousness, and it also pointed to the collective nature of mind and intuition in the new vision. For Alcott, the vision came, too—if Arthur Versluis is right—through an immersion in the theosophy of Jacob Boehme, especially as mediated through the seventeenth-century English mystic John Pordage, and it brought with it a fascination with alchemy.[130]

For Emerson, Alcott, and others, the collective quality of intuition and its full emergence in community were mirrored most directly in the ritual of conversation. Beginning in September, a group that came to be known as the Transcendental Club began to meet on an irregular basis, pursuing group explorations on high-minded and grandiose themes such as "American genius," the "education of humanity," law, truth, mysticism, and worship. (There were sometimes more specific sessions on topics like Harvard College and Emerson's journals.) The roster of the club's developing membership included all of the 1836 authors and more—some twenty-six persons who became linked to the group and among them seventeen who could be counted Unitarian ministers.[131] In addition to those already noted, the Transcendental label marked such figures—both clergy and lay—as Theodore Parker, Henry David Thoreau, Margaret Fuller, James Freeman Clarke, Frederic Henry Hedge, Orestes Brownson, Elizabeth Palmer Peabody, Jones Very, and William Henry Channing and the younger (William) Ellery Channing, both nephews of the celebrated Unitarian leader.

In the conversations of the club and in the public writing that appeared, self-culture now was accompanied by increasingly exalted views of the inner landscape to be cultivated. Miracles had gone under-soul, and the way was opened to a new—and different—manifestation of external miracles that emanated from spirit powers within. It remained for Emerson to read the signs and chart the connections. This he did in his small book *Nature*, also published in 1836, the year that, with all its literary productions, has come down in Transcendental lore as the *annus mirabilis* of the movement. Emerson's work was predicated on the age-old theory of correspondence between the human project and its cosmic referent, between microcosm and macrocosm. He argued their linkage in a religiopoetic logic that sought the traces of spirit in the natural world. Here, nature meant all that was "NOT ME," with the "me" in question being consciousness, since even one's own body needed to be thought of as "nature." Given that operating premise, Emerson's project in his book-length essay (actually, two essays that he had more or less successfully joined together) was to demonstrate the "kingdom of man over nature." It was also to issue a resounding call to readers to reclaim their inheritance and manifest once more the vast extent of their powers as once, long ago, they had done.[132] Four years before Emerson wrote *Nature* he had resigned as Unitarian minister to the Second Church in Boston, and now he was offering his alternative to what he regarded as the desiccated forms of the church. His words, in fact, announced what was meant as a revolution. Significantly, it was a revolution in which revelation continued and illumination could not be relegated to past times and ancient authorities: "Embosomed for a season in nature, whose floods of life stream around and through us, and invite us by the powers they supply, to action proportioned to nature, why should we grope among the dry bones of the past, or put the living generation into masquerade out of its faded wardrobe? The sun shines to-day also. There is more wool and flax in the fields. There are new lands, new men, new thoughts. Let us demand our own works and laws and worship."[133]

The spirit moved through nature, and it was there that Emerson would seek for it, enjoining others to follow—to achieve their action "proportioned it to" and so show forth the powers and perfections of the divine. This "NOT ME" of nature was breathed by the one mind or spirit dwelling in the human soul and in the realm of ideas. In large part Emerson's reading of nature was Platonic and, more, Neoplatonic. His essay existed in a tension between nature as palpable and real and nature as, finally, an idea, a cosmic one among the many. Discerning the traces of that divine idea in the natural world, Emerson read it as a hieroglyphic of symbols. ("Every man's condition is a solution in hieroglyphic to those inquiries he would put.")[134] Through the secret language of the hieroglyphs, Reason—here a metapower that enabled the mind to function, and a capacity typically contrasted to the more penurious "Understanding"—could find the encoding of spirit in matter and experience its revelation. Likewise, Imagination—again a transcending power—moved beyond the more limited Fancy to see beyond surface finery to the depth and truth of things and bring them to be. Thus Emerson's *Nature* expressed an enthusiasm for what can be called magic and miracle, bringing the power of the inner life outward in startling demonstrations. If Emerson talked of the secret, it was to bring it into the democratic open; in a new Masonry of the spirit, the open secret lay within the self of each reader but moved inexorably from self to world.[135]

That acknowledged, the sensuousness and rhetorical artistry of *Nature* as prose poetry can function as a masquerade of its own—deflecting attention away from the pragmatic cast of much of the work. Read with metaphysical religion in mind, the structure of Emerson's essay as a kind of higher-order how-to book begins to emerge. Indeed, as I have already suggested, there were two parts to the essay and a bridge across what Emerson himself called its "crack . . . not easy to be soldered or welded."[136] The craft metaphor was appropriate. In the first and longest section of his work—a section in which Platonism seemed for a season put to bed and Emerson reveled in the tangible reality of nature and the sense delight it bestowed—mysticism and manipulation were conjoined. The mysticism—clear to see and often quoted—celebrated nature as *real* estate. "Standing on the bare ground," Emerson wrote, with his "head bathed by the blithe air, and uplifted into infinite space," he saw the end to all "mean egotism." "I become a transparent eye-ball," he testified. "I am nothing. I see all. The currents of the Universal Being circulate through me; I am part or particle of God."[137] This was well enough, but the announcement that followed brought would-be mystics back in a different way to the bare ground. Nature existed, in Emerson's reading, to be used. In what followed, he lectured readers on the uses to which it was being put.

For Emerson nature's uses were fourfold, with nature assisting humans as a commodity, as beauty, as language, and as a discipline. As a commodity, nature benefited humans in material ways that were obvious and direct, but, as Emerson wrote, nature was also "the process and the result." Beyond the crucial usefulness of nature as commodity, however, nature benefited humans as beauty. It fed their higher nature by the delight that natural forms occasioned and, also, by the "spiritual element" that was "essential to its perfection"—a perfection that humans could take in through the "energy" of "thought and will" and express in acts of virtue. But there was still a third aspect of beauty that nature conveyed, and this it did as "an object of the intellect." "Beside the relation of things to virtue," Emerson declared, "they have a relation to thought." Nature's beauty reconstituted itself in the mind and there led not to "barren contemplation" but to "new creation." "Thus is Art, a nature passed through the alembic of man."[138]

The higher use of nature in human creativity led Emerson to the third use of nature. It provided a model for language. In a reading that owed much to Swedenborgian thought, especially as articulated by American Swedenborgian Sampson Reed (as, indeed, did the "uses" of nature and much of the entire essay),[139] Emerson argued that words are "signs of natural facts" that are themselves "symbols of particular spiritual facts." In an important clue to the metaphysical power of language, Emerson, like a latter-day American Confucius, linked the "corruption" of humanity to the "corruption of language," with the second the result of the first. It followed that an uncompromised human—a "poet" or an "orator, bred in the woods, whose senses have been nourished by their fair and appeasing changes"—held "the keys of power." Thus right language did not simply bring contact with spirit and illuminate with truth. In Emerson's scheme, the noetic moved quickly, inevitably, into the active. Language carried power. More than that, language, as Emerson inscribed it, hinted at what was to come in the emerging metaphysical religion of America. "That which was unconscious truth, becomes, when interpreted and defined in an object, a part of the domain of knowledge,—a new weapon in the magazine of power."[140] Here, in seed form, were the affirmations of later New Thought, and here was an early statement about human ability to fashion the world, to "create reality."

Emerson's mental magic—a derivative use of nature—led on, however, to a final use. Ever a moralist, Emerson looked to nature as a discipline. In his vision, objective limits could be drawn around human ability to fashion a world. Nature demanded that the mind conform itself to the hard facticity of the world's presence, to the objective status of things. It also demanded that the human will acknowledge the moral law that lay implicit within the order of nature. And yet, and yet—always the argument returned to issues of power and human agency in claiming it. The very nature that disciplined the understanding with its intellectual truths that were so hard and "out there" was receptive to the "exercise of the Will or the lesson of power . . . taught in every event." The statement that followed was surely startling. "From the child's successive possession of his several senses up to the hour when he saith, 'thy will be done,'" Emerson declared, "he is learning the secret, that he can reduce under his will, not only particular events, but great classes, nay the whole series of events, and so conform all facts to his character." Nor was Emerson shy about the sheer baldness of the statement: "Nature is thoroughly mediate. It is made to serve. It receives the dominion of man as meekly as the ass on which the Saviour rode." If we follow the moral logic of the equation, Emerson was connecting human will to a higher source of will and desire, and he was arguing for the release of self into that vastness—a thoroughly metaphysical logic that would come to characterize some late-nineteenth-century American spirituality. Indeed, underlining the practical direction of the argument, Emerson had his own prognosticating line on health: "What a searching preacher of self-command is the varying phenomenon of Health!"[141]

Launched on the pragmatic ground of nature, Emerson came to his bridge—the construct that would lead him into the more classically Platonic and Neoplatonic part of his small book. The "bridge" was Emerson's chapter called "Idealism." Caught betwixt the world as sensuous presence and the world as illusion, Emerson let his worry show. He acknowledged something "ungrateful" in his preoccupation with "the general proposition, that all culture tends to imbue us with idealism." "I have no hostility to nature," he wrote defensively, "but a child's love to it. I expand and live in the warm day like corn and melons. Let us speak her fair. I do not wish to fling stones at my beautiful mother, nor soil my gentle nest."[142] What tipped the scales for Emerson, though, was again the pragmatic; he saw, above all, "the advantage of the ideal theory over the popular faith," an advantage both "speculative and practical." "Idealism," he asserted confidently, "sees the world in God. It beholds the whole circle of persons and things, of actions and events, of country and religion, not as painfully accumulated, atom after atom, act after act, in an aged creeping Past, but as one vast picture, which God paints on the instant eternity, for the contemplation of the soul."[143] The mysticism of presence, of continuing revelation, that came with idealism turned the world to be contemplated into a divine gift—a safe and delightful port for the human gaze, but also, as the rest of the essay made plain, a divine gift that was also a tool.

Idealism progressed to spirit, and Emerson demanded the same—for a "true theory of nature and of man" needed to "contain somewhat progressive." "All the uses of nature admit of being summed in one," he confided, and this one gave to "the activity of man an infinite scope." Nature always spoke of "Spirit" and suggested the "absolute." Nature, in fact, was "a perpetual effect," a "great shadow pointing always to the sun behind us." Still, nature and spirit were ineradicably linked. Spirit was not just *behind* nature but *throughout* it, and it was also "through ourselves." "Therefore," declared Emerson, "that spirit, that is, the Supreme Being, does not build up nature around us, but puts it forth through us, as the life of the tree puts forth new branches and leaves through the pores of the old." He seemed to be tarrying in a garden of the spirit, where contemplation and mystical unitive consciousness held sway. Yet, as of old in Eden, danger lurked in Emerson's garden, and the requirement of self-culture and the moral life would not go away. Nature, it turned out, was also the human "house," and it was a house from which it was possible to become more and more estranged. "As we degenerate, the contrast between us and our house is more evident. We are as much strangers in nature, as we are aliens from God."[144]

The mystical-moral analysis carried, still again, a pragmatic thrust, and it led to a program for action. Emerson's final chapter was "Prospects." One needed to learn the human relationship to the world and learn it intuitively—"by untaught sallies of the spirit, by a continual self-recovery, and by entire humility." Such learning would make one "sensible of a certain occult recognition and sympathy in regard to the most unwieldy and eccentric forms of beast, fish, and insect." But it would do more, and it would do it astoundingly. Those who sought the wisdom Emerson was distilling needed to align themselves with the message of a "certain poet," and it was this message with which Emerson concluded *Nature*.[145] The message carried a panentheistic Platonism with a latter-day moralist tinge fully into view. This message was already in some ways grasped in the Freemasonry of the early Republic and in the developing Mormon world of Joseph Smith. And it was hinted, too, in the universalist teachings of rural New England.

Emerson's enlightenment of the spirit announced an American gospel of divinization in which higher self and ego self worked together and moved comfortably into each other's territory. Humans were meant to be "as gods," as they were for Joseph Smith, and—in a new miracles doctrine that made biblical miracles pale by comparison—the world became malleable to will and idea. First, though, there was the bad news of shrinkage. "'Man,'" lamented Emerson's poet, "'is the dwarf of himself. Once he was permeated and dissolved by spirit. He filled nature with his overflowing currents. Out from him sprang the sun and moon.'" Now, however, things were grossly different, and "'having made for himself this huge shell, his waters retired; he no longer fills the veins and veinlets; he is shrunk to a drop.'" Applying to nature "but half his force" and working on himself "by his understanding alone," wrote Emerson—leaving the poet and resuming the narrative on his own—man operated out of a "penny-wisdom" and was at best "but a half-man." In the midst of the putative darkness, Emerson saw gleams of light, which—as cosmic optimist—he could share. His short list of "occasional examples of the action of man upon nature with his entire force,—with reason as well as understanding" reads like a page from a metaphysical affirmative action catalog: "Such examples are; the traditions of miracles in the earliest antiquity of all nations; the history of Jesus Christ; the achievements of a principle, as in religious and political revolutions, and in the abolition of the Slave-trade; the miracles of enthusiasm, as those reported of Swedenborg, Hohenlohe, and the Shakers; many obscure and yet contested facts, now arranged under the name of Animal Magnetism; prayer; eloquence; self-healing; and the wisdom of children. These are examples of Reason's momentary grasp of the sceptre; the exertions of a power which exists not in time or space, but an instantaneous in-streaming causing power."[146]

For Emerson, it was restoring, or redeeming, the soul that would restore the world. As his "poet" said, the world was "'fluid'" and malleable to spirit. Nature, in short, obeyed. The world existed for humans—for Emerson's reading public. Build your own world, he told them in the words of his poet. The results suggested that the restoration of the world meant its subjection to an enhanced ego-self, an ego-self that used the power of higher spiritual energies to advance this-worldly projects and delights. When men and women conformed their lives to the "'pure idea'" in their minds, there would be "'a correspondent revolution in things.'" "'So fast will disagreeable appearances, swine, spiders, snakes, pests, mad-houses, prisons, enemies, vanish.'" Then would come the final denouement: "'The kingdom of man over nature, which cometh not with observation,—a dominion such as now is beyond his dream of God,—he shall enter without more wonder than the blind man feels who is gradually restored to perfect sight.'"[147]

The message was memorable, and it would be noticed by readers who continued to find in Emerson an American seer for a growing metaphysical religion. Meanwhile, the Emersonian rhetoric carried the ring of deeply felt personal conviction and spiritual discovery, but it also came with clues of company attached. Its sources lay, in good part, in the broad Hermetic tradition of Europe. The Swedenborgian "influx" that fed through Emerson's reading of idealism was only one presence among a series with which the metaphysical gospel was conveyed. In fact, it is possible to invoke an "occult Emerson" through the pages of *Nature,* especially if we follow the literary trail of his many allusions—allusions that in typical nineteenth-century fashion were only loosely ascribed, if that. Emerson's Platonism came strongly colored with Neoplatonism, since he read Plato through the Englishman Thomas Taylor's Neoplatonizing translations. But Emerson also quoted and cited the Neoplatonic philosopher Plotinus directly, and he knew Porphyry's life of Plotinus. He quoted such figures as the English metaphysical poet George Herbert and recalled Sir Henry Vane ("Sir Harry Vane"). His distinction between the Reason and the Understanding came from the English Romanticist Samuel Taylor Coleridge, who had misread it creatively from its Kantian source. Emerson named the pre-Socratic Greek philosophers Pythagoras and Xenophanes, and he quoted the French ex-Catholic Swedenborgian philosopher Guillaume Oegger, whose writings explored mystical and metaphysical Christian themes. He quoted Quaker founder George Fox as well. He linked the Irish idealist philosopher and cleric George Berkeley to "Viasa" (Vyasa), the arranger of the Indian Vedas and compiler of the great Indian epic the *Mahabharata.* He referenced theosophists and acknowledged the Manichean.[148]

Emerson's *Nature*—the early proclamation of Transcendental good news—was a charter document and, as such, a representative one. The "esoteric Emerson," as Richard Geldard has called him, continued to explore the implications of *Nature's* teachings in open public lectures, later reworked into essays and published for an eager American audience.[149] Children of the Puritans and the Unitarians, Emerson and the others who shared his new Transcendental views had acquired their name in derision, as perhaps half-comprehending step-children of Europe. The German philosopher Immanuel Kant had employed the term *transcendental* in his *Critique of Pure Reason* (1781) to point to ideas that came through intuition rather than the experience of the senses. In their zeal for German, and specifically Kantian, idealism, critics said, the American Transcendentalists followed vagaries and mists, walking with their heads in the clouds and their feet scarcely touching the earth. But more than the carefully argued pages of Kant's philosophy, Emerson and the other American Transcendentalists embraced a broad Romanticism. This Romanticism encompassed German thinkers like Friedrich H. Jacobi, Johann G. Fichte, Johann Wolfgang von Goethe, and Novalis (Friedrich von Hardenberg); German religionists like Jacob Boehme and Friedrich Schleiermacher; English Romanticists like the already noted Samuel Taylor Coleridge, Thomas Carlyle, and William Wordsworth; and French eclectics like Victor Cousin and Théodore Jouffroy. Always, for the early Transcendentalists, there was Emanuel Swedenborg, even if, later, Emerson at least grew decidedly lukewarm. And increasingly, among the Transcendentalists, there was Asia—a theme to which I shall return in a later chapter.

Still further, Transcendental Romanticism was a clue to the radically individualistic and, at the same time, radically connective nature of the new vision. In the Transcendental version of creating one's own reality, the deep recesses from which intuition welled were also the deep recesses that connected people with one another. The human cosmos, like the natural one, was a grand collective of the spirit. Transcendentalism, in short, had a corporate vision. We have already gained a glimpse of that corporate vision in the Transcendental Club with its formal ritual of conversation. We gain another in the communal movements that the Transcendentalists created—the Fruitlands of Bronson Alcott and the Brook Farm of George Ripley—and, behind Brook Farm in its developed state, the half-understood mystical communitarianism of the French utopian Charles Fourier (1772–1837). Self-culture, it turned out, meant the culture of the whole.

Alcott's Fruitlands was only a brief fling into the culture of the whole, an experiment of seven months. On the ninety-acre farm at Harvard, Massachusetts, purchased for Alcott by English fellow traveler Charles Lane in 1843, Alcott's Transcendental individualism stood beside totalitarian directives that pointed toward a nineteenth-century reading of Pythagorean asceticism. In the mystical pursuit of total purity, the new being—and a new and harmonial form of living—would emerge. Here "outward abstinence" was "the sign of inward fullness," and for "divine growth," the "only source of true progress" was "inward." "Our diet is therefore strictly of the pure and bloodless kind," wrote Charles Lane. "No animal substances, neither flesh, butter, cheese, eggs nor milk, pollute our tables or corrupt our bodies, neither tea, coffee, molasses, nor rice, tempts us beyond the bounds of indigenous productions. Our sole beverage is pure fountain water. The native grains, fruits, herbs and roots, dressed with the utmost cleanliness, and regard to their purpose of edifying a healthful body, furnish the pleasantest refections and in the greatest variety requisite to the supply of the various organs."[150] Alongside this dietary rigor, cotton and wool garments were banished because they were the results of slave labor—cotton the slavery of blacks in the American South and wool the slavery of sheep. The community rose and retired with the sun, and cold-water bathing was required. The overt primitivism of Fruitlands, however, belied its literary grounding in the Hermetic tradition. Charles Lane, who had been a follower of the English Boehmian theosopher James Pierrepont Greaves, met Alcott just after Greaves died. Together Lane and Alcott brought Greaves's large library of almost a thousand books, and other works that they added, to Fruitlands—replete with Boehmian and Hermetic titles, including works on magic and alchemy. Hermes Trismegistus was certainly there, and so was Cornelius Agrippa. The library offered a large hint about where the Fruitlands founders' passion lay. With its erudite preoccupations, the small community was never successful at farming. Then, when—beyond its lack of viability as a working farm—Charles Lane attempted to introduce celibacy, Bronson and Abigail Alcott balked. Fruitlands had its coup de grâce and came to a swift end.[151]

Fruitlands amused a number of people at the time and through the years.[152] It stands, however, as a testimony to the idealism of the Transcendental vision as well as the absoluteness with which individual Transcendentalists could seize an enterprise. As Anne C. Rose has argued, the social anarchism of Fruitlands "made it possible to deny the world completely and yet leave society intact."[153] Still for all that, Fruitlands embodied a project of lived metaphysical religion, an attempt to bring envisioned heavens down to earth and to make them work in the world. This was *practical* metaphysics, even if the experiment failed and even if, perhaps, it was a prognosticator for later communal experiments among metaphysicians, projecting idealism onto historical landscapes with at best mixed results. Meanwhile, at Brook Farm, another Transcendental community was engaging in its own complex and transformative project as it grew into a quasi-Fourierist phalanx.

Brook Farm was the brainchild of, by this time, former Unitarian minister George Ripley, already notorious for his views on miracles. In 1841, the same year he withdrew from the ministry after his half decade and more battling what he regarded as Unitarian conservatism, Ripley formed a joint-stock company. He aimed to plant his vision of the New Testament social order at West Roxbury, Massachusetts, outside of Boston and not far from the wary Unitarian gaze. There a group of the Transcendental faithful repaired to try their hand at agricultural living and communitarian enterprise. Emerson was not among them, eschewing the "pretended siege of Babylon" because he had not completed the siege of his own "hencoop." Years later, in 1880, he remembered Brook Farm, significantly enough, as "a French Revolution in small, an Age of Reason in a patty-pan."[154] If so, the revolution and enlightenment emerged in a decidedly new-age form, hybridized with Romantic and, in the large sense, Hermetic seed. The Transcendental version of self-culture, for Ripley and those who joined him, encompassed ideals of economic and social democracy—but also very much else.

The church that Ripley had pastored as a Unitarian cleric stood on Purchase Street in Boston, in a deteriorating neighborhood taken over by what contemporaries called the "mud-sill" class. Ripley had not intended merely to move to the suburbs but to engage in a reform project to model what society, with some tinkering, could become. None of the mud-sills, however, joined the early Brook Farm but—until 1844 when the Fourierist remake occurred and brought a sizable working-class component—only the Transcendental middle class. Moreover, most of the Transcendental elite showed up as frequent visitors rather than full-time residents. Still, the cooperative community on the 160-acre farm, which had begun with some twenty members, did grow to close to seventy, and its early membership included five with former or existing ministerial ties, one of them— John Allen—an ex-Universalist preacher. From the first, members were told by the Brook Farm Constitution that their work would be fitted to their "capacities, habits, and tastes," and they were enjoined to "select and perform such operations of labor, whether corporal or mental" that would be "best suited" to their "own endowments and the benefit of the Association."[155] Infused with this ideal of freedom and individualism in the midst of a harmonious community, Brook Farmers worked at agrarian pursuits, crafts, and light industries, and they established a well-regarded experimental school. A culture of theater and concerts, along with games and dances, came to characterize the community, which was known for its liberal tastes, the freedom of its women, and the looseness of its courtship rituals. Ubiquitously, there were Transcendental "conversations," and people and their morale seemed to blossom alongside an enthusiasm for reform of seemingly every sort. Ripley's biographer Charles Crowe summarized the Brook Farm concerns as a veritable "reform catalogue of the age," encompassing "anti-currency men, labor reformers, Grahamites, hydropaths, Swedenborgians, and representatives of dozens of reform and religious sects."[156]

It was in this context that the community began to transform itself into a Fourierist phalanx. The utopian Charles Fourier had been an autodidact who spent his life in mercantile pursuits and, without marriage and a family, poured his vision of a new social order onto thousands of pages of manuscript books, only a portion of which were published in his lifetime. On the landscape of his imagination, Fourier created an ideal society that he called Harmony, a realm that was ruled by "natural association" and that employed human desire and passion as servants to the general good. The scheme by which this corporate Harmony would work became, in practical terms, the phalanx, an elaborated community structure in which each person would be drawn to work that was socially useful and also profoundly absorbing. In Fourier's vision, the fundamental law was erotic, and its physical, and explicitly sexual, embodiment was primary.

Gratified passion enabled the phalanx to work, and gratified passion meant attention to every detail of physical want and desire—a dissection of the passions and
emotions, and a rational plan for their satisfaction. This, however, was only the
groundwork. Fourier went on to problems of work and labor, which he regarded
as primary. For him, the solution to social evil was an erotic—a passionate—
relationship to work. In the intricate and heavily articulated mental structure of
Harmony that Fourier erected, the gratification of such desire came through a
mechanization and rationalization of passion that seemed almost a contradiction. The law of attraction was regulated down to each detail, and eroticism came
by committee.[157]

The American translation of Fourier's grand vision came through his disciple
Albert Brisbane (1809–1890), whose *Social Destiny of Man* appeared in 1840.[158]
And if in France Fourier's students were already frightened or scandalized by the
sexual aspects of his system and Fourier himself never fully published them, in
America, a still more sanitized version became available through Brisbane. Here
Fourierism became a thoroughly respectable—if radical and idiosyncratic—
system for dealing with issues of industry, economy, and human labor in a new
American order being born alongside the Industrial Revolution. Inspired by Brisbane, Ripley and the others reinvented Brook Farm as a phalanx by 1844. After
1845, Ripley's weekly newspaper *The Harbinger* spread Brisbane's Fourierism
with enthusiasm, promoting the message among a wave of experimental communities that were declaring themselves Fourierist phalanxes. "In the summer of
'43," wrote John Humphrey Noyes, "Phalanxes by the dozen were on the march
for the new world of wealth and harmony."[159] In the mood of the times and at
the hub of the Fourierist wheel, the Brook Farmers began to build a central "phalanstery" to house their enterprise. Yet there were strains between the original
Transcendental founders with their cultural elitism and the new working-class
membership that joined in the wake of the Fourierist conversion. Then, in March
1846, a fire destroyed the half-finished phalanstery, creating a financial crisis and
symbolizing, too, the community's unrest. By 1847 Brook Farm had disbanded.
The foremost American Fourierist experiment was over.

The bare facts, nonetheless, invite closer scrutiny. Even if, as Noyes stated,
"Joint-stockism manages business," Fourier's heterodox prescription for social
transformation had been seriously metaphysical. He was adamant that "unless
one wishes to regard God's providence as insufficient, limited and indifferent to
our happiness, it follows that God must have devised for us a passional code, a
system for the domestic and social organization of all humanity, which is everywhere endowed with the same passions." Like the laws of "material gravitation
and the celestial harmonies," God had a plan for humans.[160] To be sure, the

Brisbane version of the vision emphasized something other than metaphysics —as had Fourier himself. But his vision of the whole and the connection of its finely chiseled attractional parts was intrinsically spiritual, and the Brook Farmers caught its drift, whatever the translation. Moreover, they intuited the affinities between the grand vision of Fourier and the Swedenborgian gospel that Unitarians and Transcendentalists had been mutually admiring in Boston. At Brook Farm, the Fourierist-Swedenborgian connection bloomed, and metaphysical religion came quietly with the flowers.

The Brook Farmers were not alone in catching the connection. Indeed, Parke Godwin, after Brisbane the major publicizer of Fourierism in the United States, in his *Popular View of the Doctrines of Charles Fourier* (1844) gave credit to Swedenborg for promoting a similar vision of "Universal Analogy." "Emanuel Swedenborg, between whose revelations in the sphere of spiritual knowledge, and Fourier's discoveries in the sphere of science, there has been remarked the most exact and wonderful coïncidence," he enthused, "preceded him in the annunciation of the doctrine in many of its aspects, in what is termed the doctrine of correspondence." He went on to proclaim "these two great minds, the greatest beyond all comparison in our later days" to be "the instruments of Providence in bringing to light the mysteries of His Word and Works." Still more, Swedenborg and Fourier had been "commissioned by the Great Leader of the Christian Israel, to spy out the promised land of peace and blessedness." Closer to Brook Farm, William Henry Channing—a frequent visitor to the farm and part-time inhabitant—had noticed an "extraordinary resemblance between the views of Fourier and Swedenborg." "Their doctrine of Correspondence and Universal Unity accords with all the profoundest thought of the age," he averred. Indeed, in Ripley's Fourierist *Harbinger*, John Humphrey Noyes counted "between thirty and forty articles on Swedenborg and Swedenborgian subjects," with their continuing message "the unity of Swedenborgianism and Fourierism." With this kind of evidence, Noyes could conclude pithily: "Unitarianism produced Transcendentalism; Transcendentalism produced Brook Farm; Brook Farm married and propagated Fourierism; Fourierism had Swedenborgianism for its religion; and Swedenborgianism led the way to Modern Spiritualism."[161]

Meanwhile, among the Brook Farmers, the so-called "symbol of universal unity" became a ritual for solemn and auspicious times. Here, as Lindsay Swift described, "the entire company would rise, join hands, thus forming a circle, and vow truth to the cause of God and humanity." "Association" became a myth and a mystique for the West Roxbury residents, for whom Transcendental self-culture had also become the culture of the whole.[162] Emerson, in his first series of essays, published in 1841, had invoked the whole—or the divine mind—as the

Oversoul in ways that are memorable. "Our being is descending into us from we know not whence," he declared to readers. Communication of that truth, which Emerson understood as revelation, brought "an influx of the Divine mind into our mind," and it came with a "fire, vital, consecrating, celestial, which burns until it shall dissolve all things into the waves and surges of an ocean of light." As individuals came into contact with that divine mind, that Oversoul, they would discover their intrinsic connection, their "one blood" rolling "uninterruptedly, an endless circulation through all men." If there were Platonic and Neoplatonic echoes, there was a clear Swedenborgianism here; and, in fact, Emerson (later to be far more tempered in his judgment) had quoted Swedenborg in his essay, alluding to "the greatness of that man's perception."[163] The Brook Farmers had felt the waves of the ocean and wanted the experience of the one blood. They sought the mental magic as a collective miracle of lived unity.

Thus the "Transcendental Brethren of the Common Life," as Swift dubbed the Farmers, shared some of the rudiments of a monastic discipline, rising at half-past six, retiring at nine, and eating a meal together.[164] There was apparently enough grumbling, but the ideal of unity made present continued to bring together the diverse personalities who flowed in and out of the community. Nor can we ignore the mildly erotic quality that ran through the Fourierist-Swedenborgian spirituality of the Brook Farmers. Swedenborg, after all, had taught that there was sex in heaven (and so had Joseph Smith), and even in American translation, the attractional universe of Charles Fourier sat well with the freedom of Transcendental women and the liberality of Brook Farm courtship customs. There was here a potent mix: Enlightenment and Romance went hand in hand, and a proto-metaphysical religiosity pervaded both. The Transcendental revolution was installing a different religious future. It was catalyzing vernacular and elite currents in a higher pragmatism that was quintessentially American and that brought blessing and delight to ego-selves on a this-worldly landscape. In so doing, it was articulating—in a different key that mediated both high and ordinary culture—the good news that Royal Arch Masons, Mormons, and Universalists were also exploring. Correspondence controlled the theoretical register; mind and imagination congealed in symbol and social arrangement; energy was raised and kept rising to mend the lives of one and all. What came next was to turn the page that Noyes had already partially opened. What came next was "modern spiritualism."

4

COMMUNION OF SPIRITS

Adin Ballou's third son, Adin Augustus Ballou, was born 30 June 1833, nearly a decade before the Ballous moved to Hopedale. Since the two older sons in the Ballou household had died, the birth came attended with high hope and deep anxiety. At first Adin Augustus's infant cries echoed "the moans of his languishing brothers," but—to the great relief and joy of his parents—he grew to be a happy child, youth, and then late teenager who pleased them mightily with his character and his contributions at Hopedale. After a year at the State Normal School at Bridgewater, Massachusetts, Adin Augustus studied for a supplementary term and then was invited to stay on as junior assistant teacher at the end of 1851. Meanwhile, acknowledging his character and maturity, the Universalist Hopedale Community formally admitted him to membership two weeks before his December teaching duties began. Adin Augustus was not yet nineteen. Two months later, on 8 February 1852, he died of typhoid fever, expiring "in the arms of his agonized parents." The Ballous were utterly overcome. "Down into his grave went all the cherished plans whose fruition depended so largely on his earthly life, genius, and ministry," wrote the grieving father. "The shock of our bereavement almost crushed the fondly doting mother, and was all that my own stronger energies could endure. Neither of us ever entirely recovered from its desolating effect."[1]

At the time of his third son's passing, the elder Ballou was already a confirmed spiritualist, and indeed, the death and bereavement spurred him to publish a carefully argued volume tempering defense of spiritualism with judicious warnings against fraud and extremism.[2] Spiritualism, however, did something more for Ballou than provide a compelling literary task to distract him from his sorrow. It brought him the conviction that he and his wife could be in touch with his beloved son again. Through Elizabeth Alice Reed, a writing medium at Hopedale, the parents learned that Adin Augustus was operating from the fourth after-death sphere and, between communications, had progressed to the fifth. They were told that he did not spend time in the more immediate spheres, thus suggesting the higher order of character that they had already imputed to him. They learned, too, that Adin Augustus's new "Spirit Home" was a social place and that their son was busily engaged in teaching the spirits of young children. In the account that unfolded, Adin Augustus's conversation ranged from describing the mechanics of spirit communication and its relative success or failure, to comforting his grieving parents in their loss, to speaking words of spirit wisdom that also seemed somewhat airy and perhaps banal. The son explained and half-apologized to his mother that "when we shall be able to control mediums entirely, so that their thoughts and ours shall not be mixed, we shall have much more to say." He found it "strange" that his father and mother were "sad and desponding" when he himself was in a place of such light, peace, and joy. "Oh, rapture divine!" he soliloquized, invoking "the Infinite Author of these blessings." He continued with his good word for the work of Hopedale: "I look, and all *good* spirits look, with peculiar pleasure on the great work of Social Reform." Confronted by vanity, vice, and sensuality in the world, by pursuits of wealth and power that led to human oppression and enslavement of other humans, the spirits were "made to rejoice" by looking "to this Dale."[3]

Even as the Ballous felt themselves reunited with their son through a medium's automatic writing, far across the country spiritualism could be found in Mormon circles in the West. Amasa Lyman was reading spiritualist books and participating in séances in southern California in 1852. Later he would be declared an apostate because of his universalist dismissal of the atonement of Jesus as a requisite for salvation. By the next decade in Utah, the Godbeites—Mormon followers of William Godbe who objected to church theocracy—were also fully immersed in spiritualism. They sat at séances, convinced that they were talking to deceased kin and to spirits who were formerly authorities in the church from which, by 1869, the Godbeites would be excommunicated. More speculatively, early Mormon leader, theologian, and amateur scientist Orson Pratt by the 1850s was echoing Hermetic doctrine and contemporary spiritualist discourse in writings that defended the Latter-day Saints. The spiritual matter of Mormon teaching achieved new concreteness when Pratt argued that the Holy Spirit was a permeating spiritual fluid: "Heat, light, electricity, and all the varied and grand displays of nature, are but the tremblings, the vibrations, the energetic powers of a living, all-pervading, and most wonderful fluid, full of wisdom and knowledge, called the HOLY SPIRIT." Pratt went even further into the discourse world of spiritualism as he invoked a "spiritual telegraph" for communication between minds to ex-

plain the spiritual fluid he had named. To operate in this world of spirit communion, one needed "a proper condition to receive the impression," and this meant
possession of a special spiritual sense. Spiritual sight would characterize life in
the world beyond, while in this one, "as the electric fluid passes through bodies
opaque to the natural light, and conveys its message thousands of miles almost instantaneously, so does the still more powerful spiritual fluid convey its message."[4]

Among the Transcendentalists, the report on spiritualist phenomena was
mixed. In the wake of the spirit rappings at Hydesville, New York, in 1848, which
began a spiritualist furor in the nation, Emerson expressed contempt and disgust—"Rat-revelation, the gospel that comes by taps in the wall, and thumps in
the table-drawer." From 1852, when he confided his thoughts to his private journal, through at least the next twenty-five years, he found ways to praise the mysticism of figures like William Blake and Emanuel Swedenborg and of religious
traditions like Hinduism and Zoroastrianism, but he looked askance at American mass spiritualism. "The whole world is an omen and a sign," he had declared
as early as 1839, well before the era of the Hydesville Fox sisters. "Why look wist-
fully in a corner? Man is the Image of God. Why run after a ghost or a dream?"
He thought the same in 1877 when he revised his early lecture "Demonology"
for publication in the *North American Review*.[5]

Thoreau, in turn, was positively vitriolic about spirits in his private correspondence: "Concord is just as idiotic as ever in relation to the spirits and their knockings. Most people here believe in a spiritual world which no respectable junk-
bottle which had not met with a slip would condescend to for a moment." By
1854, Orestes Brownson—already a Catholic for a decade—was vitriolic in public. In *The Spirit-Rapper: An Autobiography*, Brownson was shrill in his condemnation of spiritualist ethics and the free-love ethos of the movement. He
saw Mormonism as a form of spiritualism, linked the spirits to women's rights,
and also linked them to Satan. By contrast, the Transcendentalist minister James
Freeman Clarke showed himself to be, as Robert S. Cox has characterized him,
a "Unitarian-cum-Spiritualist." He attended séances and evaluated spirit visits
for evidence of authenticity. Clarke found in the spirit benevolences expressed
through the language of mediums a model for extending human sympathy beyond one's local orbit. By the time he published *Ten Great Religions* in 1871, he
had linked at least the term *spiritualism* to an exalted and mystical music of the
spheres. And he compared Brahmanism and Christianity for their "divine strains
of spiritualism, of God all in all," identifying spirit as "infinite unlimited substance."[6]

Like Clarke, Bronson Alcott was interested in spirits. In a letter to his mother,
Anna Alcott, in 1848, he told her that "as we are *Spirits in Bodies*, so we com-

municate with the Spirits in our own, or friends' Bodies, as we seek to become pure—which is but another name for being spiritual." He quoted Andrew Jackson Davis, the spiritualist seer from Poughkeepsie, New York, in the same letter and later visited Davis and his wife in New York City in 1856, attending a dinner with them about a week later when Fourier and freedom were discussed. More visiting and conversation on spiritualism with Davis came the following month, and afterwards Alcott continued to meet Davis and other spiritualists. Clearly, he was fascinated by their talk and ideas, and as Frederick C. Dahlstrand has noted, Alcott found links between his own magnetic theories of spiritual energy and the discourse of spiritualism. Yet in the end, Alcott would come to repudiate the widespread practice of spiritualism as superstition and to find the populace at large credulous and their pursuit of spirits paganizing.[7]

Clearly, Universalists, Mormons, and Transcendentalists had heard of the spirits—and, we may presume, so had Freemasons. The events to which they were responding were linked in the public mind to the mysterious rappings that Margaret and Kate Fox—the one a teenager and the other not yet twelve—claimed to hear at their ramshackle home in upstate New York in 1848. In the fabled "burned-over district," the two kindled a new fire when they announced that the raps were communications from a murdered peddler, whose body had been interred in their cellar. With a spate of publicity from intrigued neighbors and others who flocked to the house and with little peace from the rappings, the Fox family left, and their two daughters went to Rochester to live with their older sister, Ann Leah Fish. Here their story and their practice of contacting spirits were embraced by a community of Quaker activists, including especially Isaac and Amy Post. With the Posts involved in the Underground Railroad to aid the escape of fugitive slaves from the South, the incipient spiritualist movement was already being connected to the cutting edge of the period's reform movement.

The Foxes had linked themselves, among the Friends, to the Quaker radical edge. With Amy Post a cousin to Elias Hicks, the Posts had joined with the Hicksite faction of 1827, which—discontent with changes in the nineteenth-century Society of Friends—aimed to restore the original practice of cultivating the "truth" that revealed itself in and through the inner light. Such cultivation meant, at least theoretically, freedom in the social world to express and enact the truth that individual Quakers believed the light was mediating. When, however, the hierarchically organized Hicksites rebuked the Posts for their antislavery work because it involved their presence in societies with non-Quakers, the couple withdrew to form the Congregational Friends. By 1850, the small Quaker congregation based in Waterloo, New York, used language that echoed the Freemasonic ethos of the classic American Enlightenment to find in each person "a limited transcript of the perfect Architect." The Friends also thought that "between the Infinite and all beings" there existed "an unbroken chain of communication."[8] Clearly, they had set their theological compass in a direction that could point comfortably toward spirit communication.

So it was that, from the first, the American séance spiritualism that became a major phenomenon at midcentury, and for the next decade at least, came attached to a quasi-Quaker theology of inner light, inner truth, and outer action to reform society according to spirit principles of grand connection. Spiritualism, however, had flourished in America long before the séances of the Fox sisters drew the "hundreds of thousands of sentient beings" whom New York State Supreme Court judge and convinced spiritualist John Edmonds cited in the *New York Herald* in 1853.[9] Early American reports of the activity of Indian powwows already conduct us into a spiritualist landscape; indeed, the perceived link between Indians and spirits became a pervasive motif in the ritualized séances that evolved in the major Anglo-American spiritualist movement. Before the reported communications of the Fox sisters catalyzed this major spiritualist presence, however, Anglo-American Shakers were convinced that they were contacting spirits, including a large number of Indians who, the Shakers reported, were "taken in." Still more, developments within American mesmerism and its linkage, for some, to Swedenborgian themes mediated a thought world that pointed ever more comfortably toward a spiritualist cosmology. And at least a year or more before the Fox sisters announced the spirit rappings, a more speculative Anglo-American spiritualism was emerging through the trance productions of Andrew Jackson Davis and the harmonial metaphysic that he elaborated to explain them.

This chapter explores the mid-nineteenth-century spiritualist movement within this larger context, looking to spiritualism as a site for the growth of American metaphysical religion. In this account the emergent theology of a communion of spirits replicates the social fact of combination. Here are the vernacular practices of different peoples (whites, Indians, blacks) and their ideas (disguised Hermeticism; the Quakerism of inner light and truth; mesmerism, Swedenborgianism, and Davis harmonialism; universalism and a popularized Transcendentalism; progressivism and social reform; a rationalized scientism). Here, too, are renewed themes of correspondence, energy, mind and imagination, and healing, all coming together to create the later metaphysical religion of the century. As Howard Kerr and Charles L. Crow describe this cultural moment, it was, in fact, "a historical hourglass in which the sands of witchcraft, popular ghostlore, mesmerism, Swedenborgianism, and scientism pour[ed] through the channel of spiritualism, then to disperse into Theosophy and parapsychology."[10] What became of the dispersal, it should be added, could also be found in Christian

Science, New Thought, and, by the twentieth century and after, a metaphysical-ized Asian presence and then the movement for a New Age and the new spiri-tuality that followed. All the while, the American Enlightenment made friends with an expansive Romanticism. The two together brought sophisticates and credulous folk alike to the embrace of a metaphysic that explained the disruptive phenomena of death and profound social slippage at midcentury, even as it be-queathed a piety that tread softly between the Bible and a fully scientific world.[11]

SHAKER SPIRIT MANIFESTATIONS

A small band of English Shakers led by Ann Lee (1736–1784) appeared in the New York colony on the eve of the American Revolution in 1774. These were not good times to be British or unorthodox. The small group—given to the practice of celibacy, to the confession of sins, and to ecstatic experiences that included visions, spirit possession, and spirit communication—suffered persecution. The Shakers, however, survived. As the community consolidated its identity, by the early nineteenth century it had developed an authoritative account of its founder and past. According to this narrative, Mother Ann, as they called her, had been a visionary from the time of her childhood in Manchester, England. Married to Abraham Standerin (Standley), recounted the Shakers, she saw her four children die in infancy. At the time of her marriage, she was already linking the root of all sin to sexual activity, and the infant deaths only underlined her conviction. She had joined an ecstatic group, led by the charismatic James and Jane Ward-ley, known as Shaking Quakers or Shakers because of the physical signs of their ecstatic experience, and in 1770 she received a vision of the original sin in Eden and thereafter began to teach celibacy. A later vision convinced her to leave En-gland for the British North Atlantic colonies, and so it was that, with seven other believers, Mother Ann took ship and arrived in New York.[12]

The scholarly account is different. Burial records for only one infant have been located, and what can be known of Lee's activity in the Wardley society is less about the content of visions than about origins and behavior. On origins, histori-ans have found little certainty regarding the Wardley group, which in character and conviction resembled early Quakers and, still more, a group of émigré en-thusiasts known as the French Prophets or Camisards. Suppressed by the French king in the early eighteenth century, the visionary Camisards created religious excitement in England with their message of doom and judgment and a Last Day soon to come. Still further, in the Manchester of Ann Lee's day Boehmian interest was visible, and so was Swedenborgianism. All of this suggests the com-binativeness of the ecstatic milieu in which Lee and her associates practiced and proclaimed their beliefs. Meanwhile, Stephen Stein's definitive reconstruction of early Shaker history has told a story of confrontational tactics on the part of the Wardley group, including Ann Lee, that brought them into trouble with authorities and in and out of jail. "Lee's decision to leave England in the spring of 1774 with her husband and a few fellow Shakers was eminently prudent," Stein writes, "based on limited success in Manchester, growing pressures on the sect, and the promise of different circumstances in North America."[13]

What is clear from both the traditional Shaker story and contemporary revisionist history is the significance and importance for the early group of altered religious states and, specifically, the conviction of contact with spirits. As early as 1782, for example, the New Hampshire lawyer and rationalist William Plumer visited the Shakers at Harvard, Massachusetts, and remarked on their ecstatic behavior, and the following year at Canterbury, New Hampshire, he recorded similar phenomena. For the early nineteenth century, Stein has summarized the Shaker testimonial report of visions and spirit contact, including especially with Ann Lee. In 1837, however, the Shaker involvement with spirit communication intensified in ways so noticeable that historians have called the period from the late 1830s into the 1850s the Era of Manifestations. Members of the United Society of Believers (the name the Shakers officially adopted for themselves in the 1820s) called this Era of Manifestations the time of "Mother Ann's Work." As Stein has noted, no segment of Shaker history "has attracted more attention and speculation than the years of spiritualistic activity."[14]

The inaugural series of ecstatic visitations echoed in a different key the possession stories of the mostly teenage girls who in 1692 began the notorious Salem witchcraft episode. Now at Watervliet, New York, three girls aged between ten and fourteen fell under a power that Shakers linked to the work of the Holy Spirit and, alternately, to Mother Ann. Fourteen-year-old Ann Mariah Goff testified that before the community worship service she had seen a "female spirit" dressed in white. Later, during worship, the spirit appeared and worked among the Shaker sisters as they danced in ritual, kissing them, and singing songs that mourned sin and encouraged believers. Goff had traveled, she reported, with a spirit sister into the city of Paradise, with its four hundred buildings set in four rows. She had seen its huge white meeting house in the center and had also seen Jesus and Mother Ann.[15]

Before a month had passed, the spirit visitations were multiplying. Goff told Believers that, in her initial spirit experience, she had gone to the spirit world with the help of one Beulah Downs, a Shaker sister who had, about eight months previously, died. "We mean your people shall know what there is in another world," the Downs of Goff's vision said. As the spirit experiences spread, Shakers claimed that they were visited by spirits of the dead and that spirits often showed up at their own funerals to comfort the mourners. "In these wonderful days," wrote a member of the New Lebanon ministry, the dead "generally and frequently return in spirit, and minister comfort and consolation to their surviving friends."[16]

Clarke Garrett summarizes what happened in the charged time that followed: "Some of the inspired young people brought heavenly messages from the departed 'spiritual parents,' Ann Lee, Joseph Meacham, and Lucy Wright [Meacham and Wright were earlier Shaker leaders]. Others drew pictures of what they had seen in their visions. Lafayette visited the Shakers. . . . So did George Washington, Napoleon, and some Indians. There were new songs, dances, and ceremonies, all introduced by divine inspiration."[17] Spiritual gifts came ever more frequently, including objects visible only to spiritual eyes and other objects that were, in fact, material. Tours of paradise by spirits were reported with relish. In effect, a new generation of Shakers—young people who had never lived with the founding generation and their immediate heirs—went through a season of revival, a revitalization experience to bring to the community a renewed spiritual intensity and excitement evoking the time of origins. The means to return to the vital energy of the beginning was spiritualism. As in the mass movement of séance spiritualism in the next decade, death had lost some of its sting. At Mount Lebanon, New York, Rufus Bishop reflected on the impending deaths of two of the sisters in 1839 and observed that "neither they nor we have anything to mourn about for the veil between us and the spiritual world has become so transparent, in these days, that our good friends seem much more active after laying aside the clay tabernacle than they did when they were bound and fettered by it."[18]

So it was that mediums—or, as the Shakers called them, "instruments"—who felt themselves to be in communication with spirits became important ritual leaders in Shaker communities, where worship already involved forms of sacred dance and ecstatic behavior. Fed by a burst of spiritual creativity, the instruments presided over new rituals—characterized by Clarke Garrett as "sacred theater"—that led to the closing of Shaker meetings to the curious public for a seven-year period beginning in 1842. In what Edward Deming Andrews called "the most remarkable year in Shaker history," newly introduced rituals included the "midnight cry," the "sweeping gift," and a series of mountain meetings. In each—and in other and similar rituals—Shaker brothers and sisters sang new songs, engaged in new forms of ritual behavior, and often mimed objects, attire, foods—and actions that involved these items. In the midnight cry, for example, Shakers, led by their mediums, marched in the night, lamps in hand, through all the rooms of their buildings. On the third night, at midnight, they woke all sleeping community members, who then joined ranks and followed the leaders in an enacted metaphor for the vigilance necessary to the spiritual life. In the sweeping gift, on an appointed day and with mediumistic leadership, Shakers tramped through their premises armed with spiritual brooms to cleanse away evil spirits, even as other Shakers, with real brooms, engaged in a frenzy of housecleaning on property already known for its cleanliness. Mountain meetings, held twice annually, in May and September, involved the clearing of land on a hill or mountain top, its enclosure, and the creation of what was called a "fountain." Here, after fasting, confession, and prayer in silence, Shakers made their way as in pilgrimage, wearing elaborate mimed costumes and accoutrements to celebrate an equally elaborate Passover feast (also mimed). Significantly, as the Shakers reported, the spirits of the famous came and offered gifts of love—at Hancock Village, Massachusetts, Napoleon, Washington, Queen Esther, and Queen Isabella all appeared for the ceremonies.[19]

Of such Shaker ritual behavior and the Shaker spiritualist phenomena in general, Stephen Stein notes that "there was no satisfactory way to settle the argument between those who regarded the revival as silly and those who saw it as an outpouring of divine blessings."[20] The same, of course, could be observed for the vastly larger séance spiritualist movement that was to follow. Here, though, it needs to be noticed that spirit ecstasies and elaborately mimed rituals came accompanied by a profoundly mystical, and Hermetic, theology. Indeed, we gain some purchase on this Shaker theology of the period through the reported visitations of Heavenly Father and, especially, Holy Mother Wisdom—the female aspect of God, whose first spirit visit came in 1841, inaugurated by an intense round of ritual preparation.

The theological edifice that had been erected by early-nineteenth-century Shakers was replicated in the spirit visitations. First had come Jesus and Mother Ann, and now, at the height of the revival, Heavenly Father and Holy Mother Wisdom. In their particularized reprise of an essentially Hermetic and Boehmian vision, the Shakers understood Jesus and Mother Ann to be, respectively, the male and female manifestations of a male-female deity. The bisexual nature of this God signaled the completion and perfection of a humanity made in the divine image. "The dual God, male and female, called Heavenly Father and Holy Mother Wisdom, Christ being the son and Ann Lee the daughter in the new creation, were to come among us and draw a dividing line between the precious and the vile," recalled one former Shaker sister in the late 1840s. Now the spirits, and the mediums who talked to them, were carrying the message. The instrument Paulina Bates, in her widely influential *Divine Book of Holy and Eternal Wisdom* (1849), affirmed that "*Holy Mother Wisdom declares herself to be, in nature and essence, One with Eternal Power.*" And always, connected to Holy

Mother Wisdom in high and solemn fashion, was Mother Ann: "The Wisdom of God is revealed from on high and the image of her eternal brightness is brought forth in the female of God's own choice." When, beginning in 1842 and continuing until at least 1857, mediums began to present members of the community with "spirit drawings" as gifts from the heavenly realm, Holy Mother Wisdom was often claimed as author and inspirer of the gift drawings. Still more, symbols of the Father-Mother God pervaded the drawings, specified in a series of motifs that became recognized in the community for their mystical signification.[21]

It was noticeable, too, in the reports from the Era of Manifestations that, as in the mass movement of séance spiritualism that would begin in 1848, the spirits most often came to women. Hervey Elkins, raised among the Shakers at Enfield, New Hampshire, recalled after he left the United Society that he had "seen males, but more frequently females, in a superinduced condition, apparently unconscious of earthly things, and declaring in the name of departed spirits important and convincing revelations." In his own twentieth-century reconstruction of the revival, Andrews noted that as it moved from Watervliet (New York) to Canterbury and Enfield (New Hampshire), Hancock (Massachusetts), and even North Union (Ohio), the excitement was generated "first, in most instances, by groups of Shaker girls in the impressionable stages of early adolescence." More recently, Jean M. Humez has documented the pervasive role of women in the spiritualist phenomena of the Era of Manifestations. Putting the female preponderance into statistical terms for the communities at Mount Lebanon, Watervliet, Hancock, and Enfield, Louis J. Kern found that for visions unaccompanied by spiritual gifts, about 67 percent came through female instruments and only about 33 percent through men, and in visions linked to gifts, nearly all of the instruments were female. He also provided more concrete evidence regarding age for the same communities: female mediums, on average, were 24.8 years old, and males 37.5 years.[22]

Shaker spiritualism thus signaled a female deity and the prominence of actual women in the facilitation of religious experience—women who were also young and who now felt a new connection with Shaker founders. In so doing, Shaker spiritualism offered an early harbinger for the visibility, in American metaphysical religion in general, of feminized spiritual teaching and the actual leadership role of women. Meanwhile, as the Shaker sisters worked as instruments, it was especially remarkable that, as this account has already suggested, they not only reported visits from the great and famous; they also frequently played host to spirit Indians and, in some cases, spirit blacks. There were subalterns, apparently, in the spiritland—a point to which I shall return later.

What connection can be drawn between this Shaker spiritualism and the more well-known séance spiritualism catalyzed by the Fox sisters in upstate New York —home, by the 1840s, to three Shaker communities? Shaker scholar Jean M. Humez provides the beginnings of an answer when she observes that "the fundamental basis of spiritualism—the belief in the ability of the living and dead to communicate—remained a vital current in Shaker religion throughout the nineteenth century." Certainly, beyond this obvious shared conviction, there are other clear structural parallels—location and the prominent role of adolescent girls and female mediums. The roster of reported spirit visitors is also decidedly similar—the dead who were known at an intimate level, the historically great and famous, hordes of Indians and other subalterns. Likewise, the creation of a comfort zone in the face of death seems to characterize both. Finally, for both, the excitement generated by reputed spirit visitors was accompanied by institutionalization of sorts. The case is clearer for the Shakers, who experienced the spirits always in a community context and through the active involvement of Shaker leaders in controlling instruments and in functioning as instruments themselves. But in the later spiritualism inaugurated by the rappings of 1848, the heavily ritualized activities of the séance stood the test of decades to bring a measure of order and organization to the movement.[23]

In a world as intimately linked as this nineteenth-century American one, however, it is hard to stop at parallels. The argument for influence and catalytic energy is difficult to resist. Certainly, contemporary nineteenth-century observers were willing to connect the dots. Consider, for example, Frederick W. Evans. The Shaker elder—an autodidact, socialist, and progressive at the North Family in Mount Lebanon, New York—linked Shaker spiritualism, and all modern spiritualism, to Emanuel Swedenborg and then to Mother Ann. Swedenborg "was contemporary with Ann, who said he was her John the Baptist," wrote Evans in his autobiography, declaring, "He, *not* the Fox girls was the angel of modern Spiritualism." Such spiritualism had "always been an element of Shakerism," he insisted, and he saw it "as a bayou flowing out from the great River of Divine Revelation, in Shakerism, to the sea—world." For Evans, the divine trajectory was clear. "The spirits then declared, again and again, that, when they had done their work amongst the inhabitants of Zion, they would do a work in the world, of such magnitude, that not a palace nor a hamlet upon earth should remain unvisited by them." The Shaker leader counted the years of spirit influx in the Shaker Zion from 1837 to 1844, and thereafter, he thought, "we had to wait four years before the work began, as it finally did, at Rochester, N.Y.," a work that, he owned, had "far exceeded the predictions."[24]

Nor did Evans confine his opinions to his autobiography. When Charles Nordhoff (who later called the Shakers "pronounced Spiritualists") visited the Mount

Lebanon community, Evans told him that "the 'spiritual' manifestations were known among the Shakers many years before Kate Fox was born."[25] Meanwhile, John Humphrey Noyes remarked that Evans, in more than one article in the *Atlantic Monthly*, had called Shakerism "the actual mother of Spiritualism." Noyes did not disagree—in fact, he alluded later in his work to the "historical secret which connects Shakerism with 'modern Spiritualism'"—but he subsumed the Evans perspective into his own, still more combinative one. Calling the Shaker experiences "the first stage of Modern Spiritualism," he went on to make a sweeping historical point that linked Shakers to Fourierists to Swedenborgians to Transcendentalists to Spiritualists:

> The reader will note that the date of these [Shaker] manifestations—the winter of 1842–3—coïncides with the focal period of the Fourier excitement (which . . . lapsed into Swedenborgianism, as that did into Spiritualism); also that, on the larger scale, the seven years of manifestations and closed doors designated by Evans, from 1837 to 1844, coincide with the epoch of Transcendentalism. In the times of the *Dial* there was a noticeable liking for Shakerism among the Transcendentalists; and some of their leaders have lately shown signs of preferring Shakerism to Fourierism. We mention these coïncidences only as affording glimpses of connections and mysterious affinities, that we do not pretend to understand. Only we see that both forms of Socialism favored by the Transcendentalists—Shakerism and Fourierism—have contributed their whole volume to swell the flood of Spiritualism.[26]

Noyes was perceptive. In the era of the most celebrated Transcendentalist periodical, *The Dial*, for Transcendentalist leaders Shakers proved good to think. This was especially so for Bronson Alcott, who was fascinated, like Charles Lane, by the Shaker community at Harvard, Massachusetts, where the two had created Fruitlands. And, as we shall see, Andrew Jackson Davis's connection both to Swedenborgianism and to Fourierism had major implications for his harmonial philosophy and the brand of speculative spiritualism it fostered.

For their part, séance spiritualists, or phenomenal spiritualists (to use the term favored by Davis and, very much later, historian Robert Delp), could on occasion acknowledge their Shaker predecessors. Judge John W. Edmonds, who with the physician George T. Dexter published a book on spiritualism in 1853, observed in his introduction that the Shakers "for sixty or seventy years" had "lived in the full belief, and the frequent manifestation of, spiritual-intercourse as it is now displaying itself abroad throughout the world." (He went on to discover in Shaker cleanliness, good order, and efficiency a refutation of the charge that spiritualism led to insanity.)[27] Later, looking back from the vantage point of 1869, the medical doctor, sometime Universalist minister, and spiritualist James M. Peebles—who had often appeared at Shaker villages to lecture—included Shakerism in admiring terms in his history of spiritualism. Peebles linked the Shakers to the lineage of Jacob Boehme, George Fox, William Blake, and Emanuel Swedenborg, thus identifying the Hermetic ambience that surrounded them.[28] And no other than contemporary spiritualist historian Emma Hardinge remembered her visit to an unnamed Shaker village where a resident read an account of the coming to the Shakers of "guardian spirits." Hardinge was clearly excited by what she heard.

> It seemed that manifestations of spiritual presence, through rappings, movings of furniture, visions, trance, clairaudience, and clairvoyance, had been common amongst the Shakers since the time of their foundation, some seventy years ago; but the particular visitation to which the visitors desired to call attention, took place about 1830, when a multitude of spiritual beings, with the most solemn and forcible tokens of their presence, in a variety of phenomenal ways indicated the approach of a great spiritual crisis, in which they designed for a season to withdraw the special gifts enjoyed by the Shakers, and pour them out in mighty floods upon the "world's people," who, for the realization of certain divine purposes, faintly shadowed forth, were to be visited by unlooked-for and stupendous tokens of spiritual presence.[29]

For Hardinge, the Shakers were "John the Baptists" for the manifestations she celebrated.[30] As time passed, the Shakers seemed to agree. The record of the Shaker communities after 1848 tells of the enthusiastic involvement of community members in the cultural practice of séance spiritualism. "The Believers eagerly joined forces with the larger spiritualist movement in America," Stein writes, "affirming the reality of spirit and the significance of this belief." Moreover, Shaker leaders themselves were generous in supplying details. Frederick Evans, for example, by 1878 told of séances at Mount Lebanon during which "*thirty-one* different materialised spirits issued." Earlier, in 1872, Shakers reported that two of their elders, John Whiteley and William Leonard, had traveled to Troy, New York, for a "Shaker and Spiritualist Convention." Shakers also traveled out of their villages to visit spiritualist mediums, and likewise they brought the mediums home at Hancock, Mount Lebanon, and other communities. As far back as 1850, they had gone so far as to invite the Fox sisters to Mount Lebanon.[31]

Over half a century later, in their 1904 account of American Shaker history, eldresses Anna White and Leila S. Taylor read the saga of the United Society in familiar terms that linked it to the mass-movement manifestations after 1848. Shakers were the "First Modern Spiritualists" and Shakerism itself was the "Parent of Modern Spiritualism," captions in their text announced. Again, they recounted the story of how the spirits, after about ten years of intense visitation among the Shakers, told them that "they were about to leave them and go out into the world." In the face of much that they considered "disorderly and repellant" in séance spiritualism, White—who apparently regularly read the well-known séance spiritualist *Banner of Light*—and Taylor, her co-author, still thought that recent new Shakers recognized their community as a haven for "modern" spiritualism. There, under the authority and control of the "Visible Order," spirit contact was "safe, mediumship natural, controlled and protected." It was significant, thereafter, that White and Taylor ended their two-chapter reprise on spiritualism with a lengthy extract from the writing of none other than James M. Peebles.[32]

What Stein has called the Shaker "tension between gift and order" brought a balancing act to the United Society's experience of spiritualism.[33] The quest for control of spirit gifts may, indeed, be one reason why Shakers were not closely linked either by the general public of the time or by later scholars to mass-movement spiritualism. Still more, indices to scholarly studies of the Shakers draw a blank for "mesmerism" or "magnetism." That absence constitutes one of the major differences between Shaker spirit gifts and séance spiritualism. Only one year before the Shaker spirit revival started at Watervliet in 1837, the visiting Frenchman Charles Poyen began a lecture tour through New England. He brought to eager American consumers the good news of mesmerism and its sweeping mental miracles accomplished by letting go and being out of control. Much less concerned about order than the Shakers, American mesmerists would soon be selling their wares to their enthusiastic compatriots.

OF MAGNETISM—ANIMAL AND SPIRITUAL

If Shaker spiritualism affirmed the possibility of experiential contact with both the luminous and ordinary dead, it did not theorize about how, in a law-bound universe, the manifestations came to be. Shakers had "instruments," and the instruments mediated between the worlds for communities of Believers. By contrast, mesmerists promoted altered forms of consciousness with little initial attention to the dead but with—from the first—an abiding concern for theory. Indeed, for Franz Anton Mesmer (1734–1815), theory preceded experience, even though each built on the other and Mesmer revised theory even as he experimented. Standing at a crossroads between a Hermetic and a scientific universe, Mesmer, as a scientist, aspired to explanations that were intellectually compelling. He was persuaded by Isaac Newton's new (1687) science of universal gravitation. Moreover, he understood himself to be following in the footsteps of Newton's friend Richard Mead, whose work insisting on the "influence of the stars" Mesmer acknowledged in the opening lines of his doctoral dissertation of 1766.³⁴ From the first, Mesmer was preoccupied with the transfer of energy from bodies to other bodies, and as—mesmerism evolved—the transferring agent came more and more to be understood as mind.

Born on the shores of Lake Constance, Mesmer took his doctorate in medicine at the University of Vienna. His dissertation "On the Influence of the Planets" employed an essentially Newtonian theory of tides and argued for the effects of the movements of sun and moon (understood as "planets") on the human body. Matter, for Mesmer, was "attractive," and the attraction extended from the highest heavens to individual material bodies, enveloping and permeating all. "There is a force," he declared, "which is the cause of universal gravitation and which is, very probably, the foundation of all corporal properties." This force, he told readers, he would call "ANIMAL GRAVITY." "Influence" was thus operative everywhere in Mesmer's universe, and—in the specifically medical application of his findings—he explained illness by universal gravitation and its source, animal gravity. The moon and sun influenced other bodies for good or for ill, and Mesmer could declare confidently that "with the facts constituted as they are, how few will be those doctors who will not know with unshakeable firmness, from the facts themselves, that the influence of the planets must not be held to be a light matter in medicine."³⁵

Mesmer, however, had also said something else. In language that evoked another discourse community alongside the scientific one of Newton, he had announced that there was, in effect, a harmony of the spheres. "The harmony established between the astral plane and the human plane ought to be admired as much as the ineffable effect of UNIVERSAL GRAVITATION by which our bodies are harmonized, not in a uniform and monotonous manner, but as with a musical instrument furnished with several strings, the exact one resonates which is in unison with a given tone." In later years, Mesmer would make good his observation by playing the glass harmonica as he treated patients. But the rhetoric of harmony signaled more than this, and later enthusiasts and critics both were willing to identify Mesmer's older, non-Newtonian sources. La Roy Sunderland's short-lived mid-nineteenth-century periodical *The Magnet*, for example, confided to its readers in 1843 that "the celebrated Paracelsus" deserved acknowledgment as "the first we know of, who ever treated upon *animal magnetism*; and his performances in that time were such as to astonish the world." Sunderland also found it not at all surprising that Mesmer, "with his full share of the somewhat mystical temperament of his nation," should have felt the "profound charm for his mind" in the teaching of "his countryman Paracelsus." Later, by the early twentieth century, the decidedly more censorious Frank Podmore stated flatly that "not only did Mesmer borrow his theories ready-made from earlier mystics, but even the name 'magnetic' was in common use in the seventeenth and eighteenth centuries to denote the sympathetic system of medicine which was founded on these mystical doctrines. Paracelsus is commonly reputed to be the founder of this magnetic philosophy."[36]

For praise or blame, Mesmer's connections to Continental Hermeticism were obvious, and in later writings he acknowledged his affinities more openly, perhaps because of his own growing awareness. By 1799, he was not averse to finding evidence to support his theoretical claims in what came to be called clairvoyance. Warning against the "incalculable hazards of drugs and their application" and disgruntled by the poor reception accorded his magnetic "discovery," he offered his own explanation for his bad reputation. "It is because my assertions regarding the processes and the visible effects of animal magnetism seem to remind people of ancient beliefs, of ancient practices justly regarded for a long time as being error and trickery."[37] Mesmer, in effect, had been caught in the paradigm shift from premodern to modern, from the late medieval culture that, among elites, found place for esotericism to the Enlightenment world of rationalism and scientific discourse.

If the changing of worlds proved a backdrop for Mesmer's views, his ideas changed with his own experimental practice, and they also changed as manipulated by his students and disciples. In Austria in 1774, Mesmer had worked with a hysterical patient, one Fräulein Oesterline, using ferromagnets attached to various parts of her body and providing her a remedy containing iron. Oesterline told of a mysterious fluid that she felt coursing through her body, and she reported the remission of symptoms for a matter of hours. As he pondered the Oesterline case, Mesmer became convinced that it was not ferromagnetism alone—or for the most part—that had elicited the favorable response. Rather, he believed, by means of his own person he had given Oesterline the mysterious fluid. He named it *animal magnetism* ("animal" meaning something like "vital" and something distinct from mineral magnetism). Thus animal magnetism, for Mesmer, became central to cure and ferromagnets simply assists. Operating on the bases of these theoretical assumptions, he at first enjoyed some success in Vienna, but he was controversial from the beginning. When one blind patient was supposedly cured and then reverted to blindness, Mesmer left Vienna hurriedly in 1777 and under unclear circumstances.[38]

The story was hardly over. Early the next year Mesmer's heyday as a fashionable and flamboyant Paris physician began. Robert Darnton's memorable descriptions of some of his practices clearly suggest their controversial nature. Mesmer magnetized actual trees and "then attached groups of patients to them by ropes in daisy-chain fashion, always avoiding knots, which created obstacles to the fluid's harmony." Alternately, he situated them indoors around community tubs in carefully arranged surroundings "designed to produce a crisis in the patient." The tubs "were usually filled with iron filings and mesmerized water contained in bottles arranged like the spokes of a wheel." Here patients sat in circles, looped together by a rope and linking thumbs and index fingers to keep the energy current flowing. Soft music came from a pianoforte or glass harmonica. Mesmer himself would draw near a patient, "dressed in a lilac taffeta robe, and drill fluid into the patient from his hands, his imperial eye, and his mesmerized wand."[39]

Immersed in this world of medical heterodoxy and outright heresy, Mesmer meanwhile promoted the Society of Universal Harmony, founded by two of his patients. There, for a price, he was happy to confide his healing secrets. He enjoyed an enthusiastic following and evident public success, but—to state the obvious—medical approval never followed. A Royal Commission (of which the American Benjamin Franklin was a member) in 1784 issued a negative report on his work, and Mesmer left Paris after that and mostly wandered from place to place until his death, a soured and somewhat cynical man. Even during the Paris period, however, we gain a glimpse of a future that would open beyond the actual life and thought of Mesmer. Darnton, for example, recounted that during the various forms of healing crisis experienced by Mesmer's patients, "some developed into deep sleeps, and some sleeps provided communication with dead or distant spirits." These spirits "sent messages by way of the fluid directly to the somnambulist's internal sixth sense, which was extraordinarily receptive to what would now be called extra-sensory perceptions."[40]

Mesmer, however, never considered somnambulism normative for a mesmeric crisis or mesmerism in general. Indeed, in his memoir of 1799, he complained that "the imitators of my method have caused many accusations to be leveled against it" and that "*somnambulism* has been confused with magnetism." "With thoughtless zeal and exaggerated enthusiasm," he reproved, "people have wished to prove the reality of the one with the astonishing effects of the other." With a different vision, the Chastenet de Puységur brothers, and especially Amand Marie Jacques de Chastenet, Marquis de Puységur—whom Robert C. Fuller calls Mesmer's "most capable disciple"—made magnetism synonymous with artificial sleep. After experiments with a peasant named Victor on the Puységur estate, the Marquis began to promote the somnambulistic state, noticing the clairvoyance that often attended it. The mesmerized could perform mental wonders in their altered state, seeing the insides of bodies, including their own; diagnosing diseases; communicating with far distant persons and the spirits of the dead.[41]

The sleepwalkers of the Marquis de Puységur brought to the fore a new model of mesmerism. Their response seemed to depend on a developed rapport, or sympathy, between the minds of magnetizer and magnetized. Influenced by another Frenchman, Louis-Claude de Saint-Martin, Puységur moved toward a view in which thought became primary. He did not himself do away with Mesmer's mysterious fluid, in fact, calling it "dephlogisticated air." (He was invoking the already dubious phlogiston theory, with phlogiston the presumed essence of fire understood as a material substance—before, by 1784, Antoine L. Lavoisier discredited the theory).[42] But Puységur's ideas and his practice possessed a momentum of their own, in which mind and its energies were assuming new significance for magnetism and a metaphysical world beyond. Even so, the compelling image of the fluid would never really disappear, resurfacing in an American future in the tangible constructions of energy that would in turn permeate metaphysical religion and practice. In the middle place between the somnambules of Puységur and the mind of the metaphysicians, the spiritualist trance mediums of the 1850s and 1860s went "sleeping." "At the core of Spiritualism as a popular movement lay the blending of the belief in spirits of the dead with the ideas and practices of animal magnetism," writes Ann Taves.[43]

The American future began in earnest in 1836, when Charles Poyen, the French follower of the Marquis de Puységur, crossed the Atlantic and began to lecture throughout New England. Earlier attempts to introduce animal magnetism promoted by the Marquis de Lafayette (Marie Joseph Paul) and, then, Joseph du Commun had never caught on, and Poyen himself was at first greeted with disdain. But when he illustrated the somnambulic state by actual demonstrations with a professional somnambule and then with audience volunteers, the American public was captivated. The Poyen brand of education-entertainment fit the lyceum model of the day, as the entranced, before the eyes of relatives, friends, and neighbors, refused to be revived from magnetic sleep by pins, prods, or sharp and clamorous noises. Meanwhile, Poyen's plan to fashion the American people through mesmerism into "the most perfect nation on earth" struck an answering chord. He was addressing, after all, a society in which Calvinism was dying, Arminianism flourishing, mechanical marvels like the steamboat and the railroad promising earthly miracles, Jacksonian democracy proclaiming the "common man," and some—like Joseph Smith—were beginning to think that humans could be "as gods." Gradually, as Fuller has argued, mesmerism moved away from being entertainment that was of medical value. It became not so much a medical healing system as "a schema demonstrating how the individual mind can establish rapport with ever more sublime levels of reality." It pointed to an internal universe in which—far from the haunting Calvinism of total depravity and inbred sin—an avenue to higher spiritual realms could be encountered. To trust oneself to the magnetizer became to trust the world of spirit and the world of mind.[44] And sometimes, as we shall see, the magnetizer could be oneself, so that self magnetized self without the aid of an external "operator."

Poyen went home to France in 1839. His lieutenants, however, swept the nation. They were converts to his doctrine who in countless small towns brought the good news of magnetic miracles to eager listeners, who in turn became other converts. Indeed, it was one such lieutenant, J. Stanley Grimes, who demonstrated magnetism before the teenager Andrew Jackson Davis in Poughkeepsie, New York, in 1843 and so changed his life and the trajectory of "modern" spiritualism (see the next section). Interest in mesmerism was, as Emma Hardinge reported, "wide-spread," and in the several years before the rise of mass spiritualism was "largely practiced over every part of America." For New England, John C. Spurlock cites some thirty lecturers on mesmerism in 1843, while in Boston alone two hundred mesmerizers were practicing and nearby, at the Transcendentalist Brook Farm, commune members privately experimented with magnetic techniques.[45]

Even as magnetic lecturers fanned out to reach the unconverted, American mesmerism began to align itself with the new intellectual theory and practice called phrenology, which was also making its rounds on the lyceum circuit. Phrenology—from the Greek word for the mind or the seat of the understanding—studied the shape and conformation of the human skull with the conviction that its various protuberances provided indications of mental faculties and moral character. Phrenologists mapped the skull to pursue their work, and reading skull maps and touching various places on the head—"bumps" in the popular parlance—became an American fashion in and out of lyceum halls. In the optimistic American reading of the discipline, excesses and deficiencies of faculty or character as revealed by the bumps could be remedied. The phrenological early warning system, accompanied by cranial massage, could help change character and so change destiny.

Phrenological ideas, like mesmeric ones, had originated on the European Continent. Before the year 1800, the German physician Franz Joseph Gall (1758–1828) had started to teach that the mind, far from being a single unit, was composed of some thirty-seven separate faculties bearing names (of his giving) such as Veneration, Amativeness, Combativeness, and Benevolence. After conjectures and observations that had begun during his student years, he had come to believe that the physiology of the skull had a distinct effect on mental action and that the brain itself was composed of "organs" localized in the different regions of the skull. Gall's student and colleague Johann Gasper Spurzheim (1776–1832) became a missionary for the phrenological news, lecturing widely on the Continent and in Great Britain. He also published in collaboration with Gall and then—as his views changed and led to his estrangement from his mentor—under his own name. In the departures that he made, Spurzheim called the new system "science of mind." Unlike Gall, who found evil to be a significant characteristic of human life and who found a region of the brain that he labeled "Murder," Spurzheim became convinced of goodness. Like a phrenological universalist, he found benevolence seemingly everywhere, seeing all of the brain's organs as intrinsically good, with evil the outcome of abuse. Armed with this understanding, Spurzheim aimed to use phrenology as a means to the betterment of humanity. With Gall disapproving strongly, Spurzheim, according to John D. Davies, "wandered into metaphysics." Here "science and religion merged," and "phrenology revealed the laws of nature which God had established, which it was man's duty as well as God's will to follow."[46]

It was Spurzheim, the zealous missionary, who traveled to the United States in 1832 to spread phrenology. Here, already from the previous decade, phrenological writings—the works of Gall and Spurzheim himself, as well as more popularizing phrenological writings by George and Andrew Combe—were becoming known. In an intense and exhausting six-week lecture campaign in the Boston area, Spurzheim literally gave his all. He was dead of a severe fever by November. Six years later, the Scotsman George Combe made the Atlantic transit to fan the flame that Spurzheim's presence and the availability of phrenological literature had already created. Disturbed by his own youthful exposure to Calvinism, the lawyer Combe had embraced phrenology enthusiastically after he heard Spurzheim lecture in Edinburgh, and now, as the foremost phrenological expert after the death of Spurzheim, he lectured in the United States until 1840. For eighteen months, he toured most of the major cities in the East and appeared before audiences of three hundred to five hundred people, even as newspapers and magazines carried transcripts of his New York presentations.[47]

In the America that welcomed Combe, the same mix of factors that encouraged interest in mesmerism was spawning enthusiasm for phrenology. In fact, before he arrived, the writings of Spurzheim had converted Henry Ward Beecher and Orson Squire Fowler, both then students at Lane Theological Seminary in Cincinnati. Beecher went on to spread his own version of liberal Protestant evangelicalism as America's most well-known pulpit orator in the late nineteenth century. Fowler, with his brother Lorenzo Niles Fowler, turned instead to the new system. Traveling to cities and towns across the nation, the "Phrenological Fowlers" made head charts and graphs of bumps and their meaning almost household items. Indeed, it was the Fowlers who began the middle-class ritual of head readings. As Arthur Wrobel remarks, they "severely damaged phrenology's hard-won reputation among the leading members of America's medical and academic communities," even as they promoted phrenology as a tool for behavior modification to an enthusiastically receptive public.[48] With their ambitious publishing house, Fowlers and Wells, they became a conduit for an emerging metaphysical point of view and its literary reflection, ranging widely over a plethora of Anglo-American enthusiasms of the period and especially embracing themes of sex, marriage, and eugenics.

Both mesmerism and phrenology could enhance human life, according to the emerging view. The mind could shape the body; the body could bring to eager Americans comfort and spiritualized pleasure. Americans, in short, were at the threshold of affirming an enhanced body-self even as they were about to turn to mass-market spiritualism. They were beginning to be metaphysicians— with minds corresponding to Mind, energies flowing, and an end to all distress. In this context, they welcomed still another European visitor. By 1836, the same year that Poyen was lecturing on mesmerism, the English physician Robert H. Collyer arrived in New York with ambitions as a popular lecturer. He had been acquainted with the late Dr. Spurzheim, and he used the connection to advance his touring goals, even traveling to the South and the West. However, his growing interest in magnetism began to shift and change the direction of his lectures, and—chagrined by what he considered to be the cultural chaos of the United States—he seized on mesmerism as an easy extension of phrenological understanding. In large East Coast cities such as Boston, New York, and Philadelphia, he began to lecture now on mesmerism. According to his own account in *Lights and Shadows of American Life*, the Americans he met sorely needed improving. Their institutions could not muster sufficient authority, and their wild enthusiasms were rampant everywhere.[49]

Collyer's mesmeric transformation and his salvific impulse continued apace, and in 1842 he was editing a new journal called *The Mesmeric Magazine*. Its introduction was instructive. For the editor, the "highest and most permanent source of interest" in mesmerism arose from "the truly amazing phenomena exhibited in that exalted and mysterious mesmeric condition, commonly denominated CLAIRVOYANCE." Collyer went on to confide to readers that he had "frequently conducted mesmerisees when in this state, to the moon, and to several of the planets" and that he had "obtained from them vivid and entertaining descriptions of the scenery, cities, inhabitants, and general state of things in these

heavenly bodies." He hoped to share the details of such adventures in his magazine. But there was more, even than this, from mesmeric practice. "By its influence," Collyer continued, "we have been permitted to draw aside, though
with reverent hands, the veil that separates the natural from the spiritual world.
Our mesmerisees have repeatedly conversed with departed spirits, and have from
them received communications of a kind that has tested and proved to us beyond doubt, the reality and truth of the intercourse."[50] This in 1842, and this in
a pattern—mesmerism, planetary visitation, and spiritualism—that, as we shall
see, later Andrew Jackson Davis, who claimed hardly ever to read, would faithfully repeat. Significantly for Davis, Swedenborg had already linked the last two
in a form readily available to American readers by 1827 or 1828 under the title
Earths in the Universe.[51]

Collyer himself stood on lineage and forebears. He offered readers a history of
mesmerism that lauded, among others, Cornelius Agrippa, "the famous astrologer, chemist, and magician," citing Agrippa's conviction that it was possible "to
communicate . . . thoughts to another, even at a great distance." He found in Jan
Baptista Van Helmont (1577–1644), the mystically inclined Flemish physician,
chemist, and physicist, even more to be praised. It was Van Helmont, Collyer
insisted, who had anticipated Mesmer's notion of "occult influence" between
bodies at a distance and had designated the "vehicle of this influence" to be
the *"magnate magnum,"* seemingly considering it "an universal fluid pervading all nature." Collyer's Van Helmont "occasionally" called the influence "ecstatic and magical, using the latter word in its more favorable signification." For
him, a magical power lay sleeping within humans, and—in an inversion of the
familiar magnetic sleep of the mid-nineteenth century—the magnetic operator
awakened the magic that the magnetic subject inherently possessed through the
power of imagination.[52]

Already Americans had been prepared for these leaps and connections. In
the 1820s and 1830s, German Romantics had come to see a link between magnetism and a mystical religiosity replete with clairvoyant insight and psychic
powers. Against this backdrop, Swedenborgian and Boehmian understandings
were being shaped into a magnetism of the spirit in the writings of Heinrich Jung-
Stilling and Justinus Kerner. Jung-Stilling had been drawn to the theme of the
psychic body, which he associated with the concept of a "luminiferous ether"
then gaining acceptance within scientific ranks. Moreover, he argued his case
for this spiritualized body and its powers from the anecdotal evidence of somnambules. Although he was himself exceedingly wary of somnambules and their
entranced communications, he thought that "Animal Magnetism undeniably
proves that we have an inward man, a soul" and that the soul was "constituted of

the divine spark" as well as of a "luminous body." He thought, too, that the soul divested of the body in the magnetic sleep was freer and more powerful, and he posited likewise the existence of a danger zone for the magnetized soul in the "boundless ether that fills the space of our solar system." This was "the element of spirits in which they live and move," and it was "the abode of fallen angels, and of such human souls as die in an unconverted state."[53]

These speculations about magnetism, the soul, and the luminous ether, based on the experience of mesmerized subjects, formed the basis, too, of the writing—still more well-known in America—of Justinus Kerner. A poet and physician, he aimed to work therapeutically with somnambules, and, in this context, in 1826 he met the remarkable Frau Frederica Hauffe, known more widely as the Seeress of Prevorst. When she died three years later, in 1829, Kerner felt free to publish an account of her life. Weak and convulsive, she did not respond to the drugs Kerner initially prescribed, and so he turned to something she had already experienced (sometimes with benefit), magnetism. The Seeress was so receptive that, according to Kerner's report, she spent most of her time entranced, and her acute clairvoyance was only part of a catalog of wonders and miracles. In fact, she spent much of her time in conversation with the spirits of the dead, to whom she freely offered guidance and advice.[54]

Stories of the Seeress and her mysticizing magnetism appeared familiarly in mid-nineteenth-century American newspapers and periodicals (an abridged English edition of Kerner's work appeared in London as early as 1845),[55] and they were to be taken up by the new spiritualizing magnetizers of the time. In this decidedly Hermetic milieu with its anticipation of séance spiritualism, Robert Collyer's phrenological past and his mesmeric present came together, even as phrenology and mesmerism, more widely, were being perceived as partners. Apparently in 1842, Collyer and several others began to stimulate the skulls—the well-known bumps—of their mesmerized clients and to produce what they believed to be remarkable results. And so phrenomagnetism was born—a much vaunted vehicle for transcribing the Romantic Hermeticism of the past into a seeming science and tool in a new technology of the spirit.[56] In the career of phrenomagnetist La Roy Sunderland (1802–1885), we can see quite clearly the combinations and connections that were being forged.

Sunderland, a Methodist minister, charismatic revival preacher, and zealous abolitionist, was by 1843 forming, with Orange Scott, the Wesleyan Methodist Church as an institution free of both bishops and slaves. But he did not stay to enjoy the change. The year before he formed and left the church, Sunderland had begun publication of *The Magnet* in New York City, only the second periodical on mesmerism in the nation—after (Dr.) Samuel Underhill's several-month ven-

ture in 1838 in Cleveland fizzled. Sunderland's first issue rehearsed for readers
the "grand design" of the new journal: "to call attention to such FACTS, connected with Physiology, Phrenology, and Living Magnetism, as may lead to the
knowledge of those laws which govern the mind." The facts were, as Sunderland
told them later, that "*Animal Life*" was "nothing more nor less than *Magnetism* in
an organized, or modified form," with "magnetic forces" producing "the conception and growth of the human system," while their "decay and separation from
the body" resulted in death. Encompassed in their own microcosmic magnetic
universes, humans could look to advanced phrenological techniques to bring
them healing when their organs went awry. "All diseases may be controled, more
or less," Sunderland announced confidently, "by magnetising the cerebral organs corresponding with the parts affected. Hence, as far as we have ascertained
the location of the different cerebral organs, which control the vital organs, we
have found magnetism to be a specific for recent diseases of every kind."[57]

For Sunderland, still technically a man of the cloth, disease was hardly the be-
all and end-all of the magnetic universe, however. Ann Taves has pointed to the
connections he was drawing between the dissociative phenomena of the revivals,
in which he had himself been a central figure, and the dissociative phenomena of
magnetism. He acknowledged in *The Magnet* that "many pious people attribute
these [revival] experiences to the powerful influence of the Holy Spirit," but he
felt that he knew better. "A knowledge of the nervous system, and the nature of
the human mind, would leave us little doubt, that these things may be rationally
accounted for in some other way." The other way, of course, was magnetism.
Sunderland, who was to become a spiritualist by the 1850s (although he would
later die a skeptic), could not, however, evade the religious question. *The Magnet*
excerpted Jung-Stilling's *Theory of Pneumatology* (in its English-language translation) and pondered the connections between religious ecstasy and the "spontaneous sympathetic sleep." Meanwhile, in stage demonstrations of mesmerism
that he offered, subjects lost in the "sympathetic sleep" would occasionally purport to converse with their relatives among the dead.[58] It was this notion of sympathy, evoking at once a discourse resonant with the magnetic universe and a
discourse congenial to religious piety, that became the linchpin in Sunderland's
evolving system. Sunderland, the church founder of 1843, published his small
book *Pathetism* the same year to articulate a carefully rationalized theory concerning the experiences of his parallel magnetic career (by 1845 he would claim
to have magnetized some fifteen hundred individuals).[59] In work that pioneered
a significant departure from the Mesmer he so admired, Sunderland's neologism
pathetism referred to the process of producing the "sympathetic" sleep. What
Fuller has called "the science of mental sympathy" meant, for Sunderland, re-

lease from the doctrine of universal fluids and adherence to the pathos (from the Greek root) of profound emotional connection. This passional link delivered the power to magnetize a fellow creature, and this passional link—this sympathy— also signaled entry into a protodiscourse that pointed the way toward a later mental magic.[60] Sunderland, in effect, was reading the mesmerist as a manipulator of spirit, and it was no surprise that phenomena such as clairvoyance, telepathy, and discourse with spirits could be produced.

Noting "the reciprocal influence of the body and mind," Sunderland found "the features and form of the body" revealed the state of the mind. Savage face, savage mind, he said, and he went on from there to expose the racialist views of Anglo-Americans of his era. Still, it is important to notice that the protomagical world that arose out of his Anglo-American moment moved beyond contiguity and touch to tell of the power of mind. In an axiomatic declaration, Sunderland announced that "PHYSICAL SYMPATHY DOES NOT DEPEND UPON CONTINUITY OF SURFACE, OR THE CONTIGUITY OF THE PARTS AFFECTED BY IT." Pathetism, he explained further, "meant *susceptibility* to the influence of an agency which is concerned in every feeling or emotion, or passion, or action which was ever felt, or put forth by any human being." It meant, indeed, "all the feelings . . . which one human being may be able to excite in the mind of another," and it could be produced in subjects "both *in the waking and sleeping state.*" The mind and what Sunderland termed "the sympathetic system" acted reciprocally on each other, with the mind using the sympathetic apparatus to do its work. In this context, establishing the connection with another became the *"first law of Pathetism,"* a connection that he argued adamantly came through no universal fluid. "I have fully shown, I think, that it is not, and cannot be, any kind of *fluid* eliminated from the operator into the subject, either magnetic, electrical, galvanic, or nervous."[61]

The moral of the story was that Americans needed to "become familiar with the laws of *mind.*"[62] In so stating, Sunderland was revealing what a long road he himself had traveled. In one sense, he carried his baggage from the past along with him. He never forgot the dramatic bodily "exercises" that accompanied the revivals and the lessons they taught him about mental influences and physical results. Yet he had surely repackaged the contents of his own mind, moving from the Holy Spirit to the human spirit, or—to be more precise—to human mentality as the stimulus for altered forms of behavior. He had sharply revised the magnetic theory of Mesmer, abolishing the universal fluid in favor of laws of mind and sympathy. More than that, by linking phrenology to magnetism, he had facilitated the acceptance of an explanatory model that would pass into spiritualism and then pass out of it as the metaphysical faith of the late nineteenth century. Although by the late 1860s, he no longer personally gave credence to phrenological demonstrations, in the cultural moment of the 1840s a significant intellectual paradigm had been born and spread.[63]

Nor had the passion for reform that made Sunderland, as a Methodist preacher, an ardent abolitionist disappeared. Already in the 1840s, he understood pathetism to be, as Bret Carroll notes, a "vehicle of moral reform." By the 1850s, he had followed the logic of his own ideas to the spirits to whom they were leading. He worked to spread spiritualism in New England (Eliab W. Capron called Sunderland and his family "the pioneers of spiritualism in Boston"), beginning the *Spiritual Philosopher* in 1850 and lecturing several nights a week as well. As Carroll has observed, Sunderland looked expectantly to "advanced spirits," who "like revival preachers, would inwardly 'influence' mortals toward harmony with each other and the universe." Mesmerism had become a technique for reaching the dead, but the lingering light of mesmeric clairvoyance meant that the dead were expected to give back the wisdom of the higher spheres to mortal seekers.[64]

Meanwhile, phrenomagnetists during the magnetic sleep "excited" the "organs" of each client's brain through the bumpy surface of the skull, awaiting improved behaviors and more congenial minds. In so doing, they offered the spiritualists of a decade later a theoretical framework for making sense of the uncanny that many would find elegant and satisfying. Moreover, magnetists of any stripe proclaimed the abiding importance of the power of mind on its own—because of the power of thought in accomplishing the actual magnetization and because of the mental powers of clairvoyance, telepathy, and so forth. The power of mind, still further, was a double power: first, to perceive what the late-nineteenth-century metaphysicians would call "Truth"; second, to emanate energy for the reform of self and society. If there was no universal fluid, what operated in its place was tangible sympathy. The ingredients for mental magic and miracle had been set in place, waiting for later operators to mix and stir well.

Sunderland's contemporary John Bovee Dods (1795–1872) was a case in point. Dods had served for a short time as the Universalist pastor to a church in Provincetown, Massachusetts, and he had distinguished himself in his thinking by rejecting the "instantism" that accompanied the revival model of conversion. By contrast, he understood spiritual growth, like natural growth, as developmental, and he pondered the elusive mystery of a spirit's entry into flesh through the subtle "connexion" between mind and body. Then, like Sunderland, he found an explanatory model and an answer to his revival-grown questioning in animal magnetism and its link to phrenology. So it was that he became one more Universalist ex-minister eking out salvation in the borderlands in which mesmerism, phrenology, and then spiritualism flourished. Preaching his new doctrine of "electrical psychology," he announced that magnetism put humans in direct touch with the electric power by means of which God was joined to the universe. God stamped divine order as well as beauty and harmony upon the creation, and each human was a "visible daguerreotype" of the divine because of the magnetism. The conclusion was that animal magnetism—not the church or its doctrines and practices—supplied continuing access to the mind of God. In turn, the human mind, in touch with the divine, was good and could be trusted, even if it needed "at all times" to be kept "positive to the surrounding impressions of nature." And if Dods's message in some ways seemed a harbinger of the New Thought model of the late nineteenth century, he was also noticing the events of his time. It was a logical next step, then, that by 1854 he produced his book *Spirit Manifestations* to explain the phenomena of spiritualism. The movement of tables and chairs, which had become standard features of the séances, could be understood as a "redundancy of electricity" in the medium's nervous system, and raps were caused by "an electro-magnetic discharge from the fingers and toes of the medium." Not surprisingly, a few years later Dods, like Sunderland, became a spiritualist.[65]

Still another case in point was Joseph Rodes Buchanan (1814–1899?).[66] A traveling lecturer on phrenology and related themes, he appeared throughout the South and the Midwest, establishing himself as a physician and professor at the Eclectic Medical College of Cincinnati. With Sunderland, he vied for recognition as the discoverer of phrenomagnetism, and like Sunderland, he reconceptualized the technology and theorization of the phrenomagnetic process—in a new system that he called "neurology" or "anthropology." Hard on the heels of neurology came Buchanan's theory of the "nervaura," an emanation from the human nervous system different for each individual and for each separate organ. Podmore's description of Buchanan's nervaura is instructive. Writing in summary of the Buchanan exposition, he explained to readers that nervaura "stood in the scale of materiality midway between electricity and caloric [heat] on the one hand and will and consciousness on the other, being indeed the mediating link between the two sets of entities. Like other mundane forces it could be transmitted from one organism to another through an iron bar; but it was so far akin to the purely spiritual energies that by means of the *Nervaura* radiating from the anterior and superior cerebral centres 'an individual operates upon a nation and transmits his influence through succeeding centuries.'"[67]

Whatever its medical utility, from the vantage of a coming mass spiritualism, the nervaura offered enticing explanatory possibilities. When (magnetizing) individuals operated not on nations but on single subjects, they did so because the brain itself, as a physical entity, was impressible—responding to information it received through the senses. But the mind was also characterized by "mental impressibility," a phenomenon found in clairvoyance and telepathy that signaled the presence of what might be termed spiritual sensations. Hence, when in 1850 the spirits began to arrive in Cincinnati, Buchanan was ready both to embrace and to explain them. In a euphoric lead article in *Buchanan's Journal of Man*, he proclaimed excitedly, "They come! They are with us!! The mysterious powers which have disturbed, astonished and confounded the people of New York during the past year, are now at work among us, and for a week past have been making distinct manifestations of their existence." There followed a series of eleven propositions concerning the power behind the manifestations, declaring it to be "not visible or tangible," "highly intelligent," "human, and not divine," usefully described as "spiritual" and the work of spirits, and "almost invariably benevolent." The spirits belonged to "deceased friends" or "remarkable characters" from long ago, were at least partly dependent on a "connecting medium," and were capable of "on some occasions great physical power." What followed propositionally walked the boundary line between spiritualism and mesmerism. Spirits had "professed" sometimes to have mesmerized "certain highly-impressible persons," and "clairvoyants" had "often recognized these spiritual beings as attendants upon the living." These phenomena stood not alone in human history but were, in fact, "corroborated in their demonstration by a vast and ancient experience, running through all ages of the world, and belonging to all countries whether savage or civilized." Most important, in an autobiographical reference, Buchanan told readers that "my own nervauric experiments on the brain have shown that all highly-impressible persons are capable of having their spiritual and intuitive faculties sufficiently excited to rise into spiritual communion, to hold mental intercourse with departed friends."[68]

Phrenomagnetists like Sunderland, Dods, and Buchanan thus shaped mesmerism into an explanatory vehicle in which the spirits could travel well. The fluid, which disappeared under the mesmerizing work of Sunderland, became increasingly etherealized—more "spiritual"—in the theoretical assays of Dods and Buchanan. In all three, though, and in the model to which the phrenomagnetic moment gave birth, whether there was fluid or not, the notion of flow was ubiquitous. Beyond that, the spiritualist medium was a higher-level clairvoyant whose bodily apparatus had achieved or manifested a refined susceptibility —or impressibility—to the energies of spirit. Streaming into the brain of the medium, each spirit, like an invisible phrenomagnetic operator, excited the "organs" and used higher energies to send messages coursing through the medium's spine, which in turn became a "celestial telegraph" for communication with a living human world. But there was more. Beneath the pragmatic question of how the spirits used the bodies of mediums to communicate their messages lurked concerns that were ultimately theological. A. W. Sprague articulated the matter succinctly in 1855. "It is a mystery which I have vainly tried to solve," he wrote from Vermont, "the dividing line, or *connecting link*, between Clairvoyance induced by minds in the body, and Clairvoyance as unfolded by invisible and spirit power. How far human power influences these conditions, where there is apparently no spirit agency, I cannot determine. Whether controlled wholly by spirits in the body, or partially by those out, one thing is evident, that the same law operates, whether applied to Animal or Spiritual Magnetism." By 1856, Joseph Buchanan, who had called spiritualism "pneumatology," was pushing at its connection to phrenology and asking metaphysical questions. "How is the soul connected with the body, and through what organs does it directly act?" he queried, confidently declaring that these questions were resolved by the "new Anthropology."[69]

Not every spiritualist agreed, and, indeed, the larger magnetic model provoked its full share of theological and instrumentalist debate in the spiritualist community of the 1850s. Even so, we gain an expanded sense of how far the model could extend in the work of the Boston spiritualist Allen Putnam (1802–1887). Positing a "common root" and a single family relationship for mesmerism, spiritualism, (New England) witchcraft, and miracles, Putnam, in his short treatise on these themes, was sure that "the *spirits of men* perform these wonders; and all of them do it, and have ever done it, by substantially the same processes." A "universal law" connected animal magnetism to spiritualism. Still further, "a ladder of *many* steps might be constructed, on which one could go, by easy and gradual ascent, from the simplest forms of Mesmerism up to the highest phases of Spiritualism." In the first, only the physical body came under the control of the mesmerizer, not the mind. In a second, sensation and consciousness were also "put to sleep," and in a third the mesmerized subject experienced clairvoyance. The fourth step brought the mesmerized subject in touch with the past so that it could be read, while in a fifth, the mesmerized, now clairvoyant, subject beheld the spirits of the dead. "We have had, in this case, a glimpse at something which seems much like Spiritualism," averred Putnam. "Yet we are disposed to call it only *ripening Mesmerism*."[70]

Now, however, a crucial transposition was at work. A sixth step introduced the phenomenon of mesmerism without a visible mesmerizer, and Putnam stumbled over how it should be defined. "The medium passed into a sleep, or trance, like the mesmeric; and he seemed to see and hear marvellous things, as mesmeric subjects do. Probably he was *mesmerized*, — mesmerized by some *spirit*, or *band of spirits*." Finally, in the seventh step, came the presence of a medium who bore no visible signs of being magnetized. Here there was "no trance, no sleep, no loss of sensation or consciousness, no abstraction of the senses from objects and sound." Rather, all was "natural and normal." How should the medium be understood — especially when there were raps, moving furniture, and the like? Putnam was willing to invoke mesmerism but thought that to do so "the common significance of that term must be enlarged." And why should it matter whether one brought spiritualism into the mesmeric camp? Whether one named it as a form of magnetism? It is here that Putnam's humanizing and scientizing enterprise becomes clear. If the cases he had surveyed added up to a bigger, better mesmerism, then spiritualism was "absolutely but an outgrowth from the application of universal *natural* laws, and should be investigated as calmly and as philosophically as . . . electricity, magnetism, chemistry, or any other natural science." A "direct path" extended from here to the Seeress of Prevorst and to Swedenborg as well as to other visionaries, and Putnam was willing to take it.[71]

What could he conclude about the distinction between mesmerism and spiritualism? Mesmerism was "something which a man does while he has his *clothes on* [i.e., the body]." By contrast, spiritualism was "a similar act of his *after his clothes have been put off* [i.e., after death when there is no longer a body]." Thus, mesmerism and spiritualism might "differ no more than the green fruit and the ripe on the same tree." In Putnam's elegant model, then, we have a naturalistic explanation for spirit claims, embracing at once the Enlightenment and the Romantic world of the occult. Since the latter pages of the treatise were effusive, too, in their Christian benediction of spiritualist phenomena, his combinativeness appeared nearly all-embracing.[72] More than that, in the evolutionary and progressive framework that he carefully sketched, he was echoing other voices who announced that a progress taking place in spirit spheres was one of the most important aspects of spirit presence.

THE HARMONIAL PHILOSOPHY

One of the voices — a commanding voice among them — belonged to Andrew Jackson Davis. Emma Hardinge hailed him as "John Baptist" to the mass spiritualist movement (a designation that, as we have seen, she also applied to the Shakers). Davis, for her, presided over an "interregnum" between the "two great movements" of mesmerism and (séance) spiritualism, movements that she saw as intimately connected. "Many of the best mediums — especially the trance speakers and magnetic operators," she declared, "have taken their first degree in Spiritualism, as experimentalists in the phenomena of mesmerism." If so, Davis was certainly one of them. She extolled him, however, as "standing alone," as "unrivalled in the marvellous character of his occult endowments, and the irresistible nature of the influence he has exercised on humanity." Communing with the "supra-mundane," at home in the world of spirits, he stood as "the culminating marvel of modern ages"; in relation to him a hodge-podge of itinerant magnetizers and their kind had heard the "divine command to 'prepare the way of the Lord.'"[73]

Davis himself, on the other hand, was cautious in his turn toward séance spiritualism and measured in his endorsements in the 1850s and 1860s. Still more, by the 1870s, he was repudiating its excesses and surgically separating harmonialism from any connection to the mass movement. Bret Carroll aptly characterizes the relationship between the Davis movement and séance spiritualism as a "tension-filled union between the cause of harmonialism and that of the spirit rappings." Still, as Carroll acknowledges echoing Hardinge, Davis and other harmonialists prepared the way for what was to come.[74]

Davis initially seemed an unlikely candidate for the powerful role that he assumed. Born in 1826 in Orange County, New York, in a poor and—in the language of the twenty-first century—dysfunctional family, Davis was named by a heavy-drinking uncle after the hero of the battle of New Orleans and soon-to-be president of the United States. With only a smattering of formal education—a matter of five months at a Lancaster school where the children taught each other—he became an impressive autodidact, although he repeatedly disclaimed any intimacy with books. As important, from 1838 he displayed an aptitude for altered states of consciousness and claimed receipt of a message that helped persuade his family to move with him to Poughkeepsie. There by 1843 he was introduced to mesmerism when J. Stanley Grimes lectured in the town. In the wake of the Grimes visit, Davis, who had been working as a shoemaker's apprentice, discovered through the mesmeric experiments of local tailor William Levingston that he was an easy magnetic subject. For nearly two years, under Levingston's magnetic control, he gained area fame and a growing reputation as a medical clairvoyant, traveling in New York and neighboring New England. A brief connection with Universalist minister Gibson Smith at this time yielded the first collection of Davis's trance utterances when Smith, in early 1845, produced *Clairmativeness*. Davis would later disown the pamphlet.[75]

The year before, in March 1844, according to his own report Davis had undergone an experience that would change his relation to magnetism and magnetic operators radically. Unable to shake off the results of earlier magnetic work with Levingston, Davis returned to his boarding house, fell into a deep sleep, and experienced a quasi-shamanic initiatory dream-vision. A voice summoned him to dress and follow; the somnambulic Davis proceeded to Poughkeepsie's Mill and Hamilton Streets and beheld, in vision, sheep and a shepherd. Subsequently he fell unconscious; awoke and ran across the icy Hudson River; after further adventures ended up in a cemetery; and there met the spirits of the ancient Greek physician Galen and the decidedly more recent Emanuel Swedenborg. Galen presented him with a magical staff, which was by the end of the evening withheld from Davis after an angry outburst. (He finally received it considerably later.) Swedenborg gave no tangible gifts but offered special instruction, telling of visits to "this and other earths" and calling the youthful Davis "an appropriate vessel for the influx and perception of truth and wisdom." Predicting that "the things thou shalt bring forth will surprise and confound those of the land who are considered deeply versed in science and metaphysics," he told the young visionary that through him a "new light" would appear. Swedenborg himself would be the instructor of Davis's "interior understanding" and teach him the "laws" that would make him a fit communicant with "the interior realities of all subordinate and elevated things."[76]

Now, as an emerging trance physician and revisionary Swedenborgian, Davis lived the Levingston years as prelude. Then, on a trip to Bridgeport, Connecticut, he met a group of Universalists, including the physician Silas Smith Lyon and two ministers, William Fishbough and Samuel Byron Brittan. Persuaded by Lyon, Davis severed his ties with Levingston and set out for New York City to begin, with the Connecticut physician, a new venture in clairvoyant healing. Fishbough soon followed — to transcribe the entranced lectures that Davis began to deliver beginning in November 1845. Lyon would magnetize the "Seer," Davis would speak, and Fishbough would act as scribe. Notables in the radical religious and social culture of the day appeared at lecture sessions, among them the Reverend George Bush, a professor of Hebrew at New York University and a prominent Swedenborgian, and Albert Brisbane, Charles Fourier's foremost American disciple. Significantly, when Davis's 157 lectures appeared in 1847 as *The Principles of Nature, Her Divine Revelations, and a Voice to Mankind*, Swedenborgianism and Fourierism functioned as major interpretive tropes. Alongside these constructs came Enlightenment rationalism and a natural-history discourse that evoked Robert Chambers's *Vestiges of Creation* (1844) and similar works.[77] The lectures, taken as a whole, were also decidedly anticlerical, and they sounded a note that would continue in Davis's relationship to organized and orthodox forms of Christianity.

Estimates of the Davis corpus varied widely in his time and in the work of subsequent commentators and critics. George Bush, who published his *Mesmer and Swedenborg* the same year, initially functioned as an ardent and enthusiastic champion but then cooled his heels — probably because of dismay expressed by co-religionists in the official (Swedenborgian) New Church at Davis's jaundiced views of organized religion. Fourierist Parke Godwin supported the book —with its nearly eight hundred pages in its first printing—and so did historian John Bartlett. Transcendentalist George Ripley reviewed it in the *Harbinger* and took more than seven pages to enthuse over "the most surpassing prodigy of literary history." But less sanguine reviewers targeted the Davis opus as a plagiarized hodge-podge of largely Swedenborgian and Fourierist material coming not from the spirits but from his own memory. As late as the 1860s, John Humphrey Noyes quoted a hostile C. W. Webber, who wondered in print why Albert Brisbane and George Bush had failed to notice that Davis's work was "merely a sympathetic reflex of their own derived systems." Still, Noyes also quoted an Oneida Community circular that called Davis, on the basis of *The Principles of Nature*, the "great American Swedenborg" (even if he added that Davis was "more flippant and superficial than Swedenborg, and less respectful toward the Bible and the past, and in these respects he suits his customers)." In the early twentieth century, Frank Podmore—hardly an uncritical friend to spiritualist themes and doctrines—pointed to the book's glaring faults but still told readers that "at its best" there was "a certain stately rhythm and grandiloquence" about it. Even more, he thought that, although "obviously the work of an imperfectly educated man," the book's "qualities" were "more remarkable than its defects."[78]

Davis's protests that up until that time he had read only one book in his life— and that a romance—did nothing to improve his credibility for critics. Indeed, the "Scribe's Introduction" to the book providing damning evidence to the contrary. The "scribe" printed a March 1847 letter from the Reverend A. R. Bartlett, formerly of Poughkeepsie, with the recollection that Davis "loved books, especially controversial religious works, which he always preferred, whenever he could borrow them and obtain leisure for their perusal." Beyond suspicions of Davis's greater intimacy with books than he was telling came the theory that Davis had prodigiously committed *The Principles of Nature* to memory. Others speculated that he clairvoyantly read the minds of those present so that his lectures were shaped by the expertise of his listeners (a Swedenborgian lecture with Bush present; a Fourierist one with Brisbane; a combined lecture with both). Meanwhile, closer to our own time historian Slater Brown by 1970 pointed to the possibility that Davis "picked up a good part of his information, not from books, but from newspapers," citing evidence for his avid interest in the daily press.[79]

Whatever its sources—and they seem assuredly human and unspiritual—*The Principles of Nature* was a complexly combinative work, proclaiming a version of nature religion and inflecting it in emphatically metaphysical directions. Moreover, even with its sources in trance dictation and sententious prose, it possessed a logic and coherence that were, in structural terms, clear. After introductory materials including Davis's brief and ambitiously titled "Address to the World," the huge book proceeded in three parts. First came a relatively short (116-page) philosophical "Key" to what followed. Then, Davis lingered over a long (more than 550-page) Swedenborgian-plus-"popular-science" section called "Nature's Divine Revelations" (which Davis considered the "soul or basis of the whole superstructure"). Finally, a third section, just over a hundred pages in length and called "The Application; or, A Voice to Mankind," invoked a Fourierist vision.[80]

In its first paragraph, Davis's "Address to the World" enjoined readers to "exercise" their "choicest gift, which is *Reason* — and fear no corruption from truth, though new." Later the "Address" declared that there were "no possible limits to social progress and spiritual attainment and elevation." This because "man" was a "*microcosm,* or a combined expression of all the perfections contained in the Divine essence that animates and preserves the harmony of the Universe." In like fashion, the "Key" echoed Enlightenment platitudes even as it shifted them onto more obscure terrain. "REASON is a principle belonging to man alone," began the "Key." "The mind can not be chained!" "Man has rights founded in principles of Nature. These rights have been perverted, crushed, and prostrated." Reason, however, led to considerations of body and brain and inexorably on to themes of magnetism and clairvoyance, so that the entranced Davis could astutely establish his credentials for what was to come. All worked according to laws of "Nature," which operated with "a steady and unchangeable progression," and ultimately this law-bound universe led to a God who was no longer an eighteenth-century Grand Architect but instead a Grand Magnet and Mind in a thoroughly magnetized universe. Natural laws had been "established by one great Positive Power and Mind." This power filled "all negative substances. Worlds, their forces, their physical existences, with their life and forces," were "all *negative* to this Positive Mind," and "all subordinate existence" was "negative."[81]

The Enlightenment faded even more when Davis explained that "one sympathetic chain, encircling all spheres of this existence, can receive impressions instantaneously of all things desired, — and with its spiritual senses, communicate with spiritual substances." He himself received "impressions" not directly from the "Great Positive Mind" but from what he called the "*second* sphere, focus, or medium, which legitimately belongs to *this globe alone.*" In the second sphere, Davis confided, he had left the world of phenomena in which only effects were present and had come to the abode of spirit, where he could perceive both cause and effect. Still more, the word from the second sphere was that spirit was actually refined matter: "To me this all is known as matter become rare and unparticled — as the *ultimate* of matter, to which is applied the word *spirit.*" Matter, for Davis, produced mind, and mind produced spirit. Nature was all in all, and the "revelation" that would follow claimed nature as its "foundation." To open that revelation, Davis announced, he would progress beyond the second sphere, moving "onward and upward" through succeeding spheres until he reached the "ultimate" seventh sphere, in which he would be "able to comprehend all others."[82]

Davis's Swedenborgian and naturalized myth of origins ("Part II; or, Nature's Divine Revelations") began with a cataclysmic vision of liquid fire.

> IN THE BEGINNING, the Univercoelum was one boundless, undefinable, and unimaginable ocean of LIQUID FIRE! The most vigorous and ambitious imagination is not capable of forming an adequate conception of the height, and depth, and length, and breadth thereof. There was one vast expanse of liquid substance. It was without bounds—inconceivable—and with qualities and essences incomprehensible. This was the original condition of MATTER. It was without forms; for it was but *one* Form. It had not motions; but it was an eternity of Motion. It was without parts; for it was a Whole. Particles did not exist; but the Whole was as *one* Particle. There were not suns, but it was one Eternal sun. It had no beginning, and it was without end. It had not length; for it was a Vortex of one Eternity. It had not circles; for it was one infinite Circle. It had not disconnected power; but it was the very essence of all Power.

That power, according to Davis was the "GREAT POSITIVE MIND," and he went on to detail the formation of a vast and spectacular universe. Always, for him, there was the "Great CENTRE from which all of these systems and Systems of systems emanated . . . an exhaustless Fountain. . . . a magnificent and glorious Sun. . . . a Vortex. . . . an everlasting and unchangeable Parent of all things. . . . an Ocean of undulated and undefinable fire, the holy emblem of Perfection."[83]

The fiery mystical vision, however, dissolved, first, into a popular-science series of lectures describing the formation of the solar system. It dissolved again into a Swedenborgian travelogue, as Davis, emulating the Swedish seer, visited the planets (he predicted an eighth—in a lecture delivered six months before the discovery of Neptune), described their flora and fauna in detail, and also learnedly discussed their inhabitants. The Martians, for example, who were "divided into associated families" (a Fourierist aside) displayed "a peculiar prominence of the top of the head, indicative [in phrenological terms] of high veneration." They were "not large," the upper part of their faces was yellowish, and the lower part "of a different color, being rather dark."[84]

Moreover, Davis was not shy about admitting that Swedenborg had been there before or claiming that he, Davis, had further and better insights than his mentor. He looked to the day when "spiritual communion" would be "established such as is now being enjoyed by the inhabitants of Mars, Jupiter, and Saturn, because of their superior refinement," confiding to readers that they could learn more on these matters "by perusing the relations made by Swedenborg during the period of his mental illumination." But the American Swedenborg also cheerfully corrected the Swedish one, explaining that he was wrong in describing "the first three Spheres as three *hells*, inhabited by lower spirits and angels: while the three higher Spheres were the three heavens in which the higher spirits and angels dwelt." Rather, according to the postuniversalist theology of Davis, the hellish designation was "true, not in the *absolute*, but rather in the *comparative* sense." Indeed, he had proved in his lectures that the "highest" was "an unfolded representative of what the lowest [had] in substance, undeveloped." Similarly, the spirits who inhabited different planets in the solar system were "in different stages of refinement," but "spirits from any sphere" might "*by permission*, descend to any earth in the Universe, and breathe sentiments in the minds of others." This could happen even when "the person in the body" was "unconscious of the influx."[85]

Once Davis left the solar system to return to earth, he grew even more confident and expansive, declaiming on the vast eras of gradual development through which the planet passed. Here Genesis was played out in another key when humanity was created "from the dust of the earth" and as a "receptacle of one of the spontaneous breathings of the Great Positive Mind." Davis duly metaphysicalized the biblical story, reading it allegorically to reflect his own naturalistic synthesis and proceeding to an account of progressive human development. He went on to declaim at length on the Old Testament and the New, reading both in comparative terms that looked to other religious systems. The Bible represented but "*partial knowledge*," and its narrowness contrasted unfavorably with the knowledge of nature. New Testament miracles were "entirely void of all that high and celestial dignity which they would naturally be expected to possess if they were of Divine origin." Organized religion fared even worse, as Davis lamented that "the whole world, physically, morally, and spiritually" appeared to him then "as being immersed in the dark and turbid waters of sectarianism, into which the light of reason and of divine truth scarcely casts one relieving ray."[86]

Whether or not Davis thought he was delivering a new Bible of Nature, his publishers, as late as the post–Civil War "thirty-fourth" edition (which was actually more likely the seventeenth), evidently did. Conveniently interspersed between the "Revelations" and the "Application," they supplied a section of unnumbered and otherwise blank pages titled "Family Record" and subtitled serially "Births," "Marriages," "Departures" (evidently deaths), and "Memoranda." The Bible of Nature, however, was a working edition, and it provided now an

application for the hundreds of pages of sermon that had preceded. At this juncture, Davis's "impressions" turned Fourierist, and "association" reigned. Beginning with a basic sociology lesson on the class structure of society, he offered a
catalog of its present organization in terms of trades and professions and identified the lack of commitment and abundance of self-serving that attended all. The
clergy stood as a collective target for special indictment. "Of all professions and
situations occupied by men," Davis declared emphatically, "none is absolutely
more unenviable and more corrupting than that sustained by CLERGYMEN." It
was, indeed, a "deplorable fact that all the miseries, the conflicts, the wars, the
devastations, and the hostile prejudices, existing in the world" had come "owing
to the corrupting situation and influence of clergymen."[87]

Readers were not to worry, however, for Davis held the solution to the world's
ills, and it was Fourierist. Podmore thought the Davis answer was perhaps based
on Albert Brisbane's *Social Destiny of Man*. The suspicion seems likely. Brisbane
had argued in Fourierist terms for the formation of cooperative communities
that would undercut the competition that produced human miseries. "Association" provided the key to true reform and unity, and it was the natural system
for social organization. Davis, for his part, followed the party line, transmuting it
even as he did so into a practical metaphysic that presaged the discourse of early
New Thought. "Homage," he insisted, was "done to the Divine Mind, not in
prayer and unmeaning supplication, but in harmonious industry and universal
ACTION." The "misdirected *passion*" of prayer needed to be redirected, instead,
toward the "constitutional and mutual affection manifested between every particle and compound in being." This was the *"law of association,"* the "rudimental principle of Nature established by God," who was "Love." Each individual
was, in fact, "but an *organ* of the great human *Body*," and harmony, as the soul
of music — which was the "representation of divine *Order*" — must be established
among them. Thus each had to be "well instructed and properly situated," so
that the movements of each person might "accord with the movements of the
whole" and all would exist "in concert."[88] The details for the formation of separate trade and professional associations followed, and in them the ghost of the
phalanx was seemingly everywhere.

Always there was love. The "agricultural, mechanical, and manufacturing" associations, indeed, constituted "the body of Love, or of reciprocal movement."
And in a Hermetic echo, love was met and linked to wisdom in the Davis rendition. The legal, medical, and clerical associations, he explained, were "a *trinity*
forming one Whole, which corresponds to Wisdom." Thus Swedenborg stood
corrected once again. His system, so "practicable and serviceable to every mind,"
could "not now be understood or applied so extensively as when the superior As-

sociation [was] formed." Still more, Jesus emerged from the shadows of a corrupt Christianity with reformist teachings that were "descriptions of *effects* to flow legitimately from such a social organization."[89]

Davis's appeal to love was more than theoretical, as his later career as a marriage and divorce reformer suggests. On a more intimate level, too, he had taken to heart Swedenborg's insistence on "conjugial" love—the existence for each person of a spiritual mate so perfectly shaped to the soul that the two together constituted one enduring and heaven-bound whole. Davis dropped the "i" and remained preoccupied, throughout his life, with "conjugal" love. With the passing years, his theoretical references to God and Nature became progressively more gendered, and more erotically so, in a mystical sexuality of Father-God and Mother-Nature. In his personal life, his growing relationship with Catherine DeWolf Dodge, perhaps twenty years his senior, had brought him the funds to produce *The Principles of Nature*. The Dodge connection began his private search for his true and abiding soulmate, she whose "celestial copulations" with him would resonate, according to the law of correspondence, with the marriage of God and Nature. Davis eventually married Dodge, who divorced her husband (after a claimed vision by Davis) to become his wife—but not before the two were involved in scandal regarding their relationship before their official union.[90]

The relationship with Dodge both assisted and nearly derailed Davis's next venture with his friends. This was the publication of *The Univercoelum and Spiritual Philosopher*, a weekly newspaper that appeared in New York City to advance Davis's views, beginning in December 1847. Standing as its creator and editor was Samuel B. Brittan—the other Universalist minister whom Davis had met in Bridgeport, Connecticut, along with the Reverend Fishbough and Dr. Lyon. Thomas Lake Harris, another ex-Universalist minister and a poet—who would go on to found the spiritualist Mountain Cove community—also joined the group. Dodge had once again helped financially, but—in that both she and Davis were living at the editor's house—the evidence that her bedroom was empty at night created consternation among the group. When Davis and Dodge married, the rift was officially healed, but relationships among the men were never the same as before.

At this juncture, Davis was hardly the sexual radical that he would become. Nonetheless, his ideas were already attracting a following of individuals who were comeouters from the churches in the Northeast and Midwest. They were interested in the paranormal or the "supernatural" but desirous of reinscribing it as natural, and their views on love and marriage exhibited the antinomian side of metaphysics. It is this group to whom, by the 1840s, the harmonial label was ascribed—harmonial because, as John Spurlock has noted, they stressed "harmony among people and between the spiritual and the carnal." Spurning the Calvinism of their past and even the Christian perfectionism of their present, proponents of the new heterodoxy proclaimed "harmony rather than sinlessness as the key to remaking the world." They spurned middle-class morals as well when they attacked the venerable institution of marriage. In contrast to the mass-movement spiritualism that was about to blossom into a culture of female mediums and trance physicians, harmonialism was, as Spurlock remarks, "a thoroughly male business, a network of 'brotherhoods.'" Embracing mesmeric experiment, Swedenborgian theology, and Fourierist notions of association, harmonial men were middle class or better, financially affluent as a group, and elitist in their notions and values. The spirit voices that attracted them, according to Spurlock, "spoke in foreign accents and recondite English."[91]

Free-love radicals that they tended to be, the harmonialists preoccupied themselves with a series of other issues that linked an emerging metaphysical religion to themes of utopian progress and reform. They adopted Davis as their spiritual leader, and they became eager subscribers to the new *Univercoelum*. There, for the nearly two years of its existence (it folded in July 1849), the paper extolled Fourierist socialism amid millennialist rhetoric of a new age dawning. It excerpted Transcendentalists (Theodore Parker was a favorite) and admired William Ellery Channing; it championed mesmerism, phrenomagnetism, and Swedenborgianism; it advanced the cause of health reform; and it assiduously recorded the theology of Andrew Jackson Davis with its homegrown species of nature religion and its anticlerical disdain for the churches. Moving beyond the earlier universalism of its editors, it found in Jesus the metaphysical leader that after the Civil War he would become, and it proclaimed the immanence of God in the world and the living Christ presence in exalted individuals. A change in the *"religious systems of the world"* was both *"necessary"* and *"inevitable,"* editor Samuel Byron Brittan authoritatively announced in the first number: "The old ideas in which we were educated; the dark mysteries and unfounded superstitions of a corrupt and fabulous theology, must pass away." In its place, Brittan celebrated the new theology of the harmonial movement: "We believe that the Supreme Divinity is essentially *in* all his works. The material universe is the Body of which he is the animating Principle. . . . We view the Deity as an all-pervading presence; as the Positive Intelligence whose volitions govern the revolving spheres."[92]

Among the spheres, it was the second that occupied immediate attention, and, in fact, the paper was unafraid to tell readers that "transition to the second or higher sphere" defined the "process of dying." If this sounds decidedly like Davis, the *Univercoelum*, as we might expect, had been unabashed in its exaltation of the Poughkeepsie Seer, whom, by 1852, the spiritualist periodical *Shekinah* would hail as "the youthful Swedenborg of our day." In the first number of the *Univercoelum*, the editors together proclaimed their belief that "the eternal laws of Nature, as unfolded and explained through the medium" (who was Davis) constituted "the only true and desirable social condition" and formed "a sufficient and only reliable ground for the highest and holiest hopes of man, for time and for eternity." The new periodical continued to emphasize that it was "a fearless advocate of the theology of Nature, irrespective of the sectarian dogmas of men." Josiah Johnson, in one article, succinctly summarized harmonial dogma, evoking Emersonian, mesmeric, and Swedenborgian language at once, even as he echoed the Enlightenment and hinted of Fourier: "MAN being a Microcosm, or Unity of all things existing below him, cannot therefore live harmoniously with himself, or with Nature, unless the streams that supply his existence are allowed to flow naturally into his being. Neither can his social relations become perfected, unless his natural rights are allowed to flow in their direct and proper channel."[93]

"Mind" was supreme in this world of nature and unity. But Mind never severed its connection to the body, which—following the law of correspondence—obeyed physical precepts of health that brought clarity to the mental function. One typical editorial by Thomas Lake Harris stated flatly that the "only way" to "Knowledge" was "Obedience to the Laws of Nature." These were the "laws of our being, the laws of God," and obedience, therefore, so quickened "spiritual sight" and unfolded the "spiritual Nature" that individuals were "placed in a position to see the Truth, to follow it—to be guided by it into all light and all happiness." So there was Mind, and there was Truth, its object. But as reflection on the life of Jesus—"an exceedingly great, good, and spiritually exalted MAN"—suggested to William Fishbough, within each person resided an "intangible spiritual essence" that was "immediately associated with the intellectual principle itself." This "organized imponderable essence" was the spirit. It could survive death, and—as it did in the person of Jesus (and Mesmer, Davis, and others)—it could see clairvoyantly and operate magnetically. Put another way, it could exert its will in the world, so that one way that Jesus could heal came "by a concentration of his thoughts upon the patient." The lesson for Fishbough and his readers was one of democratic elation. "*All men* possess intrinsically the *same elements* which in Jesus were so harmoniously organized and so highly developed," Fishbough affirmed. He continued in language that hinted already at how soon the discourse community was organizing from which, by the 1890s, New Thought congealed. "In showing, thus that there is *a Christ* in the interior nature of every man," Fishbough wrote, he aimed to "induce every one to strive to *develop* that which is within him, and to live and act like a Christ."[94] The Jesus who could be separated from "the Christ" to become the "living Christ Presence" in humans had already been conceived in his formula.

As Fishbough's essay and so many others showed, the *Univercoelum* recognized spirits familiar to Andrew Jackson Davis—spirits who, as Ernest Isaacs has remarked, were "generalized" inhabitants of the second sphere rather than the "individual, identifiable spirits" of séance spiritualism whom later mediums questioned. But the *Univercoelum* was slow to recognize the spirits who, enthusiasts claimed, were rapping in American parlors after the Fox family happenings at Hydesville. This, even though the publication continued for over a year after the spring of 1848. One brief article under the title "Strange Manifestations" appeared in the third volume, promising to investigate occurrences in Auburn, New York, and drawing no conclusions. Still, without the Fox sisters Davis's harmonialism would have had a far different trajectory, and Davis himself became convinced of the truth of the new manifestations by the spring of 1850. According to Ann Braude, during the same year he invited the Fox sisters to his New York City home. By 1853, in *The Philosophy of Spiritual Intercourse*, he produced his own explanation for the now widespread mediumistic work.[95]

"It is a great truth," Davis wrote, "that the inhabitants of the second sphere can, and do, at times, communicate their thoughts and sentiments to the inhabitants of the earth." Any spirit who communicated was *"no immaterial* substance." Rather, the "spiritual organization" was "composed of matter—such as we *see, feel, eat, smell, and inhale*—in a very high state of refinement and attenuation." How did the refined matter that was spirit manage to communicate with the gross world of matter in which humans, in their bodies, dwelled? The answer, for Davis, had nothing whatsoever to do with "a good moral or intellectual state" in the medium, but instead with the ground rules for "electrical" transmission. "Electrical vibrations" in the séance circle generated spirit communication. In one circle about which Davis commented, "an emanation of vital electricity from the physical systems of the young ladies, (who were the medium,) and the intense interest experienced by the entire circle, caused each person present to contribute largely to the general electric atmosphere." When the brain was quiet, the "electrical elements" could flow "down from the brain into the nerves, and into all the infinite ramifications of the nerves, and thence into the atmosphere which we breathe." Hence the spirits answered humans according to "conditions and principles" that were "simple and physical, philosophical and rational." "Those conditions," Davis averred, were "no more complicated or wonderful than the principles upon which the magnetic telegraph is daily operating along our great commercial avenues."[96]

It had been less than a decade before, in May 1844, that Samuel F. B. Morse had sent wire messages from Baltimore to Washington, D.C., to demonstrate to Congress the practicality of his invention. Davis's spirits operated at the cutting edge of a new America. In their modernity and materiality, they provided a smooth transition into the new age of séance spiritualism. Thus, by positioning harmonialism to take advantage of mass spiritualism and by grandfathering it, Davis gave the movement what Robert S. Cox calls a "robust theory of spiritual action that backed the tangible, empirically verifiable phenomena of the Foxes with a thick description of the structure of the spirit world and of spiritual cause and effect." Indeed, "Davis's mesmeric visions of the afterlife dovetailed so neatly into the early Spiritualism that most commentators saw only continuity."[97]

Davis in the end remained ambivalent. By 1859 at least, he was quite distinctly separating his own "philosophical" spiritualism from the (inferior) "phenomenal" spiritualism of the séances. Many who investigated phenomenal spiritualism were "*illogical* in their thoughts; therefore, also, in their actions and character." Whatever moral value phenomenal spiritualism had, he judged, was "chiefly exhibited in the demonstration of individual post-mortem existence." By contrast, "in the great work of human culture and redemption, all intelligent minds" depended on his brand of philosophical spiritualism. Using the "laws of cause and effect," "clairvoyance in the thinking faculties," and "reasonings intuitive and correspondential," philosophical spiritualism, or harmonialism, stood ready to usher in a great new age of the spirit—what Davis would later call a "REPUBLIC OF SPIRIT embosomed and gestating in the dominant political organism." By this time—in 1885 when he hailed America as the "true" and "coming spiritual Republic"—he had already denounced séance spiritualism and severed his connection with it in the context of the flamboyance and fraudulence of postbellum spiritualism.[98]

Davis continued to write prodigiously—over thirty books in his long life, with his five-volume *Great Harmonia* (1850–1859) an especially ambitious and integrated testimonial to his abiding rejection of the notion of sin and his consistent invocation of nature and its law.[99] If the title and theme of his work evoke Fourier, Davis had also made the material his own. He likewise continued to speak energetically on the "woman" question and marriage and divorce themes, even as he practiced as a trance physician. He had long learned to magnetize himself and, in his writings, he often referred to his "impressions," material he received from deep intuition that, for him, bordered the magnetic state. Dodge, his first wife— with whom, he later declared, he had enjoyed a "fraternal" but not spiritually "conjugal" marriage—died in 1853. The next year Davis encouraged Mary Fenn (Robinson) Love of western New York in her divorce from her own husband—in continuing and complicated proceedings that involved two states. In Mary Love,

Davis believed, he had found the one whom his spirit guide had been willing to show him as his "true companion," and he owned to the same love in his heart as that "between Father-God and Mother-Nature." The two married in 1855, in a union that at the time Davis thought "conjugal." But twenty-nine years later he disagreed (stating then that he almost from the first knew that he had erred).[100]

Fenn Davis was a devoted spiritualist and an ardent feminist, already in 1853 helping to call the first New York State Woman's Rights Convention. According to Ann Braude, she "quickly outstripped her husband as a public spokesperson in both movements." She saw marriage as the cause of female oppression and spoke publicly to that effect at a spiritualist convention the following year. As Davis's faithful wife, many years later, however, when Davis believed that he had discovered in Della E. Markham (a New York City magnetist and eclectic physician) his true conjugal mate, Fenn Davis—although terminally ill—agreed amicably to a divorce. Even so, the New York spiritualist community was not so amicable. Davis and his new wife of 1885 moved to Watertown, outside of Boston, where, as a trance physician, he ended his days.[101]

Davis believed he was standing on principle and advancing the union to which all were called. A conjugal marriage was evidence that "human interests are not intrinsically conflicting, but one, *and only one!*" In the mysticism of his absolute vision, "all members must suffer when one suffers. The happiness of one is the happiness of all!" The revised Swedenborgianism of his vision blended cordially into spiritualism—and, after the heightened spiritualist moment, into the continuing metaphysical religion of the late nineteenth century. The God who was an eternal Magnet bestowed an erotic quality on the mystical content of the Davis theology. Meanwhile, what Bret Carroll calls Davis's "spiritual republicanism" brought the Enlightenment ideology, in democratized form, into the spiritualist mainstream, and his reform commitments blended with those of other spiritualists in a social concern that was powerful and continuing (more on this in the next chapter). For Davis, even mediums must be rational and exhibit active minds.[102] For them and for all other humans, the divinity of the self abided. All of nature tended to "the development of MAN; the grand consummation of the Material Structure." Like a seed in the earth reproducing "its kind," so did the "Deity, as the spiritual germ, unfold, through the ten thousand processes of Nature, its own image and likeness in the moral characteristics of the human type!" The spirit in each person was "the invisible presence of the Divine in the visible human," and—in a bash at orthodox Christian theology—it was "the only and all-sufficient Incarnation." More than that, the divinity of the self meant that, in practical matters of health and disease, the "soul principle" was involved, and the human mind needed to address the "predetermining cause," which it was "the moral duty of every mind to fully comprehend and promptly overcome."[103] Davis, in short, was nailing together major planks of the metaphysical platform that continued through the nineteenth century. It is probably not too much, in fact, to call him a founder of the late-century efflorescence that emerged.

SÉANCE SPIRITUALISM

Davis's "republic of spirit," however, had to make way for a republic of spirits. After 1848, the hints and small presences of spiritualism gave way before a collective movement that brought public excitement and impassioned debate to happenings in darkened Victorian parlors. Séances became new vehicles for intimate spiritual contact among strangers and friends. There was, indeed, a communion of spirits in the séance circles—so much so that, by 1869, Emma Hardinge could define the movement as religion. "Spiritualism, with a large majority of its American adherents," she wrote, "*is a religion*, separate in all respects from any existing sect, because it bases its affirmations purely upon the demonstrations of fact, science, and natural law, and admits of no creed or denominational boundary." This, of course, should have been a definition to delight the heart of Davis and countless others of his ilk, but by that time Davis and company found spiritualism to be no religion at all.[104]

Most who called themselves spiritualists during the years of mass spiritualism's early heyday would have agreed, as Ann Taves argues, with Hardinge. Moreover, although spiritualist authors probably exaggerated numbers, believers and practitioners were certainly a numerous lot. The "hundreds of thousands of sentient beings" that Judge Edmonds wrote about in 1853 had become, in Hardinge's estimate (based, she declared, on the "last statistical accounts" that had been supplied in 1867 by "opponents" of spiritualism) "eleven millions of persons on the American continent." Later in her narrative she reminded readers that "Spiritualism numbers one-fourth at least of the population of the United States in its ranks," a percentage that she bumped upward to one-third when she cited Roman Catholic testimony at a convention in Baltimore. "*Eleven millions,*" said the Catholics, equaled "*one-third of the population of the United States.*" A decade earlier, however, when the movement was younger, the communitarian and spiritualist Robert Dale Owen quoted the author William Howitt in a late-1850s estimate of "three millions of people in America alone." Meanwhile, Eliab W. Capron parenthetically declared for two million by 1854. For New York City, at roughly the same time, former United States senator and governor of Wisconsin Nathaniel P. Tallmadge quoted an anti-spiritualist publication that claimed "at the least calculation, forty thousand sincere believers in spiritual rappings," with, for the country as a whole, a number "immense, and far greater than the public generally imagine." They came, the writer added, from "every class in society, from the highest to the lowest, and among minds of every degree of capacity and cultivation, from the most accomplished scholar to the most ignorant of the ignorant."[105]

Summarizing the situation for the mid-1850s, Frank Podmore admitted rapid growth but offered "no statistics," with difficulty finding estimates "even professedly based on anything but conjecture." He explained: "[Charles] Hammond speaks of two thousand writing mediums alone in 1852; [Charles] Partridge, writing in 1854, says that Spiritualists in America numbered over a million; [Nathaniel P.] Tallmadge, a few weeks later, says two millions; [Joel] Tiffany, in 1855, writes, 'they now number millions.'" By 1983, historian Ernest Isaacs apparently agreed with Charles Partridge, at least for the dozen or so years before Hardinge's huge claim. "By 1855," he wrote, "probably one million Americans—out of a population of twenty-eight million—identified themselves with the new religion." Even in this pared-down version for the mid-1850s, the figure is still impressive. Meanwhile, the numbers of mediums multiplied and grew. Eliab Capron, whose home was in Auburn, New York, not far from Rochester, alleged that in Auburn in the summer of 1850 there could be found "from fifty to one hundred" mediums "in different stages of development." In Providence, Rhode Island, the same year, almost forty mediums were said to be practicing, many of them from among the elite. A Cincinnati editor claimed twelve hundred in his city in 1851, of whom he could personally name more than three hundred. For roughly the same time, Hardinge, on the basis of a report from a local minister and spiritualist editor, was telling her readers that in Springfield, Massachusetts, "the number of mediums, public and private, was believed already to exceed two hundred." Jesse Hutchinson of the renowned (at the time) Hutchinson Family Singers declared that in 1852 twenty "good" mediums were practicing in San Francisco. The same year, in Woodstock, Vermont, one spiritualist found eight or ten practiced mediums and fifty who were developing their skills. And in 1859, according to John Spurlock, seventy-one could be counted in the state of New York, while there were fifty-five in Massachusetts and twenty-seven in Ohio.[106]

These anecdotal reports about mediums are especially important. If spiritualism was, in fact, a religion, then mediums were its officiants and priests, presiding in the small circles in which spiritualist communities were constituted. As Bret Carroll has reminded students of the phenomenon, the séances provided the "structure of spiritualist practice." Evidence as to size is scattered, and—like so much of the other evidence regarding spiritualist numbers—incomplete. But mediums meant circles. Still more, Carroll cites claims regarding séance circles from contemporaries—in the mid-1850s three hundred "magnetic circles" in New York City; between fifty and sixty in Philadelphia; "quite numerous" circles in Boston; "regularly constituted societies" in nearly all of the cities and towns in the Providence, Rhode Island, area; fifty-nine séance circles nightly in Cincinnati and hundreds of occasional circles there, too.[107]

Circles had come early to the mass spiritualist movement. The Fox sisters in Rochester engaged in the sittings, and Kate Fox did also when she lived for several months before that at the Capron family home in Auburn. Here there were rappings aplenty, even as furniture moved seemingly of its own accord; a guitar sailed above the heads of séance sitters on several evenings, mysteriously being played by nobody visible; spirit hands were felt on sitters' arms or shoulders or heads; hair combs were snitched from some of the women and placed on the heads of others. With Eliab Capron, investigator-turned-believer in the lead, Rochester's Corinthian Hall was rented in November 1849 for public lecture-demonstrations. Two weeks later, Leah Fox Fish accepted payment—not just a free-will offering—for a séance.[108] Then, after Capron and George Willets, another convinced spiritualist, succeeded in getting their account published in Horace Greeley's *New York Weekly Tribune*, the western New York happenings became national news. By June of 1850, the three Fox sisters, with their mother, arrived in New York City, where the sisters began holding public séances for a fee of one dollar per sitter. A national movement had been launched. Even as the Fox sisters were apparently adored by an eager public—over the next several years they demonstrated their mediumistic abilities beyond New York City in Buffalo, Pittsburgh, Philadelphia, Washington, D.C., and the state of Ohio—mass spiritualism became an engine in its own right. When, as time passed, the younger two sisters, Kate and Margaret, led more and more tawdry lives, becoming addicted to alcohol and confessing to fraud (they had made the rapping noises with their big toes by throwing them out of joint), it really did not matter.[109] Spiritualism belonged to American vernacular culture, and with its blend of Davis's revised Swedenborgianism, mesmeric explanation, universalism, Transcendentalist themes of nature and intuition, and the rest of the metaphysical synthesis then available, it was there to stay. It would wax and wane as a mass movement, but its vision of reality, both ultimate and intimate, would move on, infusing not only a continuing spiritualist movement but also Theosophy, Christian Science (although Mary Baker Eddy would adamantly deny that), New Thought, and—in our own time—the New Age movement.

In the séance circles, meetings were sometimes regular, with sitters—like members of very small churches—arriving for weekly and even more frequent sessions. They were also sometimes irregular. John Edmonds and George Dexter provided examples of both. Their circle of six met twice weekly at Dexter's home, but in between whenever Dexter visited Edmonds at the judge's residence, séance phenomena occurred. Moreover, as the chronicle of the Fox sisters already suggests, commodification proceeded apace. The services of mediums were, quite definitely, for sale; reports told that the Fox sisters earned one hundred dollars a day. Likewise, performance—often flamboyant and even outrageous—also characterized the gatherings. Juxtaposed against a background of the loss of loved ones, the yearning for experiential knowledge of an afterworld, or even plain and simple curiosity, the antics of spirits—as the early séances of the Fox sisters already suggest—transformed revelation in many cases into slapstick and entertainment.[110]

As time passed, the repertoire of spirit protocols amplified and increased. Spirits seemed to learn from other spirits. The original rappings of Hydesville became, in Rochester, an intricate system for spelling out letters of the alphabet on the newly acclaimed "spiritual telegraph." By the mid-1850s, Nathaniel Tallmadge supplied a catalog of spirit phenomena that is instructive. Besides table-moving and the movement of other "ponderables," rapping and tipping of tables and the like were widespread. There were drawing and writing mediums (whose hands were moved to produce automatic art or script) as well as trance speakers (who spoke under what was described as spirit control) and other mediums skilled at music, dancing, and singing in the trance state. Meanwhile, "seeing" mediums gave precise descriptions of spirits thought to be present, and healing mediums accomplished their work under claimed spirit guidance. Andrew Jackson Davis himself, ambitiously supplying a conceptual map of "the field occupied by the torch-bearers of the new dispensation," provided a table of some twenty-four types of mediums neatly and logically divided into groups of six, labeled respectively "outward," "inward," "onward," and "upward." A clear hierarchy of value characterized the Davis "progressive" labels, which began with the "vibratory" medium, whose body, but not mind, was partially controlled by "invisible powers," and ended with the "impressional" medium, whose mind, he declared, was totally possessed by a controlling spirit. In between came the full display of mediumistic styles and talents from table tippers, who unnerved sitters, to psychometric readers, who could disclose the contents of sealed letters. Although Davis invoked a "beautiful harmony" rather than chaos in the kinds and qualities of mediums, he was also wary of the spirit energy that visited humans through mediumistic means. The impressional medium—who most resembled himself—could be the conduit for whatever the controlling spirit desired. As he opined, "From this source, there is now flowing into the world a mass of literature—a strange combination of prose and so-called poetic verbiage—which, it seems to me, the world might easily progress without receiving."[111]

The spirits who could totally control grew, seemingly, ever more raucous and shrill. Soon they were levitating the bodies of mediums or of sitters. By the post–Civil War period, purported photographs of spirits came into vogue, and so did the materialization of the bodies of spirits out of cabinets in the séance rooms. It is easy to be dismissive of all of this and to read it as vernacular vaudeville of the spirit to distract and titillate mid- and late-nineteenth-century Americans and—on a smaller scale—their twentieth-century and continuing progeny. A deeper reading, however, points to its connections to social, economic, and religious dislocation as the nation moved inexorably into a future in which old verities no longer held and traditional communities dissolved under the impact of serious social change. For all the less-than-divine comedy of the spirits, the mediumistic prowess of many American women (more women than men were mediums—see the next section) and men points toward pervasive mystical and even perhaps shamanistic experience, as Bret Carroll has noticed. American quasi-shamanistic mediums, to be sure, were distinctly urban. To borrow language from Robert S. Ellwood, each of them functioned as a "shaman-in-civilization," a "modern magus" whose job description included aspects of ecstasy and performance, myth and sometime fraud, seamlessly connected.[112] However, what distinguished these American mediums from many other modern magi was the public character of their work, its democratic ethos, and its cultivation of personal religious experience for all—with American revivalism on its cultural horizon to show how. Mediumistic mysticism shared a pragmatic cast with the rest of American metaphysical religion. It was shaped to this-worldly concerns, providing temporary respite—not permanent escape—so that sitters who claimed they had talked to spirits went home again to claim, as well, their space as people in a workaday world.

"The circle reinforced the premium which evangelicals had placed on inner spirituality, personal experience, and direct contact with the divine," Carroll writes. He insists, too, that the circles "had an unequivocally religious function that went far beyond an interest in the phenomena of mediumship, scientific evidence of immortality, and conversation with lost loved ones." Arguably, it was the *ritual* of the séance that ordered space and time in ways that mediated what an evangelical might call "saving grace." Carroll has pointed to the elements of structure governing the circles. The very adoption, by contemporaries, of the term *circle* linked practice to cosmology (even when, in large groups, some participants might not have gathered around the table but sat elsewhere in the room), and prominence was accorded to the home as temporary sacred space. Spiritualist practice in the séances involved orderly procedures. Practitioners early produced numerous sets of instructions to govern their home-grown liturgies and to provide good order in the face of what might seem, from sensationalized reports, the chaos and confusion generated by spirit performances. Seating arrangements were thought out; hymn singing became a regular feature, and, often, so did prayer; qualities of meditative quiet in a group setting preceded spirit phenomena. Indeed, what Carroll calls the "centrality of emotional restraint" pervaded these ritual settings.[113] It may have been that the spirits behaved outrageously, but séance sitters who brought private grief and anomie to the public table did not, typically, act out their emotional states. Moreover, the continuing rhetoric of science that pervaded the sittings (more on that in the next chapter) and the analytic mindset—the critical scrutiny—that accompanied them undercut a demonstrative spirituality of excess.

Andrew Jackson Davis, for all his ambivalence toward "phenomenal" spiritualism as distinct from the philosophical version of his own practice, was interested enough to provide one set of instructions for success. The circles always needed to incorporate positive and negative elements, he thought, and—in keeping with the twelve "elements and attributes" he found in human souls—they should consist of twelve individuals, six of them male and six female (providing the positive and negative elements respectively). Distinguishing between a medium—an instrument for the sounds the spirits were said to make—and a clairvoyant who could "discern spirits," Davis situated both at the head of the séance table. To their right he called for someone whose "electrical temperament" was signaled by "cold hands" and "a mild and loving disposition"; to their left, another individual "of a magnetic or warm physical temperament," who was "positive and intellectual." In fact, in the Davis liturgy, actual gender was less important for seating arrangements and séance success than the presence of so-called "masculine" and "feminine" traits of character. Cold hands and loving hearts were feminine; warmth and intellectual prowess male. Circles should not meet more than twice a week, Davis warned, "because those things which become too familiar are thereby deprived of their sanctity, and hence also of their power." Rooms should be quiet and also darkened so that people could more easily concentrate.[114]

In the most dramatic element of his protocol, Davis advised a "magnetic cord." His directions were explicit—"five yards of a three quarter inch rope," covered in "silk or cotton velvet," and wound round by two parallel wires, one of steel and one of silver or copper, placed an inch and a half apart, and wound "about a quarter of an inch apart." Sitters would assemble around the table with the magnetic cord in their laps, "their hands upon or grasping it, and the one which is constitutionally most susceptible to spiritual influx of emotion and influence, will feel a throbbing in the hands; and ultimately, by repeated experiments, some one among the company may be rendered clairvoyant." Mediums should not hold the cord because they were the "substances or needles" that "the magnetism and electricity" of the sitters were to act upon. After an hour, the cord could be discarded and the members of the circle, instead, hold hands.[115]

Always, for Davis, it was the "vital electricity" of the séance circle that was important. By the time he produced *The Present Age and Inner Life*, he was offering readers a "new arrangement." Now the "positive and negative principles" (the men and women or those with strong masculine and feminine energy respectively) were to be placed alternately around the table "as so many zinc and copper plates in the construction of magnetic batteries." The rope's two ends were to be crossed between the two mediums who ideally would be present, and the ends were to terminate "each in a pail or jar of cold water." Meanwhile, the conductivity of the rope would now be enhanced by attaching its copper wire to a zinc plate, even as its steel wire would be joined to a copper plate. The plates themselves should be "cut with *twelve* angles or sides," because, Davis explained, the points would greatly increase "the volume of terrestrial electricity." This was necessary for "a *rudimental aura* (or atmosphere) through which spirits can approach and act upon material bodies."[116]

Davis spoke only of magnetism and electricity, but by this time some séance spiritualists had also incorporated into their explanations talk of "odyle," or "odic force," a concept derived from the work of the German chemist and metallurgist Karl, Baron von Reichenbach. In the mid-1840s, Reichenbach began arguing for a new universal force, or "effluence," possessing neither weight nor extension but having real physical effects. Odic force was, for Reichenbach and those who agreed, distinct from electricity and magnetism and produced on sensitive individuals various sensations that could be documented and explored.[117] Whether theoretically explained by the odyle, or by magnetism and electricity, the felt experience of spiritualists translated as religion. As a version of nature religion—articulated now in a borderline scientific discourse—spiritualist séance sitting was about revelation and revelations. Those who witnessed the physical manifestations in darkened rooms also heard voices and read messages that they believed had come from the spirits. In a Protestant culture of the biblical Word, even those who were seeking religion elsewhere found it in a ritually invested Word and words. Here, as in the religious experience of American blacks and Indians and in the Latter-day pronouncements of Joseph Smith, revelation was continuous, and the authority of inner experience commanded assent from sympathetically minded believers. Mind had become the minds of spirits and the answering imaginistic work of devotees.

When the séance sitters went home, they could read, and what they could read —or at least revere—were texts that, in the twenty-first century, would be called "channeled" works. At the head of the list were three books that apparently inspired the most abiding devotion. The first of these was the familiar Davis gospel in *The Principles of Nature*. The second was a two-volume collection of messages purportedly from "Sweedenborg" and Sir Francis Bacon, produced as *Spiritualism* by Judge John Edmonds and George Dexter, the first volume appearing in 1853 with long and separate introductions by each of them and a series of appendices, one of them from Governor Nathaniel Tallmadge. The third, in 1855, was a work entitled *The Healing of the Nations*, written under "spiritual influence" by the unknown Charles Linton and promoted by Governor Tallmadge with his own lengthy introduction to head the volume and, again, a copious series of appendices, one of them from Tallmadge.[118] The success of these works generated a series of similar volumes of purported spirit communications. Selling spirits was evidently easy, and a thriving market arose for messages from the afterworld.

The (first) Edmonds-Dexter volume of 1853 appeared toward the end of the year but still went through at least five editions before the year was out. It was this volume that, apparently, captured the public mind, since there is evidence of multiple editions of the volume standing alone. The work cost Edmonds his place as a judge and forced his retirement to private practice in the context of what Slater Brown termed his "incontinent credulity." Edmonds was convinced that he was being visited not merely by friends and relatives but by Francis "Lord" Bacon and Emanuel Swedenborg. In their preface to the book, Edmonds and Dexter explained how the communications came. Dexter, pencil ready, received a good many of the messages by automatic writing. When a Mrs. S. functioned as medium, the judge took down what she said in shorthand, and when Edmonds himself was the recipient, either Dexter or Owen G. Warren took notes. After each session, Judge Edmonds edited and wrote the material out in full. In the second part of the volume, too, some forty visions that came to Judge Edmonds in séance settings appeared, some of them quite lengthy, combining description of the spirit world with opinion and moral teaching. For a twenty-first-century reader, the volume seems thoroughly sententious, and it is easy to join Slater Brown in lambasting its "pontifical discourses" as "pompous, declamatory, artificial, slightly condescending in tone." Nor was Brown wrong in noticing that the communications "sound like neither Bacon nor Swedenborg but resemble the judge himself orating on the floor of the state legislature or pontificating from the bench of the supreme court."[119] Even more, the spirit messages frequently leap from their pages with all the banality of so many platitudes printed on drug-store greeting cards.

Still, for all that, the received content of the revelations claimed by Edmonds and Dexter bears further scrutiny. Set in the context of a nation still ambivalently attached to a prominently Calvinist past, the universalist teachings of "Sweeden-borg" and "Lord Bacon" and the visualizations reported in the latter part of the volume would have seemed to many nineteenth-century seekers at once liberat-ing and reassuring. Gone were hellfire and damnation. Manifestly present were a Christian discourse of amelioration and love and a free-will teaching anchor-ing personality in moral habit. From one perspective, the rhetorical world of the work echoes the anti-orthodox declamations found everywhere in Davis. In his separate introduction, for example, Judge Edmonds went out of his way to resur-rect numbers from the 1850 national census and to link them to figures regarding the number of professing Christians in the land. The population stood in 1850 at 23,191,918, he declared, and the American Almanac counted but 4,731,639 as Christian—a figure that left 18,460,279 as nonbelievers. Then, in a display of sociological acumen, he analyzed numbers of churches, how many people they held, how often they were filled, and the like, in order to argue that "a vast ma-jority of the population of our country, professing as it did to be a Christian na-tion, were not, to say the least, professed believers in the religion of the day, and perhaps not of any religion." He clearly deplored the divisions between "numer-ous sects," and he affirmed a free investigation of nature without "fear of finding a contradiction between the works and the word of God." Edmonds thought the manifestations were inspired vehicles for assuaging the needs of the unchurched and for creating a harmony that had eluded the churches. Like Davis, too, he understood them to be "the result of human progress" and meant to teach "the grand doctrine of PROGRESSION," even as he read them in terms of electricity, magnetism, and Reichenbach's odic force.[120]

Even with the antichurch rhetoric, the volume exuded a connection to liberal Christianity that is hard to gainsay. The lessons of the spirits, if they detoured around the churches, were repetitive in their insistence on a God of love and on a Christ who was ever available as teacher and way shower. The language of the book was, we might say, friendly to Jesus and gospel teaching. Yet the mes-sage pushed the received gospel in directions that must be acknowledged as thor-oughly metaphysical, prefiguring the formulations that would become part of New Thought teaching, as one case, at the end of the nineteenth century. How else, for example, can we understand this message purported to be delivered by Lord Bacon? "Jesus was a reformer. By him the first true idea of what belonged to man as of himself, and to God as the Creator, was given to the world. Christ taught nothing of himself. He called for no belief that of himself he could accomplish any thing. But he taught that man was a part of God, that in his spirit existed the elements of eternal progression, and that all that was required of him was to believe in God, to love one another, and to develop the powers and faculties with which that God had gifted him." After a brief interval, this Lord Bacon added: "One word I will say in final illustration of my views of the religion Christ taught. It is, that God is love." [121]

The Christian envelope, however, was clearly being discarded in favor of a universalism that repositioned aspects of the "simple religion of Jesus" in order to enter a cosmological stratosphere. Here a lay theology of the absolute was being written into being. God, for example, became distinctly nonlocal in ways that presage the New Age language of the late twentieth and twenty-first centuries. And ever, the message announced humans as minor deities, divinities in the making. Said "Sweedenborg": "God has no locality. His presence fills the whole universe. . . . Say what men may, teach what men may teach, still the soul of man is a part of God himself. It lives for ever, and has lived since ere the morning stars recognized the glory of the Godhead." God had destined the "body of man" to "be the dwelling-place of a portion of himself," he reiterated. [122] There was, it is true, the occasional reference to sin—but in an emerging context that charged it to "error" in ways that hint of a Christian Science to come and a doctrine of progress and gnostic self-redemption already present. Sweedenborg, for instance, cautioned that "a soul here bowed down by error, can not rise ascendingly toward the point of its ultimate and eternal home, until it shall have purged itself by its own efforts of the sin that besets it." Nor did Sweedenborg fail to allude to his planetary knowledge and travels. The spirit spheres that less spiritually advanced mediums had described in the earlier days of the manifestations, he testified, were actually other planets: "Now, I know that spirits do go to other planets. The soul is a COSMOPOLITE AMID THE ETERNITY OF WORLDS. And is it strange that it should select an abiding-place where it can be most happy?" [123]

In or out of that abiding-place, the magnetic metaphor was opening out in directions that underline historian Robert S. Cox's reading of "sympathy" and that also suggest a New Thought and New Age future in which the "energies" of spirit reigned. Lord Bacon, for example, enjoined Edmonds and Dexter to "let the electric bond which connects life with death vibrate with emotions of love, of truth, of good and noble aspirations, and the returning current shall bring back to your consciousness the certainty that you are surrounded by those whose thoughts accord with your thoughts." Sweedenborg apparently agreed—in language that is clearly magnetic and opaquely redolent of "conjugial" love. When a departing spirit passed through the spheres, he averred, it retained earthly connections "intact." Just as a magnet attracted minerals and pointed in one direction, the spirit would "attract those whose feeling and sentiments" accorded with its own on earth and keep them always. Thus, when there were "affections formed on earth," they were neither altered nor changed by death. Rather, "the soul in the spheres" developed "more extensively the love it first recognized on earth" and was "drawn to meet the spirit for whom that love was formed."[124]

One evening in June 1853, after recorded visits by Lord Bacon and Sweedenborg, Edmonds claimed a vision in which a "presiding spirit" spoke. The statement will serve as a summary of the spiritualist faith expressed through the Edmonds-Dexter volume. Bombastic and grandiose it is—but it is also a consistent statement of American metaphysical religion, echoing Hermeticism, conflating Enlightenment categories with Romance, not intrinsically unfriendly to Christianity but still existing in a theological hinterland of the spirit:

> I am that I am. Pervading all space, in every particle of matter, from its merest atom to the soul that lives forever, in the universe of worlds that roll far beyond where the human imagination can reach, the spirit of God exists. He has spoken into being this immensity of worlds. At His command laws were instituted that govern them, and through His ministering spirits those laws are executed. Vast as eternity, limitless as space, omnipotent over all created things, all-wise to design, all-powerful to achieve, God was, and is, and ever shall be. How miserable the conception that limits Him to place! How awful the error that clothes Him with the attributes of weak and unprogressing man! Love is His very existence, and it is as vast, as eternal, and immutable as is His very nature.[125]

Charles Linton's *Healing of the Nations*, sponsored and endorsed by Governor Tallmadge, stayed closer to Christian language. Linton himself, according to Tallmadge's introduction, was a Bucks County, Pennsylvania (near Philadelphia), native, about twenty-six years old as the book was going to press. Tallmadge described him as being "of good natural capacity, of limited education, having only had the advantages of a common district school in Pennsylvania, and that, too, at a time when the common schools of that State were not as far advanced as they now are." Linton did not like school; he worked as a blacksmith, then as a dry-goods clerk, and after that as a bookkeeper for lumber merchants. It was while working for the lumber company that he developed his mediumistic abilities and felt compelled, by spirit instruction, to write a book. So he bought a notebook and transcribed according to purported spirit dictates. From November 1853 to early April 1854, the work went on, with Tallmadge present, he testified, for a large part of it. Here, however, no historical worthies showed up to identify themselves as they spoke. Instead, there came "influence," with its "holy sweetness." Like Davis, Linton insisted that he never consulted books, and more than Davis he conflated the plurality of spirits so characteristic of American spiritualism into one single speaking source that hinted of a direct line to divinity.[126]

"I have never felt but *one* Presence and but one Power," Linton confided, "which is to me as distinct as my own animal feelings." The "one-Presence-one-Power" formula, as a linguistic trope, already suggests a New Thought future. Moreover, the aphoristic nature of Linton's work points clearly toward the New Thought world. Written in succeeding chapters, all of which were divided into numbered verses, or affirmations, the book took shape as a series of platitudes generously supplied with biblical-style language — "giveth," "enjoyeth," "acteth." As the text progressed, Linton moved, Fourier-like, from one occupation or profession to the next, suggesting a harmony of the whole even as he offered spirit instruction for each. "It has truly healed my spirit," he remarked concerning the work in its entirety, "and I may add that one other spirit, as dear unto mine as its own existence, hath found in the words flowing from my pen a balm most healing." This and the allusion to healing in the volume's title again point toward the post–Civil War era of mind cure.[127]

Tallmadge himself saw the Linton material in terms of the larger spiritualist movement, and he read both in biblical terms. He agreed, apparently wholeheartedly, with the protests of those spiritualists who insisted that "the manifestations prove the Bible, and that the Bible proves the manifestations." More than that, while he was willing to accept the instrumentality of electricity and magnetism in rendering the manifestations possible, he wanted to move beyond means to acknowledge "an *intelligence* to direct the force thus applied, which can only be accounted for on the spiritual theory." What was the source of the intelligence so conceived? "In answer it is *mind*," he declared. The trajectory was clear. Magnetism led to spirits, and spirits (prefiguring a New Thought future) meant mind out of the body. This mind was not subject to natural law, according to Tallmadge, but its maker.[128]

"I believe that all the truths necessary for salvation are contained in the Bible," professed Tallmadge. *The Healing of the Nations* reaffirmed and elucidated "the great truths of the Bible" and sustained "the pure doctrines which Christ preached and practiced, instead of the sectarianism established by the creeds of men." But his youthful spiritualist prodigy was receiving a different, more gnostic message. "Man is his own savior, his own redeemer," Linton transcribed. "He is in his own independent circle of existence, which, completed in all its parts, is as perfect as his Father in Heaven; for is not the circle of an atom as perfect as the boundary of the Universe? and is not God the perfect center of all things?"

Still more, there was an antinomian edge to the message: "God created thy spirit from within his own, and surely the Creator of law is above it; the Creator of essences must be above all essence created. And if thou hast what may be, or might be termed laws, they are always subservient unto thy spirit."[129]

That announced, Linton's spirit source was hardly being consistent, and as the text unfolded the traces of a dualism more compatible with orthodox Christianity could be detected. If each person's spirit was "God within . . . manifested," something else also resided in the territory. That was matter. "Man" was "a result of Spirit and Matter," and the residual effects of what traditional Christians would call original sin would not simply go away. "It is a pitiable sight to see an immortal spirit chained, as it were, to a load of error and ignorance, the fruit of unholy seed planted by corrupt passions," Linton's spirit lamented. "Thy mind being the battle-ground in which spirit and matter contend for sway, as the one succeeds, the other must fail." The deified individual of the theology of immanence had vanished, and a new, inferior spectacle stood present instead. "Behold the difference between God and man," the spirit source chastised. "The one gave existence, and therein gave all that could be given; the other, inheritor of this great gift, contracts and concentrates this existence into a thing within its own selfishness gratified!" Still more, the path of passion seemed a headlong descent into a Calvinist hell. "When by Passion the outside man becomes deadened in feeling, the spiritual power is proportionately weakened; and thence the downward course, once entered, is frequently fearfully rapid unto its darkened close." And again: "Every successive erroneous step makes the next step easier." "In the descent, the spirit checks and warns, the reason shows the hideous deformity of the debasing passions; but as the hold slips again and again, the strides become longer and more fearful, until all is extinguished in the last dying resolve!"[130]

Reading Linton's text with its juxtaposed visions, in fact, simultaneously points the twenty-first-century reader in two directions. An orthodox Christian past haunted the spirit declamations like a persistent and stubborn ghost, even as—with his language of mind and of error to be vanquished—something very much like a Christian Science future seems to beckon. "Error hath entered the Household; flesh hath encroached upon Spirit," Linton wrote. "Man was not God. Within his being was the lower creation condensed." "Reason connects spirit with matter," and, then, "they all unite and form Mind, which is but a name for the whole." Meanwhile, the Law of Progression—that byword of Davis's harmonial philosophy—turned out to be, after all, a toiling pilgrim's progress from an old-fashioned religious world. "Cease to love the Earth. Cease to covet the fruits of darkness. Cease to hinder thyself from progressing. Elevate thyself toward Heaven."[131] The healing of the nations, in the end, was the healing of so many selves by means of true moral grit, when passional beings waged their fights against the flesh in the interests of spirit. The entranced and their spirit informants could exhort a generation of séance seekers to go back to their former stations and to begin to climb Jacob's ladder.

In sum, the anti-Christian reputation of spiritualism seems overblown. For all the hostility toward organized sects and churches, the spirit messages were ambiguous—and decidedly combinative. Uncritical to be sure, they mixed and matched past with present—a little orthodoxy could pepper the postuniversalism of the God who was unending love and the humans who were minor divinities in their own right; a mix of Hermeticism, Swedenborgianism, Fourierism, and Transcendentalism could sit well with solicitous Christian spirits. Meanwhile, the democratic ethos of spiritualism meant a new social equality as judge, doctor, governor, and a host of other professionals sat around tables at which, often, uneducated female mediums presided. A sociology of the subaltern was being excavated and explored.

SUBALTERNS IN THE SPIRITLAND

A subaltern, says *Webster's Ninth New Collegiate Dictionary*, is "a person holding a subordinate position." In the vernacular American world that, by the mid-nineteenth century, was experiencing mass engagement with spiritualism, women, blacks, and Indians all counted as subalterns. The record of how, as historical persons *and* as putative spirit visitors, they interacted with the dominant culture exposes long-standing social status designations and their emotive bases. At the same time, in the nonconventional space of spiritualist acclamation and practice, a terrain was created for imagining the social world otherwise and for enacting at least some of the imaginings in ways that led to a more level playing field, if only in the case of metaphysical women, after the Civil War.

From one perspective, women hardly seem to belong among the subalterns if we assume a rough gender balance. More than that, their high visibility in situations of spiritualist practice is noticeable. This is true despite the alternate visibility of the "stars"—the male doctors, lawyers, politicians, and the like—whose names amply graced the pages of the *Banner of Light*, the *Spiritual Telegraph*, and the rest of the spiritualist press. As we shall see, women could, and did, become stars themselves in certain spiritualist venues. Nonetheless, in the context of midcentury society with its Victorian mores and manners, it is to belabor the obvious to suggest that female freedoms were curtailed and their roles circumscribed. The "cult of true womanhood," while perhaps overstated by initial twentieth-century feminist scholarship, and while more rigorously observed in the East and Northeast than elsewhere, still operated as a constraint on a public role for women.[132] Generally speaking, they did count as subalterns.

Among the Shakers, their situation was especially complex. Even before the spiritualist outpouring that began in the late 1830s, the Shaker communities had advanced women ideologically and politically. Mother Ann—as the female manifestation of the divine presence—alongside Holy Mother Wisdom—as the co-equal partner of Heavenly Father—presented an impressive metaphysical foundation on which to erect an erstwhile feminism. Moreover, the continuing presence of women in governance roles did nothing to subvert a female agenda. Still, most Shaker women (and there were many more of them than Shaker men) played out conventional domestic roles in the communities. Even further, women were excluded from early Shaker theological writing, and the principle of feminine leadership was never fully embraced among Believers. In this context, the long spiritualist interlude known as "Mother Ann's Work" may be read as a subaltern struggle to obtain and wield power. There were decidedly more female instruments than male ones, even if the men were often prominent. Nor, from one perspective, did the dominance of women seem wrong. Thus Isaac Newton Youngs in 1838 wrote from New Lebanon that "the peculiar exercises of this manifestation, and the speaking and writing of those sacred messages have been the most abundant among the females. And it appears reasonable that it should be so, when we consider that the second appearing of Christ was in the female, and that this is the second manifestation of Mother Ann."[133]

Yet as Stephen Stein argues, the strong female presence among the instruments, especially as it involved young girls, "provoked the latent hostility of some Shaker males." The central ministry at New Lebanon hastened, in fact, to appoint more male instruments in order to counterbalance the female presence. Perhaps Heavenly Father showed up in visionary episodes in a similar attempt to balance the dramatic comings of Holy Mother Wisdom. Moreover, the tension within Shakerism between female and male instruments was hardly anomalous or idiosyncratic. In his comparative study of female spirit possession, for example, anthropologist I. M. Lewis found women's "possession cults" to be "thinly disguised protest movements directed against the dominant sex." He added that "they thus play a significant part in the sex-war in traditional societies and cultures where women lack more obvious and direct means for forwarding their aims."[134]

When the mass spiritualist movement dawned after 1848, were female mediums similarly engaging in an attempt to upstage their men? It is easy to contend for an affirmative answer. However, this kind of question needs itself to be circumscribed. Whatever the social realities of unequal power and female attempts to equalize or overturn it, the fact remains that most female spiritualists, whether Shakers or mainstream American séance goers, framed their presence and participation first and foremost in religious terms. To be sure, there were some like the flamboyant Victoria Woodhull with her free-love lectures and newspaper, her stock brokerage firm, her feminism and reformist work, and her candidacy, in 1872, for the presidency of the nation. And, as we shall see, there was the feminist reform work that Ann Braude has documented among a series of formerly self-effacing mediums of the 1850s. For the mediums themselves, empowerment came from spirit, and it fell like the sun or the rain on all alike. Reform work followed but did not lead, so that overtly most midcentury spiritualists were first interested in spiritual experience and then, and often later, in contests over social power. Still, from its beginning the mass spiritualist movement presents the first major case in which women became acknowledged leaders in a *religious* milieu. The metaphysical religion of the later nineteenth century and thereafter would continue to valorize the role of women. Indeed, one reason why American metaphysical religion has been understudied and sometimes flatly disdained by scholars has arguably been its strong female presence and leadership.[135]

Who were these women who, as mediums heading the séance tables, were exercising a new style of religious leadership in the United States? R. Laurence Moore several decades ago provided the classic profile, supplying a characterology that still holds in any survey of the midcentury spiritualist world. Surprisingly, Moore found that although mediumship was, in the mid-nineteenth century and thereafter, identified with women, a considerable number of men also lent their services. One survey from 1859 came up with 121 women and 110 men who were mediums.[136] Still, the contemporary nineteenth-century estimate placed mediumship in a feminizing context. There *were*, after all, more female than male mediums, even if the ratios were close; and there was hardly any other public profession in which women could engage. More than that, the profession required no education or formal training, and—with its continuing aura of dubious respectability—there was no social bar for the poor. In fact, from a sociological point of view, mediumship could function as a way out of poverty, an up-and-coming profession for those aspiring for more and better.

From a socioreligious point of view, however, there *were* ordinary prerequisites to the profession: indicators of future mediumistic talent. The same traits that in some premodern societies encouraged the embrace of shamanism could be identified among the urban- and town-centered world of American mediums. Above all, a would-be medium needed a high proportion of passivity in her makeup. She needed to be weak, susceptible to "impressions" and "influences," and very sensitive—someone of a nervous and perhaps melancholic temperament who tended to be pale, cold, and self-effacing. Moreover, as in some traditional societies, mediumship could be preceded by an inaugural illness, a journey into altered consciousness that functioned as a veritable rite of initiation into the world of sacrifice and suffering that attendance on the spirits demanded. The subjective experience of spiritualist mediums was that the spirits chose them rather than vice versa. Spiritualist language reflected this judgment, and in the discourse community of the séance sitters people spoke of so-and-so "being developed as a medium."[137]

Mediums often had endured lonely childhoods in which they first became aware of the presence of spirits, and mediumistic abilities were particularly prone to arise during adolescence. The spirits seemed to prop up fragile personalities, to supply a ballast against the formidable requirements of life. Victorian women, with their whispered voices and equally whispered habits of mind and life, were boosted by the presence of spirits, and this in dramatic ways. Acting through the female mediums, boisterous male spirits who harassed séance sitters with flying objects, like so many missiles, provided quiet revenge for years of passive presence. Loud declamations from the lips of "feeble" women overturned and reversed the statuses that decades of social learning had bequeathed. Supposed intellectual weakness got overturned in spirit speeches by historical greats and worthies who used the bodies of women to proclaim their high-flown messages.[138]

Nowhere was the status and role reversal more the case than among the female trance speakers who traveled to various places on a lecture circuit. Braude has detailed the public lives of these trance speakers, who—with the approval of a large following—violated Victorian mores that forbade women to speak from public platforms. Qualified for their new role by "innocence, ignorance, and youth," these women were, in one way, controlled by the men who called the meetings, presided, and presented them to an admiring public that, Braude estimates, could be counted in the thousands. But in the "abnormal state," women like Emma Hardinge, Cora Hatch, Rosa Amedy, Emily Beebe, Emma Jay Bullene, Lizzie Doten, Anna Henderson, and Achsa Sprague yielded their bodies and beings—in public—to the effluence of spirit. In place of the prankishness of many of the darkened séance rooms, platform trance speakers pronounced inspirational messages, bland and sentimental in the platitudinous style of a popularized Romanticism or Transcendentalism. The spirits had learned universalism and had amply absorbed the language of love, speaking it out through the bodies of young and sexually attractive women whose persons were decidedly part of the message. "Trance speakers were the missionaries of Spiritualism, and their far-reaching itinerancy aided the rapid spread of the movement," Ann Braude summarizes for the 1850s. Their lifestyle also accorded them—like more stay-at-home mediums—opportunities for adventure that otherwise would be barred to them. With the free-love reformist aura hovering over spiritualist heads, mediums sometimes acquired a reputation for sexual looseness that linked them vaguely to one side of Fourierism.[139]

Trance speakers, and other mediums, likewise possessed greater opportunities to gain wealth, or at least a comfortable mode of living—although this should not be overstated. The work was hard and often exhausting. But for those who had come up from poverty, the economies of mediumship from the time of the Fox sisters offered the promise and often the reality of financial improvement. Always, though, the performance aspects of the profession demanded that mediums be able to deliver—consistently, regularly, and effectively. No medium could afford to have the spirits take a night off. Thus, even if they were convinced of the reality of their gifts, mediums—like tricksters in some premodern societies—engaged as necessary in duplicitous means to guarantee success. They were frequently adepts at fraud. "Professional secrets" enabled them to keep on functioning, and as R. Laurence Moore remarks, "practitioners all too commonly found that a reliance on one dishonest prop forced them to keep seeking for others."[140]

By the post–Civil War period, spiritual tricks had become almost standard, as spirits regularly materialized out of specially constructed cabinets and spoke through trumpets to assembled sitters. In a context in which Theosophy was making its way, theories of spirit bodies—made of refined matter—grew more elaborate. The spirit, said spiritualists, lowered its vibratory rate to match the resonance of the medium's body, while her astral (inner) body moved outward from its physical frame. At that point, visiting spirits employed the astral presence as a kind of scaffold upon which to shape "ectoplasm" into a material substrate for the spirit desiring to manifest itself. In a quasi-scientific positivism that would continue to characterize the formulations of metaphysical religion, spiritualists explained the ectoplasm to be composed of refined particles of matter, whitish or grayish in color, and emanating from the medium's nose and ears. When a materialization was over, ectoplasmic matter was retracted into the medium's body almost instantly. Ectoplasm also explained the construction of a "voice box" at the narrow end of the lightweight tube known as a "trumpet" that now appeared regularly in séance rooms. The thought waves of spirits were transformed into sound waves in the presence of the medium, and so the disembodied voices gave out their messages.[141]

Trickery or not, women were functioning, in religious settings, as leaders, and as Ann Braude argues, they were sooner or later functioning as reformers in non-spiritualist contexts (a point to be explored in the next chapter). If fraud was part of the operating system in any shamanistic system, women had learned the trick, and they were employing it in widespread ways, in urbanizing contexts, and as a business proposition. Sincerity and commitment accompanied the fraud in a juxtaposition that exposes the fragility of the metaphysical construct that was spiritualism, its capacities for self-aggrandizement and at the same time its zeal for social reform. Women in the spiritualist movement, through it all, felt empowered by a vision of wholeness and equality that linked the American democratic ethos to a theology of immanence teaching the godliness of all human life.

Among the ranks of women—and men—who claimed spiritualist experience African Americans could be counted. Black Shakers were few, and about their spiritualist activity we know even less. Still, Eldress Molly Goodrich of South Union, Kentucky, in a letter of 1816 alluded to "our family of black people" (a "family," in Shaker parlance, was a living unit of usually unrelated persons within the village) and a "little mulatto child." By the 1870s, when Charles Nordhoff was writing, he noted that in South Union "for many years there was a colored family, with a colored elder, living upon the same terms as the whites" and that there were still "several colored members." We know, too, that the Era of Manifestations did not bypass South Union, and "involuntary exercises" occurred there in 1838 in the spring. Thus we may surmise that the black family was drawn into the spiritualist activity of the time.[142]

The conspicuous case of black Shaker spiritualist involvement, however, is that of Rebecca Cox Jackson (1795–1871). A free black from Philadelphia, Jackson had been early introduced to the African Methodist Episcopal church, and before she ever became a spiritualist she experienced dreams and voices that led her in visionary directions. Against a backdrop of protoholiness religion and perfectionism within antebellum Methodism, Jackson committed to beliefs regarding sanctification—a second spiritual experience after conversion hailed as the work of the Holy Spirit to free the devotee from intentional sin. She had experienced conversion during a severe thunderstorm in mid-summer 1830. Six months later, she underwent what she believed was sanctification and subsequently renounced a sexual relationship with her husband, began preaching, and by 1836 broke with her husband and her brother, an A.M.E. preacher in whose home she had lived for several years. From at least the 1840s she lived and traveled with a close woman friend, Rebecca Perot, although the exact nature of their relationship is unclear. But Jackson had longed for community and "family," and so it was that, searching for a spiritual home, she found the Shakers. She had first met them at Watervliet in 1836 and felt—she later remembered—an ecstatic experience of connection with them. Seven years afterward, when she visited

Watervliet a second time, she again felt strongly attracted. From 1847 to 1851, after a four-year period mostly spent in Philadelphia, Jackson and Perot went to live among the Shakers at Watervliet. Then, convinced by an inner voice that she had, as Shaker David A. Buckingham wrote, "a mission to convert her nation," without the Shaker elders' approval, Jackson—and Perot—left Watervliet again for Philadelphia.[143]

Jackson had dwelled at Watervliet during the time of what Shakers called "Mother Ann's Work." Here Paulina Bates, the eldress whose spirit messages were published in *The Divine Book of Holy and Eternal Wisdom* (and with whom Jackson had a difficult relationship), had been one of the most prominent of the instruments. Already in March 1847, Jackson knew the other major collection of spirit communications among the Shakers—Philemon Stewart's *Holy, Sacred, and Divine Roll and Book* (1843)—and she wrote in her autobiographical reminiscences, "I, Rebecca Cox, do receive it with a thankful heart, knowing it to be His holy word of truth." Jackson herself claimed a spirit communication the following year, when she felt that she had received, probably through an instrument in the community, a message from "Father William," the natural brother of Ann Lee. "The Lord has called thee for a great work to my people, both on earth and in the world of Spirits," she recorded him saying. She testified to a communication to the community from Holy Mother Wisdom in 1849 and the same year to a personal visionary spirit visit by Indians, both American and "East Indians." The following year she was reporting a prayer given to her personally by Ann Lee and confided to her notebook, "I saw our Heavenly Parents look on me and smile, and Mother Ann gave me sweet counsel."[144]

In 1850, Eldress Paulina Bates presented Jackson with a pamphlet on the Rochester rappings. Jackson was immediately sure that the manifestations would come to the Shakers. As it turned out, she was right—and very shortly. She reported that she saw other departed Shaker elders in vision, and she detailed a long interview with her dead brother Joseph Cox in 1851. After Jackson and Perot left Watervliet for Philadelphia to gain blacks for Shakerism, the two took what Jean Humez describes as "a lively interest in séance spiritualism," attending circles and becoming themselves speaking and writing mediums. Jackson enjoined one of the séance sitters in her circle to read the well-know Edmonds-Dexter volume on spiritualism, and she spoke the language of the spiritualist spheres. She beheld the spirit of her former husband, Samuel Jackson, as he repented his sins from the spirit world, and in other ways she exhibited a spiritualist theology that conformed to her Methodist sanctified and Shaker past.[145] Did African American culture render this spiritualism somehow different? Was it inflected in distinctive ways, shaped by spiritual instincts different from those of whites whose spiritualism Jackson shared? It is difficult to answer solely in terms of race. Rather, the distinctiveness of Jackson's spiritualism seems more a function of the combinative background she brought to it—not only her blackness but also her own trance-susceptible nature; the nature of her lived experience with others (conflicts with husband, brother, and Watervliet Shaker elders, but consolation and intimacy from Rebecca Perot); her protoholiness and sanctified Methodist past; and her Shakerism. She signaled thus the plasticity that would continue to characterize post–Civil War metaphysical religion, both in and out of the spiritualist fold.

Meanwhile, white Shaker spiritualists in the Era of Manifestations revealed through their accounts of meetings with spirits the ways in which the world of the black "other" haunted their own. "Africans" and "Hottentots" numbered among those whom they encountered. But, in at least one instance, so did American blacks. Elder James S. Prescott from the North Union, Ohio, village remembered that in 1838 the children there visited different cities in the spirit world, with their guardian angels accompanying them. In a question-and-answer session as they toured, the children asked the angels about the identity of the residents of a place called "The City of Delight." "The colored population," came the response, and —in an elaboration—"those who were once slaves in the United States." Asking who was behind them, the children learned that they were "those who were once slaveholders." In a subsequent dialogue that smacked of the North and its discourse of abolition, the Ohio Shaker children asked their questions and received angelic answers about the spirits. "*Question*—What are they doing here? *Answer*—Serving the slaves, as the slaves served them while in the earth life. God is just; all wrongs have to be righted. *Question*—Who are those in the corner? *Answer*—They are those slaveholders who were unmerciful, and abused their slaves in the world, and are too proud to comply with the conditions. *Question*—What will be done with them? *Answer*—When their time expires they will be taken away and cast out, and will have to suffer until they repent; for all wrongs must be righted, either in the form or among the disembodied spirits, before souls can be happy."[146]

Other encounters with blacks were less sympathetic. Hervey Elkins, the ex-Shaker whom we have met before, recalled "the inspirations of crude and uncivilized spirits" who "were truly ludicrous," as when, among other races and nations, Shaker men acted "precisely the peculiar traits of a Negro." At Watervliet in 1842 and 1843, racism and abolitionism seemed to vie with each other when Africans could be counted among the exotic spirit visitors arriving over a several-week period. One instrument, Sarah Simons, did not like the African spirit presence that she felt was trying to take over her body. Simons "left the table and ran in hopes of getting rid of her, but she soon took possession of the body." The unwelcome black visitor identified herself as Phebe. "She lived in Africa and was related to the royal family. She said she came when she heard the great sound, and had confessed her sins to the natives [Native Americans]. . . . The natives did not like the Africans at all." An instrument named Samuel, taking the side of the blacks, thought that the Indians "ought to be as willing that the Africans should have a privilege as themselves." "There was a good many Africans attended with us," came the report, "and two Hottentots."[147]

For all the higher energies of the spirit world, Shaker spirit visitors reflected the judgments of the Shakers. Caught between their estimates of black inferiority and their northern antislavery sentiments, they fashioned spirits who mimicked themselves. The same was true—especially for estimates of inferiority—in the mass spiritualist movement that spread across the nation in the 1850s. Robert Cox has remarked that relatively few African American spirits showed up at the séances and that "many" of those who came "prattled away in comic dialect, delivering messages that convey anything but abolitionist or egalitarian ideas." A Virginia spirit slave before the Civil War referred to his "dear masters." Another, from Richmond, was confused at his spirit freedom and kept calling to his master for explanation: "Oh, bress de Lor, massa, I'se free, free, free Massa, whar dis place? I never was here, massa. It can't be so—it must be Richmond, massa. Oh, dear massa, I'se fused."[148] In a social version of the theory of correspondence, as on earth, so in heaven. Inequality and subservience persisted in the spirit realm. No revolution of consciousness with regard to race permeated mass spiritualism, and neither would it characterize postbellum metaphysics. In a spiritual orientation that would look to the divinity within and would pronounce humans limitless, the dissonance was harsh and noisy.

Segregation in the spiritland was apparently the norm. Already in 1853 Andrew Jackson Davis offered a cartography of the afterworld that divided the spheres from the second to the seventh into two hemispheres each. "Each hemisphere," he explained, was "divided into six different societies; each being characterized by a *different* race of spirits, ruled by its own affinities, with different habits, in different stages of moral culture." We can guess which race he thought had reached a higher stage. More than that, in the mix of races that characterized the United States, culture apparently rubbed off in only one direction, as Davis relayed in the mid-1860s. Blacks did not "cause the white man to be Africanized, except so far as imitation and temporary association go." The "upshot of it all" was "that the African becomes Caucasianized in his habits, tendencies, and aspirations." Thus on an evolutionary model the "human family" ascended "through the gradual development of the races, to the Caucasian world." Until the ascension came, however, the Summerland of the second sphere was organized according to canons of racial separation. "The ultimates of every race in the Summer-Land establish a community or a world of their own." Indeed, "the Negro, starting from this left side of nature, and the Caucasian from the right, will in the Summer-Land represent two great opposite races."[149]

Cox notes that in the time after the Civil War, distinctions of race grew stronger. One medium of the late nineteenth century whom he cites—S. G. Horn—for example, affirmed that sympathy for one's kind existed throughout the spirit world, and he remarked on gorilla spirits who resonated with "the barbarous tribes of Africa." The segregation continued. Nationality and race, writes Cox, "were singularly resistant to change after death." Thus by 1881 Carrie Twing could observe that "it would be out of place to see the color of an African changed while he still retained the thick lips and flat nose of his nation." Spirits, after all, were "much happier to have their spirit homes with those of their own kind." Even on Mars, according to Annie Cridge and Elizabeth Denton in 1869, four races dwelled in ranked order, with Caucasians, whose skin was a "beautiful *pink*" and whose heads were phrenologically impressive, in the high place. By contrast, an "almost black" race with hairy bodies seemed decidedly inferior, and below them were a small-headed people who were "very dark." They did not live in houses, and Cridge thought they were "the most inferior race of human beings" that she had ever seen.[150]

If black spirits announced what whites wanted to hear, historical blacks themselves claimed contact with spirits of the dead. Within the African American conjuring tradition, as Yvonne P. Chireau has observed, the religious imagination of blacks encompassed "a host of forces that intervened directly in human life and its affairs, including spirits, ghosts, and angelic personalities that were periodically summoned to assist human beings in their endeavors." Still more, as she reports, the "lack of a sharp dichotomy between the sacred and the secular realms led many African Americans to view the spiritual realm as directly impinging on human experience." It is not surprising, therefore, that the mass spiritualism of the 1850s and beyond would resonate with the African American population. With spirit possession part of the West African background and with veneration of ancestors and continuing community attachments to kin after death part of the background, too, American blacks, in general, trod a path parallel to that of séance spiritualism. Ann Braude, however, has summarized evidence that only by the twentieth century did they identify themselves "in large numbers" as spiritualists. For example, it was 1922 before African Americans achieved enough numerical strength to withdraw from the National Spiritualist Association of America and to launch the National Colored Spiritualist Association. Certainly, too, the black Spiritual churches were a twentieth-century phenomenon. But Braude also points to the existence of individual mediums among blacks in the nineteenth century. "Probably," she thinks, blacks "introduced ideas sympathetic to Spiritualism into the white population in the South." One hint to that effect comes from Emma Hardinge's lengthy history of "modern" spiritualism, in which she printed an account that she identified as authored by a "well-known spiritualist and contributor to the *Banner of Light*." The narrative, describing Memphis, Tennessee, in the midst of the Civil War, reported a "great abundance" of blacks in the area who were "virtually free." "The negro character is quite a study to the Spiritualist," the correspondent told readers. "It is so intuitive, inspirational, religious, and altogether mediumistic." The unnamed writer went on to acknowledge the presence among the blacks of "many who see spirits, foretell events and recognize influences." "From the religious training they have received as slaves," the writer added, "they believe their influences all come from God or Jesus direct, although they often see and describe the spirits of their deceased friends."[151]

Hardinge likewise printed an extract from the *Christian Spiritualist* of Macon, Georgia, from 1860 indicating more specifically the presence of black mediums in the South. The excerpt related that there was a "colored girl, who was an excellent physical medium," and she "frequently exhibited the feat of thrusting her hand amongst the blazing pine logs, and removing it after some sixty seconds without the least injury." And there was a New Orleans "negro by the name of Tom Jenkins," who was also "well known for his power of resisting fire." On one occasion (when Hardinge herself was reportedly present), he "became entranced, took off his shoes and stockings, rolled up his pantaloons to his knees, and entered the pine wood fire, literally standing in it as it blazed upon the hearth, long enough to repeat in a solemn and impressive manner the 23d, 24th, and 25th verses of the third chapter of Daniel."[152]

Whatever the local notoriety of these blacks, more prominent African Americans who were involved with spiritualism are difficult to find. One was certainly Sojourner Truth (c. 1797–1883), the freed slave who achieved renown in the North among abolitionists and women's rights advocates with her charismatic speeches for these causes. Born as "Isabella," and never able to read and write, she adopted the name Sojourner Truth after she left domestic service in New York City in 1843 and began itinerating to preach the radical reform gospel. Truth had experienced conversion earlier, with a vision and the voice of Jesus, she testified. Now she felt herself "called in spirit" to "travel east and lecture," exemplifying the revelatory tradition of African America as she followed spirit instruction. By the early 1850s, she had met and formed a friendship with the same Amy Post who had early embraced the spiritualism of the Fox sisters in Roches-

ter. Nell Painter, Sojourner Truth's biographer, has detailed the growing connections with the spiritualist Progressive Friends that brought Truth into the orbit of
séance spiritualism, in a relationship in which, at least initially, their antislavery
work and their demand for women's rights seemed far more important to her
than their spiritualism. In the first séance that she attended, in 1851, according to
Painter, Truth—who went along with Amy Post and another nationally known
feminist, Elizabeth Lukins—"made fun of the proceedings." Nor, with her apocalyptic theology of judgment to come and damnation and hellfire for sinners, did
she seem a likely convert to the universalism that linked spiritualism to its liberal
God of love. Yet by 1857 Sojourner Truth was joining the intentional spiritualist
community called Harmonia that had newly been founded near Battle Creek,
Michigan. In the three years that she spent in the racially mixed community,
she still, according to Painter, "preached revenge against slavers and bigots." At
the same time, she continued to count herself among spiritualists, and as late
as 1868 she spoke at the National Spiritualist Convention. She was also, during
the 1860s, friends with the well-known trance medium Cora Hatch (who by this
time was Cora Daniels).[153]

Even more visible as a spiritualist was Pascal Beverly Randolph (1825–1875),
who would in postbellum times move in a theosophized world as a Rosicrucian
and sex magician. Writing about his own life from the vantage point of 1860 after
he had renounced mass spiritualism, Randolph called himself a "sang melée—
a sort of compound of a variety of bloods." He was not sorry, he said. "With the
great disadvantage of an unpopular complexion, and a very meagre education
to back it, in the early days of what has since become an extended movement,
I embraced Spiritualism; rapidly passed through several stages of mediumship,
and finally settled down as a trance speaker." An apparently difficult and quix-
otic personality, Randolph had grown up on the streets of New York City, the
illegitimate son *perhaps* of William Beverly Randolph, whom the younger Randolph claimed was descended from the elite Randolph family of Virginia. Bap-
tized as a Roman Catholic at eight years of age, he later regretted the step. He
spent some time as a ship's cabin boy, afterward entered the dyeing trade, and
then became a barber in upstate New York. Meanwhile, he had obtained little
formal education, but in a pattern frequent in metaphysical spirituality he taught
and schooled himself with, evidently, noteworthy success. His biographer, John
Patrick Deveney, assesses Randolph's numerous writings as revealing a "better-
than-nodding acquaintance with the authors of the Western occult tradition."[154]

By 1852, Randolph could boast a listing in the *Utica City Directory* in New
York state as a "clairvoyant physician and psycho-phrenologist," and the title
"Doctor" preceded his name. Close in proximity to the birthplace of mass spiri-

tualism, he fell easily into the movement. Randolph was strongly influenced initially by Andrew Jackson Davis and also by spiritualist medium and Universalist minister John Murray Spear (1804–1887). From the first as well, Randolph was regarded as eccentric, known for his mercurial changes in personality—"from ecstatic bliss to extreme despondency"—as one acquaintance put it, and known, too, for his suicidal urges. Still, he was highly visible and successful in his spiritualist work as he traveled, lectured, wrote, and attained stature in the fragile spiritualist organizations of the day. By the time he publicly recanted his spiritualism, in 1858, he claimed to have delivered three thousand speeches and visited several countries. But he told a story of feeling himself possessed, in the mediumistic condition, by a "power" he believed to be "demoniac," and he denounced the free-love search for "spiritual affinities" (true soul, as well as sexual, partners) that pervaded the movement. In a fit of deep despair he had attempted suicide in 1857, and an opportune conversion to Christianity had been a strong part of what saved him. He had experienced enough of "metaphysical moonshine and transcendental twaddle," he announced, and the public confession brought the wrath of the spiritualist community upon him.[155]

We gain a sense of their outrage from Emma Hardinge, who in many ways had been his fellow traveler, as interested in what was becoming the "occult" as he was. We also gain a sense of the racialism that brooded close to the surface of spiritualist rejection.

> It was in the year 1858 that a great jubilee was proclaimed in Boston by the societies of Christendom, who make that city their headquarters, on account of the public "recantation" of an individual known as P. B. Randolph, a Spiritualist and a trance speaker. Randolph, it was acknowledged, had not been very well sustained in his career amongst the Spiritualists, and it was suggested that some of their number neither desired to sustain him nor retain his services in connection with the cause; hence, no very great alarm for its future was experienced when he came out in the form of a "recantation," throwing himself at the same time into the arms of a certain sect of Christians in Boston, by whom he was most cordially received, formally baptized, and greatly patronized and prayed over.[156]

When, in the context of his recantation, Randolph was stage-managed for an appearance at the Boston Melodeon by one Dr. Gardner, Hardinge gossiped on paper about how some thought the doctor was "just then destitute of a sensation, and was glad to accept of anything short of negro minstrelsy."[157] In the scathing irony of Hardinge's characterization, the case of the almost-minstrel Randolph revealed a seamy side to spiritualist radicalism. By displaying bad manners in public, Randolph pushed his companions to show their truth. An incipient American metaphysical religion, despite its ontological theology of immanence, had no practical answer to American racism.

If so, the racism was nowhere more revealed than in the American Indian spirits reported both by Shakers and séance spiritualists. Like so many figures who dwelled in American racialist memory, they trod out of the minds of instruments and mediums and into the lived practice of spiritualist experience, in Shaker meetings and in mass spiritualist séance circles. Whether real spirits came or not, spiritualists themselves often regretted (recall the case of Adin Augustus Ballou) that spirit messages got mixed with the mental material of the mediums through whom they communicated. If spirits came calling, they were forced into wearing heavy disguises. Or perhaps, as they progressed through the spheres in the spiritland, the spirits had still not divested themselves of their role assignments from the first sphere, the earth of Indian-haunted America.

Among the Shakers, native spirits came frequently, teasing out from Shaker sisters and brothers a "wild-child" spirit as they played at Indianness in apparent and racist delight. When, in 1842, the Shakers closed their meetings to the public at New Lebanon, their ministry made the decision just in time, for the community was subsequently inundated with the spirits of natives who wanted to be taken in. The Indian presence spread through the Shaker villages, in which instruments felt themselves possessed by the natives and began to speak their imagined part, enacting the "savage" for other Shaker spectators. Stephen Stein cites, for example, the "translated" songs and related messages that they communicated in a Shaker version of Indian talk. "Chief Contoocook" contributed a song that began, "Me love me hills and mountains. Me love me pleasant groves. Me love to ramble round as me feel as me choose." The staid mature ministry did give visiting spirit Indians a fairly chilly reception, but younger Shakers unencumbered by office were decidedly more exuberant, able to display, as "Indians," what Louis Kern calls "forbidden emotions." Clearly, the "savages" got out of hand, behaving in ways that could not be controlled and prompting a similar response from Believers.[158]

We gain a clearer sense of what, in practice, the boisterous Indian manifestations inspired in the report by an unnamed visitor to the Watervliet community who spent four months with the Shakers in the winter of 1842–1843. In an account recorded by A. J. Macdonald and extracted by John Humphrey Noyes in his *History of American Socialisms*, we learn that at one dance meeting among Believers Mother Ann sent a message through "two angels" to one of the Shaker sisters, announcing that "a tribe of Indians has been round here two days, and want the brothers and sisters to take them in." The angels were also obliging enough to explain that the Indians were "a savage tribe who had all died before Columbus discovered America." The next dancing night brought what Noyes or the Macdonald manuscript termed "Indian orgies." Invited to come in by the presiding Elder, Indian squaws possessed eight or nine of the Shaker sisters, while male Indians took over some six Shaker brothers. Thereupon came "a regular pow-wow, with whooping and yelling and strange antics." "The sisters and brothers squatted down on the floor together, Indian fashion, and the Elders and Eldresses endeavored to keep them asunder, telling the men they must be separated from the squaws, and otherwise instructing them in the rules of Shakerism. Some of the Indians then wanted some 'succotash,' which was soon brought them from the kitchen in two wooden dishes, and placed on the floor; when they commenced eating it with their fingers."[159]

The official church family meeting journal at Watervliet also left Shaker impressions of the visiting Indians, who despite their wildness were "poor natives" and victims, suitable objects of Shaker compassion. A series of squaws had been "killed by the white man," and yet, with angelic gratitude at being "taken in" to confess their sins and to receive the Shaker gospel, they brought their Indian gifts to white Shakers, who obligingly "roasted potatoes, cooked beef, and made succotash" for them. John Wampoo, a "chief from Choctaw," came with a "wigwam filled with love," into which cooperating Shaker brothers placed "those that had not took the Indians in" (that is, had not become possessed by Indian spirits), enabling some of them to receive the Indians.[160]

Meanwhile, "wild Indian tribes" were being sent to Shaker villages in Ohio, New York, and New England by a spirit George Washington and other Revolutionary War eminences who had converted to Shakerism in the spiritland. From the first spirit visits, Indians had been coming to confess and to receive "instruction in the gospel," but now the nation's founders were blessing the endeavor, themselves imbued with Shaker truth. Against the backdrop of the visiting Indian spirits, Edward Deming Andrews remarked the presence "always" of a "curious affinity between the Shakers and the Indians," recounting a series of Shaker traditions connecting Indians to Ann Lee. As he also noted, the Shakers engaged historically in missionary work among Indians in the East as well as the Shawnee in the West. Yet if the Shakers missionized on the dance nights when Indian spirits were welcomed in, they likewise enacted their racialism, played children's games, and expressed a sense of the superiority of their brand of Western Christian culture. Their catharsis may have been good news for their communities but was hardly the same for real or imagined Indians.[161]

The alternate fantasy visitation of the West—the "nobility" of the "savage"— did not escape Shaker sisters and brothers either. In one example, the Prescott account of spirit visitation at the North Union, Ohio, village extracted by Charles Nordhoff recounted a visit by young Shaker boys and girls, as well as adults, to the "Blue City." There, they were told, American Indians dwelled in the first and "most accessible" city they reached. Why was this so? "Because," came the answer, "the Indians lived more in accordance with the law of nature in their earth life, according to their knowledge, and were the most abused class by the whites except the slaves, and many of them now are in advance of the whites in 'spirituality,' and are the most powerful ministering spirits sent forth to minister to those who shall be heirs of salvation."[162]

Instead of "female instruments in uncouth habits, and in imitation of squaws," here we have a blueprint for a late-twentieth- and early-twenty-first-century embrace of Native American "spirituality" by New Age seekers and other metaphysical Americans. But we also have the abiding racialism of culture-as-usual. "Savage" or "sacred," the Indians were "other," and, as other, they continued to visit the Shakers, as Nordhoff found, even after the Civil War. By this time, too, the Indians had long been visiting séance spiritualists in the mass spiritualist movement that swept America at midcentury. Mediums, in fact, spoke strange Indian languages while in trance. In one example from 1854 in Iowa, a new-made medium claimed to be speaking as a Chippewa Indian. Another delivered a lecture, according to the eyewitness account, "on the bad treatment the Indians had received from the white people." Thereafter, both mediums, spoken through by Indians, closed with a "majestic anthem, improvising words first in some Indian dialect, then in the English language, praising God for sending messengers to proclaim glad tidings of great joy to the children of men."[163] Conveniently enough, these Indians reflected the undercurrent of guilt and apotheosis that liberal whites had invested in the image of the Indian other. Indians could be victimized, but like better Christians than the whites, in their savage nobility they sang impressive hymns and overlooked personal oppression, hailing whites as bearers of the gospel to their lands. In so doing, they excised guilt from white consciences.

Especially after the Civil War, the Indians came calling in the séances of white spiritualists. As the hymn singers already suggest, the natives often arrived as healers. They invoked the image of the magical powers of American Indians that, as we have seen, from the seventeenth century had colored white perceptions. Summarizing a wealth of materials from the 1860s and 1870s, Robert Cox notes that, above all, Indians specialized in treating "the social malady of racial animosity." "From Emma Hardinge and James Peebles to Jesse Babcock Ferguson and Fannie Conant," he writes, "Spiritualist mediums and writers drew attention to Indian spirits who, having shed their material bodies, shed with them the confinements of racial antagonism, thereby restoring a harmonious balance between the races." Sometimes the Indians did so by the hegemonic act of spirit control, as the (white) medium surrendered autonomy to a friendly takeover by a native spirit—what Cox calls a "potentially transgressive surrender to the red other" by the white medium. No less renowned a medium than Cora Hatch, for example, had been at times controlled by an Indian girl who identified herself as Shenandoah. Names such as Montezuma, Pocahontas, and Piloho were ascribed to the spirit controls of other mediums, and Emma Hardinge cited Black Hawk (who would later dominate the black Spiritual churches of the twentieth century), Osceola, King Philip, Red Jacket, Logan, and other Indian "'braves'" who functioned as "leaders of spirit bands at circles." She added that "the most wonderful phenomena and shrewd intelligence" had been "exhibited under their influence." Hardinge herself had been, apparently frequently, controlled by a "mighty war spirit" who declared his name to be "Arrow-head the terrible." His "warnings, guidance, and protection" had put her in his debt.[164]

If the act of Indian leadership in the séance circles protected mediums, restoring lost balance and assuaging white guilt, it was also practical in material ways. Hardinge testified both to the ubiquity and the effectiveness of Indian spirit presence, declaring that "nearly every medium" was "attended by one of these beneficent beings, guiding, counselling, protecting them, and using their peculiar knowledge of herbs, plants, and earthly productions, to suggest rare and invaluable medicaments for the cure of disease." "Among the healing mediums," she reiterated, "Indian spirits are ever deemed the most successful of operators." Moreover, as names like Montezuma, Black Hawk, King Philip, Red Jacket, and even Arrow-head the terrible suggest, Indian spirits also worked to deliver strong energies to "toiling mediums." Hardinge noted that "many of the once powerful and renowned chiefs amongst the redmen" attended the séances and there performed "vast feats of physical strength, for which it is alleged their strong magnetic spiritual bodies" were "eminently fitted."[165]

The while, spirit Indians accomplished their tasks for whites as beneficent beings who had unmistakably been conquered by whites. To put this another way, their spirit presence and behavior reflected an afterlife conversion process that transformed "savage" Indians into better Christians than whites—and, in the liberal universalism of the spiritualist world, into more thoroughgoing witnesses to love. At the same time, white guilt and exaltation of departed Indians masked mental acts of domination and conquest in a racialism transmuted into religious terms. Hardinge's own statement exposed the complex dynamics of what was going on. "The [historical] Indian mocks the Christian missionary, by scornfully repudiating the gentle theories of Christianity, and urges the teachings of his forefathers, which deem vengeance for injuries the virtue of the brave," she declared, in language with which her readers would have easily concurred. Then came the inversion: "But no sooner does he become a spirit, than he practically adopts the neglected duties of true Christianity, and by deeds of love and mercy shows the white man how to prove the truth of his creed." "Death," she concluded, was "the angel of transfiguration."[166] So the "savage" Indian had been wiped away after all, succumbing in the spiritland to the religion of white invaders who—even as the invaders, as séance sitters, piously contemplated Indian virtue—were reaping the rewards of Western hegemony.

Still more, the afterworld that the Indians inhabited, as reflected through mediumistic messages, disclosed other landscapes of white fantasy. Natives apparently forgot a history of Anglo-American conquest. Instead, they lived as superior spirits who bestowed on whites, living and dead, only liberal (universalistic) Christian good. Consider, for example, the spirit information received by Mary Theresa Shelhamer. From late 1878, Shelhamer—at the time a message medium for a Boston spiritualist semimonthly called the *Voice of Angels* and later better known for the same at the *Banner of Light*—became the voice of "Spirit Violet." On earth, Spirit Violet had purportedly been Katie Ammidown Kinsey (1856–1877) of Cincinnati, a single woman who died at twenty-one after a short illness and whose father had been a faithful spiritualist. As Sister Violet, she claimed conversion to spiritualism only when she reached the disembodied state. Among the places that Spirit Violet had seen in the spirit world—and, indeed, the last of a series that she carefully described—was "the happy hunting ground of the Indians." It was, she reported, a "fair, peaceful, mountainous country of the spirit world, where the Indian race find a happy home." The Romantic description that followed included references to "green fields," "mellow sunlight," tiny blossoming flowers, and a "deep blue, rolling river" named "Kanalaw, Smiling River." Here, Spirit Violet explained, whites were welcome to visit and a number lived "as teachers to their dusky friends," even though this was "exclusively an Indian country."[167]

The Indians lived in "picturesque wigwams," which stood "white and shining, embroidered with quills, feathers, and silks of every hue, hung with many-colored hangings or curtains of silken texture, and ornamented with natural flowers." All life was "glad," in a countryside dotted with "great lodges"—"schoolhouses" and "council-halls" in which "wise chiefs" guided them. Enveloped in paradisal bliss, the Indians of various tribes "mingle[d] with one another and dwell[ed] in unity." Spirit Violet confided enthusiastically that "no hate, no anger, no fears disturb their minds; they grow in harmony, and gain that strength of mind which they send back to aid and assist the pale-faces through their chosen mediums." The Indian's soul, she said, expanded "in the power of love," and knowledge came "through his intuitive faculties" and "likewise from learned and cultured beings from the higher spheres, who delight to teach the red man, and whom he in turn listens to with reverence and love." Moreover, Indians not only healed people on earth through mediums, but they also healed the dead. Spirit Violet recounted that their spirit home was "a haven of rest to many a poor, weary pale-face" who at death, "uncared for and alone," was taken by "tender spirits" to Indian country to be "cared for by the tender Indian maid."[168]

In the séance rooms of the late nineteenth century, scenes of post-conquest bliss such as this sharpened and focused into a ritual order that Indian spirits were thought to observe. On the basis of contemporary testimony, Robert Cox has pointed to their central and crucial role in materialization séances, where they "abounded," even as Africans, Asians, and other races deemed inferior did not. Meanwhile, the Indian protective function cited by Hardinge apparently grew. As early as 1856, Allen Putnam's published account reported the presence of a band of Indian spirits who welcomed desirable spirit visitors and managed a troubling spirit "Chinaman" who was keeping higher toned spirits away by his loitering behavior. As reports multiplied concerning the proliferation of spirit visitors and their increasingly rowdy and damaging behavior, the role of spirit Gate Keeper developed to guard mediums from unwelcome spirits so that only those with serious roles to play in séances could come in. In the twentieth century, Gate Keepers were American Indian spirits. Similarly, séance sitters received personal guardianship as they made contact, through the medium, with the spirits of the dead, and at least one of their guardians was always an Indian Chief.[169] Beyond that, specific Indian spirits were frequently visible to mediums as guides for individual séance goers. It became a twentieth-century trope to describe the spirit Indians standing behind or beside those seeking guidance through spiritualist mediums. When the long shadow of spiritualism extended into the late-twentieth- and twenty-first-century New Age movement a significant part of the reported metaphysical guidance came through allegedly Indian spirits.

But what of real Indians? Did the séance sitters in Victorian parlors of the nineteenth century and their progeny acknowledge the spirit contact that had been an enduring part of Indian cultures—recorded, as we saw, from the first moments of white contact in the late sixteenth and early seventeenth centuries? Did Indian and white spiritualism overlap? White séance spiritualists, as this narrative has shown, knew about Indian chiefs and all the lore of their exploits to revenge their nations. Surely, too, white séance spiritualists must have known about the most spectacular of Indian mystics and metaphysicians during the nineteenth century and before. They must have heard, for example, of the Seneca visionary Handsome Lake, who from 1799 brought his spirit-directed teachings of "Gaiwiiyo" or the "Good Word" to the defeated Iroquois. More threateningly, they must have known of the vision-inspired prophecies, in the late eighteenth century, of the Delaware Neolin, who called for dissociation from all aspects of European culture and influenced the anti-British revolt of Chief Pontiac in 1762. Or, after 1804, they must have read, in the new West, of the former Shawnee alcoholic Lalawethika, who in trance received revelation, changed his name to Tenskwatawa (the "Open Door"), and taught that whites had been fashioned by a lesser spirit than God, thus justifying their forcible expulsion from ancestral Indian lands. By 1889, when a century of prophetic Indian spiritualism culminated in the Ghost Dance of the prophet Wovoka among the Paiutes and then other Indian nations, séance spiritualists must have been aware of events. Read by fearful and militant whites as active resistance against Euro-American dominance, the dance involved intimate connection and communication with deceased relatives in spirit trances that heartened those living through times of traumatic change.[170]

With all the hordes of friendly Indian spirits at séances, would whites look askance at circles shared with live Indians to call the spirits? To be sure, there is the tantalizing reference in Emma Hardinge's history regarding the "earnest American Spiritualist" who kept current with spiritualist journals, visited every medium in his area, and joined "all the circles held there, whether in garrets, cellars, saloons, halls, steamboats, mines, woods, valleys, Indian wigwams, or amongst the ruins of the 'lost races.'" But the mingled presence of natives and whites talking together with spirits in Indian wigwams, if it existed, was nowhere in evidence in her long account. Hardinge later did note a more segregated Indian spiritualism on the "noble-savage" model. "Many noble and distinguished Indians, both male and female," she asserted, "claim to see and hold converse with the spirits of departed friends and kindred; and the faith in immortality, and the presence and ministry of ancestral spirits as guardians to mortals, might well put to shame the cold and unfaithful materialism, even of many professing churchmen."[171]

Even this Romantic vision, however, blurred before Hardinge's narrative was complete. There was, she confided to readers, "another view of Indian spiritualism, and a darker side to the picture." In this "wider field of Indian Spiritualism" lurked "beings of an unknown and doubtful character, and mixed up with rites and phenomena of a strange, occult, and repulsive character." What followed were contemporary reports that Hardinge had gleaned from a variety of print sources. These were accounts of Indian quasi-shamanistic behavior, revisiting familiar themes regarding Indians' adoption of animal personae and their wild gestures and sounds in the trance state. Tents shook, mysterious beings howled and yelped, disembodied voices were heard, potent charms were created, and frightful animal beings presented themselves to be guardian spirits to one famous clairvoyant who was consulted even by whites. Hardinge could not explain these episodes, acknowledging a superior access by native peoples to "a knowledge which all our control over the elements fails to compete with." Where did "the clue to these mysteries" lie? Hardinge found no analogue in the annals of "modern" spiritualism. After a foray into comparison with Asian and other spiritualist forms, Hardinge was still haunted by origin questions regarding American Indian spirit manifestations. "The clairvoyant faculties, prescient powers, and general results obtained through their Spiritualism correspond closely with that of their civilized neighbors," she concluded, "but the modes of invocation differ essentially, and the characteristics which seem to mark the communicating intelligences are equally repulsive and incomprehensible to the American Spiritualist." She wondered if the "intelligences" were "a race of beings hovering on the precincts of a sub-mundane sphere" or if Indian spiritualists were communicating with "undeveloped human spirits." But in the end she had no answers.[172]

If Hardinge had no ontological or theological answers, historians have no cultural answers to the degree and extent of Native American influence on white spiritualism, but surely the Indian model was there, and it did not go unnoticed. American metaphysical spirituality grew on soil in which a broadly Hermetic European esotericism had been planted. But the abiding presence of blacks and Indians would not go away. In the combinative milieu of a democratic American terrain, esotericism dissolved, and new hybrid growths everywhere sprang up. By the 1870s, the new growths—reformations and reconstitutions of mid-century and later spiritualism—carried forward the search for correspondences and acts of heightened mind and imagination, the open yearning for the influx of saving spirit energy and anxieties over healing. The new growths were taking shape as identifiable forms of American metaphysical religion.

Part Three

ARRIVALS

5

SPIRITS REFORMED AND RECONSTITUTED

Among the numerous communications that *Banner of Light* medium Mary Theresa Shelhamer reportedly received from Spirit Violet about the afterworld came one describing the "beautiful city" Zencollia. Amid its "spires and towers" stood a building designated the "temple of learning," which Spirit Violet called the "most massive building" she had ever seen. The temple included "four spacious halls," the third of which—after "Science" and "Literature"—was dedicated to "Metaphysics." Spirit Violet had visited it in company with a companion spirit, discovering there a female speaker. "The ideas she expressed were grand and beautiful," Spirit Violet acknowledged, but she also confessed that "the language with which they were clothed was almost too abstruse for me." The accompanying spirit thought that Violet was still "too familiar" with earthly discourse to understand the spirit metaphysician. But she did explain—before Ralph Waldo Emerson's death in 1882—that "Emerson will delight to frequent this place when he comes over to our side of life." There were also "scores of other places" for "such teachers as Theodore Parker, Channing, and hundreds of like noble souls," who would be occupied in "earnest utterance for the lifting up and sanctification of the people."[1]

Clearly, for Shelhamer and her spirit friends in the 1880s, metaphysics meant Transcendentalists and their kind—engaged in a higher calling that was somewhat obscure and somewhat intimidating. Yet it was eminently worthy since it was for the benefit and blessing of ordinary people. The purified atmosphere of the Hall of Metaphysics seemed a far cry from the reported excesses and vaudeville antics of the spirits who came calling in many of the séance rooms. If the air remained a little dry in the Hall of Metaphysics, the spirits themselves apparently honored it and thoroughly recognized its worth. By the post–Civil War period, a number of Americans on the earthly side of the divide were also beginning to prefer the purer, drier air of a more detached metaphysics. The heirs and progeny, perhaps, of the harmonialism of Andrew Jackson Davis, they parsed their metaphysics differently from Spirit Violet, including in it much more than Transcendentalist-style discourse. Still, many of them looked to the Transcendentalists as founders of their tribe. More than that, the emergent metaphysicians carried the reform spirit championed by Davis and other harmonialists into new expressions. The reform began, first, in a spiritualism that looked to the world and saw, in numerous intellectual and social sites, an overwhelming need and demand for change. Reform became synonymous with "progress," the great buzzword of the age, and progress came through "science." Meanwhile, science was an enterprise in which spiritualists delighted since they regarded their own spirit communications as its cutting edge. Reform came also, and most of all, through the transformation of social life as, among other things, slavery and the oppression of women fell away. A new era of equality and justice was dawning that would also be an era of social tranquility and love.

At a certain point, however, the reform spirit turned inward to what constituted spiritualism itself, and spiritualists began to part company with their former practice and to turn to new venues and concerns. We have already seen the beginnings of the process in the flamboyant Pascal Beverly Randolph who moved noisily out of the spiritualist fold and on to other metaphysical pastures. By the 1870s and 1880s he had plenty of company. Individuals as diverse as Madame Helena Blavatsky and Henry Steel Olcott (who founded the Theosophical Society), Phineas Parkhurst Quimby and Warren Felt Evans (who pointed the way toward New Thought), and Mary Baker Eddy (who established Christian Science) moved past a spiritualism that they knew at least partially and felt they understood. These reformers turned instead to what they considered more sophisticated expressions of their metaphysical inclinations, and in so doing they turned in essentially two directions. All of them harvested the ambience of the world of spirits in works of directed imagination. For some the work continued in material symbols—like Renaissance magicians or later Continental and English practitioners—in a new, mostly Anglo-American, form of "angel-summoning" that became, properly speaking, the occult. For others the work went forward mostly on a mental plane, although they expected that its effects would not remain there. Among this second group, some aimed consciously to banish matter in an exercise of denial that both diminished and exalted the physical. They invoked divine "Principle" or "Truth" to master a sin-filled, mortal body and to bestow upon the chastened physical self the goods of a kingdom of health and well-being. Still others found the ingredients for Self-transformation in a "Spirit" immanent in matter, so that—like the Hermeticists of old and the worldwide spiritual teachers they admired—they could be as gods, identified with a power of "Good" that kept on giving.

Along a spectrum from occultism to mind cure and the transformation of the Self, we can spot the familiar signature of correspondence, the drawing down of energies of Mind and Spirit, and the strong intent to heal. In the terms of this narrative, too, we can watch the easy glide from a (material) magic resonating, however unconventionally, with the magical practice of a past Hermeticism to a newer, mental magic characterizing Christian Science and New Thought. Here a simpler work of mind and imagination prevailed; and the esoteric turned—as in spiritualism—exoteric. The new metaphysical religion that flowered in these expressions and related ones, however, began with the reform principle that so much preoccupied the spiritualists.

PROGRESS, SCIENCE, AND REFORM AMONG THE SPIRIT-SEEKERS

From the time of the early manifestations of mass spiritualism in the 1840s, the so-called "Law of Progression" reigned unchallenged among believers and their spirit visitors. One way to explain the connection could be in terms of happenstance. The early alliance of the Fox sisters with Isaac and Amy Post and their formerly Hicksite radical Quaker associates began a train of associations in which reform functioned centrally and spiritualism became but one expression of the grand principle of progress. Similarly, for the men and women who turned, with Andrew Jackson Davis, to harmonialism, Fourierist enthusiasm guaranteed that ideas about reform and progress would be uppermost. No doubt happenstance was involved here, too, but once Davis elaborated his spiritualist cosmology the Law of Progression stood at the heart of the spiritualist vision. It became, in effect, the core principle of a spiritualist theology that refused to go away even in the face of a small army of defrauding mediums and their disruptive spirit companions.

Davis had begun the turn to progress as early as the trance productions that were published as *The Principles of Nature* (1847). There, as we have seen, he revised the received Swedenborgian account of the afterworld. Its three hells were transmuted into the lower three spheres of the spirit abode, beginning with the closest to earth, which came to be called the Summerland, and continuing with the former Swedenborgian heavens, which now became the outer spheres. For Davis, in accord with his planetary travels, there were other earths beside this one, but "all earths and their inhabitants" constituted the first sphere. When inhabitants died and left it, they *progressed* through succeeding spheres, so that the eternity he and other spiritualists envisioned meant pilgrimage through landscapes of ever-increasing perfection rather than eternal rest. Meanwhile, on earth, it was already incumbent on inhabitants to refine and perfect their minds. When this was "properly accomplished," the "social world" would be "correspondingly elevated, and thus be advanced to honor, goodness, and UNIVERSAL PEACE."[2]

But this was not all. As Davis's grand vision developed, he began to explain that when all spirits reached the second sphere, the "various earths and planets" would be "depopulated," and only Spirit would remain. The spirits would not stay there, however, but would continue to progress to the sixth sphere, arriving "as near the great Positive Mind as spirits can ever locally or physically approach." (Davis's spirits, remember, were highly refined matter and thus retained a certain physicality.) When all the spirits had come to the sixth sphere and "not a single atom of life" was "wandering from home in the fields and forests of immensity," the Deity contracted inward, and the "boundless vortex" was "convulsed with a new manifestation of Motion . . . passing to and from center to circumference, like mighty tides of Infinite Power." The cataclysmic contraction, in turn, brought the "law of Association or *gravitation*" to bear, so that "new suns, new planets, and new earths" appeared. Once again, the "law of progression or *refinement*" could be applied, and so could the "law of Development." Thus God created "a new Universe" and opened "new spheres of spiritual existences." "These spheres," Davis prophesied, "will be *as much* superior to the present unspeakable glories of the sixth sphere, as the *sixth* sphere is *now* above the *second* sphere; because the *highest* sphere in the *present* order of the Universe will constitute the *second* sphere in the *new* order which is to be developed." And, we may surmise, the process would continue through countless eons of earth time in a vision not unlike that of the yugas, or great years, in a vastly expansive Hindu theology that Helena Blavatsky would later invoke (see the next chapter). Davis clinched his case with the observation that the spirit would have "no 'final home,'" since "to an immortal being, *rest* would be intolerable," "next to annihilation," and worse than "the miseries of the fabled hell." "The spirit," he proclaimed, "will progress eternally!"[3]

Davis's pronouncements found echoes seemingly everywhere within the huge spiritualist community, and revered texts reiterated for their readers the canonicity of the Law of Progression. Judge Edmonds, for example, found space in his well-known work to hail the "grand doctrine of PROGRESSION, whereby we learn that as the soul of man is an emanation from the germ of the great First Cause, so its destiny is to return toward the source whence it sprang." His co-author and medium George Dexter, the doctor, left no doubts that he agreed. After his own account of spirit visits, he proclaimed as grandly, "I see *progress* stamped on every aspiration of the human mind, as it is on every part of God's universe—progress from the animal to the intellectual—from the material to the spiritual, and bestowed on the spirit . . . as the highest boon of its Almighty Creator." And in his introduction to Charles Linton's *Healing of the Nations*, Nathaniel Tallmadge was as effusive. "The great doctrine derived from spiritual communications," he testified, "is that of everlasting PROGRESSION." In his reading, too, not only did nature teach the doctrine, but it was also eminently biblical. "The Bible teaches Progression," he affirmed, and it showed "different gradations of the progressed and progressing spirit to that of the spirit of the just man made perfect."[4]

Summarizing the beliefs of mid-nineteenth-century spiritualists, R. Laurence Moore pointed to four unwavering "principles." Spiritualists rejected supernaturalism, hailed natural law as inviolable, put their premium on external occurrences rather than inward states, and saw knowledge as progressively developing and unfolding.[5] Arguably, the last of these subsumed the first three, since the séance sitters of the era saw their practice as the living demonstration of natural and scientific process. Moreover, the process was neither secret nor "occult" but —as they saw it—clearly visible and testable for right-minded, rational observers. That they, the séance sitters, had broken from centuries of superstition and mystification was paramount evidence of the law of progression and their own place at the very edge of its unfoldment. Indeed, spiritualist practice represented the prior reform of knowledge now being corroborated in the reform of life and society.

Moore, in fact, identifies the "rhetoric of denial" that spiritualists, at least by the 1870s, employed in their rejection of their ancestry. "Spiritualist publications in the last quarter of the nineteenth century," he says, "systematically repudiated black magic, white magic, Rosicrucianism, and Cabalism. They further attacked the 'musty tomes' of such individuals as Paracelsus, Cornelius Agrippa, Raymond Tully, Nostradamus, Albertus Magnus, Eugenius Philalithes, Girolamo Cardano, Robert Fludd, and Éliphas Lévi." Hermeticism, decidedly, was out, as spiritualists reformed esotericism. Ironically, among the first wave of reformers of spiritualism would be the Theosophists, who self-consciously embraced the "occult" in a global version. Spiritualists themselves, however, were livid in their declamations against "crude speculations," "spurious philosophies," and "pseudoscience."[6] And if Hermeticism was out, true science, spiritualist science, was in.

With "science" as their second buzzword alongside "progress," spiritualists used the term in various ways that were ambiguous and also sometimes contradictory. They thought that spiritualism itself was scientific, that it followed certain universal laws and represented a sure body of knowledge. We have already seen the eagerness with which those in the séance circles embraced mesmerism, phrenomagnetism, electricity, odic force, and the like to explain the spirits. The notion of spirit matter itself was not unlike the vaguely formulated concept of the "ether" that pervaded the conventional science of the period. And when the purported spirit raps were first sorted, with spirit cooperation, into alphabetical letters and, thus, verbal communication, the language of the "spiritual telegraph" was immediately born—only four years after the famous Morse wire of 1844. Work with the spiritual telegraph, spiritualists insisted, was repeatable— like a science. Moreover, even as they sought to open the secrets of ancient Hermetic wisdom to the bright light of day, their ambivalence toward the Hermetic past was clear: Overlying their Hermes was a positivism that expressed itself in frequent preoccupation with demonstration and empirical testing. As Ann Braude observes, it was the "interpretations of investigators," rather than séance manifestations by themselves, that "provided the content of the new religion."[7]

Spiritualist positivism became a game of challenge played with anyone bearing proper scientific credentials. And believers did get noticed. Ernest Isaacs wrote that "at first as curious individuals, later in groups and commissions, still later in research societies," scientists paid attention, even if most were "repelled by the purported messages of spirits and the actions of mediums." For the Fox sisters scientific investigation turned into a daytime nightmare. By 1851, after their spectacular sojourn in New York City, Margaret and Leah Fox visited Buffalo and became the subject of an investigation by three faculty members from the School of Medicine at the university there. Writing in the Buffalo *Commercial Advertiser*, the trio announced that it was by skeletal manipulation that the notorious raps were produced. Dislocated knee joints, not dislocated spirits, had caused the noises. When Leah Fox responded with a heated challenge to the professors, the examination grew more serious and extensive. The sisters were intimidated; there were tears and very few raps; and the doctors held publicly to their theory—although they owned that they could not find the "precise mechanism" that triggered the knee-joint dislocations.[8]

If respected scientists disdained the spirits, spiritualists themselves continued to display their own version of scientific positivism. Representative of widespread spiritualist attitudes, for example, was the memorial that Nathaniel Tallmadge persuaded General James Shields to present to the United States Senate on behalf of Tallmadge himself and 13,000 others. With Samuel B. Brittan involved in its composition, according to Tallmadge, the memorial requested that Congress appoint a commission of scientists for the purpose of investigating "Spiritual Manifestations." Invoking evidence of an "occult force" that could disturb "numerous ponderable bodies," of unexplained lights in dark rooms, of ubiquitous rappings and other sounds as from musical instruments, and of the entranced states of some in the presence of the "mysterious agency," the petitioners sought congressional aid. They believed, they declared, "that the process of Science and the true interests of mankind will be greatly promoted by the proposed investigation."[9] The fact that Congress tabled the memorial suggests that many in high places, like most in the scientific community, remained unconvinced. Spiritualists, however, liked to point to the convicted. Just as Judge Edmonds and Governor and ex-Senator Tallmadge epitomized those involved in public and political life who had been persuaded, the chemist Robert Hare (1781–1858) was regularly exhibited as the converted scientist. From 1819 to 1847 a professor of chemistry at the medical college of the University of Pennsylvania, Hare engaged in important work on salts and produced novel inventions such as an oxyhydrogen blowpipe and an electric furnace. His articles appeared frequently in the *American Journal of Science*, and in 1839 the Rumford Medal of the American Academy of Arts and Sciences had been awarded him. By 1852, however, well after his retirement from the university and his election as a lifetime member of the Smithsonian Institution, Hare turned his investigative skills to spiritualist phenomena.

His interest had begun innocently enough, when he was invited to a séance circle in an affluent Philadelphia home and heard the familiar rappings. Puzzled and intrigued, he tried to find their source in this and other circles, to no avail. He could not accept the conclusion that *all* of the mediums were frauds, but neither could he by conventional means explain the raps. Hence Hare constructed what he would call a "spiritoscope" to pursue his investigation. A disk with a random alphabet inscribed on it, an arrow that could point to one of the alphabet letters, and a rod passing through it and connecting it to the séance table, Hare's instrument had pulleys and weights attached so that it would turn should the table move. A screen separated it from the medium, assuring that it could not be directly seen as Hare questioned her and the disk, correspondingly, revolved and so spelled out answers to the questions asked. Rejecting electrical theories to explain the movement and also similar postulates such as Reichenbach's odic force and an argument regarding mechanical pressure by British scientist Michael Faraday, he became convinced that his device—built to debunk spiritualist explanations—proved them instead. The spirits were real and were visiting.[10]

As he continued his investigative pursuits, Hare built several versions of his spiritoscope. In so doing, he embodied in his rational positivism and empirical meticulousness the requirements for the Baconian scientist so much in vogue during his nineteenth-century time (recall the spirit of Lord Bacon whom John Edmonds and George Dexter hailed as their frequent visitor). It had taken Hare a good three months to arrive at his conclusions, he told readers in his first-person *Experimental Investigation of the Spirit Manifestations* (1855). "I did not yield the ground undisputed, and was vanquished only by the facts and reasons which, when understood or admitted, must produce in others the conviction which they created in me." His publishers were not difficult to persuade. Partridge and Brittan were none other than the well-known spiritualists Charles Partridge and Samuel B. Brittan, whom we have met before. Hare's publication overnight guaranteed his celebrity in the spiritualist community, even as it also accorded him a dubious status among his scientific colleagues then and critics thereafter. For example, historian R. Laurence Moore, reflecting a common opinion, judges that Hare "demonstrated the mental infirmities of advanced age when he turned to spiritualism." Moore observes that even the erstwhile scientist's spiritualist publishers found him "extremely difficult to handle"; they complained that in letters to the periodical *Spiritual Telegraph* Hare failed to address the scientific dimensions of spiritualist phenomena. Still, his procedural rigor needs to be noticed. If—with Edmonds, Dexter, and Tallmadge—he made the leap of faith that rendered criticism obsolete beyond a certain point, he worked to arrive at the point by using methods similar to those that he had employed in his earlier scientific studies.[11]

Hare, despite the chagrin of his former colleagues, continued to see himself as a scientist among scientists. In fact, one of the strongest reasons he was drawn to the spirits was that he believed them to be sources of advanced knowledge—well beyond what he and other earthbound mortals had discovered on their own. In both 1854 and 1855, he brought his spiritualist research to the American Association for the Advancement of Science, permitted to read his paper out of deference to his age and long scientific career in the first case and omitted from the program in the second because of his subject. Significantly, his 1854 paper did not appear in the proceedings of the association. More to the point here, in their elation at the presence of Hare in their midst, the spiritualist community was announcing in the strongest of terms how important scientifically proven spirits remained to spiritualist self-understanding. Samuel B. Brittan began a promotional campaign, drafting Hare himself to lecture and exhibit his spiritoscope in New York City to a crowded, standing audience of more than three thousand. In a lecture that must have been memorable, the Baconian gave way to the believer, and Hare testified to the theology of progress in the seven spheres, six of them beyond the earth—those "*concentric bands surrounding the earth,* commencing sixty miles above this earth and reaching out for one hundred and twenty miles." The positivism was unmitigating, even as the aging scientist confessed the truth of life in the seventh sphere to which all mortals should aspire.[12]

For Hare and other spiritualists, seventh-sphere life represented their horizon of aspiration toward the reformed life, the millennial goal they longingly sought.

Hence the third shibboleth of this spiritualist universe of perpetual improvement was reform. Spiritualist preoccupation with reform came with its roots, both through Andrew Jackson Davis and through the Fox sisters and other séance spiritualists. For Davis, Fourierism had formed the basis for the practical application of his grand spiritualist vision in his *Principles of Nature,* and he continued throughout his professional career to provide a role model of the spiritualist who was also and preeminently a reformer. Campaigning for the reform of marriage and divorce law and for equal rights for women, Davis worked to instantiate his vision of eternal progress here on earth. He also wrote toward the same end, and his five-volume *Great Harmonia* was predicated on a Fourierist scheme.[13] Meanwhile, the Quaker ambience in which early mass spiritualism flourished guaranteed its alliance with reform activism from the first. By 1859, for example, well-known abolitionist Gerrit Smith—who also affirmed the reality of spirit communication—could comment on the dual identity of other reformer-spiritualists, assessing that "in proportion to their numbers, Spiritualists cast tenfold as many votes for the Abolition and Temperance tickets, as did others." Nearly all of the well-known abolitionists believed in the spirit manifestations, and so did a series of other reformers. As R. Laurence Moore has summarized the antebellum situation, those who counted themselves spiritualists "gained their most influential defenders from men and women who managed to support the rappers with the same enthusiasm they supported Fourierism, temperance, antislavery, health reform, and women's rights."[14]

In the specific case of women's rights, Ann Braude has demonstrated that spiritualism provided the training ground for later reform activism. A cadre of well-known female trance speakers learned to deliver messages in public as mouthpieces for purported spirits and then moved on in later years to speak publicly in their own name and for the causes about which they themselves passionately cared. "Woman suffrage benefited more than any other movement from the self-confidence women gained in Spiritualism," Braude writes. When the suffrage campaign took off in the post–Civil War period, spiritualist women were there to support it. In the California of 1870, for example, Braude found that of the nine women identified as holding suffrage meetings only one could not be linked to spiritualism, while six were listed as lecturers in the *Banner of Light.* On the basis of what she discovered in the spiritualist and reform communities, Braude argues for the role of spiritualism in giving voice to a "crucial generation" of American women. By the postbellum time, an earlier millennialism and insistence on instant societal perfection—with the spirits as prophetic messengers of an imminent new age—had given way to a social gradualism influenced by notions derived from the Darwinian concept of evolution. With social improvement coming slowly and not all at once, spiritualists dug in during the 1870s and 1880s, supporting the cause of equal rights for women and other crusades as varied as American Indian rights, prison reform and an end to capital punishment, and the rights of labor.[15]

An intrinsic connection between reform practice and spiritualist cosmology reflected in the writings of Andrew Jackson Davis and other key spiritualists meant that, from the mid-nineteenth century, the alliance of spiritualists and reformers was hardly coincidental. The spiritualism built on a theology of eternal progress could hardly fail to desire the early implementation of unending betterment in the first sphere—the sphere of earth. R. Laurence Moore has, it is true, raised provocative questions about estimating spiritualist reform activism too highly, since by the early twentieth century both practically and substantively the spiritualist connection with social reform was, in effect, dead.[16] Indeed, the evidence for the grand fizzle of spiritualist hopes and dreams for social reform is hard to avoid in the period when the nineteenth century became the twentieth. The flamboyant spiritualism of the 1850s, which had enjoyed a noticeable resurgence in the 1880s, gave way to a spate of fragile organizations and sedate renditions of spiritualism that were themselves so many ghosts of the formerly vibrant movement.

Besides, judgments about a substantive connection between spiritualism and reform need to be probed more. Visions of progress in the heavenly spheres existed side by side with a spiritualist theology of sinlessness. The God that spiritualists honored was not a God of vengeance, nor did he preside over an earth in which evil held out as a concrete reality. "If there exists an Evil principle, would not that principle be an integral element in the constitution of the Divine Mind?" Davis had asked rhetorically. "God is *all-in-all.* . . . There is no principle, antagonistic to God; no empire at war with Heaven!"[17] Instead, the God of love welcomed a prepared people who were already innately good and, with free will and the spirits to guide them, getting better all the time. The moral progress of the human soul was, in such a universe, inevitable—all spirits, remember, would at some point, arrive at the second sphere and then go on to the sixth—which would then implode and be reconstituted as a new universe to be progressed through. What, then, was a reformer to do? How or why was a reformer, after all, necessary? Coupled with social Darwinian ideas of gradual amelioration, spiritualist reform principles possessed, seemingly, little intellectual ballast. Why rush to make the good better when, at its own pace, it would all get better anyway?[18]

Still, the long light of millennialism tempered the determinist implications of the cosmology. Even if the excitement of arriving spirits could not be maintained as the decade of the 1850s gave way to more troubled Civil War times and then an era of fraud and excess in a vaudeville of the spirits, the literature of the older movement had shaped the minds of leaders. So had a history of reform associations among spiritualists. Hence a linked spiritualist-reform ideology continued to operate even as its foundations began to crumble. The heirs to the reform legacy would become those who, as we shall see, would reform spiritualism itself. In the meantime, for a movement predicated on the widespread individualism of small-time religious entrepreneurs and their informal followings, spiritualism displayed a surprising quest for—not solitary talks with spirits—but encompassing communities. Bret Carroll has pointed to the séance circles as incipient communities, even as he has noticed the communal republican yearnings of spiritualists themselves, epitomized in Andrew Jackson Davis's vision of a republic of spirit.[19] The Fourierist underpinnings of spiritualism, of course, represent a utopian ideal of community writ large in social relations. Likewise, the repeated spiritualist depictions of life in the heavenly spheres always show existence there as social—organized ubiquitously in cities and institutions and social processes. Mary Theresa Shelhamer's Spirit Violet and her accounts of spirit life were not exceptional.

More than that, beyond the *dreams* of Fourierist community—as evinced, for example, in the entire third section of Davis's *Principles of Nature*,[20] intentional community life often encouraged spiritualism, even as spiritualist practice generated community. For the former, George Ripley's Brook Farm and Adin Ballou's Hopedale Community were cases in point. In the era before mass spiritualism, so were the Shaker communities of the Northeast and Midwest. In the spiritualist heyday of the 1850s, communitarians such as Robert Owen, Robert Dale Owen, and—with free-love reputations—Josiah Warren, Mary Gove Nichols, and Stephen Pearl Andrews were all hospitable to spiritualism. And by the 1870s, John Humphrey Noyes's Oneida Community of Perfectionists in upstate New York provided still another instance. Indeed, Noyes himself owned that spiritualist practice was, as Maren Lockwood Carden summarized, "consistent with his lifelong teaching about the possibility of communication with members of the primitive church."[21]

Beyond these, spiritualists formed self-conscious communities in which the theology of spiritualism could take tangible form. The earliest, on the site of the failed Clermont Phalanx in Ohio, began in 1847 through the efforts of John O. Wattles, a Fourierist converted to spiritualism, but lasted only nineteen months. By 1851, Andrew Jackson Davis was at least considering plans for a "Harmonial Brotherhood," while more concretely, the Harmonia near Battle Creek, Michigan, in which Sojourner Truth dwelled for a time from 1857, existed as a spiritualist commune. Meanwhile, in western New York state, near Kiantone Creek on

the border of Pennsylvania, John Murray Spear had established his own Harmonia Community. Located close to a muddy mineral spring that, it was claimed,
the spirits had revealed for its healing powers, the community began at Spear's
(spirit) direction with a charter for the "City of Harmonia." The government
would be one of "love with innocence as its only protector," and it would exalt
the sovereignty of each individual member. Crime was a disease that was treat-
able; marriage was a union easily entered and left, in a sexuality of mutual consent; equality between the sexes was mandatory; and private real estate holdings
were to be replaced by octagonal houses as promoted by Lorenzo Fowler, one of
the fabled phrenological Fowlers of the period (see the previous chapter). Spear
built Harmonia on a site claimed (by the spirits, he said) to be a prehistoric city
of utopian proportions. Now it would be the place where his spirit-inspired perpetual motion machine called the New Motive Power—already the subject of
a failed experiment—might flourish again because of the "peculiarly favorable
electrical emanations" of the site. But fortune did not smile. Spear spent twenty
thousand dollars—a gift to him by an area businessman—to dig for the buried
city without success, even as his New Motive Power after being brought to New
York was trashed by an unfriendly mob. Although Harmonia hosted a National
Spiritualist Convention in 1858 and promoted an expedition to New Orleans in
1859 and 1860, the community succumbed in 1863, a victim of financial losses,
internal divisiveness, and outward opposition to its sexual permissiveness.[22]

The most noticed spiritualist community, however, flourished for a time at
Mountain Cove, in western Virginia (now West Virginia), after beginnings in
Auburn, New York, a site of early spiritualist excitement connected with the Fox
sisters in 1848 and 1849. The Auburn Circle there, under the mediumship of Ann
Benedict, believed itself to be visited by spirit communications from Apostles and
Prophets, among them Paul the Apostle, who through Benedict called the minister of the Seventh Day Baptist Church in Brooklyn, New York, to Auburn. The
Reverend James L. Scott arrived as directed, and then—also called by the Apostle
—Thomas Lake Harris (1823–1906) joined him as the so-called Apostolic movement grew. Harris, a follower of Andrew Jackson Davis and his harmonialism,
had already been dubbed the "Poet" within the group that edited and promoted
the *Univercoelum*, the early spiritualist paper published by Samuel B. Brittan. A
former Universalist minister, like so many others within spiritualist ranks, he was
speedily outgrowing Davis. By early 1851, Scott and Harris had launched a (spirit)
newspaper of their own. The movement grew as Scott continued to hold forth
in Auburn and Harris traveled to New York City to evangelize on its behalf. By
the summer, Scott claimed to be experiencing visions directing him to seek an
earthly center for the "unfolding" of the "heavenly kingdom" and a "refuge" for

God's "obedient people." In due course, the "Holy Mountain" was recognized by Scott and the others at Mountain Cove in the mountains of western Virginia.[23]

The community that formed there lasted from 1851 to 1853, some one hundred or so persons believing themselves to be established on the site of the original garden of Eden and speaking the language of Christian scripture in an illuminist version that stressed the nearness of the endtime. Roots in the Millerite movement of the 1840s, with its expectation of the Second Coming of Jesus in 1843 and then in 1844, gave to Mountain Cove communitarians a premillennial vision of impending catastrophe that only heightened their spiritualist belief. Leaders and members were imbued ever more strongly with a sense that the spirits who were aiding them required obedience and that, without spirit help, in the short time that remained social perfection could not be attained. With or without the spirits, though, Mountain Cove did not prosper. Unwelcome to its Virginia neighbors for its northern doctrines of radical reform and its theological heterodoxies, it experienced persistent internal discord. As early as the close of 1851, sexual allegations against Scott for "licentiousness and adultery" orchestrated the dissension to come, even as Scott's dismissal of Benedict and her mediumship in order to claim himself as "medium absolute" increased it. When Harris joined Scott in the spring of 1852, the two assumed co-leadership in a patriarchalism that manifested first in Scott's suppression of Benedict's authority in favor of his own, and as the Scott-Harris claims escalated, many in the community chafed. The pair announced themselves the two "witnesses" in Revelation 11:3–6, divinely chosen to prophesy—with fire emanating from their mouths, power to turn water into blood, and power, as well, to visit the earth with plagues; with authority, in short, to kill. Amid these threats of blood authority and grossly inflated claims, the community came apart.[24]

For the larger spiritualist community, Mountain Cove had gone beyond the pale. The subject of extended vitriolic narrative by spiritualist historians Emma Hardinge and Eliab W. Capron, it elicited heated condemnations and a rhetoric of thoroughgoing refusal to own it. Hardinge found Mountain Cove to be "notorious"—one of the "follies and fanaticisms" that deformed "the sacred name of Spiritualism, under the pretense of 'reforms.'" She objected strenuously to the apostolic authority and divine insight that Scott claimed, and she noticed negatively his "unquestionable authority" in matters financial. Harris fared no better with his own claims to semi-divine status. "In one of his prayers, uttered about this time [the fall of 1852]," Hardinge decried, "Harris said: '*Oh Lord, thou knowest we do not wish to destroy man with fire from our mouths!*'" Nor did Eliab Capron mince words in his earlier account, commenting on the absolutist leadership of Scott and Harris and the gullibility of their followers. The Mountain Cove episode, he thought, exposed "spiritual excitement" as a "convenient hobby for men who had graduated through the old forms of theological mysticism, until there was nothing new in that field to feed their love of leadership and pretence to special calls and inspiration."[25]

Yet despite the graduation ceremonies for older forms of mysticism and the embarrassment of many spiritualists at other spiritualists, the Mountain Cove episode exposed a longing for an authoritarian society at least embryonic in the séance circles. With all the talk of individualism and radical overthrow of social constraint among spiritualists, believers who sat in the circles gave over their authority to the direction of spirits. Their form of spiritual surrender was only writ large in the social experiment that was Mountain Cove, not contradicted by it. Still more, the kind of community that Mountain Cove attempted seemed to replicate, to some extent, the visions of utopian harmony and bliss on spirit landscapes that mediums like Mary Theresa Shelhamer gave eager listeners from the Spirit Violets of their trances. Visionary metaphors like these urged toward social enactment; spiritualist communities arose as the result, themselves a "natural byproduct and a legitimate expression of Spiritualist religion," as Bret Carroll has assessed.[26]

Both Spear's Harmonia and the Scott-Harris Mountain Cove, then, uncovered within the structure of spiritualist devotionalism not hardy individualism and American self-made spiritualizers but instead spirit-hungry men and women ready to efface themselves before something bigger and grander than themselves and to do it in community. By two decades later, in the 1870s, however, part of what was bigger and grander was the melodramatic ritual of spirit presentation. Here mediums and séance sitters mutually surrendered in outlaw episodes in which spirits seemingly vied with one another to be bolder, more obstreperous, and more outrageous than their spirit neighbors. The mediums who brought them in were likewise, by this time, skillful adepts in the art of deception. But by this time, too, self-prostrations to spirit were giving way before a discontent that would bring not the end of spiritualism but its revision and reformation in a series of new religious movements. The reconstituted spiritualism of the era brought a mysticizing past together with an inventive present. In its unflagging combinativeness, it inaugurated ever more, and more creative, forms of American metaphysical religion.

THEOSOPHY AND THE REFORM OF SPIRITUALISM

Among the investigations of spiritualism that came from American publishing houses in the 1870s, one appeared in 1875 called simply *People from the*

Other World. Its title page bore what in the rational-believer tradition of Judge Edmonds, Governor Tallmadge, and scientist Hare could only be called a devout inscription, attributed to "Lord Bacon": "*We have set it down as a law to ourselves to examine things to the bottom and not to receive upon credit, or reject upon improbabilities, until there hath passed a due examination.*" In the volume's preface, its author announced himself unconcerned with moral questions but intent on examining spiritualist phenomena "only as involving a scientific question which presses upon us for instant attention." Complaining that twenty-seven years after the Rochester rappings, "we are apparently not much nearer a scientific demonstration of their cause than we were then," he wanted to spur the scientific community to proper attention to spiritualism. Rather than studying tumble-bugs and pitcher-plants in "nonsensical debates," scientists needed to address "the astounding phenomenon of 'materialization.'"[27] If the rhetoric was unexceptional given the tradition of rational inquiry that characterized the Enlightenment side of spiritualism, what followed—in the book and in life—marked a decisive break with séance spiritualism. The author of the lengthy (nearly 500-page) work was Henry Steel Olcott (1832–1907), who in the same year that the book appeared co-founded the Theosophical Society. Together with Helena Petrovna Blavatsky (1831–1891), he would remodel spiritualism into what the pair regarded as spiritual truth and high teaching from Masters who were inaugurating a new era.

The major occasion for the book was also the occasion that brought the two together—the investigation of the flamboyant spiritual mediumship of two brothers, William and Horatio Eddy (and especially the former), on their family farm and homestead in Chittenden, Vermont. Olcott appeared at the farm with a long and varied background. He had been an agriculturalist, journalist, signals officer in the Union army, civil service reformer in government employ, and lawyer. In his youth he had seen Andrew Jackson Davis demonstrating clairvoyance, and by the time Olcott was twenty he had himself become a spiritualist. He achieved notice, in 1853, as a founding member of the New York Conference of Spiritualists, an organization formed to investigate spiritualism and to give it some intellectual ballast. But now, in his early forties and among the new urban gentry in New York City, Olcott had for years been distant from spiritualism, until one day, with a sudden thought of his neglect, he purchased a copy of the *Banner of Light* and read of "certain incredible phenomena" at the Eddy farm. "I saw at once," he later recalled, "that, if it were true that visitors could see, even touch and converse with, deceased relatives who had found means to reconstruct their bodies and clothing so as to be temporarily solid, visible, and tangible, this was the most important fact in modern physical science. I determined to go and see for myself."[28]

Olcott produced an account of his visit to the farm for the *New York Sun* and was promptly asked to return to Vermont by the *New York Daily Graphic* to investigate more thoroughly, this time accompanied by an artist who would make sketches. One of the readers of the original *Sun* article had been Blavatsky, a decidedly unconventional Russian immigrant, newly arrived from Paris with a mysterious past and a long involvement with certain forms of spiritualism. Born Helena Petrovna von Hahn, at Ekaterinoslav in the Ukraine, the daughter of a Russian army officer who had descended from German petty nobility and his Russian aristocrat wife who was a novelist, she married the forty-year-old Nikifor Blavatsky, the newly appointed vice-governor of Yerivan province in Armenia, just after her seventeenth birthday. She left him after only a short time to live with her grandfather, but when he tried to send her to her father she set out for Constantinople. So began a period of over twenty years for which only conflicting accounts of Blavatsky's whereabouts and activities exist. It seems certain, however, that she traveled extensively in Europe, the Middle East including Egypt, and North America and that she was drawn to matters spiritual and occult, acquiring an extensive experiential knowledge that included spiritualism and psychic phenomena. From childhood, she had believed in the presence of invisible companions, and that belief seems not to have deserted her during this obscure time. In a judicious summary of what may be known about the period, Bruce Campbell underlines the unconventional ("Bohemian") character of her life and points to evidence for her lengthy liaison with the opera singer Agardi Metrovitch and the possibility that she may have given birth to one or two children, fathered respectively by Metrovitch and one other person. Finally, evidence suggests that, already during this period, Blavatsky was imbued with a sense of mission, feeling herself called to a great work to come.[29]

When Olcott appeared at the Eddy homestead for his second visit, he met Blavatsky there on an investigative mission of her own. The two became fast friends, both of them identifying themselves as discontented spiritualists and Blavatsky especially decrying the materialism of American spiritualism. Meanwhile, she gradually led Olcott to believe that she could produce "spirit" manifestations and other occult phenomena far in advance of the ones he was witnessing. From the perspective of the study of American metaphysical religion, Olcott's expressed concerns were even more striking (they would later be argued far more exhaustively by Blavatsky herself). Chafing under the refusal of the spirits to allow as thorough an investigation as he wanted, Olcott in *People from the Other World* noted Horatio Eddy's written admission that he and his family were "the slaves of the powers behind the phenomena." Olcott went on to inveigh against mediumistic slavery. When mediums operated " 'under control,' " they lost their free will, and "their actions, their speech, and their very consciousness" were "directed by that of another." They were as helpless as mesmeric subjects to "do, or say, or think, or see what they desire[d]." Still worse, the materialization medium was even required, it appeared, to "lend from the more ethereal portions of his frame, some of the matter that goes to form the evanescent materialized shapes of the departed."[30]

By contrast, in Blavatsky Olcott believed he had found something different. In the second part of a book that detailed the appearance of Blavatsky at Chittenden and then addressed another mediumistic episode in Philadelphia involving apparent fraud, Olcott was ready to own that Blavatsky was "one of the most remarkable mediums in the world." "Instead of being controlled by spirits to do their will," Olcott enthused, "it is she who seems to control them to do her bidding." What was the secret, and how did she gain mastery? He did not know all the answers. But he told readers that "many years of her life have been passed in Oriental lands." There what Americans called spiritualism had "for years been regarded as the mere rudimental developments of a system." In it, relationships had been set up "between mortals and the immortals as to enable certain of the former to have dominion over many of the latter." Not willing to accept an ancient priestly "knowledge of the natural sciences" as an explanation for Blavatsky's powers, he referred instead to "those higher branches of that so-called White Magic, which has been practised for countless centuries by the initiated."[31] Olcott, in short, was turning for explanation not to science, as practiced in the nineteenth century, but to Hermeticism.

As performed by Blavatsky, the older model represented humans as powerful beings possessing divine or semidivine agency, co-creators with God of the universal order and able to manifest that order at will. "There are hidden powers in man," Olcott testified, "which are capable of making a *god* of him on earth." Meanwhile, the so-called spirits on the Eddy farm and elsewhere in the American spiritualist universe were "humbugging elemental[s]." The elementals, whom or which Blavatsky controlled, were one of "two unlike classes of phenomena-working agents." They were "sub-human nature-spirits," or they were joined at times by "earth-bound ex-human elementaries." As someone with a knowledge of magic, he thought, Blavatsky could work them to her liking. Olcott duly noted that when she appeared at the Eddy farm, the numerous American Indian spirits (and some Europeans) who were materializing out of William Eddy's cabinet gave place before new arrivals of multinational provenance. "There was," he reported, "a Georgian servant boy from the Caucasus; a Mussulman merchant from Tiflis; a Russian peasant girl, . . . a Kourdish cavalier armed with scimitar, pistols and lance; a hideously ugly and devilish-looking negro sorcerer from Africa . . . and a European gentleman wearing the cross and collar of St. Anne, who was recognised by Madame Blavatsky as her uncle."[32]

At the other end of the theosophical universe that Olcott was coming to accept, however, were the "Masters." "Little by little," he confided, "H. P. B. let me know of the existence of Eastern adepts and their powers." If she controlled "the occult forces of nature," she also served and did the bidding of "these Elder Brothers of humanity." They were "indispensable for the spiritual welfare of mankind," and "their combined divine energy" was "maintained from age to age," forever refreshing "the pilgrim of Earth, who struggles on toward the Divine Reality." Blavatsky, he said, had seen the Masters in visionary episodes from her youth. She was a "faithful servant of theirs," and she had come to New York from Paris at the behest of one of the Masters, receiving a "peremptory order" and the next day dropping everything to board a ship.[33] Apparently, there were some beings before whom Blavatsky was willing to bow. Mastery could still allow taking orders from Elder Brothers.

Situated between the elementals and the Masters, the Theosophical Society in 1875 would invent itself. In effect, Olcott, the rational investigator, had become convinced that the phenomena produced at the Eddy homestead, despite the limited testing that he was allowed to undertake, could not be "accounted for on the hypothesis of fraud." The manifestations were "not trickery," but neither were they "supernatural" nor "miracles." What remained for him was to investigate in a larger theater and still more seriously, not through the continued application of scientific tests (the scientists could and should do that) but in terms of a new vision of power—of Masters and elementals and other occult phenomena —that Blavatsky had opened to him. The Theosophical Society would do just that—expanding its compass to include a host of anomalous occurrences and phenomena that the "scientific" nineteenth century had disallowed. In this context, the new society would function as a restoration movement, gliding back past the collective silence in the mass spiritualist interlude to the Hermetic tradition of the West. At the same time, the restoration would also be a revitalization and a movement forward, because the contemporary science that Olcott and fellow travelers often disdained could also tool them to expand on the past in a new age of occult and, in their view, scientific progress. In this post–Civil War period that Mark Twain and Charles Dudley Warner dubbed the Gilded Age for its sparkling surfaces of show and financial boom with corruption beneath, members of the Theosophical Society would excavate the secrets of human power and mastery that for them seemed truer and more lasting.[34]

In May of 1875, Olcott formed a secret "Miracle Club" with spiritualist séances as its apparent major activity and Blavatsky a participant, but David Dana, the medium of choice, proved unsuccessful at summoning spirits, and the New York club fizzled. Still, Blavatsky was in the habit of hosting Sunday evening sessions in her apartment for a small group of people interested in occultism. Among them were Emma Hardinge (in private life, Hardinge-Britten), the well-known spiritualist medium and historian, and her husband Dr. William Britten. Present, too, was a youthful William Quan Judge—Irish immigrant and lawyer—who would later play so large a role in theosophical affairs. In early September of 1875, the group heard the Freemason and Kabbalist George Felt speak on ancient Egyptian lore, finding the key to art and architecture in an occult reading of "The Lost Canon of Proportion of the Egyptians." Olcott spontaneously scribbled a note about starting a society for occult research and passed it to Judge, who handed it to Blavatsky. With her nod, Olcott stood up and invited those present to form a society to "diffuse information concerning those secret laws of Nature which were so familiar to the Chaldeans and Egyptians, but are totally unknown by our modern world of science."[35]

By the next evening, sixteen persons joined the group, and by ten days later, on September 18, they decided to call themselves the Theosophical Society. The president was Olcott, with Blavatsky corresponding secretary, and Judge the council to the society. Bruce Campbell has pointed to the fact that the new Theosophists were people of privilege, "solidly" middle class with "a large proportion professionals," and among them "several lawyers, doctors, and journalists, and an industrialist." All seemed to share an interest in religion and spirituality of a nontraditional sort. The society, in fact, was bringing a New York City subculture with European ties into clearer visibility. While Olcott and Blavatsky moved in a generally spiritualist context, it was, clearly, already an expanded one. Indeed, Theosophist Alvin Boyd Kuhn, who concurred in 1930 that the pair had "launched the Society from within the ranks of the [spiritualist] cult," also addressed the issue of in-betweenness. While the general public classified Theosophy with "Spiritualism, New Thought, Unity and Christian Science," it was not "modern," as they were, but instead "a summation and synthesis of many cults of all times."[36]

For all the enthusiasm of its beginnings, the society during its first three years did not continue to fare well. Blavatsky and Olcott together formed the soul of the organization, and it was they who would keep the group going, with some prodding from Judge. Eventually the pair would transform Theosophy into a vehicle for the synthesis of Western and Eastern metaphysical categories (with a strong tilt toward the Eastern) intending to enhance the powers of an elite and spiritually advanced cadre of humans. The Theosophical Society, in other words, would be sophisticated and for sophisticates. Yet from the first it displayed, as Stephen

Prothero argues, the existence of "two theosophies." Blavatsky thrived on spontaneity and upset, Olcott on order. Blavatsky spun convoluted and highly elaborated theoretical works that made her to Theosophy what Andrew Jackson Davis had been to spiritualism (although, to be sure, her enthusiasm for phenomena set her distinctly apart from the spiritualist seer). Olcott, by contrast, brought the moralism of an American Protestant—and specifically Presbyterian and Calvinist—background to bear on his theosophical vision. Blavatsky loved interior spaces and secrets; Olcott carried over from the American democratic ethos and from mass spiritualism an impulse toward public exposition in a Theosophy that was exoteric. Thus Olcott's version of Theosophy favored the *discovery* of occult laws—something in which rational individuals could democratically engage— even as Blavatsky, more hierarchically, would foster their *unveiling*. Meanwhile, Blavatsky, the woman magus who functioned as a shaman-in-civilization, enhanced the role of women; Olcott, with his dismissal of (largely female) mediums as the dupes of elementals and as licentious persons given to free love and similar practices, promoted patriarchy. Ever the aristocrat in the midst of Bohemianism, Blavatsky brought a social consciousness far different from Olcott's with his middle-class gentry past. For him, the reform of spiritualism was part of the universal reform program intimately bound to spiritualism itself and to his own biographical trajectory. For Blavatsky, social reform programs were a matter of indifference.[37]

Together, though, the two brought a sizable legacy with them from séance spiritualism and the harmonial philosophy that was its sometime partner. As Stephen Prothero has summarized:

> Most of the liberal elements in spiritualism—its critique of Calvinist predestination in the name of individual liberty, its anticlericalism and emphasis on vernacular preaching by the laity, its antidogmatism and exaltation of individual conscience, its attempt to improve the role of women in society, and, finally, its hope of fashioning something akin to the kingdom of God on earth —survived in the theosophies of both Olcott and Blavatsky. What did not survive the transmigration were certain supposed spiritualist crudities—the preoccupation with spirits of the dead, tendencies toward communalism and free love, seemingly excessive reliance on female spiritual intermediaries, etc.— that would not appeal to genteel and aristocratic markets.[38]

The communalism would make a comeback later in selected portions of theosophical history, as we will see. Moreover, the sheer combinativeness of theosophical doctrine, "thickly populated," as Robert Ellwood notes, "with hidden Masters and the lore of many ancient cultures," could already be read as a theoretical expression of "communitas." In this visionary community of the spirit, however, what drew many to spiritualism and then Theosophy was residence in a middle place between a credulous religious past and an agnostic and positivist present. Olcott hailed "a reasonable and philosophical spiritualistic belief" and thought it "as far removed from the superstition of the Seventeenth; and Eighteenth Centuries, as it is from the degrading materialism of the last quarter of the Nineteenth." The late nineteenth century, he complained, "blots God out of the Universe, strips the soul of its aspirations for a higher existence beyond the grave, and bounds the life of man" by animal limits.[39]

Beyond the riddle of rational religious belief, however, lay the riddle of mind. Tellingly, Olcott acknowledged that "especially Mind, active as WILL, was a great problem for us." Used mutually by "Eastern magus" and "Western mesmerist and psychopath," it could bring acclaim as a "hero" to one who developed it or spiritual mediumship to another who paralyzed it. Close beside mind, for Olcott, came the active imagination and the power of thought to fashion actual things. When, along with mind, "imagination is simultaneously active," he declared, "it *creates*, by giving objectivity to just-formed mind-images."[40] In his series of observations Olcott had stated the terms for the combinative metaphysical religion of the late nineteenth century and beyond. Theosophy, Christian Science, New Thought, and a series of interrelated and entangled movements—even to the New Age and the new spirituality of the late twentieth and early twenty-first century—would agree to the contract.

Meanwhile, the Theosophical Society passed through a Western-oriented era of three years until 1878. At the apex of this earlier, Western period stood Blavatsky's publication, in 1877, of her monumental first book, *Isis Unveiled*.[41] There she claimed direct dictation by the Masters—especially one with whom she most closely identified—and she incorporated virtually all of the occult corpus of the nineteenth century (nearly one hundred volumes) into a huge work of nearly thirteen hundred pages. The text was divided between a first volume devoted to "Science" and a second to "Theology," suggesting the ongoing problematic of Theosophy as it aimed to bring the two together. From the first, however, the Blavatsky synthesis was controversial. Bruce Campbell has detailed how the spiritualist (and former Theosophist) William Emmette Coleman—a member of the American Oriental Society, the Pali Text Society, and similar organizations—claimed to have uncovered some two thousand instances of serious plagiarism. Coleman also declared that he had uncovered a series of other quotations taken not from original sources but from secondary ones without acknowledgment.[42]

If so—and the evidence was there to see—Blavatsky likewise stood in the tradition of spiritualist mediumship, with its own flamboyant fraudulence, and—

with the mediums—in a quasi-shamanic tradition in which sacred tricksterism had consistently been part of the religious game. Now, though, in the Blavatsky innovation, the trickery came not merely through act and gesture but also through words. More than that, a straightforward reading of *Isis Unveiled* and later work by Blavatsky that focuses on the external event of plagiarism may oversimplify. Even if we discount the loose nineteenth-century standards of textual attribution, it may be argued that Blavatsky's tricks counted, essentially, as religious phenomena. Sacred trickery has been predicated on the assumption that unless humans see "sign and wonders" (as in John 4:48), they will not believe—and that believing is good for them. Trickery compensates for the nonproduction of magical events on demand, even in a culture of affirmation in which devotees insist that magic does happen. Trickery, however, acknowledges that it happens only some of the time, not always, and not predictably.

Attention needs to be paid, too, to the complex psychological universe in which Blavatsky's "creative" writing occurred. Robert Ellwood has pointed to the "other order" in which Blavatsky apparently spent much of her time, a place where the "universe itself" became simultaneously "subjectivity" and a "cosmic mind animated by other subjectivities, later called the Masters and the Hierarchy." According to Ellwood, evidence suggests that the key to the enigmatic Blavatsky's marginality and liminality may have been "a mild case of dissociation or multiple personality, a condition in which each personality may operate by quite different values and have different goals from the others, and may not even be aware of everything the other does." Moreover the idea of Masters on which she drew had a long history in both East and West. It is easy to point, for example, to Hindu rishis and Buddhist bodhisattvas on Asian soil. For the West, Masters had been evoked both in Neoplatonist and Rosicrucian writings. In the nineteenth century, they were acknowledged by individuals such as Éliphas Lévi [A.-L. Constant], the French magus who named Mesmer's magnetic fluid the "astral light," and the English novelist and member of the occult Golden Dawn Edward Bulwer-Lytton, whom Blavatsky so much admired.[43]

Blavatsky's Masters, however—become Mahatmas after she and Olcott left for India in 1878—brought her over the edge when they ever more plentifully supplied her associates with materialized letters. The Anglo-Indian journalist A. P. Sinnett by 1883 had published both *The Occult World* and *Esoteric Buddhism* in touch, he believed, with the Mahatmas, the former volume describing his receipt of a series of letters from them and the latter drawn from the mysteriously materialized letters themselves. Nevertheless, by the following year Emma Cutting Coulomb, a staff member in Blavatsky's household at Adyar, India, with her husband, charged in a series of articles in the local *Christian College Magazine* that the Mahatma letters had been produced by Blavatsky, with her housekeeper as assistant. Especially damaging was the revelation of sliding back panels in a cabinet in Blavatsky's shrine room adjoining her bedroom (thus enabling letters or other objects to "materialize," as if from nowhere, within the shrine). When Australian Richard Hodgson of the Society for Psychical Research came to Adyar on behalf of a society committee, evidence of fraud mounted. Hodgson concluded that Emma Coulomb's allegations stood up to scrutiny, that all the phenomena that he could unravel were contrived, and that Blavatsky herself had written the large bulk of the Mahatma letters, with a few by someone else. His published report for the society's Committee of Investigation extended to roughly two hundred pages.[44]

In 1877, however, the full mysteries of the Mahatma letters were still waiting to be manifested from what Blavatsky would in *Isis Unveiled* call the "ether" or the "astral light." Moreover, with all of the problems associated with its composition, *Isis* emerged, arguably, as a trance production, a latter-day labor in the tradition of such works among American spiritualists. As Campbell notes, its Western occultism reflects a subculture in which belief in adepts, "white" and "black" magic, "astral light," and "elemental races or nature spirits" all flourished. The Blavatsky who spoke through these pages recounted in a grand synthesis the Hermetic tradition of the West and its nineteenth-century resonances in, for example, spiritualism, mesmerism, and psychic phenomena. Along the way came forays into modern science and ancient Kabbalah, denunciations of official Christianity and expositions of the longtime Christian wisdom tradition, and—in the most Eastern-turning materials—comparisons of Christianity to Hinduism and Buddhism. Even amid the plagiarism—beyond, but perhaps related to, issues of trance production—the extent of Blavatsky's synthesis needs to be noticed. Whatever the sources of its parts and whatever the Herculean efforts (and they were) of Olcott and others to organize the manuscript for her, Blavatsky's product had become a creation in its own right. The work sold a thousand copies in ten days, and by a year later its two reprints had also sold out. Among Theosophists and sympathizers, it continued to achieve impressive sales.[45]

Behind the massive work lay Blavatsky's conviction: "Spiritualism, in the hands of an adept, becomes Magic, for he is learned in the art of blending together the laws of the Universe, without breaking any of them and thereby violating Nature." By contrast, "in the hands of an inexperienced medium," spiritualism became "UNCONSCIOUS SORCERY." Such a medium opened "unknown to himself, a door of communication between the two worlds through which emerge the blind forces of Nature lurking in the astral Light, as well as good and bad spirits." Blavatsky minced no words for readers as she called spiritualism a "strange creed" and assessed the majority of spiritual communications to be "trivial, commonplace, and often vulgar." Moreover, manifestations such as those of the "uneducated Vermont farmer" at the Eddy homestead were "*not* the forms of the persons they appeared to be" and were "simply their portrait statues, constructed, animated and operated by the elementaries" (compare the fabled statues of the *Asclepius*). Yet spiritualism alone offered a "possible last refuge of compromise" between "self-styled revealed religions and materialistic philosophies."[46]

In a work that announced, in its first sentence, "intimate acquaintance with Eastern adepts," what they taught Blavatsky was the "Hermetic philosophy, the anciently universal Wisdom Religion, as the only possible key to the Absolute in science and theology." For those who might understand Hermeticism in Western terms, it was clear that Blavatsky, already in 1877 and before, inflected the received tradition in heavily Asian ways. Spiritualist failures would continue, she stated emphatically, "*until these pretended authorities of the West go to the Brahmans and Lamaists of the far Orient, and respectfully ask them to impart the alphabet of true science.*" As significant, her Eastern adepts had taught her "an absolute and immovable faith in the omnipotence of man's own immortal self." Invoking the "kinship" between the human spirit and the "Universal Soul — God," she affirmed that "Man-spirit" proved "God-spirit, as the one drop of water prove[d] a source from which it must have come."[47] Blavatsky was keeping apparent company with the divine human. She was also, like John Dee and other Hermeticists of old, doing her share of angel-summoning.

Even as Blavatsky exalted a Platonic "middle ground" (which she linked with "the abstruse systems of old India"), she read her Platonism and philosophy in terms of practice. "*Magic was considered a divine science which led to a participation in the attributes of Divinity itself,*" she declared in language that recalled the Hermetic corpus of the Renaissance. Exalting the human will and connecting it to "manifestation," Blavatsky unraveled a tale of the akasa or akasha, the astral light known in ancient times as sacred fire and in the modern era as magnetic fluid, "nerve-aura," Reichenbach's "*od*," electricity, and so forth. For her the light was identified with the nineteenth-century "ether" — the medium and mysterious element that, according to the common theory of light as undulation or wave, transmitted transverse waves and permeated all space. This light was, indeed, an akashic *record*, for it contained all memory and was, in fact, the "MEMORY OF GOD." Humans were light beings, for it was the "astral soul" that, in accord with "Hermetic doctrine," survived the body's death. Moreover, this "energizing principle in matter" possessed magical properties. Here Blavatsky posited a "regular science of the soul" that taught "how to force the *invisible* to become visible." It taught, too, "the existence of elementary spirits; the nature and magical properties of the astral light; the power of living men to bring themselves into communication with the former through the latter."[48]

Invoking a universal spirit or world soul operative everywhere, Blavatsky turned her attention to matters of sickness and healing. Again, her remarks arose out of the discourse world of spiritualism, its healing practices, and her mission to correct the "abuses of mesmeric and magnetic powers in some healing mediums." In a statement that, with a shift, became the New Thought faith of the late nineteenth century, she declared that "*with expectency* [sic] *supplemented by faith, one can cure himself of almost any morbific condition.*" With the "influence of mind over the body . . . so powerful that it has effected miracles at all ages," Blavatsky was now but a short step away from the "mind-cure" metaphysician. If we follow the implicit logic of her exposition, the individual, as a reconstituted magus, would wrest power from the medium to use his or her own (divine) Mind as a magical instrument of healing. Meanwhile, Blavatsky instructed readers at length in the history and structure of the human species. She announced the existence of pre-Adamite races and charted the descent of spirit into matter, emanating ultimately from a "central, spiritual, and *Invisible* sun" (Gnostic and Kabbalistic in her reading but also echoing, in some respects, the occult formulation of Andrew Jackson Davis). Clearly, she testified, Charles Darwin had gotten his directions wrong—"evolution having originally begun from above and proceeded downward." Beyond that, the human task was one of "upward progress," an ascent to the "divine parent" and source from which it had come.[49]

In an anthropology that would be parsed differently in her later *Secret Doctrine* (1888), Blavatsky used the Western Hermetic tradition to articulate a testimony to the existence of subtle bodies. Nature was "triune" (visible, invisible, and spiritually sourced), and so were humans. Each person possessed "his objective, physical body; his vitalizing astral body (or soul), the real man." These two, in turn, were "brooded over and illuminated by the third—the sovereign, the immortal spirit." The success of the "real man" in the task of "merging himself" with spirit rendered him an "immortal entity." In this context, magic meant knowledge concerning all of this, and it also became the means by which control of nature's forces could be gained and applied "by the individual while still in the body." Always, magic existed in the service of mastery. The reform of spiritualism that Olcott had demanded took shape in unmistakable terms in Blavatsky's vision. Just as he had noticed that she, unlike the Chittenden mediums, could not be enslaved by the séance productions, so she proclaimed mediumship to be "the opposite of adeptship" and announced liberation for the adept who "actively controls himself and all inferior potencies." In this there was "no miracle." All that happened was "the result of law—eternal, immutable, ever active."[50]

Here, in sum, was the Western magus at the height of dominion over the secret powers of nature. Despite all the deference to Asia, despite the attestation that India was the "cradle of the race" and "Mother" to "philosophy, religion, arts and sciences," here lay no easy belief in reincarnation (a later fundamental in Blavatsky's Theosophy). "Not a rule in nature," but an "exception," reincarnation occurred for this earlier Blavatsky only if "preceded by a violation of the laws of harmony of nature." To be sure, the work was hardly friendly to Christianity, a religion that for her bore at best a derivative status. Yet Blavatsky's reading of the Pauline indwelling Christ (see, for example, 2 Cor. 5:17 and Gal. 2:20) as an "embodied idea" and "the abstract ideal of the personal divinity indwelling in man" would be echoed (and from various sources) in a continuing American metaphysical religion.[51]

Already, though, even as *Isis* was being published and read, the personal odysseys and external circumstances of Blavatsky and Olcott were beckoning them and their flagging Theosophical Society in an Asian direction. Olcott had turned over the idea of attaching the society to the Masonic order to give it stability; and, more seriously, there had been work toward a merger with the Arya Samaj, a Hindu reform movement that sought the restoration of the ancient teaching of the scriptural Vedas. But even though the society's council formally resolved to unite with the Indian organization in May 1878, further exploration suggested an Arya Samaj that looked too sectarian for theosophical tastes. It was in this context that the Theosophical Society began to discover its reconstructed self. In *Old Diary Leaves*, Olcott remembered the process and the joint circular that he and Blavatsky drafted. Within the circular's "categorical declaration of principles," he observed, were "three Declared Objects." The first was "the study of occult science"; the second, "the formation of a nucleus of universal brotherhood"; the third, "the revival of Oriental literature and philosophy."[52]

Olcott had written expansively on this third purpose in the circular, which committed the organization not only to acquainting the West with "the long-suppressed *facts* about Oriental religious philosophies, their ethics, chronology, esoterism, symbolism," but also and especially to focusing on esotericism. Theosophists thus would spread "a knowledge of the sublime teachings of that pure esoteric system of the archaic period which are mirrored in the oldest Vedas, and in the philosophy of Gautama Buddha, Zoroaster, and Confucius." Meanwhile, internal distinctions were being set up. The New York City circular acknowledged three theosophical sections—new members who still shared "worldly interests," intermediate students "who had withdrawn from the same or were ready to do so," and the Masters, or "adepts . . . who, without being actually members, were at least connected with us and concerned in our work as a potential agency for the doing of spiritual good to the world." It would, however, be a decade later—in the context of a power struggle between Olcott and Blavatsky—before he, as president, formally created the Esoteric Section of the society.[53]

Three months after the appearance of the New York circular, in December 1878, Blavatsky and Olcott set sail for India. In the three years since the inception of their society, themes of spiritualism and its reform gradually faded before a transformed sense of mission. Still, as we will see in the next chapter, spiritualism had set the terms for the new mission, and the reconstructed Theosophy of 1878 and after answered the questions that spiritualism raised. At the edge of the rational material world, who would be in charge? When the myriad landscapes of the mind were visited, who would drive the chariot? Were humans in their day-to-day lives captive specimens to be operated by their own unconscious psyches, by the mental powers of their fellows, or by the high commands of spirits? Or were they, could they be, after all secretly—and then openly and spectacularly—in charge? Was the American spiritualist interlude a heterodox episode in the grand Hermetic scheme of things? Or was it a preparation, designed by masterful adepts, for a higher, better spiritual vision? All of the late-nineteenth-century metaphysicians would find themselves compelled by this series of questions, and all of them would find answers on the side of human mastery and command (even if, at least in the case of Mary Baker Eddy's Christian Science, hedged about with testimonies to the transcendent power of God). Metaphysicians, for the most part, would chart a course through a spiritual universe in which humans were meant to dwell as gods.

CHRISTIAN SCIENCE AND THE RECONSTITUTION OF MESMERISM AND MEDIUMSHIP

The same year that Henry Steel Olcott published *People from the Other World*, Mary Baker Glover's crisply titled *Science and Health* appeared in print.[54] A work of over 450 pages, it was the culmination of a decade of metaphysical reflection and writing by a woman in her mid-fifties who counted herself thoroughly Christian. Indeed, she wrote it after she claimed a spiritual discovery that would radically reorient religion and spiritual practice for the Christian churches. Known more familiarly as Mary Baker Eddy (1821–1910)—the name she assumed after her marriage to Asa Gilbert Eddy in 1877—the author brought far less cosmopolitanism than did Olcott to a work that would go through a plethora of editions until the familiar 1906 version became the standard text.[55] *Science and Health* stood beside the Bible for Christian Scientists, and it became the scripture that was canonically read in Christian Science services everywhere. Eddy herself would look back on the work in her later years in ways that hinted of the kind of "channeled" text that numerous spiritualists, as well as Helena P. Blavatsky, claimed to produce. When Eddy wrote it, she declared, she had "consulted no other authors and read no other book but the Bible for three years." Still more, as she said, "it was not myself, but the power of Truth and love, infinitely above me, which dictated 'Science and Health with Key to the Scriptures.'"[56]

If Eddy had begun Christian Science in mid-life, she continued to preside over the fortunes of her religious foundation with a success that could be estimated by the imposing Boston Mother Church dedicated at the end of 1894. These times of abundance and fulfillment, however, had been preceded by a personal life more bleak and compromised. Born in Bow, New Hampshire, Mary Morse Baker had grown up in the shadow of the Congregational church with its Puritan past and was formally admitted to membership at twelve, even though she could not affirm her pastor's old-school doctrine of predestination. She would continue to affirm her connection to this Congregational world, and, in fact, the language of sin was woven in and out of her writings throughout her life. Arguably, she never gave up Calvinism when she embraced metaphysics. As earlier proto-metaphysical and metaphysical practice already demonstrates, commitments to mind and correspondence could encompass Christian categories. Now, in what would become Baker Eddy's Christian Science, we test the limits of such combinativeness.

A youthful Baker married Colonel George Washington Glover of Charleston, South Carolina, in 1843, lived with him in the South for a year, and then, when he succumbed to yellow fever, returned to New England and gave birth to a son. Glover was chronically ill, and her family was, for various reasons, unsupportive in helping to care for the boisterous child. When he was five—after her recently widowed father remarried—the little boy, George Jr., was sent away to live with a now-married former family servant with whom Glover herself had a warm relationship. She apparently agreed to the plan reluctantly. Her second marriage, with the philandering dentist Daniel Patterson, ended in divorce in 1873, but she had gone back to the surname Glover well before that.[57]

Hard times dogged Eddy (to use the familiar surname) as she moved from one shabby boardinghouse to the next, living with people below her social station because of the paucity of her means. Here she experienced the spiritual seeker culture of her age in a readily available world of mesmerism and spiritualism. Meanwhile, she continued to be plagued with ill health—probably mostly what

George Beard would by the 1880s label "American nervousness," or neurasthenia.[58] Eddy's physical complaints brought her to homeopathy, hydropathy (water cure), and mesmerism and eventually to the reformed magnetic medicine of Phineas Parkhurst Quimby (1802–1866), a well-known mental healer practicing in Portland, Maine. The teaching and practice of Quimby, placed beside the authoritative message of Congregational Calvinism, became a major influence that helped to catalyze Eddy's own combinative system in Christian Science after his death in 1866.

Eddy worked with Quimby not merely as a patient—for whom the "medicine" was in large part effective—but also as a student transcribing notes of conversations with him, reading his own notes and sometimes "correcting" them, and acting increasingly as an intellectual colleague to her mentor. Moreover, as a Quimby patient-student, Eddy was hardly alone. Among the others who participated in the loose Quimby community were major early leaders in the New Thought movement. Remembering the well-known mental healer's relationship with the others, his son George Quimby recalled that his father would "talk hours and hours, week in and week out . . . listening and asking questions. After these talks he would put on paper in the shape of an essay or conversation what subject his talk had covered." Eddy, as George Quimby wrote, actively participated, even as she pursued a one-on-one intellectual relationship with the doctor, and her own thinking apparently intermingled with his.[59]

Who was this Portland healer whose thriving practice had attracted Eddy, the ailing neurasthenic patient, and who became a major intellectual and spiritual influence on her life? An autodidact like Eddy herself, Quimby was making clocks in Belfast, Maine, when he attended Charles Poyen's lectures in 1838. Attracted to the medical applications of animal magnetism, he partnered with the youthful Lucius Burkmar in an itinerating stage demonstration of clairvoyance in healing. In performances that took place as the pair traveled the lyceum circuit, Quimby mesmerized Burkmar, Burkmar "read" the disease that afflicted an inquiring audience member, and then Burkmar prescribed the remedy that would heal the illness. As the process worked—even on Quimby himself—he raised critical questions about it and eventually became convinced that the true agent of healing success was the power of suggestion and the belief it fostered within each subject. Quimby had arrived, in an incipient way, at the notion of the power of mind. In the process, he also became confident that he, too, possessed clairvoyant powers. Subsequently parting ways with Burkmar, he began a practice that increasingly departed from its magnetic beginnings. By the time he settled in Portland toward the end of 1859, Quimby was styling himself a mental healer. He was also, despite his Christian heterodoxy, a cosmological seeker with compelling religious and theological questions. Robert Peel noted that he attended Unitarian and Universalist churches.[60] And Quimby surely knew the Bible, as his writings reveal. Meanwhile, his religious liberalism links him to the harmonial philosophy of Andrew Jackson Davis and other spiritualists, and some of his ideas can also be linked to those of Emanuel Swedenborg and of the American Transcendentalists.

In the American culture of Quimby's era, as we have already seen, mesmerism blended with spiritualism into a viable way to think and act, to make sense of basic problems of human life in a kind of armchair philosophy that was also a pragmatic set of principles for action. Quimby's writings, rough and opaque though they often are, record his perceptions of this nineteenth-century thought world as he constructed his own. Whatever his knowledge of Davis (and there is no evidence, of which I am aware, that he ever directly read the well-known spiritualist), Quimby was intimately acquainted with spiritualism in its phenomenal form. Ervin Seale's complete edition of Quimby's writings, published only as recently as 1988, makes Quimby's familiarity with a spiritualist discourse community abundantly clear. (Seale's work overturned the partial, sanitized 1921 edition by Horatio Dresser—son of New Thought leaders Julius and Annetta Dresser—which left out Quimby's spiritualism and idealized his materialism.)[61]

The man who emerges from the Seale edition attended séances frequently and could influence the phenomena that occurred in the circles. "I profess to be a medium myself and am admitted to be so by the spiritualists themselves," he owned in one essay and, in another, related an account of a séance at which he proved himself to be a "healing medium." He had become a medium, he claimed, but—like the Blavatsky of a decade or more later—he enjoyed a freedom not experienced by others. "I retained my own consciousness and at the same time took the feelings of my patient," he declared.[62] Yet this Quimby—on such close terms with spiritualists and their séances and so thoroughly familiar, too, with the details of mesmeric practice—admitted the phenomena but, again like Blavatsky, thoroughly disputed their cause and conditions. For him, however, what generated mesmeric success and spiritualist manifestation were not "elementals" or "elementaries" but simple human belief and opinion.

Mesmerism and spiritualism were "phenomena without any wisdom," and a spirit was "the shadow of a person's belief or imagination." A person could not "give a fair account of the phenomena of Spiritualism" because the "experiments" were "governed by ... belief and must be so." Quimby wasted no words in pronouncing "ghosts and spirits" to be "the invention of man's superstition." "So long as people think about the dead," he stated flatly, "so long there will be spirits, for thought is spirit, and that is all the spirits there are." How did the production of spirits work, and what was the mechanism of spiritualist activity? Quimby's answer lay in the generic "power of creating ideas and making them so dense that they could be seen by a subject that was mesmerized." This was the state that, in his single-source explanation, embraced "all the phenomena of spiritualism, disease, religion and everything that affect[ed] the mind." Nor did mesmerism and spiritualism essentially differ. "The word 'mesmerism,'" Quimby wrote, "embraces all the phenomena that ever were claimed by any intelligent spiritualists." Clearly, the "other world" was "in the mind." "The idea that any physical demonstration" came "from the dead" was to him "totally absurd."[63]

Still, Quimby had bought into the spiritualist universe enough to reiterate the materialist explanation for mesmeric and similar phenomena that had been popularized by Davis and others. "Spirit" was "only matter in a rarefied form, and thought, reason and knowledge" were "the same." "Mind" was "the name of a spiritual substance that can be changed" and was, in fact, "spiritual matter." "Thought" was "also matter, but not the same matter," just as the earth was not "the same matter as the seed which is put into it." Moreover, Quimby echoed the spiritualist seer in further ways. J. Stillson Judah decades ago pointed to parallels between Davis's and Quimby's etiology of disease in the discords of the human spirit and their perception of an "atmosphere" surrounding a human subject that could be affected, for good or ill, by another. He noticed, too, their mutual identification of God with Wisdom and a series of other similar (often Swedenborgian and Hermetic) beliefs regarding divine and human nature and human destiny.[64]

Regarding "spiritual matter," so pervasive was Quimby's identification between cognitive phenomena and the material realm that it is easy to read him as a thoroughgoing materialist, given his immersion in the language world of mesmerism and spiritualism. Yet this conclusion fails to notice the rather bold departure that Quimby made from mesmeric-spiritualist canons and ideas—a departure that his patient-student Mary Baker Eddy was to take and transform in terms of Calvinist Christianity to create Christian Science. In Quimby's reconstruction of the received cosmology, he combined the materialism of his sources with an idealism that at least one mid-twentieth-century scholar linked to Transcendentalism. Quimby's knowledge of the work of Ralph Waldo Emerson and other Transcendentalists was no doubt tenuous and secondhand at best, but major newspapers habitually summarized Emerson's lyceum lectures, and idealist views were clearly there for the taking.[65] Beyond that, a generalized Swedenborgianism could be argued in tandem with these ideas. Judah, for example, pointed to the essentially Swedenborgian views that Quimby held regarding what he termed the "natural" and the "spiritual man," and his preference for an analogical, or allegorical, reading of scripture in the tradition of Swedenborg.[66]

Whatever Quimby's sources (Davis? others?), his writings demonstrate thoroughgoing preoccupation with a wisdom that transcended the material world of mind and mesmeric play. Alternately cast, this wisdom operated as a metaphysical "solid" that suffused the world, like a ghost of the mesmeric fluidic ether but always elusively nonmaterial. Set in this cosmological situation, two kinds of humans inhabited the earth—the "natural man," caught in the error of a materialist mind and its attendant phenomena, and the "scientific man," who saw past the performance into the space of wisdom. Quimby argued for the wisdom world: Calling the power that governed the material mind "spirit," the Portland physician yet recognized "a Wisdom superior to the word mind, for I always apply the word mind to matter but never apply it to the First Cause."[67]

Still more, although Quimby was thoroughly anticlerical and opposed to orthodox Christianity, his familiarity with Christian scripture meant that his writings were filled with metaphysicalized biblical references to contend for his view. Indeed, in his private papers, he betrayed a kind of messianism in which he identified himself with the biblical Christ, at the same time typically separating Christ, as identical to Science, from sole attachment to the historical Jesus. "Jesus never tried to teach anything different from what I am teaching and doing every day," he testified. His statement of his own case is crucial for understanding the new production that became Eddy's Christian Science: "Now I stand as one that has risen from the dead or error into the light of truth, not that the dead or my error has risen with me, but I have shaken off the old man or my religious garment and put on the new man that is Christ or Science, and I fight these errors and show that they are all the makings of our own mind. As I stand outside of all religious belief, how do I stand alongside of my followers? I know that I, this wisdom, can go and impress a person at a distance. The world may not believe it, but to the world it is just such a belief as the belief in spirits; but to me it is a fact and this is what I shall show."[68]

Nor were Quimby's allusions to the higher wisdom, as Robert Peel argued problematically, "recurrent elements of spiritual idealism which contradict the author's basic position."[69] A clear hierarchy of error and truth, in fact, ran through all of Quimby's writings. Mind, with its beliefs and opinions, existed as part of a material order of error; wisdom rose above it; somehow Quimby—despite the morass in which all other mortals seemingly found themselves—lived as a "scientific man" in a realm beyond. Quimby, like Jesus, inhabited the wisdom world, and Eddy had discovered the connection. This was so much so that in late 1862 her enthusiasm for her new healer-teacher embarrassed him publicly, when letters that she wrote to the *Portland Courier* in the first blush of her healing experience appeared in print. Quimby stood "upon the plane of wisdom with his truth," she proclaimed in the second of these, and he healed "as never man healed since Christ." "P. P. Quimby," she exulted, "rolls away the stone from the sepulchre of error, and health is the resurrection."[70]

Mary Baker Eddy's relationship with Quimby ended abruptly in January 1866 when the doctor died. Bereft of both doctor and mentor (her father Mark Baker had also died three months before), she poured out her feelings in "Lines on the Death of Dr. P. P. Quimby, who healed with the truth that Christ taught, in contradistinction to all isms." The poem was published in the *Lynn* (Massachusetts) *Weekly Reporter* almost a month later. Meanwhile, less than two weeks after Quimby's death, Eddy fell on ice on her way to a meeting, experienced injuries that caused severe head and neck pain with possible spinal dislocation, and three days later, in the midst of pain that her homeopathic physician could not assuage, read a New Testament passage. An account of one of the healing miracles of Jesus, the narrative, she later claimed, triggered an intense experiential state of awareness. Eddy, according to her own report and denominational tradition, had "discovered" Christian Science.[71]

If so, what she took away cognitively from the experience, at least as she later constructed it, linked the wisdom discourse of Quimby to the orthodoxy of her Congregational Christian past. Now, though, instead of immersion in the world of error that pervaded most of Quimby's writings, a felt sense of God as the only reality became the key to her healing and all healing. Even as Eddy brought the unorthodox Quimby to the orthodoxy of her past, the Calvinism of her religious construction was noticeable. At least part of the attraction of the Quimby theology for Eddy was its predication of wisdom as an unchanging and *transcendent* reality. Whatever Eddy's connections to spiritualism—and, as we shall see, they were many—the theological immanence that spiritualism proclaimed was for her in the end untenable.

Eddy did, to be sure, teach what might be called a Christian version of final union with an Oversoul become God. In the first edition of her textbook *Science and Health*, for example, she wrote that "we are never Spirit until we are God; there are no individual 'spirits.'" She went on to exhort that "until we find Life Soul, and not sense, we are not sinless, harmonious, or undying. We become Spirit only as we reach being in God; not through death or any change of matter, but mind, do we reach Spirit, lose sin and death, and gain man's immortality." But the journey was decidedly one to a transcendental state and order. The published 1876 edition of Eddy's teaching pamphlet *Science of Man*, for example, declared that "Intelligence" was "circumference and not centre" and that "Soul and Spirit" were "neither in man nor matter." Similarly, the standard edition of *Science and Health* from 1906 affirmed "God as not in man but as reflected by man" and warned against "false estimates of soul as dwelling in sense and of mind as dwelling in matter." In her "new departure of metaphysics," Eddy elsewhere told followers, God was "regarded more as absolute, supreme," while "God's fatherliness as Life, Truth, and Love" made "His sovereignty glorious." In practical terms, testimonies of healing the sick through Christian Science treatment would be the means to glorify God and scale "the pinnacle of praise."[72] Thus the Eddy who rejected the predestinarian views of her childhood church still exalted the supreme majesty of God in ways that proclaimed the underlying Calvinism of her past.

Christian Science scholar Stephen Gottschalk notes these connections in his theological study of Eddy's place in American religious culture, and he notices as well the essential Calvinism of the metaphysical dualism she propounded. "In Christian Science as in Calvinism," Gottschalk observes, "one is clearly confronted with the Pauline antithesis of the Spirit and the flesh." It is arguable, too, that the warfare model that permeates so much of Eddy's writing reinscribes Calvinism with its traditional narratives of the battle between good and evil, between God and the devil, in the life of the soul. In fact, any sustained contact with the corpus of Eddy's writings reveals the periodic invocation of "sin" as a habitual way to distinguish reprehensible states of mind and life. We have already seen her identifying the loss of "sin" in "Life Soul" in the first edition of *Science and Health*. Later, both in the *Manual of the Mother Church* (1895) and in the standard (1906) edition of *Science and Health*, Scientists and seekers could find among the six "Tenets" of the Mother Church one that acknowledged "God's forgiveness of sin in the destruction of sin and the spiritual understanding that casts out evil as unreal." "Rule out of me all sin," the *Church Manual* asked Scientists to pray daily.[73]

Ostensibly committed to the unreality of sin and evil, Eddy's writings—with their warfare mentality that equaled or amplified Quimby's polemical stance— hid a Calvinist devil lurking beneath the metaphysical surface, an evil that displayed a very tangible presence. Toward the end of Eddy's life, that presence took the form of a heightened personal fear of "malicious animal magnetism" ("M.A.M."), as prayer workers stationed outside her door through the night contended against claimed magnetic onslaughts. But much earlier, it is hard not to detect a palpable sense of evil that preoccupied her. Her contentious relationships with students and former students were cast by Eddy in terms that invited, for her, a felt sense of sin (of others toward her) and the presence of Satan, even if the name itself was banished to the outer darkness of theological incorrectness. On paper, sin was "the lying supposition that life, substance, and intelligence are both material and spiritual, and yet are separate from God." But Eddy herself allowed that sin was "concrete" as well as "abstract," and in many life situations the concreteness was manifest. Sin was a "delusion" and a *"lie,"* but even if she told her followers not to fear it, she acted as though she feared it herself.[74]

More than that, in the consistent Christian Science language of "mortal mind" that Eddy created it is hard not to read a transliterated script for sin and, indeed, for the old Calvinist theology of the total depravity of humankind. Eddy herself was uneasy about the term, calling it a "solecism in language" that involved "an improper use of the word *mind.*" However, she was willing to live with the "old and imperfect" in her "new tongue." In this context, mortal mind meant "the flesh opposed to Spirit, the human mind and evil in contradistinction to the divine Mind, or Truth and good." Still further, her "Scientific Translation of Mortal Mind" announced its "first degree" to be "depravity," identifying depravity with the physical realm of "evil beliefs, passions and appetites, fear, depraved will, self-justification, pride, envy, deceit, hatred, revenge, sin, sickness, disease, death." Eddy was adamant in her insistence that, seen from and in the divine Mind, evil itself was unreal and that, therefore, mortal mind was mind existing in a state of error. Still for all that, the language of recrimination that she cast upon it, with its emotional tone of repugnance and rebuke, suggests that she was making *something* out of this nothing in her act of warfare against it. As Ann Braude has stated, Eddy "had no doubt that the mortal, human aspects of each person reflected the total depravity of Adam's legacy," and she was "preoccupied with fighting the dangerous temporal effect of the belief in evil."[75]

Eddy also feared a lifestyle that emphasized ease, relaxation, and pleasure, this expressed in tones that suggest the Calvinist ethos that shaped her. In the spring of 1906, for example, she wrote to the young John Lathrop, who formerly served as household staff, telling him of her sorrow "over the ease of Christian Scientists." She lamented that they were habituated in the "pleasures" of "sense." "Which drives out quickest the tenant you wish to get out of your house, the pleasant hours he enjoys in it or its unpleasantness?" she asked rhetorically. A few years later, toward the very end of her life, her household staff, who had typically observed a Puritan rigor, began to relax in ways that distressed her. Staff Scientists were less vigilant in protecting her against M.A.M., and they read the Boston newspapers, played golf, went for auto rides, and stopped sometimes at libraries in the neighborhood. On one late-summer occasion, recounts Stephen Gottschalk, Eddy looked out of her window as two staff members threw a ball back and forth and another attempted to walk on his hands. She endured, as Gottschalk quotes from Calvin Frye's diary, "a very disturbed night and a fear she could not live!"[76]

The perils of flesh and spirit, however, deferred to the presence of spirits when Mary Glover's first edition of *Science and Health* appeared in print in 1875. Published nine years after Quimby's death, the work displayed a woman who now spoke with an authority of her own and a sense of knowledge gained through hard-won experience. The text likewise displayed a woman at pains to separate herself from mesmeric and mediumistic phenomena, so that the new warfare of the spirit that Eddy waged was clearly directed against spiritualism and its magnetic culture. Like her former mentor Phineas Quimby and like the founders of Theosophy, she saw in mesmerism "unmitigated humbug," and her estimate of spiritualism was equally denunciatory. In the three-page preface to her ambitious first edition, Eddy (then Glover) singled out mesmerism for direct rebuke. "Some shockingly false claims" had already been made regarding the work in which she was engaged. "Mesmerism" was one, she stated flatly, and her denial was total. "Hitherto we have never in a single instance of our discovery or practice found the slightest resemblance between mesmerism and the science of Life."[77]

If Eddy seemed defensive, she had reason to be. In her Quimby years, she had surely traveled in mesmeric and spiritualist circles, and even as she took her first steps in Lynn as a practitioner of what became Christian Science many who were close to her thought of her as a medium. Her early advertisement of her new system of healing through "Moral Science" in the spiritualist *Banner of Light* in 1868 no doubt helped to fuel the assumption, and so, no doubt, did her outsider stance toward conventional medical methods.[78] That acknowledged, the vehemence of her condemnation of mesmerism and spiritualism was still startling. Eddy, by virtue of her emotional engagement, ended up affirming what she denied. Matter became real and so did mesmeric influence and spirit contact with it when she fought them so strenuously. From another point of view, Beryl Satter has suggested that Eddy's "healing process bore a family resemblance to mesmeric or hypnotic healing,"[79] and although the divine Mind that healed and mortal minds caught in the morass of error were profoundly different in her system (and so not exactly comparable), still the ghost of resemblance was there.

"Mesmerism," she told students, was "a belief constituting mortal mind," and "error" was "all there is to it, which is the very antipode of science, the immortal mind." "Mesmerism" was "a direct appeal to personal sense . . . predicated on the supposition that Life is in matter, and a nervo-vital fluid at that." It was "error and belief in conflict" and "one error at war with another"; it was "personal sense giving the lie to its own statements, denying the pains but admitting the pleasures of sense." Why was it so dangerous? The answer lay in its proximity to Spirit, its ability to function as a lying proxy for the truth. "Electricity," she wrote, "is the last boundary between personal sense and Soul, and although it stands at the threshold of Spirit it cannot enter into it, but the nearer matter approaches mind the more potent it becomes, to produce supposed good or evil; the lightning is fierce, and the electric telegram swift." Eddy's argument, in fact, replicated the theoretical model of homeopathy in which infinitesimal doses were more potent than gross ones. Homeopaths believed that the same substance that caused the symptoms of a given disease in a well person would cure the disease in a patient who was suffering from it. The key, however, was the "potentization" of remedies by increasingly radical dilutions to the point that, physically speaking, not even a trace of the original substance remained. Now, in Eddy's warning model, not only homeopathy but also the assorted healing modalities that kept it company achieved heightened power with the increased dilution of their physicality. "The more ethereal matter becomes according to accepted theories, the more powerful it is; *e.g.*, the homoeopathic drugs, steam, and electricity, until possessing less and less materiality, it passes into essence, and is admitted mortal mind; not Intelligence, but belief, not Truth, but error."[80]

Siding with the mentalists and not the fluidic theorists regarding mesmeric and related electrical phenomena, she declared electricity to be "not a vital fluid; but an element of mind, the higher link between the grosser strata of mind, named matter, and the more rarified called mind." Rarefied or gross, the danger in the magnetic world and its environs was ubiquitous. Thus phrenology fared no better in Eddy's estimate, making an individual "a thief or Christian, according to the development of bumps on the cranium." "To measure our capacities by the size or weight of our brains, and limit our strength to the use of a muscle," she admonished, "holds Life at the mercy of organization, and makes matter the status of man." Taking aim at the health reform movement of the era, which bowed "to flesh-brush, flannel, bath, diet, exercise, air, etc.," she declared "physiology" to be "anti-Christian." Meanwhile, not only magnetism but also "mediumship" and "galvanism" were "the right hands of humbug," and mediumship by itself was an "imposition" and a "catch-penny fraud."[81]

In Eddy's reading, mesmerism and mediumship were clearly intertwined, lumped together as, for practical purposes, they had functioned in the spiritualist community in which she had sometimes, if warily, participated. Moreover, she had been called a spirit medium, not a mesmerist, and so she experienced mediumship as an especially potent enemy against which she needed to contend. "We have investigated the phenomenon called mediumship both to convince ourself of its nature and cause, and to be able to explain it," she told the student readers of *Science and Health*, although she expressed some reservations about her ability to do the second. Her critique, though, was undeterred, and it was trenchant. The Rochester rappings "inaugurated a mockery destructive to order and good morals." Likewise, the "mischievous link between mind and matter, called planchette, uttering its many falsehoods," was "a prototype of the poor work some people make of the passage from their old natures up to a better man." Eddy did not deny the sincerity of many involved in the séances, enjoining readers to "make due distinction between mediumship and the individual" and affirming that there were "undoubtedly noble purposes in the hearts of noble women and men who believe themselves mediums." But like Blavatsky and Olcott at the (ironically named) Eddy farm, she pointed to the loss of mastery that accompanied mediumistic work. Mediumship, she warned, was a "belief of individualized 'spirits,' also that they do much for you, the result of which is you are capable of doing less for yourself."[82]

Eddy bristled angrily at mediumistic claims. Mediumship presupposed that "one man" was "Spirit," and that he controlled "another man" that was "matter." It taught that "bodies which return to dust or new bodies called 'spirits'" were "experiencing the old sensations, and desires material, and mesmerizing earthly mortals." It taught, too, that "shadow" was "tangible to touch" and that it produced "electricity" and similar phenomena. She found these conclusions to be "ridiculous." The spirit manifestations were the "result of tricks or belief, proceeding from the so-called mind of man, and not the mind of God." Mediumship itself overlooked "the impossibility for a sensual mind to become spirit, or to possess a spiritual body after what we term death," something that science revealed as "more inconsistent than for stygian darkness to emit a sun-beam." "To admit the so-called dead and living commune together," Eddy asserted categorically, was "to decide the unfitness of both for their separate positions." "Mediumship assigns to their dead a condition worse than blighted buds or mortal mildew, even a poor purgatory where one's chances for something narrow into nothing, or they must return to the old stand-points of matter." Its foundations lay in "secretiveness, jugglery, credulity, superstition and belief." Because of its mystical ambience, it could "do more harm than drugs."[83]

As warrior of the spirit, Eddy with her pungency equaled or exceeded the contentiousness of Quimby, making a similar case but making it now out of a heterodox Calvinism instead of her mentor's heterodox liberal Christianity. And like the unsystematic short pieces left by Quimby, her more systematic work pointed beyond the language of argument to a *lived* engagement with powerful ideas. The center of Eddy's work was practice, and the center of her healing practice was argument. In the language game that was her metaphysical system, the practitioner argued *against* the error that was matter, against the mortal mind of the patient-client in its mesmerized "Adam-dream"—until the healer broke through to Truth and Principle. The absolutism of Eddy's stance was uncompromising. The false belief in matter condemned people to the scenarios of illness and pain that they experienced. The healing role of the Christian Science practitioner was meant not so much to provide compassionate care as to demonstrate Truth in an ideal order that reduced the physical to the nothing that it was, an order that, in short, proved the claims of the Christian gospel as Eddy herself understood them. Like the utterly sovereign, utterly transcendent God of Calvinism, like the God out of the whirlwind in the book of Job, Truth brooked no compromise and demonstrated its reality by vanquishing the appearance of disease and disorder. Christian Science healing existed not to enhance matter and materially based humanity. It existed *only* to advance the Truth, the Principle, of God.

There was, of course, a cutting irony in Eddy's adamant antimaterialism—an antimaterialism that Stephen Gottschalk in recent work has noticed so clearly—when juxtaposed to the early wealth of the Christian Science Mother Church and the rising status of its mostly female practitioners.[84] But a facile coupling of the material success of the movement to the basic Eddy theology does not stand up to scrutiny when the founder's essentially Calvinist heterodoxy is understood. Still more, the easy identification of Christian Science as a species of what Sydney Ahlstrom called "harmonial religion" is problematic. Although the term has obscured more than it reveals even for New Thought, in the case of Christian Science it misreads the evidence on almost all counts. For Ahlstrom, "harmonial" religion signified "those forms of piety and belief in which spiritual composure, physical health, and even economic well-being" were "understood to flow from a person's rapport with the cosmos." But with human lives mired in sickness, sin, and death—the triadic legacy of mortal mind—Eddy's system taught no harmony at all for the material realm but instead total and uncompromising war. Moreover, when a "saved" Christian Scientist lived out of Truth and Principle, seeing evil for the nothing that it was, there was quite literally nothing with which to harmonize. One lived in Truth, or one did not. One could simply *not* harmonize nonexistence with Principle. Eddy's antimaterialist "scientific statement of being," in the familiar 1906 edition, brought home the point: "There is no life, truth, intelligence, nor substance in matter. All is infinite Mind and its infinite manifestation, for God is All-in-all. Spirit is immortal Truth; matter is mortal error. Spirit is the real and eternal; matter is the unreal and temporal. Spirit is God, and man is His image and likeness. Therefore, man is not material; he is spiritual."[85]

Christian Scientists did, of course, at times speak colloquially, as other Christians did, about getting into harmony with God. Eddy herself had taught that sickness, sin, and death were "inharmonies" and had pronounced all past, present, and future existence to be "God, and the idea of God, harmonious and eternal." "Harmonious action," she wrote, "proceeds from Principle; that is, from Soul; inharmony has no Principle." She had suggested in *Science and Health,* too, that the discovery of "Life Soul" would make one harmonious. Moreover, at the very core of a formulaic healing event lay an intense realization on the part of a Science practitioner of the unreality of the patient's particular plight or illness and the divine perfection that instead was and had been ever present. Such realizations *could* be couched in the language of harmony. But perusal of Christian Science literature reveals no preference for the term or the discourse of harmony, and, still more, Christian Science healers were accustomed to describing their healing work not only as "treatment" but also, and quite typically, as "argument." When they healed, they spoke of "demonstrating over" illness—in a metaphor that evokes science and contest at once. As Stephen Gottschalk notes, "the aims and theological standpoint of Christian Science and of harmonialism differ so markedly that the two cannot be assumed to represent the same tendency." Pointing as well to the pain and suffering that characterized Eddy's personal life, he found the harmonial ascription especially inappropriate. Eddy needed to be saved, to be born again; and she felt in her "discovery" of Christian Science that her new birth in the spirit had happened.[86]

Yet if Eddy was a decided antimaterialist, and if she fought fiercely against the lingering shadows of mesmerism and spiritualism, the connections between her new "Truth" and these former partners would not go away. In the case of mesmerism, we know that early Christian Science practice included some rubbing or touching of the afflicted area of a patient's body in the style of mesmerists (and, imitating them, spiritualist healers). This essentially followed Quimby's practice growing out of his earlier healing technique in animal magnetism, and he had typically employed water as a medium for the work. Eddy herself acknowledged that when she started teaching she had "permitted students to manipulate the head, ignorant that it could do harm, or hinder the power of mind." According to report, she at first actively instructed students to rub and touch—not for the patent efficacy of these gestures but, as Quimby did, because of the belief that they fostered in the patient: "As we believe and others believe we get nearer to them by contact and now you would rub out a belief, and this belief is located in the brain." Like a doctor's poultice applied for pain, so the healer should place her "hands where the belief is to rub it out forever."[87] Added to this, we have already seen Eddy's demonstrated fear, stronger as she aged, of malicious animal magnetism.

In the case of spiritualism, Ann Braude has pointedly noticed the overlap between Eddy's theologically driven healing method and the discursive world of the spiritualist community. Aside from the shared social context in which both flourished and the similarity of the needs that drew converts to both spiritualism and Science, the denial of evil in Christian Science from one perspective made the movement look like spiritualism because of its overt rejection of this major Calvinist category. Likewise, both spiritualism and Christian Science exalted science to deific proportions; both opposed orthodoxies in medicine as well as religion; and both encouraged egalitarianism by promoting women as leaders and by supporting lay ability to function as healers. In other words, in both systems the patient could easily take charge, and each system thus operated on a more or less level playing field. Moreover, as Braude argues, the "most significant" agreement came with the belief that there was "no change at death." True the lack of change existed, for spiritualists, as a function of the continuing material existence of spirit bodies after the change called death and, for Scientists, in the fact that there were never any real material bodies anyway. Even so, an underlying model of permanence and denial of death's edge characterized both movements.[88]

The language of the "Father-Mother God," the "Christ Principle," and God as Principle was, as we have already seen, part of the rhetorical world of spiritualism. Beyond that, Eddy's early Christian Science followers seemed to move easily in and out of the spiritualist community. Were the new practitioners— mostly women (in the ranks as well as leaders, as we will see)—former spirit mediums? Did they transpose their performances from spirits to Spirit in the same manner that the women whom Ann Braude has studied left trance mediumship on public stages for feminist speeches in their own names? Except for a few cases, no clear answers can be given. But the questions hang there for the asking. Braude has, for example, identified the combinative thrust of the Boston periodical *The Soul* in the 1880s, a periodical at home in both spiritualist and Christian Science circles. At least one medium and her husband—the later well-known Swartses—attended a Christian Science course taught by Eddy, even as the husband tried to teach what he learned from Eddy in spiritualist contexts. Beyond this, there was the over-protest of Eddy's relentless attack on spiritualism—"mesmerism, manipulation, or mediumship" as "the right hand of humbug, either a delusion or a fraud." As Braude observes, Eddy's preoccupation with separating Science from spiritualism suggests "that she viewed Spiritualism as the religion with which her own faith could be most easily confused."[89]

Still, like Blavatsky and Olcott—from whom she strenuously separated herself as well—Eddy recognized clairvoyance as fact and thought that spiritual manifestations involved mind reading on the medium's part. However, unlike Theosophists, who looked to elementals for the production of phenomena, she thought that materializations were the products of the mediumistic mind. Yet she did not think that, in theory, spirit communication was impossible. Rather, the reality of spirit communication needed to be demonstrated outside of matter since, by definition, matter was irrevocably yoked to appearance and *unreality*. Spirits, in the plural, were "supposed mixtures of Intelligence and matter" that, "science" revealed, could not "affinitize or dwell together." But Spirit itself, in the singular, was a thoroughly different case: there was "no Intelligence, no Life, no Substance, no Truth, no Love but the Spiritual." Eddy recognized, too, the existence of trance states and the power they gave to otherwise reticent speakers.[90] Finally, like the spiritualists, in her own way she supported and promoted feminism even if she had difficulties yielding authority to talented individual women who came to her.

Given all of this, the Christian Science that Eddy shaped in her mature years reconstituted spiritualism, turning it inside out to craft a monistic system based on *non*material spirit and inverting its liberalism in her lingering Calvinism. Her reconstitution achieved manifest success, shaping its metaphysics to a new and Christian organization that demonstrates the extent to which metaphysical combinativeness could reach. The formerly self-effacing Eddy spoke and acted with decisive authority as a new religious leader, and she made and unmade institutions in the service of her cause. The roster of her doings and *un*doings quickly tells the story. She established the Christian Scientists' Association in 1876 and restructured it into the Church of Christ, Scientist in 1879. By 1882, she founded the state-chartered Massachusetts Medical College in Boston and, by 1886, the National Christian Science Association. In these years of rapid growth and development, she encouraged graduates of the college to create regional institutes that would spread Christian Science throughout the nation. In the states of Iowa and Illinois alone, according to Rennie Schoepflin, sixteen institutes arose on the Eddy model in the 1880s and the 1890s. But in 1889, with divisiveness in church governance and increasing independence among former students, she dissolved the Christian Science Association, closed her college, and disbanded the Church of Christ, Scientist, all in moves to centralize and to regain control. Several months later, in 1890, she requested that the National Christian Scientist Association adjourn for a three-year period. Then, in 1892, she reorganized the Boston church, founding the "Mother Church" so that Scientists from all across the country would need to apply for membership therein to remain within the institution.[91]

Organization proceeded apace with Eddy's publication, in 1895, of the *Manual of the Mother Church*, legislating governance matters in detail, and with the creation, in 1898, of the main administrative units that would promote her teaching. So tightly did she organize governance that Stephen Gottschalk could remark, "Perhaps the most amazing thing about Mrs. Eddy's death was the fact that it had so little apparent effect on the movement."[92] At the same time, Eddy had committed her faith to the printed word as a major means to disseminate her new reading of the Christian gospels. From early on, practitioners and patients alike were urged to read *Science and Health.* Less than a decade later (in 1884), the first number of the *Journal of Christian Science* appeared (called the *Christian Science Journal* from 1885), with Eddy herself as editor until she turned the journal over to other promising women, like Emma Curtis Hopkins, who was soon fired and went on to become a prominent New Thought leader. In addition, Eddy created, in 1898, the *Christian Science Weekly,* subsequently renamed the *Christian Science Sentinel,* and the same year, too, established the Christian Science Publishing Society. When the well-known *Christian Science Monitor* was founded in 1908 to provide a Christian Science perspective on national and international news, it came under the aegis of the publishing society, as did numerous other promotional materials for the church and for Christian Science theology.

Eddy left Boston, where she had lived at the center of her movement for seven years, and in 1882 took up residence more reclusively near Concord, New Hampshire. Later, in 1908, she moved to Chestnut Hill, not far from Boston, where she ended her days. During her senior years, she oversaw a thriving movement that attracted increasing numbers of followers and received considerable notice in the press and public mind, some favorable and some decidedly less so. In Lynn, where Eddy had gathered her earliest class of students, they came mostly from the working class. But as the movement took off, this profile began to change. Stephen Gottschalk, who has pointed to occupation as an indicator of class status, notes—summarizing a Harvard doctoral dissertation—that by the year of Eddy's death Christian Scientists largely came from the middle class, a situation that Gottschalk sees as mostly "consistent" from 1900 to 1950.[93] Most had come, too, as believing Protestant Christians, although they had their quarrels with orthodoxy. Meanwhile, as the prominence of female leadership already suggests, many more women than men joined the movement. By the last decade of the nineteenth century, five times as many woman practitioners could be counted as men. By the next decade, in 1906, Christian Science membership was 72.4 percent female, at a time when all denominations together averaged 56.9 percent women in their ranks. The pattern apparently continued through the twentieth century, since in the 1970s the ratio of women to men within the denomination was eight to one.[94] Arguably, a new form of mediumship had arisen in their midst, as women mediated no longer the spirits from the second or further spheres but instead what Scientists claimed was Spirit itself—Principle, Truth, God, and (when gender references were made) Eddy's Father-Mother God. Without their "realization" as practitioners of each patient's "true" state, the Truth—and healing—would not be manifested in particular human lives. So the women put up shingles, placed advertisements, and collected set fees—professionalizing their healing work as the séance mediums had earlier professionalized their services.[95]

Nor did the women shun the mission field. They roamed widely as itinerant teachers, bridging the gap between domestic and public spaces and garnering a swiftly building membership for Christian Science. Rennie Schoepflin has cited statistics, for example, showing a net gain of an astounding 2,500 percent in Christian Science membership between 1890 and 1906, when 40,011 Scientists were claimed. Although Eddy banned the publication of membership figures after 1908, the number of practitioners continued to grow in the early twentieth century, with 5,394 globally in 1913 and 10,775 in 1934.[96] Like the earlier mediums who spoke in public when the spirits prompted, Christian Science women apparently felt compelled by their sense of Truth to spread a public gospel. The complex motivations of their missionary impulse point, once again, to the combinative milieu in which American metaphysical religion arose and flourished. In that milieu, too, despite all of Eddy's efforts to build an ecclesial edifice unmoved by religious change and reconstruction, the religious work that was Christian Science repeatedly exhibited the combinations and recombinations that were continually remaking metaphysics.

NEW THOUGHT AND THE RECONSTRUCTION OF CHRISTIAN SCIENCE AND THEOSOPHY

To some extent, Eddy's very claims to uniqueness (even if partially correct), and to permanence and impermeability, brought change to her door. As the standard narrative of the discovery of Christian Science took shape in her remembered past and its public reconstruction, the gradualism of her early healing practice gave way before Eddy's testimony to a startling single moment of Truth. The mentorship of Quimby dissolved before the direct visitation of Spirit. Others, however, did not forget. Quimby's former patient-students Warren Felt Evans, Julius Dresser, and Annetta Seabury Dresser either indirectly (Evans) or directly (the Dressers) challenged Eddy's erasure of the Quimby legacy, even as the legacy continued to function in a rising "mind-cure" movement. At the same time, disenchanted Christian Scientists left Eddy when their views conflicted with her vision or their persons with her personality. They believed that they found in the growing mental healing movement a kinder, gentler, and more expansive version of what they had learned in Eddy's world. Healers shared their skills and news with clients who, in turn, became other healers, other sharers. The term "Christian Science" was invoked freely, used in a generic sense as a description of the new vision and healing practice. Numerous periodicals showed what was happening (Gary Ward Materra discovered some 117 in existence by 1905), and so did popular books and monographs (Materra found 744 book-length works for the same period). A networking movement had begun and was spreading fast.[97]

It was not until the 1890s that a clear New Thought identity would be posited, and that would occur in the context of Eddy's copyright on the term "Christian Science" in the early part of the decade and at least partially because of it.[98] But the rift between Eddy's Christian Science and this developing "mental science" or generic Christian Science movement existed already in the tensile structure of Quimby's thought, held together, as it was, by his ability to contain paradox and anomaly in a persuasive metaphorical quasi system. Certainly his "wisdom" transcending the error-ridden minds of his patients and their sickness affirmed the ideal order that Eddy later promoted as Spirit, Substance, Intelligence, Truth, and the like. But, as we have also seen, Quimby saw wisdom not only as transcendent but also as a solid or even fluidic substance pervading all reality, much in the manner of the old magnetic fluid. He was facile enough mostly to avoid the terms *fluid* and *ether*, but nonetheless their presence remained in the characteristics that he attributed to wisdom.[99] Even as Eddy became an absolutist of the ideal, Quimby straddled both worlds—affirming a wisdom beyond sense and matter and yet introducing sensate concepts as palpable, lived metaphors for the experience of wisdom. Nowhere can this be seen more than in Quimby's home-grown speculations on smell and its relationship to a wisdom transcending the senses yet within them. Quimby *smelled* wisdom, and he *smelled* sickness. He thought of the odors that he absorbed as so many particles of the divine in a kind of etheric atmosphere surrounding a subject.[100] And he linked their diffusion as mediumistic bearers of knowledge, or wisdom, to words and language, which also functioned as mediumistic bearers of the same.

In so doing, Quimby hinted once more of his debt to spiritualism and, especially, to Andrew Jackson Davis. In his speculations on magnetism, Davis had taught that each human soul was encircled by an "atmosphere" that was "an emanation from the individual, just as flowers exhale their fragrance." Moreover, he had posited, because of the emanation, "a favorable or unfavorable influence" that one person could have over another (this last a source, perhaps, of Eddy's later notion of M.A.M.). In his turn, Quimby pushed the metaphor and materialized it further. He likened the "brain or intellect" to a rose, and he thought that intelligence came through its smells as they emanated. Again, each belief, for Quimby, contained "matter or ideas which throw off an odor like a rose." In fact, humans typically threw off "two odors: one matter and the other wisdom." Matter, identified with the human mind (not wisdom), produced an odor that was like a "polished mirror," with fear reflected in it as "the image of the belief." Wisdom was wise because it could "see the image in the mirror, held there by its fear." Quimby was the case in point, for it was his "wisdom" that disturbed his patient's reflected "opinion," deadening the mirror "till the image or disease" had disappeared. Mostly, in the terms of the analogy, Quimby focused on the smell of matter and its manifestation as illness in the life of a patient. "The mind is under the direction of a power independent of itself," he explained, "and when the mind or thought is formed into an idea, the idea throws off an odor that contains the cause and effect." The odor was "the trouble called disease," and—unlike the doctors who knew nothing about it—Quimby himself smelled the "spiritual life of the idea" that was error. From there he could launch his healing work to banish it.[101]

This was because Quimby could also smell wisdom—a different odor—which his ailing patients were unable to detect, even though the smell of wisdom could, at least theoretically, come to them. "As a rose imparts to every living creature its odor, so man become impregnated with wisdom, assumes an identity and sets up for himself," he argued. This wisdom might be called the "first cause" and might be construed, too, to exude an "essence" that pervaded "all space." Yet, in a distinction that was crucial for Quimby, the sense of smell and the other senses belonged not to the "natural man" but to his "scientific" counterpart. Such a "scientific man"—Quimby himself—knew odor to be the most potent of the senses, conveying knowledge of good (as in savory food) and of danger, for smell was an "atmosphere" that surrounded an object or subject. Thus—and this was where he was headed—the common atmosphere of humans in similar states of fear (in the presence of danger) led to "a sort of language, so that language was invented for the safety of the race." Quimby, in short, had arrived at the idea that "the sense of smell was the foundation of language" and at the overarching conviction that from the material process came the higher wisdom. "Forming thought into things or ideas became a sense," and the process was "spiritual."[102]

Moreover, if the sense of smell was, indeed, the "foundation of language," it was also itself a language. Humans, like roses, threw off odors; odors enabled Quimby to diagnose erroneous states of mind being manifested as diseases; odors also conveyed character. Still further, distance was no factor in intuiting smells and odors. Situated in wisdom, he claimed, "my senses could be affected . . . when my body was at a distance of many miles from the patient. This led me to a new discovery, and I found my senses were not in my body but that my body was in my senses, and my knowledge located my senses just according to my wisdom."[103] Quimby's thinking on these matters was often circular, muddled, and less than clear. But through his sometimes strained efforts to explain he was laying the groundwork for later New Thought theologies of immanence and pan-entheism. Profoundly different from the hauntingly Calvinist transcendent God of Eddy, with an ultimate divine alterity, the New Thought deity would beckon as the God within and the God who, like a superconscious etheric fluid, perme-ated all things.

It was Warren Felt Evans (1817–1889), Quimby's other major theological stu-dent alongside Eddy, who would articulate—much further and more clearly than Quimby—the possibilities and powers of the resident God. At the same time, like his doctor-teacher, Evans protected the twofold nature of divinity, Mind transcendent and Mind within. Son of a Vermont farming family, Evans attended Chester Academy, spent a year at Middlebury College, and then trans-ferred, in 1838, to Dartmouth in New Hampshire. He never graduated, since midway through his junior year he felt a calling to the Methodist ministry. Ac-cording to Charles Braden, he held, at various times, eleven different positions for the denomination. Then, in 1864, he joined the Swedenborgian Church of the New Jerusalem, and the profound and abiding influence of Swedenborg be-came apparent in his subsequent writings. The break from his Methodist past and his move in an unorthodox spiritual direction were probably at some level stress-ful, for he experienced both serious and chronic "nervous" disease. Close to the time he officially became a Swedenborgian, his physical condition brought him to Quimby's Portland door. Like Eddy, Evans was healed, became a Quimby student, and also felt a calling to be a healer himself. He began a mental heal-ing practice in Claremont, New Hampshire, but by 1867 had moved to the Bos-ton area, where, with his wife M. Charlotte Tinker, he spent over twenty years practicing and teaching. Unlike Eddy and other mental healing professionals, he charged no fees and accepted only free will offerings. He also apparently read copiously and wrote a series of widely influential books on mental healing in a religious context.[104] If we track the changes from the earliest to the latest of these works, we gain a sense of the shifting discourse community of American metaphysics as it transitioned from high-century phrenomagnetic and Sweden-borgian séance spiritualism to the theosophizing world of the late 1870s and 1880s.

The earliest of Evans's six mental healing books (he had previously written four short works on aspects of Swedenborgian theology) appeared in 1869 and the latest in 1886, together revealing a disciplined, ordering mind and a facility in ar-gument and exposition. Evans was bibliographically responsible in ways that sig-nal a professionalism and attention to detail not found in earlier, and especially vernacular, authors. Often, but not always, he parenthetically cited sources of quotations, giving an author's surname, a short title, and the page or pages. Aside from the general sophistication of these works and their at-homeness in both religious and scientific worlds of contemporary discourse, they were cast in a decidedly different tone from the work of either Quimby or Eddy. Instead of polemicism and battle, in Evans readers could find affirmation and a kind of irenic catholicity that consciously combined sources in an almost theosophical style.

The first of the mental healing books, *The Mental-Cure*, disclosed an Evans who was a thorough Swedenborgian and also comfortable in a spiritualist milieu that resonated with the harmonial theology of Davis. Mind was an "immaterial substance," but matter was also a substance, one associated with the sense experience of resistance and force. All humans were "incarnations of the Divinity," love was supreme, and the good lay within, with "great futurities . . . hidden in the mysterious depths of our inner being."[105] A combined Swedenborgian-spiritualist millennialism pervaded the text with its noticeable allusions to a coming (uppercase) "New Age" (of the Holy Spirit), which was "now in the order of Providence dawning upon the world." Meanwhile, its easy assumptions regarding the real existence of spirits, its familiar references to the "Seeress of Prevorst," its citation of the ubiquitous spiritualist Samuel B. Brittan, and its doctrine of spiritual spheres pointed in the same Swedenborgian-spiritualist direction. So did its understanding of death as a "transition to a higher life" and "normal process in development." References to Gall and to phrenology as well as magnetic allusions indicated Evans's familiarity with spiritualist discourse, and there was the by now well-recognized caveat regarding magnetic power and peril ("a power that can be turned to good account, or perverted to evil"). Still more, in the Swedenborgian reading that Evans gave to "modern spiritualism," we can see the easy conflation that he and so many others were making between the sources out of which they built their world. Expounding on the "Swedish philosopher" and his doctrine of spiritual influx, Evans saw inspiration and "the commerce of our spirits with the heavens above" as "the normal state of the human mind." In that context, what was "called modern spiritualism" was "only an instinctive reaction of the general mind against the unnatural condition it has been in for centuries."[106] The plan of Evan's work was generally speaking Swedenborgian, and he was hardly bashful about acknowledging his debt, for he quoted Swedenborg frequently and in admiring terms (Braden, in fact, found seventeen references).[107] Always though, Evans focused his account on the phenomenon of illness. Bodily dysfunction signaled spiritual dysfunction, and the way to correct the body lay in correction of the spirit.

Nor was there a conceptual gap between the two in the Swedenborgian universe that Evans inhabited. Citing the authority of his Swedish mentor as well as the New Testament Paul, Evans declared for the existence of a "spiritual body" bridging the gap between the "curious and wonderful" external body and the mind. The spiritual body functioned as one among innumerable "intermediates, through which influx descend[ed] from the higher to the lower"—part of a pattern in all creation. Compounded of "a substance intermediate between pure spirit and matter," it was for Evans "a sort of *tertium quid*," literally, a "third thing" that, for many in the developing New Thought movement, would seriously alter the orthodox anthropology of human body and soul. Here the (inner or interior) spiritual body became the harbinger of a series of multiplying bodily spheres that traced a path from gross matter to highest spirit. The spiritual body became, too, the harbinger of the energy pathways that traced the same route; and, already in Evans, the roadmap was ready. *"This inner form,"* he reported, *"is the prior seat of all diseased disturbances in the body."* For Blavatsky and the theosophical movement, the spiritual body (significantly, close to her "astral" body of less than a decade after Evans's book) would later be subsumed into a series of clairvoyantly visible bodies manifested with each human frame. For many in the New Thought movement, more abstractly, it would—in a transformed version—become part of the triad of body, soul, and spirit.[108]

Where was Phineas Quimby in *The Mental-Cure*? He was there as a kind of ghost among the spirits: Evans could apparently find no methodologically viable way to acknowledge his debt. (In *Mental Medicine*, Evans's second book on mental healing—published in 1872—he did acknowledge Quimby briefly.) Yet between the lines, as it were, Evans had surely inscribed his former mentor. In the magnetic-spiritualist and, specifically, Davis harmonial tradition, he had affirmed that "every material body" was "surrounded by an atmosphere generated by a subtle emanation of its own substance." He had gone on to declare that "the air enveloping the globe we inhabit" was "charged with the minute particles proceeding from the various objects of nature." But Evans's explanation of the emanation in terms of the olfactory sense, his specific use of a rose as an example, and his identification of a spiritual cause for smells and of something analogous "in the world of the mind" all smacked of Quimby—a Quimby easily conflated with Swedenborg as Evans's text progressed. Evans emulated Quimby also (and no doubt without direct control) in the quasi-shamanic quality of his sometime relationships with patients. Reflecting on his experiences with absent healing (a familiar Quimby technique), he owned that he had on occasion "been sensibly affected with their diseased state both of mind and body." "Once," he divulged, "where the patient was troubled with almost perpetual nausea, it occasioned vomiting in us." Still, as Braden noted, citing *Mental Medicine* of 1872, Evans thought that the effects of client illness on the healer were fleeting and easily dismissed—a "few minutes of tranquil sleep" would do it.[109]

For all his intellectual expansiveness, with Swedenborg and like Quimby, Evans always returned to Christian moorings to explain and affirm what was happening. According to John Teahan, well before Evans met Quimby—and fifteen years before the inaugural publication of the Glover (Eddy) book *Science and Health*—Evans had used the term "Christian Science" in print in his short work *The Happy Islands*. But more than Quimby, the early Evans evinced a clear orthodoxy regarding the person of Jesus—he was the "one and only God made flesh, and dwelling among us." Jesus healed by moving from cause to effect, in a model that Evans and other mental healers should copy, discarding the glib Baconianism of their culture for a compelling (Christian) alternative. In a particularly cogent statement that drew a line between scientific and general cultural orthodoxy, on the one hand, and the new metaphysical faith, on the other, Evans declared for principle (read "Cause," "Truth," "Mind," "Intelligence," and so forth). "We hold to the heresy," he announced, "that principles come before facts in the true order of mental growth, and the knowledge of things in their causes, is of more worth than a recognition of effects. This we acknowledge is not the Baconian method of philosophizing."[110]

Yet just as the spiritual body bridged the world of pure spirit and the material realm of the body, Evans—with a strong pragmatism—saw a bridge between principles and facts, between causes of illness and their unpleasant effects. The bridge, as a chapter title announced, was the "sanative power of words." Words functioned as "one of the principal mediums through which mind acts upon mind." They could be written or spoken, but either way they potentially could contain "the vital force of the soul." Evans went on for pages celebrating the blessings and wonders of words, proclaiming within them "a greater power . . . than men are aware of" and telling of their creative power even as he cited German Romantic philosopher Friedrich von Schlegel's *Philosophy of History* (translated in 1835) to support his views. For Evans, the case par excellence was Jesus, who "employed certain formulas or expressive sentences into which he concentrated and converged his whole mental force, and made them the means of transmitting spiritual life to the disordered mind." The moral of his story was clear; a physician's words "oftentimes" accomplished more than "his medical prescriptions." Evans had arrived at the doorstep of New Thought affirmation and affirmative prayer.[111]

By the time he published his third healing book, *Soul and Body*, in 1876, Evans was familiarly evoking his goals for the "restoration of the phrenopathic method of healing practised by Jesus, the Christ, and his primitive disciples." If the neologism *phrenopathy* hints of former Methodist minister and latter-day spiritualist La Roy Sunderland's "pathetism," it signals, too, a continuing comfort in the older spiritualist discourse community. In a work that aimed to be "*scientifi-cally religious*, without being offensively theological," Evans had already raised his Swedenborgian banner on the title page of the volume, quoting from Sweden-borg's *Arcana Coelestia* (on correspondences) to set the tone. Still, the easy allu-sions of the volume suggest that Evans was immersing himself increasingly in the Hermetic tradition that supported, if mostly covertly, "modern" spiritualism. He acclaimed "John Baptist Van [Jan Baptista van] Helmont," the seventeenth-century Flemish physician and scientist who was also a speculative mystic. He knew Jacob Boehme, and he linked his notion of the "spiritual body" to the "*perisprit*" of the French spiritualist theorist and mystic Allan Kardec (Hippolyte Leon Denizard Rivail), whose *Book of the Spirits* (1858) he had apparently read. He linked his "spiritual body" as well to the "*nerve-projected form*" of Justinus Kerner, whose work had brought the Seeress of Prevorst to public notice.[112] Yet arguably, there was nothing here that a widely read spiritualist would not cite or invoke, and the discourse world of Evans was yet conjoined to the older spiritu-alist community.

It was Evans's next book, *The Divine Law of Cure* (1881), that marked his entry into an expanded theoretical discourse to ground his metaphysical healing practice — at this juncture, however, solely in terms of the West. Now Evans was reading the Hermetic legacy in idealist terms more absolute and encompassing, grounding his increasingly philosophical idealism in the philosophy of the Con-tinent and of England. Evans's new cast of characters included Bishop George Berkeley, whose subjective idealism taught that matter did not exist indepen-dent of perception and that the apparent existence of matter was a function of the divine Mind. The new cast likewise included the German idealist philoso-phers Georg W. F. Hegel, Friedrich von Schelling, Johann Fichte, and Friedrich Jacobi, as well as the French eclectic philosopher Victor Cousin and the English Romantic poet and synthetic theorist of language Samuel Taylor Coleridge — all, significantly, beloved of the New England Transcendentalists.[113] Still, though, the idealism that Evans taught was a fudging idealism, one that could yet speak to the spiritual materialism of Davis and his sympathizers. Unlike the categori-cal denial of matter that had been spread abroad by Eddy, Evans's statement did not deny the actuality of bodily existence but instead asserted its contingency: It always and ever lived from the mind. Idealists, he told readers, did not deny "the *reality* of external things" but only that they had "any reality independent of mind." "The world of matter with all it contains," he attested, was "bound up in an indissoluble unity with the world of mind, and in fact exists in it." It fol-lowed that bodily properties were "only modifications of our minds." They were "reducible to feelings or sensations in the soul."[114] Enter Evans's phrenopathic

mental healing method to reap the pragmatic benefits of the philosophic situation. Unthought pain was unfelt pain; and disease, without wrong thought, was as
nothing. Banish the thought, and you banished the disease. Here was the "grand
remedy, the long sought panacea . . . the fundamental principle in the phrenopathic cure."[115]

The grand remedy, however, by 1885 and *The Primitive Mind-Cure* had moved
into a new theosophical world that flamboyantly blended Western philosophy
and Hermeticism with Asian texts and ideas in a dramatic recasting of Evans's
earlier gospel. Theosophy was apparently good for idealism, too, because now the
idealism had been ratcheted up a notch or two to become more uncompromising. In a facile comparative frame that pointed toward the New Thought world
to come, Evans brought together Berkeleyan idealism, Kabbalistic lore, and a
general Hermeticism that was informed by Neoplatonic, Swedenborgian, and explicitly Emersonian references. Even, in his catalog of names dropped and texts
quoted, he cited Blavatsky, whose *Isis Unveiled* had appeared in 1877. Evans, for
example, claimed her as his authority on Pythagoras and quoted her on the "universal life-principle" (Blavatsky's "ether"). But there was also very much more.
Evans joined to his expanded Western sources a series of allusions to the Indian
Vedas and Vedanta as well as to Buddhism and even to the Muslim statement of
the eleventh- and twelfth-century Persian mystical philosopher and theologian
Al-Ghazali.[116]

Isis Unveiled, although oriented to Western Hermeticism, provided relatively
generous material on Hinduism and Buddhism, and clearly Evans had been
drawn to Asia in pursuit of the evanescent substance-energy alternately styled,
in this post-spiritualist culture, as the ether, the astral light, the Hindu akasa, or
the Kabbalistic "occult air." Blavatsky's authors were Evans's authors. He cited
and quoted the English occultist "Lord Lytton" (Edward Bulwer-Lytton) and his
utopian novel *The Coming Race* (1871) with admiration, probably lifting his own
quotation from Blavatsky's work. (It was the same line that she quoted regarding
the akasa or *"vril,"* and he tellingly provided no page citation.) He also quoted
Éliphas Lévi on the "'universal substance'" (that is, the akasa) as the "'great
arcanum of being.'"[117] Hermes Trismegistus, in Blavatskian mode, uncritically
joined the truth of Asia, even as Evan's citations from the Kabbalah were ubiquitous. Always, for him, however, came the pragmatic bottom line. Change the
akasa/ether, and you change the person and, so, the outcome of the illness.

Evans's preoccupation with the ether was patent. Like Blavatsky, he sought
to blend science and Hermeticism, evoking his era's Newtonian and scientific
concept of the ether and invoking the Hermetic testimony to go beyond it. The
Hermeticists gave this universal *"aether"* "certain occult metaphysical proper-

ties" that modern science knew nothing of; they viewed it as "a divine, luminous principle or substance" permeating and also containing all things. Moreover, they called it the "*astral light*," which, Evans told readers, signified the "feminine wisdom-principle." The fire that the New Testament John the Baptist foretold (Luke 3:16) was both "identical with the Holy Spirit" and "the universal aether of occult philosophy." Citing "the Book of Hermes, called Pimander, which signifies the Divine Thought," Evans quoted, "'The light is I.'" Why did he think this important? The answer lay in Evans's conviction that a "thought impulse" could "affect and set in motion the universal *aether*, the life-principle." It could "create a current in the *astral light*," thus giving it "quality" and directing it "as a sanative influence." Few people knew of the "marvellous power" that was "latent and slumbering in human nature."[118]

Evans went on to express caution about the power of thoughts and feelings that marked the spirit of an age. He warned that the "prevailing mode of thinking and predominant feelings of an age or community" could bear people on against their will, and he linked the observation to the teachings of Jesus on the dangers of the "world." But unlike Eddy, he did not seem drawn particularly to the dangers of magnetism, and he turned instead to the "universal life-principle" as the "mother principle, the feminine creative potency, the passive power in nature" that was "co-eternal with spirit" and its "correlative opposite." He identified the mother principle with matter, found it to be reactive, and declared to readers that it could be impressed by thought. At the same time, in apparent contradiction, he called this "primal matter" an "immaterial substance," linked not only to his already-trinity of the Kabbalah, Hinduism, and the Holy Spirit but also to the Shekinah of the Hebrew Bible, the "sacred fire of the Persians," "the Astral light of the Rosicrucians," the Egyptian Isis, and the Roman Catholic Mary.[119]

It is at this point, in his vacillation between the materiality and immateriality of the cosmic ether, that Evans, like Emerson in *Nature*, struggled with the tension between pure idealism and a material model of the world. The tension was mediated, in Evans's case, by the magnetic universe he had inherited and also by the ambivalences of the Hermetic texts themselves (see chapter 1). But the idealism was softer and less absolute than Eddy's, and it resembled Quimby's in its ability to affirm and deny at once. Beyond either of them, too, lay the high Western tradition of idealism that Evans had introduced and the theosophical discourse out of which he was now reading recent Western idealist philosophers. Ideas were "the causes of the existence of all material entities"; they united "pure intellect"—the "masculine" of "Hermetic philosophy"—with "that spiritual and feminine principle" that could be designated as "feeling." Natural things were "but representations of things in the realm of ideas," and this view was "the old

Hermetic doctrine of correspondence" that had been "reproduced by Sweden-borg." The resemblance between "macrocosm" and "microcosm" was the "key note" of Evans's own "theosophical system." All things in the microcosm pre-existed "in the *unseen and real world of light,* the world of ideas," and "after their dissolution they return[ed] to that world." Evans's "transcendental medical science and practical metaphysics" were grounded on these assumptions.[120]

The shamanic quality of Evans's earlier healing experience took on new dimensions in this theosophical representation. "Silent suggestion" to cure disease was the "inner or occult word"; it was the "'lost word' which modern Masonry laments, and for which they try to find a substitute." But the "inward Word" worked as part of a process in which the healer absorbed "the morbid condition of the patient" and assumed "the psychic embryo of the disease." "We take up into ourself his [the patient's] condition," declared Evans, "in order that we may form a clear idea of it, and this idea of it is the real disease, the *ding an sich,* or thing in itself. Thus we are able to remit it or put it away from him." In the end, the healing work Evans recommended was a species of prayer, "the most intense form of the action, or influence, of one mind upon another."[121]

The reference to prayer with which Evans ended *The Primitive Mind-Cure* suggests the overriding Christian vision that informed his theosophy—unlike that of Blavatsky or Olcott. By now the historical person Jesus had become separable from the cosmic Christ, a separation that, as we saw, was adumbrated in midcentury magnetic literature of a popular nature and also in the writings of Quimby. Identical with "the Adam Kadmon of the Kabala," "the Archetypal Man of Plato," and "man as he exists in the divine Idea," this was "the Divine Man, the Christ of Paul, at the same time a divine personage and a universal *humanized principle* of life and light." All humans were included in his being, as "weak and imperfect" selves were "merged in the grand unity of the divine-human principle, the divine humanity of the Lord, which is the Christ." Still further, if all existed as part of this Christic whole, the Christ Idea aimed "to realize itself in every human being." The "Christ within" purposed to "save even the body."[122] It was no surprise, then, that hard on the heels of this book on "transcendental medicine and practical metaphysics" Evans produced, as his final work, *Esoteric Christianity and Mental Therapeutics* (1886). Here the idealism seems still more encompassing, yet ambiguous. "What we call matter, including the gross material body," he announced, "has existence only as a false seeming. The supreme reality in the universe is spirit." What would become familiar New Thought maxims abounded: "All that *is* is God, and hence is good," and "all that which *is* is included in God." "Disease, when viewed as an evil," had "no existence except as an illusion or deceptive sensuous appearance." It was "a nihility, or nothingness," and, indeed, "an empty show." "To emancipate the inward and real man from his imprisonment in matter and an illusory body" was "to cure disease." [123]

At first glance, the language of the Evans manifesto suggests a near resemblance to the absolute idealism of Eddy. From Christian Science quarters, however, the response was vitriolic. An unnamed "Christian Scientist," who may have been Eddy herself, used the lead article of one issue of *The Christian Science Journal* to inveigh against a book that looked suspiciously like "a twin of Theosophy." Evans's work was "a mad attempt to force Christianity . . . into the farcical groves of Occultism," to make the "doctrine" of Jesus "synonymous with Hindoo occultism." The reviewer was horrified to discover that, in Evans's pages, "each individual" was "a spirit, — not God, but a god" and that matter was a "divine substance." Eddy and other Christian Scientists of her school had good reason to be upset. Evans had declared that — even if what was called matter was "not matter" but "unreal and an illusion" — matter "in itself" was "not evil." He had told readers that "in its reality and inmost essence," matter was "divine — the second emanative principle from God." It was only when matter took "dominion over spirit" that it became evil, because it had usurped God's place and had thus become "idolatrous." Evans took care to underline his point: "Matter as it is in itself, and in its place, is *an invisible, divine, and immortal substance. It is the correlative of spirit* — a manifestation of spirit." [124]

Still more, Evans's affirmation of the goodness of matter was eclipsed by his emphasis on divine goodness, bringing a marked rhetorical departure to his work when compared to that of Eddy. Certainly, Eddy testified to the goodness of God, and it would be difficult to argue otherwise. That acknowledged, however, it is significant that as early as 1876, in her first published version of the "scientific statement of being," Eddy's catalog of Truth had included no reference to the goodness of God — nor did the standard 1906 statement in *Science and Health*. By contrast, Evans — with the Arminianized Christianity of his Methodist background and his Swedenborgian-spiritualist engraftment upon it — had put a large premium on the divine goodness, and he did not let readers forget. The preference would likewise come to characterize the discourse community of New Thought in ways that identify it clearly as different from Christian Science. [125] For Evans, the "manifested God" was the same as the Platonic Idea of the Good, as "the supreme and eternal Goodness," and as the "Christ of Paul." Still more, the place of this Christ was twofold — first, as "the Universal Christ" and "God of the macrocosm," and, second, as "the Christ within" and "God of the microcosmic man." Evans aimed to assist "the student of Christian Theosophy" in exploring "the inner realm of truth." Here the "unchanging I AM" dwelled as "the Christ within us, whose divine name is Ehejah, or I Am, that is the One and the Same." "So as soon as we get the true idea of our real Self, the unchanging and undying *I Am*, and that the real man is not sick," Evans exhorted, "we cannot avoid the consciousness of an impulse to act out the idea and play the part of health." Told in the language of the Hermetic tradition, the assertion of divine humanity was as striking. "It has ever been a doctrine of the esoteric philosophy and a religion of all ages and nations," wrote Evans, "that each immortal spirit is a direct emanation from the 'Unknown God.' . . . Each individual spirit is [as *The Christian Science Journal* had been dismayed to note] not God, but *a* god, and is possessed of all the attributes of its parent source, among which are omniscience and omnipotence." The human spirit possessed "deific powers." [126]

With humans as gods, Evans had biblicized the Hermetic teaching as he articulated the "I Am" consciousness. The formula would continue in New Thought throughout the twentieth century and into the twenty-first, even as it also functioned in theosophical culture in, for example, the early-twentieth-century Guy Ballard movement and, later, in the work of Elizabeth Clare Prophet.[127] Beyond that, in his proclamation of the divine humanity, Evans had arguably undercut his idealism once more and brought to it a further degree of conceptual ambiguity. New Thought would continue to live with the conceptual crack as its language community and its practice affirmed and dissolved idealism at once, teaching illusion and the divine goodness of creation at the same time. There was an ironic symmetry in the eagerness with which the New Thought community embraced Emerson as a founder and way-shower since he, too, had been caught in the conceptual crack between idealism and a wholehearted affirmation of the natural order.

Meanwhile, Evans had also articulated what became the New Thought language of "the silence." Recommending "tranquil and silent trust in the Christ," he countenanced silence for the sick as he invoked the "ancient wisdom, 'Be still, and know that I am God.'" The healer, too, "should wait in the silence that lies at the heart of things." Evans recommended deep breathing, evoking the Holy Spirit as the "breath of God" and likewise pointing to the Hermetic "Universal Aether" and the Kabbalah. Almost he seemed a yogi as he encouraged following the breath calmly, as close as possible to "the passive attitude of sleep." And if his mentalism did not preclude attention to the physiological process of breathing, in still another stance he signaled New Thought practice to come and separated it from Eddy's Christian Science. Evans found a place, if auxiliary, for the regular physician. "No *intelligent* practitioner of the mind-cure will ignore wholly all medical science," he admonished. "Mind is the only active principle in the universe. The mind of a skillful surgeon performs marvels in saving the lives of people."[128]

How influential were Evans's books? How did they affect the New Thought community that, by the mid-1880s, when Evans published his last two, was just beginning to take shape? We get some, if indirect, answers in the little we know of their publishing history. Charles Braden found a seventh edition of Evans's first book, *The Mental-Cure* of 1869, published in 1885, and also reference to a ninth edition without a publication date. And according to Beryl Satter, this work was translated into several foreign languages. Braden noted, too, that the copy of *Mental Medicine* (1872), Evans's second book, held by the Library of Congress was the fifteenth edition, also issued in 1885. There was at least one other edition of *The Divine Law of Cure* (1881) available in 1884. The copy of *The Primitive Mind-Cure* (1885) that I have used announces itself to be a fifth edition published in 1886 — just one year after the first edition. Although we do not know the size of any of these editions, the reprintings (for they apparently were that) are remarkable for a man who built no organization and, from reports of meetings and activities of the era, kept a low public profile. As Braden observed, Eddy's *Science and Health* of 1875 reached its thirteenth edition a decade later in 1885 — with "the advantage of a rapidly expanding organization to aid in its circulation during a part of this period, while Evans had at most only a small sanitarium where he carried on his healing work." Advertisements for Evans's books appeared in New Thought periodicals from the late 1880s (when the periodicals themselves began to appear) until at least the close of the nineteenth century. Major public libraries acquired the titles, and they could be found as well in the libraries of most New Thought centers and leaders. As one example of their role, H. Emilie Cady — whose own works were later to achieve an authoritative status in the Unity School of Christianity founded by Charles and Myrtle Fillmore — was converted to New Thought by reading Evans's books. Meanwhile, evidence of the reliance of Emma Curtis Hopkins on Evans is compelling, and Fillmore himself called Evans's works "the most complete of all metaphysical compilations."[129]

At the very least, Evans modeled the transformation of the thought world of parts of an aging spiritualist community as it entered a new era under the joint impress of Christian Science and Theosophy. His emphases and ideas — divine goodness, the ambiguous maternity of God, the "I Am" presence and the Christ (who was separable from Jesus) within, the silence, affirmative prayer and mental suggestion, the spiritual body — all of these presaged a coming New Thought universe and discourse community. Evans's ambivalent idealism, with its real and yet illusory natural order, sought to embrace both science and spirit, both the

Hermetic tradition of the West and Hindu, Buddhist, and even Muslim sources in ways that would mark a new metaphysical discourse in the waning nineteenth century and beyond.

Others, however, were advancing the conversation through more organized healing work. Quimby's students Julius Dresser and Annetta Seabury Dresser made their way to Boston and began to teach and practice there, even as Eddy's star was rising in the East Coast city. For Julius Dresser, at least, the mental healing ministry he now took up represented a decided about-face. Not two weeks after Eddy's catalytic fall on the ice in Lynn, she had written to Dresser for mental healing support, but—in Yarmouth, Maine, working as a journalist—he had expressed a remoteness from Quimby and a disregard for his work. Sixteen years later, however, and living in California, Julius Dresser changed his mind. He came back east and took Christian Science lessons with his wife, Annetta, from Edward J. Arens, Eddy's former student and now strong enemy. For whatever reasons (Eddy's recent biographer Gillian Gill suggests greed; the New Thought account, anger and upset that Eddy was no longer acknowledging Quimby), the Dressers immersed themselves in the work. They did so in a Boston that, by the 1880s, was rife with metaphysical healers, numbers of them former Eddy students. It was this mix of independent mental healers and former Eddyites, often now assuming the generic Christian Science name, that coalesced as New Thought in the decade that followed.[130]

Exchanges between the Eddy group and the looser mental healing community were generally conflictual, with controversy over Quimby dominating much of the public discourse. (At least this is the story as it was later reconstructed in the nonprofessional first history of New Thought by the philosopher son of the Dressers, Horatio Dresser.) But the healing work went on—lessons, practice, and wider public lectures. So did the work of an emerging New Thought press, with books and periodicals that underlined the cognizing instincts of the mental science confraternity. The Dressers produced a circular in 1884, and by 1887 Julius Dresser saw the publication of his book *The True History of Mental Science*. The comprehensive nature of the movement's purview was indicated by some of these early works. For example, Mathilda J. Barnett's *Practical Metaphysics* (1887), according to J. Stillson Judah, reflected theosophical principles in its exposition of metaphysics; William J. Colville's *Spiritual Science of Health and Healing* the same year expressed his own background in spiritualism with the "inspirational" suggestion of its extended title.[131]

The Church of the Divine Unity (where Dresser—himself once a candidate for the Calvinist Baptist ministry—had delivered the lectures later incorporated into his mental-science book) became one of the first of the quasi–New Thought churches. It had been founded in 1886 by Jonathan W. Winkley, once a Unitarian minister and also an Eddy follower, who would later, in 1900, inaugurate the journal *Practical Ideals.* A year earlier, from 1885, Elizabeth Stuart—an Arens student (after he had broken with Eddy) who went on to take a Christian Science course from Eddy in 1881—became the catalyst for the formation of "Light, Love, Truth" in Massachusetts and New York. A Connecticut group was brought under the aegis of the organization in 1888, and in each of its locations, according to Gary Ward Materra, all of the known officers were women.[132]

From its early beginnings, however, the emerging New Thought movement was national in scope—a reality obscured by the East Coast orientation of Horatio Dresser's pioneering history (with its preoccupation with the Quimby-Eddy controversy) and its shaping influence on subsequent scholarship. Newer work, though, has told a different story of widespread New Thought foundations, beginning in the 1880s in the Midwest and Far West and spreading to numerous locations. "The movement's heart and soul lay in the western states," Beryl Satter has observed. In a networking pattern that imitated séance spiritualism and, on a smaller scale, Theosophy and that augured the future of metaphysics, New Thought women and men fanned out as independent healer-teachers in places large and small. By 1902, an article in the *American Monthly Review of Reviews* claimed over a million followers. If any one figure could be identified as a major influence on the early phases of this growth, that person was Emma Curtis Hopkins (1849–1925). Indeed, both J. Gordon Melton and Gail M. Harley have read her as the "founder" of New Thought, and although that assessment arguably oversimplifies the complexity of an act of foundation, it does point to the abiding importance of Hopkins's role. Even in the 1960s, Charles Braden acknowledged her reputation in New Thought circles as "the teacher's teacher."[133]

Who was Emma Curtis Hopkins? What did she do for New Thought theology and practice to suggest the titles that scholars have conferred on her, and how did she do it? Born in a Connecticut farming family as Josephine Emma Curtis, she acquired some education and married George Irving Hopkins, a high-school English teacher, in 1874. Their son John Carver Hopkins lived until 1905, but by that time his parents had long been separated, and his father had divorced his mother for "abandonment." What Hopkins had abandoned her husband for was the Christian Science teaching of Mary Baker Eddy. She had met Eddy in Manchester, New Hampshire, where Hopkins was living, had listened to Eddy testify to Christian Science, and had experienced a healing that she attributed to the work of the local Christian Science practitioner. After an exchange of letters, Hopkins traveled to Boston, enrolled in an Eddy class at the end of 1883, and by 1884 was listed as a practitioner in *The Journal of Christian Science*. The same year she resigned from the Congregational church of her childhood to become a member of the First Church of Christ, Scientist, in Boston. A few months later she was working without pay as editor of Eddy's journal.[134]

But the honeymoon period in Hopkins's relationship with Eddy was soon over. For reasons that are shrouded and unclear but that suggest, most persuasively, her 1885 editorial "Teachers of Metaphysics," Hopkins was dismissed after some thirteen months and ordered out of her (Christian Science) lodging. Satter has noted Hopkins's mystical language in the piece, with the editor—after contact with Eddy's teaching on "Spiritual Being"—claiming to know God "face to face" and thus implying, at least for Eddy, that Hopkins was her peer. Hopkins wrote that she had "realized the reward 'to him that overcometh' for an interval brief but long enough to fix forever in my mind the sweet consummation of faithful endeavor." Others have pointed to Hopkins's friendship with another student, Mary Plunkett, who for a variety of reasons was troubling Eddy.[135] At any rate, Hopkins was never given any explanation, and she never publicly repudiated Eddy; in fact she wrote her letters, even after the firing, to express her regard for her former teacher. Still, from the first, Hopkins had been moving to a drumbeat different from the one that Eddy heard. Her earliest article for Eddy's Christian Science journal already signaled her theosophical interests, and her theology would develop in the immanentist and mystical directions that marked New Thought. Hopkins was also decidedly feminist, interested in social-action causes, intimate —especially in her later New York years—with a literary and artistic community, and considerably tolerant of views other than her own. Publicly, she continued to maintain the low profile that made her barely visible in earlier histories of New Thought.

Hopkins moved to Chicago after leaving Eddy, first editing Andrew J. Swarts's *Mind Cure Journal* and then, with Mary Plunkett, establishing the Emma Curtis Hopkins College of Christian Science in 1886. One report from the 1920s claimed that some six hundred students participated in Hopkins's classes within a year. Meanwhile, the students formed the Hopkins Metaphysical Association, which spawned branches in numerous other places. Even with her teaching responsibilities, Hopkins did not stay home but traveled around the country to offer classes and form further outposts for her organization. For example, in 1887 she was in San Francisco, where she met Malinda Cramer, who later went on to found, with Nona Brooks, the Church of Divine Science. Later in the year Hopkins taught in Milwaukee and then in New York City, where her class included H. Emilie Cady. Hopkins and Plunkett together created *Truth* magazine as the official voice of the local Hopkins Metaphysical Associations, the national convention of which they held in Boston toward the end of 1887. By the end of that year, according to Materra, the Hopkins groups numbered twenty-one, extending from Maine to California and functioning as the earliest national New Thought organization.[136]

Plunkett (and her husband) subsequently moved to New York City, taking *Truth* with them and changing its name to *The International Magazine of Christian Science*. There followed a period of some cooperation and also the birth of a new Chicago journal called *Christian Science*, edited by Ida Nichols with much support from Hopkins. But Mary Plunkett's "spiritual marriage" to A. Bentley Worthington (later exposed as a bigamist with at least eight wives)—while she was legally married to John Plunkett—heaped scandal on the New Thought effort in New York. Plunkett and Worthington found it opportune to resettle in Christchurch, New Zealand, and to carry on their New Thought work there. In Chicago, however, Hopkins and her teaching remained relatively unscathed. More important, it had become independent, and, in the context of the upheaval, Hopkins converted her college into a seminary and ordained its graduates, overwhelmingly women. "Christian Science is not a business or profession," she was reported to have said. "It is a ministry."[137] Her Christian Science Theological Seminary functioned successfully until 1894, when—fatigued by her efforts on many fronts and by infighting at the seminary—she moved to New York City. She conducted classes and did healing work there, traveling on the East Coast and also to England and Italy. During her Chicago time, Hopkins taught Charles and Myrtle Fillmore, who founded Unity, and during her New York years, she taught Ernest Holmes, who founded Religious Science. Nona Brooks, who studied with Hopkins, co-founded Divine Science with Cramer; still another student, Annie Rix Militz, founded the Homes of Truth; and yet another, Frances Lord, carried New Thought to England. Hopkins's student Helen (Nellie) Van Anderson in 1894 began the self-consciously New Thought group in Boston called the "Church of the Higher Life." A series of other Hopkins students, well known in movement circles, spread out across the nation, bringing the Hopkins brand of metaphysics to numerous local communities.

We get a rare vignette of the Hopkins teaching style during the Chicago years in one news report from the Kansas City *Christian Science Thought* for 1890. There Hopkins, who was teaching a class at the Kansas City College of Christian Science, is portrayed as a charismatic woman with extraordinary powers. The unnamed author (was it Charles Fillmore, who edited the journal?) told readers: "After an eloquent burst of oratory, the teacher said with a peculiar quiet vehemence, '*God is Life, Love and Truth,*' long tongues of flame shot out from her vicinity and filled the room with a rosy light that continued throughout the remainder of the lecture to roll over the class in waves and ripples of what seemed golden sunlight." The writer apparently had checked with others. "Many saw it plainly while others sensed its uplifting presence in the room. We felt that we had almost experienced a modern day of Pentacost [*sic*]."[138]

Gail Harley, however, has distinguished between Hopkins's Chicago years and her New York period, and the distinction is a useful one.[139] The Chicago Hopkins followed the Eddy gospel more faithfully, although, to be sure, she departed from it in marked and consistent ways. In the New York years, by contrast, Hopkins barely reiterated the basic Christian Science formula regarding the nonexistence of matter and mostly soared into a mystical stratosphere that seemed to reflect direct experience as well as—most likely—Evans, Blavatsky, and similar sources. In both periods, though, Hopkins's material was mostly derivative—one reason why the "founder" attribution seems strained at best—although, as we will see, in at least two ways she did introduce new material or emphases into the theological mix that became New Thought. Beryl Satter has argued that Hopkins attracted people with quite different perspectives because she brought together both Eddy and Evans, and Hopkins certainly did that. Even here, however, she had probably been preceded in uniting Eddy with Evans by the former Methodist minister and spiritualist Andrew J. Swarts and his mediumistic wife, Katie L. Swarts, in their Mental Science school in Chicago. More than that, in Hopkins's work the alliance of Eddy and Evans was far more uneasy than the Satter analysis allows.[140] The tensions in the theological constructions of Quimby and Evans emerge from their work as somewhat soft and malleable—cracks in the structure on the order of the now-classic crack in Emerson's *Nature*. By contrast, Eddy opted for greater consistency and greater absolutism. It remained for Hopkins to attempt a union of the absolutism of the Eddy Christian Science message with the plasticity of the Evans construction. In brief, Evans was theosophical; Eddy was not. Hopkins did not unify their teaching but rather juxtaposed it. If there was a resolution at all, it came only in the New York period when Hopkins's *High Mysticism* paid lip service to Eddy but mostly spent its energies (and readers') in an impassioned declaration of what, by the mid-twentieth century and after Aldous Huxley, would become known as the perennial philosophy.[141]

Hopkins's publishing habits made it difficult for later admirers to gather her corpus effectively. Often, she produced pamphlets that constitute brief monograph lessons—almost sermons—on selected themes. Her Bible lessons appeared in the *Chicago Inter-Ocean* (newspaper) from 1890 through 1898. Other publications include class lessons that she had used in her teachings and her ordination addresses. Thus her publishing history is hard at best to reconstruct. For all that, enough material is available to provide snapshots of the Hopkins theology at key points in her metaphysical career, and these snapshots tell us that through the teaching of Hopkins, gradually Mary Baker Eddy quietly shifted backstage in the New Thought community and a more globally inclusive Evans style moved to the center. This is true even if in later New Thought, as we will see, only one of two major wings of the movement could trace its instincts to the Hopkins theology—a situation that, again, makes the attribution of New Thought foundation to Hopkins problematic.

Hopkins's first article in Eddy's *Journal of Christian Science* (April 1884) provides already an important clue to the different (from Eddy) cultural world in which she lived. In a piece of eleven brief paragraphs, Hopkins managed to cite "Buddhist Nirvana," "Algazel, a Mohammedan philosopher of the twelfth century," Spinoza, Confucius, the Persian "Zend-Avest," the Chandogya Upanishad, the "Persian Desatir," and the Hebrews. She sometimes quoted from these sources, no doubt as they were quoted in other works—Evans?—she had been reading. Her point was God's omnipresence and the "blessed evidence" she found of "universal goodness" and divine "impartiality" in the manifestation of God "to every people and nation of the earth." By November of the same year, for all God's universality, she was hailing the special manifestation of the divine in the Christian Science founder. Eddy's direct predecessor in giving the world a "system of ethics" with health as its "practical application" was "Jesus, the Christ." And in an apparent allusion to the Quimby controversy, Hopkins defended Eddy in remarkably feminist terms. From "many quarters" came "the bold denial of her right to her own work." Why was this so? "Because it is a woman whom God hath chosen, this time, to be His messenger, and not Jesus or Saul." Hopkins pushed on to the general conclusion: "But Woman's hour has struck. Who can doubt it? The motherhood of God beats in the bosom of time, with waking energy, today."[142]

As Gail Harley has shown, the Mother God—more noticeably than the Father-Mother God of Eddy—was a distinct (and new) Hopkins emphasis. In a millennialist division of history that echoed the twelfth-century Joachim of Fiore or the later Emanuel Swedenborg with his announcement, reiterated in Evans, of a New Age, Hopkins proclaimed a coming third age of the Holy Ghost. This Holy Ghost, however, was distinctly feminine—identified with the Shekinah of the Hebrew Bible as well as with the New Testament Spirit—and was also a sign of a feminist future to be. The coming age would be a better era than before, and Hopkins—far more than Eddy—avidly supported social reform causes. Meanwhile, her pamphlet essay *The Ministry of the Holy Mother* appeared during her Chicago years. In it the divine Mother was conjoined to both the Spirit and ministry of God in a mystical statement that was also a declaration about service and about Hopkins's conviction that any adequate idea of God required the feminine.[143] Likewise, her ordination addresses during these years regularly invoked the motherhood of God in the Holy Spirit. The Father-Mother God was still in charge, for Hopkins, and was never eclipsed by a sole reliance on the Mother. Still, the Mother received her due in Hopkins's thinking more than the divine feminine ever would later in New Thought. After the leadership of women in the initiating years of the movement, by the early decades of the twentieth century a new generation of men would rise to prominence as leaders, and the Mother would recede.

A second new emphasis in Hopkins survived—indeed blatantly—in the New Thought movement. This was Hopkins's evolving gospel of prosperity, a teaching that may have been related to her own struggle with poverty in the early years of her failed marriage with George Irving Hopkins. In fact, when Hopkins first negotiated with Eddy to become part of a Christian Science class in Boston, she had to explain her husband's indebtedness and her inability to come up with funding to support her educational goals. She worked out a special arrangement with Eddy.[144] Hence, as early as Hopkins's "Ordination Address" to her first graduating class of seminarians published in 1889, she was subtly noticing more than divine healing activity. She saw her graduates among those who were "ministers of the gospel of The Good," and she pointed to the work of Jesus in which "the poor were helped and fed." She linked her class with those who proclaimed a "New Dispensation of the Holy Spirit," a new order "wherein the poor may be taught and befriended, women walk fearless and glad, and childhood be safe and free." Christian Scientists, for her, declared "the omnipresence of God the Good and deny the presence or working power of any other Principle but the Good." More than that, it was women, linked to the "Mother God" in "the Holy Spirit of Scripture," who especially pointed toward the emphatic reading of God as good. "Woman's voice—the mother heart of the world," Hopkins told her graduates, was now proclaiming "the omnipresence, omnipotence and omniscience of The Good."[145]

These suggestions grew less subtle in Hopkins's formal lecture from the Chicago period "How to Attain Your Good." Cast in a markedly different frame from Eddy's Christian Science, Hopkins's work began with a theosophical and Evans-style "fine etheric Substance pervading all the worlds of the universe." Hopkins called it "Cosmic Substance" and supplied as synonyms for it "Mother" or "Mother-Principle" as well as "God-Substance." The human mind was "made out of this omnipresent Mother," and the "etheric substance" that "the common thought and word use" was "only a rough shadowing forth of the truly omnipresent Substance." The ancient Egyptians (not the Hebrews) called it "the *I Am* of the world," and Jesus called it "Spirit" and a series of other titles including "God," "Father," and "Love." Hopkins herself said it was the "Good-Substance."

She went on to invoke, like a mantra, a repeated affirmation: *"There is good for me, and I ought to have it."* What did the good mean for the aspiring Truth student? Among the series of explanations, many of them generic and noetic, Hopkins found her way to tangibility and profit. "Everything is really full of love for you. You love the good that is for you," she told students. "You can make the connection between yourself and prosperity by saying that the good that is for you is love." With God equated with "Love" and "Good," "all things poured down blessings into the lap of Jesus Christ because he knew everything loved him."[146] So, apparently, would it happen for Truth students. If the New Thought Statement of Being posited Good at its center, it followed that abundance on earth was one result.

In *Scientific Christian Mental Practice*, also a product of the Chicago years, Hopkins continued to weave a gospel of prosperity quietly into her teaching. Here was none of the flamboyance that would come to characterize the later New Thought pursuit of the prosperous, nor any of the mechanical formulas that would by then accompany the prosperity message. In a work structured—like Eddy's own work—on denials, first, and then affirmations, Hopkins announced to readers a series of five "universal affirmations." Here the first began "my Good is my God," and the others moved in increasingly mystical directions, invoking identity with Spirit, with the "I AM" presence, and with an absence of the ability to sin. With the use of the "right word" and the proclamation of one's freedom, she told readers, each of them would "soon be more prosperous." Scientists should experience neither poverty nor grief, and one of the things they should do was to "talk for prosperity," using the affirmation *"I believe in prosperity and success."* They should "covenant with Spirit" for support and do nothing for it, because support was "the providence of the Spirit." In a negative example, Hopkins held up one pastor of an English mission who "was very much pleased that he got his expenses paid by praying for them, and had about $14.00 left over." Her unflattering conclusion: "As all the wealth of the earth was offered him you can see that he was not especially honoring God by having such a little bit at his disposal." By contrast, Hopkins's good news of prosperity was predictive. "Men may gather all the gold into a lump, and say you cannot have any, but by some way of the Spirit you will come out with more abundant riches than all the rest put together."[147]

By the time Hopkins wrote the material in *High Mysticism*, healing, prosperity, and similar concerns receded before a unitive consciousness that dominates the studies that formed the book. Evoking "John the Revelator" in a series of twelve visionary explorations probably first published separately, Hopkins's work illustrates why the harmonial label is problematic not only for Christian Science but also for a major lineage of New Thought. If the word *harmony* appears from time to time in Hopkins's discourse, her message is hardly one of "rapport with the cosmos." Instead, a radical immanence prevails in these studies, in which the language of Self-recognition and the God-Self translates the theosophized religiosity of a dizzying catalog of traditions into an American New Thought argot. These were surely traditions imbibed at second hand—from Evans and perhaps Blavatsky (Hopkins at least once referred to the "secret doctrine," the title of Blavatsky's seminal work to be examined in the next chapter) and similar authors. What is important here, however, is how Hopkins shaped them into American metaphysics. "When half gods go the gods arrive," announced Hopkins, and she staked out the required denials (no evil, matter, loss or lack or deprivation, fearful thing, sin or sickness or death). But they cleared the way for affirmations that— while they certainly reproduce the health and blessing of New Thought expectation—are something more: mystical statements of divine identity that mince no words and leave no space for human failure. "Highest God and inmost God is One God," Hopkins declared. "Our own Soul, our own free Spirit forever says, in bold faith, 'I am Truth, I am God—Omnipresence, Omnipotence, Omniscience.'"[148]

Hopkins was evoking what I am calling the enlightened body-self, a construction of human personality and life that had been presaged in a vernacular American context as far back as the early Mormonism of Joseph Smith with its message of a divine future for humans. For Hopkins and the new American metaphysics, however, the future was now, and the future was here on earth. If the transcendent had become immanent in this Christian world gone theosophical, where the mystical language of many traditions pointed toward a secret Self that moved the world, somehow the ego—ennobled, transfigured, and exalted, but still the ego—had tiptoed behind the Self. What resulted was not quite the crass and glib formula that has been applied dismissively to New Thought—"health and wealth and metaphysics." What followed, still, was something more tangible, more practical and concrete, than the already-pragmatism of the Hermetic past—and this because it more boldly championed the garden of delight on an earth properly viewed and employed. Beryl Satter's reading of a debate and then a shift from an anti-desire rhetoric in New Thought to a clear language of desire in the early twentieth century surely speaks to the point here.[149] The secret and this-worldly history of the Self would be a leading reason why, by the twentieth century, as we shall see, some Americans became interested in South Asian tantrism. And this was why, too, in their unitive consciousness many metaphysicians turned— like earlier spiritualists and Theosophists—to concerns about social reform. As New Thought read the script, the soul's journey in the hereafter paled before the significance of a mystical present that could be paradise.

The New Thought Hermeticists were mostly white and middle class, and they linked their vision of paradise to the progressivism of their era. Interest in woman suffrage and a general feminist agenda ran high, as it had for Hopkins, but metaphysicians branched out to embrace other issues and causes as well. In fact, Gary Ward Materra has argued that the Hopkins brand of New Thought represented one of two divergent styles in the early movement. Materra identifies it as "affective" in orientation, characterized by "emphasis on the Bible, healing, and the needs of families and communities." Hopkins and those who imitated her understood their enterprise as religion through and through. They held to a vision of unity among all things and people, thought about relational ethics, and were concerned, for example, about their children as well as about church building and networking. Predominantly women, they were often feminists and social activists, unabashed in their criticism of prevailing social and economic mores and willing to entertain ideas of social reconstruction that extended, sometimes, even to socialism. A number of New Thought women found fault with capitalism in its unrelieved pursuit of profit for its own sake, even as they worked to improve the conditions of the poor.[150]

Examples abound within the Hopkins Metaphysical Association and outside it. Helen van Anderson, in Boston, used the church she formed to encourage a Young People's Club as a service organization for "hospitals, reformatories, or private homes," while a different committee brought New Thought teachings to poor and sick people in their own communities. The Circle of Divine Ministry in New York City in 1897 decided to open a room "in the lower part of the city," so that "some much-neglected classes of its inhabitants, boys and so-called criminals" could be reached. The Denver-based Church of Divine Science staffed a day nursery for the children of working-class mothers, and the church also aided a group that worked with tuberculosis-ridden men without means. Nona Brooks, its co-founder, spent seven years as the secretary of the Colorado Prison Association. In San Francisco, the earliest Home of Truth offered free meals and clothing to the poor through a branch office. The San Francisco Home of Truth also for a time created a shelter for homeless men.[151]

New Thought people threw themselves into the settlement house movement of the end of the century, beginning a metaphysical version of a settlement house in 1895 in the Roxbury District of Boston. They also moved to riskier public stances, as, for instance, in the outspoken antiwar rhetoric of Catherine Barton and Elizabeth Towne. Nor were analyses of social problems simplistic and naive. Barton, for example, commented on crime and criminals with the observation of shared guilt on the part of all: "We have so constructed our social, ethical, and religious fabric that crime is a natural outcome." Anita Trueman did not think that New Thought, with its prosperity thinking, would by itself cure the condition of a man out of a job because of economic depression. Rather, New Thought believers needed to "readjust those conditions which enrich the monopolist while he robs the people of even the opportunity to work."[152] Meanwhile, as Beryl Satter notes, individuals with New Thought ties, such as Abby Morton Diaz and Mary Livermore, embraced the form of socialism advocated by Edward Bellamy's novel *Looking Backward* (1888), which brought in its train a series of Bellamy Clubs across the nation. Former Episcopalian pastor R. Heber Newton in 1885 had joined Richard Ely's American Economic Association with its advocacy of government intervention on behalf of the disadvantaged but by 1899 found in New Thought a religion that buttressed his politics better than Episcopalianism had. He presided over the International Metaphysical League in 1900, 1902, and 1906, and he served as an officer in the New Thought Federation in 1904. Congregationalist minister Benjamin Fay Mills, with a history of attacking monopolies and praising socialism, likewise became a New Thought fellow traveler by 1905, founding a Los Angeles "Fellowship," which Satter describes as "indistinguishable" in its beliefs and goals from New Thought. Other reforming clergy among Protestants also moved into New Thought—among them Hugh O. Pentecost, Henry Frank, J. Stitt Wilson, and George Herron. They sought, as Satter recounts, the victory of "'altruism over selfism'" as well as the pursuit of human perfection.[153]

Ralph Waldo Trine, author of the classic *In Tune with the Infinite* (1897), was an out-and-out New Thought socialist. But he was hardly alone, and much of his company was female. Indeed, Materra concludes on the basis of his study that "women forged the primary links between New Thought and socialism." Thus Malinda Cramer, who co-founded Divine Science, castigated the "competitive system" as the "offspring of brute evolution" that bore "no relation to the divine methods of 'each for all, and all for each.'" Josephine Conger, who spent two years at radical Ruskin College in Trenton, Missouri, and there converted to socialism, later threw herself into the socialist women's movement. She functioned as its leading editor and at the same time acknowledged her New Thought commitments in the socialist print periodical world. "All the great men and women of the world have believed in what we call New Thought," she told readers of a 1903 issue of *Appeal to Reason*. Moreover, if a socialist organ such as *Appeal to Reason* could missionize for New Thought, at least one New Thought paper, *Social Ethics*, was also the official mouthpiece of the Socialist party in the state of Kansas. Similarly, *The New Life* of Lewiston, Idaho, straddled the line between its New Thought origins and its later socialist testimonies.[154]

What was it about New Thought that fostered socialism and a social action agenda, in general? Part of the answer lies in the vernacular environment in which early New Thought flourished—with its historic roots in midcentury spiritualism and the reform commitments that came as part of spiritualist social culture. When the cultural turn of the 1870s occurred and a generalized theosophical perspective was born, reform commitments continued to run high, as the official Theosophical Society rhetoric of the "brotherhood of man" suggests. The midwestern and western spread of New Thought—to areas less immured in tradition than the bastions of East Coast conservatism—also brought with it a populace more likely to turn in liberal, and radical, social directions. Kansas, after all, had not acquired a reputation as a radical state for nothing. However, beyond these social reasons for a New Thought–socialist and social-reform alliance, the theological vision of the New Thought movement needs to be noticed. A message of divine immanence and unity, of all as children of the one God the Good, from one perspective sat well with social reform for a more even distribution of goods. Put another way, socialism provided a better conceptual fit for New Thought than did laissez-faire or capitalist pursuit of individual aggrandizement, pace Donald Meyer's well-known reading of the "mind-cure" gospel of success.[155]

For all this social-action agenda within New Thought, however, a second style —one that made Meyer at least partly right—came to dominate New Thought after the new century began. Materra calls it "noetic." In some sense, even this style could be laid, technically, at the feet of Hopkins, because its early representative—with whom Materra associates the noetic wing initially—was Helen Wilmans (1832?–1907), who had begun her New Thought career as a Hopkins student. Wilmans, however, struck out on her own and never acknowledged a debt to her Chicago teacher. For her, New Thought counted as a business and a science of self-mastery—she called it Mental Science—and Wilmans used the mails so ostentatiously for her absent-healing business that she spent years in court fighting mail fraud charges (she was acquitted, but her work never recovered).[156]

We gain some purchase on what this noetic New Thought signaled and how it sat with Hopkins devotees in a revelatory editorial by Charles Fillmore, cofounder of Unity, in one number of his periodical *Thought*. "Helen Wilmans," he confessed to readers, "objects to my use of the words God, Father, etc. . . . She says 'Why not credit the power spoken of to *man's* creativeness and the source of supply to nature instead of God?'" He went on, after the gentlemanly courtesies, to tell readers that a "great deal" hinged "on *Words*," with their use "worthy our careful consideration." Fillmore voted for a theistic language and told readers why. By contrast, the noetic style of Wilmans and a series of others, including New Thought women Julia Seton Sears and Elizabeth Towne, points toward more secular concerns, emphasizing entry into a "privileged male world as full participants." This style encouraged prosperity thinking much more than Hopkins and the affective wing of New Thought did, and it saw the new ideas as supports for greater self-reliance and business success. Here the individualism of adults in worlds of their own making took the place of a spiritual community at prayer and in service. A social agenda fell away, and so did the Bible and traditional religious discourse, including a felt concern over sin or evil.[157] The last chapter will take a closer look at this style of New Thought, especially prominent in the twentieth century.

As the New Thought movement grew and expanded, according to Materra, the majority of the men embraced its noetic version, while the majority of the women identified with the affective style. This division meant that—with so many women in the overall movement—the noetic organizations generally attracted equal or near-equal numbers of men and women, while affective networks were strongly populated by women. Periodicals and monographs advanced the case for each in almost a feeding frenzy of press activity as new literature came and went, and new statements appeared, vanished, and were re-created in slightly different guises. If New Thought put its premium on the word and its power, divinely guided, to change earthly conditions and situations, it made good on its commitment in the written, as well as the spoken, word. Periodicals enhanced the national presence for groups like Mental Science and Unity, even as the travels of Hopkins and her disciples on a burgeoning and efficient rail system added to the nationwide spread of New Thought ideas and structures. By 1905 and the beginning of the middle years of the movement, New Thought could be found in twenty-three states as well as in England, Mexico, and Australia. The states with the greatest presence were New York, Massachusetts, Illinois, California, and Colorado.[158]

As the movement grew into these middle years, too, New Thought denominations came to flourish—some like Unity, Religious Science, and Divine Science, to stay; and others, like Annie Rix Militz's West Coast Homes of Truth and Wilmans's scattered Mental Science Temples, to disappear. Ordinations were easy to come by, and—with the movement celebrating diversity—decentralization was a major feature of organizational life. In fact, the idea of establishing separate churches and denominations was quite foreign to this late century–early century New Thought and, as in the case of the Unity movement, was resisted throughout the twentieth century and on, even when all the evidence belied the nondenominational declaration. The children of the one God preferred, despite their obvious communitarian practices, to preserve ideologies of seeking only the God within. Thus, as this sketch already suggests, attempts to organize were fraught with difficulty. Finally, though, by 1914, the International New Thought Alliance was formed. It had been preceded by a series of meetings and organizational attempts, with the earliest meeting that announced itself explicitly as a "New Thought Convention" held in 1899 in Hartford, Connecticut. Thereafter, in Boston, the International Metaphysical League called a convention, and organization—and name changes—proceeded apace. Always, New Thought people aimed for comprehensiveness, reaching out to embrace sympathizers in an erasure of difference that was theological as well as social. Malinda Cramer's early periodical *Harmony* spoke for all. Its cover page announced it to be "a monthly magazine of philosophy, devoted to TRUTH, Science of Spirit, Theosophy, Metaphysics, and to the Christ method of healing." But always, with the individualism, New Thought ecumenical organizing was tenuous at best. Charles and Myrtle Fillmore's Unity School of Christianity, for example, had only a brief and tense time of inclusion in the International New Thought Alliance, from 1919 until 1922, with Charles Fillmore for many years considering the Unity movement "practical Christianity" and different from New Thought.[159]

The Reverend Solon Lauer made the case for resemblance and inclusivity at a convention as early as 1889, explicitly naming spiritualism, Theosophy, and Christian Science and declaring that there were "no very distinct lines of demarcation between them." All of them, he thought, shared "certain things in common," and he thought, too, that "perhaps a broad and generous interpretation of each would remove most of the points of seeming antagonism." What he said next was even more telling: "Certain it is that there are thousands of persons who read the literature and attend the public meetings of all of these movements, and who find much to love and admire in them."[160] We catch a glimpse of how this process worked in the personal spiritual odyssey of Charles Fillmore (1854–1948). Even with his difficulties with the International New Thought Alliance (suggesting more narrowness on his part?), Fillmore's case is, in fact, representative. His years of religious exploration illustrate how, in an expansive time and nation, the habit of combination nudged Americans to forge out of the Hermetic and related legacies of past and present the metaphysical synthesis of New Thought.

Born on a Chippewa Indian reservation in northern Minnesota, Fillmore grew up in an Indian territory in conflict, with Chippewa, Sioux, and whites all contesting for the land. Besides being a farmer, his father worked as an Indian agent, and from early on that fact must have translated into as much intimacy with Indian culture as a white in a frontier locale could normally expect to acquire. Still more, according to Fillmore's report, when he was six and alone with his mother at the trading post his family operated, a roaming band of Sioux came and spirited him away. The kidnapping did not last a day, for a few hours later the child was returned unharmed. According to James Gaither, Fillmore later said that he thought the Indians had used him for some sort of religious ceremony.[161] How much the Indian haunting affected his later life is difficult to determine, but the early contact with difference would be replicated in the religious quest of his mature years, functioning perhaps as a kind of horizon of spiritual possibility. At any rate, by 1889 and the beginning years of the Unity movement, Fillmore could confide to readers of his new journal *Modern Thought* that he had spent twenty years in the ranks of "*progressive* Spiritualists." He thought that spiritualism had "done a noble work in bringing light to the world," even as he deplored the practice of the majority of contemporary adherents. "This majority," he complained, were "phenomenalists." Their "tendency" was "to materialize the spirit world, instead of spiritualizing the material world." Half of the mediums were "unconscious subjects of some other mind." By contrast, metaphysics was "the panacea for all such," because it taught the "soul" how it might become a "spiritual center."[162]

Fillmore had gone beyond spiritualism, but clearly he regarded spiritualists as metaphysical cousins who had gotten things at least half right. Rather open in his autobiographical reminiscences, by 1894 he was telling *Thought* readers that he had been "born and raised in the wilderness of the west" and had obtained only a "quite limited" religious education, with God an "unknown factor" in his "conscious mind" until his last few years. He added significantly, "I was always drawn to the mysterious and occult, however, and in youth took great interest in Spiritualism and afterward, in branches of the Hermetic philosophy." If so, Fillmore was still trying to bring others to the Hermetic fold. As summarized by Braden, advertisements for the first issue of *Modern Thought* included books and periodicals displaying interest in "the occult, Spiritualism, theosophy, Rosicrucianism, Hermeticism, and other subjects as well as in [generic] Christian Science." Hermeticism likewise continued to influence Fillmore, for his distinctive teaching on the "twelve powers of man"—based on the notion that twelve seats of (spiritual) power exist throughout the human body—was shaped by Rosicrucian ideas. In another example, the winged globe that became Unity's symbol grew out of a Rosicrucian ambience, when Fillmore responded to Freeman Benjamin Dowd's book *The Temple of the Rosy Cross*.[163]

Fillmore never officially joined the Theosophical Society, and the names of neither he nor his wife, Myrtle Fillmore, can be found on its membership rolls. Still, he observed in one article that he had been "a very earnest student of Theosophy for several years," describing himself as "quite familiar with its literature" within which he had found "much truth." He was also, he said, "personally acquainted with several who are considered in the inner circle of the Theosophical

Society in America." He had "studied them carefully, both from the exoteric and esoteric standpoints," and he boasted, especially, of his "near friend," who was among "the first members of the society in America" and "now right in the front of the work." This man had studied Sanskrit for years, had the "sacred writings of the Hindus" "at his tongue's end," and had "developed quite remarkable occult powers." As in the case of the spiritualists, Fillmore found the Theosophists half right. They were "so loaded up with head learning" and they had so made "of Karma a great Moloch" that they did not realize that by "mental application" one could "wipe out . . . present conditions and make *now* a new environment." Fillmore's theosophical enthusiasm was apparent, as Neal Vahle has noted, in the large number of reviews of books on Theosophy in the first (1889) issue of *Modern Thought*—thirteen, among them Blavatsky's *Isis Unveiled*—all of them recommended reading. Meanwhile, Fillmore, with Theosophists, continued to embrace reincarnation beliefs (he once told Charles Braden that he had been St. Paul in a previous life). Likewise, his connections to Christian Science and its thought world were obvious, since he had been an Emma Curtis Hopkins student and had brought her to Kansas City to teach several classes.[164] The largest difference between the Christian Science world of Eddy and the New Thought one of Fillmore was the direction of their combinations. Eddy combined Platonized Hermeticism and spiritualist-magnetic lingerings with Calvinism; Fillmore combined similar materials with Christian liberalism and Theosophy instead of Calvinism.

Fillmore's comfort in this blended and reconstructed world of differing metaphysical possibilities was hardly remarkable. His articulateness and his outreach suggest what numerous others in the metaphysical culture of the time were thinking, experiencing, and doing. Especially to be noticed in all of this is how much the comfort zone had extended to Asia. As Fillmore and so many Americans looked eastward for spiritual inspiration and solace, however, what they found was scarcely the unadulterated Asia of their (Romantic) vision. What they found, instead, was the metaphysical Asia (mind, correspondences, energy, and healing all there) that they had molded out of a Hermetic and vernacular magical past and the pluralism of an American present. Meanwhile, as we will see, the Asia of their discovery had also been mediated to them by the European West and an East itself undergoing selective westernization.

6

METAPHYSICAL ASIA

Writing in the up-and-coming *Metaphysical Magazine* (founded and edited by former Eddy Christian Scientist Leander Edmund Whipple in 1895), Detroit lawyer Hamilton Gay Howard addressed the theme of personal attraction and repulsion. With familiar nods to magnetism and electricity, Howard sententiously looked east, cloaking his argument with the authority of ancient and modern adepts. "This theory of electric or psychic wave currents pervading our atmosphere" had been "accepted by all Oriental philosophers," he informed readers, and it had also been "taught for hundreds of years in the School of Adepts, at Thebes, which Lord Bulwer Lytton is said to have attended for three and a half years—half the course." "The whole course, requiring great self-denial and continued physical trials was taken," he believed, "by the late Madame Blavatsky, and by Colonel Olcott, of Massachusetts, the advanced free-thinker and theosophist." Howard especially wanted to underscore his conviction that the "wisdom of the East" needed to be noticed, and so he excerpted a piece from a newspaper that he identified only as the *Pittsburg Dispatch*. Inviting readers into a new—and for them exotic—world, its unnamed author boasted of having before him "an English translation of a very old tantric work from the original Sanscrit, by the Hindu pandit, Rama Prasad," a work that contained "the ancient Hindu philosophy as regards the finer forces of nature." In its pages the author found, with evident enthusiasm, references and explanations for "such things as the interstellar ether; its general properties and subdivisions; the laws of vibration; the circulation of the blood and of the nervous fluid; the nervous centres and the general anatomy of the body; *the rationale of psychometry and of occult phenomena,* and a good many other things of which modern science as yet knows little or nothing."[1]

What neither Howard nor the *Dispatch* writer apparently knew was that Rama

Prasad's book had originally appeared as a series of articles in the Indian-based periodical *The Theosophist*, which had been launched in Bombay by none other than Helena Blavatsky and Colonel Henry Steel Olcott in 1879. Prasad himself was a decidedly Westernized Hindu and a Theosophist, a man who moved in a discourse community that had heavily invested in reinscribing the traditional lore of India in the scientific terms of the modern, British-inspired West. For Prasad and those who followed him, yogic pranayama had become the "science of breath." In the lengthy exposition that preceded Prasad's translation of the short text from the Sanskrit, he in fact took on the famed German scholar Max Müller for reading the Chandogya Upanishad as in places "more or less fanciful." By contrast, in Prasad's account, none of the Upanishads could be "very intelligible" without knowing something of "the ancient Science of Breath," which was "said to be the secret doctrine of all secret doctrines" and "the key of all that is taught in the Upanishads." Prasad's allusion was a double entendre. First, the Indian Theosophist had affirmed that traditional Indian religious thought was scientific, and he had rendered the Sanskrit title of the work he had translated as "The *Science* of Breath and the Philosophy of the Tattvas." The "Tattvas" of his title—literally "thatnesses"—were, in the classical dualistic Samkyha philosophy of India, the twenty-five principles constitutive of the material universe. In Prasad's usage, however—influenced probably by Helena Blavatsky's invocation of the "Great Breath" in her enormous 1888 book *The Secret Doctrine* (see below) —they referred specifically to the "five modifications of the Great Breath."[2] Thus Prasad's allusion to the "secret doctrine of all secret doctrines" pointed to Blavatsky's book and, so, to Theosophy.

Both the Howard article and the *Dispatch* excerpt that was part of it provide windows into a late-nineteenth-century American world in which the imagined otherness of Asia was redirected and rechanneled into culturally available templates for making sense of difference. Arguably, these templates were supplied by a borderlands discourse that arose on the fringes of liberal Protestantism as it existed in constant commerce with a revived and reconstructed Hermeticism— this available in theosophical, New Thought, and similar versions, and often in combinations of these. If there was any one public event that signaled the process and its continuing reinventions of the East, that event was the World's Parliament of Religions of 1893, held in conjunction with the huge Columbian Exposition in Chicago. A world's fair staged to celebrate the four-hundredth anniversary of the European arrival in the Americas, the exposition, with its displays and attendant events, celebrated, too, American economic and cultural "progress" in a triumphalist spirit that masked an unexamined racism and imperialism.[3] The parliament did not and could not disentangle itself from the cultural climate of its era, even if, with liberal Protestant leadership, its site was physically removed from that of the larger event. In the downtown Chicago Loop during the month of September, representatives of the world's religious traditions came together under the sign of progress, aiming to assess the religious status of the century and to plan for the future.

Viewed with an eye toward American metaphysical religion, the group that assembled under the liberal auspices of the parliament was decidedly congenial to the new spirituality. The combinative instinct of parliament organizers and presenters reproduced a central trope of American metaphysics. At the same time, the canons that governed the selection process brought speakers who promised to function in keeping with the conference's theosophizing agenda—that is, an agenda that promoted perennialism under the rubric of comparative religions. True enough, Roman Catholic James Cardinal Gibbons led the assembled representatives in an Our Father prayer at the Parliament's opening session, and Dionysios Latas, Greek Orthodox archbishop of Zante, had come from Athens. But the unitive theme of the parliament did not go unnoticed by some traditionalists. The General Assembly of the Presbyterian Church refused to sanction the event, this despite the fact that John Henry Barrows, who headed the parliament's organizing committee, was pastor of Chicago's First Presbyterian Church. The Anglican Archbishop of Canterbury and the Muslim sultan of Turkey also refused endorsement. At the other end of the spectrum, among Asian representatives a clear theosophical presence could be found. G. N. Chakravarti, an Indian scholar there to defend Hinduism, was a convert to Theosophy. So was the Buddhist Anagarika Dharmapala from Ceylon (present-day Sri Lanka), who had been encouraged by Blavatsky herself to become a scholar of Buddhist Pali-language texts. Kinza Hirai, a lay Buddhist from Japan, similarly had been a Theosophist. Swami Vivekananda, a Neo-Vedantin from Bengal (transformed overnight by the media and popular acclaim into a celebrity), thought along lines congenial to Theosophy. Among non-Asians, the American Alexander Russell Webb (or Mohammed Webb), who had converted to Islam, still told Henry Steel Olcott that he "had not ceased to be an ardent Theosophist." Other theosophical names also could be found among the delegates—Americans William Q. Judge and J. D. Buck and, from England, Annie Besant and Isabel Cooper-Oakley.[4]

Meanwhile, the Theosophical Society, along with Christian Science, had been accorded a separate "denominational congress" in conjunction with the parliament, a recognition given only to some three dozen separate groups. Both Theosophists and Christian Scientists were elated by attendance at their meetings. Theosophists glowed their way through two special sessions held on weekends to accommodate public interest, reporting that at the final one, with seats for four thousand, hundreds more were standing in the aisles and along the walls. An anecdote recounted how a Presbyterian minister and parliament manager interrupted William Q. Judge's speech on reincarnation to tell stray Presbyterians that their own meeting was empty and that perhaps they were confused regarding its location and should leave immediately. Supposedly, no one followed his advice. In their turn, Christian Scientists filled the hall of four thousand to hear an address by "Rev. Mary Baker G. Eddy, discoverer and founder of Christian Science," read to them in absentia, and to listen, too, to other Christian Science speakers. The next day they basked in the publicity that the *Chicago Inter-Ocean* provided them: "One of the best congresses yet held in connection with the Parliament of Religions, judged by number and interest, was that of the Christian Scientists. . . . For two hours before the hall opened crowds besieged the doors eager to gain admission. At two o'clock, the time set for opening the proceedings, the house was filled to the roof, no seats being available for love or money."[5]

The parliament was the brainchild of Charles Carroll Bonney (1831–1903), a Chicago lawyer interested in comparative religions who was also, significantly, a Swedenborgian. Bonney's faith in the theology of divine influx shaped his idea and subsequent participation in parliament proceedings in which he functioned as president. He told Christian Scientists, for example, that "no more striking manifestation of the interposition of Divine Providence in human affairs has come in recent years than that shown in the raising up of the body of people known as Christian Scientists." They, indeed, were "called to declare the real harmony between religion and science, and to restore the waning faith of many in the verities of the sacred Scriptures."[6] Nor was Bonney alone in his ecumenism and his belief in the all-pervading presence of Spirit. Something akin to the immanential theology of Swedenborg and most of the metaphysicians ran through the organizing ideology of the entire World's Parliament event.

As John Henry Barrows, chair of the parliament, introduced his massive, two-volume edition recounting its background and transcribing its speeches, he sounded the theme that appeared repeatedly in the messages of the various delegates. "Faith in a Divine Power to whom men believe they owe service and worship" had been "like the sun, a life-giving and fructifying potency in man's intellectual and moral development." But Barrows followed up the good news of divine immanence with the bad that delegates were aiming to correct. "Religion, like the white light of Heaven," had been "broken into many-colored fragments by the prisms of men." So the parliament aimed, as one of its objects, "to change this many-colored radiance back into the white light of heavenly truth." Its promoters, like closet Theosophists, were "striking the noble chord of universal human brotherhood" and evoking a "starry music which will yet drown the miserable discords of earth." To be sure, a Christian ethos surrounded the universal brotherhood, since it was "embodied in an Asiatic Peasant who was the Son of God." Still, the aims of the parliament stretched the liberal fabric of the Protestant umbrella in directions that, at least potentially, wore thin the Christian certitude of possessing the unique—and most highly evolved—religious truth. The parliament intended "to show to men, in the most impressive way, what and how many important truths the various Religions hold and teach in common."[7]

To that end, organizers imported "leading scholars, representing the Brahman, Buddhist, Confucian, Parsee, Mohammedan, Jewish and other Faiths," placed them alongside representatives of the Christian churches, and allowed these others time and a platform. The results, as Richard Seager argues, were not quite what the Chicago leaders intended. Instead, non-Christian representatives upended the liberal Christian project and exposed its tenuousness in a discourse intended to display the wisdom and integrity of the East.[8] In so doing, the Asians flattened Christian peaks not only for themselves but also, potentially, for Americans. And in so doing, they also underlined a way of talking, thinking, and being in the world that promoted the project of metaphysical religion. Now, though, metaphysics appeared under the banner of an intercepted Asia, caught in complex thickets between separate Asian pasts, Westernized Asian presents, and American polysemous perceptions. By this time, too, American metaphysics had already reached a watershed in its appropriation of global faiths to advance its homegrown spirituality. Theosophical prominence at the World's Parliament of Religions was theologically and poetically appropriate. It was the Asian turn of the Theosophical Society that had brought the universalizing discourse of the 1870s and 1880s to the authoritative statement of the 1890s. In this 1890s statement, the power of mind took on new proportions, correspondence ruled religious perceptions, and healing energies came from new (to non-Asian Americans) Asian wisdoms. This chapter looks first to the Asia mediated to the West by Theosophy and then to metaphysical American versions of yoga and Buddhism, with the presence of Theosophy—and its partner New Thought—never far away.

THEOSOPHICAL ASIA

Helena Blavatsky and Henry Steel Olcott traveled to India in late 1878, and they never returned to this country to stay. The Asian years of Theosophy and its increasingly close ties with England, the growing rift of the founders with each other, Blavatsky's European and English sojourn, her trials and tribulations over fraud charges, and her death in England in 1891—these do not concern my narrative directly. Important here, instead, are the literary products of these years and their effects on an evolving metaphysical religion in the United States. *Isis Unveiled* had played a significant role in shifting an older spiritualist language into new and more expansive vocabularies and grammars, and now the continuing work of the theosophical leaders received an eager reception in America. These writings model a reading of Asia that colonized it to suit American metaphysical requirements. In so doing, as Stephen Prothero argues in the specific case of Olcott, they "creolized" Asian cultural worlds with already combinative American discourses.[9]

Olcott's literary creolization project was apparent as early as 1881 when he first produced his *Buddhist Catechism*, a work to be considered later. Blavatsky herself provided the more far-reaching metaphysical scripture in her monumental (nearly fifteen hundred pages in two volumes exclusive of front matter and index) *Secret Doctrine* of 1888.[10] Bruce Campbell—who calls it "a, perhaps *the*, major work of occultism" in the nineteenth century—has recounted its publication history, with the new book—a reconsideration and elaboration of *Isis Unveiled*—announced as early as 1884. Blavatsky first planned to use *The Theosophist* to issue the book, publishing it in monthly installments of the same length. But by 1885 she left India for Europe, and so that specific project folded. But Blavatsky reportedly wrote—prodigiously—as she traveled and remained for a time in Italy, Switzerland, Germany, and Belgium. Her handwritten material was transferred for her into typescript, but when he saw it, Subba Row, the Indian Theosophist who had promised to edit it, withdrew before what he regarded an impossible task. Eventually, after Blavatsky moved to London in 1887, Archibald and Bertram Keightley—the two Theosophists most responsible for her presence there—created an outline for a manuscript that by then purportedly stood over a yard high. Of the four volumes that the Keightleys suggested, only two were eventually published as *The Secret Doctrine*—a first subtitled *Cosmogenesis* and dealing with the evolution of the cosmos, and a second called *Anthropogenesis* and addressing the theme of human evolution. Two others, Ed Fawcett and Richard Harte, supplied help for aspects of the project.[11]

As in the case of *Isis Unveiled* (see the previous chapter), William Emmette Coleman charged Blavatsky with plagiarism—a charge that was old news, given her previous publishing history. She claimed that her volumes—and "the Secret Doctrine of the Archaic ages"—were built around stanzas from the "Book of Dzyan," a work that Blavatsky introduced as a fragment from a Tibetan Buddhist text called the *Mani Koumboum*, the sacred writing of the Dzungarians, in the northern part of the country. While she was in Tibet, she explained, she was allowed to memorize the stanzas. But the text was "not in the possession of European Libraries" and was "utterly unknown to our Philologists, or at any rate was never heard of by them under its present name." On these points, Coleman and Blavatsky agreed, and he added that the language of Senzar, the professed original language of the work, was completely unknown. As in the case of her first huge work, he accused her of unacknowledged reliance on nineteenth-century sources from which she had compiled her work. Chief among them were H. H. Wilson's *Vishnu Purána* (1840), Alexander Winchell's *World-Life; or, Comparative Geology* (1883), and John Dowson's Hindu *Classical Dictionary* (1879). Nor was he alone in speculating on her big book's composition. René Guénon believed it was based on Tibetan fragments, but different from the ones Blavatsky herself claimed. Jewish mystical scholar Gershom Scholem thought its origins lay in the Jewish Kabbalah. And according to Alvin Boyd Kuhn, Max Müller sardonically observed that Blavatsky was either a "remarkable forger" or the contributor of "the most valuable gift to archaeological research in the Orient."[12]

Yet, granted evidence for the charge of plagiarism, Blavatsky's facility in joining the South Asian discourse to a series of other cultural conversations—Hermetic, Western scientific, and even Christian—marks her work with a synthetic originality that needs to be noticed.[13] Indeed, gun-shy perhaps from her experience with *Isis Unveiled*, she herself indirectly acknowledged the extent of her dependence (and also her estimate of what she had done) in her upper-case quotation from the French essayist Michel de Montaigne in her introduction: "'I HAVE HERE MADE ONLY A NOSEGAY OF CULLED FLOWERS, AND HAVE BROUGHT NOTHING OF MY OWN BUT THE STRING THAT TIES THEM.'" "Pull the 'string' to pieces and cut it up in shreds, if you will," she added. "As for the nosegay of FACTS—you will never be able to make away with these."[14] Still further, for all the scholarly dismissal, Blavatsky's work would shape language not only in theosophical circles but also—as Campbell's assessment of it has already suggested—well beyond them. Its statement of the "secret doctrine" of Asia would provide the vocabulary and grammar for a generic metaphysical discourse. In it Asian historical particularity was effaced, and the universalizing potential of concepts like reincarnation, karma, and subtle bodies was amplified many times over. Arguably, the general American metaphysical project of the late twentieth and twenty-first centuries would continue to sound themes and enact Asias that originated in the Blavatsky opus.

Beyond that, in the elaborate sacred tale of origins that *The Secret Doctrine* constructed, Blavatsky provided a story of cosmic and human origins that, whatever it told about Asia, surely imitated the West. In its overall modeling, her narrative resembled ancient Gnostic mythic material or Kabbalistic lore from the Middle Ages. Like Gnostic and Kabbalistic mythologies, Blavatsky's ambitious theodicy explained the predicament of humans by elaborating a series of events and entities that, in effect, harmfully separated things human from their divine or originating source. As in older Gnostic and Kabbalistic forays, the Blavatskian version of the order of the universe complicated human origins—as if interlarding an explanation with numerous layers could prove the intrinsic sacrality of humans and account for evil without alleging a flaw in the source of all. Hermes Trismegistus stayed present in this account. Blavatsky thought the "Divine Pymander" and the "hermetic Fragments" to be echoes of the "Esoteric philosophy and the Hindu Purânas," an order historians might well want to reverse and a connection they might want to challenge on other grounds.[15] In the context of the late nineteenth century's preoccupation with Darwinian evolution (and Blavatsky's own engagement with it), *The Secret Doctrine*—worlds away from what by the early twentieth century would become Protestant fundamentalism—posited a human devolution from the divine that represented also an evolution.

"Kosmos" existed in eternity "before the re-awakening of still slumbering Energy," which became "the emanation of the Word in later systems." The cosmic system was characterized by a perpetual periodicity, a latency and activity by turns. Always, there had been the "ONE LIFE, eternal, invisible, yet Omnipresent, without beginning or end, yet periodical in its regular manifestations, between which periods reigns the dark mystery of non-Being; unconscious, yet absolute Consciousness; unrealisable, yet the one self-existing reality; truly, 'a chaos to the sense, a Kosmos to the reason.' Its one absolute attribute, which is ITSELF, eternal, ceaseless Motion, is called in esoteric parlance the 'Great Breath,' which is the perpetual motion of the universe, in the sense of limitless, ever-present SPACE. That which is motionless cannot be Divine."[16]

If the divine was motion and energy, the divine was also Mind or Thought, the "Word" from which all things emanated and in which lay concealed the "plan of every future Cosmogony and Theogony." Moreover, in the Blavatskian synthesis—as throughout American metaphysical religion—the third abiding feature became the correspondence that ran through the layers of reality, so that spiritual anthropology replicated the eternal patterning of the universe. God was, in one way, neither close nor intimate; in another, the divine was alive and resonant in every cell. The "Great Breath" kept on breathing, and what it breathed was people. If this sounds like an overture in the direction of the contemplative mind, Blavatsky's own etymology suggests the same. She thought that "Dzyan" (also spelled "Dzyn" or "Dzen") was a corrupt form of Sanskrit *Dhyana*, which means meditation. Beyond that, with all the preoccupation with science (both Books I and II include a Part III titled "Science and the Secret Doctrine Contrasted") that Blavatsky displayed, she was demonstrably as concerned about aesthetics. The secret wisdom of Dzyan came packaged in "stanzas." She titled the prelude to her first volume "Proem." And her preoccupations with correspondence took the form, often, of attention to numerical symmetries akin to those in mathematics or music. Alluding to her doctrine of seven human races and also to the dangerous power hidden within the symmetries, she told readers that "doctrines such as the planetary chain, or the seven races, at once give a clue to the seven-fold nature of man." "Each principle," she continued, was "correlated to a plane, a planet, and a race; and the human principles are, on every plane, correlated to seven-fold occult forces—those of the higher planes being of tremendous power."[17]

Blavatsky's statement of a mind-energy-correspondence triad is instructive. Carl Jackson identifies it with "traditional Hindu philosophy" and suggests that concepts of "*Brahman, maya, atman,* and karma" had been "reformulated in Theosophical terminology," with connections especially to Vedanta. But if this was the case, it is also true that Blavatsky announced the message in ways that—intended or not—were congenial to American metaphysicians schooled in the moralism and work ethic of their culture's Protestant moorings. A confirmed perennialist, Blavatsky proclaimed her "Secret Doctrine" as "the universally diffused religion of the ancient and prehistoric world," and she quickly elaborated its propositions. First came the "metaphysical ONE ABSOLUTE — BE-NESS," the "rootless root" that could only be known by negation, "beyond all thought or speculation" and symbolized both as "absolute abstract Space" and "absolute Abstract Motion." Second came an affirmation of the eternity of the universe as a "boundless plane," a "playground" for countless appearing and disappearing universes, so that the "law of periodicity, of flux and reflux, ebb and flow" ruled absolutely. Third—and the existential concern that drove the first two—came the "fundamental identity of all Souls with the Universal Over-Soul," which was "an aspect of the Unknown Root." There was, therefore, an "obligatory pilgrimage for every Soul—a spark of the former—through the Cycle of Incarnation (or 'Necessity') in accordance with Cyclic and Karmic law." Blavatsky's world emerged as a hard-work universe in which there were "no privileges or special gifts in man" except for "those won by his own Ego through personal effort and merit throughout a long series of metempsychoses and reincarnations."[18] This multiplication of incarnations (beyond the Asian sources)—the cycle of seemingly endless returns for still more growth (for the soul on a "spiritual" path)—became a hallmark of later theosophical discourse into the twenty-first century. Souls on earth went to school and learned metaphysical lessons as they journeyed.

Blavatsky's "slanderers" would generate "bad Karma," but for those on the path the aesthetics of contemplation opened out into vast expanses. Here space, "THE ETERNAL PARENT WRAPPED IN HER EVER INVISIBLE ROBES HAD SLUM-

BERED ONCE AGAIN FOR SEVEN ETERNITIES." Eventually, though, the spatial "MOTHER" swelled and expanded "LIKE THE BUD OF THE LOTUS." Her vibration touched the light in the midst of darkness; a single ray entered the "MOTHER-DEEP"; and the egg therein became the "WORLD-EGG." So it went, as already the number seven began to be manifested both inside and outside the egg. The "GREAT MOTHER," who was at least once called the "FATHER-MOTHER," was the eternal cosmic source from which the divine, the spiritual, and all of the "MIND-BORN" emanated. We need not follow Blavatsky's narrative further to glimpse behind its overproduction what Alvin Kuhn called "a recital of the scheme according to which the primal unity of unmanifest Being breaks up into differentiation and multiformity and so fills space with conscious evolving beings."[19]

It is, however, worth marking the points in the narrative that reinforce the Hermeticism of the past and reconstitute it as a new statement for the times—a statement that, for Americans, domesticated Asia as a function of vernacularized Western mystical categories. Indian sacred lore in the *Vishnu Purana* told of a vast egg that floated on cosmic waters. Vishnu entered the egg as the creator Brahma—to produce the three worlds of earth, atmosphere, and heaven; he, in turn, preserved them through countless ages and finally destroyed them with flames as Rudra. Then rain fell to form one vast ocean, and, like a coiled snake, Vishnu slept on the waters. The time from Brahma's initial act of creation to the time of destruction was called a day of Brahma, or a Kalpa. Within each Kalpa, a thousand cycles passed. These were known as Maha Yugas (literally, "great years"), with each extending for 4,320,000 human years or 12,000 years of the gods (a year of the gods being 360 human years, and a day of the gods being a single human year). Every Maha Yuga was in turn subdivided into four lesser Yugas, with each shorter than the previous one. During these increasingly shorter Yugas observance of law declined and humankind grew ever more corrupt, with the shortest and most devolved of them being the Kali Yuga of 1,800 years. After the thousand Maha Yugas, Vishnu's sleep upon the ocean lasted as long. Finally, at the end of this protracted night, Vishnu woke up and re-created the worlds as Brahma; and so a distinct day of Brahma began anew. But that was not all. Brahma had a life span, and thus there were 100 years of 360 days and nights of Brahma respectively, whereupon the original evolution of life and worlds reversed itself and Vishnu returned to the contemplation of his Supreme Self, alone with eternal Time (Kala), Spirit (Purusha), and Primary Matter (Prakriti). When Vishnu decided that he wanted to play once more, the vast drama of creation again unfolded.[20]

In the midst of this cosmic theater of epic proportions, the *Vishnu Purana* warned that humans were living in the Kali Yuga, the most devolved state of its current Maha Yuga. Blavatsky, at least manifestly, followed its narrative. The Kali Yuga that the West had reached was "an age BLACK WITH HORRORS." "Man" was "his own destroyer" in a Kali Yuga that reigned "supreme" not only in India but also there. Yet more than the *Vishnu Purana*, Blavatsky historicized freely and pointedly. She predicted that "about nine years" from the time she was writing, "the first cycle of the first five millenniums, that began with the great cycle of the Kali-Yuga" would end. More apocalyptically, she declared that humans stood "at the very close of the cycle of 5,000 years of the present Aryan Kaliyuga; and between this time and 1897" there would be "a large rent made in the Veil of Nature," with "materialistic science" receiving a "death-blow." Still further, in Blavatsky's opus the language of the Yugas receded, and, in fact, at least one extended reference to the Kali Yuga read it decidedly more positively. At the Kali Yuga's close, Blavatsky announced, quoting one source at length, the minds of the living would be awakened, becoming clear as crystal. They would give birth to a new race who would be truly human beings, following the laws of the age of purity. Blavatsky thought that the *"blessings"* of the Kali Yuga were "well described" and that they "fit in admirably even with that which one sees and hears in Europe and other civilized and Christian lands in full XIXth, and at the dawn of the XXth century of our great era of ENLIGHTENMENT." As important here, working between what she claimed were esoteric Buddhist and Vedantic (Raja Yoga) sources as interpreted already in theosophical writings, she regarded the Kalpas as "Rounds." Indeed, what preoccupied her—more than Kalpas and Yugas—were "Rounds," with each "Round" in the human saga "composed of the Yugas of the seven periods of Humanity."[21]

Since all things traveled in sevens in Blavatsky's universe, every star or planet was linked to six "companion globes." Life proceeded on the seven globes in seven rounds or cycles, with rest periods or times of "obscuration" between, and in a complex rebirthing process each globe had to "transfer its life and energy to another planet." Into this cosmic scenario of action and rest, Blavatsky inserted the earth, and in so doing she historicized her narrative in ways that hinted more of Western occultism than Eastern puranas. The earth, as the "visible representative of its invisible superior fellow globes," was required to live through seven rounds. For the first three, it formed and consolidated; for the fourth, it settled and hardened; and in the final three, it returned "to its first ethereal form . . . spiritualised, so to say." Significantly, in the fourth round humanity came to be, and in the later rounds the human race would be "ever tending to reassume its primeval form." "Man" would become "*a* God and then—GOD, like every other atom in the Universe."[22]

Here, in the fourth round, a series of "root-races" had sprung up in succession, each of them dwelling on a particular continent. As Blavatsky plotted their history, in what Bruce Campbell has called a "process of involution and evolution," she invoked "Ethereal" beginnings and a "spiritual" end. The earliest (prehistoric) root-race, the "Self-born," arose on a continent called "The Imperishable Sacred Land." Thereafter came a second race on the "Hyperborean" continent, a third on Lemuria, and a fourth on Atlantis. After that, the fifth root-race, the Aryan, appeared, and it was this race that flourished in most of recorded history, including Blavatsky's nineteenth century. She had first identified its continent as "America" but went on to explain that, as it was "situated at the Antipodes," it was "Europe and Asia Minor, almost coeval with it" and then simply Europe as the "fifth great Continent."[23]

From whence had Blavatsky synthesized this material that took shape as a dissident history of the human species? If a reconstructed (which to a degree she acknowledged) metaphysical Asia supplied a part and Western Hermeticism contributed another part, a third came from a mix of novelistic sources with popular science accounts of the period. Plato, of course, had been the ancient literary source for Atlantean speculation in his *Timaeus* and his unfinished *Critias*. But by Blavatsky's time Jules Verne's *Twenty Thousand Leagues under the Sea* (with an English translation in 1873) and Edward Bulwer-Lytton's *The Coming Race* (with, in its publication year, 1871, five editions) brought Atlantean themes— and the notion of hidden, forgotten human history—to the fore. By 1882, however, these science fiction sources were eclipsed by Ignatius Donnelly's *Atlantis: The Antediluvian World*, the work of a former Republican lieutenant governor of Minnesota, United States congressman, and continuing civil servant and politician. With seven editions in the year of its publication and accolades from William Gladstone, prime minister of England, the work was translated into Swedish the year after it appeared and by 1890 had been printed in twenty-three American and twenty-six English editions. Donnelly had immersed himself in the latest findings of his era's science and had summarized the material. Here Plato's description of the island-continent of Atlantis could be read historically, with the natural catastrophe that destroyed it obliterating a spectacular human civilization. Still more, some of the Atlanteans had managed to escape and survive. England's civilization was Atlantean in its origins and that of the United States thus derivatively so.[24]

Blavatsky's third root-race of Lemurians looked even more credible in terms of the science of the time. The Pacific "land of lemurs" had first been proposed by Philip Lutley Sclater, former secretary of the London Zoological Society, fellow of the Royal Society, and friend of Thomas Huxley and Charles Darwin. Interested in ornithology and the fauna of Central and South America, he theorized species distribution in evolutionary terms, invoking a land bridge that began in Madagascar, moved through southern India, and ended in the Malay Peninsula, and calling it Lemuria. Later, the well-known German evolutionary biologist Ernst Heinrich Haeckel argued for Sclater's Lemuria as the original home of humankind, even if he later changed his mind. Like Atlantis, Lemuria had sunk into the sea, well below the surface of the Indian Ocean. Its former existence, however, helped Haeckel in explaining the way that migration assisted the geographical distribution of humans.[25]

Blavatsky absorbed it all—Vishnu, Hermes, popularized science, and even the Christian narrative of the original sin and fall of humanity—in the comprehensive unity of her account. The Atlanteans of her telling had fallen into sin and begotten monsters. In the racialism characteristic of her time, she reported that they had started out being brown-colored but later became "black with sin," degenerating into "magical practices and gross animality." They were "the first 'Sacrificers' to the *gods of matter*," and their worship devolved into "*self-worship*" and "phallicism." "Marked with a character of SORCERY," they had lost the ability to use their "third eye." Still, the shadow of Atlantean evil was swept away for Blavatsky in the ebb and flow of the law of periodicity. The Atlanteans, in effect, had died because their time had come, not—she stated specifically—because of their depravity or because they had become "black with sin." And in yet another apparent contradiction, their development as "giants whose physical beauty and strength reached their climax" followed evolutionary law.[26]

Read another—Asian and Hermetic—way, however, the fall that began human history meant the "descent" onto earth of the gods who became incarnate in human beings. Every avatar (or, Blavatsky said, "incarnation") meant "the fall of a God into generation," and she went on to cite the Upanishads for support. There was a loss of purity here, a compromise with perfection rather than a moral decision by a weak and disobedient human pair. But the "Fall of Spirit into generation" was necessary for self-consciousness, for Atman by itself would pass into "'NON-BEING, which is absolute Being.'" At the same time, the universe of humans was an illusory affair; it was Maya, with everything "temporary therein." Evil came with thought, which introduced a principle of finitude and separation, and it was related, too, to karmic law in which over countless eons of time humans worked out their destiny. Blavatsky orchestrated a complex choreography between this destiny and human freedom, rejecting notions of fatalism and invoking free agency for humans in their earthly sojourn. No individual could escape what she called a "*ruling* Destiny," but always a choice of paths to it existed. Karma neither created nor designed. Rather, each human planned and created "causes," and the law of karma adjusted "the effects." "Those who believe in *Karma* have to believe in *destiny*," she declared, "which, from birth to death, every man is weaving thread by thread around himself, as a spider does his cobweb."²⁷ According to *The Secret Doctrine*'s report, Atlanteans and Lemurians had done so, and likewise members of the Aryan race were presently so engaged.

Given all of this—and the exotic call of lost worlds and ancient, unknown peoples—the metaphysical afterlife of Blavatsky's Atlantis and Lemuria proved as extensive as her reinscription of the law of karma and reincarnation. Meanwhile, Asia beckoned again in her doctrine of the subtle bodies. Newly impressed (since *Isis Unveiled*) with the all-encompassing "sevenfold principle," which she found everywhere in nature, she discovered the seven once more. Whereas previously in *Isis* she had found nature and humanity to be triune—each human had a physical, astral, and spiritual body (or body, soul, and spirit)—now a grand multiplication of subtle bodies took place. Just as the visible planets and their rulers (the planetary gods) numbered the fabled seven, "principles in Man" corresponded. Seven bodies existed on "three material planes and one spiritual plane," and they boasted Asian-sounding names that had already been divulged to A. P. Sinnett in *Esoteric Buddhism* (by the Mahatmas, he claimed). The highest body was the "atma" (Hindu Atman, or "Universal Spirit"); the lowest, the "gross Matter" of the physical body. On an ascending scale in between came the "life" body, or the "Prana" (literally, "breath" as the "active power producing all vital phenomena"); the astral body, or Linga-Sarira (an "inert vehicle or form on which the body [was] moulded"); the animal soul, or "Kama-rupa" (the "principle of animal desire"); the "Manas" (Mind, or human soul); and the "Buddhi" (spiritual soul). In this ambitious and overarching schema, Blavatsky had provided a tour de force on the "Septenary Element in the Vedas," but she was also backtracking toward the West. She told readers that, in the ancient world, "so-called Christian Gnostics had adopted this time-honoured system" and that she had found Kabbalistic borrowings, too.²⁸

Not all the parts of the septenary human were fully developed, however, and this, too, supported Blavatsky's earlier threefold designation. As Kuhn summarized, for her humans were "sevenfold potentially, threefold actually," and this meant that of the "seven principles only the lower three have been brought from latency to activity." Blavatsky employed the term *Monad* to describe the Atma-Buddhi, the last two—and highest—"principles" within the septenary human, and she called the Monad the "dual soul." She also called the human Monad, in its "informing principle," the "HIGHER SELF," and saw it as "one and the same" with an "animal Monad," even if the first was "endowed with *divine* intelligence" and the second "with *instinctual* faculty alone." Human Monads participated in a far vaster monadic universe, since individual Monads were "*spontaneously self-active*" units characteristic of nature. In an echo of the mid-nineteenth-century spiritualist cosmology, all "Matter" was "Spirit, and *vice versâ*"; and "the Universe and the Deity which informs it" were "unthinkable apart from each other." Monads evolved through succeeding incarnations to become human, but Blavatsky distinguished the process from Darwinian biological evolution or even metaphysical descriptions of external evolution of the Monad through many forms. Instead, the "evolution of the internal or real MAN" was "purely spiritual"; it represented a "journey of the 'pilgrim-soul' through various *states* of *not only matter* but Self-consciousness and self-perception." It stopped being human only when it became *"absolutely divine."*[29]

Absoluteness, however, was the far goal. As in Andrew Jackson Davis's mid-century cosmology of eternal progress and imploding worlds, Blavatsky's human-made-god was, indeed, a "pilgrim-soul." Theosophist Alvin Kuhn, commenting on *The Secret Doctrine*, pointed to "the far-off summit" of human life "in the seventh Round," when all seven human principles would exist in "full flower" and each human would be "the divine man he was before — only now conscious of his divinity." But on the way, there was much to be done and achieved. He especially noted how, in the Blavatskian schema, when all that was evolving attained the seventh globe of a round, a return to the originating condition followed — yet with wisdom gained through experience and, so, a superior state of consciousness.[30] Here, in effect, was a Western gloss on the materials from which Blavatsky constructed her metaphysical universe. Asia had been read and, at least historically speaking, misread many times over. But the misreadings themselves constituted the creative aspect of Blavatsky's work, and the theosophical misreadings continued. The Asia of historical essentialism arguably never existed, and historical revisionism, at least in the West, re-created Asia again and again. The theosophical Asia molded by Americans and Anglophiles in general bent South Asian history and traditional lore — however much it was already bent by Asians to their own needs — into a new metaphysical version with a shape distinctly Victorian and moralistic.[31]

By 1890, for example, the children of American Theosophists in New York and elsewhere could discover from a theosophical "catechism" in William Q. Judge's periodical *The Path* that the "Secret Doctrine" was most like "the Buddhist religion and the religion of the Brahmans," which included "more than two-thirds of all mankind." They could discover, too, that Jesus Christ had also taught the same truths esoterically but that the "Secret Doctrine" contained "more theosophical knowledge than any other body of teaching." It was "the Science-Religion," in that it searched "for facts or laws in nature," and it rested on the three principles of "Being or Life," the "law of periodicity," and the "identity of all souls with the Oversoul." Learning by rote or by teacher's paraphrase, theosophical children could absorb a theology in which all nature was "ensouled," with the "world soul" entering "into the elements, such as air, fire, water, and then into the mineral, vegetable, animal, and human worlds." Each "soul spark," they would learn, went "through all things thus" and slowly reached "perfection," with "soul-union with the all" as the "only real state." Meanwhile, they were assured that the "Life Principle" that flowed through all could be called "the living Breath of the unknown Eternal One" and that its "great Law" was "Karma." Matter, or "Substance," said the catechism, was that into which the "Great Breath" breathed, and they could identify it as the "World Mother or the Oversoul." When they asked what next, the stock children's answers explained that "after a long period, The Great Breath" was "drawn in again" and that then the world "all dissolved back again into The Breath." The "Breath," however, moved "to and fro," and young readers were brought back to the law of Karma, with its "strict justice" as "the eternal nature of all being" and "Universal Brotherhood" as the moral of the tale. Where could "an example of this in human life" be found? The answer came swift and sure. "If I speak an angry word to any one at the beginning of the day, it makes both him and me feel differently for some time. This affects what we say to others, changes them to us, and so all are injured by the one selfish deed."[32]

The practical simplicity of the teaching was inescapable, suited more to the urbanized American Northeast with its Anglo-Protestant culture of moralism than a putative South Asian ashram. The progress of the soul-spark through the forms—the return of the Monad to the One—not only performed itself as agency but, ever and especially, as *moral* agency. Several readings away from Blavatsky's Hindu and Hermetic sources, Judge's Theosophy functioned as a distinct species of American metaphysical religion. Meanwhile, the American lodges flourished. The same year that the children of would-be adepts were learning their theosophical catechism, *The Path* was reporting some thirty-four American branches of the Theosophical Society, with lodges not only in obvious places like New York, Chicago, San Francisco, Los Angeles, and Boston but also in medium-sized cities such as Cincinnati, Minneapolis, Philadelphia, and St. Louis and smaller ones like Grand Island (Nebraska), Bridgeport (Connecticut), Decorah (Iowa), Santa Cruz (California), and Muskegon (Michigan). A year later, the magazine counted fifty-four lodges in North America, including one in Toronto, Canada, a sizable number of the 258 lodges worldwide. By the next year (1892), there were sixty North American lodges, including the single Canadian lodge. The pattern was similar for the next two years. There were seventy-seven North American lodges in 1893 and eighty-four the following year, including three in Canada for both years.[33]

By this time, Judge was heavily embroiled in the conflict with Henry Steel Olcott that would lead to rupture and independence for what became the Theosophical Society in America. Beginning after Blavatsky's death in 1891, Judge claimed esoteric privileges and declared his personal contact with the Masters or Mahatmas of theosophical lore (see the previous chapter). In a bitter feud between the two men continents apart (Olcott, the president of the Theosophical Society, was in India), judicial proceedings were launched against Judge, who was vice president. Accused of deception on a series of matters, of falsely claiming communication with Masters, and of also falsely sending personal messages and orders as if authorized by Masters, Judge faced a council and committee of the Theosophical Society that first found grounds not to act against him. However, when evidence contained in the private papers of the Englishwoman Annie Besant—who would later head the society—was made public without her consent, matters came to a head. A convention of the society in 1894 resolved, after Olcott's urging, that Judge should resign as vice president and go through a re-election process. The American section responded quickly. Meeting in a Boston convention the following year, members voted to secede, declaring their autonomy and changing the name of the American section to "The Theosophical Society in America." Then they elected Judge president for life—a role he held only for a year until his death in 1896. In his turn, Olcott expelled Judge from the parent Theosophical Society. No winner took all. Most of the American lodges followed Judge, but later—with lecturing and organizing efforts on the part of Besant and Countess Constance Wachtmeister, the widow of a former Swedish ambassador to London—some of the American work of the parent body was recouped.[34]

For both branches of the society in the United States, American readings of Asia continued to mold it to metaphysical categories already abroad in the nation. Here could be found roots both in the Hermetic tradition of the West and in the polyglot and combinative culture of the land, in which Native American and African American memory and practice functioned as the repressed knowledge of white Americans. And here, too, could be found a spirituality that, however much and however vociferously it protested, was engrafted on the Anglo-Protestant base that had shaped public culture. We need not subscribe to an essentialism that posits a one true reading of Asia to notice that Americans were creating an Asia to their own visionary requirements, an Asia of their dreams that would facilitate the shaping of their waking selves and Selves.

THE METAPHYSICS OF AMERICAN YOGA

Metaphysical Self-fashioning, strongly influenced by theosophical representations of Asia, grew apace as the nineteenth century wound down and the new century dawned. It spilled out of self-conscious metaphysical categories and became more general ways of talking and acting. Nowhere was this more the case than in the national appropriation of the "Brahmanism" Blavatsky loved in the American experience of yoga. The process of appropriation and the shift in public language and perception over time were remarkable. Americans moved from a thorough revulsion, in the early to mid years of the nineteenth century, toward anything remotely yogic (this among the most liberal elites) to a cautious acceptance of certain aspects of meditation yoga (again among the most liberal and now, usually, Theosophists). But in all of this, disdain for hatha, or physical, yoga continued. In the twentieth century, the theosophical legacy combined with aspects of New Thought, with already Westernized South Asian discourses, and with growing interest in South Asian tantra to create a new and American yogic product. This American yoga increasingly came to value the physical as a route to the transcendent. Along the way, it began to pay attention to the all but overlooked language of the Self in earlier American transcriptions of the Atman-Brahman equation until, by the early and middle twentieth century, American yoga gave fuller—though still limited—acknowledgment to the Self. In the midst of this, what I have already called the enlightened body-self became, more and more, the approved cultural transcription of metaphysical "mind."

The most useful place to begin following this story of American transformation is with the Transcendentalists. Nineteenth-century statements that figured this Self had spoken in terms of the Oversoul; and, as we have already seen, American language of the Oversoul preceded Blavatsky and needs to be laid at Transcendental doors. In his well-known essay on the theme in 1841, Ralph Waldo Emerson had announced that "man" was a "stream whose source is hidden" and had pointed to the soul that declared "I am born into the great, the universal mind." He had also affirmed that the person so lived by the Oversoul would "cease from what is base and frivolous in his life, and be content with all places and with any service he can render." As Frederic Ives Carpenter long ago showed, this forthright declaration of American mysticism originated not in Asian sources but in Western Neoplatonism with its idea of a World Soul in which all discrete and individual souls were joined. It was Souls, not Selves, that Emerson affirmed, and—even though he already knew that Atman equaled Brahman—his rhetorical choices were Western. It could be said that a grand enlargement of the individual soul ran through Emerson's statement, and that is certainly true. But the call was one to asceticism (cease from the "base and frivolous"), to nonattachment (be content wherever you are), and to nonpreferential service (give any service you can). Peace and tranquility, more than radical transformation, characterized Emerson's vision of the soul in union with the Oversoul: "He will calmly front the morrow in the negligency of that trust which carries God with it, and so hath already the whole future in the bottom of the heart," Emerson concluded.[35]

Emerson's younger friend, the second-generation Transcendentalist Henry David Thoreau, at first glance seems more forthcoming in making explicit yogic connections. There is at least one tantalizing letter, written in 1849, in which Thoreau invoked yoga, quoting passages from his South Asian reading and affirming that he "would fain practice the yoga faithfully." "To some extent, and at rare intervals," he confided, "even I am a yogin." By the time he lived at Walden Pond and then wrote about his sojourn there, Thoreau had immersed himself in Asian classics. His language in Walden was a veritable catalog of his reading, and he knew all about the "conscious penance" of the Brahmins of India, "sitting exposed to four fires and looking in the face of the sun; or hanging suspended with their heads downward, over flames." More affirmatively, later in the text he was quoting a "Hindoo philosopher" on how the soul, with the help of a "'holy teacher,'" finally "'knows itself to be *Brahme.*'" Nor is it difficult to find an evocation of meditation yoga in Thoreau's well-known account of how he spent his days at the pond: "In the morning," he wrote, he bathed his "intellect in the stupendous and cosmogonal philosophy of the Bhagvat Geeta." After he put his book down, he went to his well for water. What followed next was reverie, or meditation, or mysticism. "There," he remembered, he would "meet the servant of the Brahmin, priest of Brahma and Vishnu and Indra, who still sits in his temple on the Ganges reading the Vedas, or dwells at the root of a tree with his crust and water jug. I meet his servant come to draw water for his master, and our buckets as it were grate together in the same well. The pure Walden water is mingled with the sacred water of the Ganges." For Thoreau, the message was clear. The old Puritan covenant of works and the "conscious penance" of the Brahmins had both disappeared in a new and more persuasive vision. "I realized what the Orientals mean by contemplation and the forsaking of works."[36]

For all that, the complex texture of Thoreau's literary work and his thinking in general make it overambitious to call him fully a yogi.[37] In the specific case of *Walden*, for example, the Hindu references interspersed through the substantial text exist side by side with a plethora of literary allusions to Western, Islamic, and East Asian texts. Thoreau read voraciously and apparently forgot little. His work was an encyclopedic record of his intellectual and spiritual project, and to elevate one set of references above the others hints of misreading and does not make good critical sense. Like all complex thinkers, Thoreau expressed considerable ambivalence about religious and philosophical wisdom and where it lay: There was a tensile quality to his Asia. Still more, if Thoreau celebrated Asia, in the end he pruned it for planting in the domestic soil of Concord, Massachusetts, grafting it to Puritan-Calvinist roots. If Asia knew the bliss of the contemplative life, and if it was "infinitely wise," it was also "infinitely stagnant." The break-through had come, for him, not in India but in the "western part" of Asia, where there "appeared a youth, wholly unforetold by them,—not being absorbed into Brahm, but bringing Brahm down to earth and to mankind." As Arthur Versluis has argued, Thoreau's views were "essentially Unitarian," and the Harvard moral philosophy had shaped his spirituality in abiding ways.[38]

Walden first appeared in 1854, and by a year later Lydia Maria Child, the sister of Transcendentalist minister Convers Francis and a notable author in her own right, was publishing her huge three-volume *Progress of Religious Ideas, through Successive Ages.* The first comprehensive American account of comparative religions (outside of Hannah Adams's more limited 1817 *Dictionary of All Religions;* see below), Child's work was intended, as she wrote in the preface, to treat "all religions with reverence." Its index was innocent of references to the Atman or to yoga, and the most germane references, in its opening chapter on "Hindostan, or India," were to "Brahm." "Brahm" was for Child the "one invisible God," the "invisible Supreme Being," one with Nature, and evidence of "Hindoo" pantheism. "They believe that all life, whether in essence or form, proceeds constantly from Brahm," she explained. In this context, Child told of the union of the soul with the divine, at least in the case of the Brahmin who turned his back to society to become the classic forest dweller. "He must renounce his family," she told readers, "give up every species of property, sleep on the ground, and annihilate his body by such self-torments as ingenuity can devise. By this process he may finally attain absorption into the Divine Soul, which is the great object of devotional efforts among the Hindoos."[39] The message for Child was clear, and it was a works righteousness of asceticism—not the sensual delight of the self finding its Self—that ruled her Hindu mystic.

There was neither Atman nor yoga, either, in the index references of Transcendentalist (Unitarian) minister James Freeman Clarke, who published *Ten Great Religions* some sixteen years later, in 1871. Nor was his message uncritical: "An ultra, one-sided idealism is the central tendency of the Hindoo mind. The God of Brahmanism is an intelligence, absorbed in the rest of profound contemplation. The good man of this religion is he who withdraws from an evil world into abstract thought." Thus the first problem of Hindu spirituality was the lack of a service orientation on the part of the yogi (or, for Clarke, simply the "Hindoo" contemplative). The second—and from the rhetoric, worse—problem was the extreme asceticism and denigration of this world that accompanied the Hindu seeker. Clarke's existential horror was consummate: "They torture themselves with self-inflicted torments; for the body is the great enemy of the soul's salvation, and they must beat it down by ascetic mortifications. . . . In one part of India, therefore, devotees are swinging on hooks in honor of Siva, hanging themselves by the feet, head downwards over a fire, rolling on a bed of prickly thorns, jumping on a couch filled with sharp knives, boring holes in their tongues, and sticking their bodies full of pins and needles, or perhaps holding the arms over the head till they stiffen in that position." While some beat their flesh into submission (with evocations of the Catholic Middle Ages), perhaps worst of all for Clarke was the third problem. "Meantime in other places whole regions are given over to sensual indulgences, and companies of abandoned women are connected with different temples and consecrate their gains to the support of their worship."[40] Tantra on stage, we may surmise.

Members of the Transcendental circle had thus brought Asia to American notice—or at least to the notice of the Americans who read their texts and, especially in Emerson's case, heard them speak. But it was an Asia that, for all the metaphysical admiration that Emerson and Thoreau in particular evinced, got mixed marks and was ultimately found wanting. Significantly, Child had titled her work *The Progress of Religious Ideas.* Over the accounts of Asia hovered Romantic notions of progress toward the Good and the Better and hovered, too, an incipient form of the doctrine of evolution. This was hardly Darwinism yet, except perhaps in the case of Clarke: *The Origin of Species* did not appear until 1858. But Emerson, already in the first (1836) edition of his little book *Nature,* prefaced his introduction with an epigraph declaring that "striving to be man, the worm / Mounts through all the spires of form."[41] Here was Lamarckian evolution, with its insistence that all life forms were continuous, that they had arisen gradually over ages, and that characteristics acquired because of need were passed on to progeny. As for humans, so for their religions. The Christian faith stood at the pinnacle of the world's spiritual traditions, and the Transcendentalists, for all their Asiatic tours, knew that home ground was best ground. Failures of servanthood, extreme asceticism, and—at least for Clarke—an equally extreme libertinism marred South Asian spirituality. In the horrified descriptions of yogis hanging head downwards over fires and in other excruciating postures, we can read, perhaps, early-warning reports on the dangerous asanas of hatha yoga. The Brahm who spent his existence contemplating his own navel was not the Brahm in whose company mid-nineteenth-century Americans felt particularly comfortable.

If there were few full-time yogis in Transcendental forests, the Theosophical Society has already introduced us to a different reading of Asia. Blavatsky had clearly used South Asian classics as a major part of a complex theological synthesis that provided, for Theosophists, an intricate roadmap to mark their spiritual

path. As we will see for Olcott, especially concerning Buddhism, he was enthusiastic about these classics, too. Even in *Isis Unveiled*, Blavatsky knew the Atman
and knew it in Indian terms as the Self. More than that, she displayed considerable admiration for yogis, whom she portrayed as spiritual athletes who readily
performed miracles and generally evidenced awesome physical and psychological prowess. In the face of typical criticism of yogis as "obscene ascetics" who
shocked Western sensibilities by going naked, she warmly defended them. By
the time she wrote *The Secret Doctrine*, she was calling yoga itself "mystic meditation" and the source of "Supreme Wisdom," preferring Raja Yoga—which she
identified with the classical system ascribed to Patanjali as well as with two other
schools—as the "best and simplest." She continued to be fascinated by the so-
called siddhi powers, the esoteric abilities that conferred supernormal control of
physical and psychological reality. Quoting a Hindu text, she saw the ultimate
wisdom of "Yogism" in perceiving " 'by means of the SELF the seat abiding in the
SELF' where dwells the Brahman free from all." Yet the world of hatha yoga—
the physical yoga to ready the body for meditative practice—remained an alien
and uninviting realm. Blavatsky saw it as a "lower" form and linked it to "torture
and self-maceration"—language that echoed the earlier reports of yogis hanging
downwards over fires. Moreover, even pranayama, or control of the breath, belonged, for Blavatsky, to the "lower Yoga." "The *Hatha* so called," she warned,
"was and still is discountenanced by the Arhats. It is injurious to the health and
alone can never develop into Raj Yoga."[42]

Blavatsky's *Key to Theosophy* (1889) offered readers the clearest explication of
her distinctive reading of the Atman, now transposed from South Asia to function
as part of an eclectic and synthetic theological edifice. In her schema of seven
bodies in which only the first was fully physical, she had identified the "Atma" as
the seventh and highest metaphysical body, "one with the Absolute, as its radiation." She thought that the "Atma-Buddhi" was not to be identified with the
Universal World Soul of ancient Greek mystical philosophy. Yet she clearly—
if provisionally—saw the Atma(n) as the Higher Self, "inseparable from its one
and absolute *Meta*-Spirit as the sunbeam is inseparable from sunlight." And significantly, she declared the Atma, "the inseparable ray of the Universal and ONE
SELF," to be the "God *above*, more than within, us."[43]

The same year that Blavatsky published her *Key to Theosophy*, William Judge
produced his reading of the *Yoga Sutras* traditionally attributed to Patanjali.
Using an English translation produced in Bombay in 1885 by Tookeram Tatya,
an Indian member of the Theosophical Society, Judge emphasized a distinction
between hatha and raja yoga already suggested by Blavatsky. His preface clearly
explained the difference he saw between the two and warned readers of the dan-

gers of hatha yoga, quoting from the words of Henry Steel Olcott in the earlier Bombay edition. Hatha yoga worked to establish health and train the will, wrote Olcott, but "the processes prescribed to arrive at this end are so difficult that only a few resolute souls go through all the stages of its practice, while many have failed and died in the attempt. It is therefore strongly denounced by all the philosophers." Minimizing allusions to "postures" (the asanas) in the *Yoga Sutras*, Judge went on to laud raja yoga, which, he said, was "certainly spiritual." Hatha was distinctly not. Instead, it resulted in "psychic development at the delay or expense of the spiritual nature." When the Patanjali text announced, in translation, "A posture assumed by a Yogee must be steady and pleasant," Judge was quick to explain that the "postures" of the various yogic systems were "not absolutely essential to the successful pursuit of the practice of concentration and attainment of its ultimate fruits." More than that, he found them "only possible for Hindus," who had practiced them from childhood and who knew their physiological effects. Still, Judge was fairly complacent about the dangers: "These last named practices and results may allure the Western student, but from our knowledge of inherent racial difficulties there is not much fear that many will persist in them."[44]

What appealed to a late-nineteenth-century Anglo-American about the *Yoga Sutras*, we can guess, was the moral inscription that the text—and Judge's presentation of it—wrote over yogic practice. As in the theosophical children's catechism that he had published in *The Path*, Judge insisted on virtue. The Patanjali yogi developed such qualities as "harmlessness and kindness," "veracity," "abstinence from theft," "continence," the elimination of "covetousness," and similar virtues along the way to the proverbial flight of the Alone to the Alone. There was no discourse of the Self in this rendering, no prevailing language that Atman *was* Brahman, but instead a translation that hailed the "Isolation" of the soul. Judge was quick to explain that the translated text did not mean "that a man is isolated from his fellows, becoming cold and dead, but only that the Soul is isolated or freed from the bondage of matter and desire." His anti-isolationist reading accorded well with readings by later translators, but the reasons for Judge's caveat were neither textual nor linguistic. For him, instead, theosophical (and Christian) brotherhood had become Hindu righteousness. Beyond that, in the original *Yoga Sutras* there were the tantalizing allusions to the siddhi powers. The accomplished yogi, for example, could "move his body from one place to another with the quickness of thought, to extend the operations of his senses beyond the trammels of place or the obstructions of matter, and to alter any natural object from one form to another." Judge remained ambivalent about what he understood as these exploits of "Will." He was clearly fascinated, but he worried over the inextricable bond, for most, between will and desire, and he seemed grateful, or at least relieved, at the circumspection of the Patanjali text. "Patanjali and his school well knew that the secret of directing the will with ten times the ordinary force might be discovered if they outlined the method, and then bad men whose desires were strong and conscience wanting, would use it with impunity against their fellows."[45] Malicious animal magnetism, or its near relative, apparently inhabited the East as well as the West.

Judge's work elicited at least one (fairly negative) review in the *New York Times*, suggesting some awareness of yoga, however minimal, among American readers ("those who love to be muddled may be safely recommended this little book"). Even further, by the 1890s Theosophists were exempting pranayama (yogic breathing) from their strictures against hatha yoga—different from Blavatsky who had found both to be "lower." Prasad's *Nature's Finer Forces* was making its mark—in what may have been, as J. Gordon Melton has suggested, "the first book to explain and advocate the practice of yoga." Significantly, in Prasad's work along with the much-vaunted "Science of Breath" came chapters on "Evolution," "The Mind," and "The Manifestations of Psychic Force." These are themes that at once evoke the preoccupations of the theosophical world and point the way toward a later American history of yoga as a transformed metaphysic.[46]

Theosophical interest in meditation yoga, however, would continue under the rubric of raja yoga—a term that became current in American metaphysical circles after 1896 when Swami Vivekananda's *Raja-Yoga* first appeared (see below). Raja yoga, in general, had already made its appeal, if vaguely, among Theosophists, since—as we saw—Blavatsky had invoked the term. After Vivekananda's pathbreaking work, though, Theosophists learned more clearly that the "aphorisms" of Patanjali they so admired were, in fact, an exposition of raja yoga, containing techniques for stilling the fluctuations of the mind and promoting mental concentration in order to attain *samadhi*, participation in the bliss of the divine consciousness. What they did not realize in this new learning was that they were being encouraged to read the dualistic Patanjali work in ways that were monistic. They were learning, in effect, no longer the isolation of the soul from matter and desire but the presence of a divine source of bliss within an embodied individual consciousness.

Judge's successor as the head of the Theosophical Society in America (the American branch of the Theosophical Society that had broken away from the international organization) was Katherine Tingley (1847–1929), whose colony at Point Loma, California, with its "applied Theosophy," became a showcase for the raja. But it was a raja decidedly changed, even from the moral transformation already part of the Judge reading. Tingley used raja yoga as a new descriptive term for the work of socializing children in her experimental school. Her Raja Yoga School opened in 1900, including American and Cuban children, and from the first it aimed at creating a "pure moral atmosphere" for its (resident) students. Reading, especially of newspapers and magazines, was censored, daily silence was observed, sexual activity (that is, masturbation) was severely proscribed, and physical activities—but not hatha yoga—were encouraged. Since the body housed the "spiritual Ego," hygiene and physical health became preoccupations. As W. Michael Ashcraft has summarized, Point Loma raja yoga meant "a lifestyle of faculty coordination, uniting all of the faculties to achieve spiritual and moral maturity."[47] Under this regime, in effect, to be metaphysical meant, first and primarily, to be moral.

Meanwhile, Swami Vivekananda (1863–1902), the now-famed South Asian "other" who had helped Theosophists think more, and more precisely, about raja yoga, was broadcasting his views to a wider audience. After participating in the World's Parliament of Religions, he stayed to tour and lecture, visiting major cities not only in the East but also in the Midwest and the South. Even Christian Scientists welcomed him; in 1894 he offered a lecture series in Maine under their sponsorship. (He called them "Vedantins" in a letter to other monastics back in India, telling them that the Scientists had grafted the teaching of the nondualist Advaita onto the Bible.) By 1895, he had founded the Vedanta Society in New York and subsequently, in 1897, the Ramakrishna Mission and the Ramakrishna Order in India. In the midst of this activity, Vivekananda produced four books on yoga—essentially stenographed transcriptions of his lectures. The first three accorded with the classical tradition—karma (the yoga of works), bhakti (the yoga of devotion), and jnana (the yoga of knowledge). The last concerned raja yoga (the meditation yoga that Theosophists had already identified with the Patanjali *Yoga Sutras*, although it was not explicitly named there). The book that Vivekananda produced under the title *Raja-Yoga* sold out in a matter of months in 1896 and was ready for a new edition by November.[48]

There was no separate work from Vivekananda on hatha yoga, but as Elizabeth De Michelis has argued, his reconfiguration of the *Yoga Sutras* in *Raja-Yoga* both reflected and augmented an emerging spirituality significantly different from Indian classical spiritual teaching. De Michelis links the spirituality to individualism and, following Dutch scholar Wouter Hanegraaff, to a "New Age religion" of the late nineteenth and early twentieth centuries and then to the New Age movement of the later century and continuing.[49] The designation "New Age religion" is somewhat misleading here, with a presentism that minimizes connections to an earlier America. Instead, what should be clear in this

context are the patent lines of connection to American metaphysical religion—
to its lengthy history and its evolving reinvention of discourse and practice.

Vivekananda, in his late-nineteenth-century moment, became a major conversation partner in the discourse, epitomizing the revolving doors that were already connecting East with West with East again in British India. De Michelis
has noted that his relationship with the fabled Indian mystic Ramakrishna (1836–
1886) was far more ambiguous than it has been read to be in the devotional
literature of India and the American Vedanta movement. She has also pointed
to his connections with the Hindu reformist body the Brahmo Samaj. A religious and social movement of elite Bengalis, from 1828 it had moved through a
series of phases, influenced by Western contacts with Unitarian Christianity, with
ideas about science, and eventually with Theosophy (when Blavatsky and Olcott
settled in Bombay). Vivekananda's debt to the Brahmo Samaj, De Michelis estimates, cannot "be overstated." Meanwhile, Bengal itself welcomed Romantic,
Transcendental, occult, and theosophical ideas that were spread by literature,
public lectures, and personal contacts. None other than William Judge, for example, lectured there in a tour during the summer of 1884.[50]

Making his way in the metaphysical culture of the United States, which lion-
ized him after 1893, Vivekananda quickly learned the American metaphysical
dialect, and he creolized his presentation of an already combinative Indian-
Western spirituality to please American ears and tastes. His highly influential
Raja-Yoga exhibited the skill with which he blended his own message with the
discourse of his American hosts. In semantic choices already familiar to his Indian milieu *and* also true to metaphysical form, he hailed the "science" of raja-
yoga, which—unlike the "unpardonable manner of some modern scientists"—
did not "deny the existence of facts" that were "difficult to explain." This meant
"miracles, and answers to prayers, and powers of faith." Instead of the "superstitious explanation of attributing them to the agency of a being, or beings, above
the clouds," he posited an explanation that could be read with familiarity and
recognition by metaphysically inclined Americans. Raja-yoga (like Theosophy
and New Thought) taught that "each man is only a conduit for the infinite ocean
of knowledge and power that lies behind mankind." If "desires and wants" were
"in man," likewise the "power of supply" (a metaphysical term that marked the
presence of divine abundance) was also there. "Wherever and whenever a desire,
a want, a prayer has been fulfilled," Vivekananda emphasized, "it was out of this
infinite magazine that the supply came, and not from any supernatural being."[51]

Nor did Vivekananda confine himself to using jargon and code, dropping
buzzwords into metaphysical ears or minds. Success in meditation began with

establishing a strong physiological foundation, and he countenanced this for American listeners and readers by specifically citing metaphysical practitioners. "Always use a mental effort, what is usually called 'Christian Science,' to keep the body strong," he enjoined. When he approached the subject of pranayama, he linked the discipline of the breath to various species of metaphysical practice, all of them suggesting that he read them in terms congenial to "noetic" New Thought. "Sects in every country" had attempted "control of Prana." In America, he reminded readers, there were "Mind-healers, Faith-healers, Spiritualists, Christian Scientists, Hypnotists, etc.," and, whether they were aware or not, "at the back of each" lay "this control of the Prana." De Michelis has pointed both to a "prana model" (breath) and a "samadhi model" (bliss) in the text, each of them a significant reinterpretation of traditional Indian teaching in terms congenial to Vivekananda's audience. In her reading, his text linked the energy of prana to mesmeric belief and practice—and, it can be added, to notions of subtle electricity and Blavatsky's language of ether and Great Breath already abroad in the metaphysical community. Likewise, samadhi became transformed from the Patanjali radical flight of liberation in isolation from the world, with which Judge had struggled. Instead, De Michelis argues, the samadhi theme should be read in terms of "God-realization" become "Self-realization" and likewise "realization of human potential."[52] In other words, American yoga was making the choice—congenial to Theosophy and New Thought and surely influenced by them—for a philosophy of monism and a theology of immanence.

We can add, too, a bliss consciousness that already hinted of the tantric reading to come. Indeed, Vivekananda explicitly cited the kundalini, in tantrism the powerful but latent spiritual energy "asleep" at the base of the spine that, when awakened, traveled upward and brought transformative meditation states. He called it "psychic prana" and the "'Lotus of the Kundalini,'" telling how on its journey to the "thousand-petalled lotus in the brain" the Yogi would experience "layer after layer of the mind" opening and "all the different visions and wonderful powers." It was significant, too, that he likened the energy and "vibration" of pranayama to electric current, with its aim "to rouse the coiled-up power . . . called the Kundalini." On arrival in the brain, the result became "the full blaze of illumination, the perception of the Self." The aroused kundalini brought "all knowledge" and represented "the one and only way to attaining Divine Wisdom, superconscious perception, the realization of the spirit." Here all prayers were answered, for when a person received a positive response the "fulfilment" came "from his own nature." The individual had "succeeded by the mental attitude of prayer in waking up a bit of this infinite power which is coiled up within himself."

Raja-yoga was "the science of religion, the rationale of all worship, all prayers, forms, ceremonies, and miracles."[53]

In the psychologized context of his meditation yoga, Vivekananda had few things to say about the hatha. Pranayama and the transformed consciousness it evoked did require attention to posture (as did the cultivation of the kundalini)— sitting with spine erect and in a straight line with the neck and head. "Let the whole weight of the body be supported by the ribs," Vivekananda advised, "and then you will have an easy natural posture, with the spine straight. You will easily see that you cannot think very high thoughts with the chest in." But like Blavatsky and Judge, he skirted away from an embrace of the purely physical. Hatha yoga, he thought, aimed entirely at making the body "very strong." "We have nothing to do with it here," he explained both pragmatically and condescendingly, "be-cause its practices are very difficult, and cannot be learned in a day, and, after all, do not lead to much spiritual growth." For all that, De Michelis has argued his seminal role as "creator" of what she terms "fully-fledged Modern Yoga," which for her includes, but is not limited to, "Modern Postural Yoga." In a designation that encompasses not only the United States but all of the West in interaction with the Indian Subcontinent, she credits Vivekananda's *Raja-Yoga* with "im-mediately" starting "something of a 'yoga renaissance' both in India and in the West."[54] Yet as important as Vivekananda was, it needs to be noticed that among American metaphysicians and the public at large the yogic turn was more com-plex, beginning gradually and growing because of a series of players and perfor-mances yet to be staged.

By the time *Raja-Yoga* appeared, public awareness, even of hatha, had already begun. In 1893, for example, at least one spoof on "A Western Yoga" had appeared in the columns of the *New York Times*, complete with theosophical allusions to the astral body, progress, and "Yoga" as the "science of the soul" and "holy sor-cery" (an apparent allusion to siddhis). "The power comes from meditation and concentration of the mind. One must posture in silence and abstraction. And this can be best attained . . . by standing on one leg and looking at the tip of the nose."[55] Still, as the tone of the *Times* piece suggests, after the World's Par-liament and even after the 1896 appearance of Vivekananda's *Raja-Yoga*, the American experience of yoga remained guarded. Meditation yoga signaled ex-oticism and the promise of something that was spiritually more. It also fed into evolving discourses of the mind and its powers—a point to which I shall return— and it suggested a "scientific" perspective that could address religiophilosophi-cal themes rationally and pragmatically. At the cutting edge of this discourse, the yogic *practice* of pranayama had begun to bring some idealizing American devotees of religious liberalism back to their senses and their bodies. The mind had a home, and the house itself would need to be dusted and swept, even by metaphysicians. More than that, a clean house could bring the body—and the mind—to a state of delight.

Given this nineteenth-century history and its ambivalences, however—given the tortured bodies of its yogis hanging upside down—how did hatha yoga (and the body and mind of delight) come to prevail as preferred American yogic practice? If Vivekananda alone was not enough, how else did Americans incorporate into their discourse and practice the translated language of the Self in union with the universe—and, in the American context, the (lower-case) self and selves? Against the backdrop of hatha yoga's ascendancy, what, in general, happened to the metaphysical mind and to forms of meditation yoga? Any satisfactory answer to these questions must begin with the recognition, already suggested, that the route to the enlightened body-self and its American metaphysical entourage was circuitous. Yet the *American* teachers pointing toward an American yogic future were there, and they supplied important hints of what was to come. J. Gordon Melton has identified two such early twentieth-century figures in William Walker Atkinson and Pierre Bernard, both of them teachers of hatha who located it in a larger yogic context.[56] What is intriguing about the pair is that between them they introduced the major themes that have come to characterize American yoga with its covert metaphysical content.

William Walker Atkinson (1862–1932), who had a business background, was drawn to the American metaphysical tradition and became a leading New Thought author. He apparently moved to Chicago around the beginning of the twentieth century and from there produced a prodigious set of titles, one after another, book after book. As they are reproduced in the on-line library catalog of the University of California, they clearly display Atkinson's preoccupation with a series of themes. They speak of subconscious and superconscious planes of the mind, of the powers of mind and thought, of the attainability of health and success, of the exercise of will and its effects in the American pragmatic version of psychic forces. Here was New Thought in its brashest, least Christianized and God-dependent version; here was the rationalist—the noetic— tradition that Gary Ward Materra distinguishes from the more affective and socially concerned version taught by Emma Curtis Hopkins and her students. Titles such as these, for example, carry the argument in unambiguous witness: *The Law of the New Thought* (1902); *Thought-Force in Business and Everyday Life* (18th ed., 1903); *Dynamic Thought; or, The Law of Vibrant Energy* (1906); *Self-Healing by Thought Force* (1907); *The Inner Consciousness* (1908); *The Secret of Success* (1908); *The Will: Its Nature, Power, and Development* (1909);

Mind and Body; or, Mental States and Physical Conditions (1910); *Mind-Power: The Secret of Mental Magic* (1912).[57]

Readers of these books, however, likely did not know that Atkinson was also the author of another series of works on yoga under a pseudonym designed to suggest their South Asian provenance. From 1902, as Yogi Ramacharaka, Atkinson published a different set of titles. Significantly, along with books on "Yogi philosophy and Oriental mysticism," by 1904 his *Hatha Yoga; or, The Yoga Philosophy of Physical Well-Being* appeared, and by a year later the related *Science of Breath*, with again the next year *A Series of Lessons in Raja Yoga* and *The Science of Psychic Healing*. Apparently, Atkinson wrote from experience. Gordon Melton remarks that he "became an accomplished student of yoga, so much so that his books circulated and were well received in India." Whatever his personal yogic success, Ramacharaka's titles already suggest the influence of Theosophy (and likely Vivekananda) in their evocation of raja yoga, siddhi powers, and pranayama. Linked to Atkinson's New Thought themes—with, in his case, their theosophical tilt toward ideas of magical and occult powers of mind—the conceptual frame is not hard to read. Ramacharaka cited and quoted from Mabel Collins's theosophical devotional classic *Light on the Path* in his work on raja yoga, and his general teaching throughout was theosophical.[58]

Each human being was composed of a series of five hierarchical planes from the lowest, which was vegetative, through to the instinctive, the intellectual, the intuitive, and finally the plane of Cosmic Knowing. "Man is a Centre of Consciousness in the great One Life of the Universe," Ramacharaka wrote. He continued in an evolutionary declaration: "His soul has climbed a great many steps before it reached its present position and stage of unfoldment. And it will pass through many more steps until it is entirely free and delivered from the necessity of its swaddling clothes." According to the "Yogi philosophy," even the "atoms of matter" had "life and an elementary manifestation of mind," while at the highest level "the higher regions of the mind, while belonging to the individual, and a part of himself, are so far above his ordinary consciousness that to all intents and purposes messages from them are as orders from another and higher soul." Still, there were the "confining sheaths"—in an evocation of the lower bodies of which Blavatsky had written—and the "Higher Self" had to do the best that it could. If one could reach the cosmic plane, the fortunate individual would be "able to see fully, plainly and completely that there is One Great Life underlying all the countless forms and shapes of manifestation." Separateness was "'the working fiction of the universe.'" In this context, mental healing was but the restoration of "normal conditions" on the vegetative plane, so that this level of consciousness could "do its work without the hindrance of adverse conscious thought."[59]

With this anthropology as backdrop, Yogi Ramacharaka conceived the work of yogic adepts to be awakening their consciousness of the "Real Self," a process that, he explained, the Yogi Masters taught in two steps. The first was the "Consciousness of the I," with a life not dependent on the body; and the second—familiar in a New Thought context—was the "Consciousness of the 'I AM,'" identified with the "Universal Life." Thus, before one sought mastery of the secrets of the universe outside, one "should master the Universe within—the Kingdom of the Self." In the world within could be found "that wonderful thing, the Will," which was "but faintly understood by those ignorant of the Yogi Philosophy—the Power of the Ego—its birthright from the Absolute." Emersonian echoes could be heard in the allusion to Will (Emerson's Transcendental gospel *Nature* in 1836 had announced its power) and also in Ramacharaka's instructions about distinguishing between the "I" and the "Not I." But the "Real Self of Man" was "the Divine Spark sent forth from the Sacred Flame." It was the "Child of the Divine Parent.... Immortal—Eternal—Indestructible—Invincible." For Ramacharaka, in the progression that was raja yoga, the Real Self, "setting aside first this, and then that . . . finally discards all of the 'Not I' leaving the Real Self free and delivered from its bondage to its appendages." Pragmatically (and tellingly), however: "Then it returns to the discarded appendages, and makes use of them."[60]

The Ramacharaka-Atkinson synthesis was smooth and seamless. Here was Theosophy yoked to the ancient texts of India in their Westernized Neo-Vedantin transmission and yoked as well to an American celebration of will and control. Higher Self and ego self played in not-too-distant fields, ready to join to enhance the waking, everyday existence of the body in which they dwelled. For what was decidedly new about Ramacharaka's American yoga was the body. His works on hatha, on the breath, and on psychic healing were companion books that pointed toward the enhancement of the high self through enhancement of its earthly residence. Given all of this, the results were meager. The claims that Yogi Ramacharaka made for hatha yoga seem strikingly spare, and his description of the asanas suggests instead their continuity with simple calisthenics. If his books went to India, as Melton reports, we have to wonder who was reading them.

Meanwhile, in the United States, in the context of late-century and new-century worry regarding "overcivilization" and of Theodore Roosevelt's widely influential celebration of "the strenuous life" (as he titled his 1901 book), a new moral crusade was championing bodily vigor, direct action, and experience over the learning that could be gleaned from books. The natural environment, far from the corruption and debilitating ethos of cities, became an object of cultus. By 1903 *Outlook* magazine was describing nature as the "middle ground between God and man" and the "playground of the soul." Camping and scouting would institutionalize these sentiments, as physical training assumed new ascendancy as part of moral education. At the same time, natural hygiene and physical culture—older nineteenth-century currents in the health reform movement—had joined forces to lead to the gymnasium. Calisthenics were in, and they beckoned with the promise of glowing health for those who would be zealous. Will power became equated with muscle power and, in a culture characterized by the language of "muscular Christianity," became a force for public and private good order. "The identification of morality with muscularity was to grow as an article of hygienic faith through the final third of the [nineteenth] century and the Progressive years," explains James C. Whorton in his landmark *Crusaders for Fitness*. "The arena would become congested with competing programs of health building."[61]

Ramacharaka was a thorough child of his times. "Hatha yoga," he wrote, "is that branch of the Yoga philosophy which deals with the physical body—its care—its well being—its health—its strengths—and all that tends to keep it in its natural and normal state of health." It could appeal to American denizens of the "strenuous life" because it was "first, nature; second, *nature,* and last NATURE." "By all means," Ramacharaka encouraged readers, "apply the nature test to all theories of this kind—our own included—and if they do not square with nature, discard them." Not a "doctor book," his work was instead concerned with "the Healthy Man—its main purpose to help people conform to the standard of the normal man." The asanas that followed were listed as "yogi physical exercises," and, to be sure, they were generally active and aerobic. They did not resemble the classical postures that have been identified with hatha yoga. "Swing back the hands until the arms stand out straight. . . . The arms should be swung with a rapid movement, and with animation and life. Do not go to sleep over the work, or rather play."[62]

What did this yogic workout have to do with the meditative and mystical pursuit that characterized raja yoga? Ramacharaka's answer was fairly trite and perfunctory. The body was "necessary" for human "manifestation and growth"; it was the "Temple of the Spirit"; its care and development constituted a "worthy task" since an "unhealthy and imperfectly developed physical body" would obstruct the proper functioning of the mind. The "instrument" could not be "used to the best advantage by its master, the Spirit." The closest Ramacharaka came to later and standard explanations of quieting the body to prepare it for meditation or altering consciousness through certain yogic asanas—inversions, forward bends, for example—was his appeal to instrumentalism. The body was the instrument for the "real part" of a person "in the work of Soul growth." The yogic devotee would "feel as proud [of his body] as does the master violinist of the

Stradivarius which responds almost with intelligence to the touch of his bow." More than that, Ramacharaka was at pains to separate his teaching from the American knowledge of yoga that we have already met in Transcendentalist and theosophical circles. "In India," explained Ramacharaka, "there exists a horde of ignorant mendicants of the lower fakir class, who pose as Hatha Yogis, but who have not the slightest conception of the underlying principles of that branch of Yoga." They engaged in "tricks," such as reversing the peristaltic action of their intestines to eject items introduced into the colon from "the gullet." "Rank frauds or self-deluded fanatics," these people were "akin to the class of fanatics in India . . . who refuse to wash the body, for religious reasons; or who sit with up-lifted arm until it is withered; or who allow their finger nails to grow until they pierce their hands; or who sit so still that their birds build nests in their hair; or who perform other ridiculous feats, in order to pose as 'holy men.'" [63]

Yogi Ramacharaka did tell readers that they needed to "throw some mind" into their hatha yoga. He also offered a tantalizing discussion, surrounded by late-Victorian caveats and veiled allusions, of "transmuting reproductive energy" through pranayama (raising energy from the sexual organs at the base of the spine to the crown of the head to be used in meditation, as in the discourse of kundalini). "Keep the mind fixed on the idea of Energy, and away from ordinary sexual thoughts and imaginings," cautioned Ramacharaka. In essence, however, Ramacharaka/Atkinson had communicated a yoga of Will and self-efforting, a self-construction that called on a Higher (divine) Self to achieve enhanced ego goals. In so doing, he had effectively linked the language and intent of New Thought to that of Theosophy. He had also succeeded in joining hatha yoga—at least in his hatha yoga book—to raja and other forms of yoga as a venerable and respected branch. But the enlightened body-self was more a devotee of the strenuous life than of the bliss of yogic connection. A brisk "yogi bath" and body rub were partners to the active asanas of Ramacharaka's yogic world. The chapters in his text point toward natural hygiene and physical culture and toward the mantra that characterized the devotees of the health building movement—a sound mind in a sound body. [64]

Six years after Ramacharaka was urging devotees to the yogi bath and body rub, however, New York City could boast its own tantric master. Pierre Bernard (1875–1955), or Perry Arnold Baker as he was born, came from a middle-class family in Leon, Iowa (although he went by several assumed names, probably partly for protection from the law). When he met Sylvais Hamati, a Syrian-Indian man who taught yoga in Lincoln, Nebraska, in the 1880s and 1890s, his new teacher changed his life. With Hamati and others, he moved to California, where his attraction to metaphysical themes led him to conduct an academy in San

Francisco dedicated to hypnosis until, probably because of legal hassles, he left the area. Around 1905, Bernard founded his "Tantrik" order and published the first and only issue of his *International Journal of the Tantrik Order in America: Vira Sadhana* in New York City. There, with the name Pierre Arnold Bernard (used already in his San Francisco days and to which he at some point prefixed a "Dr."), he opened the New York Sanskrit College. According to reports, hatha yoga was taught on the first floor, while upstairs tantric initiates were ushered into deeper secrets. Dogged by sex scandals and hounded by the press as Oom the Omnipotent, he was apparently as flamboyant as the name suggests, reportedly sitting enthroned in the upstairs room before his wealthy initiates and receiving their worshipful adulation. His wife, Blanche deVries, was also a student, an "Oriental" dancer, and a teacher of hatha yoga. She taught, too, it was said, a softer form of tantrism than her husband's more provocative version.[65]

Yet there was telling evidence that Bernard was still a serious student of South Asian yogic themes. By 1924, he had purchased a seventy-acre estate in Nyack, New York, which became a colony for his elite and socially well-placed devotees. Here he located his impressive library, described by a website devoted to him as the "finest collection of Sanskrit works (original texts, manuscripts and translations) in the United States at the time." Indeed, the library contained "approximately 7000 volumes on the subjects of philosophy, ethics, psychology, education and metaphysics as well as much collateral material on physiology, medicine and related sciences." Students flocked to Nyack, and Asian teachers visited. Eventually, Bernard purchased more property in the area, and he also opened a series of tantric centers in Cleveland, Philadelphia, Chicago, and New York City as well as a men's camp for tantra on Long Island. Unlike Atkinson-Ramacharaka, who seemed rarely to have an unpublished thought, Bernard left little in writing. Nevertheless, as Gordon Melton has estimated, his work in shaping American yoga was "immense." This work looked to the human body as aesthetic and pleasurable in ways that went beyond the more muscular approach of the natural hygiene movement and the traditional tantrism of India. As Bernard announced in the lone issue of his journal, "The trained imagination no longer worships before the shrines of churches, pagodas and mosques or there would be blaspheming the greatest, grandest and most sublime temple in the universe, the miracle of miracles, the human body." In the specific case of hatha yoga, we gain a few clues to the substance and direction of Bernard's work through his journal's stylized illustration of an "American tantrik in the practice of his yoga." Here the American yogi sits in padmasana (lotus posture), spine erect, with hands held in special mudras or hand gestures. Evidently, too, Bernard knew about inversions and was practicing headstands, at least, at Nyack, invoking the "Art of Reversion" and enjoining students to "reverse your circulation, not once but several times a day."[66]

If we move beyond the early-twentieth-century teachers that Melton cites, we find that Bernard's legacy continued thematically in part in the doctoral dissertation completed by his nephew Theos Bernard (d. 1947) in 1943 at Columbia University. Published as *Hatha Yoga: The Report of a Personal Experience* (1950), this work boasted thirty-seven full-page glossy black and white plates, including a frontispiece—photographs of Bernard in classical hatha yoga postures. In the first American work to include such representations, here were, among others, padmasana (lotus), sarvangasana (shoulderstand), halasana (the plough—a shoulderstand variation), pascimotanasana (seated forward bend), bhujangasana (cobra), sirsasana (headstand), and other asanas familiar to twenty-first-century students of hatha yoga. Bernard's published bibliography, divided with scholarly correctness into primary and secondary sources, was instructive. In addition to primary sources such as the Patanjali *Yoga Sutras*, the *Hatha Yoga Pradipika*, the *Gheranda Samhita,* and the *Siva Samhita,* the bibliography tellingly listed among secondary works a number ascribed to the popular and controversial pseudonymous Arthur Avalon. These included the well-known *Serpent Power*—a major conduit for Western knowledge of tantrism and kundalini, identifying—with more precision and elaboration than Vivekananda—the energy coiled at the base of the spine as sexually charged and emphasizing its power to bring samadhi. Here samadhi, true to form, was understood as the bliss-inducing ecstasy of the self contemplating its Self. Secondary sources also listed works by the mysticizing scholar of Tibetan lore W. Y. Evans-Wentz and by Sir John Woodroffe (as distinct from Arthur Avalon). One work, by V. G. Rele, was titled provocatively enough *The Mysterious Kundalini,* and several—S. Sundaram's *Yoga Physical Culture,* Yogi Vithaldas's *The Yoga System of Health,* and Shri Yogendra's *Yoga Personal Hygiene*—pointed unmistakably toward hatha.[67] There will be more to say about Shri Yogendra, who would make his way to the United States and exert significant influence in the nation.

What is of concern here, however, is the substance and tenor of the Bernard text. Theos Bernard did not offer distanced learning acquired from his reading and family influence. On the contrary, he went to India, and he went native. "When I went to India, I did not present myself as an academic research student, trying to probe into the intimacies of ancient cultural patterns; instead, I became a disciple." Beyond that, he understood the hatha yoga he was presenting to readers as thoroughly tantric. Hatha yoga, he explained, was predicated centrally on the control of the breath, and he went on to link the term *hatha* itself to "the flowing of breath in the right nostril, called the 'sun breath,' and the flowing of breath in the left nostril, called the 'moon breath.'" Hatha yoga meant the union of these two breaths to "induce a mental condition called samadhi." "This," he went on to assure readers, "is not an imaginary or mythical state, though it is explained by myths, but is an actual condition that can be subjectively experienced and objectively observed." How did yogis reach this condition? The answer lay in the purification of the body and the physical techniques of yoga—intended "to make dynamic a latent force in the body called Kundalini." Kundalini yoga led in turn to laya yoga, in which the "single aim" was "stilling the mind," while finally the mind's complete subjection, understood as the "Royal Road," was raja yoga. This, not surprisingly, was the scheme laid out by the formidable Arthur Avalon, whom Bernard identified, according to the era's conventional wisdom, with Sir John Woodroffe. Thus, following Avalon, he told readers that "all these forms are often classified under the general heading Tantrik Yoga, since they represent the practical discipline based on tantrik philosophy."[68]

What Bernard described thereafter in this very personal account was surely startling—seeming almost to confirm long-ago Transcendentalist descriptions of yogic excess but inverting them to celebrate the physical feats he could eventually perform. He claimed that he held three-hour headstands and that he practiced a series of kriyas ("actions" or, as he called them, "duties") recommended in the *Hatha Yoga Pradipika*, including the purificatory dhauti karma in which he swallowed a three-foot length of cloth to cleanse his digestive tract.

> Begin with a small piece of cloth about three feet long. I found that an ordinary four-inch surgeon's gauze met every requirement. First put the cloth in a basin of water, and after it is thoroughly saturated insert one end of it as far back in the throat as possible and go through the motions of eating and swallowing. This will encourage the throat to take hold. There may be some spasms, but they will soon pass, as will all soreness that is experienced. It will take only a few days for the throat and stomach to accommodate themselves. Do not try to accomplish the feat on the first day. I began with a few inches and increased the length a little each day until I had swallowed the required twenty-two and one-half feet. With a little patience, anyone can master the technique in about three weeks.[69]

Bernard's text progressed through detailed instructions for pranayama and body locks (mudras, bandhas), disclosing purported yogic secrets and quoting (translated) texts generously along the way. There were practices of listening to internal sound and seeing inner light; there was a candle exercise—staring into its light to create a retinal afterimage. Thereafter came a series of other rigorous purifications, pranayamas, and hatha yoga exercises. As he introduced these, Bernard embellished his account with the claim of a three-month retreat to gain samadhi, although Paul G. Hackett has concluded from "substantial evidence" that the retreat never happened. The "retreat," however, functioned as a useful teaching tool. Complete with an initiatory ceremony to induce the awakening of kundalini and a warning by Bernard's teacher that no ceremony could actually achieve that goal, the narrative could at once discipline and mystify a generation of seeker-readers. Bernard would confess to them that, indeed, the ceremony had brought him a foretaste of samadhi—but not the experience itself. What was the lesson? "During my studies of the science of Yoga I found that it holds no magic, performs no miracles, and reveals nothing supernatural. I was directed at every stage to practice if I wanted to know its secrets." It was practice alone that could bring the "Knowledge of the True," and the nature of that knowledge remained for him and his readers a "mystery."[70]

If Theos Bernard had, in fact, discovered tantra, it was a tantra that in practice operated far differently from all reports of the elder Bernard's tantrism. It also contrasted strikingly with the "tantric" practice that would emerge in the New Age movement and new spirituality, in general, by the late twentieth century. Bernard's "Tantrik philosophy" and practice meant rigorous asceticism, flight from the world, totalitarian dedication, and various inscriptions on the body that looked remarkably similar to those that had been written off with disgust and revulsion in nineteenth-century accounts. The Self that Bernard could find through the awakened kundalini and samadhi seemed a far cry from the softer, kinder, ego-friendlier Self that later flourished as the enlightened body-self in the American practice of yoga. At the same time, Pierre Bernard and Theos Bernard, along with William Walker Atkinson/Yogi Ramacharaka had set important directions for an American yogic future, and they had underlined its connections to American metaphysical religion. Here siddhi powers had become Will Power; the world was Will and (health-building and/or ascetic) Desire; Will could succeed, and Desire could find fulfillment. The body could be liberated into a state of never-dreamed-of health and well-being. Even if attained through harshness and asceticism, there was a (disciplined and discipline-producing) pleasure that surpassed all knowledge in this body's pleasure, and Will, Desire, Health, and Pleasure could all lead into the highest spiritual realities that humans might experience and receive. Best of all, in the American mode, humans could achieve all of this for and in themselves. In the noetic style of one side of the New Thought movement and in echoes of an inherited Hermeticism and earlier nineteenth-century reinventions of the theme, they could be as gods.

That acknowledged, just as in the earlier heyday of Vivekananda, Americans did not always need to work alone, with only books as teachers. Nor did they need to travel, like Theos Bernard, to South Asia (although, to be sure, they sometimes did and in increasing numbers as the twentieth century progressed). Well before the 1965 change in the immigration law—which brought more Asians and more elite Asians to the nation—the East kept coming to the West. Yogic teachers were announcing that they possessed healing knowledge for American disciples. Shri Yogendra was a major case in point. During his research stay in India in 1937, the younger Bernard had made his way to the Yoga Institute of Bombay, where the already metaphysical Yogendra taught his "scientific" yoga— the man whom Melton credits with being "largely responsible for the revival and spread of hatha yoga in the twentieth century." Now Yogendra came to other American seekers. A disciple of Paramahansa Madhavadasaji of Malsar, Shri Yogendra (born in 1897 as Manibhai Haribhai Desai) after a several-year sojourn with his guru returned to the householder life, marrying instead of becoming a renunciant and swami. He had learned from his teacher, especially, the study and practice of hatha yoga, and he would thereafter work to put it on an academic footing and to establish its "scientific" basis. In this context, according to his biographer, Yogendra came to America at the end of 1919 with the aim of "popularizing yoga." He was already a man with a mission. One anecdote had it that just before Madhavadasaji's death in 1922 the aged teacher wrote Yogendra saying that his American task was akin to Vivekananda's in spreading the fame of Ramakrishna. Yogendra went back to India less than five years after he came, however, intending to return to the United States but thwarted by the restrictive immigration legislation of 1924. Still, he had managed to found his Yoga Institute at Santa Cruz, California, and he had written four works on yoga.[71]

We glean some sense of Yogendra's teaching from these works, and in general they resonate more with the natural hygiene/physical culture orientation of Yogi Ramacharaka than with the tantric ambience of the Bernards. For Yogendra, hatha was the "primal yoga effort" and "the methodical approach to the attainment of the highest in Yoga." It recognized "the concept of the wholeness of Man," and it proposed "to achieve psychosomatic sublimation through a system of physical culture." This included "physical education, hygiene, therapy, and biologic control of the autonomous nervous system affecting the hygiene of the mind and moral behaviour." Allusions to what Avalon and Bernard had called the kundalini were careful and restrained: "The hathayogins have laid down various practices for the methodical sublimation not only of sex but also of all baser instincts." Seemingly more important than samadhi was the basic biological goal of survival and longevity. "If yoga succeeds with the yogins in the present as it did in the past, it can hardly be doubted *why any man* following the yoga code of controlled biological living *should not live more than a hundred years.*" (His teacher purportedly died at the age of 122, so Yogendra no doubt wrote confidently.)[72]

Yogendra's yoga was based on the *Hatha Yoga Pradipika*, and that text's concern for purification, which we have already seen in the yogic experiment of
Theos Bernard, became for Yogendra a question of health and hygiene. "Even
the civilized society has been sick, to a more or less extent, *throughout history*,"
he would later write in *Why Yoga*, "because human civilization and culture did
not fully succeed in weeding out the grass roots of savage inherited potentials."
He was thoroughly committed to the science that grounded the health-building
enterprise; he worked with medical professionals in New York; and he knew such
natural health celebrities as Bernarr Macfadden, Benedict Lust, and John Harvey
Kellogg. Still, the science he preached was a science of the spiritual. Hatha yoga
would put its students "in the direct touch with the Reality (of objects on which
they contemplate)." Moreover, the physical body that demanded the rigorous
discipline of natural hygiene was but one of a series of bodies. In the textual tradition of South Asia and in the language that Theosophists were continuing to
invoke, he could insist that "yoga recognizes more subtle bodies or sheaths . . .
than one."[73]

Clearly, Yogendra belonged to a new and nontraditional cadre of Asian teachers. Neither an ancient chanter of texts nor a renunciant hidden away for years
in Himalayan hills, like Vivekananda he was already partially a Westerner before
he ever came to the United States. Growing up in British India, matriculating—
before he met his guru—at St. Xavier's College in Bombay, translating the yogic
message into a scientific argot, linking his religiophilosophical views to those of
Plotinus and Henri Bergson, Yogendra was a blended product of East and West.
He was a transnational before the term and the concept became current.[74] As
with Vivekananda, it is too simple to say that East (Yogendra) met West (Americans) in the United States in the 1920s. More complexly, East-West met West,
and, as we have seen, the West that got met was already textually in touch with
Asian sources and some of its seekers had traveled to sit at the feet of South Asian
masters.

The combinative habit was, if anything, even more prominent in the celebrated Bengali Paramahansa Yogananda (1893–1952), who came to America in
1920 to attend, as India's delegate, the International Congress of Religious Liberals in Boston. He remained to lecture and teach on the East Coast and then to
establish the headquarters of the Self-Realization Fellowship, which he founded
in 1920, in Los Angeles. As the name he chose for his American organization already suggests, it is in Yogananda that we get a thoroughly conscious language
of the Self to refer to the Atman and its long-hailed union with Brahman. But
Yogananda's language of the Self was hardly incessant, and, indeed, he spoke as
much, or more, of the Christ within. Born as Mukunda Lal Ghosh in Gorakhpur

in northeastern India, close to the Himalayas, Yogananda—like his guru Sri Yuk-teswar Giri and his guru's guru (who was also his father's guru) Lahiri Mahasaya —was a Westernized Hindu long before he made his way to the West Coast of the United States. His father had been a railroad official, and the younger Ghosh's attempts to run away to the Himalayas were thwarted and disdained. When, in 1910, Mukunda Ghosh met and came under the tutelage of Sri Yukteswar, he was urged by his guru to attend Calcutta University. He graduated in 1915. It was only thereafter that he took formal vows as a swami and renunciant.

Yogananda's *Autobiography of a Yogi* (1946) is an important document in con-structing any account of what happened to Yogananda, to yoga, and to its meta-physical American form. A complex and enormously skillful hybrid of traditional Indic elements, combinative Hindu-Western culture in India, and self-fashioning and posturing, Yogananda's work appealed to American readers even as it drew them into an alternate world. Thus the autobiography provides clues to an im-portant transition time for American yoga. On the one side stood the fascina-tion of marvel and miracle, of the siddhi powers that the yogic tradition encom-passed. Here was the mysterious Mahavatar Babaji, hailed by Yogananda as the founding guru from which his lineage descended. This Babaji was hundreds of years old, materialized and dematerialized at will (and in so doing supplied in-direct insight into the possible sources of Madame Blavatsky's Mahatmas), and had appeared to Yogananda to commission him to spread his kriya yoga to the West. On the other side came the running barrage of footnotes with its Christian gospel references and theological points regarding Christ, its copious supply of quotations from Emerson, and its steady commentary on what Yogananda con-sidered cutting-edge science (to establish yoga's scientific credentials).[75]

Indeed, what Paramahansa Yogananda stressed about kriya yoga was its un-equaled utility as a "scientific" path to the attainment of samadhi—with practi-cal details revealed only after an initiatory period in the Self-Realization Fellow-ship.[76] His Boston address to the conference of religious liberals, as revised and expanded in 1924, is instructive. Ambitiously titled "The Science of Religion" and so evoking Christian Science, Religious Science, Divine Science, and a modest army of self-conscious metaphysicians, Yogananda's address pronounced the universality and oneness of religion. It hailed the nature of God as bliss and declared the existence of four fundamental religious methods to reach God. Three of them—intellectual, devotional, meditative—were less good. The fourth—the "scientific method" or "yoga"—would lead to "bliss-consciousness." This method would separate the "Self" from the body without death and smacked of the mysterious kundalini power already admired by Theosophists. "The scientific method teaches a process enabling us to draw to our *central part*

—spine and brain—the life current distributed throughout the organs and other parts of our body. The process consists of magnetizing the spinal column and the brain, which contain the seven main centers, with the result that the distributed life electricity is drawn back to the original centers of discharge and is experienced in the form of light. In this state the spiritual Self can consciously free itself from its bodily and mental distractions."[77]

The combinative habit was unmistakable. Here was Vivekananda's raja yoga transmuted, with the metaphysical assistance of Arthur Avalon and company, into a new, more tantric version. And here, too, were echoes of animal magnetism and phrenomagnetic electricity imported from the nineteenth century along with Blavatsky's astral light and ether. Nor had physical culture left the equation. Kriya yoga flourished, for Yogananda, in a context in which the physical body became active and energized. In 1918, he had opened a school for boys in Ranchi, a town in Bihar, some two hundred miles from Calcutta. Students there not only learned yoga meditation but also what Yogananda called "a unique system of health and physical development, *Yogoda*," the principles of which he believed he had discovered two years earlier. "Realizing that man's body is like an electric battery," he wrote, "I reasoned that it could be recharged with energy through the direct agency of the human will." He went on to describe the effects at Ranchi. The boys "responded well to Yogoda training, developing extraordinary ability to shift the life force from one part of the body to another part and to sit in perfect poise in difficult *asanas* (postures). They performed feats of strength and endurance that many powerful adults could not equal." If the language of energy and electricity, even for the boys, hinted of tantrism—perhaps disguised for an American audience and surely already reinvented in India in a Westernized Hindu milieu—Yogananda was a sign of evolving times.[78] He had brought tantric themes in touch with an American language of science that circled New Thought and theosophical themes and that coexisted comfortably with liberal versions of Christianity. The kundalini had met the Self, and the Self was discovered to be the living Christ presence within.

After Yogendra and Yogananda a series of yogic teachers—of hatha and meditation yoga and both of them combined—came and went in the American yogic world. Kriya yoga itself fractured into a series of competing forms and teachers. As for others, there is not space here to tarry even on leading names, although some do come to mind—Indra Devi (Eugenie Petersen), who was healed in India by the famed Krishnamacharya and studied with him; Yogi Grupta, who followed Swami Sivananda Saraswati, founder of the Divine Life Society; Swami Satchidananda, also a popularizer of Sivananda's "integral yoga"; Richard Hittleman, who authored numerous popular books and introduced hatha yoga to television in the 1960s. Meanwhile, with the publication of B. K. S. Iyengar's *Light on Yoga* (1966), which became a Bible to the hatha yoga world, with his visits to America, and with the ambitious worldwide certification process for Iyengar teachers, a canonicity was emerging.[79] Along the way, yoga got feminized, and women became the major producers and consumers of yogic asanas. In meditation yoga, likewise, divine mothers and female spiritual teachers proliferated—and kundalini prevailed as their general message. Against the backdrop of the civil rights movement, the Vietnam War, second-wave feminism, and rising ethnic consciousness, more and more non-Asian Americans were turning east and refashioning what they found there. New forms of spirituality were abounding, in the New Age movement and beyond.

Among meditation yoga teachers, the Maharishi Mahesh Yogi achieved celebrity during the 1960s when, discovered by the Beatles, he taught the simple silent mantra practice that he called Transcendental Meditation. Tellingly, it brought with it promises not of samadhi but of lowered blood pressure, increased intelligence, relief from stress, and reduction of crime in locales inhabited by a critical mass of meditators. By the 1970s, Swami Muktananda visited the United States, preaching a "meditation revolution." His American disciples in Siddha Yoga practiced and, under his successor Swami Chidvilasananda (Gurumayi), rationalized and domesticated a form of tantric yoga. Important here, Muktananda's message told of interior consciousness and bliss, of the divinity of the Self that echoed, in stronger, more insistent language, the earlier teaching of the Self-Realization Fellowship. "Honor your Self, worship your Self, meditate on your Self," Muktananda enjoined. "God dwells within you as you." Still further, at South Fallsburg, New York, in Muktananda's American ashram, hatha yoga was in. Between them, the Maharishi and Muktananda spelled out for devotees the new Americanized version of ancient India—a world bathed in spiritual consciousness and bliss that also had become a pleasure-dome and abode of this-worldly good health, good fortune, and thorough enjoyment.[80]

On the other side of the continent, at Esalen in Big Sur country along the California coast, the message was theorized and practiced with new self-consciousness at the height of the human potential movement of the 1960s and beyond. Esalen's co-founder Michael Murphy as a young man had traveled to India in 1956 and spent sixteen months at the Pondicherry ashram of the decidedly Westernized and metaphysically inclined guru Sri Aurobindo (1872–1950). Even though Aurobindo by then was dead, Murphy—who had devoured his philosophy at Stanford—never forgot. His Esalen Institute acted as an important culture broker, a model of certain metaphysical themes, and a broadcaster of the new-enlightenment message of the Self/self and its embodied blissfulness. It was

Esalen that gave the word to many Americans who otherwise might not have heard the news—or, at least, not heard it so clearly and authoritatively. Esalen understood the human potential to reside in the enlightened body-self. Its body-work brigade, its lush beachside ceremonies of nudity and hot tub, its elusively present marijuana, its evolving humanistic and transpersonal psychologies for the self-in-relation, its social vision of one interconnected, interracial, and inter-ethnic world—all of these beg for a metaphysical reading. From Murphy's side, they selectively re-present American metaphysical religion as it encountered, in Aurobindo, a metaphysical Asia. Esalen Self-fashioning taught a cross-section of Americans, and it led them to sacrality in a secular world, to their realization as new American gods who walked a pleasurable earth, and to yogic regimes that subverted religion-as-usual.[81]

If in surveying this late-twentieth-century spiritual landscape we pronounce this transformed American yoga simply a reinscribed version of Vivekananda or a transliterated form of Indian tantrism, arguably we obscure more than we inform. It is true that if we single out hatha yoga, scholars of yogic India have pointed unmistakably to its tantric origins, and likewise, in another context, De Michelis has pointed to the influence of Vivekananda.[82] As practiced in twentieth- and twenty-first-century America, however, it would be glib to call hatha yoga a tantric practice or to invoke Vivekananda too strenuously as its ideological buttress. Nor, despite the popularity of kundalini in numerous contexts, can meditation forms of yoga prevalent in New Age, or simply new, spirituality be described, in uncontested ways, as tantric. Rather, the enlightened body-self has functioned at the center of both hatha and meditation yogas. In so doing, it has re-presented the home-grown metaphysical and practice-oriented religiosity of Theosophy and New Thought as they met new, more expansive times—in touch with an already combinative metaphysical Asia. If Americans inherited Transcendentalist idealism with its Oversoul gone Indic and if unawares they also absorbed a revised Hermeticism and spiritualism, more concretely they had at hand pragmatic schemes for transformation in Theosophy and New Thought. They might never name the movements nor know their sources, but they had learned techniques that promised access to their own hidden mental powers and their body-selves in Will and Desire, health and positive thinking, wealth and metaphysics. They could imprint their new yogic practice—their strategy for sacred success—with their own made-in-America history. They could also, it turned out, look to another form of metaphysical Asia in the exoticized re-presentations of Buddhism that Americans had been encountering, beginning from the early nineteenth century.

METAPHYSICAL RELIGION AND BUDDHIST MYSTERY

Still earlier than this, in 1784, Massachusetts resident Hannah Adams (1755–1831) published what must be counted the first attempt at a comparative religions survey in the United States. The work went through second and third editions in 1791 and 1801 respectively, and in 1817 the fourth and most inclusive version appeared as *A Dictionary of All Religions and Religious Denominations.* Along the way, the work had twice changed its title, and it had also seen publication in two British editions.[83] Adams's book really *was* a dictionary, and entries appeared in uninflected alphabetical order, with no separate article on Buddhism at all. Instead, "Birmans"—in Burma—worshiped the "Boodh," while in Japan a religion called "Budso" had been introduced from China and Siam, begun by "Budha," who represented the ninth appearance of the Hindu Vishnu. Among the "Chinese," people worshiped "Foe" (the Buddha). Among the "Thibetians," however, Adams lingered with the "Grand Lama," in what was by far the longest Buddhist entry, captivated apparently by the doctrinal and ritual embroidery that her sources provided. She dwelled on divine claims for the Lama, confiding that he was "their Sovereign Pontiff," and she remarked on the mysticizing practices that surrounded the choice of successor. She reported, too, that, among others, the inhabitants of "Thibet," especially, accepted the near-universal Eastern doctrine of metempsychosis or "transmigration of the soul." And she closed still more emphatically on the "Thibetians" as the Roman Catholics of Asia, quoting sources regarding holy water, song, alms, prayers, sacrifices for the dead, convents of monks and friars, the use of beads, and the wearing of mitres and caps.[84] There seemed little in this catalog of wide-eyed wonder to create a metaphysical American future for Buddhism—even if, reading the past from a later perspective, a gloss on practical mysticism might be deciphered in the account of Tibet.

By the mid-nineteenth century, matters had not much changed. Whereas the Transcendentalists had discovered South Asian classics like the *Bhagavad-Gita* and the *Laws of Manu*, no comparable Buddhist text stirred non-Asian Americans so strongly. True, Elizabeth Palmer Peabody had translated a short part of Eugène Burnouf's French translation of the Lotus Sutra for the Transcendental periodical *The Dial* in 1844. But confusion reigned among the Transcendental elite regarding Buddhism, and they apparently conflated it with the traditional South Asian religious culture known to Westerners as Hinduism. In a letter to Elizabeth Hoar, for example, Emerson hailed the arrival in Concord of the "Bhagvat-Geeta," which he identified as "the much renowned book of Buddhism, extracts of which I have often admired."[85] Later, even as Chinese immigrants brought Buddhism to the nation, and especially to the West Coast, between the 1850s and 1880s, their religious practice did not attract significant non-Asian notice. When the Japanese arrived in California at the end of the 1890s, the pattern was similar. Immigrant presence, clearly, did not signal religious transfer.

It should not be surprising, then, that at midcentury Buddhism seemed the quintessential religion of the unknown and exotic other. Webster's *American Dictionary of the English Language* for 1849, for example, acknowledged that "one third of the human race" followed the religion of "Boodhism." It went on to explain—in what seemed a muddled account of the yugas and the sleep of Vishnu—that at far intervals "a *Boodh*, or deity" appeared "to restore the world from a state of ignorance and decay" and then sank "into a state of entire non-existence, or rather, perhaps, of bare existence without attributes, action, or consciousness." The entry called nirvana "the ultimate supreme good" and explained that there had been four "Boodhs," with the last "Gaudama." By 1864, however, Webster's Buddhism had changed its American stripes, now emerging as the doctrine taught by "the Hindu sage, Gautama, surnamed Buddha, 'the awakened or enlightened.'" It was "at first atheistic" and aimed at "release from existence" (nirvana), but it also exhibited "admirable humanity and morality," even if it involved "idolatrous worship of its founder and of other supposed kindred beings." Still, there was not much here, even in the 1864 definition, to entice a metaphysician. Nor was there seven years later, when James Freeman Clarke published his theologically driven comparative religions survey *Ten Great Religions*. There he read Buddhism as the "Protestantism of the East," with "forms" that resembled "Romanism" but a "spirit" that, in its revolt and protest against Brahmanism and in its affirmation of law and humanity, looked to him decidedly Protestant. Buddhism was rational and humane, he thought, but in the end he found it wanting. It represented a "doctrine of works" in contrast to the Christian teaching of "grace."[86]

Did a metaphysical Buddhism ever emerge on American shores? Did anything similar to the process of the reinvention of South Asian yoga among non-Asian Americans occur? And if so, what and how? The questions are particularly timely for the narrative here because scholars have pointed to the late nineteenth century as the era when Buddhism at last began to attract significant attention among non-Asians. Historian Carl Jackson, for instance, characterizes the last two decades of the century in terms of its "Buddhist vogue," when the tradition became "almost fashionable." He also alludes, for 1900, to contemporary skeptical aspersions on what some perceived as a "'Neo-Buddhist' craze." Meanwhile, American religious historian Thomas Tweed identifies the years from 1879 to

1912 as an age of "significant interest" in Buddhism.[87] Given this acknowledgment, the vogue and the interest may be charted in two ways. Together the two serve to illumine a non-Asian attraction to Buddhism that was mediated in large measure by American metaphysical religion and that subsumed Asian discourses and practices into familiar metaphysical categories. The first approach—the one explored more extensively here—looks to a literary history of American engagement with Buddhism as the tradition was reshaped to Western and metaphysical liking. The second tracks non-Asian American Buddhist sympathizers or converts through the latter part of the nineteenth century and into the early twentieth according to the same or similar canons of interpretation.

For the literary history, Carl Jackson has pointed to Charles D. B. Mills's *The Indian Saint* of 1876 as the first full-length treatment of the life of the Buddha by an American. The work boasted a Transcendentalist link, since Bronson Alcott had functioned as an intellectual and spiritual mentor for Mills and had also contacted publishers to help him get his manuscript into print. Mills openly advocated Buddhism in the work, and his critics were none too friendly. And although he lectured and published short pieces thereafter, suggesting perhaps some following, his book could not be characterized as a galvanizing text for American spiritual seekers nor as particularly metaphysical. It was in 1879, however, in a book published first in England, that the American public encountered a life of the Buddha that successfully captured a significant number of them. Sir Edwin Arnold's *The Light of Asia* became the first of a trilogy of overseas works that offered complexly combinative and metaphysical readings of the Buddha and the Buddhist tradition. Arnold's *Light* provided a free-verse rendering that softened Asian rough edges and refashioned the Buddha along lines that were ideologically congenial to Westerners. According to Jackson, estimates suggest that Arnold's poem appeared in sixty English and eighty American editions, with sales of between 500,000 and 1 million copies in Britain and the United States. Arnold had been helped in promoting his book by his Transcendental connections in the states. A widower, he had married again, and his second wife was the daughter of Transcendentalist William Henry Channing, who enthusiastically worked to publicize the volume and enlisted the aid of friends. Bronson Alcott himself saw the initial American edition through to print and worked to get early reviews of it by George Ripley and other friendly critics. Beyond that, the first American edition boasted a letter from Channing and reviews that read as endorsements. But much more than Transcendentalism was at work. "Enthusiastically reviewed and widely quoted, hotly attacked and passionately defended," says Jackson, "perhaps no work on Buddhism has ever approached its popular success." Suddenly, after years of almost invisibility, Buddhism was achieving marked American notice.[88]

The Siddhartha (Gautama) of Arnold's poem was inserted into a Christian template in the narrative of his beginnings. However, as the narrative unfolded Arnold subtly shaped it in metaphysical directions. For the Christian template, there was, to begin, his mother Queen Maya's "strange dream" of impregnation by a heavenly star. Then came the "dream-readers" who predicted a child of "wondrous wisdom," "Devas singing songs" at his birth, and the "grey-haired saint, Asita," confessing "Thou art Buddh, / And thou wilt preach the Law and save all flesh / Who learn the Law." Merchants arrived, "bringing, on tidings of this birth, rich gifts." When the young prince was eight, he astounded the teachers who asked him to transcribe the sacred Gayatri (Light) mantra by writing in many languages and then engaging in equally dazzling numerical feats "beyond their learning taught." Siddhartha already knew that his mission was to "teach compassion unto men." Despite his aging royal father's attempts to keep him in a state of "forgetting," with no mention made at court "of death or age, / Sorrow, or pain, or sickness," he took the steps that led to his encounter with all of them. So the prince renounced his heritage and left his young wife, Yasodhara, and child yet unborn, announcing to her that his chariot would not "roll with bloody wheels / From victory to victory." Instead he would be a wanderer "clad in no prouder garb than outcasts wear, / Fed with no meats save what the charitable / Give of their will, sheltered with no more pomp / Than the dim cave lends or the jungle-bush." He would give "all, laying it down for love of men." And— significant for the metaphysically inclined—he would spend himself "to search for truth, / Wringing the secret of deliverance forth, / Whether it lurk in hells or hide in heavens." Searching thus, "Death might find him conqueror of death," since he would seek "for all men's sake" until the truth was found.[89]

In the lavishness of his origins as well as in his marriage and his announced need to search for truth, Siddhartha parted company with the man from Nazareth. He also confessed a different gospel as he left palace precincts, instructing that his father, the king, be told "there is hope for man only in man" and that therefore he would "cast away" his "world" in order to "save" it. Still, he shunned the yogis in their forest austerities (which Arnold described according to the familiar conventions of horror that were part of earlier nineteenth-century discourse) and instead operated as a veritable Asian Jesus. When he saw a lamb that was lame, "our Lord . . . full tenderly / . . . took the limping lamb upon his neck," exhorting that "'twere all as good to ease one beast of grief / As sit and watch the sorrows of the world / In yonder caverns with the priests who pray." He also ignored caste law, seeking "that light which somewhere shines / To lighten all men's darkness."[90]

Finally, under the Bodhi-tree, the "Tree of Wisdom," tempted (like Jesus)—

but by "the fiends who war with Wisdom and the Light"—he withstood the "ten chief Sins." Then, in the "third watch," surprising things happened:

> Our Lord . . . saw
> By light which shines beyond our mortal ken
> The line of all his lives in all the worlds,
> Far back and farther back and farthest yet,
> Five hundred lives and fifty.

He saw "how new life reaps what the old life did sow," and

> in the middle watch
> Our Lord attained *Abhidjna*—insight vast
> Ranging beyond this sphere to spheres unnamed,
> System on system, countless worlds and suns
> Moving in splendid measures, band by band.

With "unsealed vision," he "saw those Lords of Light who hold their worlds / By bonds invisible, how they themselves / Circle obedient round mightier orbs." At the "fourth watch," the "secret came," and he learned the "noble truth" of sorrow, broke through delusion, and saw past "the aching craze to live" until he reached

> nameless quiet, nameless joy,
> Blessed NIRVANA—sinless, stirless rest—
> That change which never changes!

So it was that the "Dawn" came "with Buddh's Victory." He was "glorified with the Conquest gained for all / And lightened by a Light greater than Day's." Disciples came, and they acknowledged "a Buddh / Who doth deliver men and save all flesh." But this savior, unlike the one from Nazareth, taught "how man hath no fate except past deeds, / No Hell but what he makes, no Heaven too high." "Pray not!" he enjoined, "the Darkness will not brighten." "Within yourselves deliverance must be sought; / Each man his prison makes." Yet, in a theistic moment, he could proclaim that there was "fixed a Power divine which moves to good, / Only its laws endure." And he could confess that the Dharma Law, "the Law which moves to righteousness, / which none at last can turn aside or stay; / The heart of it is Love."[91]

Arguably, Arnold had deftly conducted readers into a territory into which they might not otherwise have walked, assuring them with unmistakable analogical references that the Buddha was actually a lot like Jesus. This was true in the major outlines of Siddhartha's life, in his teachings of compassion and love, and in the moralism of the "eightfold path" to which his teachings led. Moreover, the spectacular narrative of his enlightenment let out all stops in its mysticizing narrative that revealed the earnest heart and soul of a true devotee. However, it also cast the devotee—the Buddha—into a speculative metaphysical context that morphed the East into Western notions of the grandiose. Still further, it read the Buddha's enlightenment in humanizing terms that, as in the Hermetic tradition of the West, proclaimed a subtle message of individual mastery and control. If Arnold's Buddha was a savior, he saved people by teaching them to save themselves. Tellingly, Theosophists loved Arnold, and he obligingly returned the favor. Asked once in an interview if he had ever met Blavatsky, he replied that he knew her "very well" and was "acquainted with Col. Olcott and A. P. Sinnett [the theosophical author of *Esoteric Buddhism*]." Arnold believed there was "no doubt that the theosophical movement . . . had an excellent effect upon humanity." It had, he said, "made a large number of people understand what all India always understood, . . . the importance of invisible things." Blavatsky, though, had the final word. According to the terms of her will, Theosophists were to gather annually on her death day and read from *The Light of Asia* along with any edition of the *Bhagavad Gita*.[92]

Olcott had met Arnold at a dinner in 1884, calling the event "one of the notable incidents of that London summer." Afterwards Arnold invited him to lunch at his house, where the poet presented him with pages from the original manuscript of *The Light of Asia*. Two years later, in Ceylon where Arnold, his wife, and daughter were visiting, Olcott "set to work to organise a fitting public reception to one who had laid the whole Buddhist world under deep obligations by the writing of his *Light of Asia*." By this time, Olcott had published his own short and metaphysical work on Buddhism. His deceptively simple *Buddhist Catechism* of 1881, in traditional question-and-answer format, was already moving through its numerous editions, some forty in Olcott's lifetime and, by 1970, forty-five. Still more, by 1888 Olcott could declare in his historical diary that the catechism had been printed in "English, French, German, Sinhalese, Japanese, Arabic, and Burmese," and by 1895 he could express satisfaction that it was "circulating in nearly twenty languages."[93] Olcott's catechism had clearly *not* been written for an American audience. He produced it for use in the schools that he had created to foster educational reform in Ceylon; at first appearance it was available in both Sinhalese and English. At the heart of the "Buddhist revival" on the island, the catechism's "Protestant Buddhism" of the middle class continued as part of the curriculum of Sri Lankan schools through the twentieth century. Meanwhile, many of the subsequent editions and translations of Olcott's *Buddhist Catechism* were created for use in Asia, and a series of London editions and at least two French editions appeared as well during Olcott's lifetime. The first

American edition (from the Sinhalese) came in 1885, edited with notes by the Theosophist Elliott Coues, a professor and scientist attached to the Smithsonian in Washington, D.C., who also wrote in New Thought journals. By 1887, Coues's version had become available in a third edition. From what can be determined, a New York edition appeared, too, in 1897, and another in Talent, Oregon, in 1915. Later American editions continued to be produced.[94]

All of this limns out a large international, and especially Asian, following (with print runs in the tens of thousands and more) for Olcott's small volume. It suggests as well a substantial American audience that created enough demand to keep the book in print. But what was it that Olcott was telling the world about Buddhism? How was he reading the tradition, and what did that reading have to do with metaphysics? For this last, there was already reason to suspect a connection. The year before he produced the catechism, Olcott and Blavatsky had gone through a public ceremony in Ceylon as an Asian acknowledgment of their Buddhism. The pair had, even while still in America, both publicly and privately declared themselves Buddhists, and as Olcott explained in *Old Diary Leaves* the pansil ceremony was "but a formal confirmation of our previous professions." He hastened, however, to define the kind of Buddhism that he and Blavatsky had embraced. Not that of "a debased modern Buddhist sectarian," he declared, but rather "our Buddhism was that of the Master-Adept Gautama Buddha, which was identically the Wisdom Religion of the Aryan Upanishads, and the soul of all the ancient world-faiths. Our Buddhism was, in a word, a philosophy, not a creed." Moreover, even as Olcott called it a philosophy and a *moral* philosophy (see below), it was also, as his allusions reveal, an emphatically mysticizing philosophy. Years later, in 1893, he would receive a letter from Max Müller thoroughly debunking an "esoteric" reading of Buddhism, and Olcott would as thoroughly repudiate the missive, regretting that Müller had never been able to visit India and talk for himself to Indian pandits.[95]

If metaphysics structured the subtext of Olcott's *Buddhist Catechism*, the metaphysical construction was already decidedly complex and manifestly combinative. Stephen Prothero has recounted the circumstances that surrounded the catechism's initial publication, complete with a prepublication wrangle with Hikkaduve Sumangala, an influential Sinhalese scholar monk, over Olcott's treatment of nirvana. Olcott was forced to yield on the matter of publicly acknowledging Theravada and Mahayana disagreements over nirvana (which Olcott wanted to air) in order to gain Sulmangala's stamp of approval. However, as Prothero has argued, that was a superficial matter in terms of the overall creolization that the project represented. "If the lexicon of this creole catechism was Buddhist," Prothero maintains, "its grammar or deep structure was Christian, and its accent, clearly theosophical." Indeed, although not overtly, the catechism was *anti*-Christian. The questions it posed to Sinhalese Buddhist children arose out of a polemic meant to demean Christianity by exalting Buddhism in a subtly comparative context directed by Christian concerns and categories. It purported to understand Buddhism within that (Christian) frame, citing, for example, themes of salvation and missionization dear to the hearts of American Protestant Christians. However, the Buddhism it taught was a religion of the texts, and with post-Reformation and anti-Catholic dudgeon, it valorized beliefs and minimized rituals, employing American Protestant primitivist categories that read the "real" Buddhism as its earliest manifestations and forms. Of the five chapters in the thirty-third edition that Olcott was working on in 1897, one was devoted to a history of Buddhism as chronicled by the scholarly Orientalists of the period and another to "Buddhism and Science."[96]

From its first official page, the catechism's revisionary intent was apparent. Later editions carried a subtext of notes hardly suited to the children who were its purported audience, with the first of them announcing that Olcott had been brought "under protest" to employ the term *religion* for Buddhism, which was actually a (noble) "moral philosophy." Buddhism really meant "'an approach or coming to enlightenment'" or, possibly, "a following of the Doctrine of Sakyamuni" (the Buddha). It was the Christian missionaries (read "bad") who conferred the inept title of "religion" on Buddhism. Religion was out; philosophy was in. But in Olcott's version of the latter, philosophy took a quintessentially American Christian twist. It was, as Olcott said, "moral," and a great part of the doctrinal exposition thereafter preoccupied itself with rules of morality and right living. Thus it revised the practiced Buddhism, the "lived religion" of Ceylon, to meet primitivist, textualist, and morally righteous requirements as demanded by Olcott's own conceptual frame. Buddhist dates were computed on a Christian grid (so many years "before the Christian era"), and Sakyamuni himself, like a Horatio Alger hero, had earned his title as the Buddha by good, hard work. The title described a mental state after the mind had "reached the culmination of development," and it signaled enlightenment, or "all-perfect wisdom." Knowledge must be gained not by asceticism but by the "opening of the mind." In the midst of the moralism and the loving concern of the Buddha for suffering and spiritually hungry people, it brought the potential for control of the "Iddhi" (that is, siddhi), the "exceptional spiritual powers" not unlike those conferred by Western adeptship. These, Olcott assured the children, were "natural to all men and capable of being developed by a certain course of training."[97]

He also told them that the whole spirit of Buddhism could be expressed in the word *justice*, and that the *"other good words"* that expressed *"the essence of Bud-*

dhism" were "self-culture and universal love." This, manifestly, did not include conventional worship experience. "External worship" was "a fetter that one has to break if he is to advance higher." "From the beginning," declared Olcott, the Buddha "condemned the observance of ceremonies and other external practices, which only tend to increase our spiritual blindness and our clinging to mere life-less forms." By contrast, instead of a "creating God" and "vicarious Savior" to be attended to, instead of "rites, prayers, penances, priests or intercessory saints," one redeemed oneself. Here, in the hinterland of the spirit, one perceived the highest truths not by reason but by intuition—"a mental state in which any desired truth" was "instantaneously grasped." But in the final state of jnana ("knowledge") and samadhi, was the mind *"a blank"* and thought *"arrested"*? Resoundingly not, for—like a practiced Hermetic adept with American cultural instincts—it was "then that one's consciousness" was "most intensely active, and one's power to gain knowledge correspondingly vast."[98]

Meanwhile, the Buddha himself, with his attained knowledge of the highest states, was a light being, with "a divine radiance sent forth from within by the power of his holiness." This light, however, was hardly his sole possession. Rather, all Arhats (the finally enlightened) emitted shining light, "stronger and brighter in proportion to the spiritual development of the person." Europeans called it "the human aura," and the *"great scientist"* Baron Von Reichenbach had "fully described" it "in his *Researches*, published in 1844–5." The light, in Olcott's mantric refrain, was "natural," possessed not only by "all human beings but [also] animals, trees, plants and even stones." In the case of the Buddha or an Arhat, it was simply "immensely brighter and more extended" as "evidence of their superior development in the power of *Iddhi*."[99]

Arhats—like theosophical Mahatmas or the elementals who created spiritualist manifestations—could impress "pictures" by their "thought and trained will-power" on the minds of others. Olcott did not make the theosophical or spiritualist connections in print, but he was hardly shy about noticing "hypnotic suggestion" and adding that the power to create illusion was "familiar to all students of mesmerism and hypnotism." Did Buddhism *admit that man has in his nature any latent powers for the production of phenomena commonly called 'miracles'*? Yes, and they were, of course, "natural, not supernatural," able to be "developed by a certain system" laid down in Buddhist sacred writings. Always, for Olcott, matters of spirit led to matters of will and mastery. Thus, for obtaining iddhi, four things were necessary: "The will, its exertion, mental development, and [in a bow to Protestant Christian moralism] discrimination between right and wrong." And, in a not-so-obscure reference (for the initiated) to spiritualist elementals, Buddhist children learned that *"elemental invisible beings"* could be brought to their feet. The "Buddhist doctrine" was "that, by interior self-development and conquest over his baser nature, the Arhat becomes superior to even the most formidable of the Devas, and may subject and control the lower orders."[100]

Amidst this opening of Buddhist mystery for the luminous gaze of the enlightened body-self (to be sure, a troubled construct for traditional Buddhism), the abiding theosophical message of tolerance and universal brotherhood could be found intact. Buddhism was (unlike Christianity?) "a religion of noble tolerance, of universal brotherhood, of righteousness and justice." It possessed "no taint of selfishness, sectarianism or intolerance." Still further (and unastonishing in light of continued theosophical teaching), its *two leading ideas* that were *chiefly taking hold upon the western mind*" were "those of Karma and Reincarnation," with "the rapidity of their acceptance . . . very surprising."[101] Olcott, in short, had refashioned Buddhism to his own American Protestant *and* metaphysical needs. Whatever Sinhalese children may have thought of their revised tradition as a result, on the American side of the waters his Buddhist reinvention would instruct a cohort of spiritual seekers in ways that corroborated their developed and developing metaphysical instincts. Moral they would be (at least that was the ideal), but also masters—in a mastery that echoed their own Hermetic heritage now combined many times over with the impress of newer times and peoples.

Olcott, however, was not alone as a theosophical insider with a reconstruction of Buddhism that reached American readers. In fact, before his *Buddhist Catechism* saw its first American edition in 1885, A. P. Sinnett's *Esoteric Buddhism* had already been available in Boston for two years. The book had been published the same year (1883) in London by Trübner. In the United States, Houghton, Mifflin took it on and apparently did well with the title, since it was reprinted annually through at least 1888 and appeared at least four times more through the 1890s. The 1885 and 1886 editions both called themselves the fifth edition; an 1895 printing styled itself the sixth; and by 1898 Houghton, Mifflin told readers it was presenting them with a "New American Edition."[102] Anglo-Indian Sinnett, editor of the British Indian newspaper *The Pioneer*, openly acknowledged what he considered his true sources in the preface to the original edition. The "secret doctrine" that he was "now enabled to expound" had been "given out to the world at last by the free grace of those in whose keeping" it had "hitherto lain." It had come from "esoteric teachers" who had "chosen to work" through him, and especially from one of them, as he confided later. In short, his material had come through Blavatsky's Mahatmas. Some of it had also come, as his exposition and appended bibliography made clear, from Orientalists T. W. Rhys Davids, Arthur Lillie, Hermann Oldenberg, and Robert Spence Hardy, as well as from the French magus Éliphas Lévi, among others. Moreover, Sinnett explained that part of the material had been published earlier in the theosophical monthly the *Theosophist*. There and in its later book form in *Esoteric Buddhism*, it functioned as what Charles J. Ryan has called a "harbinger" of Blavatsky's *Secret Doctrine*. In fact, it might almost be assessed as a rough draft for some sections of Blavatsky's huge work—a rough draft that she freely criticized and corrected in her later exposition and about which she seemed flustered even at its initial publication.[103]

The reflecting hall of mirrors within the theosophical community meant, in effect, that American readers were eagerly—and in much briefer and more manageable compass—imbibing the metaphysical theology that would shape *The Secret Doctrine*. As they did so, after Sinnett's initial (and tendentious) discussion of "Esoteric Teachers," they were introduced to three separate discourses. The first and framing one rehearsed the future Blavatskian cosmology of rounds and root races, complete with an exposition of the septenary "constitution of man," with the seven "bodies"—or "principles," as Sinnett termed them—listed as "The Body," "Vitality," "Astral Body," "Animal Soul," "Human Soul," "Spiritual Soul," and "Spirit." Still more, as Sinnett explored the terrain that Blavatsky would later visit more exhaustively, he probed a perceived distinction between "personality" and "individuality" that would weave its way into later New Thought discourse. Linking his work with Olcott's *Buddhist Catechism*, in which a lengthy note explained to readers that when humans were reborn they came with a succession of personalities, Sinnett followed the logic of difference even further. Olcott had declared that "though personalities ever shift, the one line of life along which they are strung like beads, runs unbroken," and he had called the line an "individual vital undulation." Now Sinnett pursued the theme especially in terms of issues of personal immortality, quoting Blavatsky's earlier *Isis Unveiled*, in which she was already trying to sort out terms. To gain a sense of how well the Asian theosophical inoculation took in the American metaphysical world, we need only cast a glance at Charles Fillmore as he duly observed the theosophical distinction. "God has but one Son, the Christ, the one ideal man. This divine conjunction was accomplished by Jesus, and the Christ shone out through His mortal self and illumined it, until it lost its personality and disappeared into divine individuality."[104]

As for Sinnett, he knew about Atlantis and Lemuria, about "periodic cataclysm" and "cyclic law," and he saw it all in the familiar Blavatskian mode that at once disdained and affirmed Darwinian evolution. The scientific spin was "simply an independent discovery of a portion—unhappily but a small portion—of the vast natural truth." This planet's evolution was "linked with the life and evolutionary processes of several other planets"; there was more, far more, than Darwin dreamed. Rather than the limited Darwinian narrative, announced

Sinnett, evolution happened "by a *spiral progress* through the worlds." He was expounding Blavatskian globes and chains—and a process of mastery and god-making that body-selves on the path to enlightenment could internalize imaginatively and with apparent ease.[105] This, however, was the far side of Blavatsky.

On her near side, in the early 1880s, she was still rehashing old preoccupations with spiritualism, and the Mahatma guidance of Sinnett obligingly fed him portions of the conversation. Sinnett's second discourse in *Esoteric Buddhism*, inserted in the fifth and sixth chapters on "Devachan" and "Kama Loca," revisited the Blavatskian adjustments to the reconstituted spiritualist universe. Devachan—which Sinnett had encountered in the Mahatma letter known among Theosophists as the "Devachan Letter"—became Buddhist heaven in theosophical lore, although Sinnett and other Theosophists were quick to point to differences. What survived in Devachan, according to Sinnett, was "man's own self-conscious personality, under some restrictions" but still "the same personality as regards its higher feelings, aspirations, affections, and even tastes, as it was on earth." The spirits there were so absorbed in their bliss world that they were mostly impervious to earthly overtures, and so they offered very little to spiritualist interaction. They did not themselves visit the earth, and the only viable way to get in touch was for a medium to get "odylized" in contact with "the aura of the spirit in the Devachan" and thus become, however briefly, "that departed personality." How did it happen? The answer lay in the *"rapport"* that was plainly "an identity of molecular vibration between the astral part of the incarnate medium and the astral part of the disincarnate personality." Devachan functioned as a rest home for the recently dead, but a rest home to which they repaired for a very long time. Sinnett reported that "re-birth in less than fifteen hundred years" was "spoken of as almost impossible."[106]

By contrast, Kama loca was the "region of desire." Linked, in Buddhist lore, to domains in which desire and attachment ruled, it there extended to humans and animals as well as to the devas (the gods of Vedic and later India) and the asuras (their demonic younger brothers and inexorable enemies), and it included hell. Sinnett's Blavatskian gloss expanded on Buddhist tradition to provide readers with an extended polemic against the spiritualism of his nineteenth-century time. He associated Kama loca with the animal soul, a principle (the fourth) of will and desire in the human constitution that was deactivated by death. "This fact" explained "many, though by no means all, of the phenomena of spiritualistic mediumship." Indeed, the "astral shell" could be "galvanized for a time in the mediumistic current into a state of consciousness and life." Hence the spirits in Kama loca in some sense fed on mediums, taking energy out instead of putting it in. Sinnett went on to explore the behavior of these spirits, their difference from the "semi-intelligent creatures of the astral light" called "elementals," and the limits of their power in using mediums. (They could not be guaranteed recovery of their earthly personalities but instead were "just as likely to reflect some quite different personality, caught from the suggestions of the medium's mind.") The animal soul, or fourth principle, that inhabited Kama loca characteristically drew to itself the fifth principle in the human constitution—the human soul—dragging it down and separating it from the two higher elements of the self (the sixth and seventh) that dwelled instead in Devachan. The "Kama loca entity" thus was "not truly master of his own acts" but "rather the sport of his own already established affinities." Still, lamentable as this was, such a one was "on his way to Devachan." All of this meant that, from the point of view of spiritual progress, spiritualist engagement with mediums was a hindrance and a distraction, "at war" with the spirit's "higher impulses." The more frequent the spirit's visits to the séances, the more it would be drawn back to "physical life," even as "the more serious the retardation of its spiritual progress." Meanwhile, since the Kama loca sojourner was anyway preoccupied with what was happening in this new abode, spiritualism offered only dull-edged contact with the former earthbound person.[107]

Sinnett expanded on the anti-spiritualist theme, warning effusively of the harm done to the Kama loca spirit. His rhetoric, in fact, was more than a clue and provided an unambiguous announcement: "Esoteric Buddhism" was a synonym for Theosophy. When Sinnett finally devoted his third discourse, in the ninth and tenth chapters, to more immediately recognizable Buddhist themes—"Buddha" and "Nirvana"—they read almost as interpolations, abrupt departures from the cosmic and anti-spiritualist discourses of the Blavatsky synthesis. Buddha, however, manifestly belonged in this theosophical universe, even as his historical existence as Siddhartha Gautama was downplayed by being cast against a Hinduized cosmic scheme. A Buddha visited earth "for each of the seven races of the great planetary period," and Gautama was "the fourth of the series." Here and elsewhere, Sinnett turned to the work of Rhys Davids to buttress his assertions, but the historical Buddha of Sinnett emerged not according to Orientalist canons but instead as a Theosophist. Gautama was an adept, and his lived experience on earth dissolved in Sinnett's speculation on his initiatory prowess. Serious exposition of the life of Siddhartha was manifestly out. "To know when Gautama Buddha was born, what is recorded of his teaching, and what popular legends have gathered round his biography, is to know next to nothing of the real Buddha, so much greater than either the historical moral teacher, or the fantastic demi-god of tradition."[108]

As for nirvana—the ultimate spiritual goal in Buddhist systems—the "sublimely blessed state" required a finessed reading from Sinnett. In the "no-self" teaching of early Buddhism, nirvana of necessity meant a state of selflessness, in which there was no subject (no self) to be the enjoyer. In later Buddhism of the Mahayana school, nirvana was emphasized less than the idea of postponing one's final enlightenment in order to help to enlighten others. Either way—and in variations—nirvana could best be described in Western terms through notions of negative theology (not this, not that); etymologically, it meant the "blowing out" or "expiration" (as of a flame). By contrast, Sinnett had been telling readers that the "supreme development of individuality" was the "great reward" reserved not only for adepts but also for those who demonstrated more good than evil in their incarnations. Thus his nirvana, if it reflected South Asia at all, reflected Hindu, and perhaps Neo-Vedantin, notions of the realization of the essential oneness of Atman with Brahman, Self with universe. "All that words can convey is that Nirvana is a sublime state of conscious rest in omniscience," Sinnett wrote.[109]

The question of whether nirvana was "held by Buddhism to be equivalent to annihilation" was extravagant. Rather, the Buddha had experienced "the passing of his own Ego-spirit into the ineffable condition of Nirvana." Although Sinnett owned that he only had "stray hints" about the experience, he thought that it exacted "a total suspension of animation in the body for periods of time compared to which the longest cataleptic trances known to ordinary science" were "insignificant." It was a state that tempted one to stay and not return. By contrast, the Buddha had returned: he had come back "for duty's sake" in order to finish his earthly life. Thereafter he had kept coming back in "a supererogatory series of incarnations for the sake of humanity at large." Still, nirvana was a state to which all of humankind should ultimately progress. Nirvana was "truly the key-note of esoteric Buddhism, as of the hitherto rather misdirected studies of external scholars." It was "the great end of the whole stupendous evolution of humanity." And it had to do, finally, with mind—with a state of all-knowing, of "that which we ordinarily describe as omniscience." Goodness without wisdom was not enough. It was by "a steady pursuit of, and desire for, real spiritual truth, not by an idle, however well-meaning acquiescence in the fashionable dogmas of the nearest church, that men launch their souls into the subjective state."[110] Somehow, Sinnett had glossed nirvana inside out, or better, had engrafted it onto a Western-style progressivism. His call to progress through mind had transformed nirvana into the goal of a modern religious seeker who, in the American context, could blend its identity fluidly with New Thought categories and a generalized spirituality of the enlightened body-self.

In that American context, it needs to be asked how many Buddhists or Buddhist sympathizers there actually were and what sort of Buddhism they embraced in the late nineteenth and early twentieth centuries. If the "Buddhist" texts that

Americans were reading came with Theosophy and metaphysics embedded, what did that condition signal for Buddhism itself? Thomas Tweed's study of early American Buddhists and Buddhism has pointed toward some general answers to these questions. Using the subscription list of the San Francisco–based *Light of Dharma*, published from 1901 to 1907 by the Japanese Pure Land Buddhist Mission (with prominent Asian Buddhists as well as noted Western Buddhist scholars such as T. W. Rhys Davids contributing articles), Tweed could demonstrate the presence of Buddhists or Buddhist sympathizers in twenty-four states and two U. S. possessions. He was also willing to estimate the number of Euro-American Buddhists or Buddhist sympathizers in the United States during what he regarded as the peak years of American interest, 1893 to 1907. He thought that for each of these years "probably two or three thousand" Americans with European roots considered themselves "primarily or secondarily" Buddhist and "tens of thousands more" sympathized to some degree with the tradition. Much earlier, in 1889, Henry Steel Olcott had more expansively recorded that "there must be at least 50,000" *professed* Buddhists in the United States.[111]

Tweed, however, was not content with judging numbers. He went on to distinguish among types of American Buddhist sympathizers and adherents during the last quarter of the nineteenth century and on until 1912. Extrapolating from what he encountered, he identified those he termed esoterics, rationalists, and romantics, although he found most of his advocates to be mixed types in their lived experience. Buddhist esoterics, for Tweed, were "occult" and were "characterized, in part, by an emphasis on hidden sources of religious truth and meaning and by belief in a spiritual or nonmaterial realm that [was] populated by a plurality of nonhuman or suprahuman realities." These could be contacted through various sacralizing practices or altered states of mind. By contrast, Buddhist rationalists had roots in the Enlightenment and its deism, in Unitarianism and Transcendentalism, and later in the Free Religious Association and Ethical Culture Society. These individuals, he said, "focused on rational-discursive means of attaining religious truth and meaning as opposed to revelational or experiential means," and they found in the self the source of authority. Finally, Buddhist romantics signaled a more cultural approach to Buddhism. They were, as Tweed described them, "the exotic-culture type." Their attraction to Buddhism came as "part of an immersion in, and attachment to, a Buddhist culture as a whole — its art, architecture, music, drama, customs, language, and literature as well as its religion." Often, it happened, their focus was on a specific Buddhist nation. Perhaps surprisingly, too, among the types that he found, Tweed was willing to argue that, whatever might be assumed about the prevalence of Buddhist romantics, "the majority were not romantics but esoterics."[112]

Still more, when we look for a metaphysical Asia in the neo-Buddhist minds of the Americans that Tweed has studied, we can find it in *both* the esoteric and rational types. If metaphysical religion found expression in America in both material and mental versions of magic—if transformation of mind involved alternately miracle or positivist reconstruction of the self—then the enlightened body-selves of Americans could enact their owners' differing choices. As in the earlier heyday of spiritualism, they could move toward the more flamboyant phenomenal manifestations of mind (as in Blavatsky's esoteric version of Theosophy). Or they could move toward the more philosophical and speculative perspectives advanced especially by the noetic side of New Thought. In the blended world in which students of Theosophy, New Thought, and new American Asia dwelled, boundary lines were effaced or fuzzed over, and appropriation was a habitual, unremarkable, and even unconscious strategy.

In Olcott and Sinnett, the theosophical and esoteric Buddhist connections were, as we have seen, unambiguous (although, to be sure, something might be said as well for Olcott's tilt toward rationalism in his abiding interest in moral philosophy). If an example of the metaphysical inclinations of Tweed's Buddhist rationalists—his second type—be sought, Paul Carus offers a striking case. A Buddhist sympathizer (he never converted), Carus (1852–1919) was German-born and German-educated, with a doctorate from Tübingen. As an American philosopher, he edited the magazine *Open Court*, founded to succeed *The Index*, which had been the periodical voice of the Free Religious Association. Carus became identified with the Open Court Publishing Company in rural LaSalle, Illinois, outside Chicago, where—as head—he promoted a metaphysical Asian connection. His philosophical monism was reflected in the title of a second periodical he edited for many years, *The Monist*. Carus had been drawn especially to Buddhism at the World's Parliament of Religions, where he formed a personal connection with Anagarika Dharmapala of Ceylon and with Zen Master Soyen Shaku of Japan. Later, the connection extended to Soyen's well-known disciple Daisetz T. Suzuki, who worked for Open Court, even as Carus's ties to Japanese Buddhism would continue throughout his life. At the parliament itself, however, he was already addressing his audience in a speech significantly titled "Science: A Religious Revelation."[113]

There Carus disputed the notion that religion would eventually disappear, averring instead that it had "so penetrated our life that we have ceased to notice it as an independent power." Linking religion to morality, he called God not personal but "superpersonal," and he named science "a revelation of God," as the printed title of his address already suggests. But Carus's focus quickly shifted to "truth," in his view the foundation for both science and legitimate religion, and he thought that religion had "often, in former ages, by instinct, as it were, found truths, and boldly stated their practical applications, while the science of the time was not sufficiently advanced to prove them." Similarly, religion had taught moral truths before humans could rationally argue their way to them. "Almost all religions" had "drawn upon that wondrous resource of human insight, inspiration, which reveals a truth, not in a systematic and scientific way, but at a glance, as it were, and by divination." Now, however, science was on the scene, and antipathy toward it was a "grievous fault" and "moral error," indeed, an "irreligious attitude." Both religion and science, Carus concluded, were "indestructible." "Science," he declared, was "the method of searching for the truth," and religion was "the enthusiasm and good will to live a life of truth."[114]

Within the brief compass of Carus's address, he had expressed the same concerns for science and truth that preoccupied New Thought practitioners and shaped their language. But there was more. The year after the parliament, Carus published the work that would guarantee him an abiding American reputation and seal his connection to the discourse community of New Thought. He was talking the talk that these other sorts of believers did, and his Buddhist rationalism would find congenial resonances with their conversations. Carus's *The Gospel of Buddha*, produced by his own press, made its mark on American publishing, going through thirteen editions by 1910 and already, in 1894, at least fifteen printings. It offered not a Buddhism emancipated from dogma and "superstition," as its author thought, but a Buddhism that reinvented Edwin Arnold in American terms and—in the midst of doing so—introduced Americans to a Christianized Buddha who sounded remarkably like a New Thought pundit. "Truth" was Carus's mantra. And "truth," in his rendering, transformed Buddhism's Four Noble Truths into the preamble to an identity discourse speaking more of Carus's metaphysical context than of an uninflected Buddhist Asia.[115]

Like Arnold's *Light of Asia*, Carus's work presented itself as a free-verse narrative. In physical format, it obligingly went further to call attention to its poetic genre, with marginal numbers added to the verses in each of its one hundred chapters, even if most of the chapters read more like prose than Arnold's did. Beyond that, if the text told Americans in more emphatic terms "I am a poem," it also told them more emphatically "I am a poem for Christians." Its title invocation of the "Gospel" was hardly subtle. Still more, Carus conveniently supplied readers with a three-column "Table of Reference," the first column citing chapter and verse in *The Gospel of Buddha*, the second—in much abbreviated form— his sources, and the third, "Parallelisms," mostly to New Testament gospels and other biblical sources. Carus had worked hard, and he gave readers seventy-five Gospel citations, some of them double and triple references to Synoptic Gospel narratives. His smattering of other references—to New Testament epistles, to the Old Testament book of Exodus, to the theory of evolution and the Christian doctrine of the Trinity, to an occasional contemporary work—likewise revealed his concerns and sense of audience.[116] Yet Carus's table of Gospels was, in fact, a work of supererogation. Any nineteenth- or early-twentieth-century reader plunging into the text would have needed to be totally innocent of New Testament narrative to ignore his message that the Buddha strikingly resembled Jesus.

For all the Christian dress in which the Buddha made his appearance, however, this Buddha acted as a subversive agent, undercutting the Christianity of mainstream America in favor of something that hinted strongly of New Thought. Here was a pointed kinship to the "truth" teaching of the latest American version of metaphysical religion—just at the time when it was coming fully into its American identity. Carus began by acknowledging the no-atman teaching of Buddhism as a denial of a "mysterious ego-entity" sometimes linked to "a kind of soul-monad." However, this meant, for Carus, that Buddhist teaching was "monistic" and that "the thoughts of a man" constituted his "soul" and were "if anything . . . his self." The Buddha's nirvana was an "ideal state" in which the human soul, "cleansed of all selfishness and sin," became "a habitation of the truth." Already oriented by these remarks before they ever got to the life of the Buddha, Carus's readers encountered a three-chapter introduction that formed an effusive paean to truth (not coldly "rational," but instead with emotional registers turned on and turned high). Truth was "wealth," and a "life of truth" was "happiness." Truth knew "neither birth nor death" and, indestructible, it had "no beginning and no end." "Hail the truth," Carus enjoined. "The Truth is the immortal part of the mind," and, conversely, "you attain to immortality by filling your minds with truth." Still more, wary of the self, like a dutiful Buddhist sympathizer, Carus was yet a good enough American metaphysician to distinguish between the "false self and the true self." The ego constituted the false; the soul, the true; and Carus had Buddhism and metaphysics as well. As his third chapter clearly announced, truth was the "saviour from sin and misery."[117]

Nor were preface and introduction sufficient for Carus to make his point. As the narrative life of the Buddha unfolded, readers learned that Queen Maya, his mother, became impregnated when "the spirit of truth descended upon her." Later, Prince Siddhartha as a young man still in his palace but troubled by the problem of evil "beheld with his mind's eye" a "celestial visitor" who told him that "'only the truth abideth forever.'" Urged to follow the path of this truth, Siddhartha—after the vision disappeared—told himself that he had "'awakened to the truth'" and was "'resolved'" to accomplish his purpose. Intent already (in Carus's reading) on becoming a Buddha, Siddhartha affirmed that there was "'no departure from truth'" in the speech of the Buddhas. Later, after he attained Buddhahood, in the renowned Benares sermon of traditional lore, Carus's Buddha preached the message of truth with a metaphysical vengeance:

"Happy is he who has found the truth.

The truth is noble and sweet; the truth can deliver you from evil. There is no saviour in the world except the truth.

Have confidence in the truth, although you may not be able to comprehend it, although you may suppose its sweetness to be bitter, although you may shrink from it at first. Trust in the truth.

The truth is best as it is. No one can alter it; neither can any one improve it. Have faith in the truth and live it."[118]

Like Jesus, Buddha gave his disciples his Great Commission, but this commission was distinctly metaphysical. After the "devas and saints and all the good spirits of the departed generations" had shouted their joy that "'the kingdom of Truth will be preached upon earth,'" he directed his followers to "'spread the truth and preach the doctrine in all quarters of the world.'" When he visited his aged father in the midst of his preaching career, Buddha told the old king that his son was gone and in his place was "'the teacher of truth'" and "'preacher of righteousness.'" He taught his disciple Ananda "'the mirror of truth'" that was "'the straightest way to enlightenment,'" and in his farewell sermon Carus's Buddha declared significantly (to Ananda again) that he had "'preached the truth without making any distinction between exoteric and esoteric doctrine.'" After his death, or passage to nirvana, as disciples told one another what the Buddha meant, one of them called him the "'visible appearance'" and "'bodily incarnation'" of truth, remembering that the Buddha had said that he himself was the truth.[119]

In the midst of this unremitting truth in the world of Carus's Buddha, what of self—which some Americans had learned to rely on and enjoy for its inmost divinity? In a semantic exercise that took away and simultaneously gave back, this Buddha taught that the truth was "'large enough to receive the yearnings and aspirations of all selfs.'" When the selves broke apart "'like soap-bubbles,'" their future was yet intact, with the Buddha telling his disciples that "'their contents will be preserved and in the truth they will lead a life everlasting.'" There was no self, to be sure, if the soul was the self, but "'on the other hand,'" said this Buddha, there was "'mind.'" The person who understood the soul to be the mind and acknowledged the existence of mind taught "'the truth which leads to clearness and enlightenment.'" With the body subject to dissolution, incapable of being saved by any sacrifice, Buddha enjoined his followers to seek "'the life that is of the mind.'" Carus, however, had still not had enough of truth. As he summarized for readers the meaning of his constructed Buddha and testified effusively to his own admiration for him, he closed by reiterating his truth claims once again. The truth had "appeared upon earth," and the "kingdom of truth" had been "founded." There was "no room for truth in space," even though it was "infinite." Nor was there room for truth "in sentiency." Surprisingly, there was no room for truth either in "rationality." "Rationality," wrote Carus, was a "two-edged sword" that could serve both love and hatred. It was the "platform" on which the truth stood, with no truth "attainable" without it. "Nevertheless," he warned, "in mere rationality there is no room for truth, though it be the instrument that masters the things of the world."[120]

The Buddhist rationalist had perhaps clipped his own wings. In the process, he had done very much more — proclaiming a Buddha and a Buddhist teaching that resonated with the metaphysical vocabulary of New Thought. The point is not that Asian Buddhism was not metaphysically inclined already — even if Americans chose selectively from their Asian mentors, largely discarding the ritual and ceremonial life of practical religion as so much superstition. The point is, rather, that Carus had executed a tour de force for truth teaching, in the process translating the Christian gospel itself, in its neo-Buddhist guise, into a metaphysical version that corroborated the major theological confession of New Thought. "Truth teaching" was in; evangelical religion-as-usual was out. For Carus, there was nothing esoteric about any of this, whatever the testimonials of Theosophists and run-of-the-mill occultists of any stripe. He was wary of mystical overdrive, but his more sedate and controlled metaphysic still led him to a territory that neighbored the theosophical world.

The success of Carus's work lingered into the twentieth century. Yet with the new century Buddhism itself began to shift, following a path that, as Victorian culture waned, departed significantly from that of American yoga. Only after the quota reforms initiated by the immigration law of 1965 did large numbers of South Asians begin to enter the country, juxtaposing their reality to the constructed images of non-South-Asian Americans. Earlier, the Johnson-Reed Act of 1924 had limited immigration to 2 percent of the nationals from any country who lived in the United States at the time of the 1890 Census. By contrast, the late nineteenth century and early twentieth had seen a significant immigration of East Asians from Japan and China. Asian contact limited the American imaginary, as did contact with Asians in the nation's wars. Meanwhile, different from the American yogic world — in which fluidity and guru-like followings begot networks of practitioners — American Buddhism saw a significant institutional presence as the twentieth century progressed. By its second half, as Thomas Tweed has noted, non-Asian Americans could find Buddhist organizations and authori-

tative Asian teachers.[121] Teachers, institutions, and supports for a sustained practice all added up to a self-conscious identity that distinguished this American
Buddhism and marked its separation from the more diffuse world of American
metaphysical religion. A fellow traveler this conversionist, export Buddhism certainly became, and in a series of versions—Zen, Tibetan, Vipassana—a close and
intimate fellow traveler, too. However, institutions, teachers, and rubrics of practice all worked to shift discourse and to imprint it with a life of its own, distinct
from the larger world of American metaphysics. At the very least, Buddhism—
with its no-self doctrine—raised compelling questions and fostered pragmatic
compromises for those inclined to pursue private quests for the enlightenment
of body-*selves*. Nineteenth-century Buddhist best sellers in the United States had
largely fudged the problem. But denial could not dissolve it. The construction
of an American Buddhist religious universe distinct from a more diffuse metaphysical religion went a long way toward positioning Buddhism in spaces that
kept the enlightened body-self within talking distance without full embrace.

Meanwhile, the larger world of American metaphysics would grow incremen-
tally in the new times dawning. From a series of perspectives and operational directions, Americans would converge on the received discourse and practice that
Theosophy and New Thought had broadcast widely. Not bound by the sectarian strictures that controlled Christian Science, Theosophy and New Thought
seemed happiest shaping language at large and inserting themselves as the secret
doctrine that fed the religious rationales of people who never joined or even perhaps knew them. Mind and correspondence, energy and healing—they could
come in many guises. Metaphysical religion flourished, took new forms, in its
dominant variant appropriated the ethnic versions of Indians, blacks, Latinos,
and others, and reemerged before century's end as the religion of the New Age,
continuing on after. Actually, though, the term—and the movement—deceived.
There were, in truth, new ages for all, and to single out one New Age is decidedly to miss the point. Americans, who had always loved newness, celebrated it
yet again, in the twentieth and twenty-first centuries, in multiple incarnations.

7

NEW AGES FOR ALL

Ralph Waldo Trine—born in 1866, the same year that Phineas Quimby died —could count himself a midwesterner by birth and most of his education. He had come from Mt. Morris, Illinois, and had attended Knox College in his home state, where, in 1891, he took his bachelor's degree. After that, came the University of Wisconsin until he matriculated at Johns Hopkins in Baltimore. Drawn to history and political science, he reportedly once won a hundred-dollar essay prize for a piece on the prevention of crime through a "humane education." Before the new century, however, Trine had turned to New Thought, although the circumstances that led to his embrace of metaphysics remain unclear. Still, we know that most probably they worked in tandem with his social and political concerns. By 1902, he had become a socialist and was planning a book that linked socialism as the basis of social organization to New Thought as a religious system. For society, government, and industry, thought Trine, socialism was *the* logical deduction from New Thought teaching on the "fatherhood" of God and the "brotherhood" of humans.[1]

By then, however, five years had passed since he had produced the short book that would guarantee him perhaps *the* leading position among metaphysical authors. Writing in the early 1960s, Charles Braden assessed Trine's *In Tune with the Infinite* as the single most successful New Thought book. By that time, Braden reported, its English-language sales had "gone well beyond a million and a half copies." Translations of the work had appeared in twenty languages "including Japanese and Esperanto," and they had sold exceedingly well. A Braille edition for the blind was available, and with that version included among total sales, Trine's book had been distributed in "well over two million copies." Most important of all, buyers and readers were not limited to the New Thought community. Rather, Braden declared, *In Tune with the Infinite*—along with "three or four" other books by Trine—had reached the public at large. People had absorbed its message without ever knowing anything of its New Thought origins.[2]

By this time, however, the old New Thought of the nineteenth century was giving way before a later version, one that—like the message brought by metaphysical Asia—was at once buttressing and liberating the enlightened body-selves of numbers of Americans. Horatio Dresser, New Thought savant and son of the well-known Dressers, did not like the new version so well as the old, and he named Trine as one of its protagonists. Trine's revised message had exalted "thought" in its human form beyond its carrying capacity, he complained. The causes of disease were spiritual, not purely mental. Trine and others had forgotten the deeper, truer tidings about divine wisdom and the "light of the divine idea" that Phineas Quimby had announced.[3] From the perspective of the twenty-first century, however, what is startling about the Dresser criticism is how much its statement of difference misses the larger paradigm shift that Trine represented. If metaphysical religion encompassed themes of mind, correspondence, and energy, in its healing/saving endeavors, arguably its earliest New Thought expressions were modeling mind and correspondence more than energy. Similarly, across the aisle in metaphysical Asia, leaders like Paul Carus and others were hailing the abiding stasis they called "truth" with an enthusiasm that was marked. By contrast, Trine glided smoothly into the twentieth century on a flow of divine energy.

In one sense, Trine was doing nothing new. Ralph Waldo Emerson, whom New Thought people loved to quote and listed proudly as their "founder," had long ago proclaimed that nature was "not fixed but fluid. Spirit alters, moulds, makes it." Emanuel Swedenborg had taught the divine influx as one of his cardinal doctrines. And spiritualism's A. J. Davis had pronounced on "fountains" and "jets of new meanings" even in 1870.[4] Nor is it hard to cross-read even the most static declarations of the early New Thought metaphysicians for their energy quotient. For all that, however, stepping into the discourse world of Trine means entering a different kind of verbal territory or, closer to his own usage, stepping into a different kind of linguistic stream. For Trine's favored theme is just that— a stream, a fountain, a divine reservoir overflowing toward earth dwellers who gladly expose themselves to its flow. If "truth" had been Paul Carus's mantra, "flow" was clearly Trine's.

In Tune with the Infinite from the start proclaimed as the "Supreme Fact of the Universe" the "Spirit of Infinite Life and Power . . . from which all is continually coming." In keeping with the model—and with language anticipated by the Unity-oriented H. Emilie Cady—Trine invoked a "reservoir in a valley which receives its supply from an inexhaustible reservoir on the mountainside."

He was not slow to make the application. *"The great central fact in human life,"* he emphatically affirmed, *"is the coming into a conscious, vital realization of our oneness with this Infinite Life, and the opening of ourselves fully to this divine flow."* Here at last is the much-vaunted harmonialism of Sydney Ahlstrom and others, as Trine exhorted readers on the need for harmonizing their lives with the flow. Moreover, if mind had power—which it decidedly did—its power came from its *attractive* force, as it stimulated energies that corresponded to its own vibration. The "drawing power of the mind" meant that humans were "continually attracting" to themselves, "from both the seen and the unseen side of life, forces and conditions most akin" to their thoughts. With God not only transcendent but also immanent, openness to the *"inflowing tide"* enabled humans to become *"channels through which the Infinite Intelligence and Power can work."* This happened through the "inner guiding" of intuition, and it worked itself out in all domains and all ways. Trine's chapters serially treated of health, love, wisdom, peace, power, and prosperity—always finding the key to the maximization of human life in openness to the divine flow.[5]

Fear and worry had "the effect of closing up the channels of the body, so that the life forces flow[ed] in a slow and sluggish manner." Emotions, passions, and mental states all had their effects, and the moral of the unhappy report was the dominance of sickness and disease. That admitted, the solution followed. Health was *"contagious as well as disease."* All readers had to do for the contagion to spread was to clean out their muddy waters and open their troughs: "There is a trough through which a stream of muddy water has been flowing for many days. The dirt has gradually collected on its sides and bottom, and it continues to collect as long as the muddy water flows through it. Change this. Open the trough to a swift-flowing stream of clear, crystal water, and in a very little while even the very dirt that has collected on its sides and bottom will be carried away. The trough will be entirely cleansed."[6]

The message was similar in other aspects of life. Debris had to be cleared, and the streambed kept open so that the divine inflow could and would happen. Or alternately, realization of one's indwelling divine nature generated magnetic power—a formulation that, silently and without acknowledgment, subverted the order of initiative away from divine benevolence and toward personal will. Still more, when it came to the "law of prosperity," the person who lived "in the realization of his oneness with this Infinite Power" became "a magnet to attract to himself a continual supply" of things desired. As for the clearing out, it came through getting rid of the extraneous and refusing to hoard (these ideas the ideological support for later metaphysical exhortations to tithing). "Then not by hoarding but by wisely using and ridding ourselves of things as they come," taught Trine, "an ever-renewing supply will be ours." "In this way we not only come into possession of the richest treasures of the Infinite Good ourselves, but we also become open channels through which they can flow to others." Trine cheerfully cited the "highly illumined seer, Emanuel Swedenborg" on "divine influx" and "the inspired one, the seer who when with us lived at Concord [that is, Emerson]" on humans as "all inlets to the great sea of life." The human task, Trine counseled, was simply to open the gate for the divine inflow. "It is like opening the gate of the trough which conducts the water from the reservoir above into the field below. The water, by virtue of its very nature, will rush in and irrigate the field if the gate is but opened."[7]

The reiterative quality of Trine's prose simplified theology and practice so that readers of many persuasions could absorb and enact the message. Meanwhile, in the midst of the authorial exercise, Trine was enacting a practice of his own that distinctly separated him from the older metaphysical culture. It is no surprise, therefore, that Gary Ward Materra sees him as an embodiment of the noetic style of New Thought.[8] While Horatio Dresser dwelled comfortably in the affective New Thought that had flourished as strongly in the initial years, now the more instrumentalist version was promising mastery to denizens of a new twentieth-century world. In it, ego and Atman (or a New Thought "Christ presence") had become friends and partners instead of enemies. The instrumentalism guaranteed that New Thought was not for gazing at immutable truths and contemplating their beauty unalloyed. New Thought principles were energy formulas that got the practitioner from one inner place to another and so, often, from one outer place to another. Still further, it turned out, the most powerful energy formula was the one that proclaimed that all there was in the first place was Energy. God, in twentieth-century and later metaphysical religion, was Motion.

Two years before Trine's influential New Thought book appeared, another energy formula had begun its trajectory toward scientific fame and fortune. It was in 1895 that the German physicist Max Planck (1858–1947) began his black-box experiments that led the way to quantum theory. Earlier nineteenth-century work had explained light as a wave on the basis of then-accepted experimental testimony. Now Planck was finding, from his own experiments, that Newtonian mechanics could not account for the behavior of light. By 1900 Planck read a paper to the German Physical Society, telling colleagues his tale of the strange activity of light, which, he announced, could be emitted and absorbed not continuously but only in discrete and discontinuous energy bundles, or packets, which he named "quanta." Later, in 1905, Albert Einstein pushed the Newtonian gospel still further away, hypothesizing that the energy of light was composed of particles, or photons, repeatedly speeding and colliding into one another. Oscillating atoms had a secret inner life, and that life—of mysterious particles and energies—was a life in motion even as it was a life in matter. Einstein, Niels Bohr, Werner Heisenberg, Erwin Schrödinger, and others all would refine the formula, as the early twentieth century saw the theory rise to an elegance and persuasive power that signaled the end of the Newtonian world and the dawn of a new scientific era.[9]

The mathematical language of the quantum worked to convince professionals. Nonscientists, however, had to be content with imagistic efficacy. At the level of metaphor and imagination, the quantum introduced a world in which, sub-atomically, electrons—which were parts of atoms—acted at times like particles and at times like waves. Matter and energy seemed to play tirelessly with one another, and—even in science, when the mass-accelerator came along to change energy back into matter—their connection could be noticed as palpable and real. While practicing scientists learned to state the behavior of electrons in terms of mathematical probabilities, metaphysical religionists—who garnered aspects of the new science from vernacular culture—began a series of ascriptions that provided them with their own elegant "scientific" theory to authorize an evolving spirituality. German physicist Werner Heisenberg's "unsharpness principle," or principle of uncertainty, by 1927 authorized the spirituality more. The observer altered the experiment; by extension, consciousness and its inquiries could change the path of metaphysics and its experience of spirit. In fact, when matter and energy played their particle-wave game, in metaphysical terms matter and *spirit* played. In the preferred language of metaphysical Asia, Prakriti and Purusha played, and when the play could not go on—when matter got too stuck in its guise as "frozen light" (to invoke the language of one twentieth-century physician-metaphysician)—the energy of spirit suffered. Moving out of the community of professional scientists the quantum took on moral dimensions that the behavior of light had not previously acquired. Energy was good; matter more dubious. At the very least, to free up matter, to make enlightened body-selves respond to spirit's impulse and message, became the new metaphysical task for consciousness, since the observer, indeed, could alter the game. There is no evidence that Ralph Waldo Trine knew about black-box experiments, but he had set an agenda decidedly congenial to the secret life of light—or better, to a reformed secret life of light. Meanwhile, light, after all, had always been a cherished category for mystics and metaphysicians. Now they could mark the speed or the slowness of its vibrations and measure their success in the world of spirit.[10]

In one sense, they had simply found a new scientific language to perpetuate the rhetorical capital of the old mesmeric world and the now-defunct nineteenth-century theory of the ether. The ghosts of Blavatsky and company could rest content as, in the quantum, a replacement scientific world became available. Indeed, even scientists seemed to support metaphysical acts of piracy. Werner Heisenberg himself thought that, when it came to philosophical models, contemporary physicists were corroborating Plato. The most basic grid of matter was made not of physical objects in the vernacular sense but of entities that could be understood and expressed best as ideas—as mathematical variations in an ever-changing field. The world and the I could no longer be sharply separated—in fact, that was "impossible." Quantum physics functioned within a "general historical process" that moved toward "a unification and a widening of our present world."[11]

The overriding news of the twentieth century and after was that metaphysical light escaped from its own black box. Even as nineteenth-century spiritualists had created a mass movement in vernacular culture, twentieth-century and later metaphysicians would do the same, creating an *exoteric* spirituality and dissolving it so thoroughly into society at large that it became, in some versions, simply part of America as usual. We look, first, at late-nineteenth- and early-twentieth-century versions of the great dissolve at both ends of the matter-spirit spectrum. Here a closet metaphysics originally grounded continuing practices as varied as osteopathy and chiropractic, on the one hand, and pragmatic philosophy, with its legacy of idealism, on the other. In more condensed and consciously religious form, general New Thought principles shaped the confident living propounded by several small New Thought denominations, the largest among them Unity. By midcentury, still another path of diffusion came through the movement for positive thinking, even as theosophical lineages, then and before, transmuted into new and persisting forms. Nor did an ethnic presence disappear from metaphysics. We can find it even in the newest incarnation of metaphysical Asia, the American Daoism of the late twentieth century and after. Besides the New Age movement of the late twentieth and early twenty-first century, there were many other new ages.

BODY MECHANICS AND SPIRIT PHILOSOPHY

If quantum mechanics detailed the energetic structure of the universe and all its dwellers for the twentieth century and after, there had been other mechanics—and of a metaphysical sort—in the late nineteenth. Andrew Taylor Still (1828–1917), the founder of osteopathy, taught one of them. A Virginian and the son of a Methodist circuit rider, by 1837 Still was in Missouri with his father, who was also farming and practicing medicine to supplement his income. When, in 1851, the father set out for the Kansas Territory as a missionary to the Shawnee

Indians, the son and his young family eventually joined him at the Wakarusa Mission, where he began to study medicine with his father. The younger Still's first patients were Indians. Moving beyond medicine, he became an ardent abolitionist and a Union soldier in the Civil War thereafter, but subsequently he returned to Kansas to practice as an orthodox physician. There alternative medicine flourished all around him, and—a reflective man and homespun philosopher—Still noticed (in the era of "heroic" bleedings, purges, and mercuric calomel) that alternative practice did less damage than the "drugging" regimen in which he had been trained. He was drawn to certain aspects of magnetic healing, especially its notions of health as a free and unhampered fluidic flow.[12]

By 1874, Still had broken all ties with regular medicine and was advertising himself as a magnetic healer. As his practice evolved, too, he found himself attracted to the manipulative therapy known as bone setting, by this time a mostly folk practice of forcing displaced bones back where they belonged. Next Still synthesized magnetism with manipulation in a unified-field theory and practice, and by about 1880, he began to treat patients osteopathically, focusing on bones and muscles as a way to restore a natural somatic flow. For Still and his followers, most sickness came from structural disorganization or disarrangement within the body. Repetitive strains to bones, muscles, and cartilage, small though the strains might be, could create the misalignments that osteopaths called lesions. Osteopathic manipulation was intended to correct these conditions and thus, it followed, liberate the body so that its natural processes could defeat illness. To advance these goals, Still founded his osteopathic school in Kirksville, Missouri, in 1892. At first it functioned as another alternative to the growing scientific medicine of his era, challenging class and gender norms to welcome rural students from the South and the Midwest, among them an impressive number of women. But osteopathy over the years changed, as Still's brand of healing made its slow social pilgrimage from what Norman Gevitz has called "deviance" to a more conventional state of "difference." Osteopaths gradually won licenses to practice medicine, including prescribing drugs and performing surgery; they became available in mainstream hospital settings; and there they functioned simply as physicians with a different history.[13]

That history does not concern us here. What does concern, however, is the ideational imprint that Still left on osteopathic philosophy and the vision that it imparted to practitioners and, to some extent, patients. This is because the philosophy and the vision attached them to a diffuse but unmistakable version of metaphysical spirituality. For Still, the mechanical habit of manipulating bones had its complement in an old-fashioned God of Nature who was also an orderly Great Manipulator. Translated into the language of the vernacular Enlightenment, this meant a God of "truth," whose works were "harmonious" and whose law for "animal life" could be called "absolute." Translated further into the language of early osteopathy, the cure for every discomfort and infirmity lay within —"a whole system of drugs in abundance" that had been "deposited" in the body by its "Maker."[14] Here was a practical metaphysic to theorize and explain healing success, a metaphysic that combined the eighteenth-century Enlightenment's "nature's God" with the immanent deity of the Romantic era whose law and power worked from the inside out. And significantly, through his connections among practicing spiritualists Still, the former magnetic healer, almost surely had more than a passing acquaintance with the immanent God. Historian of osteopathy Norman Gevitz discovered that Still co-signed a letter that appeared in the spiritualist *Banner of Light* in 1875, appealing for help with a grasshopper invasion afflicting Kirksville. The letter alluded to "a few workers here" but complained that they were "looked upon as 'crazy' and 'worse than infidels.'" Moreover, as late as 1903 Still was in Clinton, Iowa, to attend a spiritualist meeting, and thereafter he told his osteopathic students that spiritualists' (negative) assessments of the use of drugs ran parallel to his own.[15]

Still's apparent congeniality with spiritualism is itself a clue to what his own writings thoroughly reflect. The God who grounded osteopathy was an embodied deity, and the implication—as in spiritualism's received, though obscured, Hermetic teaching—was that divinity resided in creation as its very life. More than that, a progressive quality in Still's formulation (like spiritualism but more strongly) pushed it toward its twentieth-century future. If "God had certainly placed the remedy within the material house in which the spirit of life dwells," Still's response invoked a determined agency. "With this thought I trimmed my sail and launched my craft as an explorer." The results were bountiful. "Soon I saw the green islands of health all over the seas of reason. Ever since then I have watched the driftwood and course of the wind, and I have never failed to find the source whence the drifting came."[16]

By 1897, when Still wrote these words, he could look back on twenty years of voyaging success. Meanwhile, as Still wrote them, Nature's God—for all his law-bound presence—seemed to act in ways remarkably similar to the God of flow that Trine had modeled in his own 1897 work. In one romanticized characterization, not untypical of Still, for example, he waxed expansively: "In close range, and directly in view of the most ordinary field-glass, stands the mountain of Reason, from which is rolling down in our presence the greatest nuggets of gold that the human mind ever saw coming down as from the very bosom of God Himself. All this fertility we believe is intended for the human race and benefit of man." Here was New Thought prosperity wedded to New Thought flow, both of them the effluence of an Enlightenment God who had merged with the God of divine Supply. More than that, here was conscious rejection of traditional churches in favor of the flow. Still, son of the Methodist circuit rider and intimately acquainted with evangelical revivals, was hardly diffident about declaring that he had "no use for the churches of the world." "To be a Methodist" meant "to hate a Campbellite." "To be a Campbellite" was "to hate the Baptist, and so on." All, however, would "unite as one to fight the Roman Catholic," and he saw "rivers of blood running" from most of the churches and "more coming." By contrast, he affirmed his belief in a "principle" that was "above all churches" and that was "the law and gift of God to man." What was it? In his preferred language of agency, Still testified for "bloodless rivers of love given for man to drink in all time and eternity." Always, the model was clear: God was an Enlightenment mechanic all right, but this God had created a moving machine and fueled it—impersonally—with something more than pure reason, for all Still's plentiful talk of the same. Beyond that, the something hinted of magnetic laws. The body was "a machine run by the unseen force called life"; for its harmonious operation, there had to be "liberty of blood, nerves, and arteries from the generating-point to destination." In contrast to the wasted blood of feuding religious sects, Still taught that the conserved-but-free flow, especially, of the blood guaranteed health and prevented disease.[17]

Still's model, we know, was overlaid for many later osteopaths by mainstream medicine. Yet the energetic (and magnetic) template persisted in some osteopathic quarters. If we fast forward to osteopathy a century after Still, we can catch a glimpse of what his traditional-yet-transformed vision became in the career of Robert C. Fulford, D.O., whose near-legendary life spanned the twentieth century (he flourished well into his nineties). Known for his mentorship of others and for his own reputed gifts, Fulford found time, in later life, to reflect on his nearly sixty years of osteopathic practice. He told his readers in *Dr. Fulford's Touch of Life* that the human body was "more complicated" than conventional anatomy suggested. "Besides the systems and processes well known to everyone," he confided, "the body is also composed of a complex interflowing stream of moving energy. When these energy streams become blocked or constricted, we lose the physical, emotional, and mental fluidity potentially available to us. If the blockage lasts long enough or is great enough, the result is pain, discomfort, illness, and distress." Fulford confessed autobiographically that he liked to work with children better than adults because adults emitted "less energy" than children did, took away his own energy when he treated them, and made him feel "depleted." By contrast, children, who were "more radiant," did not absorb his energy so completely. Fulford was making the same affirmations that founder Still had made—

the universe was "run by specific laws," and osteopathy was predicated on a "philosophy" that reflected these "universal laws" and applied them to human beings. What did this mean in concrete terms? Fulford's answer is instructive, seamlessly connecting Still's original vision to late-twentieth-century energetic formulations that tell of the dominance of the agential model and of the metaphysical spirituality that promotes it. The body, declared Fulford, was surrounded by what he called a "life field."[18]

What followed brought not only Still but also Helena Blavatsky up to end-of-century speed. "This life field thoroughly permeates the physical body and actually reaches beyond it by many inches. To imagine what it might look like, you might want to think of a colored aura surrounding the body, one that might appear green or red or yellow, or any other color, depending on the individual. . . . If you could see the field, it would resemble a human shadow: the field's pattern surrounds the head, spreading out around the shoulders and becoming narrower by the waist, and then tapering down the legs to the feet. In some ways, the life field could be considered the body's other half: the spatial part is the portion we commonly think of as the material human being, while the other half is this invisible field." Fulford cited electromagnetic phenomena associated with the "aura," invoking Harold Saxon Burr, a former Yale professor of neuroanatomy, to make his case. The "life field" was "an electric field with a high frequency," and so, for a popular book, it was scientific, with a highly credentialed scientific authority to buttress it. But Fulford's way of conceptualizing life field and electromagnetic activity reveals, too, a different sort of inspiration, hinting of the older spiritualist world of the ectoplasm, the mysterious substance emanating from a medium's body that enabled the spirits to manifest themselves in perceptible ways. "In a sense," explained Fulford, "the electromagnetic pattern creates a mold, which is eventually filled by matter, giving rise to a tangible, material body." If so or not, Fulford's combinativeness suggests a mental habit that had begun with osteopathy's foundation and the evidence of Still's own comfort in the spiritualist world. But now there were new dots to connect in the combinative osteopathic universe, and Fulford turned to Asia to add in the "vital energy" of the East: "The Chinese call it *chi*, the Japanese call it *ki*, and the Hindus *prana*."[19]

In the body, the "life field" became the "life force." As a practicing osteopath, Fulford claimed that he could feel the force with his hand as a prickling sensation and that it was stronger or weaker in his patients depending on whether and how much blockage was present. It was significant that the human mind played a pivotal role in the life force's presence and distribution. Much of its "flow" was "regulated by the mind." Thoughts had "physical consequences," changing the life field and its color radiations in terms of passing patterns and general spiritual evolution. This was because thinking caused energy to be emitted from the body—so much so that humans lived through their minds and not their bodies. It was mind that created reality, and any "discord or disharmony" harbored in the mind was "likely to produce an unfortunate effect in the physical body." As in other metaphysical systems, too, mind led to spirit and to God. What was "spiritual in the world" was "the universal source of this cosmic electrical energy, this life force that keeps us all alive." Fulford told readers that he suspected that the "universal life force" might be "another name for God." The conclusion for him was obvious: "God, therefore, exists within all of us, embodied in this energy."[20] The Hermetic gospel was back, and humans, as Fulford estimated them, should be living as gods.

More than that, as Fulford quoted from Still and clearly agreed with him, he brought to the fore the early theosophical teaching about the triune nature of humans. Body, soul, and spirit meant for Still "first, the material body; second the spiritual being; third, a being of mind which is far superior to all vital motions and material forms." This material-mental-spiritual being accorded with other sources of Fulford's knowledge in Asian thought and, especially, in Daoism. Even the material body pointed toward spirit; Fulford reiterated that it was "composed of electric waves of light" in what he had called the life field. That the same waves also brought light to houses and pictures and sounds to television sets suggested the divinized status of all material productions rather than their secularity. Indeed, Fulford could find no evil in the divinized world. Even though evil could happen, it did not exist—meaning, in effect, that it possessed no substantial reality. In tandem with the privative doctrine that marked nineteenth-century metaphysics, he called it the "absence of the spiritual force" and declared that people became evil by blocking off "that purity, that life-giving universal flow of energy, from their being."[21]

Other late-twentieth-century physicians followed Still's metaphysical lead toward energetic constructions of reality, especially in the cranial-sacral systems of manipulative therapy that arose from osteopathic roots. William Sutherland, for example, who originated the theory and technique of manipulation of the skull bones to unblock and regulate the flow of cerebro-spinal fluid between skull and sacrum, had studied under Still himself.[22] Cranial-sacral therapists claimed—and continue to claim—that freeing blockages and allowing natural flow to proceed unimpeded has corrected a host of seemingly unrelated maladies. More important here than details of the therapy, however, the old mesmeric model —sifted through spiritualist and theosophical registers, still carrying Enlightenment motifs — could be seen as mingling with ideas ranging from quantum theories about light to metaphysical Asian representations. A comprehensive vernacular theory had been found, and it had become persuasive.

The process had been aided by another version of body mechanics inherited from the late nineteenth century. This was chiropractic, with roots in the Hermetic tradition even more obvious than osteopathy's. Daniel David (D. D.) Palmer (1845–1913), who founded chiropractic, immigrated from Canada, taught school in Iowa and Illinois, and tried his hand at horticulture and beekeeping. He created a national market for his "Sweet Home raspberry" (a large blackraspberry variety that bore abundant fruit), and then in What Cheer, Iowa, he began a grocery business and also sold goldfish. Eventually he settled in Davenport, Iowa, where his version of body manipulation flourished. Like Still (and like Phineas Quimby), Palmer's path to physical manipulation led through spiritualism and animal magnetism. Indeed, with spiritualist friends and earnest discussions on spiritualist themes an important part of his world, it was probably not surprising that — in an evangelically oriented nation — he decided to testify to spiritualist faith on the front and inside covers of a nursery catalog he produced. Palmer expressed his commitments to the village Enlightenment when he argued against fraud within spiritualist ranks, but the spirits did not leave when he embraced magnetism. As historian of chiropractic J. Stuart Moore has noted, "assimilating spirit to science" became a persistent theme in Palmer's professional life. "By eventually traveling a path from spiritualism through magnetic healing to his innovation of chiropractic," Moore summarizes, "Palmer tapped into the harmonial tradition . . . an impulse with certain affinities to the centuries-old hermetic tradition."[23]

Like Still and Quimby, too, Palmer's appropriation of the vernacular Enlightenment brought no conflict as it mingled with newer Romantic currents that by the nineteenth century's end had transmuted mesmerism and spiritualism into Theosophy and, more, New Thought. The brief aphorisms Palmer inscribed in his personal journal provide transparent testimony to his mental world. "Vehemently and forcibly if necessary awaken your patient from his dream of suffering." "Patients suffer only as the insane suffer, from mere belief." "Disease, disarrangement, is disturbed harmony." "Mind produces all action, conscious or unconscious." Palmer invoked the "Metaphysician the soul or spirit" and thought that "the mind must be cured as well as body," since "as the mind so is the body." In full agreement with Quimby and Christian Science, he declared that disease was "only the manifestation of error or wrong doing, wrong thots." In fact, thoughts were "real substance" and modified all they touched. Still more, Palmer kept company with New Thought practices of affirmation and denial. "Enquire what state of mind at time of taking disease or accident," he exhorted himself in his journal, "then deny the cause."[24]

Palmer's small personal pamphlet library tells a similar story. Here titles range from mesmerism and spiritualism to Theosophy and New Thought. On magnetism, for example, there was popular healer Edwin Dwight Babbitt's *Vital Magnetism* (1874), which cited a series of maladies that could be addressed through spinal treatment and spoke the language of auras, health reform, and even something like prayerful meditation. Here, too, was magnetic doctor C. A. De-Groodt's *Hygeio-Therapeutic Institute and Magnetic Infirmary* (c. 1882–1883), which blended biblical writ with its invocation of "the grandest, the most subtile and refined force operating in human affairs—the vital Aura, the direct interpreter of life itself—the force called MAGNETISM." Professor J. W. Cadwell's *How to Mesmerize*, bound with *Is Spiritualism True?* in a revised 1885 edition, and James Victor Wilson's *How to Magnetize; or, Magnetism and Clairvoyance*, in a new and revised 1886 edition, also provide compelling evidence about Palmer's world. Straddling the line into Theosophy was *Psychometry and Thought-Transference*, written by an unidentified medical Theosophist ("N. C.") and introduced by Henry Steel Olcott himself. From the camp of Freethought and sexual radicalism came the Boston physician Charles Knowlton's *Fruits of Philosophy*, with its advocacy of contraception for population control, first published in England in 1832 by James Watson and now republished by Charles Bradlaugh and Annie Besant in 1877 to test suppression laws. (Besant would later succeed Olcott at the helm of the Theosophical Society.) Palmer's eclectic collection also contained a second work promoting "sexual self-government" (E. H. Heywood's *Cupid's Yokes*), and—although there is no evidence that Palmer himself followed free-love practice—Moore has reviewed the Palmer journal entries that suggest he was providing contraceptive advice to women.[25]

In Palmer's pamphlet collection as well were two published lectures by Juliet H. Severance, with an "M.D." duly attached to her name. Severance, from Wisconsin, was a well-known spiritualist, hydropathic (water-cure) doctor, magnetic healer, outspoken health reformer, and women's rights advocate. The presence of two of her lectures among the short list of Palmer pamphlets—one of them on spiritualist themes (1882) and one on magnetism (1883)—suggests the radical mental company he kept. As if to underline that assessment, Palmer's oldest pamphlet was Marcenus R. K. Wright's 1870 *Moral Aphorisms and Terseological Teachings of Confucius*, the work itself an early sign that Orientalism was beginning to cut a path through metaphysical vernacular culture. Moreover, from Palmer's Illinois days there was William Denton's 1872 pamphlet *The Deluge in the Light of Modern Science*. This piece sought to make science the arbiter of the truth or falsehood of the Bible; it concluded that the scriptural account was a fable and thus assigned the Bible "its place with all other human fallible productions." "For knowledge," Denton proclaimed, "we go to Nature, our universal mother, who gives her Bible to every soul, and preaches her everlasting gospel to all people."[26]

Palmer would, indeed, go to Nature, like Still combining a metaphysical spirituality that exalted it with techniques of physical manipulation. He would acknowledge auras ("all observers realize that we are surrounded with an aura"), but also, insofar as he understood it, embrace science. The pamphlet library represented the furniture of Palmer's own mind, and its contents bespoke the mental and physical practice he promoted. That practice crystallized and took self-conscious shape in 1895, according to Palmer—the same year that, in Germany, Wilhelm Conrad Roentgen discovered the X-ray and Max Planck began his black-box experiments. While the Germans looked to energetic forms of light, in his vernacular world Palmer likewise performed experiments with energy, conceived and practiced according to his homespun metaphysical formulation. His near-legendary account of how his spinal adjustment enabled black janitor Harvey Lillard, deaf for seventeen years, to hear described a dramatically effective intervention. Like Mary Baker Eddy's account of her "discovery" of Christian Science, the Palmer story was most likely a serial "discovery," with repeated experiments on Lillard's back. Sudden or sequential, however, Harvey Lillard's cure and the new practice of chiropractic became interventions in search of an explanation. In the metaphysical world in which he had for many years happily dwelled, Palmer found it. In fact, the name he chose for his new technique— chiropractic (reportedly suggested by Presbyterian minister and Greek student Samuel H. Weed)—no doubt appealed over other choices because of Palmer's familiarity with the term *cheiromancy* or *chiromancy* (that is, palmistry) from metaphysical literature.[27] Chiropractic was surely "done with the hands," as the Greek etymological roots suggest, but it was done with hands that had held theosophical and New Thought texts.

Moreover, if the hands that played on the spinal vertebrae in Palmer's chiropractic were metaphysical ones, the theory Palmer evolved to support his new technique combined the age-old doctrine of correspondence with magnetic models of tides and their blockages. These models were now updated in a theosophized New Thought universe in which, with Trine and others, divine reservoirs were flowing and human troughs and dams needed to be cleaned and unblocked to receive the waters. Even here, though, there were remnants of evangelical theories of sin, original and directly made, for how else to explain the blockages?

In Palmer's version of the discourse, what flowed into human embodied spirits was the end-century/new-century successor to magnetic tides that he called "Innate." In its new monism and — in the words of H. Stuart Moore — chiropractic's "impulse to reinvest science with spirit," Palmer's Innate cut a path between the rationalism of mainstream science and the Christian Science practice that effaced matter totally for spirit. *Innate* meant "born with," explained Palmer, and it was shorthand for the "individualized intelligence" that ran "through all the functions of our bodies during our wakeful and sleeping hours." As such, it was a "part or portion of that All Wise, Almighty, Universal Intelligence, the Great Spirit, the Greek's Theos, the Christian's God, the Hebrew's Helohim, the Mahometan's Allah, Hahneman's [homeopathic] Vital Force, new thot's Divine Spark, the Indian's Great Spirit, the Christian Scientist's All Goodness, the Allopath's Vis Medicatrix Naturae — the healing power of nature." Meanwhile, Palmer's theosophical Innate was not unrelated to Still's osteopathic conceptions. Palmer had visited Kirksville and learned from what Still was doing there, although later he denied that he had done so. Yet there were differences: Still was interested in the free flow of blood; Palmer, more in the flow of nerve force. Still operated on bones and muscles and promoted massage; Palmer's focus was the spine and its "subluxations," using the spinal and transverse processes as levers to correct slippages and abnormalities.[28] However, it was on the level of theory that Palmer's statement refined and elaborated the fluidic model with a sophistication that marked its greatest difference from Still's work — and perhaps contributed to the nonmedical future of chiropractic.

Palmer's Innate ran through healthy bodies on the path of freedom, but it did so in tandem with another energy called Educated. With "spirit, soul, and body" as an identifying tag to mark the connection of his ideas to Theosophy and New Thought, Palmer declared that the three composed "the being, the source of mentality" and that "Innate and Educated, two mentalities," attended to "the welfare of the body physically and its surrounding environments." By contrast to Innate, Educated was intimately connected to the life history of the individual, shaped by education and experience. It started out knowing nothing "except as it [was] acquired." Innate was part of a metaworld; it had "been thinking ever since spirit and matter began an existence." Educated began and ended with a person's historical existence. But, perhaps surprisingly, Innate took back to eternity what Educated had learned. In the life trajectory of an individual, the two worked together, one tending to the body's inner welfare and the other to "outer well-being." Still, the mutual assistance between Innate and Educated was only "more or less," and they could be "antagonistic." A "displaced portion of the osseous structure" could, for example, press "against a sensory nerve causing the information received by Educated, which is transferred to Innate, to be abnormal." It was no wonder, then, that in a short text that still read as a mission statement for chiropractic, Palmer legitimated his work by testifying that "our physical health and intellectual progress of this world and the next depends largely upon the proper alignment of our skeletal frames."[29]

In Palmer's expansive vision of the role of chiropractic, fixing a spine and physical body could mean fixing an eternity. The chiropractor, as Hermetic priest, released the stuckness and freed the spirit. Not only did the chiropractic intervention allow Innate to move everywhere in the physical frame, guaranteeing health and well-being. It also operated as a moral and spiritual practice to affect the future of the spirit, whose acquired learning during an earthly lifetime could change spiritual status in the life to come. In fact, oral tradition among Palmerites had it that D. D. Palmer initially pondered whether he should present his new system of spinal adjustment as a religion. Still more, discourse on the spiritual would continue to characterize the tradition. Palmer's son B. J. (Bartlett Joshua) Palmer (1882–1961) pointed the way for twentieth-century changes. The son was clearly a more thoroughgoing materialist than his father, localizing the operations of Innate to the physical brain and dwelling on the materiality of the spiritual process. By 1907, he had purchased his father's struggling school in Davenport, paid its debts, and incorporated it. Expansive and charismatic, he drew students and staff to him and promoted loyalty among the devout. He also had a bitterly contentious relationship with his father, and the two became rivals in the evolving trajectory of chiropractic.[30] All the same, the son built on the metaphysical religiosity of his father.

We gain perhaps the most succinct statement of these connections and differences in an essay by Joy M. Loban, D. D. Palmer's associate and teacher at his school, later teacher and head of B. J. Palmer's rival Universal Chiropractic College, and eventual executor of the father's estate. Here the "philosophy" expressed became clearly a philosophy of religion. Chiropractic had "investigated and explained that mysterious and elusive thing men call[ed] the Soul," and it elucidated "the 'Nature' which [had] been used for generations as a name for the unknowable." The model that Loban unfolded was thoroughly agential. He wrote expansively that chiropractic had "taken the forces and energies which move and wield and reconstruct the elements" and had shown how they acted "in absolute obedience to an Intelligence" that was "all-pervading." It ventured "into the realm of (so-called) occult phenomena" and proved them "to be simply action in obedience to easily understood laws." Chiropractic philosophy was, in Loban's words, "the Philosophy of Cause." "The study of Chiropractic properly begins with a knowledge or conception of the ABSOLUTE and proceeds by successive steps through the various steps that intervene before we arrive at a consideration of the ultimate expression of Energy in the tissue cells of man."[31]

What followed in Loban's exposition seems thoroughly Blavatskian. Each "individualized intelligence, or Entity called Ego, soul, etc." appeared to develop "only" through education, and it was "only through knowledge" that perfection could be reached. That stated, Loban thought that the "Entity" needed to "inhabit, in turn, the various stages of physical development (for the physical body of man has passed through ages of evolution) in order that it may reach perfection." Why would not one physical body suffice? Loban answered sententiously, invoking the "law that no portion of matter exists forever without changing from one state to another"; the physical, thus, had to "be dissolved and scattered." In keeping with D. D. Palmer's notions of the role of Educated in transforming Innate, Loban declared that as the mind passed from physical life to the "void" to physical life again it retained "all the knowledge it [had] already gained in previous existences." It used the knowledge "in the operation of the new medium for the acquisition of more knowledge." "Just as matter is dependent upon the Mind for its existence in organized form, so is the Mind dependent upon Matter for its development."[32] In Hermetic and theosophical vein, always, humans would walk the earth as gods, but the twist on reincarnation was unmistakably Palmerian. Now they would walk as enlightened body-selves, with perfected flesh the prerequisite for perfected spirit.

As Loban went on to track the action of Innate Intelligence in "the creation, transmission and expression of Power," however, the new physicality and energy emphasis of B. J. Palmer became apparent. First, purpose had to be present, but then "energy," which was "gathered in the brain" and "akin to electricity" but with "a higher rate of vibration." "Mental impulses" traveled through the nerves from brain to body and were there "expressed as life," impulses that were "sent out in a series of vibrations—a current continually flowing from the brain outward." The only thing that could interfere would be an obstacle in the path of transmission; in other words, a subluxation of the spine that interfered with the exit of the nerve from the spinal column. Thus the task of the chiropractor was clear and specific—to remove the blockage or the slippage. Chiropractic *philosophy*, by contrast, was grand and "all-comprehensive." It encompassed "all things created, and back of all the ABSOLUTE." In it could be found "the germs of every truth which is now and always has been." From this perspective, the "true Chiropractor" was "neither a Mental Scientist nor a Physicist"; the healing discipline included "both Physics and Metaphysics—and the relation between the two."[33]

Loban was not shy about invoking B. J. Palmer, and his words to that effect were effusive in their overinvestment, astounding in their silence. He had quoted

freely, he said, "from the utterances of B. J. Palmer," even engaged in "bold plagiarism" of the younger Palmer, whom he acclaimed as the "originator" of chiropractic philosophy. About D. D. Palmer, Loban had nothing to say, even though
later, as executor of the elder Palmer's estate, he would file suit against the son on
grounds that he had maliciously driven his auto into his father during a parade
in 1913. Meanwhile, B. J. Palmer was as caught as Loban between confession
and silence. The father thought the son's brain theories to be "anatomical non-
sense," according to Moore. These theories, in effect, reduced the role of Innate
and turned the body into a machine run by the brain. From a historical perspective, however, it is not hard to see that the shift between father and son restated
the shift between the older, more "spiritualized" and affective New Thought that
Horatio Dresser admired and the newer, more mentalistic and noetic version ex-
emplified by Trine and later New Thought writers. Meanwhile, although B. J.
Palmer's valorization of the brain was probably not original (Moore pointed to
its sources in a 1906 textbook), the younger man did love machines.[34]

By 1909, Palmer was promoting the use of the X-ray, and by 1923 a device
called the Neurocalometer, which he claimed could find spinal subluxations
by detecting changes in nerve transmission. Mechanical electricity was replacing the sensitized palm of the chiropractor. Whereas D. D. Palmer had insisted
that no electrical gadgets should be used for adjustments, now a series of new
tools beckoned the enterprising chiropractor. Yet, arguably, the gadgetry fed
seamlessly into a chiropractic worldview premised on metaphysical notions of
energy, and chiropractors operated them to open conduits and generate streams
of power ultimately spiritual. By 1937, for example, chiropractors could employ
the Chromoray, using spectral colors in an instrument developed in keeping
with the *Principles of Light and Color*, the 1878 work of Edwin Dwight Babbitt,
whose magnetism had influenced D. D. Palmer. Chromopathy, as the therapy
was called, turned on the metaphysical notion that each color in the spectrum
vibrated according to a signature pattern corresponding to that of a particular
illness. By selecting and mixing appropriate colors, the causes of illnesses—not
just their consequences—could be addressed by employing "the higher forces of
nature." Similarly, other devices used electricity to provide stimulation to ailing
patients and thus unblock the healing forces of nature.[35]

Some chiropractors were "straight," adhering strictly to the protocols of spinal
adjustment advanced from the first days of chiropractic. Others were "mixers,"
freely combining spinal adjustment with other modalities including instruments,
nutritional supplements, (homeopathic) flower remedies, and the like. Intersect-
ing these divisions, however, some became mechanics who aspired to membership in the modern scientific community. Others, with or without acknowledg-

ment, were metaphysicians, continuing to subscribe to notions of blockage and flow and thus to the spiritual model behind the ideas. The changes that these twentieth-century chiropractors embraced returned them, again and again, to their origins. Thus, when the New Age came along and they freely joined, they did so in touch with their own roots. To cite but one example, California chiropractor John F. Thie and his "Touch for Health" technique (a kinesiological approach based on the work of chiropractor George Goodheart) revisited the Palmer model in New Age dress. Using acupressure (finger pressure to acupuncture points) along with chiropractic, Thie taught a practice that combined metaphysical Asia with metaphysical America. He explained to readers of his textbook/workbook that the chiropractor believed "that the innate intelligence that runs the body is connected to universal intelligence that runs the world, so each person is plugged into the universal intelligence through the nervous system." Turning to Goodheart's work that had preceded his own, he read the development of kinesiology for the restoration of muscular balance as a blend of Western and Eastern modalities. Goodheart had used "earlier chiropractic work and the ancient Oriental practices in the activation of energies in the body." Adopting the methods that Thie now taught would "help prevent malfunctions and pains from developing, as well as correct the reason for the pain and allow the life force to flow uninterrupted throughout the body." Always, he saw his patient/client holistically—"as a whole structural, chemical, and psychological or spiritual being."[36]

Spirit philosophy, however, was the property not only of chiropractors, osteopaths, and other denizens of the vernacular world. At the other end of the cultural spectrum, among the elite, another brand of metaphysics thrived. As early as 1872, a group of young intellectuals began meeting in the shadow of Harvard University at Cambridge, styling themselves, apparently, the Metaphysical Club. The logician and scientist Charles Sanders Peirce was the only one of the group who actually used the name—chosen, he said, "to alienate such as it would alienate"—as he recalled the fortnightly meetings of the club many years later. Still, the name rang historically true. Metaphysics, for the conventional intellectual society of the era, was a pariah term, and—as Louis Menand has written—"agnosticism was then riding its high horse, and was frowning superbly upon all metaphysics." Besides Peirce, members of the "club" included a roster of later luminaries in American intellectual history—men like lawyer and jurist Oliver Wendell Holmes Jr., mathematician and philosopher Chauncey Wright, historian and philosopher John Fiske, and psychologist and philosopher William James. The club soon dissolved (in less than a year), and members went their separate ways, although intersections and friendships continued among them at various points in their careers. Like the earlier Transcendental Club, the talkers in this one (as their putative name suggests) had wanted in their own way to rattle cultural sabers, arming themselves with ideas that challenged the orthodoxies of the day. In science, religion, and philosophy, the Cambridge metaphysicians had found the themes of their discourse. They sought to retain the values associated with traditional religious culture but threw their energies into the confrontation between religion and science and a martial reconstruction of the relationship between the two. Looking for a basis for certainty, they could no longer find it in received religious formulas nor in scientific theories. Rather, it was in scientific *method* that they found the best resource for approaching certainty. They parried with the Darwinian theory of evolution in the midst of their discussions, and out of their discourse came the beginnings of pragmatism in philosophy.[37]

Charles Peirce (1839–1914) had used the term *pragmatism* in a paper for club members, operating on a cue he received from reading Immanuel Kant's classic *Critique of Pure Reason* (1781). He had told them that the intellectual significance of belief lay in its impact and effect on their actions. Very much later, in the first decade of the twentieth century, he would explain that the term *pragmatism* was "invented to express a certain maxim of logic," which would "furnish a method for the analysis of concepts." The method involved tracing out imaginatively "the conceivable practical consequences . . . of the affirmation or denial of the concept" and acknowledging that "herein lies the *whole* of the purport of the word, the *entire* concept." By that time, Peirce's reflections had been stimulated by his felt need to distinguish his ideas from those of his longtime friend William James, who in a lecture in 1898 had used the word *pragmatism* and credited it to Peirce.[38] It is on James's reading of pragmatism and, more, on his deployment of the idea in his encounter with the metaphysical religionists he met that my narrative dwells. As the Cambridge-trained and then Harvard professor James left the earlier Metaphysical Club behind and met the vernacular metaphysicians of his late-century, new-century era, he found that they were worthy enough partners for parrying and that out of the interaction something good could come. His philosophical construct of pragmatism, in fact, was an ideational tool that reflected the religious labor in which they and others were engaged.

William James (1842–1910) had been shaped from childhood to be a religious seeker. His father, Henry James Sr., had been converted in the Second Great Awakening and then reconverted to Swedenborgianism in 1844. The elder James was friends with Ralph Waldo Emerson, knew (the poet) Ellery Channing and Henry David Thoreau, and could match words with Amos Bronson Alcott. He was also a Platonist and had read his share of Charles Fourier, whose thinking probably influenced him enough to name Plato's invisible world of ideas the realm of Divine Love—for a time the elder James was, in fact, an advocate of free love.[39] His oldest son spent his life re-answering the questions his father's seeking raised. But, ironically, William James's contrary answers to his father's world ended by affirming what they denied.

Years before that, however, Henry James Sr.'s religious questing demonstrated for his son the authority of a self uninhibited by received convention. In the educational experience that he gave his son, he replicated the lesson. James Sr. moved William and his brother Henry James Jr. in and out of a series of schools, so that the two together had been enrolled in ten different institutions by 1855. After that, William James experienced several versions of Continental schooling until, in 1861, he matriculated at the Lawrence Scientific School at Harvard. It was 1869, however, before he lasted through an entire degree program and received his M.D. from Harvard (he never practiced as a physician). The effect of what Louis Menand calls this "international hopscotch" was profound. James never learned what it was like to think inside a box. He approached intellectual problems, as Menand argues, "uninhibited by received academic wisdom."[40] Indeed, James had been primed, in the midst of elite culture and with the respected and credentialed status that it gave him, to acknowledge in some ways his simultaneous participation in vernacular culture. Like the New England Transcendentalists who played so important a role in the coalescence of American metaphysical religion, he operated as a professional nonprofessional in religion, cutting a path identifiably separate from received and inherited orthodoxies.

It was at Harvard that James met Peirce and Holmes, with whom he became close friends and with whom he took the initial steps that led to his later philosophy of pragmatism. But after he received his medical degree, he was dogged by depression and illness, both to be chronic visitors in James's later life. Personal psychology thus continued to push him to raise existential questions, using the methods of science to forge a philosophy that could enable him (and others) to live in a world in which the old order no longer held. By 1872 he had begun his long career at Harvard (until 1907), joining the Harvard faculty ostensibly as a lecturer in physiology and anatomy. With an interest in physiological psychology, however, he transferred into philosophy, there creating the charter psychological laboratory in the nation. When his *Principles of Psychology* appeared in 1890, its central concept of a nonseparable link between body and mind, with the mind functioning (pragmatically) as the body's tool, enabled him to achieve his academic reputation. Already the germ of his later philosophy was visible in the textbook, and his later works—often the written versions of his frequent invited lectures—established his authority as the leading voice in American philosophy in his era and perhaps afterward. If so, it was a philosophy that took on the religious questions his culture was asking. *The Will to Believe* (1897), *The Varieties of*

Religious Experience (1902), *Pragmatism* (1907), *A Pluralistic Universe* (1909), and *The Meaning of Truth* (1909) all suggest in their titles the spiritual tenor of his work and ideas.[41]

Important here, the religious questions that James was asking—questions that intersected complexly with the spiritual seeking of his own life—reflect the agenda of American metaphysical religion as it turned toward themes of energy and agency. James had clearly noticed metaphysical religionists before the nineteenth century's end, and he was almost a quiet fellow traveler in their world. Ann Taves notes that James "shared much with new religious movements, such as Spiritualism, Theosophy, and, especially New Thought." She assesses, too, that with "metaphysically informed efforts at mediation" that were "vastly more sophisticated than theirs," he gave "a new legitimacy and prestige to these popular movements." More specifically, as Henry Samuel Levinson remarks, James gleaned his knowledge of the World's Parliament of Religions through Paul Carus's exuberant reports in the *Monist*, a journal that James read "thoroughly." Levinson also notes James's literary acquaintance with Phineas Quimby, about whom he read "curiously." James had apparently made his way through Ralph Waldo Trine's *In Tune with the Infinite*, and he liked it enough to give the book to his son Henry as a birthday present. In 1898, when a medical licensing bill would have prevented mental healers from practicing in the state of Massachusetts, James testified in court on their behalf, arguing that the bill would quash the acquisition of a new kind of medical experience. For all this, he possessed a certain wariness in the face of the new religious orientation, especially when it presented itself with an Asian overlay. He never, for example, visited the Young Men's Buddhist Association when he was in San Francisco, and he continued to express a fear that Asia was a cultural threat to the West.[42]

Yet the metaphysical version of Asia clearly fascinated James. Late in his life, in a lecture significantly titled "The Energies of Men," he cited his own guardedly positive rendition of its spirituality. He thought the "most venerable ascetic system," and the one with "the most voluminous experimental corroboration" for its results, was "undoubtedly the Yoga system in Hindustan." He could bandy yogic terms—Hatha Yoga, Raja Yoga (had he read Blavatsky and/or Swami Vivekananda?), and Karma Yoga—and could declare that the practice of yogic discipline "for years" brought "strength of character, personal power, unshakability of soul." Even further, he told readers about a "very gifted European friend" who for several months fasted "from food and sleep," performed yogic "exercises in breathing and thought-concentration, and its fantastic posture-gymnastics." Thereby he "succeeded in waking up deeper and deeper levels of will and moral and intellectual power in himself" and escaped from a chronic brain condition that had troubled him. But James's friend was a man of "very peculiar temperament," and James judged that few would have the will power to begin his kind of practice.[43]

Hence James himself backed away from metaphysical Asia and turned to metaphysical America to mark the role of ideas in unblocking energies: "We are just now witnessing a very copious unlocking of energies by ideas in the persons of those converts to 'New Thought,' 'Christian Science,' 'Metaphysical Healing,' or other forms of spiritual philosophy, who are so numerous among us to-day. The ideas here are healthy-minded and optimistic; and it is quite obvious that a wave of religious activity, analogous in some respects to the spread of early Christianity, Buddhism, and Mohammedanism, is passing over our American world. The common feature of these optimistic faiths is that they all tend to the suppression of . . . 'fearthought.'"[44]

By the time he wrote these words, James had already, since 1902 and his *Varieties of Religious Experience,* established his definition of healthy-mindedness and explored New Thought under that rubric. There, as in "The Energies of Men," his inquiry operated on the premise of his pragmatism, and in his philosophical stance he modeled, in a sharper, clearer formula, what New Thought people were thinking and doing. James's achievement in *Varieties* was such that the work stood at once as a highly impersonal and highly personal book. As Ann Taves summarizes, it abstracted the mystical core of Christianity.[45] It operated studiously out of scientific canons of disciplined inquiry in psychology, and it used a series of examples to reach its general conclusions. But the intimacies of its lengthy narratives of religious experience belied its scientism, and James's forays into meaning as he assessed his confessional data, especially in his conclusion and postscript, led him to candid revelations of his own religious quest. For unmistakably, what James found in the experiential narratives of his subjects spoke to more than his rationalism.

As a psychologist James had at hand the new category of the subconscious to take the place of the magnetism of trance states and the mediating world of spirit visitors as conduits for revelation. He could explain clairvoyance and suggestion without recourse to supernaturalism or even the blurry naturalism of earlier intellectualizing theories. But James's subconscious—his "transmarginal or subliminal region"—was the gateway to a vaster, larger realm, and it functioned as a container for the kind of material that had formed the substance of religious and mystical revelation. It was "the abode of everything that is latent and the reservoir of everything that passes unrecorded or unobserved." It was "also the fountain-head of much that feeds our religion." "In persons deep in the religious life," he concluded, "the door into this region seems unusually wide open;

at any rate, experiences making their entrance through that door have had emphatic influence in shaping religious history." The language of "reservoir" and "fountain-head" was striking in James's formulation. These were, as we have seen, the chosen metaphors of Ralph Waldo Trine and H. Emilie Cady, at least, and James had used them, in New Thought fashion, to posit a divinizing force and source of revelation within. As he had declared, "metaphysical revelation" was the "farther office of religion."[46]

James's general understanding of religion replicated the theory of correspondence so cherished by metaphysicians. "Were one asked to characterize the life of religion in the broadest and most general terms possible, one might say that it consists of the belief that there is an unseen order, and that our supreme good lies in harmoniously adjusting ourselves thereto." Moreover, as his conclusions about the subliminal already reveal, like the New Thought writers whom he read, James's God was immanent. In a passage that began with a consideration of God in nature and the world around, he turned abruptly to a God-haunted world within: "It is as if there were in the human consciousness *a sense of reality, a feeling of objective presence, a perception* of what we may call 'something there,' more deep and more general than any of the special and particular 'senses' by which the current psychology supposes existent realities to be originally revealed." When he turned specifically to New Thought in what he called the "religion of healthy-mindedness," he cited and quoted New Thought authors Horatio Dresser and Henry Wood, quoted Horace Fletcher on "fearthought," and excerpted several lengthy passages from Ralph Waldo Trine.[47]

Following Francis W. Newman's distinction between the "once-born" and the "twice-born," James identified the mental healers of his day with the once-born.[48] They were optimists, he thought, even in some cases cut off from sadness by a "congenital anaesthesia." They experienced "no element of morbid compunction or crisis," and hence they did not require another and better world to make sense of the one in which they lived. Although this summary ignored the way that metaphysical religion decreed the presence of divine power and plenitude in situations that were often quite the reverse, it did distinguish a habit of discourse in the New Thought community. As James noted, the "advance" of liberal Christianity over a fifty-year period could "be called a victory of healthy-mindedness within the church over the morbidness with which the old hell-fire theology was more harmoniously related." But he was clearly drawn to the "Mind-cure movement" as his case par excellence. Within it, he had noticed "various sects of this 'New Thought'" but found their agreements "so profound" that their differences could be "neglected." (Although he cited Christian Science only once —for its radical denial of evil—he missed the Calvinist-leaning exclusionism of

Mary Baker Eddy's church and linked it, generically, with New Thought as a species of mind-cure.)[49]

James thought the New Thought movement impressively large—"a genuine religious power." He added astutely that it had "reached the stage, for example, when the demand for its literature is great enough for insincere stuff, mechanically produced for the market, to be to a certain extent supplied by publishers." More than that, he could begin to trace the process of cultural diffusion. "The indirect influence of this has been great. The mind-cure principles are beginning so to pervade the air that one catches their spirit at second-hand. One hears of the 'Gospel of Relaxation,' of the 'Don't Worry Movement,' of people who repeat to themselves, 'Youth, health, vigor!' when dressing in the morning, as their motto for the day." James could play the intellectual historian, too, and he cited origins in the Christian Gospels, in "Emersonianism or New England transcendentalism," in "Berkeleyan idealism," and in "spiritism, with its messages of 'law' and 'progress' and 'development.'" Likewise he pointed to "optimistic popular science evolutionism" and Hinduism as movement sources. (In a specific turn to New Thought teachings of divine immanence, he found within them "traces of Christian mysticism, of transcendental idealism, of vedantism, and of the modern psychology of the subliminal self.") But the bottom line, for James, was the sheer practicality of the movement. Mind-cure had spread because of its results, its "practical fruits," which suited the "extremely practical turn of character of the American people." So much so that "their only decidedly original contribution to the systematic philosophy of life" was "intimately knit up with concrete therapeutics."[50]

James quoted the aphorisms of the movement to point to New Thought's message of agency. "'Pessimism leads to weakness. Optimism leads to power.'" "Most mind-curers here bring in a doctrine that thoughts are 'forces,' and that, by virtue of a law that like attracts like, one man's thoughts draw to themselves as allies all the thoughts of the same character that exist the world over. Thus one gets, by one's thinking, reinforcements from elsewhere for the realization of one's desires; and the great point in the conduct of life is to get the heavenly forces on one's side by opening one's own mind to their influx." Yet the paradox of the agency and the flow was that, at its epicenter, it required stillness, "passivity." James had posited a mystical core that implicitly countered the "Don't Worry Movement." Success came through surrender and letting go; it meant resigning "the care of your destiny to higher powers" and "the passage into *nothing* of which Jacob Behmen writes." Mind-curers had, without a conviction of sin, ended in religious states similar to Lutherans and Wesleyans, demonstrating "regeneration by relaxing, by letting go"; giving their "little private convulsive self a rest, and finding that a greater Self is there." Always, though, thoughts were suggestions; they were ideas *with power*, ideas that assumed for individuals "the force of a revelation." For James, the point was that the revelation worked. "The mind-cure movement spreads as it does, not by proclamation and assertion simply, but by palpable experiential results." Totally unscientific and at war with scientific positivism, it yet adopted scientific method in adhering to rule and expecting concrete effects.[51]

Was New Thought then true thought? Were the purveyors of metaphysical Truth, in everyday terms, correct? These questions push the argument into a Jamesian corner where pragmatism sits waiting. For in his pragmatic theory of truth, James in effect gave carte blanche to New Thought practitioners and a host of religionists of other and distinctive stripes. He had told them to keep on doing what they were doing because it led them somewhere that they experienced as good. It would be half a decade more before James's lectures on pragmatism appeared as a book, but he had clearly been thinking and writing under the aegis of pragmatism in his *Varieties* already. When the lectures on pragmatism did come, they captured succinctly his actional theory of truth, which in its outline reflected the agency-based universe of metaphysical religion. In James's theory, as in metaphysical religiosity, energy abounded if a person opened out to it and allowed it to carry the individual to further regions of the mind and back again to this-worldly blessing.

Thus, what needs to be noticed most about James's pragmatic theory of truth is its moral character. It is, quite simply, a moral theory of truth, and as a moral theory of truth it carries the implicit quality of agency. In his essay "What Pragmatism Means," from the collection he called simply *Pragmatism*, James associated his concerns with "the pragmatic method"—a way of "settling metaphysical [here meaning "philosophical"] disputes that otherwise might be interminable." In this context, pragmatic method meant trying to "interpret each notion by tracing its respective practical consequences." What difference would it make if one thing were true rather than another? Citing the Greek derivation of the term *pragmatism*—from the word for "action"—and citing, too, his friend Charles Peirce as the first to introduce the term, he said that, for Peirce, beliefs were "really rules for action." They led to certain forms of conduct, and conduct was their "sole significance." James took Peirce's belief about belief (or at least his understanding of it) and made his own promotion of it something of a cottage industry after 1898. Now he was summarizing his position. In a reading of metaphysics that straddled the worlds of professional philosophy and American metaphysical religion, he linked historic metaphysics (philosophy) to magic because of the power of incantatory words to control a situation—a "spirit, genie, afrite, or whatever the power may be." In the presence of a mysterious universe, words operated to resolve its enigma and so to control and bind, leading the mind to rest. Words like "'God,' 'Matter,' 'Reason,' 'the Absolute,' 'Energy'" were "so many solving names."[52]

By contrast, James pushed toward science and away from what he regarded as magic and its (seductive) restfulness. If a person followed James's pragmatic injunctions, there would be no closing of the metaphysical quest. "You must bring out of each word its practical cash-value, set it at work within the stream of your experience. It appears less as a solution, then, than as a program for more work, and more particularly as an indication of the ways in which existing realities may be *changed*." Theories thus understood became *"instruments not answers to enigmas, in which we can rest."* Here was a resoundingly Protestant reading of value—associated not with contemplation and quietistic gaze but instead with forthright action toward a goal. Drawn to mystical acts of mind that fused far goals with present endeavors, James spoke them in the cultural language of action and effort. Philosophy, like religion, was hard work. The work appeared more spacious, however, when James cited the (later often-noted) corridor theory of truth, borrowed from Italian pragmatist Giovanni Papini. Pragmatism, like a hotel corridor, opened out into numbers of dramatically different "chambers." There could be an atheistic writer in one, a devotee in prayer on his knees in a second, a chemist in a third, an idealist metaphysician in a fourth, an anti-metaphysician in a fifth. All, however, owned the corridor and had to go through it to get to their rooms. Hence James wanted to look away from first things and origins to *"last things, fruits, consequences, facts."*[53]

That established, he went on to call pragmatism not only a method but also "a certain *theory of truth*." Summarizing the position of other logicians as well as his own stance, James was ready now to define: "*Ideas (which themselves are but parts of our experience) become true just in so far as they help us to get into satisfactory relations with other parts of our experience.*" James was also ready to carry his view into the bastions of theology. "*If theological ideas prove to have a value for concrete life,*" he declared, "*they will be true, for pragmatism, in the sense of being good for so much. For how much more they are true, will depend entirely on their relations to the other truths that also have be to acknowledged.*" Still more, James was bent on conflating the age-old Platonic ideas of the good and the true. Truth, he insisted, was "*one species of good*, and not, as is usually supposed, a category distinct from good, and co-ordinate with it. *The true is the name of whatever proves itself to be good in the way of belief, and good, too, for definite, assignable reasons.*"[54] It was patently clear that value—the good—was primary. Psychologist and philosopher James was working as an ethicist.

Read against James's profile of the New Thought universe in *Varieties*, it is likewise clear why James could endorse the New Thought position and run with it. New Thought people were quintessential pragmatists in method and behavior, and James had anyway concluded in *Varieties* that God was "real" because he produced "real effects." Moreover, James's own philosophical method, from one point of view, had mimed the metaphysical reflections of New Thinkers: His subliminal self was their immanent God; his instrumentalism in method was their practice of affirmation and denial; his moralism matched theirs; his option for action resonated with their unblocked energies; his typologizing echoed their theories of correspondence; his mentalism sat easily beside theirs. In the end, though, and ironically, the once-born world was not a place in which he personally—with his life of chronic depression and unease—could reside. His long account of the religion of the "sick-soul" and "morbid-mindedness" plumbed the religion of those who had deeply experienced the evil of their worldly plight and been reborn into a nonnaturalistic realm. Whatever their religious background (but especially in the American revival tradition), he declared for the greater completeness of their world. "The completest religions would therefore seem to be those in which the pessimistic elements are best developed."[55]

Still, at the very least, James had taken a vernacular culture that other professionals of his time and later were ready to discard, had found it worthy of his curiosity, and had begun to investigate its categories and to use them as his thinking tools. The seriousness of that endeavor was revealed in the last two decades of his life in his connection with the London-based Society for Psychical Research, founded in 1882 with an Anglo-American following. James, in fact, had helped to form an American branch of the society in 1884, and by 1890 he was issuing a call to researchers to study trance comparatively. Impressed by the complexity of psychic phenomena, he also, by 1909, acknowledged that the study of psychics themselves was "tedious, repellent, and undignified." That, however, did not stop him from persisting. He was willing to estimate that "in good mediums *there is a residuum of knowledge displayed* that can only be called supernormal." And he thought that there was "a cosmic environment of *other consciousness* of some sort," which was "able to work upon them." He had, he wrote, arrived at "one fixed conclusion" from his experience with psychic phenomena. Humans were like "islands in the sea, or like trees in the forest." Whatever their surface connections, the trees joined roots "in the darkness underground," and so did the islands "through the ocean's bottom." "Just so," there existed "a continuum of cosmic consciousness, against which our individuality builds but accidental fences, and into which our several minds plunge as into a mother-sea or reservoir." James had reversed the New Thought metaphor. But he went on to diagnose the separate selves of his own society and to link his findings to a wider

investigative field that reversed his reversal. "Our 'normal' consciousness is circumscribed for adaptation to our external earthly environment, but the fence is
weak in spots, and fitful influences from beyond leak in, showing the otherwise
unverifiable common connection. Not only psychic research, but metaphysical
philosophy, and speculative biology are led in their own ways to look with favor
on some such 'panpsychic' view of the universe as this."[56]

Seven years earlier, in *Varieties*, James had speculated on the *"farther"* side of
human consciousness after he had explored its nearer side in the personal aspects of the subconscious mind. He had spoken of "over-beliefs" and confessed
his own. Invoking the common testimony of the religious people who had been
his subjects and provided his data, he posited the axiom that they had identified their "real being" with a "germinal higher part." In turn, he had linked the
higher part to *"a* MORE *of the same quality, which is operative in the universe outside."* James wanted to know whether the "more" was "merely our own notion"
or if it really existed, and he had rested the case for its reality on his pragmatism.
The "more" produced effects, and his own over-belief in the God of Christian
culture could proceed apace. Strikingly, like Trine and his New Thought deity,
this God was a God of Energy and Action. The "divine facts" that James could
acknowledge concerned "the actual inflow of energy in the faith-state and the
prayer-state." But there was still a beyond. "The whole drift of my education goes
to persuade me that the world of our present consciousness is only one out of
many worlds of consciousness that exist, and that those other worlds must contain experiences which have a meaning for our life also; and that although in the
main their experiences and those of this world keep discrete, yet the two become
continuous at certain points, and higher energies filter in."[57]

More than that, it followed from the pragmatic rubric that there were plural
worlds of meaning that different people tapped and so that there were different
truths that could be owned. In his exposition of healthy-mindedness, James had
already pronounced the universe "a more many-sided affair than any sect, even
the scientific sect, allows for." He wondered "why in the name of common sense"
he and others needed to "assume that only one such system of ideas can be true."
"Truth *happens* to an idea," he had written in *Pragmatism.* "It *becomes* true, is
made true by events." He had gone on to notice that his narrative was "an account
of truths in the plural, or processes of leading," with only the common quality
that they paid off. It was only the drawing out of the obvious, then, when James
published his Hibbert Lectures at Manchester College under the title *A Pluralistic Universe.* Countering, on this point, the monisms of metaphysical Asia and
metaphysical America alike, James yet ultimately affirmed metaphysical believers. His brief for pluralism and distributiveness ("pluralism lets things really exist

in the each-form or distributively") was also a brief for the habitual practice of combinativeness so cherished among religious metaphysicians.[58]

James was, in one sense, ahead of their game. He was playing affirmatively with the notion that the "each-form" might be "the eternal form of reality no less than it is the form of temporal appearance." And he was finding his "multiverse" still a "coherent world," not a "block-universe" but instead "a universe only strung-along, not rounded in and closed."[59] In so doing, he was, in fact, playing out the premises of his pragmatism, guaranteeing to each and all an equal place in the heavenly kingdom. Unlike Andrew Taylor Still and the Palmers, father and son, who believed that there was only one truth and they had it, James had discovered a metaphysical manyness at the heart of things. If he also smuggled in another monism in the monism of his pragmatic method, he had still played his game memorably. Whatever the philosophical conundrum of circularity with which he contended, his spirit philosophy, like the spirit philosophy of body mechanics, bore the mark of encounter with American metaphysical religion and suggested tellingly its diffusion in national culture and society. The twentieth-century-and-after story was the story of how far the metaphysical flow actually did extend.

CONFIDENT LIVING AND POSITIVE THINKING

"Confident living rights every wrong; / Dynamic power helps me be strong. / Confident living comforts my heart; / From such a blessing I can't depart." "Confident living fulfills my way, / Opens my channels without delay." So runs the refrain and part of one verse of a favorite hymn in Unity churches. The practice-oriented cast of the words, with their references to "dynamic power," comfort, and open channels, points to the payoff that James had found in New Thought metaphysics. That payoff was appropriated by a series of New Thought institutions in the twentieth century and after. These were small denominations, by any measure, and by 2004 they had, quite startlingly, neither been acknowledged nor included in the *Yearbook of American and Canadian Churches*. (Christian Science is also nowhere present.) This in itself is blatant testimony to cultural invisibility. (In recent volumes a "Directory of Selected Faith Traditions in America" lists Jews, Muslims, Baha'is, Buddhists, Hindus, Jains, Sikhs, and even Native American spiritual traditions.)[60] Moreover, it is testimony that may speak to the sociological myopia of the editors or to the apparent unconcern of these groups about being known—or to both. Yet the strongest among the groups—Divine Science, Religious Science, and Unity—all thrived through the twentieth century and into the twenty-first, bringing their versions of confident living to pragmatically tuned metaphysical believers and practitioners.

Divine Science—officially Divine Science Federation International—is based in Denver, Colorado, and is the smallest of the three denominations, with, by the last decade of the twentieth century, only thirty plus congregations in the United States and some centers in Canada, New Zealand, and South Africa.[61] A strong example of the facile networking that characterized New Thought from its beginnings, Divine Science could boast a series of founders—the three Colorado-based Brooks sisters, Alethea Brooks Small, Fannie Brooks James, and, foremost, Nona Lovell Brooks (1862–1945), as well as Malinda Cramer (1844–1906), who gave the movement its name. In 1885 in San Francisco, Cramer, who had been an invalid for twenty-five years, gave up on doctors and determined to get well on her own. After that, according to her own report, she had a felt experience of the omnipresence of God and experienced, too, a sense that she herself was in God. She got well and by 1887 began teaching and also attended a class offered by Emma Curtis Hopkins in the Bay City. Cramer had likewise formed an association with a former Mary Baker Eddy student named Miranda Rice, so she must have been aware of Eddy's teaching.

The same year that Cramer took the Hopkins class, in Pueblo, Colorado, two of the Brooks sisters—Nona and Alethea—became students of Kate Bingham, a teacher who had returned from Chicago, where, she claimed, she had been healed by Hopkins. Bingham's classes, too (and not surprisingly in light of the Hopkins connection), stressed the omnipresence of God. Nona Brooks, who had a troubling throat condition unresponsive to medical treatment, took the Bingham classes and in the course of one of them claimed an experience of white light and sheer presence that left her instantly and completely healed. Meanwhile, the third sister, Fannie Brooks James, studied under Mabel MacCoy, a former Chicago Hopkins student who had first sent Bingham to her teacher there. Immersed in Hopkins teaching and teachers, the three at the same time moved away from the denials of the reality of the material order characteristic of Christian Science and Hopkins-style New Thought, affirming the creation as an expression of God that shared in the divine substance. When Cramer traveled to Denver to teach New Thought classes, Nona Brooks attended, and the two women felt a connection. The name Divine Science came from Cramer, and the Brooks sisters received permission to use it for their teaching. The two streams converged. To the Statement of Being found in one form or another in both Christian Science and New Thought groups (there is no reality but God), Divine Science added the Law of Expression—an agency-oriented formula that stressed the *act* of the creator as manifested in creation. The shift was subtle, but it suggests once again the preoccupation with energy that Trine had signaled and that marked the twentieth-century-and-continuing version of metaphysics so strongly.

In 1892, Nona Brooks formed the International Divine Science Federation, and in 1898 the Divine Science College was incorporated in Denver. With networking intrinsic to its style and with Brooks a prominent speaker at New Thought conventions, by 1922 Divine Science had become part of the International New Thought Alliance. By then, too, its churches were flourishing in West Coast cities and also in midwestern locations like Illinois, Kansas, Missouri, and Ohio, while, in the East, Boston, New York, and Washington, D.C., all became sites for Divine Science churches. The relatively independent congregations in the movement became more formally organized in 1957 with the creation of the Divine Science Federation International. Meanwhile, Divine Science publications kept coming. In former Irish Catholic and Jesuit-trained Emmet Fox (1886–1951), with his metaphysical readings of the Bible and his "Golden Key" of reflecting on God instead of present difficulty, the movement produced one of the most well-known New Thought authors of the Depression years. Tantalizing hints in earlier Divine Science publications, however, suggest extrabiblical sources for its affirmations. Although Cramer—a former Quaker— insisted on personal spiritual experience as the origin of her teachings, J. Stillson Judah long ago pointed to evidence of her acquaintance with Christian Science, Kabbalah, Hermeticism, Theosophy, and Indian philosophy. For Nona Brooks, Hazel Deane's biography cited her awareness of the writings of Phineas Quimby, Warren Felt Evans, Helena Blavatsky, H. Emilie Cady, Ralph Waldo Trine, Henry Wood, and similar authors. But the official story, once again, was that Brooks and her sisters operated with personal experience primary: They picked and chose what supported their intuitions and their work.[62]

By contrast to Divine Science, the roots of Religious Science lay in the experience and teaching of one man. Ernest Holmes (1887–1960), however, in his combinativeness thoroughly reflected the New Thought desire for synthesis that Divine Science also hinted. Holmes, like a series of metaphysical religious leaders before him, did not come to his task equipped with professional training. He never went to college, although his brother Fenwicke Holmes graduated from Colby College in Maine, went on to Hartford Theological Seminary, and became a Congregationalist minister on the West Coast. Fenwicke Holmes, however, would eventually leave the ministry to work with his brother, and it was Ernest Holmes who took the lead in the movement that became Religious Science. Important here, from early on he was apparently an insatiable reader. J. Stillson Judah detailed a series of authors whom Holmes knew, including Emerson and especially his classic essay "Self-Reliance." The future Religious Science founder was familiar with Eddy's *Science and Health*, had read New Thought authors like the affective Hopkins and Cady and the more noetic

Christopher D. Larson and Orison Swett Marden, and was drawn as well to the "Hindu" mysticism of Swami Ramacharaka. By 1915, he had turned his attention to Hermetic materials, the Bhagavad Gita, and even the Persian Zend-Avesta. He was also seeking to synthesize these widely different materials with an Anglo-American literary tradition of reflection that included Emerson, Walt Whitman, William Wordsworth, and Robert Browning. Most of all, he found himself attracted to the English metaphysical writer Thomas Troward (1847–1916), with his triadic understanding of body, conscious mind, and spirit as the stuff of human existence. For Troward and for Holmes, spirit represented both the Universal Mind (God) and the subjective, or unconscious, mind of humans. This subjective mind mediated God's creative power, and it responded to suggestions from the conscious mind to manifest health or illness. Indeed, there was a mechanical quality to the divine operation in this activity, since Universal Mind produced a form in the objective world to match each idea — in Troward's conscious application of what he saw as the Swedenborgian law of correspondences.[63]

As the rationalism of this statement already suggests, Holmes — unlike Cramer and the Brooks sisters — represented a noetic version of New Thought. For him "science" functioned like clockwork and yielded expected results in what Religious Science practitioners later liked to call "scientific prayer." At the same time Holmes had reportedly experienced what was by then being called — after the appearance of the work of Richard Maurice Bucke — "cosmic consciousness." Moreover, by 1924 when he moved to New York for a brief period, he began to visit the elderly Emma Curtis Hopkins and became her last student. Hopkins had by this time, of course, turned thoroughly toward the mysticism that had attracted her throughout her long career, and her mysticism confirmed and intensified the direction in which Holmes was already headed. Charles Braden wrote, in fact, that Holmes considered Hopkins, alongside the thirteenth-to-fourteenth-century German Meister Eckhart, the "greatest of the mystics."[64]

Meanwhile, Holmes's pen had not been idle. He and his brother had early begun the magazine *Uplift*, and they also published their share of books. Ernest Holmes's ambitious work that would become the textbook of Religious Science, however, appeared in 1926, after his turn to mysticism; in its revised and expanded version of 1938 it grew to well over six hundred pages. The work systematically used Holmes's synthesis of Troward and a series of other sources in his own combinative religious declaration. From the start, he had ratcheted up the degree of abstraction in a mode characteristic of noetic New Thought writers. Scriptural quotations and text citations, while present, were minimal. (Much later, in 1957, when J. Stillson Judah asked Holmes if he considered his teaching to be Christian, Holmes hesitated before replying that he was not sure that this was the case.) "There is nothing supernatural about the study of Life from the metaphysical viewpoint," Holmes announced in his introduction. Hailing the "subconscious mind" as the "mental law of our being, and the *creative factor* within us," he affirmed to readers that there was "a *mental law*, working out the will and purposes of our conscious thoughts. This can be no other than *our individual use of that Greater* SUBJECTIVE MIND, *which is the seat of all mental law and action*, and is 'The Servant of the Eternal Spirit throughout the ages.'" Holmes had read Sigmund Freud, and that was apparent. But the formulation was also, in its own way, Jamesian—emphasizing agency, with the subjective, or subliminal, self opened out to an All (although I am aware of no direct evidence that Holmes read William James). At the same time, there was a will-power gloss on the access a person could have to the subliminal, or subjective, and it iterated the message of the enlightened body-self, the enhanced and divinized ego-self that an exoteric American Hermeticism was constructing.[65]

"No mystery" obscured the operation of the Subjective Mind and its mental law, and the "road to freedom" lay "not through mysteries or occult performances, but through the intelligent use of Nature's forces and laws." "Conscious intelligence" marked the spiritual world, and the Subjective functioned as "a world of Law and of mechanical order." It worked in peoples' lives as "largely a reaction, an effect, a way."[66] It was not a person (there went the biblical God), even though often it seemed to act personally. Mind, then, could be approached scientifically because it worked by (old-style, Newtonian) laws. Learn the law and how to manipulate it, and you learned a miracle. Distinguishing between the conscious mind and the subjective mind, Holmes thought that both echoed the "'Eternal Thing' Itself," and he was willing to accord to it the qualities that had traditionally been associated with a divine Person; indeed, he was quite willing to call it God. But God was Energy, and Energy existed to be used: "This Universal Life and Energy finds an outlet in and through all that is energized, and through everything that lives. There is One Energy back of all that is energized. This Energy is in everything. . . . Our thought and emotion is the use we make— consciously or unconsciously—of this original creative Thing that is the Cause of everything." With the "seed of perfection" hidden within, Spirit worked for people by working through them. Surrounded by Mind or Intelligence, humans also existed within it and might "draw from It." However, what was drawn had to come "THROUGH THE CHANNEL OF OUR OWN MINDS." Holmes added that Emerson had advised others to get their "*bloated nothingness* out of the way of the divine circuits."[67]

How did people use these seemingly rarefied propositions? The answer is that they gave themselves "treatments"—with each treatment a strategy of mental interruption and reversal that was expected to alter the course of external events and circumstances. (Both Religious Science and Divine Science practitioners — but not Unity students — spoke of treatments, although people in all three worked in much the same mode.) Holmes explained that a treatment was "a spiritual entity in the mental world" and was "equipped with power and volition." "Operating through the Law," it knew "exactly how to work and what methods to use and just how to use them." The methods, it turned out, were strenuous denials (of undesired conditions) and affirmations (of desired ones), but — and this was the difficult part — experienced not through a clenched determination put into the word but through the opening that the word produced. "We *do not put the power* into this word, but we do let the power of the Law flow through it, and the one who most completely believes in this power will produce the best results."[68] Holmes, for all his abstraction, was willing to provide an example:

> One finds himself impoverished. He wishes to change this condition. He knows that it is not in accord with Ultimate Reality; that the Spirit imposes no limitations. . . . First, he realizes that the Law of Life is a Law of Liberty, of Freedom. He now states that this Law of Liberty is flowing through him and into all his affairs. But the image of his limitation persists. . . .
>
> Right here, he must stop and declare that these images of limitation are neither person, place nor thing; that they have no power, personality nor presence and no real law to support them. He does not believe in them and they cannot operate through him. He is free from their influence, forever. He then begins to fill his thought with the idea of faith, the expectancy of good and the realization of plenty. He senses, and mentally sees, right action in his life. He puts his whole trust in the Law of Good, and It becomes very real to him as he definitely speaks It into being — into his being and into the being of his affairs.[69]

What had happened? For Holmes and Religious Science practitioners, science had triumphed over sense. Looked at from another point of view, though, mental magic had happened — the manipulation of consciousness (instead of the maneuvering of material ritual accoutrements) to obtain a desired result *in the material world*. At the same time, Holmes was recommending mystics to his followers — calling a mystic "one who intuitively perceives Truth and, without mental process, arrives at Spiritual Realization." For nonmystics, (spiritual) evolution advanced similar goals in the "awakening of the soul to a recognition of its unity with the Whole." Its aim was to produce an individual who might "completely manifest the whole idea of life," thus bringing "Unity to the point of particularization." And like Helena Blavatsky and Theosophists, Holmes saw material evolution as the effect of this spiritual evolution. "This reverses the popular belief, declaring that *evolution is the result of* intelligence, rather than intelligence being the result of evolution!"[70] Holmes and his students were having life both ways—drawing energy from mystical systems and, through the mental transformers of will and intent, lighting up lives for enhanced ego-selves. On grounds like this, living could, indeed, be confident, and Religious Science did grow confidently through a series of organizational changes.

As early as 1917, Holmes and his brother had begun what they called the Metaphysical Institute, and Ernest Holmes was ordained to carry on his work by the Denver Divine Science Church. A year after he published *Science of Mind*, however, he established the Institute of Religious Science and Philosophy in Los Angeles. Affiliated institutes sprang up in a loose organizational structure, and eventually the groups began to call themselves churches and the Religious Science Church. By 1949, the International Association of Religious Science Churches was incorporated. However, as the Church of Religious Science took shape out of the older Los Angeles institute alongside other groups and centers, divisiveness erupted over issues of democracy versus central control. Should all—on a Christian Science model—be legal affiliates of the Los Angeles Religious Science Church? Or should a more congregational polity persist? Some—the larger group—chose the first model, and others the second, so that separate organizations resulted and continued. By the last decade of the twentieth century, those in the International Association of Religious Science Churches, which had resisted formal affiliation with the Los Angeles Church of Religious Science and insisted on local control, had become Religious Science International. This organization included over one hundred churches in the United States and five in Canada as members, and it offered enthusiastic support to the International New Thought Alliance. Meanwhile, the Religious Science Church, organized along the lines desired by Holmes and now known as the United Church of Religious Science, had become the majority body. Like Religious Science International a strong supporter of the International New Thought Alliance, it claimed some 270 churches and related groups not only in the United States and Canada but also in thirteen other countries from Central and South America and western Europe (including Britain) to Africa, India, Australia, and the Philippines.[71]

The Unity School of Christianity, however, was at least twice as large. Moreover, the size of its formal organization—both as Unity School and, from 1966, as the Association of Unity Churches—was only a minimal statement of its influence by the last decade of the twentieth century. Melton reported that the Association of Unity Churches could count approximately seventy thousand members, with nearly 550 congregations and over one hundred affiliated study groups in North America alone, while in other countries there were fifty-five congregations and fifty study groups. Still, Unity—even in the early twenty-first century—remained uncomfortable thinking of itself as a denomination. Local churches often pronounced themselves "nondenominational," and the national leadership preferred to think of Unity as a movement.[72] Such ambivalence toward, and even rejection of, denominational status only reiterated Unity's early history. From the first, Unity had invented itself as a broadcast beacon for the printed word, and with its numerous publications—most notably its *Daily Word* (from 1924)—it reached a far wider audience than self-conscious metaphysical believers. Unity's message of confident living, innocuously presented, made its way even into evangelical and fundamentalist households without causing alarm or concern. As we have seen, Unity was the late-nineteenth-century creation of Charles and Myrtle Fillmore in Kansas City, Missouri, and thus—like Divine Science—considerably older than Holmes's movement. It also shared with Divine Science a set of identifications that continued, throughout the twentieth century, to place it squarely within the affective, Hopkins-style New Thought community. Beyond that—unlike Holmes and many Religious Scientists—it always understood itself as thoroughly Christian. Yet, with Charles Fillmore, it absorbed teachings from nineteenth-century Theosophy to turn-of-the-century metaphysical Asia and then, in Fillmore's style, the late-twentieth-century-and-continuing New Age and new spirituality movements.

For all Charles Fillmore's theological facility later, Myrtle Fillmore (1845–1931) led in bringing the pair into the Hopkins orbit and, so, into New Thought (although, like Hopkins, they originally called themselves Christian Scientists). Born Mary Caroline Page of Methodist parents, a graduate of Oberlin College, and later a teacher in Clinton, Missouri, she was nine years Charles Fillmore's senior. The two met in Texas, married, and settled in Colorado in 1881. They moved to Kansas City, Missouri, three years later, and Charles Fillmore began selling real estate there. By 1886, according to her recollection, Myrtle Fillmore believed that she was dying of an inherited tubercular condition along with intestinal and related problems. Medical remedies failed, and Fillmore thought her prospects bleak. Then, however, Eugene B. Weeks, a non-Eddy Christian Science practitioner, came from Chicago to Kansas City to present a course of lectures. Both Fillmores attended, but it was Myrtle Fillmore who was riveted by what she heard. Instead of a familiar tale of family genetics and health weakness, she listened to a new and different account of her ancestry. She was God's child, and that was her "hereditary parentage." "The truth came to me—a great revelation, showing me that I am a child of the one whole and perfect mind, created to express the health that God is." She took the message and, instead of being healed by Weeks, did with it what later became central to Unity teaching: She "applied" it—in a series of persistent affirmations that straddled a line between the will-power teaching of noetic New Thought and a warmer, more affiliative brand of Christianity. "It flashed upon me that I might talk to the life in every part of my body and have it do just what I wanted. I began to teach my body and got marvelous results. . . . I told my heart that the pure love of Jesus Christ flowed in and out through its beatings and that all the world felt its joyous pulsation. I went to all the life centers in my body and spoke words of Truth to them—words of strength and power. . . . until the organs responded."[73]

Charles Fillmore was initially more skeptical, but—already a student of Theosophy and Hermetica—he was impressed by his wife's improvement and gradually came to accept the new metaphysics. He began using affirmative-style prayer for a hip dislocated since a skating accident in his childhood and a stunted leg that had plagued him afterward. (He was later to point to a slow improvement over the years in the condition of the leg and the hip, until, he said, both legs were nearly the same length.) By 1889, he had left his real estate business and begun publishing the magazine *Modern Thought*. The next year he invited Emma Curtis Hopkins to Kansas City to lecture, and then both Fillmores went to Chicago to study at her Christian Science Theological Seminary. They were ordained by Hopkins in 1891. By then, Charles Fillmore had renamed his magazine *Christian Science Thought* and, soon thereafter, simply *Thought*, because of Eddy's legal objections to generic uses of the Christian Science name. By this time, too, Myrtle Fillmore, who had been operating as a spiritual-healing practitioner since her own restoration to health, had thrown herself into the work of prayer ministry, becoming co-central secretary to the Society of Silent Help, which her husband had founded as early as 1889. The pair took the name Unity for their work; a new magazine called *Unity* was begun (*Thought* was incorporated into it four years later); and the prayer ministry became the Society of Silent Unity and later simply Silent Unity. The Fillmores encouraged the formation of local societies of Silent Unity (there were some six thousand members by the mid-1890s), and a message of affirmative prayer and study became the business of Unity. With a growing list of publications and other experiments (the Fillmores started the vegetarian Unity Inn, for example, in 1905), the Unity School of Christianity was incorporated in 1914. By 1922, Unity was on the radio, and two years later it had purchased its own radio station, which operated for a decade, with Charles Fillmore devoting considerable time to radio lecturing. (A radio and television program would be launched again in 1969.) By 1949, Unity headquarters had been shifted to a fourteen-hundred-acre location outside Kansas City, which was developed as Unity Village and continued into the twenty-first century.[74]

If Unity people did not think they belonged to a denomination, they thought of themselves as students, and what they thought they studied in their metaphysical (that is, allegorical) readings of the Bible was practical Christianity. For example, the Unity churches that sprang up considered themselves to be dedicated not to Jesus Christ but to the *teachings* of Jesus Christ. The low Christology of the Unity movement rendered it difficult, anyway, to focus exclusively on the person of Jesus. The man from Nazareth was an elder brother and way-shower, and Unity students believed that the living Christ presence had anointed him and could take over their lives as well. Still more, the discourse community of the movement emphasized that practitioners were, indeed, students. Ministers wore no ministerial robes for Sunday services and provided "lessons," not sermons, for their congregants. Church bulletins sometimes conveniently supplied space for taking notes. Within the churches, organs were out, and pianos and other, lighter instruments were in.

Unity's basic textbook came to be—perhaps surprisingly—not the work of one of the Fillmores but instead the production of the homeopathic physician and student of Emma Curtis Hopkins, H. Emilie Cady (1848–1941). Cady's *Lessons in Truth* began in an invitation from the Fillmores in 1894 to publish a course of lectures on "truth principles" in *Unity* magazine. By 1901, because of a steady demand for the material, it appeared as a book, and so began a history of enduring demand and reprinting. According to Russell A. Kemp, by 1975 it had been translated into eleven languages as well as Braille, and according to Neal Vahle by 2002 it had sold more than 1.6 million copies, thus outselling every other Unity book. Through the years, Unity played fast and loose with the text, altering the order of the chapters and removing material—like a section on "chemicalization" (an Eddy term that signals an agitation and aggravation of old beliefs on their way to dissolution)—that seemed unsuited to a changed and changing time. Unity likewise supplied chapter and verse for biblical texts (which left their King James English for the New Revised Standard Version), whereas Cady did not, and Unity editors even transformed references like "man" to more politically correct language in the late twentieth century.[75]

The somewhat old-fashioned title *Lessons in Truth*, with its suggestion of a fixed order of the universe and an absolute reality, substantial and unchanging, belied to some extent its message of action and energy. Cady, in keeping with metaphysical idealism, did her share of affirming a divine unchangeability, calling God "the underlying substance of all things" and a "principle" that was "unchanging" and "forever uncognizant of and unmoved by the changing things of time and sense." That acknowledged, the reader needed only to turn to Cady's first lesson, "Statement of Being," to find another version of the divine. "God is Spirit, or the creative energy which is the cause of all visible things," Cady announced. "Man," in turn, was "the last and highest manifestation of divine energy, the fullest and most complete expression (or pressing out) of God." Meanwhile, the moving waters Cady had invoked as early as 1891 were there, too. The "one Source of being" was the "fountainhead" and "the living fountain of all good." In metaphors and images that had initially preceded Trine's, God was a "great reservoir"—one that led into "innumerable small rivulets or channels," each of which opened out "into a small fountain." "Continually filled and replenished from the reservoir," each fountain was "itself a radiating center." "The love, the life, and the power which are God," Cady emphasized, were "ready and waiting with longing impulse to flow out through us in unlimited degree." "Stagnation," by contrast, was "death."[76]

Parallels in Cady's language to Trine's images of cleaning out a trough suggest more than a simple transference from one to the other but instead a metaphysical discourse community widely congenial to these metaphors. "A pool cannot be kept clean and sweet and renewed unless there is an outlet as well as an inlet. It is our business to keep the outlet open, and God's business to keep the stream flowing in and through us." "Your greatest work," Cady counseled, "will be done in your own God-appointed channel." Unity students who pored over these agency-oriented dimensions of "Truth" had learned from the start Noah Webster's definition for *spirit* in the contemporary dictionary that Cady was using. "'Spirit is life. . . . It is vital essence, force, energy, as distinct from matter.'" Studying these lessons with the aid of "Question Helps" for each of the chapters, they could arrive at a perception of metaphysical teaching in which the unchanging was yet the ever-moving.[77] They would be primed for the active work of prayer.

For besides studying, Unity students prayed. For them, prayer meant, first, "entering the silence," in which—as in the hymn—they sought to have their "channels" opened and receptive to a divine presence within. Only after they experienced a felt sense of connection were they instructed to continue to the next stage of prayer—the denials (of what was undesirable) and affirmations of the desired outcomes that they considered to be aligned with Truth. Like other mental healing practitioners, they decreed what they regarded as good and expected outworkings and manifestations. On these terms, Silent Unity was drawn into a national prayer ministry, using a developing technology to advance its work. By the late twentieth century, a twenty-four-hour prayer telephone line was available (and more recently a website), and people who had no formal relationship to Unity were often users. A cadre of Silent Unity prayer workers held requests in prayer for thirty days, sent letters to callers, and encouraged people in general to engage in prayer, as in the annual World Day of Prayer that by the end of the century was being promoted. Prayer workers, from the time of the Fillmores, stopped all activity to engage in regular periods of prayer throughout the day. There were legendary tales about how May Rowland, director of Silent Unity from 1916 to 1971, refused to leave the Silent Unity prayer tower during a tornado alert. Prayer, for Rowland and other students of Unity, was the chief vehicle for harnessing their own divine energy and bringing it to bear on practical situations.

Unity's *Daily Word*—a small monthly pamphlet with a daily affirmation, short related discourse, and scriptural verse—above all promoted affirmative prayer and practice. From the first, it touched a popular core, with a circulation totaling over 144,000 by 1928, some 182,000 a decade later, and nearly 400,000 in 1948. By 2002, according to Neal Vahle, it had 1.2 million subscribers and was available in eight languages and in Braille. These readers, obviously, had to be mostly non-Unity students, since, as we saw, the membership rolls of Unity churches have been vastly smaller. English-language editions of the *Daily Word*, at least, came in regular and large-type versions, and subscription rates were nominal. Always, the telephone number for the Silent Unity prayer line was prominently printed on the inside front cover, along with, in the computer age, the Unity website address. One recent "word," for example, begins with the affirmation "God's healing love is flowing through me as forgiveness." Providing the word "Forgive" as a brief marginal keyword for practice, the short affirmative meditation—written in the first person—ends with the declaration "My heart is once again a clear, unobstructed channel for God's healing love that flows through me and from me." The scriptural verse that follows (Luke 23:34) quotes Jesus asking his father to forgive his persecutors.[78] Clearly, the reader is being asked to emulate Jesus the teacher, putting the message into practice for the day at hand.

Indeed, a short list of Unity beliefs—ideas about the one presence and power of God everywhere, about a living Christ presence within, about the creative power of thought and the demonstrable effects of prayer—always includes an emphasis on practice. Unity principles *work*, devotees have insisted. Their insistence has linked them to the energy metaphors and preferences of twentieth-century New Thought even if, for most of the century, their official organization had no formal connection with the International New Thought Alliance. Charles Fillmore, for example, thought the divine energy within to be so powerful that physical immortality could result, and early Unity students embraced reincarnation beliefs as a first step toward their immortal futures. After the smashing of the atom and the demonstrated power of the bomb, Fillmore wrote that "the next achievement of science will be the understanding of the mental and spiritual abilities latent in man through which to develop and release these tremendous electrons, protons, and neutrons secreted in the trillions of cells in the physical organism. . . . It is through release of these hidden life forces in his organism that man is to achieve immortal life, and in no other way."[79]

Fillmore read the Gospel accounts of Jesus in analogous terms, using notions of the atom that he had conceived at least as early as 1912 and interpolating them with theosophical ideas. For the resurrection, Fillmore could explain the narrative in natural terms because Jesus had "simply unloosed the dynamic atoms of His whole body and released their electrical energy. This threw Him into the fourth dimension of substance, which He called the 'kingdom of the heavens.'" (The *"fourth dimension,"* reported Fillmore, was "a state of existence that popular material science says must be, in order to account for the effects that are being expressed on every side.") At the same time, in a theosophical gloss on Christian teaching, Fillmore invoked the "twelve powers of man"—what he called aspects of the "Subconscious realm" that were correlated to twelve centers in an idealized male body, much on the order of occult renditions of Kabbalistic charts depicting the power centers of the Sephiroth. Always, Jesus provided the metaphysical template, and the "soul development" of Jesus demonstrated what human growth and development should be. The highest center in Fillmore's Christian scheme was an "I Am" center at the crown of the head ("where phrenology locates spirituality," he explained). Humans could look toward the "second coming of Christ" in "the awakening and the regeneration of the subconscious mind through the superconscious or Christ Mind."[80]

The sacred technology for awakening and regeneration, in turn, came through the power of words. In Fillmore's first book, *Christian Healing* (1909), he pointed to the Genesis account of God's "original creative Word" and declared that humans could not know "how the thought, or Word, works" except through their own consciousness. From there he invoked the spoken word, which, he told readers, "carries vibrations through the universal ether, and also moves the intelligence inherent in every form, animate or inanimate." This power of the word, he said, was given to be used, and humans had the power "to deny and dissolve all disintegrating, discordant, and disease-forming words." "It is your duty as expresser of the divine law," he enjoined, "to speak forth the Logos, the very word of God, and cause the Garden of Eden, the everywhere present Mind-Substance, to manifest for you and in you in its innate perfection." Always, in circular fashion, the word led back to prayer. Writing about her long experience as director of Silent Unity, May Rowland remarked in 1961, "We feel that our prayers are effective because we speak the truth about you." Fillmore himself had long before written that "the secret of demonstration is to conceive what is true in Being and to carry out the concept in thought, word, and act." Thus Fillmore's prayer became, in the terms of this narrative, the highest form of mental magic: "If I can conceive a truth, there must be a way by which I can make that truth apparent. If I can conceive of an inexhaustible supply existing in the omnipresent ethers, there is a way by which I can make that supply manifest." Again and again, the path to realization came through the articulated word, the word of prayer: "Every word is a thought in activity, and when spoken it goes out as a vibratory force that is registered in the all-providing substance."[81]

Fillmore could have added, by extension, the printed word. Unity's steady supply of the same—often, as we have seen, to an audience only peripherally related to Unity School—became an important factor in the spread of New Thought belief and practice in society at large. It did so by providing a word with an identity tag that could not be recognized, a word that consorted amicably with whatever else resided in peoples' minds. But in this Unity was not alone. If all of New Thought was thoroughly inept in producing denominations, in the end it found a better way to spread its spirituality. It disappeared. It became a part of general culture, so that by effacing its own logo it successfully shaped American mentality in marked and continuing ways. This is not to say that, through some vast conscious or unconscious missionary plot, it benumbed and beguiled an unsuspecting populace. Rather, New Thought had goods for sale that Americans wanted. It told them what they were inclined to hear, confirming them in their already-present suspicion of the divine status of their secret selves. Now New Thought was inviting them to make the secret public. Thoroughly discounting the dark recesses of the Freudian unconscious, New Thought's inner halls of light only confirmed the exoterics of American identity. Purveyors of democracy and freedom for all, leaders of the world's first and most successful revolution, Americans thought well of themselves, and the message of inner divinity and outer power supported their self-conceptions.

Positive thinking took over where confident living left off. Gradually, outside the denominations especially, the affective side of New Thought began to yield to an aggressive noetic presence, as New Thought authors and their imitators did exactly what William James said they were doing: Because of the size of the demand, they flooded the market with readily available and repetitive instruction manuals for success, "mechanically produced" and driven by the pecuniary desires of publishers. Whether or not it was "insincere stuff," as James alleged, is more difficult to tell. There was an easy glide from conviction and enthusiasm into the comfortable company of a cash cow. At the same time, drawing the line from the perspective of the twenty-first century for authors about whose lives little is known seems perverse and wrongheaded. Still, early-twentieth-century contemporaries were certainly making their judgments about right and wrong, with affective and Christian-identified metaphysical religionists casting critical glances at their brasher neighbors. Charles Fillmore, for example, warned against selfish use of his "electronic fire." Employed for self-serving purposes, it became "destructive" because of the "crosscurrents" that it set up "in the nervous system."

He adamantly opposed encouraging "those who still have worldly ambitions to take up the development of the twelve powers of man." Readers would be "disappointed" if they sought "to use these superpowers to gain money" or "control others" or "make a display of . . . power."[82]

One of the brasher New Thought neighbors was surely William Walker Atkinson, whom we have met before with his Anglo-American surname and also as Swami Ramacharaka. His titles did indeed flood the market of his day as commodities selling other commodities—success, happiness, and health achieved through the power of thought and will. Even at this writing Amazon.com advertises twenty-one works by Atkinson (as Atkinson) readily available in inexpensive reprints through Kessinger Publishing. A master of combinative discourse, Atkinson in his agency-oriented titles and their contents straddled lines between New Thought, Theosophy, magical practice, metaphysical Asia (here as Atkinson *without* the Ramacharaka pen name), and what would later emerge as positive thinking. Consider, for instance, his *Thought-Force in Business and Everyday Life,* evidently his first published book and suggestive of a background that included business. Published in both Chicago and London in 1901, it was reprinted in Chicago and New York in 1903, reprinted again in 1911 and 1913, and available in Russian by 1910. According to Atkinson's counting, the New York edition of 1903 was the eighteenth. Be that as it may, the short work of just over one hundred pages announced itself to be a "Series of Lessons in Personal Magnetism, Psychic Influence, Thought-Force Concentration, Will Power, and Practical Mental Science." Its partial contents included the topics of vegetarianism, celibacy, and deep breathing (suggesting a yogic influence), but also sections on the power of the eye and magnetic gaze as well as "volic force" (that is, will power) and direct and telepathic "volation." Atkinson wanted to show readers how "thought force" could aid them, and he was interested in "character building" by the use of "mental control" gained through the "art and practice of concentering." His notions of gaze and will hinted, too, of an older mesmeric model transformed for new times and situations.[83]

Atkinson's *Thought Vibration* (1906), subtitled evocatively enough *The Law of Attraction in the Thought World,* in another short work (less than 150 pages) aimed to instruct readers on thought waves and their reproduction, conflating notions of "mind building" and secrets of the "will."[84] Using the law of gravity as model, Atkinson explained thought waves in the context of waves of light, heat, magnetism, and electricity, finding the difference that marked these diverse waves of energy to be in their vibratory rates. For Atkinson, hidden frequencies existed in the world of light and sound vibration, and humans had only to wait the day when better honed scientific tools could locate them. Against this backdrop, the task became to raise the level of one's inner mental vibrations through the exercise of will power. Training was required to attain mastery, and mastery would mean that the "I" could command the mind with the will as its tool. How did a person do that? The answer came through the New Thought technique of affirmation. It all worked by law, and by working in concert with law a person could become immune to injurious thoughts and negative feelings.

Atkinson's habit of combination had led him to a remarkable synthesis between Theosophy and New Thought. The theosophical disdain for control of trance mediums by spirits had transmuted into an active war against control of the mind by an undisciplined and destructive internal dialogue. The New Thought weapon to still the assault was the practical technique of affirmation. Between the two—Theosophy and New Thought—lay a universe of blended discourse about magnetism and science and also about the occult and magic. For Atkinson was headed toward a conscious espousal of mental magic—the manipulation of (subconscious) mind by the overt control and intention of the (conscious) mind to attain ego goals and desires. The enlightened body-self of metaphysical Asia and its erstwhile enthusiasts were being led seductively down a primrose path of desire, vulnerable to the goals of a self-aggrandizing and less-than-enlightened ego even as it understood itself to be building "character."

Atkinson rendered the magical ambience of his work still more explicit in the title of a book he published the following year. *The Secret of Mental Magic* provided seven lessons to teach readers how to become mental magicians, experts at mental healing and suggestion. He speedily followed up the same year with *Mental Fascination*, which declared itself a "supplement or sequel" and purported to give "special instruction" to "students" of the earlier book. It was in *Mind-Power* (1912), however, that Atkinson produced probably the most comprehensive work (it was nearly 450 pages long) that dealt with his version of mental magic. Here the energy quotient was raised to new heights as he invoked the "mental dynamo," explained the nature of mental power and "mentative induction," and pursued the issue of "mental magic" in animal and human life. Atkinson was interested in "personal magnetism" and "channels of influence," and he offered readers four varieties of suggestion to assist them. As in other works, he traveled with an awareness of danger. The "malicious animal magnetism" of the late-nineteenth-century world had entered a new domain of occultism, and Atkinson solicitously provided a "glimpse" of the "occult worlds," even as he taught self-protection in dangerous territory and gave instruction on mental healing and "mind-building."[85]

"Entering the silence" did not function as a rhetorical trope in Atkinson's world. Nor did lengthy disquisitions on the divine source of all. Instead, he had discovered divinity at first hand, and it was mostly male and pointedly operative in a world of ego-driven goals and successes. If Hermeticism had gone exoteric in the mass spiritualism of the nineteenth century, it was becoming thoroughly secular in Atkinson's rendition, in which the secrets of revelation had become affirmations of agency and control. The ego-friendly manipulation of success would continue as other and later business enthusiasts latched onto his formulas and those of a small army of similar New Thought authors. Together they provide one expression, at the margin, of what happened to New Thought. In fact, the experience of Ralph Waldo Trine when he visited Henry Ford in 1928 already suggests what could result. Trine, the old socialist, found himself swept into the orbit of the charismatic capitalist and reported billionaire who had read *In Tune with the Infinite* and declared for its efficacious support when he was struggling to build the Ford Motor Company. Trine's published account of their meeting shows that he was transfixed—even mesmerized—by the objectified emblem of what his book had apparently done.[86]

We gain some insight into the runaway transformation of the New Thought gospel if we contrast the Depression-era work of Charles Fillmore called simply *Prosperity* (1936) with Napoleon Hill's *Think and Grow Rich* (1937), which promised to reveal the (Andrew) Carnegie "secret" of getting rich. Like his teacher Emma Curtis Hopkins, Fillmore remained essentially unconcerned about acquisition but expected the divine Supply to provide all that he needed, with some to spare. In a covenant that he and Myrtle Fillmore had signed as early as 1892, they had dedicated themselves and their money to the "spirit of Truth" and the "Society of Silent Unity." They understood and agreed "that the Said Spirit of Truth shall render unto us an equivalent for this dedication, in peace of mind, health of body, wisdom, understanding, love, life and an abundant supply of all things necessary to meet every want without our making any of these things the object of our existence." In 1936, Fillmore's teaching was much the same, if elaborated considerably more. The lessons in his book *Prosperity*, he volunteered, were intended "to explain man's lawful appropriation of the supplies spiritually and electrically provided by God." "When we understand and adjust our mind to the realm or kingdom where these rich ideas and their electrical thought forms exist we shall experience in our temporal affairs what is called 'prosperity.'" It was all scientific, and it was all based on vibratory laws, as Fillmore saw it. The ether existed as an "emanation of mind," and Jesus had anticipated these discoveries of modern science, calling the ether the "kingdom of the heavens," which it was the divine "good pleasure" to bequeath to humans.[87]

What did all of this mean in practice? With "man" as "the inlet and outlet" of the divine mind, humans needed to begin to liquidate their debts first mentally.

Debts had been "produced by thoughts of lack, impatient desire, and covetous-ness." When these thoughts were "overcome," a new train of events would be set in motion. Avoiding "'easy-payment plans,'" a debtor should bless creditors "with the thought of abundance," knowing that God was the "unfailing resource" and "infinite and unfailing supply." Change your thinking, Fillmore instructed, and you changed your outer situation, since "outer things" conformed "to the inner pattern." Still more (and suggesting the evangelical world from which many New Thought converts no doubt came), one should tithe, providing one tenth of one's resources "for the upkeep of some spiritual work or workers. . . . set apart first even before one's personal expenses" were "taken out." Far from it being "unthink-able to connect the teaching of Jesus with the counting house and the market place," the "lofty teachings" of the Gospels were "the most practical rules for daily living." In that context, an idea had "the power of building thought structures, which in turn materialize in the outer environment and affairs and determine every detail of . . . existence." In Fillmore's version of the by-now-familiar New Thought metaphor, he told readers, "Your consciousness is like a stream of water. If the stream is in any way dammed up, the water settles in all the low places and becomes stagnant. The quickest way to purify and reclaim the low, 'swampy' places in your consciousness is to let in the flood from above by opening the dam." Nor, once the waters came, should people try to contain them. In his own theoretical expression of the socialism of the early Trine and a series of other early New Thought leaders with affective leanings, Fillmore cast his vote for an eco-nomic order that went considerably beyond Franklin Delano Roosevelt's New Deal. "The divine law holds that the earth is the Lord's and the fullness thereof. If this truth were thoroughly understood, men would begin at once to make all property public, available for the use and enjoyment of all the people."[88]

By contrast to Fillmore's law of flow and electrical energy with the (tithed) abundance of the kingdom distributed to all, Napoleon Hill gave his "Andrew Carnegie" version a year later in *Think and Grow Rich*, a book that, according to Donald Meyer, in twenty-one years went through twenty-eight printings. Meyer, calling the Hill work an example of a drift toward "magical psycho-science," has pointed to a "matching audience" of "men on the fringe" for this and similar efforts.[89] If these men were down, author Hill was decidedly upbeat. He had from early life been drawn to the achievements of Carnegie as well as other icons of the times such as Thomas Edison and Alexander Graham Bell. Hill's Hermetic secret had been confided to him over half a century before by Carnegie and had also been passed to thousands of others.

The secret was a secret for success at *accumulation*. It concerned the basic idea behind a series of techniques and strategies that would enable practitioners to acquire "vast fortunes through the aid of the Carnegie secret." Like Fillmore and all of the New Thought metaphysicians, Hill considered thoughts to be "things" and things with agency. They were "powerful things" when they were "mixed with definiteness of purpose, persistence, and a burning desire for their translation into riches, or other material objects." Indeed, desire represented the "starting point of all achievement" and the "first step toward riches." But the second step, perhaps surprisingly, was faith, and it was here that the metaphysical overlay of Hill's method became apparent. If faith was the "head chemist of the mind," as he declared, when it was "blended with thought," the "subconscious mind" got the "vibration" and transmitted it to "Infinite Intelligence, as in the case of prayer." More than that, when faith was blended with the emotions of love and sex, the three together had "the effect of 'coloring' thought" so that it immediately reached "the subconscious mind, where it [was] changed into its spiritual equivalent, the only form that induces a response from Infinite Intelligence." The Almighty, or its New Thought equivalent, was, in effect, being programmed to respond according to (business) plan. How was faith developed in order to start the action of the Infinite? The answer was familiar: It was accomplished by "autosuggestion," and autosuggestion happened through the disciplined use of affirmations. "*Repetition of affirmation of orders to your subconscious mind is the only known method of voluntary development of the emotion of faith.*" When emotions were mixed with faith or any other feeling, Hill told readers, they got "magnetized" and attracted harmonizing vibrations, an assessment with which Fillmore could agree.[90] Always, however, Hill's plan was a plan of accumulation.

Hill invited readers to lie in their beds at night envisioning how much money they wanted to acquire, seeing it already in their possession, and stating, as a kind of contract with the universe, what service or merchandise they would provide in return. Meanwhile, what was needed for the successful execution of the dream was the "power of the master mind." Here knowledge and effort were to be coordinated "in a spirit of harmony, between two or more people" for attaining the financial goal. The human mind was "a form of energy," Hill explained, and part of it was "spiritual in nature." Coordinating the "spiritual units of energy of each mind" formed an "affinity," and that constituted the "'psychic' phase of the Master Mind." Why was that important? It brought the power of the many to the service of the self. In a bow to vernacular Freudianism, even sexuality could be transmuted to the service of the self's acquisitive goal, fueling it with a stimulus and energy that could provide "a super power for action." In the midst of this, prayer functioned as a necessary assist for the subconscious mind, provided that it broadcast, like a well-tuned radio, the right radio waves for Infinite Intelligence. The brain, as the "broadcasting and receiving station," could pick up the thought vibrations not only of the Infinite but also of other minds, and Hill endorsed the principle of telepathy, seeing it at work at successful conference tables. Even, for all the manipulation, there was a "sixth sense"—a "door to the temple of wisdom"—by means of which "Infinite Intelligence" might and would "communicate voluntarily, without any effort from, or demands by, the individual."[91]

Basic fears—and especially the fear of poverty—needed to be abolished. Always, however, the Carnegie secret lay in the idea.[92] And the idea, as Hill would have it, was the idea of having and holding. Arguably, metaphysical "energy" had been dammed in the Hill preoccupation with acquisition, and—while the Infinite still supervised the project—for the most part the Infinite was now subject to ego control. A balance had tilted, and the precarious enlightened body-self, with its enhanced ego goals, had been nudged toward a more focused mode of activity and toward less metaphysically oriented ego goals. Hill, in effect, had flirted with metaphysical religion and in the end kidnapped it for a marginal enterprise. Metaphysics, however, could travel a less purely acquisitive path in mid-twentieth-century America, one that looked more broadly to a series of goals that included material prosperity but also peace and tranquility of mind for millions. The purveyor par excellence of this brand of metaphysical spirituality was Norman Vincent Peale (1898–1993).

Born in small-town Ohio of Methodist parents (his father was a Methodist circuit minister), Peale graduated from Ohio Wesleyan University and, after a stint in journalism, went back to school at Boston University School of Theology. In the middle of his studies, he was ordained to the Methodist ministry in 1922 and after five years at a church in Brooklyn, New York, accepted a call to University Methodist Church in Syracuse. Then, with a growing reputation and offers from both a Methodist church in Los Angeles and the (Dutch) Reformed Church in America's Marble Collegiate Church in New York City, Peale in 1932 chose Marble. He remained there for a long and distinguished career until he retired in 1984. However, as his biographer Carol George has observed, even though Peale switched denominations officially, the traditional Methodist culture in which he had thrived never really left him. His mature message, as it took shape at Marble, brought the liberal (Arminianized) Methodist tradition together with Calvinist language, an evangelical style, and conservative politics. As important, Peale would gradually bring to the combination a clear orientation to metaphysical spirituality. As long before as his years at Ohio Wesleyan, he had been drawn to Emerson and James. Already the mystical theology of the divine presence, mediated by the personalism of Borden Parker Bowne, was part of Peale's background; in his Boston seminary days Bowne was in the ascendant. Later, by 1928 while he was at the Syracuse church, Peale became acquainted with New Thought literature, gradually moving, as George explains, "from a mystical Methodism to a form of New Thought." It would be 1949, at Marble, however, before he would publicly come to endorse positive thinking along metaphysical lines.[93]

Nor was Peale secretive about his sources. In *Spirits in Rebellion*, for example, Charles Braden recalled the rumors he had heard from New Thought friends that Ernest Holmes had once visited Marble Collegiate. According to Braden's hearsay evidence, after the service Peale greeted the founder of Religious Science "as one he knew and deeply respected from the reading of his writings." Braden had also heard of Peale's "at least indirect contacts" with Unity. With these pieces of information as background, he wrote Peale a letter querying him about his New Thought connections, and, to his surprise, he received not a letter in answer but a telephone call. Peale owned that he had read the New Thought material and had found much that he felt was valuable but—in the same combinative fashion preferred by metaphysicians—had worked it into his own system. He referred Braden to his book *The Tough-Minded Optimist*, in which one of the chapters ("Never Be Afraid of Anybody or Anything") provides autobiographical reminiscences on Peale's formation. Yes, as the account reveals, Peale had discovered a certain kind of "'spiritual literature' which he found was increasingly getting into the homes of his people." It was emanating, among other places, from Unity, Religious Science, Science of Mind, Christian Science, and a series of metaphysically inclined teachers.[94]

Marble Collegiate Church, like Peale's previous two churches, grew spectacularly during his tenure; he brought a small and declining congregation into a situation of overflow, with crowds coming to hear his preaching. He traveled, he formed organizations, and he started to write. His *Guideposts* magazine, a monthly in the style of *The Reader's Digest*, from 1945 gave what has been called "Pealeism" a public face throughout the country. With "More than a magazine" as its motto, by the 1950s it had created a national prayer center with Silent Unity as its model. Subscriptions grew apace: 200,000 before the publication of *The Power of Positive Thinking* in 1952; 500,000 in 1953; a million in 1961; 2 million in 1973. "Through contacts in religion, politics, business, and industry, he was creating circles of supporters that collectively formed a vast national network, essentially the constituent part of the Phenomenon of Pealeism," says George. "It was indeed a phenomenal creation: Like an octopus, it gradually developed tentacles that reached deeper into new areas of popular culture." Peale's career was, as George assesses it, a "bellwether for major cultural realignments in the twentieth century, his priorities more symptom than cause of great subterranean shifts at work reconstituting the social landscape." Ironically, the shifts at work had brought to Peale's huge, far-flung congregation not the solitary businessmen living out their "motel theory of existence" whom he had hoped to reach. Instead, after 1952 his audience became predominately middle-class and middle-aged women, and they mostly counted themselves mainstream evangelical Protestants.[95]

In time Peale would author well over forty books. But far and away the most widely known was his inspirational best seller *The Power of Positive Thinking*, the work accorded first-place status in Louis Schneider and Sanford Dornbusch's classic study of major American inspirational books from 1875 to 1955. (Trine's *In Tune with the Infinite* held second place.) From a set of statistics published in 1956 by Alice Payne Hackett, Schneider and Dornbusch cited 2 million copies of Peale's book sold. These mid-1950s statistics on the sales success of *The Power of Positive Thinking*, however, would be thoroughly eclipsed by the data of later years. According to Carol George, by the late 1980s the book had reached sales of over 15 million copies, and it still could be counted one of the top ten books on self-improvement on the market.[96]

What had so moved readers to keep buying the book and to recommend it, apparently, to others? To note, as J. Stillson Judah did, that—like the books with, usually, the "greatest appeal" in the Schneider-Dornbusch study—it "contained concepts like those of New Thought" is perhaps to posit a truism. It is also to miss the agential and pragmatic nature of what Peale was delivering. He was offering seekers from mainstream churches a set of simple, practical techniques that, presumably, they could readily use to change their lives miraculously. He was claiming not a theological breakthrough but an easy way to efficacy and power. In a book that he declared was written "for the plain people of this world" and "with deep concern for the pain, difficulty and struggle of human existence," Peale hoped to show them how they could cultivate "peace of mind" not as "escape" but as "a power center out of which comes driving energy for constructive personal and social living." Moreover, in a discourse style that made him seem like a veritable student of Unity, he testified that the book was conceived and delivered in a context of prayer. "This book is written to suggest techniques and to give examples," Peale had begun in his introduction. He was offering readers "simply a practical, direct-action, personal-improvement manual." Still further, the how-to principles he provided were not of his invention but given "by the greatest Teacher who ever lived and who still lives."[97]

The principles abounded. So did the examples, and—strikingly for a book that came to have a largely female audience—the examples betrayed a decidedly male bias. It did not seem to matter, though. Anecdotes ambled their way through the pages of the book as just-so stories of good times come out of bad, peace out of turmoil, success out of failure, self-discipline out of addictive behavior. Formulaic and pat, they recommended a tripartite approach to any problem: affirm the desired good; visualize it; believe it. And it would come. The metaphysical preference for affirmative prayer—with affirmations repeated many times over —controlled these pages, and so did New Thought metaphors of God as an in-streaming, activating energy that moved through individuals when they called on higher power or had it mediated to them by another. In one story of his en-counter in a midwestern city with a depressed and lethargic man in a hotel room, Peale remembered a remarkable turn of events: "I sought for guidance and found myself, quite to my surprise, standing beside him and placing my hand upon his head. I prayed, asking God to heal the man. I suddenly became aware of what seemed to be the passing of power through my hand which rested upon his head. I hasten to add that there is no healing power in my hand, but now and then a human being is used as a channel, and it was evidently so in this instance, for pres-ently the man looked up with an expression of the utmost happiness and peace and he said simply, 'He was here. He touched me. I feel entirely different.'"[98]

The Unity prayer practice of entering the silence was here: People who lacked peace of mind were enjoined to "practice emptying the mind," and they were urged to the "daily practice of silence." "Everyone should insist upon not less than a quarter of an hour of absolute quiet every twenty-four hours," Peale insisted. After the silence, or in it, came prayer and visualization. "Do not always ask when you pray, but instead affirm that God's blessings are being given, and spend most of your prayers giving thanks." In meditation, "sit relaxed," and "think of your mind as the surface of a lake in a storm" until "now the waves subside." Then "spend two or three minutes thinking of the most beautiful and peaceful scenes you have ever beheld," and "repeat slowly . . . words which express quietness and peace." After that, he told readers, they should repeat the words of Isaiah 26:3: "'Thou wilt keep him in perfect peace, whose mind is stayed on thee.'" Mean-while, the New Thought habit of denial accompanied the Peale advice: "Never mention the worst. Never think of it. Drop it out of your consciousness."[99]

Peale recommended Emerson, James, and Thoreau to his readers, and he especially noted as Emerson's "fundamental doctrine" the idea that "the human personality can be touched with Divine power and thus greatness can be released from it." Similarly, James had pointed to the power of belief, and Thoreau had evoked as the "secret of achievement" holding "a picture of the successful out-come in mind." Again and again, Peale repeated to readers his New Thought message of higher power. "This power is constantly available. If you open to it, it will rush in like a mighty tide. . . . This tremendous inflow of power is of such force that in its inrush it drives everything before it, casting out fear, hate, sick-ness, weakness, moral defeat, scattering them as though they had never touched

you, refreshing and restrengthening your life with health, happiness, and goodness."[100]

Yet for all his embrace of metaphysical discourse and his reiteration of what
were essentially Hermetic and mesmeric metaphors, Peale was careful to circum-
scribe them to the pragmatics of method. He made no announcement of direct
divine presence within, no testimony to God living within you as you, no affirmation of the great "I Am" thriving at the crown of the head and within one's
being. Peale was stealing mystical results, like a latter-day Jason stealing a golden
fleece, but the full mystical union in which humans felt themselves to be God—
the union so precarious and problematic for orthodox Christianity—was evaded
and suppressed. Instead, a doctrinally conventional biblical God came from outside to offer help and salvation to the floundering individual who called upon
him. All was, on that score, evangelical and even Calvinist, and Peale could feel
that all was well. The critics, however, could not. Clerical and academic alike,
they issued a hue and cry when Peale's book appeared seemingly everywhere
and became wildly successful in vernacular culture. What George calls a "savage
critical attack" nearly convinced him to resign from Marble Collegiate: Only his
dying father's wish persuaded him to stay.[101]

Like Mary Baker Eddy, whose Christian Science brought her the wrath of
orthodox churchmen and other contemporaries, Peale faced the disdain of the
sophisticated in church and not-so-church contexts for his plebeian efforts,
deemed corrosive to (their) culture and to theological thought. Indeed, Peale's
hard times raise questions about the easy feminist assumption that Eddy faced
the lash of culture mostly because she was a woman speaking and acting with authority. Instead, placed beside the experience of Eddy, Peale's similar problems
suggest that what drove critics was that both authors saw their work as faithfully
within the bounds of a larger orthodoxy. Both hybridized their metaphysics to
older, existing constructions within Christianity—for Eddy her Calvinist heritage, however much she rejected Calvinist predestination; for Peale his Methodist warmth and evangelicalism in a traditional Gospel culture. In Peale's case,
those outraged by the wolf within the sheepfold said that Pealeism did not really
represent religion at all but, instead, a masquerading secularism or, in George's
words, "a kind of shadow religion" that was a "distorted and dangerous adaptation." Practical Christianity could be an end in itself rather than a means to
final glory. Practice could become the center instead of existing in the service
of basic Christianity.[102] Beyond that, both Eddy and Peale, as theologians, had
been distinctly lowbrow, and as lowbrow they had, manifestly and undeniably,
trumped the learned of their respective times. Their success could not go un-

noticed among the cultured despisers of acknowledged vernacular participation. Finally, for both (and for New Thought, in general), a closet anti-Catholicism may have played a role in their rejection. Did the metaphysical invitation to the depths of the self in Protestant America smack of Catholicism, in however heterodox a variant? Was there a way in which even the invocation of an inner world, or of metaphysics, or of entering the silence raised subliminal fears of a nonrational religiosity against which the Reformers of the rational Protestant world had struggled? Could Protestant exotericism remain safe if ordinary people looked too long and too comfortably into their private selves?

Quashing Peale, however, would not end the experienced comfort of Americans with the world within. New Thought had leaked out of its community container all over American culture. Among evangelical Christians, for example, clerical leaders like Phineas F. Bresee, who founded the (Holiness) Church of the Nazarene, preached with conviction the God who was divine Supply and the source of true abundance. Robert H. Schuller (like Peale of the Reformed Church in America), built the flamboyant Crystal Cathedral from whence he televangelized his "Hour of Power," testifying for a systematic theology of self-esteem and the secret of successful living. And (Granville) Oral Roberts—the former pentecostal preacher who subsequently got ordained a Methodist minister, built the City of Faith, and televangelized to the nation—brought to mainstream notice healing powers as dramatic as those of early Christian Science and New Thought practitioners.[103] Meanwhile, outside the ranks of the clergy, New Thought made its way among physicians as notions of the psychosomatic origins of disease grew and medical professionals came to recognize stress as a factor in illness. For the holistic among them, the New Thought world became an invitation to a new kind of magical thinking—in which the power of mind imagined the body into a restored situation of health, well-being, and even spiritual transformation. To take but one late-twentieth-century example, there is holistic medical guru Deepak Chopra's popular book *The Way of the Wizard* (1995). Offering readers, as the work's subtitle promises, "twenty spiritual lessons for creating the life you want," Chopra's book hails Merlin—the renowned magician of King Arthur's legendary court—as the greatest teacher in the civilization of the West. Chopra, an Indian immigrant with an M.D. and former ties to the Maharishi Mahesh Yogi of Transcendental Meditation, encourages readers not to embrace either medicine or Asia but instead the path that Merlin trod. Chopra would show them, through Western Hermeticism, how to go beyond ordinary reality by shifting their perception and opening themselves to the spiritual transformation possible in everyday life. Such transformation, his book testifies, represents the true alchemy that the wizard possesses. Thus, if readers followed the path of Chopra, who followed Merlin, they would go questing for their wisest selves. The path to this wise self lay, not surprisingly, within: It entailed entering the silence (once again), observing the mind, awakening it, and then using it to transform everyday reality. It was all there — the action, the agency, the flow of power, the pragmatics, the mysticism, and the magic. "A *wizard*," Chopra announced, "*can turn fear to joy, frustration to fulfillment. A wizard can turn the time-bound into the timeless. A wizard can carry you beyond limitations into the boundless.*" Always, "*the cave of the heart*" was "*the home of truth*," while, simultaneously, all humans lived "*as ripples of energy in the vast ocean of energy.*"[104] And if the wizard was there and all of metaphysics was there, so — in the background — was Theosophy.

THEOSOPHICAL LINEAGES AND LEGACIES

Katherine Tingley, the "Purple Mother" (she was fond of the color), stepped into the vacuum left in the Theosophical Society in America with the death of William Judge in 1896. Her Raja Yoga School at Point Loma, California (see the preceding chapter), would be only one of a series of experiments that she carried forward. Tingley (born Westcott) came from old Massachusetts stock with, on one side, "strong members of the Congregational Church, and on the other side ... materialists." She would later recall a childhood "spent largely with nature," in which she "realized its mystery" even as she felt repelled by the religious conservatism of New England and its "revengeful" and "punishing" God. Significantly, she had enjoyed the company of a grandfather who was a Mason. She had come to Theosophy after two failed marriages, with a background already in spiritualism and Eastern occultism. But she also brought with her the influence of the American Protestant social gospel and the utopian expectancy that characterized parts of late-nineteenth-century American culture. Indeed, after she married Philo B. Tingley in 1888, she opened — by the 1890s — her Do-Good Mission on New York's East Side. "Crowds used to come there daily for soup and bread," she recollected, "and what else I could provide to help them." She felt overwhelmed by the suffering all around her, especially during a strike of the period, remembering a baby who had died in its mother's arms at the door of her mission. It was in this context that William Judge noticed her work and came calling, telling her that he could offer her something "that would go much deeper, removing the causes of misery and not merely relieving the effect." Thus, from the first, she was Judge's "convert," and she became a close and trusted ally, even nursing him during illness in his final year. She had come to believe that karmic patterns from the past explained a person's present circumstances and that present ignorance could be corrected by education to alter and prevent what gave rise to suffering.[105]

After Judge's death and the charismatic Tingley's assumption of control—not without political maneuvering and the use of mediumship to claim contact with Judge's spirit—she announced her proposal for a "School for the Revival of the Lost Mysteries of Antiquity." This was a thoroughly Blavatskian idea, but what was new was Tingley's vision of the school as part of a utopian society she would create. With a world crusade already initiated to win members for the Theosophical Society, she obtained land at Point Loma on the tip of the peninsula that forms San Diego Bay. Other Theosophists were already primed to join her. In the midst of widespread utopian interest, they had read, for example, Edward Bellamy's *Looking Backward* (1888), the popular utopian novel that argued for a new cooperative social organization based on the collective power of the state. Theosophists—like a number of New Thought people (see chapter 5)—had joined the Nationalist clubs that were spreading the Bellamy vision. Amid their shared enthusiasm, in 1897 the Point Loma Community's cornerstone was laid, and Tingley proclaimed the future. Utopianism and a subtle Masonry blended as she dedicated "this stone: a perfect square, a fitting emblem of the perfect work that will be done in the temple for the benefit of humanity and the glory of the ancient sages." Tingley's Theosophy would join a social-reform ideal to the inner quest, following the impulse of spiritualists and New Thought people but giving new concreteness to the linked projects of outer and inner work. The Point Loma Community aimed to become a new American "city upon a hill," a metaphysical showcase to advance the earthly and spiritual healing of humanity.[106]

With a Tingley lodge in Buffalo sponsoring a home for "unfortunate women" and California Theosophists holding meetings in prisons, Tingley herself began an International Brotherhood League that historian Emmett Greenwalt called "a sort of DoGood Mission on an international scale." As troops returned from the Spanish-American War in 1898, she involved herself and other Theosophists in providing medical relief, earning praise from laggard government officials who were embarrassed into recognizing theosophical efforts. Thus she was able to secure transport to Cuba from the government to continue her relief work. Meanwhile, at a theosophical convention in 1898, she secured her control by reorganizing the society as the Universal Brotherhood and Theosophical Society with a new constitution conferring extensive power on her as "Leader and Official Head" for life. Theosophists who supported her and moved to Point Loma read the convention as a millennial event, inaugurating a new world cycle with the close of the first and most terrible period of the Kali Yuga, which Blavatsky had predicted would come before the end of the century (see the previous chapter). For them, Tingley had become equal to Blavatsky and Judge, and, as W. Michael Ashcraft notes, "one of a great trinity of leaders appointed by the Masters."[107]

In the next six years, Tingley would close almost all of the lodges to focus theosophical energies on Point Loma—a move that led to a shrinking membership base and, in the end, the demise of her colony as it staggered under the weight of financial burdens. Still, in the years in which it flourished in the early twentieth century, the community became a place to notice. With two public buildings, the Temple and the Homestead, or Academy (their aquamarine and amethyst glass domes as dramatic as Tingley), community members themselves lived in assorted bungalows and tents. But they also boasted a Greek theater in the open—the first in the nation—and impressive orchards and gardens. The theosophical residents had come from middle- or upper-middle-class backgrounds, and at the community's height they were five hundred strong (with three hundred students in the Raja Yoga School). Child rearing practices were innovative: Children spent their time in a community nursery after the first few months of their lives, and parents were visible only as Sunday visitors. Like the Brook Farm and Oneida experiments of the nineteenth century, early-twentieth-century Point Loma fostered music and the arts with enthusiasm. (Tingley linked music to a "science of consciousness" and found an "immense correspondence" between music and "thought and aspiration"; similarly, she thought that "true drama points away from unrealities to the real life of the soul.") Residents could point to their horticultural achievements and the California agriculturalists who were acknowledging the community's research. They could also feel satisfactions about a Woman's Exchange and Mart and a series of crafts that recalled the Shakers. The community's print productions gained notice when Point Lomans produced the first linotype printing of Sanskrit in the United States. And at an exposition in Leipzig, Germany, in 1914, the community's exhibit of printing and graphics earned a gold prize.[108]

Always, and in the tradition of William Judge, what drove Point Loma Theosophy was moralism. This, of course, fit hand in glove with the reform commitments of Tingley, but it also expressed the particular character that the Judge foundation had already imprinted on the American movement. The moralism also kept time with Blavatsky's own ideal construction of the occult world, for she distinguished it from magic: Occultism, Blavatsky thought, was altruistic, whereas magic manipulated externals for self-centered aims and goals.[109] Tingley's own synthesis combined themes of divine transcendence and immanence, drawing on theosophical and American sources. It invoked nature as the Great Mother and yet turned clearly to a God within—and this with an outright language of the Self that bespoke the changes that metaphysical Asia was bringing. It taught a Puritan discipline of social behavior even as it commended to other Theosophists the spiritual discipline of meditation and a contemplative life. In the midst of this, it pushed Theosophists toward compassionate care for the world as the fruit of an inner life. It read a commitment to the world in American patriotic terms that smacked of a civil religion of the left even as it heralded, with Tingley apparently in charge, the millennial dawning of the new cycle.

As much as the New England Transcendentalists, Tingley had found God in nature, and her Point Loma existence overseeing the Pacific from the bluff of the spectacular theosophical property confirmed her in the habit. Nature was the "Mighty Mother" and the "Great Mother," and, as such, the place where divinity resided. "We lost touch ages ago with the Mighty Mother, Nature," she wrote, "and now need to go to her again." She hailed nature's "shining silences" and thought it the place to go to "seek aid." "Look up into the blue sky or the stars; catch in the air the feeling of her universal life." At the same time, the universe was "the outgrowth, the expression, of an infinite scheme proceeding from an Inmost Source beyond our comprehension." Humans, in turn, flowed out from it and followed "evolutionary law, passing through the many lives ordained for our growth towards perfection—we are here to work out the purposes of existence." Tingley knew about human suffering—her own, especially—and affirmed that she found in it "treasures of experience." With a complexity that belied the seeming glibness of her millennialism, she kept harking back to discipline and saw "meeting the trials from without" as a form of the same.[110] But unlike William James's twice-born souls who were sick, Tingley proclaimed a Hermetic gospel: Humans, in fact, were divine. "Godlike qualities lie sleeping within us, the spiritual things that mark us immortal. For here with the heart is the Kingdom of Heaven, and the only recompense a man needs is to become aware of his own divinity. It is there, a creative power within us, by whose virtue he who has patience to endure and work shall behold the fruit of his efforts—the human family glorified and brought to the goal his heart tells him may be reached. An order of life shall yet be established by those who have gone through the schools of experience, birth after birth, round after round, until they lifted themselves out of the strain and sorrow."[111]

For Tingley, Theosophy, with its message of inner divinity, gave the "highest law of conduct," and it led her, as ever, to the social order and to reflections on criminals, prisons, and capital punishment. Those who committed crimes lacked "the sovereign knowledge of the god within." "How then dare we condemn any man?" she asked. "How do we know what we ourselves might have done if placed as they had been, in other lives long since forgotten?" Prisons were "monuments of iniquity," since they brought no "moral correction" to their inmates. Still more, capital punishment was a "form of murder," because a person's life did not belong "only to the community" but was "part of the universal scheme of life." It was "the crime against the Holy Ghost, the higher law." Nor were matters different in the collective life of nations. "Separateness," she wrote sententiously, was the "curse" of nations, which should instead be built "on the rock of that enduring wisdom which belongs to the divine soul of man." Tingley decried the "fear and apprehension of war" that she saw as "becoming a chronic disease" and found war in the "lower" selves of humans gone collective. "Shame on the people that so distrusts its higher self and godlike abilities as to feel unable to resist invasion by any other means than brute force!" But war for her could also be righteous. There was "one true and legitimate battlefield," she declared, "the mind of man, where the duality of our nature keeps us constantly at the only rightful war there is—the war of the god in us against the lower self." [112]

America, though, had a higher destiny. It was, she believed, "the chosen spot for solving some of life's greatest problems." She could urge young people to "study the Constitution of the United States; go back to the spirit that actuated the formation of that Constitution." Yet the future of possibility that she saw at the end of 1897 when she wrote these words was inextricably bound up with her Blavatskian expectation of the new cycle dawning. An "opportunity" had been "given to humanity" that it had not experienced "for thousands of years." The "cycle" had "reached its point of swiftest momentum." In an invocation that she gave some time later, she declared that "the crucial point of the cycle" was "past" and the "fiercest ordeal . . . over." "No powers in heaven or hell can longer stay the onward progress of humanity," she proclaimed. "The hosts of Light are already victorious." [113]

The "white city" of Point Loma, however, unlike the White City at the Columbian Exposition in Chicago just a few years earlier, was a city in relative isolation. If it was a city upon a hill, it did not bring millions—or thousands—to its doors. Despite favorable press coverage and the presence of Cuban children and orphans from Buffalo at its school, it could not sustain itself economically. By 1942, the Point Loma site was abandoned and, under Tingley's successor Gottfried de Purucker, the communitarians moved to Covina, east of the city of Los Angeles. Eventually, they made their way to Altadena, near Pasadena. [114] It was other theosophical voices, however, whose messages made larger impacts on the metaphysical religion of the twentieth century and continuing. The most significant of these voices, perhaps ironically, was the textual voice of the English Theosophist Charles W. Leadbeater. It was Leadbeater's promulgation of the chakras that generated a new, more focused discourse on access to higher energies among Theosophists and reached out to a vastly larger audience. By the end of the twentieth century, the language of chakras had become taken-for-granted discourse among countless Americans who had never heard of Theosophists but who knowledgeably filed chakras away on their shelf of just-so tools for thinking.

At first glance, talk of (Indian) chakras evokes metaphysical Asia. The chakra system rests on the notion of energy centers in the physical body that function as sites for energy exchange between inner and outer. According to the lore that entered the West, there are seven major ones, and—in the context of the blended Asian-theosophical discourse—they register not merely in the physical body but in the other subtle bodies that Blavatsky's metaphysical Asian schema identified. In the twentieth century, more and more, these subtle bodies came to be seen as energy bodies, with Charles Leadbeater's book *The Chakras* first giving currency to the energy-body concept.[115] What is so surprising about the language of the chakras, however, is how quickly and easily it spun away from its Asian roots. Indeed, it became a free-floating, general discourse on energy—used by the end of the twentieth century, for example, interchangeably with talk of Chinese acupuncture points and energy meridians. Far more than the discourse of yoga—which stayed contained in sets of body-discipline and meditation practices continually fed by infusions from Asia—the chakras became an independent enterprise.

Already in 1927, when it first appeared, Leadbeater's book signaled the cultural detachment and reattachment that transformed the language of chakras into a Hermetic and metaphysical lingua franca. The publishing history of the short work (under 150 pages including front matter and index) is instructive. It includes at least twenty English-language printings with some six Spanish versions and even a Japanese one. Significantly in the case of the English-language reprints, only six of them (two in 1927 and four thereafter) were available before 1965. Beginning in 1966, however, *The Chakras* went through fourteen printings, with the last—in 2003—not by a theosophical press at all but by Kessinger Publishing of Whitefish, Montana, essentially a metaphysical reprint service that photocopies older works and binds them in softcover format. Meanwhile, by 1980 Quest Books, the imprint of the Theosophical Publishing House in Wheaton, Illinois, was claiming that "hundreds of thousands of copies" of the theosophical classic had been sold.[116] All of this, of course, suggests that the lingua franca came into its own particularly when the New Age movement and new spirituality, in general, began to make their way in American culture.

In that context, Leadbeater's book, as the virtual first word in the new discourse, pushed it strongly in a direction that encouraged its detachability from Asia. Leadbeater used Sanskrit terms in identifying each of seven chakras (and, it could be added, like Blavatsky before him thus mystified readers and added authority to his own discourse by its exotification). In the opening page of his first chapter (titled, tellingly enough, "The Force-Centres"), he also squarely situated chakras in South Asia, citing the Sanskrit meaning of the term *chakra* as "wheel" and alluding to Buddhist sources and even the Orientalist scholar T. W. Rhys Davids, so well loved by Theosophists. But South Asia swiftly fell away in favor of a short tour of the theosophical language of the "etheric double," summarizing the work of fellow Theosophist A. E. Powell in his book *The Etheric Double* (1925). The etheric double was an "invisible part of the physical body," and through it flowed the "streams of vitality" that kept the body alive. It also brought "undulations of thought and feeling from the astral to the visible denser physical matter." Then—in a reference that became transparent as the work progressed—Leadbeater explained that the etheric double was "clearly visible to the clairvoyant as a mass of faintly-luminous violet-grey mist, interpenetrating the denser part of the body, and extending very slightly beyond it." It turned out that the chakras, too, could be "easily" seen by anyone who possessed "a slight degree of clairvoyance," because they appeared "as saucer-like depressions or vortices" in the surface of the etheric double.[117]

Leadbeater could be counted among the gifted. In a work that contained ten vivid color reproductions on glossy paper, his plates and textual descriptions presented not the chakras of any classical Indian text or texts but the psychospiritual material of his own visionary experience. The circumspection was thin, and the fig leaf exquisitely transparent: "These illustrations of ours show the chakras as seen by clairvoyant sight in a fairly evolved and intelligent person, who has already brought them to some extent into working order." Leadbeater obligingly offered a few Asian, but non-Indian, allusions to images and statuary depicting, for example, the crown chakra (Borobudur in Java; Nara in Japan) and devoted a final chapter ("The Laya Yoga") to "the Hindu books." Along with some name dropping of Hindu texts, prominently in evidence were Arthur Avalon (Sir John Woodroffe in collaboration with Atul Behari Ghosh)—a theosophically favored author—along with the ubiquitous Rama Prasad (*Nature's Finer Forces*), Helena Blavatsky, and even Mabel Collins. Meanwhile, Leadbeater's comparativist inclinations in a Hermetic mode surfaced from the first. He nodded to "frequent" descriptions of the chakras "in Sanskrit literature, in some of the minor Upanishads, in the Puranas and in Tantric works" and to the use of the chakra system "today by many Indian yogis." Then he quickly turned to Europe, confiding to readers that "certain European mystics were acquainted with the chakras."[118]

Leadbeater spent ten paragraphs on one of them—Jacob Boehme's student Johann Georg Gichtel, whom he associated with the "secret society of the Rosicrucians." Gichtel's *Theosophia Practica* (1696), with—by the 1720s—the reproduction of clairvoyantly perceived "chakra" images, proved conclusively for Leadbeater that "at least some of the mystics of the seventeenth century knew of the existence and position of the seven centres in the human body." Just to be sure that readers understood, he reproduced one of Gichtel's plates, and it, indeed, looks strikingly similar to contemporary twenty-first-century representations of the energy centers. It was not a far stretch from there for Leadbeater to go to Freemasonry, claiming chakra knowledge among Freemasonic "secrets" and arguing that, in ritual, Freemasons "by utilizing them [the secrets] actually stimulate certain of these centres for the occasion and purpose of their work." Leadbeater added authoritatively that Freemasons generally knew "little or nothing" of what was occurring "beyond the range of normal sight" and alluded to his own book *The Hidden Life in Freemasonry* (1926), in which he had "mentioned as much of the matter" as was "permissible."[119]

In one sense, Leadbeater had only done as much as other Theosophists, beginning from Blavatsky and A. P. Sinnett, in offering a thoroughly metaphysical Asia to English-language readers. But by introducing the experimental data of his own subjective experience, arguably, he had gone further. He had shown more clearly how portable and culturally detachable the South Asian concepts actually were. Indeed, if we move quickly to late-century times, by 1987 in the midst of now-periodic reprintings of Leadbeater's book, at least three influential works in New Age and new spirituality circles were also trumpeting the good news of the chakras. They did so in largely, if not entirely, universalist terms that read chakras as synonyms for energy centers on the human body. Significantly, all three books arose out of personal experience, with chakras used to authorize the subjective impressions of the authors as a kind of metalanguage. For a first, Anodea Judith's *Wheels of Life* (with Judith's "Ph.D." designation prominently tagged to her name) went through seventeen printings of its initial edition in 1987 and appeared in a second, expanded version in 1999 claiming over 100,000 copies sold. It announced itself the work of a "somatic therapist, counselor, yoga teacher, and workshop leader." The preface to the first edition began with a description of how Judith came to chakras. "Once upon a time, while sitting on my sheepskin rug in deep meditation, I had a strange experience. I was quietly and consciously counting my breaths when suddenly I found myself outside of my body—looking at another me sitting here in full lotus. No sooner did I realize who I was looking at . . . than I saw a book fall into her lap. As it landed, it jarred me back into my body and I looked down and read the title: *The Chakra System* by A. Judith Mull (my name at the time)."[120]

Mull/Judith went for confirmation not to Leadbeater's work but to a remembered passage in a book by well-known New Age guru Ram Dass (the former Richard Alpert associated with Harvard University's Psychology Department). But she was later to discover Leadbeater's book and understand its significance, calling it "the standard Western classic on chakras" and "for a long time . . . the only Western book on the subject." Because information was so scarce, she explained, she had needed to develop her own theories "through self-experimentation and the scrutiny of others" in her yoga teaching and bodywork practices. "Before long, everything I saw seemed to fall into this neat little pattern of 'sevenness': colors, events, behaviors, days." She had continued to develop her theories from the "hundreds of clients" whom she had seen, and she had also "delved into Sanskrit literature, quantum physics, theosophy, magic, physiology, psychology, and personal experience to patch together a coherent system." Judith gave each of her seven chakras English names (which became quasi-canonical in the late-century, new-century metaphysical world): "survival, sex, power, love, communication, clairvoyance, and wisdom." She had forged through all of this a user-friendly tool to think energy patterns in physical, emotional, and spiritual registers. Chakras, wrote Judith, were *"organizing centers for the reception, assimilation, and transmission of life energies."*[121]

Judith, moreover, had decidedly rationalized the older model of chakras provided by Leadbeater's trance productions. The body, she explained, was a "vehicle of consciousness." Chakras were the "wheels of life" that enabled the vehicle to move "through its trials, tribulations, and transformations." For the vehicle to run "smoothly," what was needed was "an owner's manual as well as a map that tells us how to navigate the territory our vehicle can explore." With each chakra being "a step on the continuum between matter and consciousness," bridging "the gulf between matter and spirit" meant accepting one's identity as "the Rainbow Bridge that connects Earth and Heaven once again." Judith did keep Sanskrit language and terminology, made a few references to Asian sources, resurrected the much-favored Arthur Avalon, and—by the second edition, especially—dwelled to some extent on Tantrism and the kundalini experience. All of this, however, had become a convenient rhetorical instrument for a Western metaphysical spirituality that, by now, was preaching and teaching the enlightened body-self. In fact, so much was this the case that Judith included physical exercises to develop and regulate each of the chakras. She wanted open chakras if they were closed and cleared chakras if they were blocked so that they could work better, and she wanted to integrate their activity. Even further, she devoted a chapter to the interactions among chakras in dyadic relationships and in relationships with the culture as a whole. In keeping with the New Age community, she read the future in millennialist terms, invoking the "new evolutionary order" that "must encompass and combine the planes and stages of all levels of consciousness." The present age, she said, was a time of "tumultuous changes and limitless possibilities."[122]

By contrast to the ambitious Judith book, Rosalyn L. Bruyere's *Wheels of Light* was briefer and more limited. First published in a homegrown version by her Healing Light Center Church in Glendale, California, in 1987, by 1989 it was picked up for mass-market publishing by Simon and Schuster. It was Bruyere, and then Barbara Ann Brennan, who introduced a focus on the human aura into the discourse of the chakra system. With a background in spiritualism, Bruyere said that she remembered seeing auras as a young child, suppressed the seeing, and then resurrected it as an adult when her children began to talk about the "colored fuzz" surrounding people. Encouraged by a medium at the (spiritualist) Universal Church of the Master in West Hollywood and then by spiritualists in the Church of Antioch in Santa Ana, she began "reading" auras and, by 1971, was also ordained a spiritualist minister. In the end, however, it was energies and not ghosts that won her. According to her own report, "I would scan the aura, find holes, put my hands there and pump them up." Even before she spoke of chakras, she claimed to see colors, to sense "congestion," and to "run energy" to clear it.[123]

Enter, at this point, science—in the person of Valerie Hunt, a tenured professor at the University of California, Los Angeles, who was metaphysically inclined. With a grant to study a series of "energy" phenomena generated through "structural integration," or rolfing (the deep-manipulation bodywork systematized by Ida Rolf), Hunt employed Bruyere as an aura reader. Bruyere, by this time, had acquired a reputation for such work in Los Angeles, and Hunt wanted to use her for experiments to ascertain the frequencies produced by the human energy field. With electrical equipment and Bruyere working simultaneously, Hunt sought to correlate human energy frequencies with those of visible light. "From that, we concluded," wrote Bruyere, "that what science had been calling the human energy field, or the mind field, and what religious traditions had been calling the auric field were one and the same." Thereafter Bruyere began to think increasingly in terms of the chakra system. From the first her reflections were expansively comparative. India was but one port of call in a series of cultures and peoples who knew about chakras—Hopis, Egyptians, Greeks, Chinese among them—and the fact that a *Sanskrit* term defined tiny energy vortices on the body was, for Bruyere, more or less irrelevant. (She casually cited "the Reverend Charles Leadbeater and Annie Besant" in a somewhat confused historical account that also named Alice Bailey.) Bruyere was much more interested in identifying the colors of chakras; in characterizing, sometimes, entire cultures in terms of chakras that predominated (as defined by color); and in correlating what she was finding with New Age science. "When we refer to 'color of energy' (or, sometimes, *frequency*)," she declared authoritatively, "we mean the color of the energy or chakra, as defined by the wavelength of electromagnetic radiation being emitted at that location, as perceived by those who have second sight."[124]

Bruyere's chakras, experientially based and scientifically "proven," had departed far indeed from their Asian context. At the Healing Light Center Church that she founded after the spiritualists indicated their displeasure with her direction, she began to teach her healing techniques, using aura reading and the laying on of hands. One of the people who sat in her classes was Barbara Ann Brennan, an erstwhile employee of the National Aeronautics and Space Administration from the Goddard Space Flight Center in Maryland. Brennan, who styled herself a former "NASA physicist" (she had earned an M.S. in atmospheric physics at the University of Wisconsin and at NASA had studied the reflection of solar light from the earth), came to Bruyere as part of a professional and personal quest. Like a series of metaphysical leaders who have been cited in this narrative, she arrived as a self-made and entrepreneurial spiritual seeker. She went on to shape personal and professional answers that made a noticeable mark on the new metaphysical culture of the late twentieth century. Raised on a Wisconsin farm without books (except the Bible), central heating, or indoor plumbing, she, like Bruyere, spoke of seeing auras in childhood around "trees and the small animals," and, like Bruyere, as an adult she sought to reclaim her remembered experience.[125]

After she left NASA, Brennan pursued mind-body studies, worked in "bioenergetics" (predicated on the work of Freud's one-time disciple Wilhelm Reich), then "core energetics" with John Pierrakos, and later "Pathwork Helpership Training." Along the way, she gained knowledge of a variety of alternative therapies. As her own counseling work continued in this and later contexts, she became convinced that, as in childhood, she was seeing auras again—now around the bodies of her clients. Brennan went on to identify layer upon layer of energy fields in a theosophized account that ended with nine (instead of seven) energy bodies. Her *Hands of Light* (1987)—a textbook to teach the form of energy healing that she was practicing—provides a succinct account of her nonconventional scientific sources as well as her theosophically oriented spiritual ones. In its Bantam popular format of 1988, the book became a best seller and, by early 1996, with Brennan's later *Light Emerging* (1993), had sold 750,000 copies worldwide. According to the Brennan website in 2004, *Hands of Light* by then had more than a million copies in print and had been published in twenty-two languages. Moreover, alongside the books, Brennan produced audiotapes, lectured nationally, maintained the website, and had established a school—by then in South

Florida—to train other healers in her work. Nonaccredited but licensed by the State of Florida's Commission for Independent Education, the Barbara Brennan School of Healing boasted of more than one thousand graduates by June 2000, with the 2004 student body ranging in age from eighteen to seventy-five, two-thirds of them from various states throughout the United States and the remaining third from twenty-nine foreign nations. According to the website, over 15 percent of students worked in the health-care profession as physicians, registered nurses, physical therapists, psychotherapists, and nutritionists. Still more ambitiously, a Barbara Brennan School of Healing EUROPE existed in Mondsee, Austria.[126]

Given this background and the Brennan focus on auras, what is especially interesting about chakras in the Brennan account—in which they function prominently—is how much they are taken for granted. They are, as tellingly, almost completely detached from South Asia. Indeed, Brennan's first two references to chakras in her text glided over the term without any attempt at definition—as if speaking a language that readers used and understood. It was only on the third use, in a discussion of the "seven layers of the auric field," that she told readers how in the structured layers of the field (the odd-numbered layers) a "vertical flow of energy" pulsated "up and down the field in the spinal cord." She added that there were "swirling cone-shaped vortexes called chakras in the field" and that their "tips" pointed into "the main vertical power current" while their "open ends" extended "to the edge of each layer of the field" in which they were located. Brennan's explanation included a "Universal Energy Field," with "each swirling vortex of energy" (that is, chakra) sucking or entraining energy from the field, and thus engaging in processes of exchange. Exposing the combinative habit that had, by now, lost all touch with national cultures, she added that "all the major chakras, minor chakras, lesser chakras and acupuncture points are openings for energy to flow into and out of the aura."[127]

Brennan cited Leadbeater on the chakras in her bibliography (in a 1974 printing), but her text itself was innocent of references to him. Still more, nothing she had written located chakras in South Asia or in Sanskrit textual sources. At the same time, Brennan did—however briefly—give a passing nod to ancient spiritual traditions with which she felt her own work to be connected. Mystics throughout the world, she declared, had practiced "traditions" that were "consistent with the observations scientists have recently begun to make." She pointed to "ancient Indian spiritual tradition" with its discourse on "a universal energy called *Prana.*" And although her rare references to kundalini were devoid of cultural context, Brennan alluded vaguely, in one place, to "Tantric tradition." She noticed Chinese "chi" (qi) and observed that the "ancient art of acupuncture focuses on balancing the yin and the yang." Moreover, she (as vaguely) acknowledged the Jewish Kabbalah (dating it, without explanation, to "538 B.C."), connected it to the language of energies as "astral light," and pointed, too, to auras in religious paintings depicting Jesus and "other spiritual figures." "Many esoteric teachings—the ancient Hindu Vedic texts, the Theosophists, the Rosicrucians, the Native American Medicine People, the Tibetan and Indian Buddhists, the Japanese Zen Buddhists, Madame Blavatsky, and Rudolph Steiner, to mention a few—describe the Human Energy Field in detail," she affirmed. Brennan went on to cite representatives of the Hermetic energy tradition, naming Pythagoreans and other figures familiar to this account, including Paracelsus, Jan Baptista van Helmont, Franz Anton Mesmer, and Count Wilhelm von Reichenbach.[128]

She argued that diseases (her concern) for the most part originated in the body's energy system, and she sought to teach students how to identify problems in the subtle bodies and to repair and restructure them, thus preventing or reversing disease in the physical body. Brennan thus had been brought to the language of chakras to elaborate her rather elegant model—a spirit anatomy of energy bodies transferring energy from the individual to the Universal Energy Field and taking it back again, with chakras as the vehicles of transfer. If there were structured layers to these auric energy fields or bodies, there were also fluidic ones (the even layers) characterized by color and motion. Still more, Brennan instructed students on the role of chakras at birth and death, offering metaphysical glosses on reincarnation. "If the metaphysics disturbs you, please take it as a metaphor," she counseled students tolerantly. She told them, anyway, how at death people left their bodies through their crown chakra (an observation with which Andrew Jackson Davis would have agreed) and how she had "often seen them resting, surrounded by white light for some period of time after death. They appear to be taken care of in some kind of hospital on the other side."[129]

On the earthly side, energy blocks (now long familiar) closed the chakras and created illness. Healing thus meant opening the chakras. With psychology a strong suit in light of Brennan's counseling background, it was not surprising when she identified the sources of energy blocks as emotional. However, for her the emotional ultimately pointed the way to the spiritual, and problems on one register corresponded to problems on the other. The therapist functioned, in reality, as a spiritual healer, doing a work of love with a theology that smacked of Theosophy and New Thought. "The healer reaches into . . . painful areas of the soul and gently reawakens hope. S/he gently reawakens the ancient memory of who the soul is. S/he touches the spark of God in each cell of the body and gently reminds it that it is already God and, already being God, it inexorably flows with the Universal Will towards health and wholeness." Still more, the emotional work that would bring the rewards of spirit was predicated on the healing of self in human relationships. In the post-Freudian discourse community in which Brennan functioned, failed relationships pointed toward the chronic malady of "self-hatred" and led back again to more failure between self and other. If the Brennan logic is extended, unblocking and healing the self meant, in the end, building effective community—even if Brennan herself never took her ideas very far in a social direction. What is clear, though, is that, for Brennan, people failed themselves and others for a reason that was finally spiritual. They could not extend their unconditional love to the "Godself within."[130]

With chakras as channels and conduits in the free flow of energy to and from the "Godself," Brennan had arrived where Theosophists always arrived—at the divinity within themselves. Outside the discourse on chakras, other Theosophists in the early twentieth century—spin-offs from the Blavatskian tradition—created lineages that carried forward theosophical ideas in the decades that followed. Closest among them to Theosophy was Alice Bailey (1880–1949), a former Theosophist who came late to Leadbeater's language of chakras but who, in her preoccupation with "centres" and divine rays of energy, effectively demonstrated similar concerns before the appearance of his book. Born Alice La Trobe-Bateman in an upper-class British family, she went to school under private tutors and went to church in the Church of England. Her mother died when she was a child, and with a troubled adolescence and suicidal tendencies (she tried to commit suicide at least three times), she was drawn to religion and spirituality. She was also educated to a social conscience, remembering that "from the earliest possible time we were taught to care about the poor and the sick and to realise that fortunate circumstances entailed responsibility." Still more, according to her later recollections from at least 1895 the teenage La Trobe-Bateman began to experience the uncanny. On a Sunday morning that year, while she was seated in the drawing-room of her aunt's house instead of going to church, a "tall man," dressed in well-cut European clothes "with a turban on his head," visited her. She was, as she later wrote, "scared stiff," but he sat beside her and told her that work had been planned for her in the world. To do it, she needed to change her "disposition considerably." She needed to "give up being such an unpleasant little girl" and "try and get some measure of self-control." He would visit her again at intervals. Later she felt that he had done so and eventually that she knew who he was. The visitor, for whom she claimed to work in the years that followed, was "the Master K.H., the Master Koot Hoomi." He was "very close to the Christ."[131]

To be sure, Theosophists would know that Koot Hoomi counted as a theosophical mahatma with solid Blavatskian connections, but his closeness to the

"Christ" pointed toward—and prognostically resolved—another world of experience. Drawn to the high-church ritual of the Anglican part of her family, Bailey
had also experienced the narrower low-church version of the Church of England, with its foreboding visions of hellfire for the damned. She grew into something of a fundamentalist, working, in conjunction with the Young Women's
Christian Association, as a missionary to British army soldiers in places ranging
from Ireland to India. Eventually, the fundamentalism dropped away, but the
figure of the Christ remained.[132] Even in the midst of the fundamentalism, in
the Himalayan Mountains and at the Wesek commemoration of the birthday
of the Buddha, she claimed a vision of the Christ standing at the apex of a "tri-
angle" formed with two other figures. The crowd below, she recalled, seemed
in "constant movement," modeling the symbols of world spirituality with their
bodies—various forms of the cross, the circle, the five-pointed star, triangles. But
the ecumenical Christian focus of the vision gave way before something else:
As the three figures stretched out their arms, another and different one came toward the rock. She "knew in some subjective and certain fashion that it was the
Buddha," but she "knew at the same time that in no way was our Christ belittled."
There was a "Plan," and "all the Masters" were "eternally dedicated" to it.[133]

More conventional events were happening in La Trobe-Bateman's life. She
met her future husband, Walter Evans, in India, and after their marriage in 1907
moved with him to Cincinnati, Ohio, and then—after he completed his studies
at Lane Theological Seminary and was ordained an Episcopal priest—to California. Evans was physically abusive and emotionally troubled, and he left her
in 1915. But around this time she was introduced by friends in Pacific Grove to
Theosophy and eventually drawn to the American headquarters of the Theosophical Society in Krotona, California (this a branch of the Adyar-based original
Theosophical Society, not the Judge-Tingley Theosophical Society in America).
At Krotona, she became editor of the journal of the society, *The Messenger*, met
her future husband Foster Bailey (national secretary), and claimed still another
mysterious visitation in 1919. Djwhal Khul, "the Tibetan," she later confided,
had asked her to be the human conduit for his books. Initially reluctant, she
agreed when she came to believe that Koot Hoomi was supporting the project.
So began her involvement in the production of a series of metaphysical books
(some twenty of them), heavily drenched in theosophical terminology and lore
but increasingly distinctive in their thrust. The first, *Initiation, Human and Solar*
(1922), saw a few of its chapters published in *The Theosophist*, but tensions were
growing and Bailey's claim to revelation was setting other theosophical nerves
on edge. Bailey, in turn, was becoming more critical of the Esoteric Section of
the society, which she had joined. In the midst of highly politicized dissension,

both she and Foster Bailey were dismissed from the Theosophical Society. They married in New York and, in 1923, organized the Arcane School there. Yet Bailey was still a Blavatskian devotee, teaching classes on *The Secret Doctrine*, even as she worked, as she believed, as the amanuensis for the Tibetan.[134]

Initially, three aspects of theosophical teaching attracted Bailey. First, the belief that there was "a great and divine plan" for "return to God" drew her. Second, she "discovered" that there were "Masters" who were "responsible for the working out of that Plan and Who, step by step and stage by stage" had "led mankind on down the centuries." Significant for her future work, she "found that the Head of this Hierarchy of spiritual Leaders was the Christ" and so "felt that He had been given back" to her "in a nearer and more intimate way." Third, she encountered the teaching that "pulled" her "up short for a long time" — the "dual belief in the law of re-birth and the law of cause and effect, called Karma and Reincarnation."[135] She did not like the Sanskrit term *karma*, favored by "Theosophists who, so often, like[d] to sound learned." But she came to accept the idea. As her teaching evolved through the Tibetan's books, however, it became clear that a sense of the ultimacy of energy and its entry into the human world — the hallmark of twentieth-century and later metaphysical religion — shaped her vision as much. The Plan was a plan about charging the world, inundating it with divine radiance. The Masters worked fervidly to accomplish the goal, and the laws of karma and reincarnation guaranteed that there would be enough time for humanity to be saturated with the sacred and so brought back to God.

As Bailey wrote through these ideas (and with her disdain for Sanskrit name-dropping), she used the language of "centres" to refer to what Leadbeater, in 1927, called chakras, although after 1927 the term *chakras* became more frequent in her writings. As early as 1922, in her first book, she thought of these "centres" as the stuff of ordinary occult knowledge: "It has been said that in the head of every man are seven centres of force, which are linked to the other centres in the body and through which the force of the Ego is spread and circulated, thus working out the plan." She made at least one passing reference to the "utilisation of the chakras (or centres) in the palms of the hands" and, employing the language of "centres," offered readers a detailed description of their awakening in "initiation." In her later and often-cited *Treatise on Cosmic Fire* (1925), Bailey's text underlined the energy dimensions of the centers. They were "formed entirely of streams of force." "When functioning properly," they themselves formed the "body of fire," which she identified as "'the body incorruptible' or indestructible, spoken of by St. Paul" (1 Cor. 15:53). Decades before Barbara Brennan, she was affirming, too, the presence of the "centres" on subtle bodies. In humans, she testified, centers were "found on the mental plane" and could be traced from

there "to the astral level, and eventually to the etheric levels, to the fourth ether."
On the physical body, Bailey placed the centers in the traditional major chakra
locations. She also provided readers, in her *Treatise on White Magic* (1934), with
a close analysis of their working. "Each centre or chakra is composed of three
concentric interblending whorls or wheels which in the spiritual man upon the
probationary path move slowly in one direction, but gradually quicken their activity as he nears the portal of the Path of Initiation. On initiation, the centre of
the chakra (a point of latent fire) is touched, and the rotation becomes intensified, and the activity, fourth dimensional."[136]

Beyond the centres or chakras, though, what drew Bailey—and distinguished
her reading—was her attention to "rays." Blavatsky had introduced the discourse
on rays from her own occult sources in *The Secret Doctrine*; the twentieth-
century comprehensive and separately published *Index* to the mammoth work
lists close to twenty-five citations. Thus the germ of Bailey's work as, she believed,
the amanuensis of the Tibetan lay in Blavatsky's volumes. But Bailey and her
Tibetan surely ran with what she had learned. Bailey's *Treatise on the Seven Rays*
appeared in five volumes over a series of years (1936, 1942, 1951, 1953, 1960), with
the last three published posthumously. The first two dealt with esoteric psychology, the third with esoteric astrology, the fourth with esoteric healing, and the
fifth with the rays themselves and initiations.[137]

A ray, Bailey explained in the glossary to *Initiation, Human and Solar*, was
"one of the seven streams of force of the Logos," one of the "seven great lights."
Divided into three "Rays of Aspect" and four "Rays of Attribute," the rays included, for the former, "Will, or Power," "Love-Wisdom," and "Activity, or Adapt-
ability." For the latter, they encompassed "Harmony, Beauty, Art, or Unity" (as
one ray), "Concrete Knowledge or Science," "Abstract Idealism or Devotion,"
and "Ceremonial Magic, or Law." Bailey thought that there were "seven major
types of people" and that they were related to the "seven great Rays or Energies,"
which she also identified as the book of Revelation's " 'seven spirits before the
throne of God' " (Rev. 1:4). With each ray expressing "a peculiar and specialised
type of force," for Bailey "all people" were "units of consciousness breathed forth
on one of the seven emanations from God." Hence "even their monads or spiritual aspects" were "inherently different just as in the prism (which is one) there
are the seven differentiated colours."[138] In prose that was often well nigh im-
penetrable and dense with occult terminology (despite Bailey's own castigation
of theosophical linguistic habits), she probed the dimensions and distinctions
of spiritual energy that the rays represented. Her language would continue into
the late twentieth century and on, as New Age and new spirituality aficionados
spoke of what rays they had "come in" (to the planet) on and how that distin-

guished them as persons. Whatever the ray, though, Bailey had taught them—as had twentieth-century metaphysicians across the board—that they were energy beings.

Energy, moreover, was moving toward one great goal, and Bailey advanced the theosophical message of the millennium and specified it further. Blavatsky and other Theosophists—among them, Annie Besant and Charles Leadbeater—had declared for a "new age" to come, with Besant promoting her young Brahmin protégé Jiddu Krishnamurti as that age's "World Teacher" and Leadbeater calling him the vehicle of the Lord Maitreya and of the Christ. Before Krishnamurti eventually disavowed the role in 1929, Bailey remembered that "Mrs. Besant's pronouncements about Krishnamurti were splitting the society wide open."[139] Still, Bailey's own new-age pronouncements were even more emphatic, if more ideal. More than Leadbeater, she conflated the identities of the Buddha of the endtime—the Lord Maitreya—and the eschatological Christ of Christianity, fusing the figures in ways that her early vision in the Himalayan Mountains had already prefigured. Always, though, it was the Christ who was central in Bailey's account.

Indeed, one of her volumes with the Tibetan, *The Reappearance of the Christ* (1948), drew together an occultized South Asian discourse on the coming of avatars with the Christic focus that was Bailey's own.[140] Still more, it inserted both of these into a cosmology of the stars and planets in the linguistic terms of Western astrology and the action-oriented language of world service. Here Bailey bequeathed to the later New Age movement the expectation of the coming age of Aquarius. She announced the end of the age of Pisces and the dawning of the Aquarian era, with the coming Christ providing Aquarian service to all of humanity. In concert with the reappearance of the Christ, predicted Bailey, would come a major evolutionary event in the development of consciousness as humanity would be drawn away from individual needs and toward the needs of the whole. Anxiety over personal salvation would yield before the drive to world service, even as materialistic concerns would fall away before a new spiritual order. The Christ who would come, for Bailey, would arrive not only as the first Son of God but also as a kind of world executive, head of a spiritual hierarchy that represented the inner government of the earth. The example of the Christ would provide the model for a united world in which interdependence and interaction would bring a new material and spiritual order for the culture and civilization to be.

In this meeting between West and East, Bailey thought, humans had a significant role to play: It was their responsibility to advance the coming age. By 1935, the Arcane School was promoting the use of the so-named Great Invocation, a prayer believed to have potencies that were, in effect, sacramental and, as J. Stillson Judah wrote, "almost magic and divine." The Great Invocation called for the Christ who would return to earth, prayed that the "purpose" of the Masters would "guide the little wills of men," affirmed the working out of the "Plan of Love and Light" that could "seal the door where evil dwells," and prayed that "Light and Love and Power" would "restore the Plan on Earth." Later, Arcane School teachings announced that Christ himself had given humanity the Great Invocation on the full moon in June 1945, in the context of the ending of World War II. Full-moon meditations, culminating in the solemn recitation of the Great Invocation, have continued to be a practice of the Arcane School and other Bailey devotees. Meant to raise spiritual energies and to set up conditions that will bring the coming once more of the Christ, the meditations employ various ritual techniques—music, dance, speech, and gesture. They turn on the Bailey invocation, recited while visualizing the descent of the power (energy) of the hierarchy of masters.[141]

Other social-oriented programs created by Bailey's Arcane School promoted the notion of world service. As early as 1932, World Goodwill was established as the "New Group of World Servers" to bring right human relations to the world and to use the constructive power of goodwill to prepare for the return of the Christ anticipated by Bailey followers. Its work has been, in the large sense, educational, and it has functioned as an "accredited non-governmental organisation" with the Department of Public Information of the United Nations. By 1937, Triangles joined World Goodwill to carry on the work of the Bailey-affirmed "hierarchy." Considered a "service activity" for those who "believe in the power of thought," Triangles has linked groups of three individuals who each day unite mentally in "creative meditation" to radiate the light energy of goodwill to the world. At the center of the meditative action of each group stands the Great Invocation.[142] Bailey's theosophical tilt toward the figure of the Christ has thus been accompanied by a Western-style organized commitment to service, however mental the form it takes. More than that, Bailey—perhaps more than any other single teacher from the theosophical world—set the stage for the New Age movement. Her Great Invocation, her expectation of the astrological Age of Aquarius with its profound spiritual shift, her full-moon meditations, her preoccupation with continuing revelation through Masters, her incoming rays with distinctive divine energies for humans and society all have found their presence in New Age belief and practice.

Alice Bailey—or her Tibetan—however, seemed doubtful about other theosophical innovations. "The Masters portrayed in the many theosophical movements (since the time of H. P. B.) are not distinguished by intelligence and show little judgment in the choice of those whom the organisations claim are initiates or important members of the Hierarchy," the Tibetan deplored in an appendix to Bailey's autobiography. In this, the Bailey-Tibetan view accorded with that of older theosophical organizations. But like New Thought, Theosophy had spun out of (organized) control. As Bailey's words hinted, a plethora of small groups appeared and disappeared. They announced through one figure or another their corner on continuing revelation, and—with assured access to a world of spirit and ascended mastership—taught their message to whoever would listen for as long as they would listen. J. Gordon Melton's *Encyclopedia of American Religions*, with its seemingly endless catalog of groups in the "Ancient Wisdom Family," suggests the extent and diffusion of these theosophical offshoots and lineages in American general culture. To cite but one influential case, consider the I AM movement. With a name that in itself points to the presence of New Thought in the theosophical world (even as we have seen the reverse), I AM hailed its masters as enthusiastically as older Theosophists had done. By contrast, Bailey's Tibetan condemned the masters who had been "brought before the general public by such movements as the I AM movement" as a "travesty of the reality." [143]

Perhaps what Bailey and the Tibetan found so objectionable in the I AM Ascended Master Religious Activity was its easy conflation of New Thought with these theosophical masters. The I AM account of its origins, *Unveiled Mysteries*, from the first signaled hybridism. According to Guy W. Ballard (1878–1939), the author and mining "engineer" who established I AM, he had encountered the "ascended master" Saint-Germain on the slopes of Mount Shasta, in northern California, while hiking there in 1930. (The figure was identified with the Comte de Saint-Germain, an eighteenth-century French necromancer, alchemist, and mystic claiming to be several centuries old. He had been hailed by Blavatsky as "the greatest Oriental Adept Europe has seen during the last centuries" and was likewise highly esteemed by Henry Steel Olcott.) Ballard, with a background in spiritualism and mediumship and a history of poverty, was already heavily invested in occult and metaphysical lore, studying it in the "occult" library in Los Angeles in a milieu saturated with Hopkins-style New Thought. Here Annie Rix Militz, a Hopkins student, had established her Home of Truth center before the end of the nineteenth century and had used it as a base to establish other Homes of Truth on the West Coast until her death six years before Ballard's hike. Meanwhile, in Atascadero, in central California, by the 1930s William Dudley Pelley was elucidating his Liberation-Soulcraft philosophy after a claimed out-of-body experience in the Sierra Madre Mountains. He had received messages from masters, or "mentors," who taught that all humans participated in the Godhead and so were bound and connected to one another. Pelley became still more well-known, as the decade progressed, through the right-wing Silver Shirts that he founded—anti-Communist, anti-New Deal, and anti-Semitic. Ballard and his wife, Edna Ballard—a student of metaphysics and the occult, too—would maintain close contact with Pelley. It was no doubt through his influence that an exaltation of the American nation and a right-wing superpatriotism emerged in their teaching.[144]

Guy Ballard had climbed the mountain because he had heard rumors that the Great White Brotherhood—the theosophical masters—maintained a branch lodge there. So it was that Ballard's account of what transpired on a day in 1930 combined remnants of Theosophy with other remnants of New Thought in a new synthesis of his own. He had knelt to scoop some water, felt something like electricity rush through his body from head to foot, and turned to see the mysterious hiker who later revealed himself to be Saint-Germain. Significantly, the young man offered Ballard a creamy liquid that repeated the electrical effect on Ballard's mind and body. He told Ballard that the drink had come from "Universal Supply," which was everywhere available to those who loved sufficiently. Themes of poverty and prosperity intertwined in this essentially New Thought message that came in tow with the Ballard autobiography. Moreover, New Thought teaching was as generously supplied as the Universal Supply of the drink. In effect, Saint-Germain instructed Ballard in leaving behind the outer busyness of mind and body and entering the silence. In this and later reported visitations, too, after reviewing some of Ballard's previous lives, Saint-Germain began to teach that reincarnation could be avoided. (Belief in reincarnation had been taught not only by Theosophists but also by many—like Charles Fillmore and Unity students—in New Thought.) Saint-Germain himself was an *ascended* master, and the I AM Religious Activity came to teach that ascension was possible—and, indeed, the true goal of humans, instead of reincarnation. Here, again, there were New Thought connections. The Saint-Germain teaching accorded strikingly with the radical view advanced by Annie Rix Militz in her late Los Angeles years, when Militz moved away from Fillmore and began to teach "ascension," or "translation." "Like Jesus," she had written, "this can be your last incarnation, that is, the last one which has had its beginning in a flesh-birth." "The God-Self" was "never incarnated and therefore cannot be reincarnated." "Truth undeceives the ego when it gives itself up to the great Ego," Militz affirmed, "and then it begins its journey back to the Path which it left so long ago, and its arrival is the realization of Being-what-it-is, called the Ascension."[145]

Still more, the silence of a stilled body and mind—a spiritual strategy toward the growth that would bring ascension—led on into a distinctly New Thought terrain. Saint-Germain taught the use of affirmations. He also taught the use of decreeing, a practice that, according to J. Gordon Melton, had begun with Emma Curtis Hopkins during her New York years. Here a decree was a statement distinguished by its energy and focus, its concerted investment of will, in commanding—or demanding—certain outcomes for good. It was spoken from the stance of the high Self that was God within. In the I AM context, a decree came to be used for destructive as well as constructive ends, in acts of "warfare" against what believer-practitioners deemed as evil. Since decrees were, in effect, especially forceful affirmations, it followed that the denials (of negative conditions) that were also part of New Thought prayer practice could be tweaked. They could become, in the emphatic form of the decree, what looked like old-fashioned curses. Ballard's ascended masters—Saint-Germain and Jesus the leading ones, but there were others—had supplied a continuing revelation that put Ballard himself in charge. He was Saint-Germain's "Accredited Messenger," and Edna and Donald Ballard (his son) were soon added, so that the trio became the only "Accredited Messengers" of the ascended masters. As they began to teach and develop their revelation, abundance replaced their former poverty. Edna Ballard, particularly, became a commanding presence. Charles Braden wrote of the movement's appeal to "enormous numbers of people in all the great cities" with claims of "more than a million followers" (even three million in the estimate of some members). "It is a fact," he wrote, "that in the late thirties they gathered huge crowds, filling the great auditoriums of the larger cities of America, night after night, for a week or more each."[146]

With continuing revelation from ascended masters and the practice of affirmation and, especially, decreeing, the I AM Religious Activity flourished. Meanwhile, the name by which it was known—I AM—also signaled New Thought presence in the midst of Theosophy. With hints of the "I Am" language in mid-nineteenth-century spiritualism, Warren Felt Evans later promoted its use, bequeathing the verbal formula to early New Thought, as we have seen. For the Ballards, the name did not come at once. Charles Braden remarked that he had "found no single reference to the I Am in *Unveiled Mysteries*, the original text, the first revelation made by St. Germain to Guy Ballard." However, as they grew into use of the name, what the Ballards evoked in the "I Am" or the "Mighty I Am Presence" straddled the line between personal and impersonal: I Am was an "It" but also displayed personal qualities like love, wisdom, and knowledge. More than that, I Am also straddled a line between supreme source and individualized God-Self within. Again, it was Emma Curtis Hopkins—who had hybridized Christian Science with the teaching of Warren Felt Evans—who taught her students, like Annie Rix Militz in Los Angeles, to think in terms of the "radiant I Am." As Melton has summarized, "In connection with her decreeing, Hopkins and her students also used the term 'I AM' in the peculiar manner later to be identified with the 'I AM' movement." She had written a pamphlet *The Radiant "I AM,"* and one of her students—Thomas J. Shelton—developed her ideas even further in his book of *I Am Sermons.* In Los Angeles, by 1904 Militz's *Primary Lessons in Christian Living and Healing* carried a similar "radiant" message.[147]

If the radiant I Am Presence pointed toward New Thought discourse, the I AM movement's developing language of light told of abiding connections to Theosophy and, notably, to twentieth-century Theosophy, with its themes of powerful light and energy. The Ballards' Saint-Germain had taught the visualization and cultivation of a sense of the body's envelopment in a "Dazzling White Light," this as part of the process of uniting self with God. The "threefold truth" he and other ascended masters revealed included use of a violet consuming flame of divine love (the other two truths were the "Mighty I Am Presence" within and invocation of the "I Am" name for God). This violet flame was seen as a light cylinder surrounding a person as a mark of the divine presence. When a believer called forth the personal "I Am Presence" from within, taught the Ballards, they released the flame to burn up impurity and discord in the world—an activity intimately bound up with the practice of decreeing. In a declaration reminiscent of, especially, Alice Bailey's rays, I AM promoted the belief that each one of the ascended masters radiated a specific color representing a particular aspect of the divine. According to Edna Ballard, "clean, clear, bright colors" were "rivers of blessing from the realms of light, the source of all perfection." By contrast, some colors were deeply problematic: the color red "cut off the White Light," Saint-Germain warned, and black reflected hate as well as destruction and death. Members of I AM neither wore them nor kept objects in these colors close to them.[148]

In this blended Theosophy–New Thought world, lineages and lines of connection were everywhere. One formulation led to the next and on to the next; it was hard to tell when and where the line would be crossed that would lead some to object—and object strenuously—to the religious thought and practice of believers. I AM clearly crossed the line and became controversial. It experienced a prolonged period of litigation leading to two Supreme Court rulings (1944 and 1946)—in an often-cited case that raised issues regarding sincerity in religious belief and the dissemination of materials deemed fraudulent through the mails. The Court overturned lower-court convictions of Edna and Donald Ballard (Guy Ballard had died in 1939), but it was 1954 before the group could use the mails again and 1957 before its tax-exempt status returned. I AM's troubles, however, were not over. As it rebuilt—with an office building in the Chicago Loop and a retreat center near Mount Shasta—it also faced significant internal discord.

Continuing revelation meant that ascended masters could talk freely to whom they chose, and new groups and lineages could be created. Out of the splintering came, for instance, Mark L. Prophet's Summit Lighthouse, and—after his sudden death in 1973—the creation the following year of the Church Universal and Triumphant by his widow, Elizabeth Clare Prophet (the designated "Messenger" of the ascended masters), and the Summit Lighthouse's board of directors. Both I AM and spin-off groups like the now fairly well-known Church Universal and Triumphant contributed to the discourse community that became the New Age movement.[149] As we will see in this narrative's conclusion, ascended masters, once they started visiting, kept coming and—in the space age—came under new guises and assumed new roles.

ETHNIC SCRIPTS AND SUBSCRIBERS

There were, however, other new ages in which the white majority culture stood on the sidelines or entered only fitfully. We have already encountered the presence of "others" in Anglo-American spiritualist culture. Native Americans, for example, had haunted white minds from the earliest days of contact, and from the time of the Shaker manifestations of the late 1830s Indians had taken their place among the spirits who showed up for spiritualist seekers. By the heyday of séance spiritualism, their appearances had become organized, and by the end of the century the protocols for native visitors had been set. But they also visited more informally. We gain a brief glimpse in Clara Whitmore's fictionalized account of her childhood in the South in the late nineteenth century. Whitmore remembered that when she was six or seven, small and sensitive Nellie Reynolds came as a live-in helper for her mother. Reynolds, not herself well-liked, in the evenings turned medium for Indian Jo, who was large, strong, and much-liked. He brought news of relatives when snowstorms blocked communication, entertained family members who were there, and healed them. Jo was a "Christian Indian" and "friend of the Pale Faces," at a time when all the other Indians were gone. Indeed, "he seemed like a neighbor who dropped in, often three or four evenings a week." In the twentieth century, in the old and established spiritualist community Indians continued to come and go, almost like old friends and like Indian Jo. In the resident spiritualist camp at Cassadaga, Florida, for example (the oldest such religious community in the Southeast), some of the residents in the 1990s clearly favored Native American images and artifacts, while Indian guides still came by to assist mediums.[150]

Outside white minds, however, Native American metaphysicians thrived. Living Indians, in a mingled context of traditionalism and hybridism, pursued analogs to white activity on their own or with whites. Oblivious or indifferent to the blanket condemnation of Indian-white spiritual enterprises by Native American academics, some Indians accepted white clients and acted as spiritual mediums on their behalf, in effect playing the role of counselor. After she was ordained a spiritualist minister, for example, Rosalyn Bruyere's second teacher had been a Hopi elder named Grandfather David Monongya, who confided Hopi prophecy to her. Later, as a New Age healer, she regularly visited reservations for healing work, assisted clearly by her former spiritualism and the affinity it gave her to Native Americans, whose practices she sometimes adopted. However, such instances (and there were many) existed as the surface manifestation of a pervasive reality. Whether traditional or mingled with New Age beliefs and practices, Native American religiosity in the twentieth century and beyond clearly tilted toward metaphysics. Even in the strong Christian communities that flourished on the reservations and in cities with sizable American Indian populations, inherited structures of belief and practice altered the character of native Christianity. Sometimes these habitual patterns and practices existed alongside Christian practice, as in the much-reported case of the Oglala Sioux Black Elk, who was both a Catholic catechist and a Sioux traditionalist (and, later, a leader in the pan-Indian Ghost Dance). In a cultural world of combination, Indians subtly or not so subtly reinvented Christianity to accommodate their own sensibilities. Traditional ritual and ceremony had always been strongly marked by symbolism—in object, gesture, and sound—whether esoteric or transparent. Synthetic and blended ceremony operated similarly.[151]

Among African Americans, the tradition of continuing revelation, alive and well from colonial times, did not depart and leave blacks spiritless. Habits of practice flourished in the rural South, in northern and southern cities, and elsewhere throughout the nineteenth century and on into the twentieth and twenty-first. Anthropologists, sociologists, litterateurs, and religious studies scholars have provided windows into this dense culture of haunts and spirits and into the belief and practice systems that arose, paralleling white metaphysical endeavors and sometimes crossing over into them. After the Civil War, older black traditions of conjure (that is, hoodoo or root doctoring) were attacked by preachers and educators who sought to improve the lot of the freed slaves in the South. But as Yvonne Chireau has observed, anthropologists and ethnologists by the end of the century began to look again at these inherited beliefs, seeing their "mystical traits," their "unrefined spirituality," and their "racial and religious sensibility." For the twentieth century, the prominence of metaphysical religion among blacks is clear in the typology developed by Hans A. Baer and Merrill Singer to characterize all black religion in the United States. Alongside mainstream denominations and established sects, messianic-nationalist groups, and conversionist ones (like holiness and pentecostal practitioners), Baer and Singer identify "thaumaturgical sects." For them, thaumaturgy means "magico-religious" ceremonies and rituals, or the acquisition of "ecstatic knowledge" that promises seekers who come to these groups "spiritual power over themselves and others." Baer and Singer consider thaumaturgical activity expressive only, but in the terms of this narrative it is easy to see a magical instrumentalism in the quest for spiritual power.[152]

Important for the instrumentalism, rural and southern magical beliefs traveled to urban and northern areas. In his study of the survival of hoodoo beliefs and tales in northern Indiana, for example, Gilbert E. Cooley found that former southern root doctors, as northern and urban professionals, now called themselves "psychics," or "spiritualistic readers," or "prophets." "Most urban root doctors work under the guise of another name," Cooley reported. "Furthermore, they associate themselves with a particular church or at least assume the title of minister." To accommodate their practice, candles, oils, incense, roots, and other paraphernalia appeared in "religious candle shops," creating an economy predicated on magical and metaphysical work. Not only in Gary, Indiana, but also in cities like New York, Chicago, Detroit, Washington, Philadelphia, and St. Louis, black storefront churches and, especially, spiritualist churches supported a small army of mediums, psychic readers, and spiritual healers. As Chireau has summarized, "techniques such as numerology, palmistry, hypnotism, and astrology gave a veneer of legitimacy to these supernatural professionals, as did their titles: 'Professor' or 'Doctor.'" Metaphysical Asia surfaced, too, as some newspaper advertisements acquainted the public with exotic specialists who knew "Hindu" or "Oriental" secret lore. Even Christian ministers could function as entrepreneurial dispensers of magic and the occult. By the 1920s, too, blues songs sometimes carried conjure references in their titles, as in Ma Rainey's "Louisiana Hoodoo Blues," Bessie Brown's "Hoodoo Blues," and Blind Lemon Jefferson's "Low Down Mojo Blues."[153]

Nor had matters changed by the late twentieth century. Based on extensive fieldwork beginning from 1983 as she traveled the country by bus, Joyce E. Noll's *Company of Prophets* uncovered what she called "substantial and definitive psychic abilities" in a broad range of native-born blacks. Prophets came not only from the ranks of the poor but from a variety of socioeconomic classes and educational backgrounds. The range of claims and practices that Noll identified is extraordinary—mediums, spiritual healers, exorcists, ceremonial performers skilled in tarot and the use of crystals as well as in astrology and numerology, out-of-body travelers, recounters of past lives. Many of the "prophets" were still content to practice traditional Western religions, even as others turned to Asia and still others joined "New Age religions and groups." All, however, "believed in a Supreme Spirit consciousness," and their practice showed the same pragmatic and agency-oriented stance that could be found in mainstream metaphysical culture. Here was Mother Susie Booth, who lived to be 106 years old and who talked to powerful spirit guides and gave messages from the pulpit of the Upper Room, her church in Chicago. And here was Eddie Cabral, who aligned himself with three "entities" in order to create what he called a "triangular energy." More in keeping with New Thought categories and with what he knew of the East, here, too, was Chicago's Walter Nathaniel Thomas Jr., who established the Divine Light Temple and taught meditation in person and through his books *Divine Light Meditation* and *Spiritual Meditation.* In the midst of a financial struggle over a barely profitable building with a mortgage on it, he felt himself lifted into the air while meditating and decreed that he would sell the building that very day. He got a long distance phone call about two hours later with an offer to buy.[154]

In this plethora of individualized and small-group expressions, spiritualism clearly stood out. Like white spiritualists in the twentieth century, blacks found themselves in congregational settings. As early as 1913 Mother Leafy Anderson had organized the Eternal Life Spiritualist Church in Chicago, and Spiritual churches—complexly combinative groups based largely in spiritualism—began in earnest in the 1920s. Leafy Anderson herself apparently came to New Orleans around 1920, where Spiritual churches especially grew with female leadership, not unlike Christian Science and New Thought. New Orleans, however, was not alone as a spiritualist mecca, and in various cities in the nation—Chicago, Detroit, New York's Harlem, Houston, Baltimore, and Philadelphia among them —a network of congregations sprang up. Although most of them maintained a connection with a parent church if they had one, they were also highly decentralized. Beginnings often seemed informal and haphazard—typically as private businesses to advise people seeking jobs, heal them, help in their love affairs, or protect. Spiritualist advisors would eventually form congregations with their clients as members and then pastor them in storefront churches. In the Depression era, spiritualists became the fastest growing among the small and intense religious groups that arose throughout the black population. On Chicago's Southside, in "Bronxville," for example, in 1928 one church in twenty—or seventeen churches—was a Spiritual congregation; by 1938, one in ten—a total of fifty-one—could claim the same. As high as the numbers stood, they excluded a large group of unchurched spiritualists who kept home altars or worked as spiritualist advisors (thought to be over one hundred just before World War II). Meanwhile, in Harlem during the 1920s 15 percent of black churches were likewise Spiritual.[155]

Joseph Washington has described the combinative and agency-based religious culture of groups such as these as he identifies what drew people to them. Their "straightforward utilitarian use of religion" clearly appealed with its ready access to magical tools to protect from evil and attract desired good. "Spiritualists," Washington says, "combined the instinct of voodooism with Roman Catholic holy objects; Baptist and Methodist hymns were borrowed but not their fever-pitched preaching; their spiritual healing was taken over from the Holiness, Pentecostal groups, as well as their ritual of jubilant worship through swinging gospel tunes driven by the beat of secular rhythm and blues." In New Orleans, where Spiritual churches achieved special prominence and where scholars beginning with Zora Neale Hurston have paid more attention, prophecy and healing—as elsewhere—have functioned as hallmarks. Understood as biblical "gifts of the spirit," they have also conformed to major themes in metaphysical religion, and they have appeared not only in public worship but also in private client-centered therapy situations. As anthropologists Claude Jacobs and Andrew Kaslow have summarized, rituals range from conventional Christian ones like communion, baptism, and ordination to more distinctive practices like a "helping hand service," a "candle drill," and saint-day feasts. Jacobs and Kaslow point especially to the complexity of spirit possession in these churches, describing how "members may be filled by the Holy Spirit, as in Pentecostal churches, or 'entertain' spirits or spirit guides, as in Voodoo and Spiritualism."[156]

It is significant that the chief spirit guide in the New Orleans churches was—and continues to be—the Indian Black Hawk. Jacobs and Kaslow have noted the frequency of services dedicated to him as well as the number of altars and the many people who call him their spirit guide. They have also pointed to the prominent presence of representations of Black Hawk and Native Americans in the churches. Mother Leafy Anderson had begun the Black Hawk tradition, and report had it that she herself was half Mohawk and had called Black Hawk a "saint for the South." The historical Black Hawk had been a leader among the Sauk and Fox peoples of the upper Mississippi Valley in the early nineteenth century. He supported the British in the War of 1812 and later, in 1832—soured by Indian Removal west of the Mississippi and by poor land and shortages of food—led some one thousand men, women, and children to the east bank of the river. His rebellion failed, he ended up in a U.S. jail, and he was subsequently returned to Fox and Sauk loyal to the federal government. After that, he purportedly dictated his autobiography, although the authenticity of the document that claimed to be his work has been questioned. That, however, has not stopped him from occupying a ritual place of honor in Spiritual churches.[157]

Jacobs and Kaslow probe the meaning of the elaborate ritual and preeminent place accorded Black Hawk, suggesting that he has functioned as a complex symbol identified with Saint Michael (the Archangel) and also with Martin Luther King Jr. Indeed, they conclude that he was "more than an Indian spirit or powerful guide" but instead a "master symbol" like the Virgin of Guadalupe for Mexico. "As the symbol of the Virgin integrates a diverse nation," they write, "we suggest that the symbol of Black Hawk does the same for the assorted membership of the New Orleans Spiritual churches." Even, it seems, blacks had their own African American Black Hawk because, at the dawn of the twentieth century, a black bandit named Black Hawk harassed people in the Mississippi delta. Still, Jacobs and Kaslow point back again to the Indian identity of Black Hawk. For blacks separated from Africa and its ancient gods, Black Hawk, as a Native American, offered a non-European model of identity. More than that, in the Louisiana and New Orleans area the history of the two races was clearly intertwined, and mixed-race offspring were ubiquitous.[158] If blacks, like whites, experienced Indian hauntings, the haunts functioned differently and for different reasons. Blended lives were not the creations of fantasy but lived situations, and they could be celebrated.

This kind of unity between peoples—so much a part of the theoretical expression of American metaphysical religion—became a historical reality, too, in the Peace Mission Movement of Father Divine (1879–1965). In a formation that, for Baer and Singer, defies easy categorization into any one of the major types of black religion they propose, Divine's Peace Mission—like the Spiritual churches—displayed its fair share of metaphysical presence. Divine himself had been born as George Baker Jr., and he experienced the religiosity of Baltimore's storefront churches even as he grew to know something of Methodism and Catholicism there. His synthesizing habit led him to the pentecost of Los Angeles's famed Azusa Street Revival in 1906. But as Ronald White has shown, he was also strongly attracted to New Thought. Divine took the message of the God within seriously and literally, so that—in his first exploration of religious leadership—he took his place as the "Messenger," God in the degree of Sonship, in a spiritual triumvirate. Besides the mild-mannered Father Jehovia (Samuel Morris), the trio included Reverend Bishop Saint John the Vine (John A. Hickerson) whose homegrown theology displayed his familiarity with aspects of New Thought. In this, he was supported by Father Divine, who as the organizing power of the group taught the others the metaphysics he already knew.[159]

Familiarity with metaphysics existed identifiably in the black community, but

George Baker, who loved books, probably first absorbed New Thought through some of its extensive literary productions. He was especially influenced by the Unity teachings of the Fillmores and in his later life publicly expressed his admiration for Charles Fillmore and for Unity. Later, in Los Angeles in 1906, the twenty-seven-year-old Baker had still more opportunities to read metaphysical literature and to interact with whites in the movement. The message of oneness with God, of the power of mind, of God as infinite Supply, and poverty as the result of wrong thinking proved powerful, and he took it and reshaped it to his own evolving and eminently practical theology. As Jill Watts has written of blacks in general, from a New Thought perspective "blacks possessed just as much divinity as whites and, by applying mind-power, could overcome oppression and reap the benefits of American enterprise. Positive thinking allowed African Americans to assert control over their destiny and to combat their feelings of powerlessness in white America."[160]

As for Father Divine, he not only read New Thought books but he also turned to metaphysical Asia. He absorbed Jiddu Krishnamurti's *The Kingdom of Happiness* and also Baird T. Spalding's *Life and Teaching of the Masters of the Far East,* a work that had strongly influenced Guy Ballard and the I AM movement.[161] It was Charles Fillmore who affected him most deeply, but it was distinctly Fillmore in combination. Divine fused the mind-cure and prosperity teachings of Fillmore and New Thought, the reinforcements that came from the intuitionism of Krishnamurti, and the purported mind-power thinking that Spalding found among isolated Indian masters in the Himalayas. He wove them seamlessly into his own combinative religion that—like the Spiritual churches—brought together the perfectionism of holiness religion and the exuberance of the revival tradition with what New Thought had given him. Armed with his new religious synthesis, the Messenger broke from his Baltimore ministry, traveled in the South as a preacher and religious teacher, and then made his way to New York. There, in Sayville, Long Island, in 1919, he began a religious community. He had become convinced of the presence of God within each person, and he believed that spiritual and material wholeness went together. So began a long era in which he led enthusiastic devotees in a Depression-era haven of prosperity supported by his near-legendary generosity and hospitality. In a ritual that became central to the community's practice, he presided over a laden banquet table supplied with course after course and hours in which to consume them, and he even weighed his followers to be sure that they were growing fat. In the implicit theological message of the daily banquet occasions, he was the Messiah present for the messianic banquet. When his followers took the message of his divinity literally, Father Divine—whose adopted name said it all—did not deny that he was God. According to some (and like Charles Fillmore), he claimed that he would not die, and he held that the same good news could apply to the devout among his followers.[162]

Divine's enthusiastic banquets and mystical claims to divine identity, however, stood side by side with a pragmatism that also smacked of New Thought. His followers should know peace—and heaven—on earth, and he would guarantee that. He supplied food and shelter to followers at a nominal price, found employment for those who had no work, and often encouraged the formation of cooperative businesses. Nor would he abide racial segregation and disharmony. After the death of his first wife, in 1946 he married the Canadian-born Edna Rose Ritchings, who was white, and so he modeled black-white unity for devotees. God, though, was clearly black, since Father Divine was God present in the community. Blacks and whites could live in harmony, but the message was one of black priority and power in an African American liberation theology predicated on New Thought. Indeed, if we juxtapose the Father Divine message of the black empowered Self with the culture of spirit dependency embodied in Spiritual churches and a plethora of independent spiritualists, the central paradox of American metaphysical religion emerges clearly—a paradox that would be brought home sharply by the later New Age movement. On the one hand, metaphysics has spread the good news that humans are gods or gods-in-the-making. On the other, it has provided dramatic and performative scripts to ensure salvation by turning to Higher Powers—spirits, masters, mediums, and seers.

Even as Father Divine combined New Thought with other elements and reflected metaphysical paradox, in the American West and Southwest, Latinos were habitually practicing their own combinative versions of the faith. In a culture that, before recent inroads by pentecostalism and general Protestant evangelicalism, was at least nominally Catholic, several versions of vernacular metaphysics flourished throughout the twentieth century and on. In individualized forms of *curanderismo* (healing) and in organized ones as spiritualism and spiritism that emphasized curanderismo, Latinas and Latinos revealed metaphysical assumptions and enacted metaphysical scripts. They combined indigenous elements with European-derived ones to create authentic and independent versions of Mexican American metaphysics. Curanderismo—the religious folk healing system of Mexico and the American borderlands—depends on charismatic and prophetic figures who can channel more-than-natural energy into a series of corresponding registers—material, mental, and spiritual. Based on the claimed possession by the healer of a special gift for the work (*el don*), it functions in a universe of symbolic material discourse. Here the markers are such elements as the use of herbs and teas, midwifery and massage therapy, forms of divination such as card reading, and numerous spiritual cleansings, or sweepings—with food items like lemon, garlic, purple onions, and eggs. Studying its south Texas expression in the Lower Rio Grande Valley, anthropologists Robert T. Trotter and Juan Antonio Chavira have traced its historical sources to a panoply of ideas and practices. In various and fluid formations these can also be tracked in curanderismo elsewhere, and so the Trotter-Chavira statement of sources is broadly instructive: "Judeo-Christian religious beliefs, symbols, and rituals, early Arabic medicine and health practices (combined with Greek humoral medicine, revived during the Spanish Renaissance); medieval and later European witchcraft; Native American herbal lore and health practices; modern beliefs about spiritualism and psychic phenomena; and scientific medicine." "None of these influences dominates *curanderismo*," they report, "but each has had some impact on its historical development."[163]

The Spanish-Moorish engraftment on native tradition meant, already, the blending of two cultures with strong metaphysical components: We explored the metaphysical substrate in Greek theories of the four humors in the first chapter, and certainly Arab-Moorish medicine was predicated on notions of correspondence in which balance was primary and disharmony with the environment (social, spiritual, and physical) caused disease. Similarly, a native metaphysic, expressed in symbolic action, formed the basis of Mesoamerican culture. Bernard Ortiz de Montellano, who has pointed to the culture's homogeneity and paid special attention to the Aztecs, notes its strong shamanic elements and cites themes—and temple architectures—that represent connections between the human body and the universe. As in Spanish-Moorish medicine, good health reflects states of balance and equilibrium understood in the widest context and including the gods. In both systems and also in biblical ideas of healing that came through Christianity, material substances—largely botanical—provide strong assists. In curanderismo, their metaphysical properties supply a poetry of alliance with bodies in pain, as when—in the many *limpias*, or purifications, that a healer prescribes—eggs are passed over the body to absorb negative vibrations and energies.[164]

The explicitly magical universe of witchcraft also came into curanderismo through the contact culture that brought Europeans to Mesoamerican terrain. Rafaela Castro has called *brujería* (witchcraft) "an integral part of the culture of Mexico and the Southwest" and has pointed to the role of sixteenth-century conquerors and colonists in imparting European witchcraft beliefs. Here, missionary friars played a significant part with their denunciations of witches in a universe of sin, evil, and the devil. In the case of curanderismo, Trotter and Chavira cite the strong support for correct incantatory formulas, prayers, and rituals that medieval and later witchcraft bequeathed across the Atlantic—magic that the two say dated "back to Egypt, India, and pre-Christian Europe." They also note its encouragement of human attempts to control the spirits. In this regard, a *curandero* or *curandera* could acquire a reputation for power. In many cases, too, the negative reading of witchcraft that came as part of the baggage of Christian culture meant that healing power was seen as emanating from the devil. Healers would help, but healers were also to be feared. Not themselves witches (that is, *brujos* or *brujas*)—who are understood to function independently from healers and stand as "accepted facts of life" in Chicano culture—healers could still be confused with witches. Conversely, people often sought them to undo the harm that they believed a witch had caused.[165]

Combination, though, did not simply fuse multiple pasts. Emergent discourses from Europe continued to move westward and to enter Mexican and Mexican American cultural conversations. They modified the healing scripts of curanderismo and also came to function more separately in spiritualist contexts. In a Mexican American culture that Romantic glosses typically depict as isolated from Europe and Anglo-America, ideas and writings supporting "modern" spiritualism and psychic research flourished. Especially notable were the works of Allan Kardec (Leon Denizarth Hippolyte Rivail), the nineteenth-century Frenchman whom we have met briefly before. Kardec, who for semantic reasons called his beliefs about contact with spirits "spiritism" (he thought that the term *spiritualism* might be applied to any antimaterialist or extramaterialist belief), published seven works on spiritist themes as midcareer productions. Son of an old and distinguished family, he had been educated in Switzerland and returned to France to dabble in various semi-learned pursuits, translating books into German for young people, lecturing on various sciences, and participating—significantly—in the Phrenological Society of Paris and the Society of Magnetism. Like others in the evolving metaphysical community of the era, he was drawn to investigations of clairvoyance and trance, sleep walking, and similar mesmeric phenomena. When, after 1848, news of the Hydesville happenings across the Atlantic brought new excitement and interest to these and related themes, Rivail (he was not yet Kardec) engaged in a series of séance sessions. Through two young female mediums, he believed, he contacted the spirits who gave him his pen name and dictated the contents of his spiritist books.[166]

Especially, these spirits countered the anti-reincarnationist version of spiritualism that Andrew Jackson Davis and others had advanced in America earlier. For Kardec, in fact, as Frank Podmore summarized, the "leading tenet" of the "new gospel" was reincarnation, with multiple incarnations allowing the soul to progress from life to life. (This turn toward reincarnation, it should be noted, already signaled—or perhaps helped to create—the climate for the appearance of

Theosophy.) Although its English-language translation had to wait until 1875, Kardec's ground-breaking *Le Livre de Esprits* (The Spirits' Book) had appeared in French as early as 1853, and it was published again in a revised French version in 1857. As a textbook for Kardec's brand of reincarnational spiritualism, it went through at least fifty-two editions, and Kardec himself created the monopolistic journal *La Revue Spirite* to support the work. Kardec's books, in general, were popular; Podmore noted that they "sold by tens of thousands, and were trans-lated into nearly every European language." By the later twentieth century, they were surely being translated into Spanish, as even a cursory review of the Inter-net WorldCat database shows. Meanwhile, June Macklin has noted that by this time simplified digests of Kardec's teachings appeared in paperback throughout Latin America.[167]

In the United States, Kardecist spiritism and a more generalized spiritualism could be found in places as varied as south Texas, California, and Indiana, where migrant laborers came. There is confusion in the anthropological literature about what counts as spiritism and what as spiritualism, but generally the acceptance or rejection of the theological tenet of reincarnation locates a spirit-believer in the spiritist or spiritualist camp respectively. More than that, as Luis D. León has observed, based on the work of Silvia Ortíz Echániz, spiritists may have come from higher social classes than spiritualists. In Mexico, Kardec's work—which turned on the creation of spiritual healing centers and explicit ritual directions for prayer and incantation in temple ceremonies—led to the organization of spiritual temples. These grew rapidly in the late twentieth century, some explic-itly spiritist and others more broadly spiritualist. They also spread across the bor-der, as León's representative account of one such (spiritualist) temple in East Los Angeles—with its fifty mediums at various levels of training—shows.[168]

At the same time, charismatic healers came to take their places as the saints of Mexican American curanderismo, among them El Niño Fidencio, Don Pedrito Jaramillo, and Teresa Urrea. Tellingly, they are figures who in devotional fol-lowing—and for Jaramillo and Urrea in their lives as well—have straddled the Mexico–United States border. In doing so, they embody the individual and col-lective histories of Latino immigrants and the ritual "dramas of salvation" that Macklin found in the work of curanderas and curanderos. Moreover, as León in-sists, the "truly charismatic" healing gift (*el don*) was "*revealed*, not conferred." In the case of José Fidencio de Jesús Constantino Síntora, popularly called El Niño Fidencio (1898–1938), the famed healer became so strong an object of cultus that, after his death, temples sprang up in Mexico and the United States, includ-ing Chicago. Here trance mediums brought his spirit back to consult, cure, and even predict the future. According to El Niño lore, the future healer—like Alice

Bailey—received his own version of a visit from a master: Once, when he was caring for his sick younger brother, the door of his shack opened and a stranger (Jesus, he later thought, standing in the Sacred Heart position of Catholic devotionalism) handed him a book that detailed the plant and herb remedies that would cure his brother. In a second, separate incident, another calling came when he saw in vision a "tall, bearded man with a luminous halo around his venerable head" who told him of his "high destiny" as a healer. Later, from 1925 to 1927, El Niño was employed in Mexico by a German from whom he learned European spiritism. A controversial figure who alternately was accused of unwittingly creating harm and hailed as an effective healer, he kept up his healing work from his bed in 1935 when his own health declined. After his death, two annual three-day festivals sprang up to honor him, and according to an anthropological team who filmed the El Niño devotionalism in 1972, as many as fifty thousand people participated. Most of the devotees were women.[169]

With regard to the more general spiritualist movement, in the United States Luis León has pointed to the existence of "at least three highly public *espiritualista* [that is, spiritualist] temples—each with several hundred members and many more 'visitors'—in East Los Angeles alone." Numbers of temples also appeared in Southern California and in the American Southwest, where in 1981 Trotter and Chavira reported that spiritualism was growing in south Texas. They reported, too, that for the healing work of curanderismo the concept of energy functioned as the central unifying idea. Indeed, if the material, mental, and spiritual levels of healing that they detailed are scrutinized, the metaphysics of energy becomes clearly apparent. At the material level, the numerous *limpias* that they recorded (they themselves were subject to nine) absorbed the vibrations of negative energy, as we saw in the use of the egg. According to the larger theory—Trotter and Chavira call it "one prevailing theory"—all persons and animals as well as some objects could give out or take in "vibrating energy." This energy assumed either positive or negative form and led to positive or negative outcomes. The counter energy of incantation and sound could disrupt negative patterns that were concentrated in an individual's body, there to cause illness. Meanwhile, substances like water and oil could be prepared with "mental vibrations" giving them "magnetic properties" that supplied strength on contact.[170] Thus, in a real sense, healing became a process of energy balancing, using ritual accoutrements in order to perform new scripts of equilibrium for the client-patient.

At the mental level, which Trotter and Chavira reported as the least prevalent and in fact rare, the curandero or curandera worked to channel mental energy to the specific somatic site where illness existed. Healers thought that the power of their own minds could transform, at the cellular level, what was wrong—discouraging the spread of diseased cells and accelerating the growth of healthy ones. Finally, at the spiritual level—less common than material healing but more pervasive than mental energy channeling—healers entered trance states, in which they felt that they were projecting their own souls outward to make room for the entry of benevolent spirits. Especially, for the spiritual level, Trotter and Chavira noted beliefs that sickness and disease could be "caused, diagnosed, and cured by spiritual forces called *corrientes espirituales* (spiritual currents)." What constituted healing, then, was the manipulation of spiritual currents.[171]

Mexican American curanderismo and spiritism have shown no sign of abating in recent years. Quite the contrary, in the politicized climate of Chicano consciousness of *la raza* (the "race"), traditional practices and beliefs have provided scripts to perform not only the Chicano and Chicana body but also the spiritualized body politic. In the words that León applies to one healer—Don Pedrito Jaramillo—but that, arguably, may be extended to all, "healing the body . . . served as a microcosm for repairing the nation that was dismembered in colonization." There were, however, other ethnic scripts and dramas being enacted on American soil, and to notice what is perhaps obvious, some of them came as the property of different European immigrant groups. Throughout the twentieth century, for example, the Pennsylvania Dutch (that is, Germans) kept on marking their barns with hex signs to ward off evil, and pow-wowing has continued to thrive among them. Later immigrants, like Italian Americans, passed on their fear of the "evil eye" and, as late as the mid-twentieth century, some in the first generation still used garlic and various assigned objects as talismans for protection. When the garlic was abandoned, plastic evil-eye protectors and similar devices remained.[172]

Other performances, however, came from new twentieth-century embodiments of metaphysical Asia, this time metaphysical *East* Asia. Unlike African Americans, Mexican Americans, and to a considerable extent Continental Euro-Americans—and somewhat like Native Americans but much more than they—ethnic East Asians shared their dramas of salvation with non-Asians. Still more, East Asians not only shared: They missionized. In acts of religion that also functioned as acts of entrepreneurship, they sold a reconstituted and even newly invented Daoism (Taoism) to mainstream American buyers. The performances that resulted point unmistakably to the twentieth-century metaphysical themes we have been exploring. They exhibited high energy concerns—so that energy, in fact, became a mantric term. They promoted experiences of personal power in a context that exalted an enlightened body-self. They taught, if you will, a Vedanta of East Asian provenance, in which yin and yang were resolved in the harmony of the unifying principle, the Dao. All things were one thing, but the one thing lay at the service of individual need and desire. And if there were exalted teachers (the other side of the equation), the teachers never became ascended masters, and the teachers were, in some cases, subject to criticism.

Daoist practitioners did not become a noticeable presence in the United States until after the change in the immigration law in 1965 brought a visible increase in the numbers of Chinese immigrants and especially of the well-educated and privileged classes. Perhaps ironically, though, one of the first conspicuous expressions of American Daoist themes came not from China at all but arrived secondhand from Japan as part of the cultural baggage that shaped (Japanese) American macrobiotics. To complicate matters further, from almost the first macrobiotics was intimately connected to the New Age movement. Indeed, J. Gordon Melton has argued that in 1971 the Boston macrobiotic community's *East West Journal* became the first national periodical to explore the issues and themes that were being identified with the New Age.[173] Michio Kushi (1926–), a Japanese immigrant and the foremost teacher of macrobiotics in America, however, had a different, more Asian self-understanding. So, too, did the early macrobiotic community. In a metaphysical context that extended from food ways to a general religious philosophy of life, the macrobiotic movement embodied for them a distinctive spirituality with roots *not* of the New Age.

Kushi himself had not originated macrobiotics (literally, "great"—or "long"—life). Its creator was Yukikazu Sakurazawa (1893–1966), who adopted the Westernized name Georges (and later George) Ohsawa. He had shaped macrobiotics from the ideas of a lineage of Japanese food philosophers, the most immediate being his own teacher, Sagen Ishizuka. The founder of the Shoku-Yo movement in Japan at the beginning of the twentieth century, Ishizuka taught a self-conscious and systematized restoration of traditional dietary habits. Still further, from at least the time of Shoku-Yo, the food philosophy functioned, too, as a sociopolitical philosophy with distinctive spiritual overtones. On the inside cover of Ishizuka's second book, for example, an inscription announced the foundation of the world to be the nation, the foundation of the nation to be the home, of the home to be the body, of the body the spirit, and, finally, the foundation of the spirit to be food.[174] The metaphysical reversal that Ishizuka's inscription signaled continued to mark macrobiotics. Now the body was not so much in the mind (that is, controlled by it) as the mind was in the body, being shaped by it and what it was fed. Still, there would be enough inconsistency in macrobiotic circles to support the classic metaphysical position, so that even as the macrobiotic body fed the mind the metaphysical mind enjoyed its share of macrobiotic notice and privilege.

Ohsawa had become the central figure in the Shoku-Yo, and he spent years as an indefatigable lecturer and writer, organizing a Western network of macro-biotic centers. After World War II, he maintained a study house—his Student World Government Association—and it was here that Michio Kushi, a student in politics and law at Tokyo Imperial University, found him. "Have you ever considered the dialectical application of dietary principles to the problem of world peace?" Ohsawa asked Kushi when they met. Kushi was persuaded and then, encouraged by Ohsawa and endorsed by Norman Cousins, he immigrated to the United States and continued his graduate work at Columbia University in New York City. Absorbed in his experiential studies of macrobiotics, he never obtained a degree but instead moved to Boston and began a center. He had married a Japanese macrobiotic student (Tomoko Yokoyama, who became Aveline Kushi). With help from her, from the Japanese immigrant pair Herman and Cornellia Aihara on the West Coast, and from other Ohsawa students like Shizuko Yamamoto in New York City, he worked to make a movement grow. The *East West Journal*, begun in 1970, reached a circulation of near 80,000 by 1985, and by the late 1980s, conservatively, there were close to 100,000 adult macrobiotic adherents in the nation.[175]

What had these subscribers obtained through the new scripts they read and were now performing? Ohsawa had already bequeathed to his fledgling movement a religious philosophy. He taught the "order of the universe" and the "unique principle" that grounded it. He began to invoke the "Tao" (read as "way," or "spiritual path," or "practice," or "cosmic absolute" that was both transcendent and within the self), identifying his ideas with the Chinese Daoist philosopher Lao-Tsu (Laozi). But he also identified them with a world catalog of sages and seers. And as they stood, his teachings were remarkably poised to enter American metaphysical discourse. In his *Zen Macrobiotics*, Ohsawa offered readers "twelve theorems of the unique principle." He affirmed that yin and yang were the "two poles of the infinite pure expansion," that they were "produced infinitely, continuously, and forever," and that everything was "restless" because "things and phenomena" were "constantly changing their Yin and Yang components." He also propounded his "seven stages of judgment" with the "supreme" (highest) stage one of "absolute and universal love that embraces everything and turns every antagonism into complementarism." More concretely, yin and yang became a taxonomy for the classification of food, because the beginnings of spirituality lay, for Ohsawa and his movement, in human biology and its transformation through food. In a variation of conventional representations of Chinese teaching, Ohsawa had identified yin as a centrifugal, expanding energy. It was earth's force and associated with rising seeds and plant growth; it was also female, cold, (paradoxically?) passive, and spiritual (all—it should be noted in the context

here—associated with mediumistic activity). By contrast, yang represented cen-
tripetal, contracting power. As heaven's force and the energy of the contained,
sheathed seed, it carried the germ of potential life within; it was—like the familiar gendered understandings—male, hot, active, and physical. In keeping with
the order of the universe, foods should be locally grown and used in season; in the
late-twentieth-century American community, the teaching soon incorporated
the notion that they should be organically grown, free from chemical fertilizers
or pesticides. Grains and vegetables, as the most balanced foods (with equal proportions of yin and yang) got preferential treatment, and not surprisingly, brown
rice—the staple of traditional Japan—was acknowledged as the most balanced
food of all. It was these substances that could create good health and lead on and
beyond to supreme judgment and spiritual wholeness.[176]

Eating macrobiotically became a delicate balancing act. It took account of an
individual's constitution (given genetically and present from birth), condition
(what eating habits and other stresses had done to the basic constitution), location and climate, and even "dream" or purpose (a monk should eat differently
from a day laborer or business executive). More than that, macrobiotic dietary
choices were only the beginnings of a life journey predicated on a metaphysical
superstructure that, as Ohsawa's "twelve theorems" and "seven stages" already
suggest, ambitiously explained all aspects of the cosmic and human worlds. After
Ohsawa's death, Michio Kushi expanded and embellished his teaching, offering
theosophical readings of his own from his Japanese past and, it seems virtually
certain, from contact with American New Age students and American metaphysical culture in general. The combinative product of past and present, Kushi's teachings proclaimed a new-old spirituality, reinvented and reconstructed
in patterns supportive of American projects of its time. Whereas Ohsawa had
only touched on themes such as Chinese traditional thought and its practical
application in a macrobiotic way of life, Kushi taught more. He was interested,
for example, in Chinese "five-element" or "five-transformation" theory, and he
used it to intersect the canonical teachings of yin and yang. With ideas based
on *The Yellow Emperor's Classic of Internal Medicine* (dating probably from
around 500 B.C.E.), which—not without help from the macrobiotic community
—would become a popular text in American vernacular "Taoism," Kushi taught
five changes of the primal energy of life. Fire, earth, metal, water, and wood all
stood as elements, or "phases," to which seasons of the year, times of the day,
physical organs, food, and even tastes (salty, sour, and so forth) corresponded.
Under Kushi's tutelage, practitioners ate for constitution and condition, taking
note not only of yin and yang but also of the phases of energy transformation.[177]
In other words, someone in whose basic constitution one element or transforma-

tion was weak or who, through a current condition, presented a weakened profile in one element or transformation would eat to heal the problem. Someone with a weak liver or gall bladder, either because of genetics or personal history, for example, would eat foods said to strengthen and support the liver or gall bladder.

Whatever it did for diseased livers and gall bladders, the American Daoist rhetoric of Kushi's teaching—easily available because of the plethora of inexpensive books that Kushi, with the aid of his students, published—brought familiarity with Daoist language to America. (For a time, macrobiotic literature was even sold and distributed under the imprint of Tao Books.) It also taught a combinative mixture that Ronald E. Kotzsch, the leading historian of the movement, has called the "gospel according to Kushi." As one example, using the concepts of yin and yang as arbiters, Kushi taught a traditional sexuality that brought the unique principle in touch with family values. Sexual pleasure was greatly to be desired, but only in marriage. More than that, children were to be desired, and artificial restraints on childbearing carried not only moral but also and especially physical consequences. These caveats, from one perspective, could keep company with even a Roman Catholic natural-law ethic. From another—with its celebration of sensuality as an assist to and result of optimum health, and with its preoccupation with the physical consequences of obstructing the natural order—the Kushi way parted practical company with Catholicism and similar orientations quickly.[178]

In terms of metaphysical religiosity, though, the theosophizing speculations of Kushi deserve notice. Kushi himself was attracted to Gnosticism, as his growing endorsement of the Gnostic *Gospel of Thomas* shows. Kushi knew, too, about such staples of the American metaphysical discourse community as auras and chakras. In his *Gentle Art of Making Love*, for example, he advised on "stimulating" the chakras and activating them during sexual play. Far and above all of this, however, he theorized on a grand scale about cosmogony and anthropology, building on Ohsawa's synthesis but going well beyond it. For instance, he took Ohsawa's gnostic diagrammatic statement of the order of the universe depicting its evolution as a logarithmic spiral and—in the shadow of the New Age appropriation of quantum physics—elaborated it further. Now Kushi invoked everything from DNA helices, star formations, and seashell construction, to hair-growth patterns and the direction of water down the kitchen sink. "The substance of the Great Life / completely follows Tao," he quoted from Lao-Tzu (Laozi), and he declared for "spirals of everlasting change."[179]

Kushi's expansive narrative of cosmic, earthly (that is, natural), and human history emerged as a gnostic tale of grand proportions, intricately thought through and thought out, with myriad correspondences between material, historical, and spiritual stages of development. It included attention, for example, to a prehistoric period in which extraterrestrials bolstered the level of cultural achievement, both technological and spiritual, and in which, as Venus moved closer to the sun, emigrants from that planet were forced to make their way to our earth. In a variation of the master theme that linked earth to space beings (as we shall see later, a characteristic New Age marker), he also thought that intelligent visitors had come to our planet to teach and intermarry with earthlings. (He has continued to be interested in unidentified flying objects—UFOs—to the present.) Kushi's extraterrestrials knew the laws of yin and yang and so could control natural energies and use mind powers like clairvoyance and telepathic communication. Meanwhile, in the Kushi account ancient architectural remains, like the pyramids and other megaliths, had been designed to attract and control the energies of the cosmos. Kushi knew about Blavatsky's lost continents of Atlantis and Lemuria and pronounced them destroyed by the flooding that attended a shifting earth axis. Moreover, he taught that humans had manifested themselves through stages, coming from the "one infinity," or "universal spirit," through a world of "radiation," where spirits dwelled, and then a world of "vibration," or "energy," inhabited by souls, ghosts, and astral bodies. From there, soon-to-be humans entered the atmosphere, the waters of embryonic life, and finally the earth. "Our roots as human beings are in heaven," Kushi wrote, "and the *ki* or electromagnetic energy that animates us comes primarily from above through the chakras before branching out to the [acupuncture] meridians and then to trillions of cells. Each cell has spirit, nourished constantly by energy and vibration from heaven and earth. We are fully spiritualized when these cells are activated."[180]

What did humans come for? In Kushi's optimistic reading (not far from New Thought formulations), they came to live out a dream and to be "trained" on the "playground" of earth. Those who ate macrobiotically and shared the "same blood quality" could "act and play together to realize humanity's common dream of building One Peaceful World" and continue their "endless journey through the stars." "We play in this universe, living our eternal life, transforming ourselves constantly, manifesting ourselves into various forms," he summarized. If the element of tragedy seems missing, those who know Kushi can point to his often dire prognostications for the future and his warnings of peril in the first decade of the twenty-first century. He has counseled personal transformation through "meditation, self-reflection, and prayer," but the more elementary—and collective— message was to work to transform the planet by beginning with its biological base, missionizing for food in order to missionize for spirit.[181]

Spirit, though, always seemed to register as energy in American Daoist circles, as in twentieth-century and later metaphysical religiosity in general. If Kushi and the macrobiotic movement had provided early introductions to what American and metaphysical Daoist themes could be, it remained for a series of Chinese immigrants to supply their own performances. They did so on different stage sets and with a different, albeit sometimes overlapping, cast of characters. Elijah Siegler, who has studied American Daoism, has called it a "new religious movement that may have some connection to the Daoist tradition in China, but has less connection than claimed from within the movement itself." His evidence for the assessment has come largely from examining self-conscious statements of Daoist identity as expressed through a series of practices. These include reading and study of ancient texts believed to constitute the foundations of Daoism—the *Daodejing* (*Tao Te Ching*) and the *Yijing* (*I Ching*). They also encompass performance of the physical movements taught in taijiquan (t'ai-chi ch'uan) and qigong (ch'i-kung), and use of traditional Chinese medicine with its acupuncture and herbalism. And, it could be added, they extend to the cultivation of distinctive types of meditation practice that aim, like the physical movements and the medicine, to augment and direct the flow of *qi*. (The mysterious and much-sought qi signals something like South Asian prana and something like Western "breath" that opens out toward spirit—suggesting, again, the enlightened body-self.) For Siegler, American Daoism originated from a confluence of Western intellectual and East Asian immigrant histories, from a "collaboration between progressive elements in American society, and elite, lettered Chinese immigrants, nostalgic for their own displaced childhoods." (The "Tao," in popular parlance, was mother of us all.) As in the case of metaphysical South Asia, the metaphysical East Asia of American Daoism arose in a world in which the West was hardly absent from the East. Like a series of reflecting mirrors, each culture replayed again and again what the other had constructed it to be—in a combining of images that endlessly reproduced themselves to create the fluid set of practices deemed in America to be Daoist. American Daoism, says Siegler, was "not merely influenced by moments of contact but constituted by them."[182]

With Daoism for the West, in the words of intellectual historian J. J. Clarke, "not so much a living tradition as a collection of writings," it was the vernacular entry of culturally facile and educated ethnic Chinese that brought Daoism into the territory of the body and, so, the enlightened body-self. What Siegler calls a "statistically miniscule" but "culturally significant" number of American spiritual seekers found in a Daoist vocabulary of correspondence a discourse that satisfied. It conformed for them to long-held American metaphysical notions of correspondence between macrocosm and microcosm. Especially, in concert with the twentieth-century and later emphasis of American metaphysical religion, they could read it in terms of energy, for qi was but another term for the ubiquitously desired metaphysical "energy." Here their views of Daoism derived from older, romanticized Western representations of Daoism in an Orientalist mode—work unsupported by current critical scholarship. Uninformed by that knowledge, their new American Daoism became a nonexclusive religion recognizing Lao Tzu (Laozi) as its founder and promoting few written texts. Unspecific geographically (no central shrines; portable sacred space in nature and the self), it remained historically indifferent and uninvolved in politics or social ethics. Its only divisions arose from traditionalist or more free-floating readings of what constituted Daoism.[183]

The Daoism in the minds of American seekers had been shaped not only by an older cohort of Western scholars and their popularizers but also by enthusiasm for the "perennial philosophy" and the human potential movement. As in the case of American yoga, Esalen Institute in Big Sur, California, played a significant role. So did the idealized figure of the Oriental monk, part of American vernacular culture through such images as that of the Dalai Lama and fictive portrayals of martial arts mastership and of inscrutable Daoist masters with magical powers. In this climate of expectation, the new ethnic Chinese Daoist masters of America, sometimes with bona fide acting backgrounds, simply performed themselves. Teachers claimed lineages (a Chinese requirement for authenticity) or invented them. They cultivated personal followings but did not create institutions. Curricula could not be replicated because the master, in effect, was the curriculum. The Chinese masters thus cultivated mystification, and their students cultivated practice—in a discourse community in which the "energy" of qi became both the desired good and the fluid and ever-changing absolute.[184]

American Daoists in the late twentieth century and after have been well-educated, middle class, white, and about equally divided between genders. Their introduction to Daoism usually comes through taiji or qigong or similar disciplines, through contact with acupuncturists or Chinese herbalists because of health problems, or through "Daoist" texts, often read in college or even high school. Age has varied widely, with no particular bias toward youth. (This last is unsurprising, since taiji and qigong are particularly well-adapted to seniors and alternative medicine is often favored for the chronic diseases that especially plague older people.) Figures for the number of Daoists in the late-century United States and Canada range from a low of just over 11,000 to more ambitious estimates of 30,000 and even 45,000. Still these are small numbers, even if a huge traffic in Daoist websites exists on the Internet (Siegler cites "hundreds if not thousands"). If scholars could not link this American Daoism to a Chinese counterpart, U.S. practitioners remained oblivious. They were innocent of an evolving scholarship that painted Daoism as exclusivist and intolerant, distinct from the vulgarities of ordinary culture, and related to a specific Chinese geography of sacred mountains. Nor did they seek to recover and periodize a history of Daoism, going beyond the time of Laozi and Zuangzi (Chuang Tzu) to explore a later saga during a series of Chinese dynasties. They were unaware that Daoism was a religion of books, which in its first (fifth-century) canon numbered more than 1,400 titles in some 5,305 volumes—larger than the canon of any religion save Buddhism. And they had no idea of the political role that Daoist sects played in China as revolutionaries who succeeded in creating a theocracy for at least several decades during the Han dynasty. They did not know that for a large part of Chinese history Daoism had been state-sponsored. Nor did they know anything of the rigor of its conventional moral precepts and the elaborateness of its ritual life. Americans drawn to Daoism have dwelled instead in a Daoism of their minds and imaginations.[185]

The Daoism of their imagining, though, like the New Thought universe of a century earlier, has been inherently unstable. Its nonsectarian universalism pushed it toward a larger metaphysical community, in which Daoism became a Daoism of language and the Daoism of language blurred into the general rhetoric of spiritual "energy" in contemporary American metaphysics and especially the New Age. Taiji, qigong, and traditional Chinese medicine had other takers besides self-conscious Daoists. Moreover, even the writings of charismatic Daoist teachers were read widely by sympathizers who never assumed Daoist identities but instead maintained more hybrid and combinative ones. Take, for example, the work of Mantak Chia (1944–), a Thai businessman in Hong Kong and China with a diverse educational background, much of it in meditative and martial arts techniques. Chia has pitched his teaching to Americans with a national seminar circuit since 1981. He has also advertised widely in New Age publications, developed an international organization, created a network of healers working under him, and—with American Michael Winn directing—offered instruction regularly at a summer camp/retreat in upstate New York.

In 1981, Chia's book *Awaken Healing Energy through the Tao* appeared in its first edition. Billed as "Taoist Esoteric Yoga," it succeeded so well that it appeared only two years later in a more widely marketed imprint. With direct and textbook style, Chia immediately positioned what he offered as a third alternative to Zen silent sitting and Hindu mantric meditation. Instead, he presented a "system stressing the circulation of energy called 'chi' along certain pathways inside the body." "These pathways," he informed readers, "help direct the 'chi'—also known as prana, sperm or ovarian power, the warm current, or kundalini power —to successively higher power centers (chakras) of the body." Secret knowledge of this system had been "transmitted for thousands of years in China," and there it had brought "extraordinary improvements in health and life." "Chi" was the "primordial life force itself," and its flow proceeded in ideal order in the human fetus, with its navel point the starting place for the movement of energy and "the point of strongest energy storage and circulation in the adult." Age, however, brought blockage, and the "perfect energy circulation we enjoyed as babies" was disrupted. What could adults do? They could turn to the specific type of meditation that Chia taught, which would bring reawakening so that the "healing power of the Tao—the life energy in its original, pure, undivided form"—would flow unimpeded once again.[186]

Chia had evoked a combinative catalog of buzz words and ideas from American metaphysical religion, and he had announced a meditative form that involved the mind in the (mysticized) physicality of the body in order to heal and enliven it. With theosophical acumen, he pointed to the "etheric body." Still more, he introduced the language of the body's "microcosmic orbit"—its route for the flow of energy that seemed like a vastly simplified acupuncture meridian (Chia, in fact, acknowledged the same in the subtitle to the first edition of his book and in the text of his second edition). The microcosmic orbit began at the perineum and moved up the back of the spine to the tongue, with its tip on the roof of the mouth acting like a "switch" to send energy back down the front of the body. This seems like a decidedly esoteric technique—except that it was being mass-marketed to a sizable audience of American readers. (In fact, Michael Winn, who wrote an introduction to the second edition, reported that "students of various Chinese arts" were "shocked to see his book sold in a store." The "circulation of the microcosmic orbit was the 'highest secret' to gaining internal power in the mind and body.")[187]

With all of this preparatory cultivation of the sophisticated would-be Daoist, what Chia taught next was a seemingly childlike instruction in the "inner smile." After creating a calm and quiet environment in which to begin the practice of meditation, after relaxing mentally and taking thirty-six (a multiple of nine and a favored Chinese number) deep abdominal breaths, the meditator needed to relax the internal organs. So the "ancient Taoist masters" recommended the exercise of smiling "love" into the vital organs. With closed eyes, the meditator smiled "sincerely" into them and proceeded from there to smile down a "front," "middle," and "back" line, thus reaching all major organs and even the inside of the vertebrae of the spine. What the meditator smiled was "chi energy," and when the task was about to be finished he or she collected the energy at the navel—so that there would be no excess energy to cause trouble in the head. How could a person be sure? "To collect the energy simply concentrate your mind on your navel and imagine your energy spinning like a slow top inside, spiralling outward movement." Men should spiral first in a clockwise direction; women counter clockwise.[188] In effect, Chia was recommending putting the mind in the body. He was selling acts of disciplined imagination that came from a mentalist perspective, and he was teaching metaphysics, using breath and sensation as magical tools halfway between the mental and the material.

With already its open "secrecy" in a popular book, Chia's inner smile meditation gained a decidedly exoteric following. It became a friendly New Age practice that crept into settings as varied as acupuncture offices, Unity churches, and secular-seeming relaxation workshops. It smiled beckoningly, and people bought it. Inner smiles were so easy to perform and, at the very least, so nondenominational and so harmless. They did not seem occult or esoteric at all. Like Norman Vincent Peale's positive thinking, inner smiles and other energy practices spilled out of their cultural containers to become anybody's property who wanted them. If there were "nightstand Buddhists"—people who kept a Buddhist book beside their bed and sometimes dipped into it—there were also numbers of nightstand or workshop Daoists. Still, the message of the power of mind in a set of ostensibly physical practices bears scrutiny for its metaphysical content. Chia's performative strategy was hardly isolated. It came with a long prehistory, and throughout the cultural world that touched a self-conscious American Daoism, the message of the mind in the body was seemingly everywhere.

To take an example from the practice of taiji, we need only look at a canonical text for the Yang-style taiji that has become the most practiced style in the United States. The classic *Tai-Chi Ch'uan* (1947) was putatively the work of Chen Yen-lin, a wealthy Chinese merchant—known in the West as Yearning K. Chen—who had studied under the transmitter of the Yang family's style. Indeed, in the climate of exalted regard for lineage claims, the report was that he had, in effect, stolen Yang family secrets by borrowing transcripts one evening, hiring seven transcribers to copy them all night long, and then in 1932 publishing the results in Chinese. But Chen's text contained entire sections, not present in the original Chinese, that were probably the work of his translator Cheng Man-ch'ing. Moreover, the solo form instructions and explanations did not match up identically with the Chinese, and the work had probably been reshaped to tell Western students what the translator thought would appeal. Still, with its intricately precise directions and figures for the performance of the long-form (108-posture) "right side" movements, the text began with a crisp and slightly quaint introduction to orient readers and about-to-be doers. "T'ai-chi Ch'üan," the translated Chen told readers, would rebuild their "spirit and body," and it was "closely related to Meditation." In fact, it was better, because the long practice of meditation could "hinder blood circulation," but the "t'ai-chi" movements helped to "quicken it." "T'ai-chi" was predicated on a "subtle system of Chinese philosophy" called the

"Grand Terminus." "From the Negative Terminus to the Grand Terminus," the text explained, were "comprehended the theories of all created things in the universe, and the principles of the formation of *Yin* and *Yang*." Since all things in the universe were composed of yin and yang elements and since science itself agreed (Chen cited the "electron theory" of "positive and negative electricity"), the practitioner enacted the "theories of the Grand Terminus." In so doing, he or she entered upon a moving meditation: "Give up all thoughts. Set your eyes forward, directed to the spot just in front of the outgoing hand. Close your mouth and breathe through your nose. Press your tongue against your palate. . . . Raise your spirit and breathe down from the navel psychic-centre, so that you may feel at ease in every part of your body and the blood may circulate smoothly."[189]

Even more explicit for metaphysically inclined Americans was the taiji instruction on mind-intent ascribed, once more problematically, to Chen—this time under his pseudonym Chen Kung. Published originally in Chinese in 1932, according to compiler and translator Stuart Alve Olson, the text in which this instruction formed a part had mostly emanated from Wu Ho-ching, a student of the founder of the Yang family style. Here discourse on "ch'i" mingled with discourse on mind and "mind intent." The "efficacy of the T'ai Chi Ch'uan exercise" was "very great." The movements nourished the "ch'i," which purified the blood. Purified blood made the body strong, and the strength of the body brought strength to the mind. But the mind likewise had its master, and that was "mind-intent." In fact, the mind acted "as only an assistant to the mind-intent," and—in a reversal—the quality of the mind governed the quality of the "ch'i." All three were "interconnected" and worked "in a rotational manner," Chen Kung told readers. "When the mind is confused the mind-intent will disperse. When the mind-intent is dispersed the ch'i will become insubstantial (weak)."[190] The message was one of constant circulation, constant changing—all points responsible, all points creating. It beckoned with a promise of late-breaking metaphysics with an East Asian veneer.

Clearly, the Chen-ascribed texts were telling some Americans what they wanted to hear and know. If American Daoism and its attendant practices were growing and thriving in late-twentieth-century America and after, success had come in large part because the energy discourse of East Asian teachers and their followers replicated a longstanding, and now especially emphasized, discourse habit of American metaphysicians. In exotic (for non-Asian Americans) dress—a dress performatively enhanced by ethnic masters who had newly discovered and/or invented themselves—American Daoism replayed American metaphysical religion with substance and style. In so doing, American Daoism was part of an explosion of variants of old-style American metaphysics. A large number of these variants came to be recognized, however loosely, as part of what the media began calling the New Age movement by the 1970s. But even the New Age movement could not contain the spiritual efflorescence and overflow of American metaphysical religion—an efflorescence and overflow that kept Pealeism company and that went even further in colonizing American minds and hearts. Still, the New Age movement became a phenomenon to be noticed, and in itself it provided useful instruction on the dimensions and dilemmas of American metaphysical religion in the late twentieth century and on. Like all of American metaphysical religion, it rested on combinative notions of the power of mind and the pervasiveness of correspondences, both in quests to heal and save. Like all twentieth- and twenty-first-century American metaphysical religion, it discovered that the no-longer-secret name of God was Energy.

CODA

The New New Age

From one point of view, the New Age movement began when enough people who thought about a dawning "new age" began to use upper instead of lower case letters to refer to the time. Put another way, the New Age movement happened when participants and observers who had identified a certain kind of emergent community began to reify it. This occurred sometime in the early-to-mid 1970s, and, arguably, it occurred because the media had noticed and sought to name the apparent whirlwind. It is instructive to browse through "old" books from the years before designations and attitudes became fixed. Doug Boyd's 1974 account of the celebrated Cherokee and adopted Shoshone shaman Rolling Thunder, for example, contains this casual reference: "Many Indians were returning to the tradition. Many new-age young people were developing awareness of the Indian way. These people could help the Indian to reverse the present pattern of polluting, exploiting and destroying nature." Boyd himself, who first heard Rolling Thunder address a small white professional audience in 1971, located him for readers in a continuum that told them how to think Rolling Thunder and how to think spirit. "Rolling Thunder expressed ideas and concepts that I had heard from spokesmen from India, Japan and Tibet. He said there was a law of nature that causes all things to be balanced, a law that says that nothing comes free, that all things must be paid for, that all wrongs must be righted. Teachers from all over the world have spoken of this law of karma. Rolling Thunder told how medicine men and others of similar practices communicate without words. Practitioners of all times and places from witch doctors to shamans to yogis, swamis and sages, have had this ability."[1]

As Boyd made clear, whatever else this lower-case "new age" was, it had been marked by a grand ecumenicity, a combinativeness that made the old-style "perennial philosophy" look effete and elitist beside it. A similar comprehensiveness marked Marilyn Ferguson's *Aquarian Conspiracy* (1980), which by the time of its second edition in 1987 had sold one-half million copies and which has often been cited as a basic statement of New Age views. Ferguson's original edition, though, contains no index entry for the term, and—so far as I can tell—it appears nowhere in her text. Instead, Ferguson was ebullient over an exploding interest in "consciousness" since the 1970s and over the phenomenon of networking (her "conspiracy") that she found seemingly everywhere. Her text gave no index entry to Alice Bailey either. But in its introduction Ferguson confessed that she was "drawn to the symbolic power of the pervasive dream in our popular culture: that after a dark, violent age, the Piscean, we are entering a millennium of love and light—in the words of the popular song [from the Broadway musical *Hair*], 'The Age of Aquarius,' the time of 'the mind's true liberation.'"[2]

Seven years later, when the second edition appeared, however, its paperback cover excerpted *American Bookseller*'s review of the book as the "New Age watershed classic." Ferguson herself, in an afterword for the new edition, noted a series of "breaking stories." Among them was *increasing media coverage of metaphysical/spiritual news.*" Then, citing a *New York Times* front-page feature in September 1986 on the "growing number of adherents to spiritual views," Ferguson—one time only—used the much-repeated term: "Over the next few months other major features on the 'New Age,' some positive, appeared in publications like *Time, U.S. News and World Report, The Los Angeles Times*, and on television ('20–20,' 'Sixty Minutes,' network morning shows). Soon virtually all the popular magazines, major newspapers, and television networks were providing ongoing coverage. Since then, the emerging views and values have become the topic of TV dramas, even situation comedies."[3]

Ferguson had noticed that the New Age movement was, in large part, constructed as a media event. When numbers of metaphysically inclined spiritual seekers who were calling themselves "new-age" discovered themselves in print to be part of the New Age movement, they found that their ranks, seemingly overnight, swelled and augmented. Named by an independent and authoritative arbiter (the media), they grew surer of their own identity and the attitudes out of which it was formed. And if any one media "moment" shifted perception to this upper-case New Age, it was probably the publication of film star and political activist Shirley MacLaine's autobiographical *Out on a Limb* in 1983, with its video version by 1986.[4] *Out on a Limb* was translated into Spanish, Italian, German, and Polish as well as Chinese, Japanese, and Korean. Meanwhile, in its video format, its made-for-television friendliness captured a huge American audience that, in many cases, may not have had significant prior exposure to her new-age concerns. MacLaine's story, with herself as star, invited the same kind of study of important texts that American Daoism would promote. It also thrust the actress and many of her readers into novel (for them) practices such as channeling. Most startling of all for most, it pushed MacLaine into a secondhand encounter, in a different hemisphere, with a reported space visitor—who seemed a reconstituted theosophical master and who was, like MacLaine, a woman.

This is not, of course, to ignore perceptions of a coming new age (we began there) before Shirley MacLaine discovered the New Age and the media cooperatively evangelized for her. More precisely, by the 1960s a major shift in the metaphysical discourse community was taking place regarding a new age, and it was probably easiest to locate among Theosophists. J. Gordon Melton has pointed to the role played by the several hundred organizations that can be traced to the parent Theosophical Society. Continuing revelation kept continuing; and ascended masters apparently kept finding new people with whom to converse. Moreover, as Melton notes, the beginnings of what became the New Age movement could be tracked to Britain. There a confluence of spiritualists and Bailey-style Theosophists (Bailey had predicted the new age would come late in the twentieth century) flourished in a context made still more metaphysically congenial by the arrival of Eastern teachers after World War II. Concepts of "spiritual energy" to come at the dawn of the Aquarian age fed into a mood of general millennial expectation. At Findhorn near Inverness in Scotland, Peter and Eileen Caddy and Dorothy Maclean from 1965 built an experimental community, claiming that the aid of nature spirits was enabling them to grow spectacularly large and lush produce on ground that could hardly be expected to yield at all. As they reported their communings with the land and its spirits, they taught a theology of immanence. At the same time, others of a metaphysical bent began to talk of spiritual "light" as they recalled theosophical teachings on the coming of a new age. In the process, they came to see their own gatherings as points of light. Linked to one another, they believed—as in the old Alice Bailey vision—that they could bring new and greater light, channeling it to the world and engaging in a work of global transformation. Supported by small organizations such as, from 1971, Sir George Trevelyan's Wrekin Trust for exploring metaphysical themes, study groups networked with one another and spread the mood of expectation. "The message of the New Age swept through the ranks of the psychically attuned in much the same way that the charismatic movement did at the same time through ranks of evangelical Christians," Melton observes.[5]

The British new age hardly stayed home, and by the close of the 1960s it had spread internationally and linked itself to metaphysical discourse communities in North America. "Light" groups were in, and so were crystals. In a world in which vernacular readings of the new quantum science had taught people how to think light, mystical and scientific light mingled and fused in crystals: Crystals were crucial in technological applications in the dawning computer age and crucial as well, for believers, in focusing and transmitting spiritual intention and energy. Worn as a pendant around the neck, a crystal became a new and Western lingam, a source of ever-available energy to infuse life into life. Placed at strategic locations to mark boundaries and enhance the flow of spirit, crystals protected and augmented the life force of believers and, in their view, all to which they extended. Even before the light groups, however, theosophical influence encouraged other stateside believers to expect an imminent new age in a context of expanding light. The new age, they thought, would be ushered in by space brothers or space-age ascended masters.

As early as June 1947, private pilot Kenneth Arnold claimed to have sighted nine silvery disks near Mount Rainier in Washington state, disks that he estimated to be flying at 1,200 miles per hour. Arnold made sure to tell a news reporter, describing the objects as moving like saucers that skipped across water. So began the era of unidentified flying objects (UFOs), spotted by a series of observers and provoking continued speculation. In one notably metaphysical explanation, for example, Swiss psychologist Carl Jung argued that the sightings were the result of displaced psychic contents—the "self" in space. Some, however, were not so sure, and they were not content to gaze at the unexplained and speculate on origins. They felt that they were making contact with space vehicles and whoever was flying them. The claim of contact with extraterrestrials, as we saw, had already been made in the eighteenth century by Emanuel Swedenborg, and spiritualists like Andrew Jackson Davis had felt no apparent qualms about describing life on other planets. Now, however, in an age of heightened technology and sophisticated flying objects of human construction, claims of contact with space beings gained new immediacy and plausibility. Tellingly, many of those who reported contacts with extraterrestrials ("contactees") displayed, as a group, backgrounds of immersion in theosophical and/or spiritualist lore.[6]

When in 1952 Polish-born George Adamski claimed conversations with a Venusian named Orthon, he had already, since the 1930s, been working as a metaphysical teacher, issuing publications from the "Royal Order of Tibet," for whom, he said, he was lecturing. Adamski hastened to produce books on his contactee experiences in 1953 and 1955 (as well as later ones), and he attracted a following. Plagued by allegations of fraud, he still had contributed an important word to a conversation that continued. Unlike ufologists, who saw the "saucers" as scientific mysteries to be clarified, contactees like Adamski and their devotees thought that they were dealing in mysteries that were metaphysical. The outlines of the message of the space brothers were clear: Humans were being warned to reform their evil ways, to "fly right," in so many words. As Jerome Clark summarizes, "What the contactees created was a space-age version of an occult visionary religion, with roots in theosophy, the I AM movement, and other supernatural belief systems in which wise extraterrestrials played a role."[7]

Examples of the theosophical and spiritualist pasts of contactees abound. George King, for instance, who founded the Aetherius Society in London in 1954 and then settled himself and his center in Los Angeles, had been a medium, a yogi, and a student of theosophical lore before his space-age experiences. After the beginning of his reported revelations from Master Aetherius of Venus in 1955, who—according to King—named him the "primary terrestrial mental channel," King delivered trance lectures from "masters." Robert Ellwood thought them to be "identical to the 'Great White Lodge' of Theosophy." In the late 1950s, with their project Operation Starlight fully unfolding, members of the society traveled to Holdstone Down in England—to behold Master Jesus in cosmic light—and then to nine English mountains called by the Cosmic Masters through King "New Age Power Centers." Later, in the 1960s, they conducted Operation Karmalight, suggesting once again the prevalence of theosophical discourse and the continuing significance of light. In still another case, George Hunt Williamson, an archaeologist and also a student of Theosophy, published his account of contact with Martians through automatic writing from as early as 1952. But Williamson also claimed contact with ascended masters, and he later became associated with the Brotherhood of the Seven Rays, the name of the organization alluding to the full spectrum of light rays associated with ascended masters. According to Williamson, the brotherhood had first been established when the lost continent of Lemuria was destroyed between 10,000 and 12,000 B.C.[E.], and now, in 1956, it was being resuscitated as a monastic system in the Andes Mountains of Peru.[8]

The new high-tech ascended masters—now no longer earthlings but still functionally persons and profoundly wise ones at that—provided what Robert Ellwood has called "symbols of mediation." Like the multiplied forms and beings guaranteeing complexity to old Gnostic and Kabbalistic myths, these new answers for the Hermetic imagination announced that the universe was hardly vacant and that humans were not at all alone in it. Those who received their messages did so through a reconstructed form of mediumship that came to be called channeling. "Channels"—as on radios, television sets, and advanced technological gadgetry considered to be communication devices on spaceships—brought information and wisdom to believers. Now, though, the communicators—Ellwood's "symbols of mediation"—were no longer only or mostly the spirits of the intimate departed, or of historic scientific and political professionals, or of American Indians or African Americans or even Russian Cossacks. Instead, they were space brothers or extraterrestrial masters, and—as time passed—they became "entities," beings who had never been human or—as in the case of later well-known channel JZ Knight's Ramtha—came from lost civilizations (like Ramtha's Atlantis). Alternatively, they were collective beings representing "group souls."[9]

Contactees, however, soon had public company. In 1970, when writer Jane Roberts published *The Seth Material,* she launched an era of nationwide awareness. Communication with other-than-human entities had now left the boundaries of the contactee community and its followers to spread in the larger culture. Roberts was Jane Roberts Butts, a former Skidmore College student and now housewife who had taken different jobs during her married life and even published a novel in 1963. "Seth," the being with whom she claimed contact, had emerged when, experimenting alongside her husband with a Ouija board, they both received messages from the mysterious communicator. Thereafter Roberts found that she could become entranced and that Seth came channeling through while she was in trance states. He apparently had very much to tell, and Roberts produced book after book, some sixteen in all. The Seth writings became enormously popular in metaphysical circles, contributing to the self-identity of an emergent New Age movement and also augmenting its ranks.[10]

Roberts herself, despite all the fanfare, led a quiet life even as she questioned the source of the phenomenon, calling Seth a "dramatization of the unconscious" but implying that the unconscious in question was different from her own. In the second of the Seth books, for example, Seth announced concerning his mysterious identity: "I can quite literally be called a ghost writer, though I do not approve of the term 'ghost.' It is true that I am usually not seen in physical terms. I do not like the word 'spirit,' either; and yet if your definition of that word implies the idea of a personality without a physical body, then I would have to agree that the description fits me." Seth also boasted that he had "donned and discarded" more bodies than he cared to tell. "Consciousness," he declared sententiously, "creates form. It is not the other way around."[11]

Channeling and contact with space visitors—probably the two most flamboyant themes that marked this early New Age—had functioned as metaphysical harbor lights for MacLaine's 1983 *Out on a Limb.* She had dutifully, at the behest of a friend, visited the huge and well-stocked Bodhi Tree, the fabled metaphysical bookstore on Melrose Avenue in Los Angeles, and had begun to read the books recommended to her. They provided a short course on the metaphysical tradition, with special attention to reincarnation, and soon she was supplementing them with contacts with a series of trance channels, including the well-known Kevin Ryerson. She knew about Alice Bailey and Jane Roberts, and she was well aware of Roberts's doubts about and resistance to the channeling phenomenon. When MacLaine met Ryerson, he was adamant about not being religious. "What church would have me?" he answered in reply to MacLaine's question. He explained, though, that "two, three, or maybe four spiritual entities" used him "to channel information." Then, in trance as the entity "John," Ryerson told the actress that he had information both about her and about the cosmos based on "that which ye would term the Akashic Records." "Akasha," he continued, "is that which ye might term the collective unconscious of mankind, stored in ethereal energy. This energy could be termed as the mind of God."[12]

MacLaine's spiritual journey reached a new point when David, her California metaphysical friend, invited her to Peru and the Andes Mountains (Peru and the Andes, as we have seen, were already favored by devotees of ascended masters and space contacts). Up in the Andes, "in the sulphur baths and along the banks of the bubbling Mantaro," David told MacLaine about "a girl called Mayan." Mysterious and beautiful, she transmitted vast reservoirs of knowledge and insisted that "the most important relationship was between each soul and God." But he had trouble telling MacLaine about her origins. "Where could she be from that's so hard to say? Another planet." "You got it!" David said. "You guessed it. You're right." Later, MacLaine learned that the locals routinely spotted UFOs. "'Shirley,' said David, 'everyone I've talked to up here has a flying-disc story. *Every single one.*'" He also told her that Mayan had come from the Pleiades (a theme that the Swiss farmer Edouard ["Billy"] Meier had introduced into the contactee literature in the 1970s, although Meier himself was trailed by numerous allegations of hoax). From what Mayan had told David, he confided, extraterrestrials were "*superior* because they understand the process of the *spiritual* domain of life." The mysterious woman from the Pleiades was reaching out to MacLaine through David because the actress was meant to be a "teacher" on a "much wider scale" than her mentor and friend. She was appointed to write the "simple truth" that was the "Big Truth." "'The simple truth,' he said, 'of knowing yourself. And to know yourself is to know God.'"[13]

It was an odd message, given the twin bookends of the MacLaine account. Trance channels and space visitors came from outside. They got consulted for guidance and direction, and they assumed the authority, for seekers, that institutions had for many who were perhaps less questioning and certainly more conventional. It was as if the Hermetic legacy had been turned inside out in this new New Age—as if the tensions and contradictions that had plagued American metaphysical religion since its nineteenth-century appearances had been ratcheted to new heights in the continuing quest for spiritual energy. The people who would be "as gods" found it necessary to consult. Americans who sought to create their own reality had discovered that they needed to get directions—both on the reality and on the programmatic strategies for obtaining it—from somebody else. Moreover, when they consulted and got directions, they did so on a cosmic scale. That was perhaps appropriate, for there was nothing secret, or esoteric, in what Americans were pursuing. The nonsecrecy had been a fact since the mid-nineteenth century, when mass spiritualism—with its collection of trance-produced books seemingly a dime a dozen—had opened Hermetic secrets to American takers. Now the media had made even surer of the *exotericism* of what was transpiring, and New Age people cooperated enthusiastically. MacLaine was not alone in her instinct for grand announcement when she wrote a book that built to its Peruvian denouement with a woman from the Pleiades.

Still, for all that, Shirley MacLaine's outland gospel could not withstand the domesticating onslaught of the barrage of media coverage that rendered the secret public and exoteric. Americans grew more comfortable with extraordinary visitors and their messages, even as those who considered themselves New Age in the later 1980s and after often skirted past preoccupation with channeling and visits with space people. Increasingly, in the combinative habit intrinsic to metaphysical religion New Age Americans moved on to amplify numerous themes that were already woven into the texture of their synthesis. If they were "Star People," descended from benevolent space beings, as contactee Brad Steiger had declared, they were also heirs to a panoply of metaphysical and related themes bequeathed them by their American experience. The post-1983 MacLaine provides an instructive example. If she had been enthralled by channeling and space contact in 1983, a check-in six years later shows her teaching the gospel of the God-self as Mayan, through David, had desired her to do, but complexifying it in noticeable ways and also reading it largely as therapy. Several books after *Out on a Limb*, in her new autobiographical advice manual *Going Within*, the reconstructed MacLaine still acknowledged UFOs and space contacts, but her strongest interests lay elsewhere. The inside front and end papers of the book are telling. Both portray a stylized woman in yoga attire seated in lotus posture with seven appropriately colored circles—the chakras—illuminating the figure. On the opposite page a full-colored circle for each chakra sits centered between text describing its nature and function. In the book itself, MacLaine announced to readers that there was "nothing new about the New Age," told them that the New Age was "about *self*-responsibility," and displayed concern about personal and social healing. She instructed them in meditating and chanting and explained how she herself used meditation to allow her "Higher Self" to "reveal itself." "Directions coming from the Higher Self," she testified, were "by their very definition attuned to harmonious love and light energy." [14]

This "Higher Self" was the "personalized reflection of the Divine spark." Still further, with the end papers of her book telling the story already, MacLaine learned about "a specific power of aligning with certain energies." The physical body was "but the reflection of a series of more subtle bodies of energy within." These reflected "the vibration of the God Source"—at the disposal of humans if they but knew "how to access it." Everybody seemingly agreed. "The Egyptians, the Chinese, the Greeks, the North American Indian and African tribes, the Incas, the early Christians, the Hindus of India, the Buddhists of Asia, and today's metaphysicists and mystics everywhere in the world share, to some degree, a common belief." What was it? They all thought that the body was "only a physical manifestation of energies that together create an entity beyond that which can be seen." They believed that "those levels of existence, those energies, that entity, reflect the nature of God and the universe." MacLaine had discovered chakras, and she had found auras. She meditated on the proverbial "wheels," visualized them, and used sound to free up emotions and heal. Confident in her enlightened body-self, she explored other means of healing as well—experiencing psychic surgery from Filipino Alex Orbito and pondering how it could be. "There was no doubt in my mind that his hands had entered my body. I had felt it and seen it, not only in myself but in others as I stood over them and observed." She invoked "all the spiritual masters," who testified that the "physical" was "fundamentally a coagulation of molecules" that were "a product of our consciousness."[15]

MacLaine explained for readers: "If my body is made up of molecules determined by my consciousness to take the human form and all of it is actually composed of immortal God-like energy, I can accept the concept that psychic surgery is performed through a spiritual connection with the Divine." The connection, she thought, separated "living atoms one from another with an energy that doesn't violate, but simply and gently slips *through* the physical, much as a hand slips gently, without violation, through liquid." Humans were all "part of God," and within the "profound realization" of the "God within," they could "trust the loving and well-ordered magic" of who they were "meant to be."[16] So the New Age, for MacLaine and many other believer-practitioners, was about healing false beliefs and getting out of their own way to allow changes in consciousness to change the physical order. If the message seemed distinctly similar to New Thought (even Christian Science) and to a more diffused rendition in positive thinking, it was: The metaphysical ballast supplied by older metaphysicians shaped the New Age pragmatically. Alternative healing became the order of the New Age day, even as the psychology of Carl Jung and the human potential movement being celebrated at Esalen Institute helped to shape it. So there was energy and there was healing; there was the power of mind and the correspondence between body-self, Higher Self, nature, universe, and God.

All the pieces of American metaphysical history came together in the New Age—Transcendentalism and spiritualism, mesmerism and Swedenborgianism, Christian Science and New Thought, Theosophy and its ubiquitous spin-offs, and especially metaphysical Asia. Quantum physics provided a horizon of discourse that could enable MacLaine and others to engage in mystical-scientific speculation about spiritual healing and psychic surgery. Parapsychology pushed the scientific argot toward the paranormal. Astrology—with its millennial expectation of the dawning age of Aquarius—charted quasi-scientific star maps to explain, according to principles of correspondence, the relationships between personality, destiny, and an individual's place in the universal scheme. Astrological dispensationalism, paralleling the Protestant fundamentalist version, told of coming ages, or dispensations, and their character and consequences.[17]

Meanwhile, as the example of Rolling Thunder already suggests, Native American shamans and teachers were hardly shy about sharing spiritual goods with white takers. The Chippewa Sun Bear, to the consternation of more traditionalist Indians as well as (later) Native American academics, gave the store away when he founded the (white) Bear Tribe Medicine Society and regularly sponsored Medicine Wheel gatherings from 1966. New Age people appropriated Native American rituals with enthusiasm, holding sweats, using rattles and drums, wearing feathers, beads, and gemstones in ceremonial ways, and adopting sacred-pipe ceremonies as well. From Indians they learned to make pilgrimages to sacred sites, often native ones, and they also learned to engage in mental journeying on a shamanic model. Imitating the Native America (and the Asia) of their imagining, they revered nature and exalted ecology. Earth became a living being, and environmental concerns—alongside other concerns for peace and a harmonious and holistic feminism—began to shape a social ethic.

The term "New Age"—now loosened from its ties to Theosophy, UFOs, contactees, and even channels and crystals—became a catch-all designation for an alternative collection of beliefs and behaviors. No one participant in the movement necessarily endorsed and supported all of them—or even knew about them all. Andrew Jackson Davis's mid-nineteenth-century distinction between a philosophical, or speculative, form of spiritualism (his own harmonial philosophy) and a phenomenal one (séances and their enthusiasts) became strikingly appropriate for this mature New Age. A new generation of metaphysical thinkers emerged with pragmatic agendas for everything from mystical practice to environmental needs, from pursuit of the divine feminine to international peace, and from promoting true science and holistic health to spiritual and psychological transformation. To take a leading example, New Age teacher-prophet Ken Wilber, with strong interests in the relationship between science and spirituality, rose to prominence when he placed transpersonal psychology on a New Age intellectual map in his 1977 *Spectrum of Consciousness*. Working in a field that came to be called "noetic studies" (that is, studies of consciousness), Wilber produced book after book—which all seemed one book. From one point of view, he was teaching, for a new time, mid-twentieth-century perennialism. From another, he was supplying it with a distinctive psycho-physical tilt in an advance portrait of the enlightened body-self. In *Spectrum of Consciousness*, for instance, he invoked dualistic and nondualistic modes of thinking with the expected conclusion. It was "of the utmost significance," Wilbur wrote, "that, of the vast number of scientists, philosophers, psychologists, and theologians that have fully and deeply understood these two modes of knowing, their unmistakable and unanimous conclusion is that the non-dual mode alone is capable of giving . . . 'knowledge of Reality.'" He had already discovered Asian sources, and he blended them facilely with Western ones to teach the supreme virtue of the "Now-moment." For Wilber, it was "in this moment, right now, we are . . . always arriving at Mind, we are always arriving at WHAT IS NOW, whether that be suffering, seeking, pain, joy, or simple confusion." The journey did not "start Now," but instead it ended "Now, with whatever state of consciousness is present at this moment." "That," Wilber flatly declared, was "the mystical state, and that we are." He preached (for it was such) a "future-less Present," in which what came was "mortification, this Great Death, this total dying to the future by seeing Now-only." Paradoxically, with no future in sight what was missing, too, was the past; and with the absence of both came "no beginning in time" and "no end in time." Instead, traveling from the mystical horizon came an "awakening" to "that which is Unborn, and therefore to that which is Undying."[18]

The problem, as Wilber saw it, was that humans erected for themselves a "boundary," and so they could not reach the unitive state that represented the truest expansion into personal growth. Once "primal resistance" began to "dissolve," a person's "separate self" dissolved with it. In teachings that drew copiously on an approved short list of Asian metaphysical teachers—Ramana Maharshi, Chögyam Trungpa, Tarthang Tulku, Suzuki Roshi, and Jiddu Krishnamurti, for example—Wilber pushed for the "no-boundary" state. "As you begin to see that everything you do is a resistance, you start to see that even your feeling of being a separate self 'in here' is also nothing but a resistance. . . . But as this becomes obvious, there are no longer *two* different feelings here, no longer an experiencer on the one hand having an experience on the other hand, but only one, single, all-pervasive feeling—the feeling of resistance. . . . The feeling of self condenses into the feeling of resistance, and both dissolve."[19]

This New Age mysticism, to be sure, seems like classic teaching, rewritten (and often not elegantly) with the discourse community of contemporary alternative science in mind, and rewritten as well with the body-self and its transpersonal psychology in mind. Apparently, too, some contemporary religious professionals did not object. Jesuit David Toolan's "journey into New Age consciousness," for instance, opened with the baths at Esalen (the enlightened *body*-self, with clothing an anomaly) and progressed to India. It returned west to a rediscovered account of Genesis, in which new physics—with its "tantric thermodynamics"—brought order through fluctuation, and it traveled the path of meditation in ways that climaxed in Jean Houston's ritual theater. To prime the "neural system" and the "kinesthetic body" became keys to transpersonal reality and a new natural theology. "You have to travel far and hear the meaning of the journey from a stranger," Toolan wrote, "perhaps from a[n] Israeli physiotherapist, a clairvoyant Californian, a Sufi clown, or a reincarnate Tibetan wise man. Spirit is like the wind; you never know where it's coming from or when." Toolan, as a Jesuit, freely acknowledged the tension with Catholicism that his pilgrimage brought. He was "grateful for the internal resistance" that his Catholicism gave to "Neoplatonism," grateful that it saved him from "quick-fix transcendence and gnostic escapes." Still, he had made the journey, and using the language of theoretical physicist David Bohm on the implicate order and the hologram for support, Toolan found the whole in the part and the part in his body. "If this is true, the body is silent metaphor, habitation of soul, a reservoir of prophetic dreams, our depth probe into the abyss of God's will."[20]

From a more academic perspective, process theologian and ethicist David Ray Griffin's explorations of religion, science, and postmodernity have invoked New Age teaching without attaching a New Age label. Griffin sought a reenchanted science and a reenchantment of the world—a return to a sense of subjectivity, experience, and feeling within nature—and he argued that reenchanted science was different from "sacred" science, immune to criticism. He found the ingredients for the reenchantment in a certain reading of quantum physics, one that was not its "dominant interpretation . . . limited to rules of calculation to predict the content of observations." Nor was Griffin happy with the usual New Age glide from quantum physics to mysticism. Perhaps surprisingly, though, to support his more nuanced account, Griffin turned to Ken Wilber, citing Wilber's argument that quantum physics promoted mysticism but did so indirectly. "As these physicists became aware that physical theory gave them only shadows and symbols of reality, rather than reality itself, they became freed from the materialistic worldview and hence open to taking their own conscious experience as real and revelatory." Griffin likewise cited J. E. Lovelock and Lynn Margulis for their "Gaia hypothesis" of the earth as a living organism, carefully separating himself from overreadings of the same. He went on to point to David Bohm and his view that "every natural unit, as an act of enfoldment, in some sense enfolds the activity of the universe as a whole within it," with the universe "as an active whole" that could be seen as "divine." Bohm, Griffin thought, was "suggesting that postmodern science, in speaking of the implicate order, would include reference to divine activity."[21]

These kinds of issues, raised by elites and intellectuals, seem a far cry from ordinary practice among those who, in one way or another, thought of themselves as New Age. Phenomenal practice in the New Age was always—as we have seen for metaphysical religion in general—practice grounded in ordinary procedures and sacred technologies that, in the large sense, could be called magical. As this narrative has elsewhere suggested, magic means a noncausative transformation of a practitioner's self and environment in the direction of a good desired. It is accomplished either through material means (the cultivation of active imagination through symbolism, ritual, and alternative forms of energy work) or purely mentalist operations (meditation and directed mental processes, such as New Thought affirmations and denials). In the pursuit of such magic, New Age metaphysicians combined freely from many sources to find the techniques and practices that worked for them. With healing so prominent, for example, energy healing practices such as Reiki flourished. Here, in a Japanese initiatory form of palm healing, a practitioner through a series of "attunements" felt himself or herself to be a conduit for universal life-force energy directed to a client. Or there was Therapeutic Touch, publicized by Dolores Krieger from ideas and practices supplied by Theosophist Dora Kunz. Tellingly, Kunz—who claimed perception of subtle energies from childhood—would become president of the Theosophical Society in America (the Blavatsky-Olcott society) from 1975 to 1987, and she traced her lineage to British Theosophist Charles W. Leadbeater, with whom she studied in Australia. By contrast, Krieger, the publicist, was a registered nurse with a Ph.D. She began to teach Kunz's method at New York University, meanwhile also lecturing widely at other American and Canadian universities and professional organizations. Almost missionary in her effort, she systematized what she had learned for general consumption, using radio and television to effect, giving workshops, publishing essays, and, especially, publishing her book *The Therapeutic Touch*. Here she wrote familiarly of South Asian prana, teaching that people in good health had an excess of the same and that they could transfer it to another less blessed. The process of transfer, she declared, did not usually deplete the giver because the healer was "in constant energy flux," in a "continued constant flow." It was clear, too, that the "touch" was a touch of energy and that no physical contact was involved. The healer's hands stood several inches away from the client; auras and chakras—carefully disguised for in-hospital use and consumption—were the covert order of the day.[22]

Various forms of New Age shamanism cultivated active imagination in other venues, and so did an array of related practices, such as the appropriation by some of the Chinese art of placement—furniture, accoutrements, and similar objects—in a person's local environment. Feng shui practices changed energy, practitioners and their clients said, and rendered a disagreeable environment into a harmonious one. Everywhere, seemingly, the enlightened body-self found new niches that required transformation; everywhere the New Age world got up-ended and reconstructed. Still, the time for relative quiet came in the work of meditation. Even here, though, the preference for agency encouraged meditative techniques that promoted energy shifts and augmentations. Kundalini and microcosmic orbits were congenial; so was visualization in extensive formats that made real a desired good. Nor were practices so disorganized as at first they might seem. The combinative leanings of those who pursued the New Age, their valorization of change, and their fear of the lackluster imprisonment of institutions —none of these would lend themselves to the creation of strong organizations. Instead, as this narrative has already noticed, more fluid forms of community available through networks and networking predominated. Here, as sociologist Paul Heelas has observed, it is best to notice different levels of commitment. Individuals could express strong affiliation, working on the inside as New Age service providers; or they could be strong followers—people who showed up at a series of workshops, participated regularly in one or another small group, or the like. Or, finally—in a variation of the now-proverbial "nightstand Buddhists," they could be "nightstand" New Age people, reading occasional books, attending infrequent lectures or even conferences.[23]

Who were these New Age people? Sociological and demographic clues have been sketchy and general, but there is enough, for the late twentieth century, to suggest a pattern. Those who have identified with the movement are often unaware of their connections to a metaphysical path but sometimes not. Either way, they share a series of characteristics with earlier American metaphysical religionists from the Anglo-American mainstream. They have been mostly white, more female than male, often middle-aged, sometimes young, and frequently urban dwellers. Although media have often overstressed their wealth by focusing on expensive weekend workshops and seminars and the entrepreneurial goods and services that movement people provide, the New Age population has seemed to be middle class and upwardly mobile, better educated than average, and not especially alienated from society. Still, a strong working-class component of the New Age cannot be written off, even if it is quieter and less noticeable. In terms of the formal religious backgrounds from which New Age people have come, evidence again is less than totally persuasive, but it does suggest representative participation by mainstream American Protestants, Catholics, and Jews. Sometimes the protestations of Jewish rabbis seem to point to a New Age overinhabited by Jews, but the protests can be read as more a function of Jewish fears of disappearance than of demographic realities. Similarly, sometimes the mystically oriented practices of the New Age seem to attract more than an even share of Catholics—perhaps caught between their sacramentalism, which honors materiality, and their sexual ethic, which fears and reproves it. (Jesuit David Toolan's narrative hints at this, and a generation of Catholic New Age nuns also suggests the same.) But again, there are no real demographics to support the characterization.[24] Still more, with the fine line that can be drawn between entrepreneurship and evangelization—and with the self-help enthusiasm evident in many evangelical circles—it can be argued that Protestant evangelicals provide a backbone to the New Age. Again, the evidence is largely impressionistic, and the contrary arguments for Jews and Catholics point to the presence of sizable representation from all three traditions.

Given the fluid profile of "members" in a changing network of believers and practitioners, can anything at all be said about numbers? Criteria for "membership" have been clearly disputable, and data to support any given set of criteria seem often as dubious. In 1993, for example, Barry Kosmin and Seymour Lachman announced confidently that twenty thousand Americans could be counted in the New Age. On the basis of impressionistic evidence alone, that estimate seems untenably low. At the other end of the spectrum, literary critic Harold Bloom—on the basis of his decidedly nonsociological survey of the field—has argued that "Gnosticism" (that is, metaphysics) has been the real religion of Americans. And, in fact, even if survey data seriously delimit the all-expansiveness of a Bloom, it can still yield very large numbers of New Age sympathizers. Consider, for example, data suggesting that perhaps 25 percent of Americans accepted reincarnation beliefs in the late 1980s. Meanwhile, if we want to return to the camp of the narrow, we can limit membership to people who have subscribed to major New Age periodicals, listed themselves in movement directories, or signed up as participants in New Age–identified events such as the Whole Life Expos held in a series of cities as annual gatherings and emporia. Or, as another strategy, we can sweep most of the unchurched into a catch-all New Age designation— with roughly 7 percent of the populace in the category by the mid-1980s, and among baby boomers and those younger noticeably more. To be safe, we could add some crossover members from traditional religions.[25]

None of these strategies has seemed entirely persuasive, and sociological estimates themselves have moved from the Kosmin-Lachman twenty thousand to a high of sixty million believer-practitioners for the United States alone. In this context, the most sophisticated guess for the American situation may have come from British sociologist Paul Heelas, with his tripartite reading of levels of New Age involvement—"fully-engaged," "serious part-timer," and "casual part-timer." On the basis of all three, Heelas was willing to offer his view in the mid-1990s. "Thinking of the USA," he wrote, it was "safe to say that well in excess of 10 million people currently have *some* contact with what is on supply. But we neither know the total figure, nor the numbers—over the 10 million figure—for whom the contact is, to varying degrees, significant."[26]

Still, with the thorough combinativeness of New Age aficionados—with the readiness with which all universalist metaphysical beliefs expand and incorporate others—the attempt to segregate a New Age community can never fully persuade. New Age beliefs, by definition, merge into general American beliefs and values, and the generalization is especially cogent for the philosophical side of the movement. More than that, signs of the decline of an ebullient New Age movement, by the early twenty-first century, are marked. The millennium happened, and it had not happened. The new world of the New Age was still clearly encased in the old. New Age people themselves declared the movement to be over, and so did some scholars. On the basis of media coverage alone, it is clear that the story has not been so compelling as it had been two decades earlier. Decline, however, is hardly the end. From the first bursts of upper-case enthusiasm for the New Age, some in the metaphysical community—with all the requisite beliefs and practices—resisted the designation. Indeed, sometimes it seemed that those who accepted the New Age label functioned as counterparts to self-styled fundamentalists among conservative Protestant evangelicals: Not everybody whom scholars would call fundamentalists called themselves that, and those who did had their reasons. From a far different perspective, the distinct repertoire of beliefs and practices that acquired the New Age label tumbled over boundaries—as had the beliefs and practices of an earlier New Thought—to become more or less public property. In the early twenty-first century, arguably, a renewed and far more encompassing metaphysical spirituality was abroad in the land.

For an example of resistance to New Age characterization, consider the neo-pagan community of the late twentieth century. In his huge and literature-based study of New Age religion, Dutch scholar Wouter J. Hanegraaff sets aside an entire chapter to discuss the phenomenon of neopaganism and its status as a form of magic. He sees neopaganism as one of the major trends in New Age religion—channeling, healing, and New Age science being others—and he clearly has grounds for the argument. In his reading, neopagan magic is "different from traditional magic" because the magical worldview is "*purposely adopted* as a reaction to the 'disenchanted' world of modern western society." Hanegraaff cites major historical markers for any discussion of American and English neopaganism—the presence of Wicca, its foundation in 1939 by Britisher Gerald Gardner, evocations of medieval witch persecutions by Margaret Murray in her *Witch-Cult in Western Europe*, the ritual magic of another Britisher, Aleister Crowley, "spiritually-oriented feminism" resulting in the Goddess movement, and the like.[27]

This might all seem unexceptional, save that American neopagans have themselves resisted New Age categorization. With comments on neopagans' rather extensive cultural borrowing, for instance, religious studies scholar Sarah M. Pike has alluded to the general neopagan disdain for New Age people as "inauthentic." Admitting that neopagans find it hard to distinguish themselves from the New Age community, she observes that clearly, for neopagans, the boundary is "very significant" because people persist in "making the attempt" to separate the two. One neopagan whom Pike quotes writes that the New Age is "a very shallow approach to everything, taken without any real context or understanding of **anything**. It also seems to have been stripped of anything that might really challenge people or make them uncomfortable—yes, you too can achieve Total Enlightenment in about an Hour!" New Agers are "superficial" and pursue "worry-free knowledge." Unlike pagans who attend festivals to draw closer to the natural world, New Age people "hypocritically" avoid "any real contact." Neopagans feel that those who identify as New Age do not like the community of witches any better than the witches like New Agers. Moreover, neopagans complain of New Age financial exploitation. All of this, of course, hardly adds up to a clear and analytically cogent set of distinctions, and it is not material that is easily falsifiable. Even more, a set of shared beliefs and practices can be identified, as Pike notes. Both pagans and New Age people, she observes, share "beliefs and practices that many conservative Christians find dangerous: visualization, sacralization of nature, 'occult' techniques such as divination and astrology, and interest in American Indian and other non-European religions."[28] Still, the refusal to connect with the New Age agenda continues to point to an abiding sense of separation and distance in the self-perception of pagans. The simple fact that one can distinguish semantically—the New Age, the neopagan—itself speaks volumes.

Yet if neopagans were issuing a call to separation from New Age metaphysicians, even as they read their manifestos a counter-process was occurring. Against the backdrop of the new millennium, the *old* millennialism of the late-twentieth-century New Age was coming apart. The early and lower-case new age had come largely out of theosophical splinter groups of Baileyite and I AM provenance and later. It had transformed ascended masters into space-age extraterrestrial visitors of superior wisdom and had reinvented spirit communication as entity channeling in a technological new-science milieu with the energy of light and crystals carrying multiple significations. The mature New Age, with its upper-case authority and media blitzes, had folded space commander-teachers, channels, and crystals under a larger, looser canopy of holistic healing. It had included among its blessings not only physical, emotional, and spiritual health but also pleasure and prosperity, magic and metaphysics. And it was fed more evenhandedly by New Thought and Theosophy, and also by Transcendentalism, quantum physics, human-potential discourses that opened to transpersonal psychology and parapsychology, environmentalism and Native Americana, astrology, and very much more. Its habit of combination only grew stronger as, like a vast cultural sponge, it absorbed whatever spiritual moisture was available. The postmillennial New Age, however, found the moisture disintegrating the medium. New Age became old age, the relic of a slightly unfashionable past—still around to be sure but beginning to seem a little too musty and precious. Like Ken Wilber's "now," the media-promoted New Age was dying to its own past and to a future.

The slow and continuing death of the New Age, however, was the beginning of its rise and future. Just as Theosophy and New Thought, in the early twentieth century, had dissolved into more and more diffuse renderings, just as their spin-offs and ideational contents spread outside their cultural containers into America at large, the New Age began to do the same. Now it was "new spirituality"—a new spirituality that went its way innocuously and underlabeled. Meditation became a property that even mainstream churches promoted. Environmentalism brought sacred sensibilities into the offices of lobbyists. Alternative healing, to the consternation of mainstream medical professionals, became a majority practice alongside the work of credentialed physicians. Psychics found their niches as service professionals, helping police, for example, to identify criminals. Hypnotherapists helped people to lose weight, curb their smoking, cut their alcoholism or their drug habit, and succeed in testing situations in which previously they had been frozen. Testimonies to the creative power of thought were everywhere, and motivational speakers made them their paycheck. Life coaches became fashionable. Indian-style jewelry and crystals seemed mostly unremarkable. Even past lives could provide the stuff of accepted party conversations, while references to a person's karma did not raise eyebrows. Chakras functioned as part of a new spiritual vocabulary. The New Age was stepping aside for a new and exoteric spiritual America.

In this new spiritual America, metaphysical religiosity—found already in its proto form among the mix of peoples in North America in the early seventeenth century—was showing itself the resilient, chameleonlike, and pervasive reality that it was. By refusing to be separated out into a set of organizations or discrete identities, by disengaging its own discourse community in favor of generalization, metaphysical religion made itself a lingua franca that could be shared, even for those who self-consciously identified with one or another organized religious body. Metaphysicians could exist both in and outside Christianity, or Judaism, or other inherited traditions. Still further, the lingua franca did promote certain semantic choices, and it did provide a vocabulary of engagement that marked its late-twentieth/early-twenty-first-century time. Metaphysical religiosity—in the declining New Age and in the new spirituality that was succeeding it—was different from the metaphysical religion of a century previous. The old teaching of correspondence was there, and so was the discourse of the power of mind—whether God's or a person's own. A disguised Hermeticism still prevailed. But the mind had manifestly acquired a body, and the body refused to stay out of metaphysical discourse. It was the enlightened *body*-self that twenty-first-century metaphysicians and their immediate forebears hailed. More than that, it was an enlightened body-self in seemingly perpetual need of energy. Was the world racing too fast? Were there too many tasks to be done? Was there not enough time or space for contemplation? Whatever the spiritual and practical dilemmas, the sense of exhaustion and the need to be charged with a divinizing energy were ubiquitous. New spirituality in America meant energy spirituality, and the energies of mesmerists and ether vibrations were only preparation for what had transpired.

In its exotericism the new spirituality had also taken the mid-nineteenth-century spiritualist impulse for mass marketing and run with it in new and more sophisticated ways. As the media grew in a computer-age technological universe, so did the mystical capacity for exotericism keep pace. Metaphysicians had come out of their closets to make headline news, and clearly they were loving it. Secrets had gone public by a mile or a beer keg, and nobody seemed to mind. In this atmosphere of public scrutiny and public property, too, the old social agendas of metaphysicians assumed new cogency. Alice Bailey's Triangles could function under the shadow of the United Nations in quiet ways, but—more noticeably— new-spirituality advocates learned their politics in order to work concretely for environmentalism, peace, and feminism. They could side with political candidates—Greens, Natural Law, and even old-fashioned Democrats and Republicans—as issues and values warranted. Out of the closet meant entry into history, and metaphysicians—who had always known that there was a social order—by the twenty-first century knew it more. Their religious history had been a history of combinative belief and practice, and they unabashedly continued their combinative ways as they preached behavioral sermons, unawares, on the exchange meaning of community. Indeed, what befell the New Age was also befalling the new spirituality. Both combined themselves so habitually and unremarkably that, as regular fare, they tended to lose themselves and find themselves reinvented.

For the American religious historian, though, the metaphysical habit of combination provides a large historiographical clue about how to make sense of the spiritual life of the nation. Seen from the perspective of early-twenty-first-century metaphysical religion, combinative practices supply an important insight about what everybody had been doing all along. If consensus historiography needed to be long gone in the face of the ongoing demise of a central Protestant consensus, the historiography of pluralism seems also to limp. Americans were neither purely and simply tolerating one another nor contesting one another for limited goods, as the standard interpretive tropes of the pluralist historiographical model suggest.[29] Rather, from a religious perspective, they were begging, borrowing, and stealing from one another, and they were doing it in broad historiographical daylight with little or no apology. Catholics and Protestants did it, and so did Jews. When Muslims became new neighbors on the block, they did it as well, and so did South and East Asians. Native Americans and African Americans had long since made their appropriations, and the public secret that was now emerging was that whites had all along borrowed from Indians and from blacks as well. Americans, in short, were—and had long been—reinventing their spiritual selves and communities to produce transformed religious worlds. Hence they require a historiography of connection, one noticing that contact is much of what there is to tell and that contact demands a new emplotment as a comprehensive American religious narrative. Religion in the United States, in general, needs to be noticed for its overlapping between and among cultural worlds.

For metaphysical religiosity itself and its contemporary presence as new spirituality, its embrace of mental and material magic has pointed one way toward a reenchantment of the world. If as Jonathan Z. Smith has argued, religion is a process of human labor—and labor that, in ritual terms, goes on in the struggle with incongruity—the religious work of magical presence needs to be recognized for its access to the powers of human imagination and, so, for its theological power.[30] Metaphysicians, through the course of American religious history, struggled with human incongruity—intellectual, emotional, environmental, practical, spiritual. They felt the pain that others felt and—in their vernacular community—took a hands-on approach to finding solutions. So they created—stories, more sophisticated narratives, theologies. It was labor, indeed—often hard work; and its results were likewise often uneven. When creations did not function smoothly, metaphysicians sometimes hyperinvented them, and thus they perpetrated hoax and fraud. When the creations needed novelty to arrest and attract, metaphysicians sometimes also hyperinvented those, and the results were absurdities. Even when they exalted themselves as gods in the making or already made, metaphysicians still found that they needed to consult and that often the consultations came as revelations from beings who were higher than their godly selves. But metaphysicians had gifts for persuasion, and they found ready niches in the imaginations of their friends and neighbors. Sometimes their work turned out well, and sometimes it became mightily persuasive. Whether they produced art or kitsch, however, they did labor at religion outside the box. In their openness and vulnerability, their failures and successes, a magic still dwells.

NOTES

INTRODUCTION

1. Work especially over the last decade or so has explored the transatlantic character of revivalism. See, e.g., Mark A. Noll, David W. Bebbington, George A. Rawlyk, eds., *Evangelicalism: Comparative Studies of Popular Protestantism in North America, the British Isles, and Beyond, 1700–1990* (New York: Oxford University Press, 1994); W. R. Ward, *The Protestant Evangelical Awakening* (Cambridge: Cambridge University Press, 1992); and Michael J. Crawford, *Seasons of Grace: Colonial New England's Revival Tradition in Its British Context* (New York: Oxford University Press, 1991).

2. William G. McLoughlin, *Revivals, Awakenings, and Reform: An Essay on Religion and Social Change in America, 1607–1977* (Chicago: University of Chicago Press, 1978), xiii–xiv.

3. Jon Butler, "Born-Again History?" Unpublished paper presented before the American Historical Association and the American Society of Church History, December 1992, 2, 14.

4. Jon Butler, "Historiographical Heresy: Catholicism as a Model for American Religious History," in Thomas Kselman, ed., *Belief in History: Innovative Approaches to European and American Religion* (Notre Dame: University of Notre Dame Press, 1991), 286–309.

5. On church historians, one thinks, e.g., of classic works such as Robert Baird, *Religion in America* (1843), with its revised edition (1856) abridged and edited by Henry Warner Bowden (New York: Harper and Row, 1970); William Warren Sweet, *Religion on the American Frontier*, vol. 1: *The Baptists* (New York: Henry Holt, 1931); vol. 2: *The Presbyterians* (New York: Harper, 1936); vol. 3: *The Congregationalists* (Chicago: University of Chicago Press, 1939); vol. 4: *The Methodists* (Chicago: University of Chicago Press, 1946); and, more recently and expansively, Winthrop S. Hudson, *Religion in America* (New York: Scribner's, 1965), now in its seventh edition with John Corrigan (Upper Saddle River, N.J.: Pearson/Prentice Hall, 2004); and Mark A. Noll, A His-

tory of Christianity in the United States and Canada (Grand Rapids, Mich.: Eerdmans, 1992); see Sydney E. Ahlstrom, *A Religious History of the American People* (New Haven: Yale University Press, 1972), 488–90, 1019–47.

6. Butler, *Awash in a Sea of Faith*, 88–97.

7. Donald G. Mathews, "The Second Great Awakening as an Organizing Process, 1780–1830," *American Quarterly* 21 (1969): 23–43. I develop a tripartite typology and expand on one of the types—evangelicalism, or "knowing through the heart"—to add still a fourth type not discussed here (prophecy, or "knowing through the will") in Catherine L. Albanese, ed., *American Spiritualities: A Reader* (Bloomington: Indiana University Press, 2001).

8. See William James, *The Varieties of Religious Experience: A Study in Human Nature* (1902; rpt., London: Collier-Macmillan, 1961), 143. James took his categories of the "once-born" and "twice-born" from Francis W. Newman (see ibid., 80).

9. For "popular religion" and its problems as a term, see Charles H. Long, "Popular Religion," in Mircea Eliade, ed., *The Encyclopedia of Religion* (New York: Macmillan, 1987), 11: 442–52; and Catherine L. Albanese, "Religion and Popular American Culture: An Introductory Essay," *Journal of the American Academy of Religion* 64, no. 4 (1996): 733–42. For "vernacular religion," see Leonard Norman Primiano, "Vernacular Religion and the Search for Method in Religious Folklife," *Western Folklore* 54, no. 1 (1995): 40–44, esp. 44; and Leonard Norman Primiano, "Intrinsically Catholic: Vernacular Religion and Philadelphia's 'Dignity,'" (Ph.D. diss., University of Pennsylvania, 1993). For discussions that raise some of the same issues and inflect them in somewhat similar and related ways, see David D. Hall's "Introduction," in David D. Hall, ed., *Lived Religion in America: Toward a History of Practice* (Princeton: Princeton University Press, 1997), vii–xiii; and Robert Orsi, "Everyday Miracles: The Study of Lived Religion," in Hall, ed., *Lived Religion in America*, 3–21.

10. Charles S. Braden, *Spirits in Rebellion: The Rise and Development of New Thought* (Dallas: Southern Methodist University Press, 1963), 4.

11. J. Stillson Judah, *The History and Philosophy of the Metaphysical Movements in America* (Philadelphia: Westminster, 1967), 21, 11.

12. For medieval European metaphysics, see Frederick Copleston, *A History of Philosophy*, vol. 2, *Mediaeval Philosophy*, Part I, *Augustine to Bonaventure*, and Part II, *Albert the Great to Duns Scotus* (1950; rpt., Garden City, N.Y.: Doubleday, 1962); Maurice De Wulf, *An Introduction to Scholastic Philosophy, Medieval and Modern* (originally *Scholasticism Old and New*), trans. P. Coffey (1907; rpt., New York: Dover, 1956); David Knowles, *The Evolution of Medieval Thought* (New York: Vintage, 1962); and Gordon Leff, *Medieval Thought: St. Augustine to Ockham* (1958; rpt., Baltimore: Penguin, 1968).

13. See Herbert Hovenkamp, *Science and Religion in America, 1800–1860* (Philadelphia: University of Pennsylvania Press, 1978), esp. 23–24; and see, also, Theodore Dwight Bozeman, *Protestants in an Age of Science: The Baconian Ideal and Antebellum American Religious Thought* (Chapel Hill: University of North Carolina Press, 1977).

14. Nathan O. Hatch, *The Democratization of American Christianity* (New Haven: Yale University Press, 1989); for a discussion that focuses on some of these themes in the

context of New England, see David Jaffee, "The Village Enlightenment in New England, 1760–1820," *William and Mary Quarterly*, 3d series, 47, no. 3 (July 1990): esp. 327–28.

15. For textbook preferences in the nineteenth century, see Ruth Miller Elson, *Guardians of Tradition: American Schoolbooks of the Nineteenth Century* (Lincoln: University of Nebraska Press, 1964).

16. On esotericism, see Antoine Faivre, *Access to Western Esotericism* (Albany: State University of New York Press, 1994), 10–13. Scholars in the "esoteric" school besides Faivre include, among the most well-known, Wouter J. Hanegraaff, Pierre A. Riffard, Arthur Versluis, and Allison P. Coudert. See, e.g., Wouter J. Hanegraaff, "On the Construction of 'Esoteric' Traditions," in Antoine Faivre and Wouter J. Hanegraaff, eds., *Western Esotericism and the Science of Religion: Selected Papers Presented at the Seventeenth Congress of the International Association for the History of Religions, Mexico City, 1995* (Leuven, Belgium: Peeter, 1998), esp. 11–16, 28 (on a "hidden tradition"), 43; and Pierre A. Riffard, *L'ésotérisme: qu'est-ce que l'ésoterisme?: anthologie de l'ésotérisme occidental* (Paris: R. Laffont, 1990), esp. on secrecy ("La Discipline de l'Arcane"), 245–306.

17. On dissident history, see Catherine L. Albanese, "Dissident History: American Religious Culture and the Emergence of the Metaphysical Tradition," in Walter H. Conser Jr. and Sumner B. Twiss, eds., *Religious Diversity and American Religious History: Studies in Traditions and Cultures* (Athens: University of Georgia Press, 1997), 157–88.

18. Ann Taves, *Fits, Trances, and Visions: Experiencing Religion and Explaining Experience from Wesley to James* (Princeton: Princeton University Press, 1999).

1. EUROPEAN LEGACIES

1. See Wouter J. Hanegraaff, "Lodovico Lazzarelli and the Hermetic Christ: At the Sources of Renaissance Hermetism," in Wouter J. Hanegraaff and Ruud M. Bouthoorn, eds., *Lodovico Lazzarelli (1447–1500): The Hermetic Writings and Related Documents* (Phoenix, Ariz.: Arizona State University, Arizona Center for Medieval and Renaissance Studies, 2005), 1–104. I am grateful for Hanegraaff's extraordinarily close and helpful reading of an earlier draft of this chapter and for his textual suggestions.

2. For these and related details, consult Antoine Faivre, "Hermetism," in Mircea Eliade, ed., *The Encyclopedia of Religion* (New York: Macmillan, 1987), 6: 295–96; Frances A. Yates, *Giordano Bruno and the Hermetic Tradition* (1964; rpt., Chicago: University of Chicago Press, 1991), 12–13; and Brian P. Copenhaver, trans., "Introduction," in *Hermetica: The Greek Corpus Hermeticum and the Latin Asclepius in a New English Translation, with Notes and Introduction* (1992; rpt., New York: Cambridge University Press, 1997), xli, xlvii–xlviii.

3. See Peter Kingsley, "Poimandres: The Etymology of the Name and the Origins of the Hermetica," in Roelof van den Broek and Cis van Heertum, eds., *From Poimandres to Jacob Böhme: Gnosis, Hermetism, and the Christian Tradition* (Amsterdam: In de Pelikaan, 2000), 41–76. Kingsley writes that the name Poimandres "referred to Thoth

in his role as the creative intelligence of the supreme god, the delegate and representative of Re who—at least on some occasions and in some cult contexts"—seemed "to have merged with Re himself" (ibid., 52).

4. The best brief synopsis of the various opinions concerning the identity of Hermes Trismegistus may be found in Copenhaver, *Hermetica*, xiii–xvi, xxxiii–xxxv, xl–xliii, xlv–lvi and passim, xv.

5. Faivre, "Hermetism," 296; Yates, *Giordano Bruno*, 13–14.

6. In a strong statement of the relationship between philosophical and technical Hermetica, Garth Fowden has argued, not without controversy, that in effect Renaissance and later commentators artificially segregated the *Corpus* and its teachings by severing their connection with the practical Hermetic texts. All of these belong together, he observes, as "technical" and "philosophical" books that are "related aspects" of "a practical spiritual 'way.'" See Garth Fowden, *The Egyptian Hermes: A Historical Approach to the Late Pagan Mind* (New York: Cambridge University Press, 1986), xvi, as quoted in Copenhaver, *Hermetica*, xxxvi.

7. Copenhaver, *Hermetica*, xxxvii.

8. André-Jean Festugière, *La Révélation d'Hermès Trismégiste*, 4 vols. (Paris: J. Gabalda, 1950–54), has argued strongly for the primacy of Greek influence. By contrast, Jean-Pierre Mahé, *Hermès en Haute-Égypte*, 2 vols. (Québec: Presses de l'Université, 1978–82), has emphasized the Egyptian character of the writings, as has Fowden in *The Egyptian Hermes*, even though he also thinks that Mahé overestimated the importance of Egyptian materials. Strongly emphasizing Egyptian elements, too, is Peter Kingsley, who declares that "the time is long gone when we can afford to believe that because the Hermetica use Greek philosophical language they have no Egyptian prehistory" ("Poimandres," 72). Hans Jonas has pointed to the Near Eastern and Gnostic overtones of Hermetic literature, arguing that "in certain portions" it "reflects gnostic spirit" and that especially the *Poimandres* of the *Corpus Hermeticum* "is an outstanding document of gnostic cosmogony and anthropogony independent of the speculations of the Christian Gnostics" (Hans Jonas, *The Gnostic Religion: The Message of the Alien God and the Beginnings of Christianity*, 2d ed., rev. (Boston: Beacon Press, 1963), 41, 147. For a brief and useful survey of the scholarship, see Copenhaver, *Hermetica*, xiv–lix.

9. Festugière, *Révélation*, 1:84; as quoted in Copenhaver, *Hermetica*, lv; Yates, *Giordano Bruno*, 22.

10. See the discussion of Fowden in Copenhaver, *Hermetica*, xxxix; Roelof van den Broek, "Gnosticism and Hermetism in Antiquity: Two Roads to Salvation," in Roelof van den Broek and Wouter J. Hanegraaff, eds., *Gnosis and Hermeticism: From Antiquity to Modern Times* (Albany: State University of New York Press, 1998), 4, 6, 9–10.

11. See the paraphrase of Ficino's *argumentum* in Yates, *Giordano Bruno*, 16.

12. See the short synopsis in Jean-Pierre Mahé, "Hermes Trismegistos," in Mircea Eliade, ed., *The Encyclopedia of Religion*, 6: 290, 292; Kingsley, "Poimandres," 56.

13. Copenhaver, *Hermetica*, 21–23, 15.

14. Ibid., 20, 3, 28, 20; on the Hermetic idea of God, see Van den Broek, "Gnosticism and Hermetism in Antiquity," 7–9.

15. Copenhaver, *Hermetica*, 2, 24 (my emphasis), 33, 50, 52, 41.

16. Ibid., 67, 69, 78, 88.

17. Ibid., 90.

18. The practice of animating a statue by drawing an intelligent being into it may also be found in other religious contexts. See, e.g., Joanne Punzo Waghorne and Norman Cutler, *Gods of Flesh, Gods of Stone: The Embodiment of Divinity in India* (New York: Columbia University Press, 1996). I owe this observation to Wouter J. Hanegraaff.

19. Ibid., 62, 60.

20. Yates, *Giordano Bruno*, 41; Stephen Wilson, *The Magical Universe: Everyday Ritual and Magic in Pre-Modern Europe* (London: Hambledon and London, 2000), xxvi. Yates argued in what may be an exaggeration that "the rehabilitation of the *Asclepius*, through the discovery of the *Corpus Hermeticum*" became "one of the chief factors in the Renaissance revival of magic" (Yates, *Giordano Bruno*, 41); see Hanegraaff, "Lodovico Lazzarelli and the Hermetic Christ," 102 n281, 73 n193.

21. See Joseph Dan, ed., *The Christian Kabbalah: Jewish Mystical Books and Their Christian Interpreters* (Cambridge: Harvard College Library, 1997), 13; Yates, *Giordano Bruno*, 84, 92, 111.

22. See Frances A. Yates, *The Occult Philosophy in the Elizabethan Age* (London: Routledge and Kegan Paul, 1979), esp. 33–34.

23. Antoine Faivre makes just this point in another way in his authoritative discussion of the related domain of esotericism, which he identifies as having four "intrinsic" characteristics and, among them, an interconnection of "imagination" and "mediations." "These two notions are linked and complementary," he writes. "The idea of correspondence presumes already a form of imagination inclined to reveal and use mediations of all kinds, such as rituals, symbolic images, mandalas, intermediary spirits." He adds that "it is especially under the inspiration of the *Corpus Hermeticum* . . . that memory and imagination are associated to the extent of blending together. After all, a part of the teaching of Hermes Trismegistus consisted of 'interiorizing' the world in our *mens*, from whence the 'arts of memory' cultivated in the light of magic, during and after the Renaissance." See Antoine Faivre, *Access to Western Esotericism* (Albany: State University of New York Press, 1994), 10, 12–13. See, also, Antoine Faivre, "Introduction I," in Antoine Faivre and Jacob Needleman, eds., *Modern Esoteric Spirituality* (New York: Crossroad, 1992), xv, xvii.

24. Copenhaver, *Hermetica*, xxxii, xvi (Copenhaver cites Festugière and Walter Scott as modern scholars who "distinguished the 'popular' occultist writings attributed to Hermes from the 'learned' or 'philosophical' treatises" [ibid., xxxii]); Kingsley, "Poimandres," 68.

25. See Jonas, *Gnostic Religion*, esp. 34–37, 41, 147–73; Van den Broek, "Gnosticism and Hermetism in Antiquity," 1.

26. On translations from the Arabic, see Faivre, "Hermetism," 296–97; and on medieval ritual magic, see Claire Fanger, ed., *Conjuring Spirits: Texts and Traditions of Medieval Ritual Magic* (University Park: Pennsylvania State University Press, 1998).

27. Faivre, "Hermetism," 295; Allison Coudert, "Renaissance Alchemy," in Mircea Eliade, ed., *The Encyclopedia of Religion*, 1: 200–201.

28. Andrew Weeks, *German Mysticism from Hildegard of Bingen to Ludwig Wittgenstein: A Literary and Intellectual History* (Albany: State University of New York Press, 1993), 122. See, also, Marc van der Poel, *Cornelius Agrippa: The Humanist Theologian and His Declamations* (New York: Köln, 1997); Joseph Dan, ed., *Christian Kabbalah*, 13.

29. G. Mallory Masters, "Renaissance Kabbalah," in Faivre and Needleman, *Modern Esoteric Spirituality*, 143.

30. For the misreading of Agrippa, see Van der Poel, *Cornelius Agrippa, the Humanist Theologian*, 1–3; Yates, *Occult Philosophy*, 37; Weeks, *German Mysticism*, 120.

31. Weeks, *German Mysticism*, 120; Van der Poel, *Cornelius Agrippa, the Humanist Theologian*, 54, 10.

32. Andrew Weeks, *Paracelsus: Speculative Theory and the Crisis of the Early Reformation* (Albany: State University of New York Press, 1997), 185; Allison Coudert, "Paracelsus," in Mircea Eliade, ed., *The Encyclopedia of Religion*, 11: 183. For the comparison of Paracelsus to Luther, see the brief but lucid summary in Coudert, ibid.

33. Weeks, *Paracelsus*, 185; Faivre, "Hermetism," 300; Faivre, *Access to Western Esotericism*, 62.

34. Heinrich Schipperges, "Paracelsus and His Followers," trans. John Bowden, in Faivre and Needleman, eds., *Modern Esoteric Spirituality*, 155; Paracelsus, *Septem Defensiones*, IX: 568 and VIII: 321, as quoted in ibid., 161–62; Schipperges, "Paracelsus and His Followers," 166, 162 (emphasis in original).

35. Yates's controversial work is *The Rosicrucian Enlightenment* (London: Routledge and Kegan Paul, 1972). For the scholarly demolition of the work, see, especially, Brian Vickers, "Frances Yates and the Writing of History," *Journal of Modern History* 51, no. 2 (June 1979): 287–316; and for a more tempered disavowal of the Yatesian "grand narrative" from the perspective of religious studies, see Wouter J. Hanegraaff, "Beyond the Yates Paradigm: The Study of Western Esotericism between Counterculture and New Complexity," *Aries* 1, no. 1 (2001): 5–37.

36. Frances A. Yates, *The Rosicrucian Enlightenment* (1972; rpt., Boulder: Shambhala, 1978), xi; Roland Edighoffer, "Rosicrucianism: From the Seventeenth to the Twentieth Century," in Faivre and Needleman, eds., *Modern Esoteric Spirituality*, 187; Faivre, *Access to Western Esotericism*, 64; Roland Edighoffer, "Hermeticism in Early Rosicrucianism," in Van den Broek and Hanegraaff, eds., *Gnosis and Hermeticism*, 197–215, 211.

37. See Yates, *Rosicrucian Enlightenment*, 207 ("so far as my own researches have gone, I have found no evidence of a real secret society calling itself 'Rosicrucian,' and really in existence as an organized group at the time the manifestos were published and during the time of the [Rosicrucian] furore"); Faivre, *Access to Western Esotericism*, 65 ("this Rosicrucian myth"); Edighoffer, "Hermeticism in Early Rosicrucianism," 197 ("so-called Early Rosicrucianism").

38. Faivre, *Access to Western Esotericism*, 65.

39. Roland Edighoffer has recounted how suspicions of being the author of the *Fama* and *Confessio* dogged Andreae during his life, and he has detailed the Lutheran theologian's continuing responses to the documents. Edighoffer argues persuasively that, in the context of the religious and political currents of the times, "uncertain about

his future, wounded in his self-esteem, the young Andreae without doubt imagined a legendary, all-powerful character, one who rights wrongs and heralds a new age. The name of this hero, this Christian Hercules, was inspired both by the coat of arms of the Andreae family and by that of Luther, each of which bore the double motif of the rose and the cross. . . . One may therefore legitimately propose the hypothesis that the young Andreae invented the eponymous character, although Tobias Hess [a man eighteen years senior to Andreae; a jurist, physician, theologian, and Kabbalist whose friendship Andreae cultivated] would have supplied the kabbalistic, Paracelsian, and Joachimite infrastructure of the original manifestos" (Edighoffer, "Rosicrucianism," 201–2).

40. Edighoffer, "Hermeticism in Early Rosicrucianism," 212.

41. Yates, *Rosicrucian Enlightenment,* 42.

42. Arthur Versluis, *The Esoteric Origins of the American Renaissance* (New York: Oxford University Press, 2001), 14–15. See, also, Peter C. Erb, "Jakob Boehme," in Mircea Eliade, ed., *The Encyclopedia of Religion,* 2: 275–76.

43. See Ingrid Merkel, "*Aurora*; or, The Rising Sun of Allegory: Hermetic Imagery in the Work of Jakob Böhme," in Ingrid Merkel and Allen G. Debus, eds., *Hermeticism and the Renaissance: Intellectual History and the Occult in Early Modern Europe* (Washington, D.C.: Folger Shakespeare Library, 1988), 303–4; see, also, R. H. Hvolbek, "Was Jacob Boehme a Paracelsian?" *Hermetic Journal* 19 (Spring 1983): 6–17; and for a useful discussion of Boehme's personal spirituality, see Peter Erb, "Introduction," in Jacob Boehme, *The Way to Christ,* trans. Peter Erb (New York: Paulist, 1978), esp. 4–21.

44. Arthur Versluis, *Theosophia: Hidden Dimensions of Christianity* (Hudson, N.Y.: Lindisfarne, 1994), 60 n3, 58; Erb, "Introduction," in Boehme, *Way to Christ,* 10; see, also, Peter C. Erb, "Jakob Boehme," in Mircea Eliade, ed., *The Encyclopedia of Religion,* 2: 275–76; and for book-length studies of Boehme, see Andrew Weeks, *Boehme: An Intellectual Biography of the Seventeenth-Century Philosopher and Mystic* (Albany: State University of New York Press, 1991), and Cyril O'Regan, *Gnostic Apocalypse: Jacob Boehme's Haunted Narrative* (Albany: State University of New York Press, 2002).

45. Merkel, "*Aurora,*" 303; for a useful summary, on which this one is based, see the exposition in B. J. Gibbons, *Gender in Mystical and Occult Thought: Behmenism and Its Development in England* (Cambridge: Cambridge University Press, 1996), 89–90.

46. Erb, "Jakob Boehme," 276; Erb, "Introduction," in Boehme, *Way to Christ,* 9.

47. Merkel, "*Aurora,*" 302; Versluis, *Theosophia,* 60–61, 65; on the "new orthodoxy" that disappointed Protestants after the first generation of Lutheran reform, see Merkel, "*Aurora,*" 304.

48. Yates, *Occult Philosophy,* 75.

49. William H. Sherman, *John Dee: The Politics of Reading and Writing in the English Renaissance* (Amherst: University of Massachusetts Press, 1995), 51, 89. Sherman estimates the library collection, on the basis of a 1583 catalog, as between 3,000 and 4,000 books "representing virtually every aspect of classical, medieval, and Renaissance learning," adding that "the library was especially rich in scientific and histori-

cal manuscripts, and its unsurpassed Hermetic, navigational, artistic, Paracelsian, and Semitic holdings have long attracted scholarly attention" (ibid., 31). More conservatively, Nicholas Clulee cites over 2,000 book titles and 198 manuscripts, in Nicholas H. Clulee, *John Dee's Natural Philosophy: Between Science and Religion* (London: Routledge, 1988), 12.

50. See Peter J. French, *John Dee: The World of an Elizabethan Magus* (London: Routledge and Kegan Paul, 1972), 113–19; György E. Szönyi, "John Dee and Early Modern Occult Philosophy," *Aries* 2, no. 1 (2002): 77.

51. Meric Casaubon, as quoted in French, *John Dee*, 11; Yates, *Occult Philosophy*, 104, 95, 103–4, 108, 89, 170; French, *John Dee*.

52. Clulee, *John Dee's Natural Philosophy*, esp. 16; Sherman, *John Dee*, 13, xii, 20, 25; and, for later work, see, e.g., Deborah Harkness, *Talking with Angels: John Dee and the End of Nature* (Cambridge: Cambridge University Press, 1999); Håkan Håkansson, *Seeing the Word: John Dee and Renaissance Occultism* (Lund: Lunds Universitet, 2001); and Benjamin Woolley, *The Queen's Conjurer: The Science and Magic of Dr. John Dee, Adviser to Queen Elizabeth I* (New York: Henry Holt, 2001)—all three cited in Szönyi's review article "John Dee and Early Modern Occult Philosophy," 76–87.

53. Sherman, *John Dee*, 42.

54. These were Fludd's *Apologia* (for the "Fraternity of the Rosy Cross"), a work that appeared in Leyden in 1616, and his *Tractatus*, a Rosicrucian defense that appeared in Oppenheim in 1617.

55. See Christopher McIntosh, *The Rose Cross and the Age of Reason: Eighteenth-Century Rosicrucianism in Central Europe and Its Relationship to the Enlightenment* (Leiden: E. J. Brill, 1992), 27; William H. Huffman, *Robert Fludd and the End of the Renaissance* (London: Routledge, 1988), esp. 160–61.

56. This is the judgment, too, of Joscelyn Godwin in *Robert Fludd: Hermetic Philosopher and Surveyor of Two Worlds* (London: Thames and Hudson, 1979), 10.

57. Huffman, *Robert Fludd and the End of the Renaissance*, 3; Godwin, *Robert Fludd*, 7; Dan, ed., *Christian Kabbalah*, 13.

58. McIntosh, *The Rose Cross and the Age of Reason*, 77; B. J. Gibbons, *Spirituality and the Occult: From the Renaissance to the Modern Age* (London: Routledge, 2001), 103.

59. Huffman, *Robert Fludd and the End of the Renaissance*, 105–6; Gibbons, *Spirituality and the Occult*, 45, 9.

60. See Godwin, *Robert Fludd*, 14; Robert Fludd, "The Philosophical Key," as quoted in Huffman, *Robert Fludd and the End of the Renaissance*, 115–16; on Fludd and high magic, see Huffman, *Robert Fludd and the End of the Renaissance*, 117–21.

61. This is a judgment in which Huffman (*Robert Fludd and the End of the Renaissance*, 1) and Godwin (*Robert Fludd*, 5) concur; for a sampling of Fludd's diagrammatic teaching illustrations, see Godwin, *Robert Fludd*, a work that is for the most part a reproduction of some 126 of the engravings.

62. Frances A. Yates, *Theatre of the World* (Chicago: University of Chicago Press, 1969), 186; Huffman, *Robert Fludd and the End of the Renaissance*, 160; on literary influences, see, e.g., Yates, *Occult Philosophy*, 115–33, 147–63, 177–81.

63. For a brief but useful discussion of these views, see Herbert Leventhal, *In the Shadow of the Enlightenment: Occultism and Renaissance Science in Eighteenth-Century America* (New York: New York University Press, 1976), 5–7. My discussion in the paragraphs that follow is also generally shaped by Leventhal's work. See, also, E[ustace]. M[andeville]. W[estenhall]. Tillyard, *The Elizabethan World Picture* (1943; rpt., London: Chatto and Windus, 1958).

64. Keith Thomas, *Religion and the Decline of Magic* (New York: Scribner's, 1971), 288, 291–92.

65. Ibid., 8; John Donne, "The Extasie," as quoted in Leventhal, *Shadow of the Enlightenment*, 8.

66. Antoine Faivre, "Ancient and Medieval Sources of Modern Esoteric Movements," in Faivre and Needleman, *Modern Esoteric Spirituality*, 50–51; Yates, *Rosicrucian Enlightenment*, esp. 207–8. Edmond Mazet points to class issues in the formation of speculative Masonry in his article "Freemasonry and Esotericism," in Faivre and Needleman, *Modern Esoteric Spirituality*, 250.

67. As quoted in Yates, *Rosicrucian Enlightenment*, 211 (emphasis in Yates).

68. See Yates, *Rosicrucian Enlightenment*, 193–94.

69. Jon Butler, *Awash in a Sea of Faith: Christianizing the American People* (Cambridge: Harvard University Press, 1990), esp. 83–97.

70. See Hanegraaff, "Lodovico Lazzarelli and the Hermetic Christ," from which this account is taken.

71. Faivre, "Hermetism," 297; see Hanegraaff, "Lodovico Lazzarelli and the Hermetic Christ."

72. Faivre, "Hermetism," 296.

73. Yates identified Bruno's faith as that of "a Renaissance Neoplatonic Hermetist" and wrote, e.g., "Bruno's philosophy cannot be separated from his religion. It *was* his religion, the 'religion of the world,' which he saw in this expanded form of the infinite universe and the innumerable worlds as an expanded gnosis, a new revelation of the divinity from the 'vestiges.' Copernicanism was a symbol of the new revelation, which was to mean a return to the natural religion of the Egyptians, and its magic, within a framework which he so strangely supposed could be a Catholic framework" (Yates, *Giordano Bruno*, 350, 355, 354). See, also, Maurice A. Finocchiaro, "Philosophy versus Religion and Science versus Religion: The Trials of Bruno and Galileo," in Hilary Gatti, ed., *Giordano Bruno: Philosopher of the Renaissance* (Burlington, Vt.: Ashgate, 2002), 51–96.

74. See Emmanuel Le Roy Ladurie, *Montaillou: The Promised Land of Error*, trans. Barbara Bray (New York: Vintage, 1979).

75. The quotations are taken from the English edition of Ginzburg's *Il formaggio e i vermi* (1976): Carlo Ginzburg, *The Cheese and the Worms: The Cosmos of a Sixteenth-Century Miller*, trans. John and Anne Tedeschi (1980; rpt., New York: Penguin, 1985), 5–6, 107.

76. Wilson, *Magical Universe*, esp. xvii–xxx.

77. See Carlo Ginzburg, *I Benandanti: Stregoneria e culti agrari tra Cinquecento e Sei-*

cento (1966), published in English as *The Night Battles: Witchcraft and Agrarian Cults in the Sixteenth and Seventeenth Centuries*, trans. John and Anne Tedeschi (1983; rpt., New York: Penguin, 1985).

78.	Gregory Zilboorg, *The Medical Man and the Witch during the Renaissance: The Hideyo Noguchi Lectures* (Baltimore: Johns Hopkins Press, 1935), 8–9.

79.	Ibid., 42. The quotation from the *Malleus Maleficarum* comes from Zilboorg, ibid.

80.	Margaret Murray, *The Witch-Cult in Western Europe: A Study in Anthropology* (Oxford: Clarendon Press, 1921); see, also, Margaret A. Murray, *The God of the Witches* (1931; rpt., New York: Oxford University Press, 1970). The literature on western European witchcraft is vast, a good portion of it not in English. Among older English-language studies, especially noteworthy are Norman Cohn, *Europe's Inner Demons: An Enquiry Inspired by the Great Witch-Hunt* (New York: Basic Books, 1975); Richard Kieckhefer, *European Witch Trials: Their Foundation in Popular and Learned Culture* (Berkeley: University of California Press, 1976); and H[ugh]. R[edwold]. Trevor-Roper, *The European Witch-Craze of the Sixteenth and Seventeenth Centuries* (New York: Harper, 1969). The explosion of interest has come especially from the late 1980s into the 1990s. Among these (English-language) works, see Anne Llewellyn Barstow, *Witchcraze: A New History of the European Witch Hunts* (San Francisco: Pandora, 1994); Robin Briggs, *Witches and Neighbors: The Social and Cultural Context of European Witchcraft* (New York: Viking, 1996); Stuart Clark, *Thinking with Demons: The Idea of Witchcraft in Early Modern Europe* (New York: Oxford University Press, 1997); Eugene D. Dukes, *Magic and Witchcraft in the Dark Ages* (Lanham, Md.: University Press of America, 1996); Gabor Klaniczay, *The Uses of Supernatural Power: The Transformation of Popular Religion in Medieval and Early Modern Europe*, trans. Susan Singerman (Princeton: Princeton University Press, 1990); Brian P. Levack, *The Witch-Hunt in Early Modern Europe*, 2d ed. (New York: Longman, 1995); Eva Pocs, *Between the Living and the Dead: A Perspective on Witches and Seers in the Early Modern Age*, trans. Silvia Redey and Michael Webb (Ithaca: Cornell University Press, 1999); G. F. Quaife, *Godly Zeal and Furious Rage: The Witch in Early Modern Europe* (New York: St. Martin's, 1987); and Geoffrey Scarre, *Witchcraft and Magic in Sixteenth and Seventeenth Century Europe* (Atlantic Highlands, N.J.: Humanities Press International, 1987).

81.	See Wilson, *Magical Universe*.

82.	John Bale, *A Comedy concernynge Three Lawes, of Nature, Moses and Christ* (1538), as summarized, with quotations, in George Lyman Kittredge, *Witchcraft in Old and New England* (1929; rpt., New York: Russell and Russell, 1956), 34–35.

83.	*Sermons by Hugh Latimer*, ed. G. E. Corrie (1844), as quoted in Kittredge, *Witchcraft in Old and New England*, 71; Hildred Geertz, "An Anthropology of Religion and Magic, I," *Journal of Interdisciplinary History* 6 (1975): 71–89, cited in Ellen Badone, ed., "Introduction," in *Religious Orthodoxy and Popular Faith in European Society* (Princeton: Princeton University Press, 1990), 9.

84.	Thomas, *Religion and the Decline of Magic*, 245; Alan Macfarlane, *Witchcraft in Tudor and Stuart England: A Regional and Comparative Study* (London: Routledge and Kegan Paul, 1970), 115–17, 120–21.

85. Thomas, *Religion and the Decline of Magic*, 229, 227; Frank Klaassen, "English Manuscripts of Magic, 1300–1500: A Preliminary Survey," in Fanger, ed., *Conjuring Spirits*, 3–31.

86. Macfarlane, *Witchcraft in Tudor and Stuart England*, 126, 130. Macfarlane quoted George Gifford, *A Dialogue Concerning Witches and Witchcrafts* (1593).

87. Robert C. Fuller, *Americans and the Unconscious* (New York: Oxford University Press, 1986).

88. Thomas, *Religion and the Decline of Magic*, 227, 89, 107, 84–96.

89. John L. Brooke, *The Refiner's Fire: The Making of Mormon Cosmology, 1644–1844* (New York: Cambridge University Press, 1994), 19, 20, 21.

90. Thomas, *Religion and the Decline of Magic*, 292, 294.

91. Ibid., 293.

92. Ibid., 371, 375, 378, 381.

93. W. Vaughan, *The Golden-Grove* (1600), as quoted in Thomas, *Religion and the Decline of Magic*, 227.

2. ATLANTIC JOURNEYS, NATIVE GROUNDS

1. David Hackett Fischer, *Albion's Seed: Four British Folkways in America* (New York: Oxford University Press, 1989). (Albion was the earliest name recorded for the island of Britain.)

2. Ibid., 6.

3. Ibid., 6–7.

4. Ibid., 31, 33; Alan Macfarlane, *Witchcraft in Tudor and Stuart England: A Regional and Comparative Study* (London: Routledge and Kegan Paul, 1970); Fischer, *Albion's Seed*, 127.

5. See John Hale's deposition in *Records of Salem Witchcraft, Copied from the Original Documents* (1864; rpt., New York: Da Capo, 1969), 1: 246. Hale also alludes to Hoar ("D.H.") in his *A Modest Enquiry into the Nature of Witchcraft* (1702; rpt. with an introduction by Richard Trask, Bainbridge, N.Y.: York Mail-Print, 1973), 29–30, but he mentions neither fortune telling nor palmistry there. Hoar confessed to witchcraft and was condemned, but—because of "potent friends"—she received a stay of execution. See George Lincoln Burr, ed., *Narratives of the Witchcraft Cases, 1648–1706* (New York: Scribner's, 1914), 366n.

6. John Putnam Demos, *Entertaining Satan: Witchcraft and the Culture of Early New England* (New York: Oxford University Press, 1982), 12 (significantly, Demos is quoted, too, in Fischer, *Albion's Seed*, 128); Samuel G. Drake, *Annals of Witchcraft in New England and Elsewhere in the United States, from Their First Settlement* (1869; rpt., New York: Benjamin Blom, 1967), vii–viii, x.

7. Demos, *Entertaining Satan*, 81; Jon Butler, *Awash in a Sea of Faith: Christianizing the American People* (Cambridge: Harvard University Press, 1990), 87–88; Drake, *Annals of Witchcraft in New England*, viii.

8. Increase Mather, *An Essay for the Recording of Illustrious Providences* (1684), reprinted as *Remarkable Providences Illustrative of the Earlier Days of American Colo-*

nisation, introduced by George Offor (London: Reeves and Turner, 1890), 129 (emphasis in original).

9. Butler, *Awash in a Sea of Faith*, 75; Arthur Versluis, *The Esoteric Origins of the American Renaissance* (New York: Oxford University Press, 2001), 32–35; George Starkey, as quoted ibid., 34.

10. Butler, *Awash in a Sea of Faith*, 76; Charles Morton, *Compendium Physicae*, as quoted ibid., 76; Versluis, *Esoteric Origins of the American Renaissance*, 35, 29, 11, 30.

11. See Walter J. Ong, "Ramus, Petrus," in Paul Edwards, ed., *The Encyclopedia of Philosophy* (New York: Macmillan, 1967), 7: 66–68; Perry Miller, *The New England Mind: The Seventeenth Century* (1954; rpt., Cambridge: Harvard University Press, 1963), 116.

12. See Ong, "Ramus," 67; and Walter J. Ong, *Ramus, Method, and the Decay of Dialogue: From the Art of Discourse to the Art of Reason* (Cambridge: Harvard University Press, 1958), 30, 199, 205–7. Ong connected the application of the term *Methodist* to John Wesley and his followers to the fashion for "method" introduced by Ramus and his disciples (see Ong, "Ramus," 67).

13. Petrus Ramus, as quoted in Wilbur Samuel Howell, *Logic and Rhetoric in England, 1500–1700* (Princeton: Princeton University Press, 1956), 157.

14. P[etrus] Ramus, *The Logike of the Moste Excellent Philosopher P. Ramus, Martyr*, trans. Roland MacIlmaine (1574), ed. Catherine M. Dunn (Northridge, Calif.: San Fernando Valley State College, 1969), 54. On MacIlmaine's emphasis on "natural method," see Howell, *Logic and Rhetoric in England*, 183; and for the "natural moral order" in Ramus and the Puritans, see John C. Adams, "Ramus, Illustrations, and the Puritan Movement," *Journal of Medieval and Renaissance Studies* 17, no. 2 (1987): 209.

15. Howell, *Logic and Rhetoric in England*, 189, 192–93, 206.

16. Alexander Richardson, *The Logicians School-Master, Or a Comment upon Ramus Logick* (London: Gertrude Dawson and Samuel Thomson, 1657), 82.

17. Miller, *New England Mind*, 168, 214; Ong, "Ramus," 67. Miller's evocation of aesthetics and beauty in Puritan contexts was echoed later by William A. Clebsch in *American Religious Thought: A History* (Chicago: University of Chicago Press, 1973), wherein Clebsch argued for a lineage of American thinkers, especially Jonathan Edwards, Ralph Waldo Emerson, and William James, who moved from ethics and moralism to aesthetics and a sense of at-homeness in the universe; i.e., being in "place," just as — here — the Ramean logic ordered mental space by visualizing it. To be logical meant to find one's proper home amid mental mansions by drawing their blueprints on paper.

18. This formulation owes something to Michel Foucault. See, especially, his dissection of the medical "gaze" in *The Birth of the Clinic: An Archaeology of Medical Perception* (1963), trans. A. M. Sheridan Smith (London: Tavistock, 1973).

19. Fischer, *Albion's Seed*, 310.

20. Ibid., 341.

21. Ibid., 342–43 (emphasis in original).

22. Butler, *Awash in a Sea of Faith*, 77–78, 80.

23. See Mechal Sobel, *The World They Made Together: Black and White Values in Eighteenth-Century Virginia* (Princeton: Princeton University Press, 1987), 84–85.

24. See Fischer, *Albion's Seed*, 526–30.

25. See the summary in John L. Brooke, *The Refiner's Fire: The Making of Mormon Cosmology, 1644–1844* (New York: Cambridge University Press, 1994), 25, 40.

26. Fischer, *Albion's Seed*, 527–29; Butler, *Awash in a Sea of Faith*, 74–75.

27. See Versluis, *Esoteric Origins of the American Renaissance*, 22–23.

28. Fischer, *Albion's Seed*, 529–30.

29. Ibid., 529.

30. See Catherine L. Albanese, *America: Religions and Religion*, 3d ed. (Belmont, Calif.: Wadsworth, 1999), 340.

31. Herbert Leventhal, *In the Shadow of the Enlightenment: Occultism and Renaissance Science in Eighteenth-Century America* (New York: New York University Press, 1976), 13–65, 64.

32. Butler, *Awash in a Sea of Faith*, 82–83.

33. Brooke, *Refiner's Fire*, 33, 34, 38–39.

34. On the Society of the Woman in the Wilderness, see Albanese, *America*, 258–59; Brooke, *Refiner's Fire*, 40–41; Versluis, *Esoteric Origins of the American Renaissance*, 38–40; Butler, *Awash in a Sea of Faith*, 76.

35. Brooke, *Refiner's Fire*, 41.

36. Ibid., 42; Conrad Beissel, *Mysterion Anomias: The Mystery of Lawlessness; or, Lawless Anti-Christ Discover'd & Disclosed*, trans. Michael Wohlfarth (Philadelphia: Bradford, 1729), as quoted in Versluis, *Esoteric Origins of the American Renaissance*, 42–43.

37. Brooke, *Refiner's Fire*, 42 (emphasis in original).

38. Versluis, *Esoteric Origins of the American Renaissance*, 44; Brooke, *Refiner's Fire*, 44.

39. Brooke, *Refiner's Fire*, 45, 50, 362 n68, 55.

40. Albert J. Raboteau, *African American Religion* (New York: Oxford University Press, 1999), 12–14; Michael A. Gomez, *Exchanging Our Country Marks: The Transformation of African Identities in the Colonial and Antebellum South* (Chapel Hill: University of North Carolina Press, 1998), 18, 9. Gomez's figures come from the classic study by Philip D. Curtin, *The Atlantic Slave Trade: A Census* (Madison: University of Wisconsin Press, 1969).

41. As quoted in Winthrop D. Jordan, *White over Black: American Attitudes toward the Negro, 1550–1812* (1968; rpt., Baltimore: Penguin Books, 1969), 73, 3–4; Gomez, *Exchanging Our Country Marks*, 20–22.

42. William D. Piersen, *Black Yankees: The Development of an Afro-American Subculture in Eighteenth-Century New England* (Amherst: University of Massachusetts Press, 1988), 3–4 (quotations), 166–67.

43. Gomez, *Exchanging Our Country Marks*, 19–20.

44. Ibid., 27–34.

45. Ibid., 22, 26; Peter H. Wood, *Black Majority: Negroes in Colonial South Carolina from 1670 through the Stono Rebellion* (New York: Knopf, 1974), 43–46; Piersen, *Black Yankees*, 3–5.

46. Gomez, *Exchanging Our Country Marks*, 66.

47. Leonard E. Barrett, *Soul-Force: African Heritage in Afro-American Religion* (Garden City, N.Y.: Doubleday, Anchor, 1974), 17.

48. Maulana Karenga, "Black Religion: The African Model" (1993), in Larry G. Murphy, ed., *Down by the Riverside: Readings in African American Religion* (New York: New York University Press, 2000), 42–44.

49. Mechal Sobel, *Trabelin' On: The Slave Journey to an Afro-Baptist Faith* (1979; rpt., Princeton: Princeton University Press, 1988), ix, 10–21, 58; for Thomas Luckman, see *The Invisible Religion: The Problem of Religion in Modern Society* (New York: Macmillan, 1967).

50. Sobel, *Trabelin' On*, 58, 66–67, 75.

51. John Thornton, *Africa and Africans in the Making of the Atlantic World, 1400–1680* (Cambridge: Cambridge University Press, 1992), 255, passim.

52. Ibid., 236–38. Robert A. Orsi has argued for a relational, rather than meaning-driven, understanding of religion and religiosity in his collection of essays *Between Heaven and Earth* (Princeton: Princeton University Press, 2005).

53. Thornton, *Africa and Africans in the Making of the Atlantic World*, 238–39, 243.

54. Ibid., 249.

55. Ibid., 254.

56. Ibid., 246.

57. Leonard Barrett, "African Religions in the Americas" (1974), in C. Eric Lincoln, ed., *The Black Experience in Religion* (Garden City, N.Y.: Doubleday, Anchor, 1974), 313 (emphasis in original).

58. Ibid., 314. See, also, John W. Blassingame, *The Slave Community: Plantation Life in the Antebellum South*, rev. ed. (New York: Oxford University Press, 1979), 114.

59. See M. Drake Patten, "African-American Spiritual Beliefs: An Archaeological Testimony from the Slave Quarter," in Peter Benes, ed., *Wonders of the Invisible World: 1600–1900* (The Dublin Seminar for New England Folklife, Annual Proceedings 1992) (Boston: Boston University, 1995), 45.

60. Barrett, *Soul-Force*, 64, 65; Herbert G. DeLisser, *Twentieth-Century Jamaica* (1913), as quoted in Barrett, *Soul-Force*, 63–64.

61. Bryan Edwards, *An Abridgment of Mr. Edwards's Civil and Commercial History of the British West Indies in Two Volumes* (London: J. Parsons and J. Bell, 1794), vol. 2, in Milton C. Sernett, ed., *Afro-American Religious History: A Documentary Witness* (Durham: Duke University Press, 1985), 20 (emphasis in original), 21; Barrett, *Soul-Force*, 66–67.

62. Edwards, *Abridgment*, in Sernett, ed., *Afro-American Religious History*, 20; Edward Long, *The History of Jamaica* (1774), cited in Barrett, *Soul-Force*, 69.

63. Barrett, *Soul-Force*, 71–72; Edwards, *Abridgment*, in Sernett, ed., *Afro-American Religious History*, 21 (emphasis in Sarnett).

64. For Barbardos, see the account in Elaine G. Breslaw, *Tituba, Reluctant Witch of Salem: Devilish Indians and Puritan Fantasies* (New York: New York University Press, 1996), 46, 48.

65. Cotton Mather, *The Negro Christianized: An Essay to Excite and Assist That Good*

Work, the Instruction of Negro-servants in Christianity (Boston: B. Green, 1706), 15 (emphasis in original).

66. See Breslaw's book-length argument in *Tituba, Reluctant Witch of Salem.*

67. See Piersen, *Black Yankees,* 81.

68. Alice Morse Earle, *In Old Narragansett: Romances and Realities* (New York: Scribner's, 1898), 79–80.

69. Ibid., vi–vii.

70. Sylvia R. Frey and Betty Wood, *Come Shouting to Zion: African American Protestantism in the American South and British Caribbean to 1810* (Chapel Hill: University of North Carolina Press, 1998), 56.

71. Gomez, *Exchanging Our Country Marks,* 246.

72. As quoted and cited in Frey and Wood, *Come Shouting to Zion,* 47 (emphasis in Frey and Wood), 60.

73. Frey and Wood, *Come Shouting to Zion,* 59–60.

74. On South Carolina bowls, see Leland Ferguson, *Uncommon Ground* (Washington, D.C.: Smithsonian Institution, 1992); Patten, "African-American Spiritual Beliefs," 49; and William D. Piersen, *From Africa to America: African American History from the Colonial Era to the Early Republic, 1526–1790* (New York: Twayne, 1996), 97. On Virginia and Maryland, see Mark P. Leone and Gladys-Marie Fry, "Conjuring in the Big House Kitchen: An Interpretation of African American Belief Systems Based on the Uses of Archaeology and Folklore Sources," *Journal of American Folklore* 112, no. 445 (1999): 377–80, 383; on minkisi, see, also, Theophus H. Smith, *Conjuring Culture: Biblical Formations of Black America* (New York: Oxford University Press, 1994), 39–42; and on conjure as the formalization of the knowledge and use of charms, see Patten, "African-American Spiritual Beliefs," 50.

75. Sobel, *Trabelin' On,* 41, 48.

76. Piersen, *From Africa to America,* 98; Sobel, *Trabelin' On,* 48; Blassingame, *Slave Community,* 110, 113.

77. Henry Bibb, *Narrative of the Life and Adventures of Henry Bibb, An American Slave,* ed. Lucius C. Matlack (1850), introduced by Charles C. Heglar (Madison: University of Wisconsin Press, 2001), 26–28.

78. W. E. B. Du Bois, "The Religion of the American Negro," *New World* 9 (1900): 618, as quoted in Blassingame, *Slave Community,* 40–41.

79. See the discussion in Albanese, *America,* 25; Colin G. Calloway, *New Worlds for All: Indians, Europeans, and the Remaking of Early America* (Baltimore: Johns Hopkins University Press, 1997), 40; Henry W. Bowden and James P. Ronda, eds., "Introduction," in *John Eliot's Indian Dialogues: A Study in Cultural Interaction* (Westport, Conn.: Greenwood, 1980), 4. The master narrative of demographic decimation begins with anthropologist Henry F. Dobyns, in his "Estimating Aboriginal American Population: An Appraisal of Techniques with a New Hemispheric Estimate," *Current Anthropology* 7 (1966): 395–416.

80. Calloway, *New Worlds for All,* 33, 37. On hepatitis, see Kathleen J. Bragdon, *Native People of Southern New England, 1500–1650* (Norman: University of Oklahoma Press, 1996), 26.

81. Nancy Oestreich Lurie, "Indian Cultural Adjustment to European Civilization," in James Morton Smith, ed., *Seventeenth-Century America: Essays in Colonial History* (Chapel Hill: University of North Carolina Press, 1959), 34.

82. On Roanoke and Thomas Hariot, see Karen Ordahl Kupperman, *Roanoke: The Abandoned Colony* (Totowa, N.J.: Rowman and Allanheld, 1984), esp. 159.

83. Thomas Hariot, *A Briefe and True Report of the New Found Land of Virginia* (1588), in David Beers Quinn, ed., *The Roanoke Voyages, 1584–1590: Documents to Illustrate the English Voyages to North America under the Patent Granted to Walter Raleigh in 1584* (London: Hakluyt Society, 1955), 1: 372–73 (emphasis in original), 345.

84. Thomas Hariot, *A Briefe and True Report of the New Found Land of Virginia* (Frankfurt a/Main: Johann Wechtel for Theodor de Bry, 1590); reprinted as Thomas Harriot [*sic*], *A Briefe and True Report of the New Found Land of Virginia*, introduced by Paul Hulton (New York: Dover, 1972), 54, 62–65.

85. [John Smith], *A Trve Relation of Such Occurrences and Accidents of Noate as Hath Hapned in Virginia* (London: Iohn Tappe, 1608), in *Travels and Works of Captain John Smith, President of Virginia, and Admiral of New England, 1580–1631*, ed. Edward Arber, new ed. by A. G. Bradley (Edinburgh: John Grant, 1910), 1: 21 (emphasis in original).

86. Ibid., 22; [John] Smith, *A Map of Virginia. With a Description of the Covntrey, the Commodities, People, Government and Religion* (Oxford: Joseph Barnes, 1612), in *Travels and Works of Captain John Smith*, 1: 76–77; [Smith], *Trve Relation*, in *Travels and Works of Captain John Smith*, 1: 22.

87. See William S. Simmons, *Spirit of the New England Tribes: Indian History and Folklore, 1620–1984* (Hanover, N.H.: University Press of New England, 1986), 11–12; Bragdon, *Native People of Southern New England*, 26; Daniel Gookin, *Historical Collections of the Indians in New England* (1674), with notes by Jeffrey H. Fiske (N.p.: Towtaid, 1970), 7–12; Alden T. Vaughan, *New England Frontier: Puritans and Indians, 1620–1675*, 3d ed. (Norman: University of Oklahoma Press, 1994), 28, 54.

88. Winthrop to Sir Simonds D'Ewes, 21 July 1634, in Everett Emerson, ed., *Letters from New England: The Massachusetts Bay Colony, 1629–1638* (Amherst: University of Massachusetts Press, 1976), 119.

89. Higginson to his friends at Leicester, England, September 1629, in Emerson, ed., *Letters from New England*, 38 (emphasis in original); William Wood, *New England's Prospect* (1634), ed. Alden T. Vaughan (Amherst: University of Massachusetts Press, 1977), 100–101; Gookin, *Historical Collections*, 20. On rain making, see, also, Bragdon, *Native People of Southern New England*, 207.

90. See the discussion in Simmons, *Spirit of the New England Tribes*, 38–39; and, for Hobbamock, tutelary deity of the powwows, William S. Simmons, "Southern New England Shamanism: An Ethnographic Reconstruction," in William Cowan, ed., *Papers of the Seventh Algonquian Conference, 1975* (Ottawa: Carleton University, 1967), 217–56. There was some variety in English reports on ascriptions. For example, John Josselyn, who published an account of his voyages to New England, reported that the Indians "acknowledge a God who they call *Squantum*, but worship him they do not, because (they say) he will do them no harm," thus presenting Squantum as a

good, not an evil, deity—in contrast to "*Abbomacho* or *Cheepie*," who "many times smites them with incurable Diseases, scares them with his Apparitions and pannick Terrours, by reason whereof they live in a wretched consternation worshipping the Devil for fear" (John Josselyn, *An Account of Two Voyages to New-England, Made during the Years 1638, 1663* [1674], 2d ed. [1675; rpt., Boston: Veazie, 1865], 103 [emphasis in original]).

91. Simmons, *Spirit of the New England Tribes*, 118.

92. Gookin, *Historical Collections*, 20; Roger Williams, *A Key into the Language of America* (1643), ed. James Hammond Trumbull, in Roger Williams, *The Complete Writings of Roger Williams* (New York: Russell and Russell, 1963), 1: 147–51 (emphasis in original); on thirty-eight deities, see ibid., 148, n269.

93. Wood, *New England's Prospect*, 101; Williams, *Key into the Language*, 152.

94. Josselyn, *Account of Two Voyages*, 102–3, 104 (emphasis in original).

95. William Bradford, *Of Plymouth Plantation, 1620–1647*, ed. Samuel Eliot Morison (New York: Knopf, 1952), 84; A Merchant of Boston [Anon.], *The Present State of New-England with Respect to the Indian War*, in Samuel G. Drake, ed., *Old Indian Chronicle; Being a Collection of Exceeding Rare Tracts, Written and Published in the Time of King Philip's War* (Boston: Samuel A. Drake, 1867), 158 (emphasis in original). The Bradford incident is most probably the same one that is recorded, also for March 1621, in the anonymous seventeenth-century tract *Origin of Indian Wars*, included in Drake, ed., *Old Indian Chronicle*, 19. Roger Williams also noticed Indian prayer for rain, without specifically citing the role of the powwow, in Williams, *Key to the Language*, 94.

96. Gookin, *Historical Collections*, 20.

97. Bragdon, *Native People of Southern New England*, 201, 203.

98. Edward Johnson, *Wonder Working Providence, 1628–1651* (1654), as quoted in Simmons, *Spirit of the New England Tribes*, 39; Edward Winslow, *Good Newes from New-England* (1624), as quoted in Simmons, *Spirit of the New England Tribes*, 39; Simmons, *Spirit of the New England Tribes*, 39–41. On powwows, see Vaughan, *New England Frontier*, 36.

99. Henry Whitfield, *Strength Out of Weaknesse: Or A Glorious Manifestation of the Further Progresse of the Gospel among the Indians in New-England*, as quoted in Simmons, *Spirit of the New England Tribes*, 41–42.

100. Simmons, *Spirit of the New England Tribes*, 249; Josselyn, *Account of Two Voyages*, 104 (emphasis in original). See, also, the discussion of Indian lights at death in Simmons, *Spirit of the New England Tribes*, 120.

101. Calloway, *New Worlds for All*, 68. On Jesuit reports on Iroquoian peoples' dreams, see the helpful overview in Robert Moss, "Missionaries and Magicians: The Jesuit Encounter with Native American Shamans on New England's Colonial Frontier," in Benes, ed., *Wonders of the Invisible World*, 17–33.

102. Jacques Frémin, as quoted in Anthony F. C. Wallace, *Death and Rebirth of the Seneca* (1969; rpt., New York: Vintage, 1972), 59–60.

103. Paul Ragueneau, as quoted in Wallace, *Death and Rebirth of the Seneca*, 61–62.

104. Halliday Jackson, *Sketch of the Manners, Customs, Religion, and Government of the*

Seneca Indians in 1800 (1830), as quoted in Wallace, *Death and Rebirth of the Seneca*, 60–61.

105. Wallace, *Death and Rebirth of the Seneca*, 73.

106. William Penn, *A Letter from William Penn, Proprietor and Governor of Pennsilvania in America, to The Committee of the Free Society of Traders* (1683), in William Penn, *The Select Works of William Penn*, 4th ed., (1825; rpt., New York: Kraus, 1971), 3: 230.

107. John Heckewelder, *An Account of the History, Manners, and Customs of the Indian Nations, Who Once Inhabited Pennsylvania and the Neighbouring States* (1819; rpt. in revised ed. with intro. and notes by William C. Reichel, Philadelphia: Historical Society of Pennsylvania, 1876), 228, 231–32.

108. Ibid., 232–33.

109. Ibid., 236–38.

110. Ibid., 240 (emphasis in original), 249. Heckewelder's account, of essentially late-eighteenth-century provenance, sheds challenging light on the controversial thesis of Sam D. Gill in *Mother Earth: An American Story* (Chicago: University of Chicago Press, 1987) that the Native American earth mother was a nineteenth-century artifact, a product of the Romantic archetype of the earth mother emanating essentially from European and Euro-American scholarship. So, too, does the seventeenth-century Wampanoag chief Massasoit's alleged speech questioning the notion of land ownership and exclaiming that "the earth is our mother, nourishing all her children, bears, birds, fish, and all men." See Russell Bourne, *Gods of War, Gods of Peace: How the Meeting of Native and Colonial Religions Shaped Early America* (New York: Harcourt, 2002), 33.

111. Heckewelder, *Account of the History, Manners, and Customs of the Indian Nations*, 250–51 (emphasis in original), 254.

112. Ibid., 255.

113. See James Axtell, "The White Indians of Colonial America," in James Axtell, *The European and the Indian: Essays in the Ethnohistory of Colonial North America* (1981; rpt., New York: Oxford University Press, 1982), 168–206.

114. Thomas Morton, *New English Canaan; or, New Canaan: Containing an Abstract of New England Composed in Three Bookes* (Amsterdam: J. F. Stam, 1637). Peter Force, in his *Tracts and Other Papers*, 2, no. 5 (Washington, D.C.: Peter Force, 1838), lists C[harles]. Green of London as printer in 1632, but this is dubious. For a useful reading of Morton, see Richard Slotkin, *Regeneration through Violence: The Mythology of the American Frontier, 1600–1860* (Middletown, Conn.: Wesleyan University Press, 1973), although Slotkin stresses the erotic quality of Morton's reading more than I do here.

115. See, e.g., Gary B. Nash, *Red, White, and Black: The Peoples of Early America* (Englewood Cliffs, N.J.: Prentice-Hall, 1974); Karen Ordahl Kupperman, *Settling with the Indians: The Meeting of English and Indian Cultures in America, 1580–1640* (Totowa, N.J.: Rowman and Littlefield, 1980); Axtell, *The European and the Indian* (1981); Neal Salisbury, *Manitou and Providence: Indians, Europeans, and the Making of New England, 1500–1643* (New York: Oxford University Press, 1982); Sobel, *World They Made Together* (1987); James Axtell, *After Columbus: Essays in the Ethnohistory of Colonial North America* (New York: Oxford University Press, 1988); James Axtell, *Be-*

yond 1492: *Encounters in Colonial North America* (New York: Oxford University 1992); Frank Shuffelton, ed., *A Mixed Race: Ethnicity in Early America* (New ' Oxford University Press, 1993); Vaughan, *New England Frontier* (3d ed., 1994); Ca way, *New Worlds for All* (1997).

116. Kupperman, *Roanoke*, 56–57.

117. Simmons, *Spirit of the New England Tribes*, 37; Calloway, *New Worlds for All*, 32.

118. Drake, *Present State of New-England*, in *Old Indian Chronicle*, 158–59, n172; Cotton Mather, *The Wonders of the Invisible World; Being an Account of the Tryals of Several Witches, Lately Executed in New-England* (Boston: Govenour of the Province of the Massachusetts-Bay in New-England, 1693). (Mather's work was reprinted in London at the same time.)

119. Kupperman, *Settling with the Indians*, 116.

120. Ezra Stiles, 13 June 1773, in *The Literary Diary of Ezra Stiles*, ed. Franklin Bowditch Dexter, 3 vols. (New York: Scribner's, 1901), 1: 385–86.

121. Williams, *Key to the Language*, 147, 153, 152 (emphasis in original).

122. Penn, *Letter from William Penn*, 230.

123. Kupperman, *Roanoke*, 131–40; Ralph Hamor, *A True Discourse of the Present Estate of Virginia* (1615), as quoted in Kupperman, *Settling with the Indians*, 113; Kupperman, *Settling with the Indians*, 156.

124. [J. Hector] St. John de Crèvecoeur, *Sketches of Eighteenth-Century America: More "Letters from an American Farmer,"* ed. Henri L. Bourdin, Ralph H. Gabriel, and Stanley T. Williams (New Haven: Yale University Press, 1925), 193–94 (the manuscript from which the excerpts are taken ["The Wyoming Massacre"] was most probably composed in July 1778 [see Bourdin, ed., in Crèvecoeur, *Sketches*, 23]); and J. Hector St. John Crèvecoeur, *Letters from an American Farmer* (1782; rpt., Gloucester, Mass.: Peter Smith, 1968), 203–35. And see the discussion of this revealing Crèvecoeur letter in Bourne, *Gods of War, Gods of Peace*, 14–18.

125. Crèvecoeur, *Sketches*, 194–95; William M. Beauchamp, ed., *Moravian Journals Relating to Central New York, 1745–66* (1916; rpt., New York: AMS, 1976), 13, 23 (the other chief explanation for the Black Prince's name was that he was so heavily tattooed; the explanation of the name comes from William Beauchamp's commentary, not from Spangenberg); Simmons, *Spirit of the New England Tribes*, 252.

126. Calloway, *New Worlds for All*, 28–31; Crèvecoeur, *Sketches of Eighteenth-Century America*, 70–71.

127. Heckewelder, *Account of the History, Manners, and Customs of the Indian Nations*, 229; Jack Weatherford, *Indian Givers: How the Indians of the Americas Transformed the World* (New York: Crown, 1988), 192–93; Harold E. Driver, *Indians of North America*, 2d ed. (Chicago: University of Chicago Press, 1969), 557; Virgil J. Vogel, *American Indian Medicine* (New York: Ballantine, 1973), 3. *The Indian Doctor's Dispensatory* is the work of Peter Smith (Cincinnati: Browne and Looker). By 1855, Daniel Smith produced *The Reformed Botanic and Indian Physician: A Complete Guide to Health* (Utica, N.Y.: Curtiss and White), and by 1857, Richard Foreman had published *The Cherokee Physician; or, Indian Guide to Health* (New York: J. M. Edney), which promised in its subtitle to supply "general rules for preserving health

without the use of medicines" but also announced, "To which is added a short dispensatory by Jas. W. Mahoney." On white "Indian doctors" and Pennsylvania German "powwowing," see Vogel, *American Indian Medicine*, 117–38. See, too, John George Hohman, *Pow-Wows; or, Long Lost Friend: A Collection of Mysterious and Invaluable Arts and Remedies for Man as Well as Animals* (1820), reprinted in A. Monroe Aurand Jr., *The "Pow-Wow" Book: A Treatise on the Art of "Healing by Prayer" and "Laying on of Hands," Etc., Practiced by the Pennsylvania-Germans and Others* (Harrisburg, Pa.: Aurand, 1929). Hohman's book was originally published in German as Georg Johann Hohman, *Der Lange Verborgene Freund; oder, Getreuer und Christlicher Unterricht für Jedermann, Enthaltend: Wunderbare und Probmässige Mittel und Künste, Sowohl für die Menschen als das Vieh* (Reading, Pa.: Gedruckt für den Verfasser, 1820).

128. Kupperman, *Settling with the Indians*, 117; Calloway, *New Worlds for All*, 28, 30. On Ockett and her ministrations to whites, see the excerpt from the autobiography of Henry Tufts, *A Narrative of the Life, Adventures, and Sufferings of Henry Tufts*, (1807), in Colin C. Calloway, ed., *Dawnland Encounters: Indians and Europeans in Northern New England* (Hanover, N.H.: University Press of New England, 1991), 208–11.

129. Matthew Mayhew, *The Conquests and Triumphs of Grace: Being a Brief Narrative of the Success Which the Gospel Hath Had among the Indians of Martha's Vineyard (and the Places Adjacent) in New-England* (London: Printed for Nath. Hiller, 1695), 18. I am grateful to Ann Marie Plane for calling Mayhew's anecdote to my attention.

130. Drake, *Annals of Witchcraft in New England*, 136–37; the New York governor as quoted in Burr, ed., *Narratives of the Witchcraft Cases*, 42.

131. Piersen, *From Africa to America*, 98.

132. Phillis Wheatley, *Poems on Various Subjects, Religious and Moral* (London: A. Bell, 1773); see Betsy Erkkila, "Phillis Wheatley and the Black American Revolution," in Shuffelton, ed., *Mixed Race*, 228–29.

133. Phillis Wheatley, "On Imagination," from *Poems on Various Subjects*, quoted in Erkkila, "Phillis Wheatley," 236.

3. REVOLUTIONS AND ENLIGHTENMENTS

1. John Greenleaf Whittier, *The Supernaturalism of New England* (New York: Wiley and Putnam, 1847). The earlier essays were "New England Superstitions," which appeared in the *New England Magazine* in July 1833, and "New England Supernaturalism," which was published in three succeeding issues of the *United States Magazine and Democratic Review* in September, October, and November 1843.

2. John Greenleaf Whittier, *The Supernaturalism of New England*, ed. Edward Wagenknecht (Norman: University of Oklahoma Press, 1969), 29. All subsequent references to Whittier's work are to this edition. John Josselyn's work is *New Englands Rarities Discovered: In Birds, Beasts, Fishes, Serpents, and Plants of That Country* (London: Printed for G. Widdowes, 1672).

3. Whittier, *Supernaturalism*, 30.

4. Ibid., 30–31.

5. Ibid., 32–33 (emphasis in original), 101–2.

6. Ibid., 51, 59, 83, 85, 79, 85, 87, 83 (emphasis in original). The work to which Whittier alluded was a translation into English of an astrological and magical text from the Continent. Child was named and celebrated in the dedication to the English translation.

7. Ibid., 103.

8. Ibid., 114–15.

9. See David Jaffee, "The Village Enlightenment in New England, 1760–1820," *William and Mary Quarterly*, 3d series, 47 (July 1990): 327–28. Jaffee focuses on the print revolution and, as his title indicates, on New England, while I use the term more broadly both conceptually and geographically.

10. See Steven C. Bullock, *Revolutionary Brotherhood: Freemasonry and the Transformation of the American Social Order, 1730–1840* (Chapel Hill: University of North Carolina Press, 1996), 46–47; J. Hugo Tatsch, *Freemasonry in the Thirteen Colonies* (New York: Macoy Publishing and Masonic Supply, 1929), 21–22; Dorothy Ann Lipson, *Freemasonry in Federalist Connecticut, 1789–1835* (Princeton: Princeton University Press, 1977), 31 n48, 3; Lynn Dumenil, *Freemasonry and American Culture, 1880–1930* (Princeton: Princeton University Press, 1984), 4; Sidney Morse, *Freemasonry in the American Revolution* (Washington, D.C.: Masonic Service Association, 1924), x.

11. [James Anderson], *The Constitutions of the Free-Masons: Containing the History, Charges, Regulations, &c. of That Most Ancient and Right Worshipful Fraternity* (1723; rpt., Philadelphia: Benjamin Franklin, 1734); Lipson, *Freemasonry in Federalist Connecticut*, 29, 14–29.

12. Margaret C. Jacob, *The Radical Enlightenment: Pantheists, Freemasons, and Republicans* (London: George Allen and Unwin, 1981), 115.

13. [Anderson], *Constitutions*, 48 (emphasis in original). This is, of course, the Franklin reprint.

14. On clubmen vs. social architects, see Lipson, *Freemasonry in Federalist Connecticut*, 13–30. On Masonic signers of the Declaration of Independence, see Jay Macpherson, "The Masons and the Great Seal," in R. William Weisberger, Wallace McLeod, and S. Brent Morris, eds., *Freemasonry on Both Sides of the Atlantic: Essays Concerning the Craft in the British Isles, Europe, the United States, and Mexico* (Boulder, Colo.: East European Monographs, 2002), 557; and Stephen Knight, *The Brotherhood: The Secret World of the Freemasons* (London: Granada, 1984), 34.

15. Bernard Faÿ, *Revolution and Freemasonry, 1680–1800* (Boston: Little, Brown, 1935), 229–30; Morse, *Freemasonry in the American Revolution*, xi.

16. On Prince Hall Masonry, see Charles H. Wesley, *Prince Hall: Life and Legacy* (Washington, D.C.: United Supreme Council, Southern Jurisdiction, Prince Hall Affiliation, and Philadelphia: Afro-American Historical and Cultural Museum, 1977). Wesley has debunked earlier Prince Hall histories, beginning with William Grimshaw in 1903 and George W. Crawford in 1914, for their lack of historical documentation regarding Prince Hall himself. See William H. Grimshaw, *Official History of Freemasonry among the Colored People in North America* (New York: Negro Universities Press, 1903); and George W. Crawford, *Prince Hall and His Followers: Being a Mono-*

graph on the Legitimacy of Negro Masonry (New York: Crisis, 1914). On the selec-
tivity of Prince Hall Masonry, see William A. Muraskin, *Middle-Class Blacks in a
White Society: Prince Hall Freemasonry in America* (Berkeley: University of California Press, 1975); and Loretta J. Williams, *Black Freemasonry and Middle-Class Realities* (Columbia: University of Missouri Press, 1980). On London clubmen and Freemasonry, see Lipson, *Freemasonry in Federalist Connecticut*, 13–30.

17. A Member of Royal Arch, *Hiram: Or, The Grand Master-Key to the Door of Both
Antient and Modern Free-Masonry: Being an Accurate Description of Every Degree
of the Brotherhood, as Authorized and Delivered in All Good Lodges*, 2d ed. (London: W. Griffin, 1766); [A Gentleman Belonging to the Jerusalem Lodge], *Jachin and
Boaz: Or, An Authentic Key to the Door of Free-Masonry, Both Ancient and Modern: Calculated Not Only for the Instruction of Every New-Made Mason; But Also
for the Information of All Who Intend to Become Brethren* (Boston: J. Bumstead, for
E. Larkin, 1794); Lipson, *Freemasonry in Federalist Connecticut*, 361–62 (Lipson has
listed "about a dozen" American editions before 1825, with the earliest in New York
in 1796, but I have followed the on-line catalog of the University of California for the
American story). Interestingly, the "Member of Royal Arch" did not disclose the contents of the Royal Arch degree—see below in the text—in *Hiram*.

18. A Gentleman Belonging to the Jerusalem Lodge, *Jachin and Boaz: Or, An Authentic
Key to the Door of Free-Masonry, Both Ancient and Modern* (London: E. Newbery
and W. Moore, 1795), 30 (I cite here and below from the London edition of 1795,
which has been the one available to me). On both the practical and mystical signifi-
cances of the secret word, see Bullock, *Revolutionary Brotherhood*, 11.

19. Gentleman Belonging to the Jerusalem Lodge, *Jachin and Boaz*, 31–32.

20. Bullock, *Revolutionary Brotherhood*, 16, 18.

21. Gentleman Belonging to the Jerusalem Lodge, *Jachin and Boaz*, 14, 24.

22. Ibid., 24. The text omits the reference to 1 Kings 2:21 and lists the sole scriptural verse
as 2 Chronicles 3:15, but this verse is a more general allusion to the two pillars without naming them.

23. Gentleman Belonging to the Jerusalem Lodge, *Jachin and Boaz*, 12.

24. Thomas Paine, "Origin of Freemasonry," in Thomas Paine, *The Complete Writings of
Thomas Paine*, ed. Philip S. Foner (New York: Citadel, 1945), 2: 834–36. Paine's essay
was published at first only partially, in 1810, and then more completely in 1818 (see
Foner, ed., *Complete Writings of Thomas Paine*, 830). For Smith, see George Smith,
*The Use and Abuse of Free-Masonry; A Work of the Greatest Utility to the Brethren of
the Society, to Mankind in General, and to the Ladies in Particular* (1783; rpt., New
York: Masonic Publishing and Manufacturing, 1866).

25. [Anderson], *Constitutions*, 69.

26. Gentleman Belonging to the Jerusalem Lodge, *Jachin and Boaz*, 1–2.

27. Ibid., 32.

28. Bullock, *Revolutionary Brotherhood*, esp. 85–108; Morse, *Freemasonry in the American Revolution*, 14–15.

29. Bullock, *Revolutionary Brotherhood*, 86.

30. See ibid., 90, 92, 94, 96, 98. Bullock supplies statistics for Boston from 1752 to 1775 and for Philadelphia from 1756 to 1760.

31. Ibid., 107.

32. See Richard A. Rutyna, "Tidewater Virginia Freemasons and Occupational Diversity, 1785–1815," in Weisberger, McLeod, and Morris, eds., *Freemasonry on Both Sides of the Atlantic*, 525–56.

33. See Morse, *Freemasonry in the American Revolution*, 16–17; Bullock, *Revolutionary Brotherhood*, 109, 132, 110–11.

34. For a brief and useful summary of the Morgan affair and its exploitation by politicians to fuel an Antimasonic movement, see Alice Felt Tyler, *Freedom's Ferment: Phases of American Social History from the Colonial Period to the Outbreak of the Civil War* (1944; rpt., New York: Harper and Row, 1962), 351–58. The full title of William Morgan's book was *Illustrations of Masonry by One of the Fraternity, Who Has Devoted Thirty Years to the Subject*. The book provoked an attempt to kidnap its publisher David C. Miller and to burn or destroy his printing office. Its subsequent publication history is unclear, but the on-line catalog of the University of California lists an edition published by M. Gardiner in Cincinnati, presumably in 1850.

35. See E. Cecil McGavin, *Mormonism and Masonry* (Salt Lake City: Stevens and Wallis, 1947), 163–67.

36. Tatsch, *Freemasonry in the Thirteen Colonies*, 140–41.

37. [Thomas Smith Webb], *The Freemason's Monitor; or, Illustrations of Masonry: In Two Parts. By a Royal Arch Mason* (Albany: Spencer and Webb, 1797). Reprints appeared in New York (1802) and Boston (1808), but also in Providence (1805), in Salem, Massachusetts (1808, 1812, 1816, 1818), in Andover, Massachusetts (1816), and in Montpelier, Vermont (1816).

38. Bullock, *Revolutionary Brotherhood*, 240.

39. [Webb], *Freemason's Monitor*, 2–3. William Preston's *Illustrations of Masonry* first appeared in London in 1788 and in a second edition in 1796. Written from the perspective of the "ancients," the text went through at least twelve English and several American editions, according to Dorothy Ann Lipson, before the end of the eighteenth century (Lipson, *Freemasonry in Federalist Connecticut*, 33, n51).

40. [Webb], *Freemason's Monitor*, 51–52, 153, 219.

41. Ibid., 242, 244–47.

42. Ibid., 250–56.

43. Ibid., 259–61.

44. John L. Brooke, *The Refiner's Fire: The Making of Mormon Cosmology, 1644–1844* (New York: Cambridge University Press, 1994), 140–45, 158; Jerald Tanner and Sandra Tanner, *Mormonism, Magic, and Masonry* (Salt Lake City: Utah Lighthouse Ministry, 1983), 20–21.

45. See, e.g., Brooke, *Refiner's Fire*, 168–70; and S. H. Goodwin, *Mormonism and Masonry* (Washington, D.C.: Masonic Service Association of the United States, 1924), v–vi; S. H. Goodwin, *Additional Studies in Mormonism and Masonry* (Salt Lake City: N.p., 1932), 8; E. Cecil McGavin, *Mormonism and Masonry*, enl. ed. (Salt Lake City:

Stevens and Wallis, 1947), 3–4; Fawn M. Brodie, *No Man Knows My History: The Life of Joseph Smith* (1945), 2d ed. (1971; rpt., New York: Vintage, 1995), 65–66. For a different reading, see Richard L. Bushman, *Joseph Smith and the Beginnings of Mormonism* (Urbana: University of Illinois Press, 1984), 128–31; and D. Michael Quinn, *Early Mormonism and the Magic World View* (Salt Lake City: Signature, 1987), 160–65. (Quinn's book was published in a second edition by Signature in 1998, but I use the first, somewhat shorter and more available, edition here and elsewhere. Revisions in the second edition are largely directed toward Mormon critics.)

46. See Jerald Tanner and Sandra Tanner, *The Changing World of Mormonism: A Condensation of "Mormonism: Shadow or Reality?"* (Chicago: Moody Press, 1980), 535–36; and Goodwin, *Mormonism and Masonry*, 34–36.

47. See John Stanford, *Urim and Thummim: A Discourse Delivered before Hiram Lodge, No. 72, on St. John's Day, Dec. 27, 1800* (Mount Pleasant, N.Y.: Russell Canfield, n.d.). See, also, Exod. 28:30 and Lev. 8:8. John Brooke has likewise described a series of Mormon artifacts with Freemasonic associations (see Brooke, *Refiner's Fire*, 157–58).

48. Brooke, *Refiner's Fire*, 166, 194, 198, 252 (the phrase "true Masonry" was Heber Kimball's in 1858); Michael W. Homer, "'Similarity of Priesthood in Masonry': The Relationship between Freemasonry and Mormonism," *Dialogue: A Journal of Mormon Thought* 27, no. 3 (Fall 1994): 3 (I am indebted to D. Michael Quinn for calling this article to my attention); Brooke, *Refiner's Fire*, 166–67. Jan Shipps has called Brooke's work "flawed" and has faulted its subtitle *The Making of Mormon Cosmology, 1644–1844* as an overstatement. "In failing to point to all that the Saints took from the Bible," she argues, Brooke's work neglected "definitive components of that cosmology and an ingredient in the LDS [Latter-day Saint] mix that is absolutely critical to explaining Mormonism's appeal." See Jan Shipps, *Sojourner in the Promised Land: Forty Years among the Mormons* (Urbana: University of Illinois Press, 2000), 11, 213.

49. Brooke, *Refiner's Fire*, 220, 253, 249; Goodwin, *Mormonism and Masonry*, 50, 54–59; Tanner and Tanner, *Changing World of Mormonism*, 536–47; Homer, "'Similarity of Priesthood in Masonry,'" 1–113.

50. Brooke, *Refiner's Fire*, 204.

51. On the Kabbalah of Isaac Luria (1534–1572), see Gershom G. Scholem, *Major Trends in Jewish Mysticism* (1941), 3d ed. (1954; rpt., New York: Schocken, 1961), 244–86.

52. Brooke, *Refiner's Fire*, 33, 45.

53. Ibid., xiii, 29.

54. See, for example, Sig Synnestvedt, "Life of Emanuel Swedenborg," in Sig Synnestvedt, ed., *The Essential Swedenborg: Basic Teachings of Emanuel Swedenborg, Scientist, Philosopher, and Theologian* (New York: Twayne, 1970), 21, 24. For another brief bibliographical view of Swedenborg, see Jane K. Williams-Hogan, "Swedenborg: A Biography," in Erland J. Brock et al., eds., *Swedenborg and His Influence* (Bryn Athyn, Pa.: Academy of the New Church, 1988), 3–27. For a full-length biography, see Inge Jonsson, *Emanuel Swedenborg*, trans. Catherine Djurklou (New York: Twayne, 1971).

55. Emanuel Swedenborg, *Heaven and Its Wonders and Hell: From Things Heard and Seen* (1758), trans. J. C. Ager (1852; rpt., New York: Swedenborg Foundation, 1964),

111; Emanuel Swedenborg, *Arcana Coelestia; or, Heavenly Mysteries* (1747–1758): 2888, in Synnestvedt, ed., *Essential Swedenborg*, 126.

56. Swedenborg, *Heaven and Its Wonders and Hell*, 39, 31, 14, 13, 17, 139. For another and fuller view of Swedenborgian heaven and its relation to modernity, see Colleen McDannell and Bernhard Lang, *Heaven: A History* (New Haven: Yale University Press, 1988), 181–227.

57. Emanuel Swedenborg, *The Delights of Wisdom Pertaining to Conjugial Love after Which Follow the Pleasures of Insanity Pertaining to Scortatory Love* (1768), trans. Samuel M. Warren and rev. trans. Louis H. Tafel (1856; rpt., New York: Swedenborg Foundation, 1980), 56.

58. Swedenborg, *Heaven and Its Wonders and Hell*, 36, 151, 291, 353.

59. Quinn, *Early Mormonism and the Magic World View*, 12–13.

60. Brooke, *Refiner's Fire*, 206.

61. See Sterling M. McMurrin, *The Theological Foundations of the Mormon Religion* (1965; rpt., Salt Lake City: University of Utah Press, 1974), 17–18.

62. Joseph Smith, *The Doctrine and Covenants of the Church of Jesus Christ of Latter-Day Saints*, ed. Orson Pratt (1880; rpt., Westport, Conn.: Greenwood, 1971), 131:7; Joseph Smith, Funeral Oration for King Follett, as recorded by Wilford Woodruff, as quoted in Brooke, *Refiner's Fire* (emphasis in Brooke), 235; Smith, *Doctrine and Covenants*, 132:20.

63. Smith, *Doctrine and Covenants*, 76:50–98. See, also, Brooke, *Refiner's Fire*, 199–200; and Quinn, *Early Mormonism and the Magic World View*, 175.

64. See Scholem, *Major Trends in Jewish Mysticism*, 156–243; Jacob Boehme, *The Three Principles of the Divine Essence*, in Jacob Boehme, *The Works of Jacob Boehme*, trans. G. Ward and T. Langcake, 4 vols. (London: M. Richardson, 1764–81), 1: 68, 171. See, also, Catherine L. Albanese, "Mormonism and the Male-Female God: An Exploration in Active Mysticism," *Sunstone* 6, no. 2 (March–April 1981): 52–58.

65. I have been able to locate three German-language productions at Ephrata: one in 1811–1812, another in 1822, and a third in 1824. See Ralph R. Shaw and Richard H. Shoemaker, *American Bibliography: A Preliminary Checklist for 1811* (New York: Scarecrow, 1962), 35–36; Richard A. Shoemaker, *A Checklist for American Imprints for 1822* (Metuchen, N.J.: Scarecrow, 1967), 31; and Richard A. Shoemaker, *A Checklist for American Imprints for 1824* (Metuchen, N.J.: Scarecrow, 1969), 37–38.

66. Brooke, *Refiner's Fire*, 258, 281, 262–63; Quinn, *Early Mormonism and the Magic World View*, 60–62.

67. See Mary Ann Meyers, *A New World Jerusalem: The Swedenborgian Experience in Community Construction* (Westport, Conn.: Greenwood, 1983), 23.

68. Brodie, *No Man Knows My History*, 118.

69. Quinn, *Early Mormonism and the Magic World View*, 22, 25, 111, 78–79. For another discussion of the magical ambience of the Smith family—and a psychologized (family systems) reading of its conflicts and their role in helping to shape Joseph Smith Jr. as a prophet, see Dan Vogel, *Joseph Smith: The Making of a Prophet* (Salt Lake City: Signature, 2004), esp. 35–52.

70. Quinn, *Early Mormonism and the Magic World View*, 44–45; Dan Vogel, *Indian Origins and the Book of Mormon: Religious Solutions from Columbus to Joseph Smith* ([Salt Lake City:] Signature, 1986), 12–13.

71. See the brief account in Stephen A. Marini, *Radical Sects in Revolutionary New England* (Cambridge: Harvard University Press, 1982), 54–55.

72. Smith, *Doctrine and Covenants*, 8:8.

73. Quinn, *Early Mormonism and the Magic World View*, 27; Jan Shipps, "The Prophet Puzzle: Suggestions Leading toward a More Comprehensive Interpretation of Joseph Smith," *Journal of Mormon History* 1 (1974): 3–20.

74. Quinn, *Early Mormonism and the Magic World View*, 114, 118–23, 122, 119.

75. Ibid., 51.

76. David Whitmer, *An Address to All Believers in Christ* (1887), as quoted in Vogel, *Indian Origins*, 16.

77. Quinn, *Early Mormonism and the Magic World View*, 191. Generally, and especially in comparison with the work of John L. Brooke (*Refiner's Fire*), Quinn has de-emphasized the explicitly Hermetic provenance of Smith's magical world.

78. Quinn, *Early Mormonism and the Magic World View*, 197, 202, 64–72; Tanner and Tanner, *Mormonism, Magic, and Masonry*, 2–5; Tanner and Tanner, *Changing World of Mormonism*, 88–91.

79. Lucy Mack Smith, *History of Joseph Smith by His Mother, Lucy Mack Smith* (1901), ed. Preston Nibley (Salt Lake City. Bookcraft, 1958), 83.

80. Vogel, *Indian Origins*, 18.

81. Ibid., 24–27. On New England, see James W. Mavor Jr. and Byron E. Dix, *Manitou: The Sacred Landscape of New England's Native Civilization* (Rochester, Vt.: Inner Traditions, 1989).

82. Vogel, *Indian Origins*, 36–37, 38–42, 62–63. For Fawn Brodie's demolition of the Spalding thesis, see Brodie, *No Man Knows My History*, 442–56.

83. See Vogel, *Indian Origins*, 66, 33, 29.

84. Harold Bloom, *The American Religion: The Emergence of the Post-Christian Nation* (New York: Simon and Schuster, 1992), 35, 103. For Jan Shipps on the question of whether Mormonism is Christian—a "complicated question," as she declares—see Shipps, *Sojourner in the Promised Land*, 335–57.

85. See Brodie, *No Man Knows My History*, 362–66.

86. For the document constituting the Tunbridge Universalist Society, see Dan Vogel, ed., *Early Mormon Documents* (Salt Lake City: Signature, 1996), 1: 633–34 (quotations from the New Hampshire Universalist convention are cited from Vogel); Brodie, *No Man Knows My History*, 118.

87. Brooke, *Refiner's Fire*, 144, 45, 132.

88. Richard Eddy, "History of Universalism," in Joseph Henry Allen and Richard Eddy, *A History of the Unitarians and the Universalists in the United States* (1894; rpt., New York: Scribner's, 1903), 255, 256–76; Peter W. Williams, "Unitarianism and Universalism," in Charles H. Lippy and Peter W. Williams, eds., *Encyclopedia of the American Religious Experience: Studies of Traditions and Movements*, 3 vols. (New York: Scribner's, 1988), 1: 580. See, also, Richard Eddy, *Universalism in America: A History*

(Boston: Universalist Publishing House, 1884–86). The Sibylline Oracles, purporting to be the utterances of the Greek Sibyls, have been assigned by modern critics mostly to Jewish and Christian authors in a period ranging from the second century B.C.E. to the second century C.E.

89. Eddy, "History of Universalism," in Allen and Eddy, *History of the Unitarians and the Universalists*, 372–75.

90. George Huntston Williams, "American Universalism: A Bicentennial Historical Essay," *Journal of the Universalist Historical Society* 9 (1971): 10–11 (emphasis in original). Williams's work was also published as an independent monograph (Boston: Beacon, 1976). See, also, Marini, *Radical Sects*, 68–69; and Ernest Cassara, ed., *Universalism in America: A Documentary History* (Boston: Beacon, 1971), 10–14.

91. Williams, *American Universalism*, 10 (emphasis in original); on these details of Winchester's life, see Elmo Arnold Robinson, *American Universalism: Its Origins, Organization, and Heritage* (New York: Exposition, 1970), 15.

92. See the discussion by Eddy in Allen and Eddy, *History of the Unitarians and the Universalists*, 314–15.

93. See ibid., 375.

94. For brief summaries of Winchester's life, see Marini, *Radical Sects*, 69–71; and Cassara, ed., *Universalism in America*, 14–17.

95. Marini, *Radical Sects*, 71.

96. See the account by Eddy in Allen and Eddy, *History of the Unitarians and the Universalists*, 375; see, also, Cassara, ed., *Universalism in America*, 7.

97. Marini, *Radical Sects*, 71–72.

98. Ibid., 73–75.

99. David Robinson, *The Unitarians and the Universalists* (Westport, Conn.: Greenwood, 1985), 313–14; Marini, *Radical Sects*, 75.

100. Robinson, *Unitarians and Universalists*, 215.

101. See the discussion in Marini, *Radical Sects*, 144–48; Eddy, "History of Universalism," in Allen and Eddy, *History of the Unitarians and the Universalists*, 435–36.

102. Ibid., 147.

103. See the discussion in Cassara, ed., *Universalism in America*, 18–22, esp. 21; see, also, Ernest Cassara, *Hosea Ballou: The Challenge to Orthodoxy* (Lanham, Md.: University Press of America, 1982).

104. Whitney R. Cross, *The Burned-Over District: The Social and Intellectual History of Enthusiastic Religion in Western New York, 1800–1850* (1950; rpt., New York: Harper and Row, 1965), 18; Cassara, ed., *Universalism in America*, 29.

105. John Coleman Adams, *Universalism and the Universalist Church* (Boston: Universalists Publishing, Murray Press, 1915), 19.

106. Cross, *Burned-Over District*, 323–25, 344; on Spear, see Williams, *American Universalism*, 59–60.

107. Cross, *Burned-Over District*, 326.

108. John Humphrey Noyes, *History of American Socialisms* (1870; rpt., New York: Dover, 1966), 119.

109. Adin Ballou, as quoted in Noyes, *History of American Socialisms*, 123–24, 125, 126.

110. Adin Ballou, *An Exposition of Views Respecting the Principal Facts, Causes, and Peculiarities Involved in Spirit Manifestations: Together with Interesting Phenomenal Statements and Communications* (Boston: Bela Marsh, 1852).

111. John Murray, *The Life of John Murray, Preacher of Universal Salvation*, ed. Thomas Whittemore (Boston: Trumpet Office, 1833), 111–14.

112. Ibid., 114–15.

113. Ibid., 116–19 (emphasis in original).

114. Ibid., 119.

115. Ibid., 119–22.

116. Ibid., 162, 234 (upper case and emphasis in original).

117. See Williams, *American Universalism*, 3; and Cassara, ed., *Universalism in America*, 6.

118. For the classic study of the rise of American Unitarianism, see Conrad Wright, *The Beginnings of Unitarianism in America* (1955; rpt., Hamden, Conn.: Shoe String, Archon, 1976).

119. For a useful and brief overview of the formation of American Unitarianism, see Williams, "Unitarianism and Universalism," 579–85.

120. Daniel Walker Howe, *The Unitarian Conscience: Harvard Moral Philosophy, 1805–1861* (Cambridge: Harvard University Press, 1970).

121. See the discussion in Conrad Wright, *The Liberal Christians: Essays on American Unitarian History* (Boston: Beacon, 1970), 1–21.

122. David Robinson, *Apostle of Culture: Emerson as Preacher and Lecturer* (Philadelphia: University of Pennsylvania Press, 1982), 9–10.

123. Ibid., 15.

124. Ibid., 29.

125. James Martineau, *The Rationale of Religious Enquiry; or, The Question Stated of Reason, the Bible, and the Church* (London: Whittaker and Co., Simpkin and Marshall, and R. Hunter, 1836).

126. George Ripley, "Martineau's *Rationale of Religious Enquiry*," *Christian Examiner* 21 (November 1836): 225–54.

127. Ralph Waldo Emerson, "An Address Delivered Before the Senior Class in Divinity College, Cambridge, Sunday Evening, 15 July, 1838," in *The Collected Works of Ralph Waldo Emerson*, ed. Alfred R. Ferguson et al., vol. 1 (Cambridge, Mass.: Harvard University Press, 1971), 81. For Norton's views, see Andrews Norton, *A Discourse on the Latest Form of Infidelity: Delivered at the Request of the "Association of the Alumni of the Cambridge Theological School," on the 19th of July, 1839* (Cambridge, Mass.: J. Owen, 1839); and Andrews Norton, *Remarks on a Pamphlet Entitled "'The Latest Form of Infidelity' Examined"* (Cambridge, Mass.: John Owen, 1839).

128. William H. Furness, *Remarks on the Four Gospels* (Philadelphia: Carey, Lea, and Blanchard, 1836); Orestes Augustus Brownson, *New Views of Christianity, Society, and the Church* (Boston: James Munroe, 1836); Convers Francis, *Christianity as a Purely Internal Principle*, in *Tracts of the American Unitarian Association*, 1st ser., 9: 105 (Boston: Leonard C. Bowles, 1836), 8.

129. Amos Bronson Alcott, *Conversations with Children on the Gospels*, 2 vols. (Boston:

James Munroe, 1836–37). For a twentieth-century reprint, see Amos Bronson Alcott, *Conversations on the Gospels*, 2 vols. (1836–37; rpt., New York: Arno, 1972).

130. Arthur Versluis, *The Esoteric Origins of the American Renaissance* (New York: Oxford University Press, 2001), 116–21.

131. For a short but useful discussion, see William R. Hutchison, *The Transcendentalist Ministers: Church Reform in the New England Renaissance* (1959; rpt., Boston: Beacon, 1965), 30–33.

132. Ralph Waldo Emerson, *Nature* (1836), in *Collected Works* 1: 8 (upper case in original), 45. On the composition of the text as two essays joined together by a narrative bridge, see the notes by Robert Spiller, ibid., 3–4.

133. Emerson, *Nature*, 7.

134. Ibid.

135. Emerson himself was preoccupied with the theme of the "open secret," a theme mediated to him especially through the German poet Novalis and his English interpreter Thomas Carlyle. For two recent studies of the theme in relation to Emerson, see Versluis, *Esoteric Origins of the American Renaissance*, 129–38 (a reading in terms of Novalis and Carlyle); and David L. Smith, "'The Sphinx Must Solve Her Own Riddle': Emerson, Secrecy, and the Self-Reflexive Method," *Journal of the American Academy of Religion* 71, no. 4 (December 2003): 835–61 (which works from a more general philosophical perspective).

136. Ralph Waldo Emerson to William Emerson, Concord, 8 August 1836, in *The Letters of Ralph Waldo Emerson*, ed. Ralph L. Rusk (New York: Columbia University Press, 1939), 2: 32.

137. Emerson, *Nature*, 10.

138. Ibid., 11, 13, 15–17.

139. Emerson was much influenced by the writings of Sampson Reed (1800–1880), especially his *Observations on the Growth of the Mind* (1826; rpt., New York: Arno, 1972) and his contributions to the *New Jerusalem Magazine*.

140. Emerson, *Nature*, 17, 20, 21, 23.

141. Ibid., 23–29, 25, 27.

142. Ibid., 35–36.

143. Ibid., 36.

144. Ibid., 36–39.

145. Ibid., 39–41. The "certain poet" was probably Amos Bronson Alcott, whose doctrine of Genesis, or Lapse (man as the "god in ruins") is reflected in the lines that follow. For a related discussion, see Odell Shepard, *Pedlar's Progress: The Life of Bronson Alcott* (1937; rpt., New York: Greenwood, 1968), 453–63.

146. Ibid., 42–43. Hohenlohe was the Roman Catholic bishop Alexander Leopold of Hohenlohe-Waldenberg-Schillingfürst (1794–1849), whose miraculous cures were linked to his prayer.

147. Emerson, *Nature*, 43–45.

148. Ibid., 22, 35, 11, 40–41, 15, 22, 27, 22–23, 23, 35. Emerson's distinctions between the Reason and the Understanding, like his distinction between the Imagination and the

Fancy, came to him from Samuel Taylor Coleridge through Calvinist cleric and University of Vermont professor James Marsh. Marsh's American edition of Coleridge's *Aids to Reflection* (1829) began with his own preliminary essay that provided a reading of Coleridge.

149. See Richard G. Geldard, *The Esoteric Emerson: The Spiritual Teachings of Ralph Waldo Emerson* (New York: Lindisfarne, 1993). Emerson's *Essays* appeared in 1841 and his *Essays, Second Series* in 1844, probably the two best-known of his collections.

150. Charles Lane and A. Bronson Alcott, "The Consociate Family Life" (1843), excerpted in Louisa May Alcott, *Transcendental Wild Oats and Excerpts from the Fruitlands Diary*, ed. William Henry Harrison (Harvard, Mass.: Harvard Common Press, 1981), 91, 89. *Transcendental Wild Oats* originally appeared in 1873. Charles Lane was the putative author of the Lane-Alcott excerpt.

151. On the library, see Versluis, *Esoteric Origins of the American Renaissance*, 120–21, 128. The classic study of Fruitlands is Clara Endicott Sears, *Bronson Alcott's Fruitlands* (1915; rpt., Philadelphia: Porcupine, 1975). See, also, Shepard, *Pedlar's Progress*, 343–80; Frederick C. Dahlstrand, *Amos Bronson Alcott: An Intellectual Biography* (Rutherford, N.J.: Fairleigh Dickinson University Press, 1982), 173–203; Anne C. Rose, *Transcendentalism as a Social Movement, 1830–1850* (New Haven: Yale University Press, 1981), 117–30.

152. Bronson Alcott's daughter Louisa May Alcott, with her *Transcendental Wild Oats* (1873), inscribed this reading of Fruitlands unforgettably in American minds. The younger Alcott had little sympathy for her father's grand schemes and wide-eyed idealism.

153. Rose, *Transcendentalism as a Social Movement*, 130.

154. Ralph Waldo Emerson, 17 October 1840, in *The Journals and Miscellaneous Notebooks of Ralph Waldo Emerson*, vol. 7, ed. A. W. Plumstead and Harrison Hayford (Cambridge, Mass.: Harvard University Press, 1969), 408; Ralph Waldo Emerson, *Historic Notes of Life and Letters in New England*, in Ralph Waldo Emerson, *The Complete Works of Ralph Waldo Emerson*, ed. Edward Waldo Emerson, centenary ed. (Boston: Houghton, Mifflin, 1903–1904), 10: 364.

155. Brook-Farm Association for Industry and Education, "Constitution," in Octavius B. Frothingham, *Transcendentalism in New England: A History* (1876; rpt., Gloucester, Mass.: Peter Smith, 1965), 161. The classic study of Brook Farm is Lindsay Swift, *Brook Farm: Its Members, Scholars, and Visitors* (1900; rpt., Secaucus, N.J.: Citadel, 1961).

156. Charles Crowe, *George Ripley: Transcendentalist and Utopian Socialist* (Athens: University of Georgia Press, 1967), 161.

157. See Jonathan Beecher and Richard Bienvenu, "Introduction," in Jonathan Beecher and Richard Bienvenu, trans. and eds., *The Utopian Vision of Charles Fourier: Selected Texts on Work, Love, and Passionate Attraction* (Boston: Beacon, 1971), 1–64.

158. Albert Brisbane, *Social Destiny of Man; or, Association and Reorganization of Industry* (Philadelphia: C. F. Stollmeyer, 1840).

159. Noyes, *History of American Socialisms*, 206; see, also, Rose, *Transcendentalism as a Social Movement*, 151, for details on the phalanxes.

160. Noyes, *History of American Socialisms*, 194; Charles Fourier, *Le Nouveau monde in-*

dustriel et sociétaire (3d ed., 1848), and Charles Fourier, *Théorie de l'unité universelles* (2d ed., 1841–43), from Charles Fourier, *Oeuvre complètes de Charles Fourier*, 12 vols. (Paris: Editions Anthropos, 1966–68), in Beecher and Bienvenu, trans. and eds., *Utopian Vision of Charles Fourier*, 211.

161. Parke Godwin, A *Popular View of the Doctrines of Charles Fourier* (New York: J. S. Redfield, 1844). The Godwin quotation is from Noyes, *History of American Socialisms*, 541. William Henry Channing, "Fourier and Swedenborg," *The Present* (April 1844), as quoted in Noyes, *History of American Socialisms*, 545; Noyes, *History of American Socialisms*, 546, 550.

162. Swift, *Brook Farm*, 66.

163. Ralph Waldo Emerson, "The Over-Soul," in Ralph Waldo Emerson, *Essays: First Series*, in *The Collected Works of Ralph Waldo Emerson*, ed. Alfred R. Ferguson et al., vol. 2 (Cambridge, Mass.: Harvard University Press, 1979), 159, 166, 169, 173, 166.

164. Swift, *Brook Farm*, 47.

4. COMMUNION OF SPIRITS

1. Adin Ballou, *Autobiography of Adin Ballou, 1803–1890*, completed and edited by William S. Heywood (1896; rpt., Philadelphia: Porcupine, 1975), 235–36, 376–79.

2. Adin Ballou, *An Exposition of Views Respecting the Principal Facts, Causes, and Peculiarities Involved in Spirit Manifestations: Together with Interesting Phenomenal Statements and Communications* (Boston: Bela Marsh, 1852).

3. Adin Ballou, *An Exposition of Views Respecting the Modern Spirit Manifestations: Together with Interesting Phenomenal Statements and Communications*, 2d ed. (1852; rpt. of the 2d American ed., Liverpool: Edward Howell, 1853), 99–110 (emphasis in original).

4. John L. Brooke, *The Refiner's Fire: The Making of Mormon Cosmology, 1644–1844* (New York: Cambridge University Press, 1994), 288, 275; Orson Pratt, *The Holy Spirit* (1856), as quoted in Craig James Hazen, *The Village Enlightenment in America: Popular Religion and Science in the Nineteenth Century* (Urbana: University of Illinois Press, 2000), 54 (upper case in Hazen); Orson Pratt, *Spiritual Gifts* (1856), as quoted and cited in Hazen, *Village Enlightenment*, 56–57.

5. John B. Wilson, "Emerson and the 'Rochester Rappings,'" *New England Quarterly* 41, no. 2 (June 1968): 248–58; Ralph Waldo Emerson, *The Journals of Ralph Waldo Emerson*, ed. Edward Waldo Emerson and Waldo Emerson Forbes, 10 vols. (Boston: Houghton Mifflin, 1909–1914), 8: 298; Ralph Waldo Emerson, "Demonology," in *The Early Lectures of Ralph Waldo Emerson*, vol. 3, 1838–1842, ed. Robert E. Spiller and Wallace E. Williams (Cambridge, Mass.: Harvard University Press, 1972), 170.

6. Henry David Thoreau, *The Correspondence of Henry David Thoreau*, ed. Walter Harding and Carl Bode (New York: New York University Press, 1958), 284, as quoted in Wilson, "Emerson and the 'Rochester Rappings,'" 249 (the comments came in a letter from Thoreau to his sister Sophia); on Brownson's *Spirit-Rapper*, see Russell M. Goldfarb and Clare M. Goldfarb, *Spiritualism and Nineteenth-Century Letters* (Rutherford, N.J.: Fairleigh Dickinson University Press, 1978), 64–65; Robert S. Cox, *Body*

and Soul: A Sympathetic History of American Spiritualism (Charlottesville: University of Virginia Press, 2003), 80, 83, 84–85; James Freeman Clarke, _Ten Great Religions: An Essay in Comparative Theology_ (1871; rpt. [34th ed.], Boston: Houghton, Mifflin, 1895), 136–37.

7. Amos Bronson Alcott to Anna Alcott, 22 April 1849, _The Letters of A. Bronson Alcott_, ed. Richard L. Herrnstadt (Ames: Iowa State University Press, 1969), 149 (emphasis in original); Amos Bronson Alcott to Mrs. A. Bronson [Abigail] Alcott, 17 October, 25 October, 13 November, 6 December, and 10 December 1856, 1 January and 17 January 1859, in _Letters_, ed. Herrnstadt, 202, 205, 210, 218, 219, 221, 240, 293; Frederick C. Dahlstrand, _Amos Bronson Alcott: An Intellectual Biography_ (Rutherford, N.J.: Fairleigh Dickinson University Press, 1982), 228–29, 248.

8. Waterloo Congregational Friends, _Proceedings_ (1850), as quoted in Ann Braude, _Radical Spirits: Spiritualism and Women's Rights in Nineteenth-Century America_, 2d ed. (Bloomington: Indiana University Press, 2001), 13; see Braude, _Radical Spirits_, 10–15, for a fuller discussion of the Quaker-Fox connection.

9. John Edmonds, _New York Herald_, 6 August 1853, as extracted in an appendix to Ballou, _Exposition of Views Respecting the Modern Spirit Manifestations_, 134.

10. Howard Kerr and Charles L. Crow, _The Occult in America: New Historical Perspectives_ (Urbana: University of Illinois Press, 1983), 4.

11. Some of these connections are suggested by R. Laurence Moore's essay "The Occult Connection? Mormonism, Christian Science, and Spiritualism," in Kerr and Crow, eds., _Occult in America_, 135–61.

12. The Shaker construction of Ann Lee may be visited in Benjamin S. Youngs, _Testimony of Christ's Second Appearing Containing a General Statement of All Things Pertaining to the Faith and Practice of the Church of God in This Latter-Day_ (Lebanon, Ohio: John M'Clean, 1808); for an early-twentieth-century Shaker account, see Anna White and Leila S. Taylor, _Shakerism: Its Meaning and Message_ (1904; rpt., New York: AMS, 1971), 14–67.

13. Stephen J. Stein, _The Shaker Experience in America: A History of the United Society of Believers_ (New Haven: Yale University Press, 1992), 3–6, 7. On Boehme and Swedenborg in Manchester, England, see Clarke Garrett, _Spirit Possession and Popular Religion: From the Camisards to the Shakers_ (Baltimore: Johns Hopkins University Press, 1987), 145–46.

14. See Garrett, _Spirit Possession and Popular Religion_, esp. 181, 189; Stein, _Shaker Experience in America_, 166–67, 165.

15. Stein, _Shaker Experience in America_, 168; Sally M. Promey, _Spiritual Spectacles: Vision and Image in Mid-Nineteenth-Century Shakerism_ (Bloomington: Indiana University Press, 1993), 9–10.

16. Promey, _Spiritual Spectacles_, 138. Quotations are from Promey's work; Downs's words were reported by the Mount Lebanon ministry.

17. Garrett, _Spirit Possession and Popular Religion_, 238–39.

18. As quoted in Promey, _Spiritual Spectacles_, 138–39.

19. Garrett, _Spirit Possession and Popular Religion_, 239. For a detailed account of the new instrument-led rituals, see Edward Deming Andrews, _The People Called Shakers: A_

Search for the Perfect Society, 2d ed. (New York: Dover, 1963), 160–72. The Shaker elder Frederick W. Evans cited a seven-year period of closing Shaker worship to the public in his *Autobiography of a Shaker* (1869), but he gave the inaugurating date as 1837, whereas the ministry decision to close the meetings actually came in 1842 (see Frederick W. Evans, *Autobiography of a Shaker, and Revelation of the Apocalypse*, enl. ed. [1888; rpt., Philadelphia: Porcupine, 1972], 40; and Stein, *Shaker Experience in America*, 175). In their 1904 work, White and Taylor list a three-year period of public closure on the Sabbath from 1842 to 1845 (see White and Taylor, *Shakerism*, 233).

20. Stein, *Shaker Experience in America*, 190.

21. As quoted in Jean M. Humez, ed., *Mother's First-Born Daughters: Early Shaker Writings on Women and Religion* (Bloomington: Indiana University Press, 1993), 219; Paulina Bates, *The Divine Book of Holy and Eternal Wisdom, Revealing the Word of God, Out of Whose Mouth Goeth a Sharp Sword* (Canterbury, N.H., 1849), as anthologized in Humez, ed., *Mother's First-Born Daughters*, 261 (emphasis in Humez), 263; on the Shaker spirit drawings, see Promey, *Spiritual Spectacles*.

22. Hervey Elkins, "Fifteen Years in the Senior Order of Shakers," as extracted in Charles Nordhoff, *The Communistic Societies of the United States: From Personal Visit and Observation* (1875; rpt., New York: Hillary House, 1961), 243; Andrews, *People Called Shakers*, 152–53; Humez, ed., *Mother's First-Born Daughters*, 209–72; Louis J. Kern, *An Ordered Love: Sex Roles and Sexuality in Victorian Utopias — the Shakers, the Mormons, and the Oneida Community* (Chapel Hill: University of North Carolina Press, 1981), 106.

23. Humez, ed., *Mother's First-Born Daughters*, 224. On Shaker institutionalization, see ibid., 209–10; and on the institutionalized ritual of the séance in mass-movement spiritualism, see Bret E. Carroll, *Spiritualism in Antebellum America* (Bloomington: Indiana University Press, 1997), 120–51.

24. Evans, *Autobiography of a Shaker*, 40–41 (emphasis in original).

25. Nordhoff, *Communistic Societies of the United States*, 118, 157.

26. John Humphrey Noyes, *History of American Socialisms* (1870; rpt., New York: Dover, 1966), 595, 612–13.

27. John W. Edmonds, "Introduction," in John W. Edmonds and George T. Dexter, *Spiritualism*, 5th ed. (New York: Partridge and Brittan, 1853), 45n. For phenomenal spiritualists, see Andrew Jackson Davis, *The Great Harmonia*, vol. 5, *Being a Progressive Revelation of the Eternal Principles Which Inspire Mind and Govern Matter* (*The Thinker*) (1859; rpt. of 1865 ed., Mokelumne Hill, Calif.: Health Research, 1973), 253–54; and Robert W. Delp, "Andrew Jackson Davis: Prophet of American Spiritualism," *Journal of American History* 54, no. 1 (1967): 51.

28. James M. Peebles, *Seers of the Ages: Embracing Spiritualism, Past and Present; Doctrines Stated and Moral Tendencies Defined* (Boston: W. White, 1869); see the synopsis in Stein, *Shaker Experience in America*, 322.

29. Emma Hardinge, *Modern American Spiritualism: A Twenty Years' Record of the Communion between Earth and the World of Spirits* (New York: The Author, 1870), 27.

30. Ibid.

31. Stein, *Shaker Experience in America*, 199–200, 320–26, 321–22; Evans, *Autobiography*

of a Shaker, 232 (emphasis in original), 232–39; Promey, *Spiritual Spectacles*, 254–55 n50. Given this evidence, Andrews's observation that "the mechanics of modern spiritualism—the automatic writings, table liftings, knockings, and ectoplasmic materializations—offended the Shaker mind" seems dubious at best (see Andrews, *People Called Shakers*, 175).

32. White and Taylor, *Shakerism*, 221, 237–38, 250–51. For White's familiarity with the *Banner of Light*, see Stein, *Shaker Experience in America*, 322.

33. Stein, *Shaker Experience in America*, 186.

34. Franz Anton Mesmer, *Physical-Medical Treatise on the Influence of the Planets* (1766), in F. A. Mesmer, *Mesmerism: A Translation of the Original Medical and Scientific Writings*, trans. George J. Bloch and introduced by Ernest R. Hilgard (Los Altos, Calif.: William Kaufmann, 1980), 3.

35. Ibid., 6, 14 (upper case in original), 20.

36. Ibid., 19 (upper case in original); [La Roy Sunderland], "Pathetism in the Fifteenth Century," *The Magnet* 10 (March 1843): 220 (this and other materials from *The Magnet* are courtesy of the American Antiquarian Society); [La Roy Sunderland], "Magnetism: Anton Frederick Mesmer," *The Magnet* 2, no. 12 (June 1844): 270 (emphasis in original; we may safely assume that all unsigned articles in *The Magnet* were written by Sunderland himself); Frank Podmore, *Modern Spiritualism: A History and a Criticism* (1902), reprinted as *Mediums of the Nineteenth Century*, 2 vols. (New Hyde Park, N.Y.: University Books, 1963), 1: 44. E. R. Hilgard, in a view that perhaps protests too much, plays down the Hermetic influence: "Despite efforts by others to show that Mesmer's ideas came from the alchemists and other practitioners of magnetic medicine, from earlier writers such as Paracelsus and [Jan Baptista] Van Helmont, he in fact drew mostly from the work of Mead. . . . There was nothing mystical, occult, or astrological in Mead's work, and there was none (intentionally) in Mesmer's" (Hilgard, "Introduction," in Mesmer, *Mesmerism*, xvii).

37. Franz Anton Mesmer, "Dissertation by F. A. Mesmer, Doctor of Medicine, on His Discoveries," in Mesmer, *Mesmerism*, 112, 120–23, 128.

38. My account here and below mostly follows E. R. Hilgard's construction of events in his introduction to F. A. Mesmer, *Mesmerism*, xii–xiv.

39. Robert Darnton, *Mesmerism and the End of the Enlightenment in France* (1968; rpt., New York: Schocken, 1970), 6, 8.

40. Ibid., 8, 10.

41. Mesmer, "Dissertation," 91 (emphasis in original); Darnton, *Mesmerism*, 58; Robert C. Fuller, *Mesmerism and the American Cure of Souls* (Philadelphia: University of Pennsylvania Press, 1982), 10.

42. See Darnton, *Mesmerism*, 68–69, 16–17; Fuller, *Mesmerism and the American Cure*, 11–13; Podmore, *Modern Spiritualism*, 1: 62.

43. Ann Taves, *Fits, Trances, and Visions: Experiencing Religion and Explaining Experience from Wesley to James* (Princeton: Princeton University Press, 1999), 127, 166.

44. See Fuller, *Mesmerism and the American Cure*, 18–19, 21, 46, 88. Fuller was quoting from Charles Poyen's personal narrative of his work in his *Progress of Animal Magnetism in New England* (Boston: Weeks, Jordan, 1837), 55; on Joseph du Commun, see

Slater Brown, *The Heyday of Spiritualism* (1970; rpt., New York: Pocket Books, 1972), 14. On the American lyceum movement for public education and entertainment in special town halls across the United States, see Carl Bode, *The American Lyceum: Town Meeting of the Mind* (1956; 2d ed., Carbondale: Southern Illinois University Press, 1968).

45. Hardinge, *Modern American Spiritualism*, 22; John C. Spurlock, *Free Love: Marriage and Middle-Class Radicalism in America, 1825–1860* (New York: New York University Press, 1988), 85.

46. John D. Davies, *Phrenology, Fad and Science: A Nineteenth-Century American Crusade* (1955; rpt., [Hamden, Conn.:] Archon, 1971), 3–9, 9.

47. Ibid., 16–17, 10, 20–21.

48. Ernest Isaacs, "A History of Nineteenth-Century American Spiritualism as a Religious and Social Movement" (Ph.D. diss., University of Wisconsin, 1975), 19; Arthur Wrobel, "Phrenology as Political Science," in Arthur Wrobel, ed., *Pseudo-Science and Society in Nineteenth-Century America* (Lexington: University Press of Kentucky, 1987), 124–25.

49. Robert H. Collyer, *Lights and Shadows of American Life* (Boston: Brainard, 1838). For a useful discussion, see Fuller, *Mesmerism and the American Cure*, 26–28.

50. "Introduction," in R[obert]. H. Collyer, *The Mesmeric Magazine; or, Journal of Animal Magnetism* 1, no. 1 (July 1842): 2 (upper case in original; this and other materials from *The Mesmeric Magazine* are courtesy of the American Antiquarian Society).

51. This was an edition of the London translation (from the Latin) of 1758. The title supplied here is from the spine of the book; the full title in English is *Concerning the Earths in Our Solar System, Which Are Called Planets: and Concerning the Earths in the Starry Heaven: Together with an Account of Their Inhabitants, and Also of the Spirits and Angels There: From What Has Been Seen and Heard*. The earliest edition I have been able to locate was published in Boston in 1828 by Adonis Howard. Slater Brown, however, cites an 1827 edition in *Heyday of Spiritualism*, 100.

52. [Robert H. Collyer], "History of Mesmerism: Part First," in *Mesmeric Magazine*, 5–6 (emphasis in original).

53. Heinrich Jung-Stilling [J. H. Jung], *Theorie der Geister-Kunde* (c. 1827), trans. Samuel Jackson as *Theory of Pneumatology* (1834), as quoted in Podmore, *Modern Spiritualism*, 1: 96–97.

54. See the account in Podmore, *Modern Spiritualism*, 1: 99–101.

55. Justinus Kerner, *The Seeress of Prevorst; Being Revelations Concerning the Inner-Life of Man, and the Inter-Diffusion of a World of Spirits in the One We Inhabit*, trans. [Catherine] Crowe (London: J. C. Moore, 1845).

56. According to Frank Podmore, Collyer would recant phrenomagnetism by the following year (see Podmore, *Modern Spiritualism*, 1: 129).

57. On Underhill, see Isaacs, "History of Nineteenth-Century American Spiritualism," 22; [La Roy Sunderland], "Preliminary," *The Magnet* 1, no. 1 (June 1842): 1 (upper case in original); [La Roy Sunderland], "Life, Health, Disease, and Death," *The Magnet* 1, no. 3 (August 1842): 57 (emphasis in original).

58. Taves, *Fits, Trances, and Visions*, 131, 127; [La Roy Sunderland], "The Magnetic Na-

ture," *The Magnet* 1, no. 5 (October 1842): 107; [La Roy Sunderland], "The Nature of Man," *The Magnet* 1, no. 7 (December 1842), 158–61; [La Roy Sunderland], "Ecstasy," *The Magnet* 1, no. 11 (April 1843): 249, 249–51; Brown, *Heyday of Spiritualism*, 23.

59. La Roy Sunderland, *Pathetism; with Practical Instructions* (New York: P. P. Good, 1843); Fuller, *Mesmerism and the American Cure*, 39, 189 n14, 191 n37.

60. Fuller, *Mesmerism and the American Cure*, 39; Sunderland, *Pathetism*, 2.

61. Sunderland, *Pathetism*, 39, 41, 68, 72, 101, 103, 231 (upper case and emphases in original). In a refinement of this statement, Frank Podmore argued that in Sunderland's system it was the pathetized person's "own anticipation or apprehension of certain results" that was crucial and that "results followed, not on the will of the operator, but on the expectation of the patient" (Podmore, *Modern Spiritualism*, 1: 157).

62. Sunderland, *Pathetism*, 237 (emphasis in original).

63. See Podmore, *Modern Spiritualism*, 1: 156–57. Podmore cited Sunderland's brief acknowledgment of his "mistake" in La Roy Sunderland, *The Trance and Correlative Phenomena* (Chicago: J. Walker, 1868), 52.

64. Carroll, *Spiritualism in Antebellum America*, 113; Fuller, *Mesmer and the American Cure*, 95, 98; E[liab]. W[ilkinson]. Capron, *Modern Spiritualism: Its Facts and Fanaticism, Its Consistencies and Contradictions* (Boston: Bela Marsh, 1855), 214.

65. John Bovee Dods, as quoted and summarized in Fuller, *Mesmer and the American Cure*, 85–89; John Bovee Dods, *Spirit Manifestations Examined and Explained* (1854), as quoted and summarized in Podmore, *Modern Spiritualism*, 1: 289.

66. Podmore stated that Buchanan was "still living (in 1899)" and added in a note that he died in 1900 (Podmore, *Modern Spiritualism*, 1: 155 and 155 n4).

67. Podmore, *Modern Spiritualism*, 1: 156 (emphasis in original).

68. See the summary in Fuller, *Mesmerism and the American Cure*, 53–54; [Joseph R. Buchanan], "The Spirit World!" *Buchanan's Journal of Man* 2, no. 5 (November 1850): 129–30 (this and other materials from *Buchanan's Journal of Man* are courtesy of the American Antiquarian Society).

69. I borrow the term *celestial telegraph* from the title of the French Swedenborgian L. Alphonse Cahagnet's work *The Celestial Telegraph; or, Secrets of the Life to Come, Revealed through Magnetism* (1848; trans. rpt., New York: J. S. Redfield, 1851); A. W. Sprague, "Clairvoyance and Immortality," *Buchanan's Journal of Man* 5, no. 11 (November 1855): 292 (emphasis in original); [Joseph R. Buchanan], "Relations of Phrenology and Spiritualism," *Buchanan's Journal of Man* 6, no. 1 (January 1856): 39.

70. Allen Putnam, *Mesmerism, Spiritualism, Witchcraft, and Miracle: A Brief Treatise, Showing That Mesmerism Is a Key Which Will Unlock Many Chambers of Mystery* (Boston: Bela Marsh, 1858), 6, 7, 8, 10, 13, 15 (emphases in original).

71. Ibid., 15, 20, 25, 27–28, 33 (emphases in original).

72. Ibid., 39 (emphasis in original), 40, 63–74.

73. Hardinge, *Modern American Spiritualism*, 27, 23, 25–26.

74. Carroll, *Spiritualism in Antebellum America*, 21.

75. Gibson Smith, *Clairmativeness; or, Human Magnetism, with an Appendix* (New York, 1845). Podmore used this spelling, *Clairmativeness*, and claimed that the volume contained four trance lectures by Davis (Podmore, *Modern Spiritualism*, 167 n1), but, as

Podmore noted, Davis himself wrote that the correct title was *Clairlativeness* — referring to a "clear production" by a spirit; see Andrew Jackson Davis, *The Present Age and Inner Life: A Sequel to Spiritual Intercourse* (Hartford: S. Andrus, 1853), 153. Davis's account of his life, on which much of mine is based, may be found in Andrew Jackson Davis, *The Magic Staff: An Autobiography* (New York: J. S. Brown, 1859); see, also, Isaacs, "History of Nineteenth-Century American Spiritualism," 26–56.

76. Davis, *Magic Staff*, 227–41, 242–43.

77. Andrew Jackson Davis, *The Principles of Nature, Her Divine Revelations, and a Voice to Mankind* (New York: S. S. Lyon and W. Fishbough, 1847).

78. Isaacs, "History of Nineteenth-Century American Spiritualism," 48–50; Brown, *Heyday of Spiritualism*, 95; Noyes, *History of American Socialisms*, 567, 539–40; Podmore, *Modern American Spiritualism*, 1: 165. The book by George Bush is *Mesmer and Swedenborg; or, The Relation of the Developments of Mesmerism to the Doctrines and Disclosures of Swedenborg* (New York: John Allen, 1847).

79. Andrew Jackson Davis, *The Principles of Nature, Her Divine Revelations, and a Voice to Mankind*, 34th ed. (Boston: Colby and Rich, 1881), ix–x (subsequent citations from *The Principles of Nature* are to this edition); Brown, *Heyday of Spiritualism*, 101. Brown cites compelling evidence that the thirty-fourth edition, first issued by Colby and Rich in 1876, was actually the seventeenth. The thirteenth edition was published in 1866, and the thirtieth was advertised in 1868 by its publishers with no extant evidence of editions between, thus suggesting a printer's error "exploited" in later editions (see Brown, *Heyday of Spiritualism*, 97n).

80. Catherine L. Albanese, *Nature Religion in America: From the Algonkian Indians to the New Age* (Chicago: University of Chicago Press, 1990); Davis, *Principles of Nature*, 1.

81. Davis, *Principles of Nature*, 1–2, 5, 25–37, 43, 40 (emphases and upper case in original).

82. Ibid., 43–44, 46, 50, 119–20 (emphases in original).

83. Ibid. 121, 122, 131 (emphases and upper case in original).

84. Ibid., 198.

85. Ibid., 675–76, 674, 675 (emphases in original).

86. Ibid., 328, 489 (emphasis in original), 511, 557.

87. Ibid., 699 (upper case in original).

88. Podmore, *Modern Spiritualism*, 1: 166; Albert Brisbane, *Social Destiny of Man: or, Association and Reorganization of Industry* (Philadelphia: C. F. Stollmeyer, 1840); Davis, *Principles of Nature*, 714–15, 734, 736–37 (emphases and upper case in original).

89. Ibid., 770, 776 (emphases in original).

90. Catherine L. Albanese, "On the Matter of Spirit: Andrew Jackson Davis and the Marriage of God and Nature," *Journal of the American Academy of Religion* 60, no. 1 (Spring 1992): 1–17; Andrew Jackson Davis, *The Penetralia; Being Harmonial Answers to Important Questions*, 4th ed. (1858; rpt., San Jose, Calif.: Aquarian Fellowship, 1970), 190.

91. Spurlock, *Free Love*, 84, 83, 94, 95, 98.

92. S[amuel]. B[yron]. B[rittan]., "The Signs of the Times," *The Univercoelum and Spiri-*

tual Philosopher 1, no. 1 (4 December 1847): 11; S[amuel]. B[yron]. B[rittan]., "Relation of Deity to the Universe," *The Univercoelum and Spiritual Philosopher* 1, no. 3 (18 December 1847): 38 (emphases in original; these and other materials from the *Univercoelum* are courtesy of the American Antiquarian Society).

93. "Death," *The Univercoelum and Spiritual Philosopher* 1, no. 4 (25 December 1847): 57; *Shekinah* 1 (1852): 119, as quoted in Carroll, *Spiritualism in Antebellum America*, 22; Editors Univercoelum, "The Univercoelum," *Univercoelum* 1, no. 1: 8–9; *The Univercoelum and Spiritual Philosopher* 1, no. 16 (18 March 1848): 256; Josiah Johnson, "Unity" [continued], *The Univercoelum and Spiritual Philosopher* 1, no. 25 (20 May 1848): 396 (upper case in original).

94. See, e.g., Samuel W. Fisher, "The Supremacy of Mind," *The Univercoelum and Spiritual Philosopher* 2, no. 14 (2 September 1848): 209–11; T[homas]. L[ake]. H[arris]., "Knowledge through Obedience," *The Univercoelum and Spiritual Philosopher* 2, no. 11 (12 August 1848): 169; William Fishbough, "The Theological Conception; Its Growth, Dependencies, &c.," *The Univercoelum and Spiritual Philosopher* 2, no. 19 (2 October 1848): 291–93 (emphases and upper case in original).

95. Isaacs, "History of Nineteenth-Century American Spiritualism," 55–56; Podmore, *Modern Spiritualism*, 1: 173, 204; Braude, *Radical Spirits*, 35, 212 n6; Andrew Jackson Davis, *The Philosophy of Spiritual Intercourse, Being an Explanation of Modern Mysteries* (New York: Fowlers and Well, 1853), 21.

96. Davis, *Philosophy of Spiritual Intercourse*, 23, 49, 25–26 (emphases in original).

97. Cox, *Body and Soul*, 7, 75.

98. Andrew Jackson Davis, *The Great Harmonia: Being a Progressive Revelation of the Eternal Principles Which Inspire Mind and Govern Matter*, vol. 5: *The Thinker* (1859), 6th ed. (New York: C. M. Plumb, 1865), 252–54 (emphasis in original); Andrew Jackson Davis, *Beyond the Valley; A Sequel to "The Magic Staff:" An Autobiography* (Boston: Colby and Rich, 1885), 64, 326 (upper case in original); see, also, the discussion in Carroll, *Spiritualism in Antebellum America*, 35–37.

99. Andrew Jackson Davis, *The Great Harmonia*, 5 vols. (Boston: Benjamin B. Mussey, 1850–59). Individual volumes carry different subtitles, and there are short titles for each volume as well: vol. 1, *The Physician*; vol. 2, *The Teacher*; vol. 3, *The Seer*; vol. 4, *The Reformer*; vol. 5, *The Thinker*.

100. Davis, *Magic Staff*, 394, 414, 416, 466, 472, 494–95, 501, 547, 545–52; Davis, *Beyond the Valley*, 96.

101. Braude, *Radical Spirits*, 58, 117; Davis, *Beyond the Valley*, 104–14, 203–4, 286–93; Robert W. Delp, "Andrew Jackson Davis and Spiritualism," in Wrobel, ed., *Pseudo-Science and Society*, 110–11.

102. Davis, *Present Age and Inner Life*, 213 (emphasis in original); Carroll, *Spiritualism in Antebellum America*, 19, 37, 117.

103. Davis, *Present Age and Inner Life*, 40 (upper case in original); Andrew Jackson Davis, *Death and the After-Life: Eight Evening Lectures on The Summer-Land*, rev. ed. (Boston: Colby and Rich, 1866), 12; Andrew Jackson Davis, *The Harbinger of Health; Containing Medical Prescriptions for the Human Body and Mind* (New York: A. J. Davis, 1862), 19, 409.

104. Hardinge, *Modern American Spiritualism*, 11 (emphasis in original); Andrew Jackson Davis, *The Fountain, with Jets of New Meaning* (Boston: William White, 1870), 210–14—and see Ann Taves's evaluation of the arguments in Taves, *Fits, Trances, and Visions*, 401 n4.

105. Taves, *Fits, Trances, and Visions*, 401 n4; Hardinge, *Modern American Spiritualism*, 13, 239, 273 (emphasis in original); Robert Dale Owen, *Footfalls on the Boundary of Another World: With Narrative Illustrations* (Philadelphia: J. B. Lippincott, 1860), 37n; Capron, *Modern Spiritualism*, 381; Nathaniel P. Tallmadge, "Introduction," in Charles Linton, *The Healing of the Nations*, 2d ed. (New York: Society for the Diffusion of Spiritual Knowledge, 1855), 10n (the first edition apparently also appeared in 1855).

106. Capron, *Modern Spiritualism*, 113; Isaacs, *History of Nineteenth-Century American Spiritualism*, 105; Podmore, *Modern Spiritualism*, 1: 303; Ernest Isaacs, "The Fox Sisters and American Spiritualism," in Kerr and Crow, eds., *Occult in America*, 95; Brown, *Heyday of Spiritualism*, 159–60; Hardinge, *Modern American Spiritualism*, 77; Braude, *Radical Spirits*, 20; Spurlock, *Free Love*, 94.

107. Carroll, *Spiritualism in Antebellum America*, 120–51, 124.

108. Isaacs, "Fox Sisters," 84–85; Brown, *Heyday of Spiritualism*, 125–27; Capron, *Modern Spiritualism*, 103–8.

109. See Isaacs, "Fox Sisters," 86–105; Braude, *Radical Spirits*, 17.

110. J[ohn]. W. Edmonds and Geo[rge]. T. Dexter, "Preface," in Edmonds and Dexter, *Spiritualism*, iii; Brown, *Heyday of Spiritualism*, 132; on commodification and performance, see Carroll, *Spiritualism in Antebellum America*, 125.

111. Brown, *Heyday of Spiritualism*, 124; Tallmadge, "Introduction," in Linton, *Healing of the Nations*, 49–62; Davis, *Present Age and Inner Life*, 128–97, 129, 130, 196.

112. Carroll, *Spiritualism in Antebellum America*, 145; Robert S. Ellwood Jr., *Religious and Spiritual Groups in Modern America* (Englewood Cliffs, N.J.: Prentice-Hall, 1973), 50; Robert S. Ellwood Jr., *Alternative Altars: Unconventional and Eastern Spirituality in America* (Chicago: University of Chicago Press, 1979), 52–57.

113. Carroll, *Spiritualism in Antebellum America*, 127, 125, 129, 130–40, 142.

114. Davis, *Philosophy of Spiritual Intercourse*, 96–98.

115. Ibid., 98–100.

116. Davis, *Present Age and Inner Life*, 76 (emphasis in original).

117. See R. Laurence Moore, *In Search of White Crows: Spiritualism, Parapsychology, and American Culture* (New York: Oxford University Press, 1977), 30; Podmore, *Modern Spiritualism*, 1: 117–19.

118. Brown, *Heyday of Spiritualism*, 236, 230–36.

119. Ibid., 231, 230; Edmonds and Dexter, "Preface," in Edmonds and Dexter, *Spiritualism*, iv; Brown, *Heyday of Spiritualism*, 230–31.

120. Edmonds, "Introduction," in Edmonds and Dexter, *Spiritualism*, 8–9, 34 (upper case in original), 39–40.

121. Edmonds and Dexter, *Spiritualism*, 216.

122. Ibid., 103, 107.

123. Ibid., 295, 123 (upper case in original).

124. Cox, *Body and Soul*; Edmonds and Dexter, *Spiritualism*, 131, 145–46.
125. Edmonds and Dexter, *Spiritualism*, 340.
126. Tallmadge, "Introduction," in Linton, *Healing of the Nations*, 3–6.
127. Ibid., 6 (emphasis in original); Tallmadge, "Introduction," in Linton, *Healing of the Nations*, 5. The one-Presence-one-Power formula, for example, was basic for Charles Fillmore, co-founder of the Unity School of Christianity.
128. Ibid., 12, 44–45 (emphases in original).
129. Ibid., 17, 71; Linton, *Healing of the Nations*, 74, 163.
130. Linton, *Healing of the Nations*, 185, 153, 154, 135–36.
131. Ibid., 215, 136, 445–46.
132. For the classic discussion, see Barbara Welter, "The Cult of True Womanhood, 1820–1860," *American Quarterly* 18 (Summer 1966): 151–74; and Nancy F. Cott, *The Bonds of Womanhood: "Woman's Sphere" in New England, 1780–1835* (New Haven: Yale University Press, 1977). For a brief discussion of an alternative view in a midwestern context, see Fran Grace, *Carry A. Nation: Retelling the Life* (Bloomington: Indiana University Press, 2001), 9, 104–6.
133. For a positive reading of the role of women among the Shakers, see Marjorie Procter-Smith, "'In the Line of the Female': Shakerism and Feminism," in Catherine Wessinger, ed., *Women's Leadership in Marginal Religions: Explorations Outside the Mainstream* (Urbana: University of Illinois Press, 1993), 23–40; on Shaker practice toward women, see Stein, *Shaker Experience in America*, 76, 52–53, 129; Humez, ed., *Mother's First-Born Daughters*, xx–xxiii; Isaac Newton Youngs, as quoted in Promey, *Spiritual Spectacles*, 46.
134. Stein, *Shaker Experience in America*, 187; I. M. Lewis, *Ecstatic Religion: An Anthropological Study of Spirit Possession and Shamanism* (1971; rpt., Baltimore: Penguin, 1975), 31.
135. On Victoria Woodhull, see Mary Gabriel, *Notorious Victoria: The Life of Victoria Woodhull, Uncensored* (Chapel Hill: Algonquin, 1998); and Barbara Goldsmith, *Other Powers: The Age of Suffrage, Spiritualism, and the Scandalous Victoria Woodhull* (New York: Knopf, 1998); and on former self-effacing female mediums as later reformers, see Braude, *Radical Spirits*. On the leadership and prominence of women in American metaphysical religion, the classic study (which includes the Shakers) is Mary Farrell Bednarowski, "Outside the Mainstream: Women's Religion and Women Religious Leaders in Nineteenth-Century America," *Journal of the American Academy of Religion* 48 (June 1980): 207–31.
136. Moore, *In Search of White Crows*, 102–29, 105.
137. Ibid., 106–7, 121; Braude, *Radical Spirits*, 83.
138. See, e.g., Moore, *In Search of White Crows*, 125, 111.
139. See Braude, *Radical Spirits*, 84–90, 88; Moore, *In Search of White Crows*, 115–16. On Fourierism, spiritualism, and free love, see Carl J. Guarneri, *The Utopian Alternative: Fourierism in Nineteenth-Century America* (Ithaca: Cornell University Press, 1991), 348–53.
140. See Moore, *In Search of White Crows*, 108, 125–26.
141. See the description, for the twentieth century, by J. Stillson Judah in *The History and*

Philosophy of the Metaphysical Movements in America (Philadelphia: Westminster, 1967), 68–69.

142. Molly Goodrich to Daniel Goodrich Jr., 30 November 1816, in Humez, ed., *Mother's First-Born Daughters*, 164, 163; Nordhoff, *Communistic Societies of the United States*, 207; Stein, *Shaker Experience in America*, 172.

143. See Jean McMahon Humez, ed., "Introduction," in Jean McMahon Humez, ed., *Gifts of Power: The Writings of Rebecca Jackson, Black Visionary, Shaker Eldress* (Amherst: University of Massachusetts Press, 1981), 10–32, 32; on Jackson's relationship with Perot, see ibid., 9, 9 n10.

144. Rebecca Cox Jackson, in Humez, ed., *Gifts of Power*, 209, 212, 215, 217–18, 220.

145. Ibid., 221, 226–27; Humez, ed., "Introduction," in ibid., 33; Jackson, in ibid., 242, 251, 253–55, 263.

146. James S. Prescott, in *Shaker and Shakeress* (1874), excerpted in Nordhoff, *Communistic Societies of the United States*, 234 (emphasis in original). *Shaker and Shakeress* was a periodical.

147. Hervey Elkins, *Fifteen Years in the Senior Order of Shakers: A Narration of Facts, Concerning That Singular People* (1853), excerpted in Nordhoff, *Communistic Societies of the United States*, 242; "Account of meetings during which the participants were inspired or experienced visions (1842–1843)," Watervliet, New York, in Humez, ed., *Mother's First-Born Daughters*, 245–46.

148. Cox, *Body and Soul*, 168.

149. Davis, *Present Age and Inner Life*, 277 (emphasis in original); Davis, *Death and the After-Life*, 181–83, 185,

150. Cox, *Body and Soul*, 195–97 (emphasis in Cox).

151. Yvonne P. Chireau, *Black Magic: Religion and the African American Conjuring Tradition* (Berkeley: University of California Press, 2003), 29, 32; Braude, *Radical Spirits*, 29, 210 n46; see, also, Cox, *Body and Soul*, 166; Hardinge, *Modern American Spiritualism*, 498.

152. Hardinge, *Modern American Spiritualism*, 205.

153. [Olive Gilbert], *Narrative of Sojourner Truth, A Bondwoman of Olden Time: With a History of Her Labors and Correspondence Drawn from Her "Book of Life,"* intro. Jeffrey C. Stewart (1878; rpt., New York: Oxford University Press, 1991), 13, 67, 65–71, 99, passim (the first edition of the *Narrative of Sojourner Truth*, without the *"Book of Life,"* appeared in 1850); Nell Irvin Painter, *Sojourner Truth* (New York: W. W. Norton, 1996), 143–48, 146, 148; Braude, *Radical Spirits*, 211 n48.

154. Pascal Beverly Randolph, *The Unveiling: or, What I Think of Spiritualism* (1860), as quoted in John Patrick Deveney, *Pascal Beverly Randolph: A Nineteenth-Century Black American Spiritualist, Rosicrucian, and Sex Magician* (Albany: State University of New York Press, 1997), 21; Deveney, *Pascal Beverly Randolph*, 1, 373 n1, 3, 8, 4.

155. Deveney, *Pascal Beverly Randolph*, 8–24, 92, 95.

156. Hardinge, *Modern American Spiritualism*, 242.

157. Ibid., 243.

158. Stein, *Shaker Experience in America*, 176; Kern, *Ordered Love*, 106. On Americans' playing Indian in general, see Philip J. Deloria, *Playing Indian* (New Haven: Yale Uni-

versity Press, 1998), and for a Delorian reading in terms of the mass spiritualist movement, see Cox, *Body and Soul*, 189–211.

159. Noyes, *History of American Socialisms*, 597, 604–5. A Shaker account of a feastday ceremony at Hancock Village, Massachusetts, in September 1842, as quoted by Edward Deming Andrews, similarly reported that "the Natives struck in, the whoop was sounded briskly, and for some time it appeared they rather carried the day. . . . After considerable exercise such as hopping upon one foot, dancing sideways, whooping, shaking hands, bowing of the head, running to and fro, catching one another, running around one another giveing and receiveing love, and diverse other simple movements of the spirit, we were called together by the Savior" (Andrews, *People Called Shakers*, 166–67).

160. "Account of meetings," in Humez, ed., *Mother's First-Born Daughters*, 243–45.

161. Noyes, *History of American Socialisms*, 611; Andrews, *People Called Shakers*, 169.

162. Nordhoff, *Communistic Societies of the United States*, 235.

163. Ibid., 242, 251; William Wittinmyer (1854), in *Telegraph Papers*, 4, as quoted in Podmore, *Modern Spiritualism*, 1: 257–58.

164. Cox, *Body and Soul*, 198, 203; Brown, *Heyday of Spiritualism*, 239; Cox, *Body and Soul*, 181; Hardinge, *Modern American Spiritualism*, 482.

165. Hardinge, *Modern American Spiritualism*, 481–82.

166. Ibid.

167. M[ary]. T[heresa]. Shelhamer, *Life and Labor in the Spirit World: Being a Description of Localities, Employments, Surroundings, and Conditions in the Spheres* (Boston: Colby and Rich, 1885), 7, 16, 19–20, 84–85.

168. Ibid., 85–86.

169. Cox, *Body and Soul*, 203; Allen Putnam, *Natty, a Spirit: His Portrait and His Life* (Boston: Bela Marsh, 1856), 91–94, as quoted and cited in Cox, *Body and Soul*, 200; Judah, *History and Philosophy of the Metaphysical Movements*, 70.

170. For a brief introduction to these and similar events of prophetic spirit contact, see Joel W. Martin, *Native American Religion* (New York: Oxford University Press, 1999), 56–62, 91–104.

171. Hardinge, *Modern American Spiritualism*, 16, 482.

172. Ibid., 483–87, 487, 489.

5. SPIRITS REFORMED AND RECONSTITUTED

1. M[ary]. T[heresa]. Shelhamer, *Life and Labor in the Spirit World* (Boston: Colby and Rich, 1885), 54–55, 57.

2. Andrew Jackson Davis, *The Principles of Nature, Her Divine Revelations, and a Voice to Mankind*, 34th ed. (Boston: Colby and Rich, 1881), 674–77 (upper case in original; see ch. 4, n79 for evidence that this was actually the seventeenth edition).

3. Andrew Jackson Davis, "Concerning the Spirit's Destiny," in Andrew Jackson Davis, *The Great Harmonia*, vol. 2, *The Teacher* (1851; rpt., Boston: Bela Marsh, 1862), 252–54 (emphases in original).

4. J[ohn]. W. Edmonds, "Introduction," in John W. Edmonds and George T. Dexter,

Spiritualism, 5th ed. (New York: Partridge and Brittan, 1853), 64–65 (upper case in original); George T. Dexter, "Introduction," in Edmonds and Dexter, *Spiritualism*, 99 (emphasis in original); Nathaniel P. Tallmadge, "Introduction," in Charles Linton, *The Healing of the Nations*, 2d ed. (New York: Society for the Diffusion of Spiritual Knowledge, 1855), 66–67 (upper case in original).

5. R. Laurence Moore, *In Search of White Crows: Spiritualism, Parapsychology, and American Culture* (New York: Oxford University Press, 1977), 19.

6. R. Laurence Moore, "The Occult Connection? Mormonism, Christian Science, and Spiritualism," in Howard Kerr and Charles L. Crow, eds., *The Occult in America: New Historical Perspectives* (Urbana: University of Illinois Press, 1983), 151; "Preface," in William Emmette Coleman, *Practical Occultism: A Course of Lectures through the Trance Mediumship of James Johnson Morse* (San Francisco: Carrier-Dove, 1888), as quoted in Moore, "The Occult Connection?" 151.

7. Ernest Isaacs, "A History of Nineteenth-Century American Spiritualism as a Religious and Social Movement" (Ph.D. diss., University of Wisconsin, 1975), 167; Moore, *In Search of White Crows*, 36; Ann Braude, *Radical Spirits: Spiritualism and Women's Rights in Nineteenth-Century America*, 2d ed. (Bloomington: Indiana University Press, 2001), 19.

8. Isaacs, "History of Nineteenth-Century American Spiritualism," 202–3; Slater Brown, *The Heyday of Spiritualism* (1970; rpt., New York: Pocket Books, 1972), 135–37.

9. See [Nathaniel P. Tallmadge] "Appendix—D" and "Appendix—O," in Linton, *Healing of the Nations*, 467–74, 534–37.

10. Isaacs, "History of Nineteenth-Century American Spiritualism," 203–5; Craig James Hazen, *The Village Enlightenment in America: Popular Religion and Science in the Nineteenth Century* (Urbana: University of Illinois Press, 2000), 86–88.

11. Robert Hare, *Experimental Investigation of the Spirit Manifestations, Demonstrating the Existence of Spirits and Their Communion with Mortals; Doctrine of the Spirit World respecting Heaven, Hell, Morality, and God. Also, the Influence of Scripture on the Morals of Christians* (New York: Partridge and Brittan, 1855), 131, as quoted in Hazen, *Village Enlightenment*, 84; Moore, *In Search of White Crows*, 32; Hazen, *Village Enlightenment*, 73. On Baconianism, see Theodore Dwight Bozeman, *Protestants in an Age of Science: The Baconian Ideal and Antebellum American Religious Thought* (Chapel Hill: University of North Carolina Press, 1977); Herbert Hovenkamp, *Science and Religion in America, 1800–1860* (Philadelphia: University of Pennsylvania Press, 1978); and Walter H. Conser Jr., *God and the Natural World: Religion and Science in Antebellum America* (Columbia: University of South Carolina Press, 1993).

12. On Hare, the spirits, his fellow scientists, and his fellow spiritualists, see the account in Hazen, *Village Enlightenment*, 91, 74, 76; Robert Hare, as quoted in Isaacs, "History of Nineteenth-Century American Spiritualism," 208 (emphasis in Isaacs).

13. Andrew Jackson Davis, *The Great Harmonia*, 5 vols. (Boston: Benjamin B. Mussey, 1850–59). Individual volumes carry different subtitles, and there are short titles for each volume as well: vol. 1, *The Physician*; vol. 2, *The Teacher*; vol. 3, *The Seer*; vol. 4, *The Reformer*; vol. 5, *The Thinker*.

14. Gerrit Smith, *Lectures on the Religion of Reason,* as quoted in Moore, *In Search of White Crows,* 70; Moore, *In Search of White Crows,* 70.
15. Braude, *Radical Spirits,* 192, 193, 201; Moore, *In Search of White Crows,* 71–73, 77–78.
16. Moore, *In Search of White Crows,* 83–87.
17. Andrew Jackson Davis, "What and Where Is God?" in Davis, *The Great Harmonia,* vol. 2, *The Teacher,* 289 (emphasis in original).
18. See the discussion in Moore, *In Search of White Crows,* 74–87.
19. Bret E. Carroll, *Spiritualism in Antebellum America* (Bloomington: Indiana University Press, 1997), 120–23, 35–39; Andrew Jackson Davis, *Beyond the Valley; A Sequel to "The Magic Staff:" An Autobiography* (Boston: Colby and Rich, 1885), 64, 326.
20. Davis, "Part III: The Application; or, A Voice to Mankind," in *Principles of Nature,* 679–782.
21. Moore, *In Search of White Crows,* 97; Maren Lockwood Carden, *Oneida: Utopian Community to Modern Corporation* (Baltimore: Johns Hopkins University Press, 1969), 122.
22. Isaacs, "History of Nineteenth-Century American Spiritualism," 243, 250–54 (with quotations from original document in Isaacs); Moore, *In Search of White Crows,* 94; Brown, *Heyday of Spiritualism,* 188.
23. Isaacs, "History of Nineteenth-Century American Spiritualism," 243–46 (with quotations from original document in Isaacs).
24. For the most perceptive account of the community from a religious-studies perspective, see Carroll, *Spiritualism in Antebellum America,* 162–76, 169–70.
25. Emma Hardinge, *Modern American Spiritualism: A Twenty Years' Record of the Communion between Earth and the World of Spirits* (New York: The Author, 1870), 207–17, 208, 209, 212 (emphasis in original); E[liab]. W[ilkinson]. Capron, *Modern Spiritualism: Its Facts and Fantasies, Its Consistencies and Contradictions* (Boston: Bela Marsh, 1855), 116–31, 131.
26. See Carroll, *Spiritualism in Antebellum America,* 164–65.
27. Henry S. Olcott, *People from the Other World* (Hartford, Conn.: American, 1875), title page (emphasis in original), iv–vii.
28. Henry Steel Olcott, *Old Diary Leaves: The True History of the Theosophical Society* (1895), reprinted as *Inside the Occult: The True Story of Madame H. P. Blavatsky* (Philadelphia: Running Press, 1975), 2.
29. Bruce F. Campbell, *Ancient Wisdom Revived: A History of the Theosophical Movement* (Berkeley: University of California Press, 1980), 4–6.
30. Olcott, *People from the Other World,* x.
31. Ibid., 453.
32. Olcott, *Old Diary Leaves,* 14 (emphasis in original), 11, 72, 8.
33. Ibid., 6, 17–20.
34. Olcott, *People from the Other World,* 406, 341; Mark Twain's and Charles Dudley Warner's novel *The Gilded Age: A Tale of To-day* was first published in 1873–74, giving historians and cultural critics a convenient label to characterize the uneasy period from after the Civil War until 1873, or—in some accounts—until roughly 1890. The period was castigated for its currency inflation and financial speculation, loose morals

in business and politics, and excessive materialism in the wake of northern victory in the Civil War.

35. Campbell, *Ancient Wisdom Revived*, 26–27.

36. Ibid., 27; Alvin Boyd Kuhn, *Theosophy: A Modern Revival of Ancient Wisdom* (New York: Henry Holt, 1930), 90, 1.

37. See the discussion in Stephen Prothero, *The White Buddhist: The Asian Odyssey of Henry Steel Olcott* (Bloomington: Indiana University Press, 1996), 51–53.

38. Ibid., 53–54.

39. Robert S. Ellwood Jr., *Alternative Altars: Unconventional and Eastern Spirituality in America* (Chicago: University of Chicago Press, 1979), 111; Olcott, *People from the Other World*, 342.

40. Olcott, *Old Diary Leaves*, 140 (upper case and emphasis in original).

41. H. P. Blavatsky, *Isis Unveiled: A Master-Key to the Mysteries of Ancient and Modern Science and Theology*, 2 vols. (New York: J. W. Bouton, 1877).

42. Campbell, *Ancient Wisdom Revived*, 32–34.

43. Ellwood, *Alternative Altars*, 109–10; Robert S. Ellwood Jr., *Religious and Spiritual Groups in Modern America* (Englewood Cliffs, N.J.: Prentice-Hall, 1973), 78.

44. A[lfred]. P[ercy]. Sinnett, *The Occult World* (London: Trübner, 1881); A[lfred]. P[ercy]. Sinnett, *Esoteric Buddhism* (Boston: Houghton Mifflin, 1883); Campbell, *Ancient Wisdom Revived*, 87–93.

45. See Campbell, *Ancient Wisdom Revived*, 32, 35.

46. Letter of Helena P. Blavatsky to Henry S. Olcott (1875), as quoted in Olcott, *Old Diary Leaves*, 110 (upper case in original); H. P. Blavatsky, *Isis Unveiled: A Master-Key to the Mysteries of Ancient and Modern Science and Theology* (1877; rpt. as centenary anniversary ed., Los Angeles: Theosophy Company, 1975), 1: x, 41, 70 (emphasis in original), x.

47. Blavatsky, *Isis Unveiled*, v, vii, xlv (emphasis in original), vi.

48. Ibid., xi, 25 (emphasis in original), 58, 125 (emphasis in original), 128, 184, 178 (upper case in original), 327, 340 (emphasis in original).

49. Ibid., 216 (emphasis in original), 299, 302 (emphasis in original), 154, 303, 319.

50. Ibid., 2: 587–88.

51. Ibid., 1: table of contents (ch. 15), 351; 2: 574.

52. Campbell, *Ancient Wisdom Revived*, 77–78; Olcott, *Old Diary Leaves*, 401.

53. Olcott, *Old Diary Leaves*, 401 (emphasis in original), 399–400; Campbell, *Ancient Wisdom Revived*, 97–98.

54. Mary Baker Glover, *Science and Health* (Boston: Christian Scientist Publishing, 1875).

55. Mary Baker G. Eddy, *Science and Health with Key to the Scriptures* (Boston: J. Armstrong, 1906). This edition would continue to appear after Eddy's death in 1910 with Trustees under the Will of Mary Baker G. Eddy listed as publisher.

56. Mary Baker Eddy, *The First Church of Christ Scientist and Miscellany* (1916), as quoted in Rennie B. Schoepflin, *Christian Science on Trial: Religious Healing in America* (Boston: Johns Hopkins University Press, 2003), 28.

57. For Eddy's theologically driven account of most of these events, see Mary Baker Eddy,

Retrospection and Introspection (1891; rpt., Boston: First Church of Christ, Scientist, n.d.), 13–14 ("Theological Reminiscence"), 19–21 ("Marriage and Parentage"). For a judicious sifting of the evidence regarding the surrender of Mary Glover's son George, see Gillian Gill, *Mary Baker Eddy* (Cambridge, Mass.: Perseus, 1998), 86–94.

58. George Miller Beard, *American Nervousness, Its Causes and Consequences: A Supplement to Nervous Exhaustion (Neurasthenia)* (New York: Putnam, 1881). On Eddy's involvement with spiritualism, see, for example, Gill, *Mary Baker Eddy*, 152–53, 172–80.

59. The construction of Eddy's Quimby years is fraught with difficulty. For a careful reading that still stresses differences between Eddy and Quimby, see Robert Peel, *Mary Baker Eddy: The Years of Discovery* (New York: Holt, Rinehart, and Winston, 1966), esp. 180–83. George Quimby is quoted in Horatio W. Dresser, ed., "Appendix," *The Quimby Manuscripts* (1921; rpt., Secaucus, N.J.: Citadel, 1969), 438.

60. Peel, *Mary Baker Eddy: The Years of Discovery*, 162.

61. Dresser, ed., *Quimby Manuscripts*; Phineas Parkhurst Quimby, *The Complete Writings*, ed. Ervin Seale, 3 vols. (Marina del Rey, Calif.: DeVorss, 1988), although this is still not a critical edition. On the general direction of Dresser's changes, see Hazen, *Village Enlightenment*, 144–45.

62. Quimby, *Complete Writings*, 2: 411; 3: 251, 248.

63. Ibid., 2: 92, 144, 148, 206, 340; 3: 246, 343.

64. Ibid., 2: 142; 3: 195–96; J. Stillson Judah, *The History and Philosophy of the Metaphysical Movements in America* (Philadelphia: Westminster, 1967), 150–54. For materialist readings of Quimby, see my earlier work, Catherine L. Albanese, *Nature Religion in America: From the Algonkian Indians to the New Age* (Chicago: University of Chicago Press, 1990), 107–15; and, still more thoroughgoing, Hazen, *Village Enlightenment*, 113–46.

65. For a sense of this process in the case of Emerson, see, e.g., Willard Thorp, "Emerson on Tour," *Quarterly Journal of Speech* 16, no. 1 (February 1930): 19–34; Hubert H. Hoeltje, "Ralph Waldo Emerson in Minnesota," *Minnesota History: A Quarterly Magazine* 11, no. 2 (June 1930): 145–59; Russel B. Nye, "Emerson in Michigan and the Northwest," *Michigan History Magazine* 26, no. 2 (Spring 1942): 159–72; and Lynda Beltz, "Emerson's Lectures in Indianapolis," *Indiana Magazine of History* 60, no. 3 (September 1964): 269–80. For a similar rehearsal regarding Henry David Thoreau, see Walter Harding, "A Check List of Thoreau's Lectures," *Bulletin of the New York Public Library* 52 (1948): 78–87. For the Transcendentalist reading of Quimby, see Stewart W. Holmes, "Phineas Parkhurst Quimby: Scientist of Transcendentalism," *New England Quarterly* 17 (September 1944): 356–80.

66. For the Swedenborgianism, see Judah, *History and Philosophy of the Metaphysical Movements*, 149–50; and, for another quick digest, see Peel, *Mary Baker Eddy: The Years of Discovery*, 162–63, 338 n26.

67. Quimby, *Complete Writings*, 3: 196; for a discussion of Quimby's notion of wisdom, see Hazen, *Village Enlightenment*, 133–43.

68. Quimby, *Complete Writings*, 3: 371. In view of the pervasive nature of Quimby's "wisdom" discourse and its consistency, I find it strained at best to read the Quimby material, as Robert Peel did, in terms of Eddy's possible interpolations as an amanuen-

sis and editor (see Peel, *Mary Baker Eddy: The Years of Discovery*, 182). Similarly, Quimby's apparent denial that he was making himself equal to Christ seems miscast, although Charles Braden took it at face value (see Charles S. Braden, *Spirits in Rebellion: The Rise and Development of New Thought* [1963; rpt., Dallas: Southern Methodist University Press, 1984], 78).

69. Peel, *Mary Baker Eddy: The Years of Discovery*, 182.

70. Mary M. Patterson to the *Portland Courier*, as quoted in Georgine Milmine, *The Life of Mary Baker G. Eddy and the History of Christian Science* (1909; rpt., Grand Rapids, Mich.: Baker, 1971), 60.

71. See Peel, *Mary Baker Eddy: The Years of Discovery*, 195–97; see, also, for a useful sifting of the evidence, Gill, *Mary Baker Eddy*, 161–65.

72. Glover, *Science and Health*, 435; Mary Baker Glover, *The Science of Man, By Which the Sick Are Healed, Embracing Questions and Answers in Moral Science* (1876; rpt., New York: Rare Book, n.d.), 5; Eddy, *Science and Health with Key to the Scriptures*, 467, 311; Mary Baker Eddy, *Miscellaneous Writings, 1883–1896* (1896; rpt., Boston: Trustees under the Will of Mary Baker G. Eddy, 1924), 234; Mary Baker Eddy, *Manual of the Mother Church* (Boston: First Church of Christ, Scientist, 1895), 47, as cited and quoted in Stephen Gottschalk, *Rolling Away the Stone: Mary Baker Eddy's Challenge to Materialism* (Bloomington: Indiana University Press, 2006), 320.

73. Stephen Gottschalk, *The Emergence of Christian Science in American Religious Life* (Berkeley: University of California Press, 1973), 48–50, 284–85, 120; Eddy, *Science and Health with Key to the Scriptures*, 497; Eddy, *Manual of the Mother Church*, 15–16; Eddy, *Manual of the Mother Church*, 41, as quoted in Gottschalk, *Rolling Away the Stone*, 196.

74. Eddy, *Retrospection and Introspection*, 67; Eddy, *Miscellaneous Writings*, 108–9 (emphasis in original). Beryl Satter has read Eddy's repudiation of matter/evil/sin in terms of the body, and especially the female body with its sexual vulnerability and social subordination. In this context, she points to an Eddy doing "apocalyptic battle, in which woman would conquer the falsehoods of the Adam-dream." See Beryl Satter, *Each Mind a Kingdom: American Women, Sexual Purity, and the New Thought Movement, 1875–1920* (Berkeley: University of California Press, 1999), 67–68.

75. Eddy, *Science and Health with Key to the Scriptures*, 114–15; see, also, Gottschalk, *Emergence of Christian Science*, 67; Braude, *Radical Spirits*, 186.

76. Mary Baker Eddy to John Lathrop, 9 May 1906, as quoted in Gottschalk, *Rolling Away the Stone*, 356; Calvin Frye Diary, 21 August 1910, as quoted in Gottschalk, *Rolling Away the Stone*, 402 (the description of the entire episode is taken from Gottschalk's account).

77. Glover, *Science and Health*, 90, 5.

78. See Schoepflin, *Christian Science on Trial*, 26, 24, 15, for her putative spirit mediumship and for quotations from her *Banner of Light* advertisement.

79. Satter, *Each Mind a Kingdom*, 65.

80. Glover, *Science and Health*, 112–13 (emphasis in original).

81. Ibid., 27, 328–29, 93, 96.

82. Ibid., 84, 92, 100, 88, 87.

83. Ibid., 71–72, 64, 65, 66, 67, 70, 74.
84. See Gottschalk, *Rolling Away the Stone.*
85. Sydney E. Ahlstrom, *A Religious History of the American People* (New Haven: Yale University Press, 1972), 1019–62; Eddy, *Science and Health with Key to the Scriptures,* 468.
86. Glover, *Science of Man,* 7, 10; Glover, *Science and Health,* 435. For formulaic utterances and typical language, see, e.g., Schoepflin, *Christian Science on Trial,* 55–72, 75–77; Stephen Gottschalk, "Christian Science and Harmonialism," in Charles H. Lippy and Peter W. Williams, eds., *Encyclopedia of the American Religious Experience,* 3 vols. (New York: Scribner's, 1988), 2: 901–2.
87. Glover, *Science of Man,* 12; Mary Baker Eddy, as remembered in 1875 by Samuel P. Bancroft from 1870 and as quoted in Schoepflin, *Christian Science on Trial,* 25.
88. Braude, *Radical Spirits,* 183–84.
89. Glover, *Science of Man,* 12; Braude, *Radical Spirits,* 185–86.
90. Braude, *Radical Spirits,* 187; Glover, *Science of Man,* 4–5.
91. Schoepflin, *Christian Science on Trial,* 47, 106; Gottschalk, *Emergence of Christian Science,* 175.
92. Gottschalk, *Emergence of Christian Science,* 175.
93. Ibid., 257. Gottschalk based this assessment on Neal DeNood, "The Diffusion of a System of Belief" (Ph.D. diss., Harvard University, 1937).
94. Gottschalk, *Emergence of Christian Science,* 234, 244; Schoepflin, *Christian Science on Trial,* 34.
95. On the business of being a Christian Science practitioner, see Schoepflin, *Christian Science on Trial,* 48–52.
96. See ibid., 53.
97. For a succinct summary of this process, see Gary Ward Materra, "Women in Early New Thought: Lives and Theology in Transition, from the Civil War to World War I" (Ph.D. diss., University of California, Santa Barbara, 1997), 64–67, 110, 117.
98. On the copyrighting and its results, see Satter, *Each Mind a Kingdom,* 96.
99. Hazen, *Village Enlightenment,* 139–41.
100. See Quimby, *Complete Writings,* 1: 186.
101. Andrew Jackson Davis, "What Is the Philosophy of Healing?" in Andrew Jackson Davis, *The Great Harmonia,* vol. 1, *The Physician* (1850), 13th ed. (Boston: Banner of Light, n.d.), 286; Quimby, *Complete Writings,* 1: 160, 240–41.
102. Quimby, *Complete Writings,* 1: 412; 2: 152–53; 3: 90, 93–95.
103. Ibid., 3: 323–24.
104. See Braden, *Spirits in Rebellion,* 90–91; and John F. Teahan, "Warren Felt Evans and Mental Healing: Romantic Idealism and Practical Mysticism in Nineteenth-Century America," *Church History* 48, no. 1 (March 1979): 90. Evans's six books on mental healing were Rev. W[arren]. F[elt]. Evans, *The Mental-Cure, Illustrating the Influence of the Mind on the Body Both in Health and Disease, and the Psychological Method of Treatment* (Boston: H. H. and T. W. Carter, 1869); W[arren]. F[elt]. Evans, *Mental Medicine: A Theoretical and Practical Treatise on Medical Psychology* (Boston: Carter and Pettee, 1872); W[arren]. F[elt]. Evans, *Soul and Body; or, The Spiritual Science*

of Health and Disease (Boston: Colby and Rich, 1876); W[arren]. F[elt]. Evans, *The Divine Law of Cure* (Boston: H. H. Carter, 1881); W[arren]. F[elt]. Evans, *The Primitive Mind-Cure: The Nature and Power of Faith; or, Elementary Lessons in Christian Philosophy and Transcendental Medicine* (Boston: H. H. Carter and Karrick, 1885); W[arren]. F[elt]. Evans, *Esoteric Christianity and Mental Therapeutics* (Boston: H. H. Carter and Karrick, 1886).

105. Evans, *Mental-Cure*, 28, 32, 45, 55. Evans was apparently at this date still styling himself a "Reverend" (perhaps an attempt to sell books?), even though it was already five years since he had left the Methodist ministry. Evans's four earlier publications, all published in Boston and none of them explicitly focused on healing, were *Divine Order in the Process of Full Salvation* (1860), *The Happy Islands; or, Paradise Restored* (1860), *The Celestial Dawn; or, Connection of Earth and Heaven* (1862), and *The New Age and Its Messenger* (1864). The "messenger" of the "New Age" (of the Holy Spirit) was Emanuel Swedenborg.

106. For the New Age, see Evans, *Mental-Cure*, 57, 119, 191, 211, 258, passim; for spirits, see, for example, ibid., 79–80, 181, 288, 360; for the Seeress of Prevorst, see ibid., 133, 136, 266, 357; Brittan is cited ibid., 291; for spiritual spheres, see ibid., 70; for death, see ibid., 108; for phrenology and magnetism, see ibid., 102, 273 passim; for modern spiritualism, see ibid., 79–80.

107. Braden, *Spirits in Rebellion*, 93. Gail Thain Parker read Evans rather superficially in terms of these Swedenborgian correspondences, focusing only on *The Mental-Cure* except for some earlier attention to his *New Age and Its Messenger*, ignoring the more complex aspects of Evans's work, and ignoring, even further, the dramatic expansion of his ideas in his five subsequent mental healing books. See Gail Thain Parker, *Mind Cure in New England: From the Civil War to World War I* (Hanover, N.H.: University Press of New England, 1973), 49–56.

108. Evans, *Mental-Cure*, 58–59, 62–63 (emphases in original).

109. Braden, *Spirits in Rebellion*, 91–92, 125; Evans, *Mental-Cure*, 68–69, 261. Braden noted that Evans's reference to Quimby in *Mental Medicine* was evidently the only one in the corpus of his patient-student's work.

110. Teahan, "Warren Felt Evans and Mental Healing," 77 (Teahan also cites the 1850 work by the Rev. William Allen, *The Elements of Christian Science*, which likewise used the term but in a different context); Evans, *Mental-Cure*, 264, 263.

111. Evans, *Mental-Cure*, 296–308, 296–97, 305–7.

112. Evans, *Soul and Body*, 3–4, title page, 22–23, 30 (emphases in original). The French title of Kardac's widely influential work is *Le livre des esprits contenant les principes de la doctrine spirite*.

113. See Braden, *Spirits in Rebellion*, 99, for the list, although the characterizations are my own.

114. Evans, *Divine Law of Cure*, 164, 168, as quoted in Braden, *Spirits in Rebellion*, 100 (emphasis in Braden).

115. Braden, *Spirits in Rebellion*, 101–2, with quotations from Evans, *Divine Law of Cure*, esp. 250–52.

116. W[arren]. F[elt]. Evans, *Primitive Mind-Cure: The Nature and Power of Faith; or, Ele-*

mentary Lessons in Christian Philosophy and Transcendental Medicine, 5th ed. (Boston: H. H. Carter and Karrick, 1886), 131, 137 (emphasis in Evans). The quotation was only slightly altered from the text of *Isis Unveiled* (1: 616)—punctuated differently and with the emphases treated differently. For Berkeley, see, e.g., Evans, *Primitive Mind-Cure*, 1, 12; for Emerson, see ibid., 20, 26, 93, 138; for Al-Ghazali, see ibid., 20.

117. Evans, *Primitive Mind-Cure*, 139–40; Edward Bulwer-Lytton, *The Coming Race* (Edinburgh: W. Blackwood, 1871), as quoted in Blavatsky, *Isis Unveiled*, 1: 126.

118. Evans, *Primitive Mind-Cure*, 142–45 (emphases in original).

119. Ibid., 145, 148–49.

120. Ibid., 3, 5, 7, 10 (emphasis in original).

121. Ibid., 87, 160–61 (italics in original), 193.

122. Ibid., 168–69 (emphasis in original), 171. John Teahan notes that ancient Gnosticism first taught a distinction between Jesus and the Christ (see Teahan, "Warren Felt Evans and Mental Healing," 69).

123. Evans, *Esoteric Christianity*, 57 (emphases in original), 53.

124. A Christian Scientist, "Evans's Esoteric Christianity," *Christian Science Journal* 4, no. 5 (August 1886): 105–6; Evans, *Esoteric Christianity*, 28 (emphasis in original).

125. Eddy, *Science of Man*, 5–6; Eddy, *Science and Health with Key to the Scriptures*, 468.

126. Evans, *Esoteric Christianity*, 57, 59, 5, 46–48 (upper case and emphasis in original), 17 (emphasis in original; see, also, 86).

127. For Guy Ballard and Elizabeth Clare Prophet, see ch. 7.

128. Evans, *Esoteric Christianity*, 141–42, 97, 153 (emphasis in original).

129. Braden, *Spirits in Rebellion*, 126–28; Satter, *Each Mind a Kingdom*, 70; Materra, "Women in Early New Thought," 74; Charles Fillmore, as quoted in Judah, *History and Philosophy of the Metaphysical Movements*, 240. To underscore the point regarding Fillmore, one advertisement from 1890 in his *Christian Science Thought*, e.g., offered five of Evans's mental healing books (all but the 1869 *Mental-Cure*). See *Christian Science Thought* 3, no. 5 (September 1890): 13. Fillmore's *Christian Science Thought* was earlier known as *Modern Thought* and later simply as *Thought*. According to H. Taylor Hines, in his unpublished paper "Personality, Service, and the New Thought Woman: The Life and Writings of H. Emilie Cady," Cady especially remembered *Mental Medicine*, *The Divine Law of Cure*, and *Esoteric Christianity and Mental Therapeutics*; Hines cites correspondence from Cady to Lowell Fillmore from 1937 (H. Emilie Cady to Lowell Fillmore, 11 November 1937, Lowell Fillmore Collection, Unity Archives).

130. See Gill, *Mary Baker Eddy*, 158–59, 312. For accounts of the early growth of New Thought in the environs of Boston, see Judah, *History and Philosophy of the Metaphysical Movements*, 169–93; and Braden, *Spirits in Rebellion*, 129–54.

131. Horatio W. Dresser, *A History of the New Thought Movement* (New York: T. Y. Crowell, 1919); Julius A. Dresser, *The True History of Mental Science: A Lecture Delivered at the Church of the Divine Unity*, rev. with additions (Boston: Alfred Budge, 1887); Judah, *History and Philosophy of the Metaphysical Movements*, 170; M[athilda]. J. Barnett, *Practical Metaphysics; or, The True Method of Healing* (Boston: H. H. Carter and Karrick, 1887); W[illiam]. J. Colville, *The Spiritual Science of Health and Heal-*

ing: *Considered in Twelve Lectures, Delivered Inspirationally, by W. J. Colville, in San Francisco and Boston, during 1886* (Chicago: Garden City Publishing, 1887).

132. Braden, *Spirits in Rebellion,* 149; Materra, "Women in Early New Thought," 80, 88, 90.

133. Satter, *Each Mind a Kingdom,* 79–80; J. Gordon Melton, "Emma Curtis Hopkins: A Feminist of the 1880s and Mother of New Thought," in Catherine Wessinger, ed., *Women's Leadership in Marginal Religions: Explorations Outside the Mainstream* (Urbana: University of Illinois Press, 1993), 88–101; Gail M. Harley, *Emma Curtis Hopkins: Forgotten Founder of New Thought* (Syracuse, N.Y.: Syracuse University Press, 2002); Braden, *Spirits in Rebellion,* 143.

134. Useful constructions of Hopkins's life may be found in Harley, *Emma Curtis Hopkins;* Melton, "Emma Curtis Hopkins," 88–101; and Materra, "Women in Early New Thought," 131–44. My own work here and in the following paragraphs especially draws on this last.

135. Satter, *Each Mind a Kingdom,* 81–82; Emma Curtis Hopkins, "Teachers of Metaphysics," *Christian Science Journal* (September 1885), in J. Gordon Melton, ed., *New Thought: A Reader* (Santa Barbara, Calif.: Institute for the Study of American Religion, 1990), 90; Harley, *Emma Curtis Hopkins,* 18–20; Robert Peel, *Mary Baker Eddy: The Years of Trial* (New York: Holt, Rinehart, and Winston, 1971), 179–80.

136. Materra, "Women in Early New Thought," 136–37.

137. As quoted ibid., 140.

138. "Kansas City College of Christian Science," *Christian Science Thought* 2, no. 1 (April 1890): 13.

139. Harley, *Emma Curtis Hopkins,* 35–129.

140. Satter, *Each Mind a Kingdom,* 86–89. Satter read Evans only in terms of his final book *Esoteric Christianity and Mental Therapeutics;* Schoepflin, *Christian Science on Trial,* 91–92. Hopkins, as an Eddy Scientist, accused A. J. Swarts of plagiarism (from Eddy) but later mended fences with him when she moved to Chicago, and she even, for a time, edited his journal. On the spiritualism of the Swartses, see Braude, *Radical Spirits,* 185–86.

141. Emma Curtis Hopkins, *High Mysticism: A Series of Twelve Studies in the Wisdom of the Sages of the Ages* (1924?; rpt., Marina del Rey, Calif.: DeVorss, [1974]); Aldous Huxley, *The Perennial Philosophy* (New York: Harper, 1945). The publishing history of *High Mysticism* (or *Higher Mysticism,* which may have been its original title) is tangled at best. Internal evidence points to 1917 or thereafter as the date of composition (see Hopkins, *High Mysticism,* 133), but the earliest listed edition I can locate — Cornwall Bridge, Conn.: High Watch Fellowship, 1914–1925 — predates the 1917 year. The on-line catalog of the University of California also lists two 1924 editions: New York: E. S. Gorham, 1924; and Baltimore: Williams and Wilkins, 1924. This last lists its title as *Studies in High Mysticism: The Magia Jesu Christi, IV. Faith,* a title important because it suggests that, as Charles Braden categorically stated (*Spirits in Rebellion,* 148), the twelve studies were originally published independently and in different years (supported by the inclusive dates of the High Watch Fellowship listing), thus explaining the 1917 reference and the 1914 first publication date. Note, too, in this last

title the evocation of Jesus as *"Magia,"* pointing to the Hermetic and theosophical influence on the work.

142. Emma Curtis Hopkins, "God's Omnipresence," *Journal of Christian Science* (April 1884), in Melton, ed., *New Thought*, 86; Emma Curtis Hopkins, "Fiat Justitia," *Journal of Christian Science* (November 1884), in Melton, ed., *New Thought*, 88.

143. Harley, *Emma Curtis Hopkins*, 82–83; Melton, "Emma Curtis Hopkins," 93–95; Emma Curtis Hopkins, *The Ministry of the Holy Mother* (Cornwall Bridge, Conn.: Emma Curtis Hopkins Fund, n.d.).

144. See Harley, *Emma Curtis Hopkins*, 11–13.

145. Emma (Curtis) Hopkins, "C. S. Ordination Address," *Christian Science* 1, no. 7 (March 1889): 173–75. I have counted at least five Hopkins ordination addresses, very similar in content, in Ida Nichols's Chicago-based *Christian Science* journal. Besides this first one, they include: Emma (Curtis) Hopkins, "C. S. Ordination Address," *Christian Science* 1, no. 10 (June 1889): 269–74; Emma Curtis Hopkins, "Ordination Address," *Christian Science* 2, no. 11 (July 1890): 342–46; Emma Curtis Hopkins, "Ordination Address," *Christian Science* 3, no. 5 (January 1891): 131–36; and Emma Curtis Hopkins, "Ordination Address," *Christian Science* 4, no. 2 (October 1891): 34–39.

146. Emma Curtis Hopkins, "How to Attain Your Good (n.d.)," in Melton, ed., *New Thought*, 96–100 (emphases in Melton), 103–4.

147. Emma Curtis Hopkins, *Scientific Christian Mental Practice* (1958; rpt., Marina del Rey, Calif.: DeVorss, n.d.), 62–63 (upper case in original), 73, 90 (emphasis in original), 94, 93, 251. There is evidence that individual chapters were first published separately.

148. Hopkins, *High Mysticism*, 33, 43, 32, 108 (on separate publication of the chapters, see n141).

149. Satter, *Each Mind a Kingdom*, esp. 13–14.

150. Materra, "Women in Early New Thought," 300, 302, 9–10, 12, 47, passim.

151. See ibid., 230–32, where Materra cites and quotes these cases.

152. See ibid., 232–34, where Materra cites and quotes these cases.

153. See Satter, *Each Mind a Kingdom*, 200–205; Edward Bellamy, *Looking Backward, 2000–1887* (Boston: Ticknor, 1888).

154. Ralph Waldo Trine, *In Tune with the Infinite; or, Fullness of Peace, Power, and Plenty* (New York: Crowell, 1897); Materra, "Women in Early New Thought," 240, 239, 241–42, 236–38.

155. Donald Meyer, *The Positive Thinkers: A Study of the American Quest for Health, Wealth, and Personal Power from Mary Baker Eddy to Norman Vincent Peale* (1965), 2d ed. as *The Positive Thinkers: Religion as Pop Psychology from Mary Baker Eddy to Oral Roberts* (New York: Pantheon, 1980).

156. Materra, "Women in Early New Thought," 101–2.

157. [Charles Fillmore], "Not an Answer, but an Opportunity," *Thought* 5, no. 11 (February 1894): 454, 454–60 (emphases in original); Materra, "Women in Early New Thought," 291, 299–301, passim.

158. See Materra, "Women in Early New Thought," esp. 302, 106.

159. See Braden, *Spirits in Rebellion*, 323 (upper case in Braden), 259–61; Judah, *History and Philosophy of the Metaphysical Movements*, 240–41.

160. Rev. Solon Lauer, "After Christianity, What?" (1889), as quoted in Judah, *History and Philosophy of the Metaphysical Movements*, 178.

161. Neal Vahle, *The Unity Movement: Its Evolution and Spiritual Teachings* (Philadelphia: Templeton Foundation, 2002), 33; James Gaither, ed., *The Essential Charles Fillmore: Collected Writings of a Missouri Mystic* (Unity Village, Mo.: Unity, 1999), 8. Vahle bases his account on an unidentified New York City newspaper article from 1934 entitled "Unity Founder Tells What It Means" (Charles Fillmore Collection, Unity Archives).

162. [Charles Fillmore], "Spiritualism and Metaphysics," *Modern Thought* 1, no. 5 (August 1889): 8 (emphasis in original).

163. [Fillmore], "Not an Answer but an Opportunity," 456–57; Judah, *History and Philosophy of the Metaphysical Movements*, 248, 235; Braden, *Spirits in Rebellion*, 332–33; Charles Fillmore, *The Twelve Powers of Man* (Kansas City, Mo.: Unity School of Christianity, 1930); Freeman Benjamin Dowd, *The Temple of the Rosy Cross: The Soul, Its Powers, Migrations, and Transmigrations* (San Francisco: Rosy Cross, 1888).

164. Leo-Virgo [Charles Fillmore], "'Let Your Light Shine,'" *Thought* 4, no. 9 (December 1892): 358–59 (emphasis in original); Vahle, *Unity Movement*, 137. On Fillmore's reincarnation beliefs, see Vahle, *Unity Movement*, 63–67, 70; Gaither, ed., *Essential Charles Fillmore*, 387–93; Braden, *Spirits in Rebellion*, 260. For Emma Curtis Hopkins's classes in Kansas City, Missouri, see "Mrs. Hopkins' Primary Class in Kansas City," *Modern Thought* 1, no. 9 (January 1890): 8; "Personal," *Modern Thought* 1, no. 11 (March 1890): 8; "Kansas City College of Christian Science," *Christian Science Thought* 2, no. 1 (April 1890): 13; "The Theological Class in Christian Science," *Christian Science Thought* 2, no. 3 (May 1890): 9. Diane Smith of Membership Services at the Theosophical Society in America, after on-line and microfiche research in the society's records at Wheaton, Illinois (for which I am indebted to her), found membership for only two persons named Fillmore—both in the San Antonio, Texas, lodge and only from February 1920 through June 1921. Neither Cap. Harston D. Fillmore, M.D., nor his wife, Annie A. Fillmore, have any known relationship to Charles and Myrtle Fillmore.

6. METAPHYSICAL ASIA

1. Hamilton Gay Howard, "Psychic Law of Attraction and Repulsion," in "Department of Psychic Experiences," *Metaphysical Magazine* 3, no. 5 (May 1896): 396–404, 402 (emphasis in *Metaphysical Magazine*). The work to which the *Pittsburg Dispatch* writer was alluding was Rama Prasad, *The Science of Breath and the Philosophy of the Tatwas: (Translated from the Sanskrit) with Fifteen Introductory and Explanatory Essays on Nature's Finer Forces (Eight Re-printed from "The Theosophist," with Modifications, and Seven New* (London: Theosophical Publishing, 1890), which appeared in a second and revised version in London in 1894 as *Nature's Finer Forces: The Science of Breath and the Philosophy of the Tattvas*, edited by G[eorge]. R[obert]. S[tow].

Mead. It is not clear from the context which edition was being cited in the newspaper nor whether the paper was published in Pittsburgh, Pennsylvania, represented in a variant spelling, or a town with a similar name (such as Pittsburg, California, which is northeast of Oakland).

2. Bruce F. Campbell, *Ancient Wisdom Revived: A History of the Theosophical Movement* (Berkeley: University of California Press, 1980), 79; Rama Prasad, *The Science of Breath and the Philosophy of the Tattvas*, 2d ed., ed. G[eorge]. R[obert]. S[tow]. Mead (1894), reprinted as *Nature's Finer Forces: The Science of Breath and Philosophy of the Tattvas* (Whitefish, Mont.: Kessinger, [1997]), 179, 1 (emphasis for "science" in the title is mine); H. P. Blavatsky, *The Secret Doctrine: The Synthesis of Science, Religion, and Philosophy*, 2 vols. (London: Theosophical Publishing, 1888). On Samkhya philosophy, see Edeltraud Harzer, "Samkhya," in Mircea Eliade, ed., *The Encyclopedia of Religion* (New York: Macmillan, 1987), 13: 47–51. I am indebted to my colleague Barbara Holdrege for pointing me toward Samkhya and toward dualism here and elsewhere.

3. See Robert W. Rydell, *All the World's a Fair: Visions of Empire at American International Exhibitions, 1876–1916* (Chicago: University of Chicago Press, 1984); and, with particular application to religion, Richard Hughes Seager, *The World's Parliament of Religions* (Indianapolis: Indiana University Press, 1995); John P. Burris, *Exhibiting Religion: Colonialism and Spectacle at International Expositions, 1851–1893* (Charlottesville: University Press of Virginia, 2001), esp. 86–166.

4. See Carl T. Jackson, *The Oriental Religions and American Thought: Nineteenth-Century Explorations* (Westport, Conn.: Greenwood, 1981), 244–45, 251–52; Sylvia Cranston, *H.P.B.: The Extraordinary Life and Influence of Helena Blavatsky, Founder of the Modern Theosophical Movement* (New York: Putnam's, 1994), 426.

5. Cranston, *H.P.B.*, 426–27; Campbell, *Ancient Wisdom Revived*, 102–3; John Henry Barrows, ed., *The World's Parliament of Religions: An Illustrated and Popular Story of the World's First Parliament of Religions, Held in Chicago in Connection with the Columbian Exposition of 1893*, 2 vols. (Chicago: Parliament Publishing, 1893), 2: 1419; *Chicago Inter-Ocean*, 21 September 1893, as quoted in Robert Peel, *Mary Baker Eddy: The Years of Authority* (New York: Holt, Rinehart, and Winston, 1977), 49.

6. Jackson, *Oriental Religions and American Thought*, 244; Eric J. Ziolkowski, ed., *A Museum of Faiths: Histories and Legacies of the 1893 World's Parliament of Religions* (Atlanta: Scholars Press, 1993), 7; Seager, *World's Parliament of Religions*, 51–52; Barrows, ed., *World's Parliament of Religions*, 2: 1419.

7. Barrows, ed., *World's Parliament of Religions*, 1: 3, viii–ix, 18.

8. Ibid., 1: 18; see Seager, *World's Parliament of Religions*, esp. 103–20.

9. See Stephen Prothero, *The White Buddhist: The Asian Odyssey of Henry Steel Olcott* (Bloomington: Indiana University Press, 1996), esp. 5–10, 176–82.

10. Henry Steel Olcott, *A Buddhist Catechism, According to the Canon of the Southern Church* (Colombo, Ceylon: Theosophical Society, Buddhist Section, 1881); Blavatsky, *Secret Doctrine*, see n2 above.

11. Campbell, *Ancient Wisdom Revived*, 48 (emphasis in original), 40–41.

12. Ibid., 41–42; Alvin Boyd Kuhn, *Theosophy: A Modern Revival of Ancient Wisdom*

(New York: Henry Holt, 1930), 195; H. P. Blavatsky, *The Secret Doctrine: The Synthesis of Science, Religion, and Philosophy*, 2 vols. (1888; rpt., Los Angeles: Theosophy Company, 1974), 1: xxii (all subsequent references are to this edition). Blavatsky's nineteenth-century sources were available in their earliest editions as H[orace]. H[ayman]. Wilson, *The Vishnu Puráná: A System of Hindu Mythology and Tradition* (London: J. Murray, 1840); Alexander Winchell, *World-Life; or, Comparative Geology* (Chicago: S. C. Griggs, 1883); John Dowson, *A Classical Dictionary of Hindu Mythology and Religion, Geography, History, and Literature* (London: Trübner, 1879).

13. It is beyond my scope here to evaluate Coleman's evidence. However, on a much smaller matter—Coleman's charge in a short essay that Blavatsky "largely" plagiarized from Ignatius Donnelly's *Atlantis: The Antediluvian World* (New York: Harper, 1882) and that she "coolly appropriated" a significant series of "detailed evidences" on the relationships between Eastern and Atlantean civilizations without giving Donnelly credit—my own comparison of Donnelly and Blavatsky suggests something different. Reading Donnelly's part 3, chapter 4, against Blavatsky's *Secret Doctrine* has revealed a comprehensive reliance not merely on this Donnelly chapter but on the whole of his book. Nor was I able to locate clear verbal dependence in a three-page series of items to which Coleman pointed, even as Blavatsky's series was different from Donnelly's. Moreover, Blavatsky quoted Donnelly once and cited him twice more. What she did not do was to credit Donnelly as her source when she cited another author purely from a quotation in Donnelly. See William Emmette Coleman, "The Sources of Madame Blavatsky's Writings," Appendix C, in Vsevolod Servyeevich Solovyoff, *A Modern Priestess of Isis*, trans. Walter Leaf (London: Longmans Green, 1895), 358. For a more extensive discussion, see Catherine L. Albanese, "Dissident History: American Religious Culture and the Emergence of the Metaphysical Tradition," in Walter H. Conser Jr. and Sumner B. Twiss, eds., *Religious Diversity and American Religious History: Studies in Traditions and Cultures* (Athens: University of Georgia Press, 1997), 186 n72.

14. Blavatsky, *Secret Doctrine*, 1: xlvi (upper case in original).

15. Ibid., 1: 285.

16. Ibid., 1: 1–2 (upper case in original).

17. Ibid., 1: 1, xxxv; Kuhn, *Theosophy*, 194.

18. Jackson, *Oriental Religions and American Thought*, 167 (emphases in original); Blavatsky, *Secret Doctrine*, 1: 14 (upper case in original), 16–19.

19. Blavatsky, *Secret Doctrine*, 1: xxxvi, 27–29, 33 (upper case in original); Kuhn, *Theosophy*, 201.

20. For a brief and useful summary, see Thomas J. Hopkins, *The Hindu Religious Tradition* (Encino, Calif.: Dickenson, 1971), 100–101.

21. Blavatsky, *Secret Doctrine*, 1: 645 (upper case in original), 644, 377, xliv, 612, 378 (emphasis and upper case in original), xliii. Blavatsky's source, she claimed, was Yamadeva Modelyar.

22. Blavatsky, *Secret Doctrine* 1: 158–59 (emphasis and upper case in original).

23. Ibid., 1: 160, 2: 6, 164, 7–8; Campbell, *Ancient Wisdom Revived*, 44; Albanese, "Dissident History," 177.

24. Jules Verne, *Twenty Thousand Leagues under the Sea; or, The Marvellous and Exciting Adventures of Pierre Aronnax, Conseil His Servant, and Ned Land, a Canadian Harpooner* (Boston: G. M. Smith, 1873); Edward Bulwer-Lytton, *The Coming Race* (Edinburgh and London: W. Blackwood, 1871) (the work was also published in New York and Toronto the same year); Donnelly, *Atlantis* (see n13 above); Albanese, "Dissident History," 172–75. For Donnelly's political career, see Martin Ridge, *Ignatius Donnelly: The Portrait of a Politician* (Chicago: University of Chicago Press, 1962); and David D. Anderson, *Ignatius Donnelly* (Boston: Twayne, 1980).

25. On Sclater, see C. Brown Goode, ed., *The Published Writings of Philip Lutley Sclater, 1844–1896*, Smithsonian Institution, Bulletin of the United States National Museum, No. 49 (Washington, D.C.: Government Printing Office, 1896), xvi–xix; Ernst Haeckel, *The History of Creation; Or, The Development of the Earth and Its Inhabitants by the Action of Natural Causes*, trans. and rev. by E. Ray Lankester, 2 vols. (New York: D. Appleton, 1876), 1: 361, 2: 325–26, 399; Albanese, "Dissident History," 178–79.

26. Blavatsky, *Secret Doctrine*, 2: 227, 785, 273, 286, 350, 319 (emphases and upper case in original); see, also, Albanese, "Dissident History," 177–78.

27. Blavatsky, *Secret Doctrine*, 2: 483–84, 1: 192–93, 274, 639 (emphasis and upper case in original), 2: 305, 1: 639 (emphases in original); see, too, Campbell, *Ancient Wisdom Revived*, 47–48.

28. Blavatsky, *Secret Doctrine*, 1: 152–54, 2: 593, 596, 604, 605–11; A[lfred]. P[ercy]. Sinnett, *Esoteric Buddhism* (London: Trübner, 1883). Blavatsky introduced some confusion in her listings regarding the hierarchical placement of the astral and life bodies, and she reversed them in different lists.

29. Kuhn, *Theosophy*, 214; Blavatsky, *Secret Doctrine*, 1: 178, 2: 102–3, 1: 631, 179, 175, 2: 185 (emphases and upper cases in original).

30. Kuhn, *Theosophy*, 214–15.

31. On misreadings, or "misprisions," see Harold Bloom, *Agon: Towards a Theory of Revisionism* (New York: Oxford University Press, 1982), esp. 16–51.

32. J. Campbell VerPlanck, "A Theosophical Catechism: For the Use of Children, Lesson I," *The Path* 5, no. 7 (October 1890): 213–16; J. Campbell VerPlanck, "A Theosophical Catechism: For the Use of Children, Lesson II," *The Path* 5, no. 8 (November 1890): 249–51; "A Theosophical Catechism: For the Use of Children, Lesson III," *The Path* 5, no. 10 (January 1891): 304–7.

33. "American Branches: Theosophical Society," *The Path* 4, no. 12 (March 1890): 390; "American Branches: Theosophical Society," *The Path* 5, no. 12 (March 1891): 394–95; "Sixteenth Annual Convention," ibid., 405; "American Branches: Theosophical Society," *The Path* 6, no. 12 (March 1892): 408–9; "American Branches: Theosophical Society," *The Path* 8, no. 3 (June 1893): 94–96; "American Branches: Theosophical Society," *The Path* 9, no. 2 (May 1894): 66–68.

34. See Campbell, *Ancient Wisdom Revived*, 103–11; Cranston, *H.P.B.*, 45.

35. Ralph Waldo Emerson, "The Over-Soul," in Ralph Waldo Emerson, *The Collected Works of Ralph Waldo Emerson*, vol. 2, *Essays: First Series*, ed. Joseph Slater et al.

(Cambridge, Mass.: Harvard University Press, 1979), 159, 175; see Frederic Ives Carpenter, *Emerson and Asia* (Cambridge: Harvard University Press, 1930), esp. 75–78, where he demonstrates clearly that Asia entered the Emersonian equation as a corroborating, not first, voice. By 1861, at least one entry in Emerson's journal in language strikingly reminiscent of the Oversoul would invoke "Hindoo theology" and its goal of restoring "that bond by which their own self (atman) was linked to the Eternal *Self* (paramatman)." For the earlier Emerson, the language of the Self was not to be found. See Ralph Waldo Emerson, *The Complete Works of Ralph Waldo Emerson*, ed. Edward Waldo Emerson (Boston: Houghton, Mifflin, 1903–6), 6: 426n (emphasis in original). See, also, Carpenter, *Emerson and Asia*, 123, where after "(paramatman)," he interpolated in square brackets "[i.e. Over-Soul]." In so doing, Carpenter echoed Emerson's son and editor Edward Waldo Emerson, who preceded his quotation from Emerson's 1861 journal entry with a discussion that linked it to the Oversoul (Emerson, *Complete Works*, 6: 425n).

36. William Harding and Carl Bode, eds., *The Correspondence of Henry David Thoreau* (New York: New York University Press, 1958), 251, as quoted in Jackson, *Oriental Religions and American Thought*, 65; Henry D. Thoreau, *Walden*, ed. J. Lyndon Shanley (Princeton: Princeton University Press, 1971), 4, 8, 96 (emphasis in original), 298, 112. Arthur E. Christy long ago acknowledged Thoreau's yogic consciousness in *The Orient in American Transcendentalism: A Study of Emerson, Thoreau, and Alcott* (1932; rpt., New York: Octagon, 1963), 199.

37. The unqualified attribution has in the past been made regarding his spirituality. In a series of articles in the 1960s and early 1970s, English scholar William Bysshe Stein made the connection, discovering Thoreau at his yogic exercises virtually everywhere and every time. See William Bysshe Stein, "Thoreau's *Walden* and the *Bhagavad Gita*," *Topic* 3 (1963): 38–55; Stein, "Thoreau's First Book, A Spoor of Yoga: The Orient in *A Week on the Concord and Merrimack Rivers*," *Emerson Society Quarterly* 41 (1965): 3–25; Stein, "The Yoga of *Walden*: Chapter 1 ('Economy')," *Literature East and West* 8, nos. 1 & 2 (June 1969): 1–26; Stein, "The Hindu Matrix of *Walden*: The King's Son," *Comparative Literature* 22, no. 4 (Fall 1970): 303–18; Stein, "Thoreau's *A Week* and *Om* Cosmography," *American Transcendental Quarterly* 11 (1971): 15–37. See, also, Jackson, *Oriental Religions and American Thought*, esp. 65–66, for a yogic reading of Thoreau.

38. Henry D. Thoreau, *A Week on the Concord and Merrimack Rivers*, ed. Carl F. Hovde et al. (Princeton: Princeton University Press, 1980), 136; Arthur Versluis, *American Transcendentalism and Asian Religions* (New York: Oxford University Press, 1993), 84. For Unitarian moralism, see Daniel Walker Howe, *The Unitarian Conscience: Harvard Moral Philosophy, 1805–1861* (Cambridge: Harvard University Press, 1970). And for an essentially Christianizing reading of Thoreau, see William J. Wolf, *Thoreau: Mystic, Prophet, Ecologist* (Philadelphia: Pilgrim, 1974).

39. Lydia Maria Child, *The Progress of Religious Ideas, through Successive Ages*, 3 vols. (New York: Francis, 1855); Hannah Adams, *A Dictionary of All Religions and Religious Denominations, Jewish, Heathen, Mahometan, and Christian, Ancient and Modern*

(New York: James Eastburn, and Boston: Cummings and Hilliard, 1817). Quotations are from the following edition of Child's work: Lydia Maria Child, *The Progress of Religious Ideas, through Successive Ages*, 4th ed. (New York: James Miller, 1855), 1: viii, 10–11, 23. For the index, see 3: 465–78.

40. James Freeman Clarke, *Ten Great Religions: An Essay in Comparative Theology* (1871), 34th ed. (Boston: Houghton, Mifflin, 1895), 519–28, 83.

41. Charles Darwin, *On the Tendency of Species to Form Varieties; and On the Perpetuation of Varieties and Species by Natural Means of Selection* (London: [Linnaean Society of London], 1858); Ralph Waldo Emerson, *Nature* (1836), in Emerson, *Collected Works*, vol. 1, *Nature, Addresses, and Lectures*, ed. Alfred R. Ferguson (Cambridge, Mass.: Harvard University Press, 1971), 7.

42. H. P. Blavatsky, *Isis Unveiled: A Master-Key to the Mysteries of Ancient and Modern Science and Theology* (1877; rpt., Los Angeles: Theosophy Company, 1975), 2: 566n, 565, 612, 620, 346; Blavatsky, *Secret Doctrine*, 1: 43, 132, 158, 293, 2: 296, 568 (upper case in original), 1: 47, 95 (emphasis in original).

43. Helena P. Blavatsky, *The Key to Theosophy: Being a Clear Exposition, in the Form of Question and Answer, of the Ethics, Science, and Philosophy for the Study of Which the Theosophical Society Has Been Founded* (London: Theosophical Publishing, 1889); quotations are from H. P. Blavatsky, *The Key to Theosophy: An Abridgement*, ed. Joy Mills (Wheaton, Ill.: Theosophical Publishing, Quest, 1972), 56, 63, 74, 81, 83 (emphases and upper case in original).

44. William Quan Judge, *The Yoga Aphorisms of Patanjali: An Interpretation*, trans. J[ames]. H[enderson]. Connelly (New York: Path, 1889); James Henderson Connelly was listed explicitly as translator in the *New York Times*, 10 June 1889, p. 3, col. 1; quotations are from William Q. Judge, *The Yoga Aphorisms of Patanjali* (1889; rpt., Los Angeles: Theosophy Company, 1973), viii–ix, 33–34, ix. Elizabeth De Michelis has argued against the easy identification of raja yoga with the Patanjali *Yoga Sutras*, calling it a "modern accretion" and identifying the Theosophical Society as the earliest group to make the connection (see Elizabeth De Michelis, *A History of Modern Yoga: Patanjali and Western Esotericism* [London: Continuum, 2004], 178).

45. Judge, *Yoga Aphorisms* (1973), 30–31, 61, xvi, 57, xiv–xv.

46. *New York Times*, 10 June 1889, p. 3, col. 1; J. Gordon Melton, "Yoga," in J. Gordon Melton, with Jerome Clark and Aidan A. Kelly, ed., *New Age Encyclopedia* (Detroit: Gale, 1990), 502. I am indebted to Melton's essay for my own initial construction of the late-nineteenth-century and early-twentieth-century history of American yoga.

47. See W. Michael Ashcraft, *The Dawn of the New Cycle: Point Loma Theosophists and American Culture* (Knoxville: University of Tennessee Press, 2002), 85–107, 95, 102. I am indebted to Sarah Whedon for bringing this work to my attention.

48. De Michelis, *History of Modern Yoga*, 112–13, 124–25, 149–50 (where De Michelis sifts the evidence for *Raja-Yoga*'s oral origins). I am grateful to David White for information on the absence of raja yoga from the *Yoga Sutras*.

49. See Swami Vivekananda, *The Complete Works of Swami Vivekananda*, Mayavati Memorial Edition, 14th ed. (Calcutta: Advaita Ashrama, 1973); De Michelis, *History of Modern Yoga*; Wouter J. Hanegraaff, *New Age Religion and Western Culture:*

Esotericism in the Mirror of Secular Thought (Leiden: E. J. Brill, 1996), 521–22. De Michelis herself is a British scholar.

50. De Michelis, *History of Modern Yoga*, 97–108, 49, 47.

51. Swami Vivekananda, *Raja-Yoga*, in Swami Vivekananda, *The Complete Works of Swami Vivekananda*, Mayavati Memorial Edition, vol. 1 (1907; 12th ed., Calcutta: Advaita Ashrama, 1965), 125–26.

52. Ibid., 139, 149–50, 168; De Michelis, *History of Modern Yoga*, 130–32, 151, 153, 159–75, 168.

53. Vivekananda, *Raja Yoga*, 160–62, 164–65; see, also, 168, 170.

54. Vivekananda, *Raja Yoga*, 138; De Michelis, *History of Modern Yoga*, 90, 1–9, 182.

55. *New York Times*, 15 October 1893, p. 22, col. 1.

56. Melton, "Yoga," 502.

57. Gary Ward Materra, "Women in Early New Thought: Lives and Theology in Transition, from the Civil War to World War I" (Ph.D. diss., University of California, Santa Barbara, 1997); William Walker Atkinson, *The Law of the New Thought: A Study of Fundamental Principles and Their Application* (Chicago: Psychic Research, 1902); William Walker Atkinson, *Thought-Force in Business and Everyday Life: Being a Series of Lessons in Personal Magnetism, Psychic Influence, Thought-Force, Concentration, Will Power, and Practical Mental Science*, 18th ed. (New York: S. Flower, 1903); William Walker Atkinson, *Dynamic Thought; or, The Law of Vibrant Energy* (Los Angeles: Segnogram, 1906); William Walker Atkinson, *Self-Healing by Thought Force* (Chicago: Library Shelf, 1907); William Walker Atkinson, *The Inner Consciousness: A Course of Lessons on the Inner Planes of the Mind, Intuition, Instinct, Automatic Mentation, and Other Wonderful Phases of Mental Phenomena* (Chicago: Advanced Thought, 1908); William Walker Atkinson, *The Secret of Success: A Course of Nine Lessons on the Subject of the Application of the Latent Powers of the Individual toward the Attainment of Success in Life* (Chicago: Advanced Thought, 1908); William Walker Atkinson, *The Will: Its Nature, Power, and Development* (Chicago: Progress, 1909); William Walker Atkinson, *Mind and Body; or, Mental States and Physical Conditions* (Chicago: Progress, 1910); William Walker Atkinson, *Mind-Power: The Secret of Mental Magic* (Chicago: Advanced Thought, 1912).

58. Yogi Ramacharaka, *Advanced Course in Yogi Philosophy and Oriental Occultism* (Chicago: Yogi Publication Society, 1905); Yogi Ramacharaka, *Hatha Yoga; or, The Yogi Philosophy of Physical Well-Being* (Chicago: Yogi Publication Society, 1904); Yogi Ramacharaka, *Science of Breath: A Complete Manual of the Oriental Breathing Philosophy of Physical, Mental, Psychic, and Spiritual Development* (Chicago: Yogi Publication Society, 1905); Yogi Ramacharaka, *A Series of Lessons in Raja Yoga* (Chicago: Yogi Publication Society, 1906); Yogi Ramacharaka, *The Science of Psychic Healing* (Chicago: Yogi Publication Society, 1906); Melton, "Yoga," 502; Mabel Collins, *Light on the Path: A Treatise Written for the Personal Use of Those Who Are Ignorant of the Eastern Wisdom, and Who Desire to Enter within Its Influence* (Boston: Cupples, Upham, 1886). Collins was a novelist and the co-editor of the London theosophical journal *Lucifer*, and—after first claiming Helena Blavatsky's Mahatma Koot Hoomi (Koot-Hoomi Lal Singh) or another Hindu adept as author—she subsequently de-

clared that she merely wrote down the words of the treatise as she saw them "written on the walls of a place I visit spiritually." See Cranston, *H.P.B.*, 371; and Kuhn, *Theosophy*, 301.

59. Yogi Ramacharaka, *A Series of Lessons in Raja Yoga* (Chicago: Yogi Publication Society, 1906), 197, 198, 216, 217–18, 202.

60. Ibid., vi, 1–3. For the Emersonianism, see Emerson, *Nature*, 23–29, 42–43, 8.

61. Theodore Roosevelt, *The Strenuous Life: Essays and Addresses* (New York: Century, 1901); "Back to Nature," *Outlook* 74 (8 June 1903): 305–6, as quoted in Clifford Putney, *Muscular Christianity: Manhood and Sports in Protestant America, 1880–1920* (Cambridge, Mass.: Harvard University Press, 2001), 35 (see Putney, *Muscular Christianity*, 33–39, for a useful general discussion of these themes); James C. Whorton, *Crusaders for Fitness: The History of American Health Reformers* (Princeton: Princeton University Press, 1982), 281–82.

62. Yogi Ramacharaka, *Hatha Yoga*, 9–10, 11, 13, 195 (emphasis and upper case in original).

63. Ibid., 17–18, 11–13.

64. Ibid., 232–33, 211–13.

65. My account of Bernard's life is based on J. Gordon Melton, "Pierre Bernard," in Melton et al., *New Age Encyclopedia*, 64–65; Hugh B. Urban, "The Omnipotent Oom: Tantra and Its Impact on Modern Western Esotericism," *Esoterica* 3 (2001): 218–59, www.esoteric.msu.edu/VolumeIII/HTML/Oom.html; [Nik Douglas?], "The Library of Pierre Arnold Bernard," www.vanderbilt.edu/~stringer/library.htm, and, especially helpful, a lecture by Paul G. Hackett, "Theos Bernard and the Early History of Tibetan Studies in America," University of California, Santa Barbara, 13 January 2006. Hackett also confirmed details concerning the life of Pierre Bernard and Theos Bernard in e-mail communications on 30 March 2006 and 31 March 2006.

66. "The Library of Pierre Arnold Bernard"; Melton, "Pierre Bernard," 65; Pierre Arnold Bernard, *International Journal of the Tantrik Order in America*, as quoted, with illustration reproduced, in Urban, "Omnipotent Oom"; Charles Boswell, "The Great Fuss and Fume over the Omnipotent Oom," *True: The Man's Magazine* (January 1965): 86. So far as I can tell, Bernard's published writing was confined to the single issue of his journal; on the differences between American and traditional Indian tantra, see Urban, "Omnipotent Oom," esp. 34–38.

67. Theos Bernard, *Hatha Yoga: The Report of a Personal Experience* (London and New York: Rider, 1950), with bibliography 97–99; John George Woodroffe [Arthur Avalon], *The Serpent Power; Being the Sat-Cakra-Nirupana and Paduka-Pañcaka: Two Works on Laya-Yoga* (London: Luzac, 1919). Arthur Avalon was actually a composite—not merely a pseudonym for Sir John Woodroffe as long thought, but a collaboration of Woodroffe and one Atul Behari Ghosh, a Bengali and Tantric scholar; see Kathleen Taylor, *Sir John Woodroffe, Tantra, and Bengal: "An Indian Soul in a European Body"?* (Richmond, Surrey, Eng.: Curxon, 2001). I am indebted to Jeffrey Kripal for this information.

68. Bernard, *Hatha Yoga*, ix, 15.

69. Ibid., 35.

70. Ibid., 75–96, 96. For Hackett, see n65 above.

71. J. Gordon Melton, "Shri Yogendra," in Melton et al., *New Age Encyclopedia*, 511; on Yogendra, see the hagiographic biography by Vijayadev Yogendra, *Shri Yogendra: The Householder Yogi* (Santa Cruz: Yoga Institute, 1977), 56, 67, passim. Vijayadev Yogendra stated that the Yoga Institute was founded at Bear Mountain, near Tuxedo Park, New York, in 1920 (*Shri Yogendra*, 64), and, indeed, Shri Yogendra did work in New York for a time. But Shri Yogendra himself identified Santa Cruz as the place where he founded the American Yoga Institute. See Shri Yogendra, *Yoga Asanas Simplified*, 7th ed. (Bombay: Yoga Institute, 1958), 10. For another hagiographic biography, useful for its transcription of primary sources, see Santan Rodrigues, *The Householder Yogi: Life of Shri Yogendra* (1982; rpt., Santa Cruz: Yoga Institute, 1997).

72. Yogendra, *Yoga Asanas Simplified*, 7, 9, 166 (emphases in original); Vijayadev Yogendra, *Shri Yogendra*, 67.

73. Shri Yogendra, *Why Yoga* (Santa Cruz: Yoga Institute, 1976), 20 (emphasis in original), 53, 51; Melton, "Yoga," 503.

74. See Melton, "Shri Yogendra," 511; Yogendra, *Why Yoga*, 54.

75. Paramahansa Yogananda, *Autobiography of a Yogi* (1946; rpt., Los Angeles: Self-Realization Fellowship, 1998).

76. For the classic description (for the uninitiated), see ibid., esp. 275–86.

77. Paramahansa Yogananda, *The Science of Religion*, rev. and exp. ed. (1924; rpt., Los Angeles: Self-Realization Fellowship, 2001), vii–viii, 61, 67 (emphases in original).

78. Yogananda, *Autobiography of a Yogi*, 288–89 (emphases in original). As for the fabled Pierre Bernard and for a string of Hindu gurus to the West, Yogananda now comes with a sex scandal attached to his name, since an elderly miner from Oregon has claimed to be his son and since Yogananda reportedly had a series of relationships with women despite his celibate swami vows. (See Carter Phipps, "In Search of Babaji," *What Is Enlightenment?* [Spring/Summer 2002]: 85; Phipps cites an interview with Marshall Govindan as well as an investigative report in the *New Times* of Los Angeles.)

79. B. K. S. Iyengar, *Light on Yoga* (New York: Schocken, 1966); for a searching analysis of Iyengar's thought and its impact, see De Michelis, *History of Modern Yoga*, 194–274.

80. On the Maharishi, see Catherine L. Albanese, *America: Religions and Religion*, 3d ed. (Belmont, Calif.: Wadsworth, 1999), 306–7; on Siddha Yoga, see Douglas Renfrew Brooks et al., *Meditation Revolution: A History and Theology of the Siddha Yoga Lineage* (South Fallsburg, N.Y.: Agama, 1997), esp. the introduction by Brooks, xix–xli, xxxvii; and, for the most responsible and believable account of Muktananda's tantra, Sarah Caldwell, "The Heart of the Secret: A Personal and Scholarly Encounter with Shakta Tantrism in Siddha Yoga," *Nova Religio* 5, no. 1 (October 2001): 9–51.

81. On Esalen, see Walter Truett Anderson, *The Upstart Spring: Esalen and the American Awakening* (Reading, Mass.: Addison-Wesley, 1983); George Leonard, *Walking on the Edge of the World: A Memoir of the Sixties and Beyond* (Boston: Houghton Mifflin, 1988), esp. 107–248; and Jeffrey J. Kripal and Glenn W. Shuck, eds., *On the Edge of the Future: Esalen and the Evolution of American Culture* (Bloomington: Indiana University Press, 2005).

82. See David Gordon White, *The Alchemical Body: Siddha Traditions in Medieval India*

(Chicago: University of Chicago Press, 1996), 140–42; Georg Feuerstein, *The Yoga Tradition: Its History, Literature, Philosophy, and Practice* (Prescott, Ariz.: Hohm, 2001), 382–87; and De Michelis, *History of Modern Yoga*.

83. Hannah Adams, *An Alphabetical Compendium of the Various Sects Which Have Appeared from the Beginning of the Christian Era to the Present Day* (Boston: B. Edes, 1784); Hannah Adams, *A View of Religions, in Two Parts* (Boston: J. W. Folsom, 1791); Hannah Adams, *A View of Religions, in Two Parts* (Boston: Manning and Loring, 1801); Adams, *Dictionary of All Religions* (1817). For a discussion of Adams and the publishing history of her book, see Thomas A. Tweed, "Introduction," in Hannah Adams, *A Dictionary of All Religions and Religious Denominations, Jewish, Heathen, Mahometan, Christian, Ancient and Modern* (1817; rpt., Atlanta: Scholars Press, 1992), vii–xvi, xxxviii.

84. Adams, *Dictionary of All Religions* (1992), 46, 49, 55–56, 288–90.

85. [Elizabeth Palmer Peabody, trans.], "The Preaching of the Buddha," *The Dial* 4 (January 1844): 391–401; Ralph Waldo Emerson to Elizabeth Hoar, 17 June 1845, in Ralph L. Rusk, ed., *The Letters of Ralph Waldo Emerson*, 6 vols. (New York: Columbia University Press, 1939), 3: 290. On the identification of Peabody as translator of the excerpt of the Lotus Sutra in *The Dial*, see Thomas A. Tweed, *The American Encounter with Buddhism, 1844–1912: Victorian Culture and the Limits of Dissent*, 2d ed. (Chapel Hill: University of North Carolina Press, 2000), xvi–xvii.

86. Noah Webster, *An American Dictionary of the English Language* (1849), and Noah Webster, *An American Dictionary of the English Language* (1864), as quoted in Thomas A. Tweed and Stephen Prothero, eds., *Asian Religions in America: A Documentary History* (New York: Oxford University Press, 1999), 111; Clarke, *Ten Great Religions*, 139, 142–43, 156–57, 168–69.

87. Jackson, *Oriental Religions and American Thought*, 141, 152; Tweed, *American Encounter with Buddhism*, 80.

88. Jackson, *Oriental Religions and American Thought*, 144, 143; Tweed, *American Encounter with Buddhism*, 46.

89. Edwin Arnold, *The Light of Asia* (1879; rpt., Whitefish, Mont.: Kessinger, n.d.), 12–13, 16–17, 19–21, 23, 26, 55, 92, 98, 101–2, 106. On the sale of Arnold's work, see the estimate given by his biographer Brooks Wright, *Interpreter of Buddhism to the West: Sir Edwin Arnold* (New York: Bookman Associates, 1957), 75; and see Tweed, *American Encounter with Buddhism*, 29, where he cites Wright.

90. Arnold, *Light of Asia*, 112, 124, 130, 133–34, 143, 149.

91. Ibid., 154, 156–57, 164–70 (emphasis and upper case in original), 174, 179, 184, 208, 211, 214.

92. As quoted in Cranston, *H.P.B.*, 428 (Cranston gives the source as the Canadian periodical *The Lamp* for December 1895 and the original from the *Alliance Forum*); ibid., 429.

93. Henry Steel Olcott, *Old Diary Leaves: The History of the Theosophical Society, Third Series, 1883–87* (1904; rpt., Wheaton, Ill.: Theosophical Publishing, 1972), 166–67, 353–54; Henry Steel Olcott, *Old Diary Leaves: The History of the Theosophical Society, Sixth Series (April, 1896–September, 1898)* (1935; rpt., Wheaton, Ill.: Theo-

sophical Publishing, 1975), 175; Campbell, *Ancient Wisdom Revived*, 84; Henry Steel Olcott, *Old Diary Leaves: The History of the Theosophical Society, Fourth Series, 1887–92* (1910; rpt., Wheaton, Ill.: Theosophical Publishing, 1975), 51; Henry Steel Olcott, *Old Diary Leaves: The History of the Theosophical Society, Fifth Series (January, 1893–April, 1896)* (1932; rpt., Wheaton, Ill.: Theosophical Publishing, 1975), 424. The edition of the *Buddhist Catechism* that I have used (Henry S. Olcott, *The Buddhist Catechism* [Wheaton, Ill.: Theosophical Publishing, 1970]) announces on the reverse of its title page that it is the forty-fifth edition. Stephen Prothero, in his *White Buddhist*, reports that he was working from an Adyar edition of 1947 that was the forty-seventh (ibid., 205 n21, 223), so some discrepancy remains about how editions were counted. Prothero also says that there were translations "into over twenty languages," but Olcott's statement of "nearly twenty" came in 1895, twelve years before his death.

94. Prothero, *White Buddhist*, 10, 101; Olcott, *Old Diary Leaves: Fourth Series*, 355–56; Henry Steel Olcott, *A Buddhist Catechism, According to the Canon of the Southern Church*, ed. with notes by Elliott Coues (Boston: Estes and Lauriat, 1885); Henry Steel Olcott, *A Buddhist Catechism, According to the Cannon of the Southern Church*, 3d ed., ed. with notes by Elliott Coues (Boston: Estes and Lauriat, 1887); Henry S. Olcott, *The Buddhist Catechism* (New York: "Theosophist" Office, 1897); Henry S. Olcott, *The Buddhist Catechism* (Talent, Oreg.: Eastern School, 1915). Sylvia Cranston describes Elliott Coues as a "professor" and "scientist" as well as, at various points in his career, "an anatomist, a historian, a naturalist, and an ornithologist." He founded a Washington, D.C., lodge of the Theosophical Society but later became embroiled in theosophical politics and intrigues and was expelled from the society in 1889 (see Cranston, *H.P.B.*, 262, 270, 370–73). My own used copy of *The Buddhist Catechism* contains, on its inside front cover, a handwritten inscription from a man to his wife (both named), dated 1971 and suggestive of the devotional ambience that came to surround the work: "May this catechism be a comfort to you and prosper you in Joy, Happiness, and Serenity as you practice your mastery of the Supreme Dharma."

95. Henry Steele [*sic*] Olcott, *Old Diary Leaves: The Only Authentic History of the Theosophical Society, Second Series, 1878–83* (1900; rpt., Adyar, India: Theosophical Publishing, 1954), 167–69; Olcott, *Old Diary Leaves: Fourth Series*, 41–44.

96. Prothero, *White Buddhist*, 101–3, 103; Olcott, *Old Diary Leaves*, 128.

97. Olcott, *Buddhist Catechism* (1970), 1–2, 97, 4–5, 15, 21 (all subsequent quotations are from this edition); I borrow the term "lived religion" from David D. Hall, ed., *Lived Religion in America: Toward a History of Practice* (Princeton: Princeton University Press, 1997).

98. Olcott, *Buddhist Catechism*, 53–54, 56, 57, 59, 93 (emphases in original; questions were italicized by Olcott's printers).

99. Ibid., 112–15 (emphases in original).

100. Ibid., 117–20, 123, 124 (emphases in original).

101. Ibid., 99–100, 101 (emphases in original).

102. I have based this summary on entries from the World Catalog Data Base, representing the Union Catalog of approximately twelve thousand libraries worldwide.

103. A[lfred]. P[ercy]. Sinnett, *Esoteric Buddhism*, 5th ed. (1885; rpt., San Diego: Wizards, 1987), xvi, xx, xxii, 8, 239, passim (all subsequent references are to this edition; see, also, in it Sinnett's "Preface to the Annotated Edition," in which he cited "the great Adept himself, from whom I obtained my instruction in the first instance" [v]); Charles J. Ryan, *H. P. Blavatsky and the Theosophical Movement*, 2d and rev. ed., ed. Grace F. Knoche (Pasadena: Theosophical University Press, 1975), 111; on Sinnett, Theosophy, and the Mahatmas, see Campbell, *Ancient Wisdom Revived*, 56–57, where he argues that Blavatsky wrote most of the letters and her "confederates" the rest. The "great Adept" (above) was "Master K. H.," or "Koot-Hoomi Lal Singh"; see A. P. Sinnett, *The Mahatma Letters*, ed. A. T. Barker, 2d ed. (1926; rpt., Pasadena: Theosophical University Press, 1992). The first edition of *The Mahatma Letters* was published posthumously in 1923; the letters themselves came from the period between 1880 and 1884. On Blavatsky's not entirely positive response to the publication of *Esoteric Buddhism*, see the reprinted "Correspondence" appended to Sinnett, *Esoteric Buddhism*, 247–54.

104. Sinnett, *Esoteric Buddhism*, 73–80, 232–34; Olcott, *Buddhist Catechism*, 74–75; Blavatsky, *Isis Unveiled*, 1: 315; Charles Fillmore, *Talks on Truth* (1926) (1934; rpt., Unity Village, Mo.: Unity School of Christianity, [1965]), 167.

105. Sinnett, *Esoteric Buddhism*, xxv, 64–65, 37, 45 (emphasis in original).

106. Ibid., 78–79, 94–95 (emphasis in original), 98. The Mahatma letter, said to be from Koot Hoomi and received in July 1882, quoted a text it named as the *Shan-Mun-yi-Tung*, in which the Buddha told his disciple Sariputra of the "Deva Chan." It was a "region of Bliss called *Sukhavati*," and it was "encircled with *seven* rows of railings, *seven* rows of vast curtains, *seven* rows of waving trees." It was the "holy abode of Arahats" and "possessed by the Bodhisatwas [*sic*]." The Buddha informed them that "myriads of Spirits" went there "for rest" and then returned "*to their own regions*." See A. T. Barker, ed., *The Mahatma Letters to A. P. Sinnett from the Mahatmas M. & K. H.*, 2d ed. (1926; rpt., Pasadena: Theosophical University Press, 1992), 100 (emphases in original; the first edition appeared in 1923); and Vicente Halo Chin Jr., ed., *The Mahatma Letters to A. P. Sinnett from the Mahatmas M. & K. H.*, *Transcribed and Compiled by A. T. Barker, in Chronological Sequence* (Adyar: Theosophical Publishing, 1998), 189–90 (this edition was mostly based on the 3d edition of 1962). The Chinese text, if extant, is obscure: My colleague in Chinese religions, William Powell, has no knowledge of the *Shan-Mun-yi-Tung*. Neither, apparently, did Edward Conze in his bibliography of Buddhist scriptures, nor did Lewis Lancaster (to whom Powell referred me), who revised it. See Edward Conze, *Buddhist Scriptures: A Bibliography*, ed. and rev. Lewis Lancaster (New York: Garland, 1982). My cursory search of Sinnett's listed and textually cited Orientalist sources in available imprints revealed neither references to Devachan nor to Kama loka, although R. Spence Hardy included a number of references to the celestial world of Dewa-loka, which seems a variant of Devachan. See R. Spence Hardy, *A Manual of Budhism* [*sic*], *in its Modern Development*, trans. (from Singhalese mss.) R. Spence Hardy (Varanasi, India: Chowkhamba Sanskrit Series Office, 1967), 2, 5, 24, 25, 28, 33, 103, 126, 448, 472, 476, 489, 491. Also cursorily examined were T. W. Rhys Davids, *Buddhism: A Sketch of the Life and Teach-*

ings of Gautama, the Buddha (London: Society for Promoting Christian Knowledge, 1890, 1903); and Hermann Oldenberg, *Buddha: His Life, His Doctrine, His Order,* trans. William Hoey (1882; rpt., Varanasi, India: Indological Book House, 1971).

107. Sinnett, *Esoteric Buddhism*, 99, 100, 103, 105–8, 110, 78, 118, 121. On kamaloka in Buddhism, see John Bowker, ed., *The Oxford Dictionary of World Religions* (New York: Oxford University Press, 1997), s.v. "Loka" (585).

108. Sinnett, *Esoteric Buddhism*, 171, 174–75, 185. The edition of Rhys Davids that Sinnett listed was T. W. Rhys Davids, *Buddhism: Being a Sketch of the Life and Teachings of Gautama, the Buddha* (New York: Society for Promoting Christian Knowledge, E. and J. B. Young, 1878).

109. Sinnett, *Esoteric Buddhism*, 188–89; *The HarperCollins Dictionary of Religion,* ed. Jonathan Z. Smith (San Francisco: HarperSanFrancisco, 1995), s.v. "nirvana," 785–86; Richard H. Robinson, *The Buddhist Religion: A Historical Introduction* (Belmont, Calif.: Dickenson, 1970), 15.

110. Sinnett, *Esoteric Buddhism*, 189–94.

111. Tweed, *American Encounter with Buddhism*, xxxiii, 31–32, 43, 163–64, 46; Olcott, *Old Diary Leaves: Fourth Series,* 117. My own reading would extend the period of high Buddhist influence back through the 1880s. The context of Olcott's estimate suggests that he was referring to white Christian converts, but—given his enthusiasm for Buddhism—it seems likely that he overestimated.

112. Tweed, *American Encounter with Buddhism*, 75, 51, 60–61, 69, 77.

113. Paul Carus, "Science: A Religious Revelation," in Barrows, ed., *World's Parliament of Religions,* 2: 978–81; for Carus himself, see Tweed and Prothero, *Asian Religions in America,* 148–49.

114. Carus, "Science," 978, 980, 981.

115. Paul Carus, *The Gospel of Buddha* (Chicago: Open Court, 1894); the copy that I have used—from the Davison Library at the University of California, Santa Barbara—announces itself to be the "fifteenth printing"; Tweed, *American Encounter with Buddhism,* 46.

116. Carus, *Gospel of Buddha,* 233–42.

117. Ibid., vi, vii, 3–5.

118. Ibid., 7, 15, 17, 18, 42.

119. Ibid., 43, 65, 199–201, 205, 226.

120. Ibid., 127–28, 130, 133, 229–30.

121. Tweed, *American Encounter with Buddhism*, 158–59.

7. NEW AGES FOR ALL

1. Charles S. Braden, *Spirits in Rebellion: The Rise and Development of New Thought* (Dallas: Southern Methodist University Press, 1963), 167. For Trine's book reflecting his vision of social and political transformation, see Ralph Waldo Trine, *In the Fire of the Heart* (New York: McClure, Phillips, 1906); Trine especially emphasized public utilities and labor.

2. Ralph Waldo Trine, *In Tune with the Infinite; or, Fullness of Peace, Power, and Plenty*

(New York: T. Y. Crowell, 1897); Braden, *Spirits in Rebellion*, 164–65 (Braden did not list the "three or four" other books).

3. See Horatio W. Dresser, *Handbook of the New Thought* (New York: Putnam's, 1917), 26–50, esp. 34 ff., 44, 47; and J. Stillson Judah, *The History and Philosophy of the Metaphysical Movements in America* (Philadelphia: Westminster, 1967), 189–90.

4. Ralph Waldo Emerson, *Nature*, in Ralph Waldo Emerson, *The Collected Works of Ralph Waldo Emerson*, ed. Alfred R. Ferguson et al., vol. 1 (Cambridge, Mass.: Harvard University Press, 1971), 44; Andrew Jackson Davis, *The Fountain; With Jets of New Meanings* (Boston: W. White, 1870).

5. Ralph Waldo Trine, *In Tune with the Infinite* (Indianapolis: Bobbs-Merrill, 1970), 15, 17–18, 19 (emphasis in original), 26, 35 (emphasis in original). All subsequent quotations are to this edition. On harmonialism, see Sydney E. Ahlstrom, *A Religious History of the American People* (New Haven: Yale University Press, 1972), 1019–20. Taylor S. Hines, in his unpublished paper "Personality, Service, and the New Thought Woman: The Life and Writings of H. Emilie Cady," has shown that, as early as 1891, H. Emilie Cady had written of a "beautiful foundation" (i.e., fountain). It was "supplied from some hidden, but inexhausible source," with "vigorous life bubbling up" at the center but displayed near motionlessness and "scum" at the circumference; she made the expected application, too, with "Spirit" at the center and "stagnation" in "man's body" (see H. Emilie Cady, "Finding the Christ in Ourselves," *Christian Science Thought* 3, no. 7 [October 1891]: 257–58).

6. Trine, *In Tune with the Infinite*, 38, 47 (emphasis in original).

7. Ibid., 135, 146, 150, 159.

8. Gary Ward Materra, "Women in Early New Thought: Lives and Theology in Transition, from the Civil War to World War I" (Ph.D. diss., University of California, Santa Barbara, 1997), 507.

9. See Catherine L. Albanese, *Nature Religion in America: From the Algonkian Indians to the New Age* (Chicago: University of Chicago Press, 1990), 150–51. Accessible narratives of the early history of quantum theory may be found in Gary Zukav, *The Dancing Wu Li Masters: An Overview of the New Physics* (New York: Bantam, 1980), and Victor Guillemin, *The Story of Quantum Mechanics* (New York: Scribner's, 1968), both background sources for my account in *Nature Religion in America* and here. See, also, George Gamow, *Thirty Years That Shook Physics: The Story of Quantum Theory* (Garden City, N.Y.: Doubleday, 1966).

10. See Albanese, *Nature Religion in America*, 151; and see, also, Werner Heisenberg, *Physics and Philosophy: The Revolution in Modern Science* (New York: Harper, 1958), 159–60; Zukav, *Dancing Wu Li Masters*, 192–95; and Fritjof Capra, *The Tao of Physics: An Exploration of the Parallels between Modern Physics and Eastern Mysticism*, 2d ed. (Boston: Shambhala, 1985), 77–99. For Heisenberg's principle of indeterminacy, see Guillemin, *Story of Quantum Mechanics*, 91–101; and see Heisenberg's statement in Werner Heisenberg, *The Physical Principles of the Quantum Theory*, trans. Carl Eckart and Frank C. Hoyt ([New York:] Dover, 1930), 3, 20, and in Heisenberg, *Physics and Philosophy*, 55–58. Prakriti (matter) and Purusha (spirit) were the two essential and different principles that grounded the thinking of the dualistic Indian Samkhya

school; see Edeltraud Harzer, "Samkhya," in Mircea Eliade, ed., *The Encyclopedia of Religion* (New York: Macmillan, 1987), 13: 47. On matter as "frozen light," see Richard Gerber, *Vibrational Medicine: New Choices for Healing Ourselves* (Santa Fe: Bear, 1988), 59 (significantly, Gerber's language throughout his work hints of a theosophical worldview; his dedication, e.g., cites *"the vast spiritual Hierarchy which silently works to uplift the human condition"* [ibid., 9; emphasis in original]).

11. Albanese, *Nature Religion in America*, 151–52; Werner Heisenberg, *Natural Law and the Structure of Matter* (London: Rebel Press, 1970), 32; Heisenberg, *Physics and Philosophy*, 81, 205.

12. See Norman Gevitz, *The D.O.'s: Osteopathic Medicine in America* (Baltimore: Johns Hopkins University Press, 1982), 1–15.

13. Ibid., 14–17; Norman Gevitz, "Osteopathic Medicine: From Deviance to Difference," in Norman Gevitz, ed., *Other Healers: Unorthodox Medicine in America* (Baltimore: Johns Hopkins University Press, 1988), 124–56.

14. Andrew Taylor Still, *Autobiography of Andrew T. Still with a History of the Discovery and Development of the Science of Osteopathy* (1897; rpt., New York: Arno Press and the New York Times, 1972), 99–100; see Catherine L. Albanese, *Reconsidering Nature Religion* (Harrisburg, Pa.: Trinity Press International, 2002), 28–29. On Still, his background, and his relationship to metaphysical themes, see, too, Robert C. Fuller, *Alternative Medicine and American Religious Life* (New York: Oxford University Press, 1989), 81–90.

15. Gevitz, *D.O.'s*, 13–14, 156 n52. The letter that Still co-signed appeared in *Banner of Light* 36 (9 January 1875): 8.

16. Still, *Autobiography*, 100–101.

17. Ibid., 195, 208, 221.

18. Robert C. Fulford with Gene Stone, *Dr. Fulford's Touch of Life: The Healing Power of the Natural Life Force* (New York: Pocket Books, 1996), 5, 17, 19, 22.

19. Ibid., 22–23, 23–25, 27 (emphasis in original).

20. Ibid., 29–30, 42–43, 46–47, 34.

21. Andrew Taylor Still, as quoted in Fulford, *Dr. Fulford's Touch of Life*, 156; Fulford, *Dr. Fulford's Touch of Life*, 157, 161, 162.

22. Fulford, *Dr. Fulford's Touch of Life*, 186.

23. J. Stuart Moore, *Chiropractic in America: The History of a Medical Alternative* (Baltimore: Johns Hopkins University Press, 1993), 5–7, 7; Vern Gielow, *Old Dad Chiro: Biography of D. D. Palmer, Founder of Chiropractic* (Davenport, Iowa: Bawden, 1981), 7–42. See, also, Fuller, *Alternative Medicine*, 68–74.

24. Daniel David Palmer, Journal (undated), as quoted in Gielow, *Old Dad Chiro*, 56.

25. E[dwin]. D[wight]. Babbitt, *Vital Magnetism: The Life-Fountain. Being an Answer to Dr. Brown-Sequard's Lectures on Nerve Force. The Magnetic Theory Defended, and a Better Philosophy of Cure Explained* (New York: E. D. Babbitt [1874]—and see the discussion of this work in Moore, *Chiropractic in America*, 12–13); C. A. De-Groodt, *Hygeio-Therapeutic Institute and Magnetic Infirmary* ([Burlington, Iowa: C. A. De-Groodt, c. 1882–1883]), 6 (upper case in original); J. W. Cadwell, *Full and Comprehensive Instructions: How to Mesmerize; Also, Is Spiritualism True?* (1883; rev. 6th ed.,

Boston: Author, 1885); James Victor Wilson, *How to Magnetize; or, Magnetism and Clairvoyance*, rev. ed. (New York: Fowler and Wells, 1886); N. C., *Psychometry and Thought-Transference, with Practical Hints for Experiments* (Boston: Esoteric Publishing, 1887)—N. C. has an attached "F.T.S." (Fellow of the Theosophical Society) on the title page of the pamphlet; for Olcott's introduction, see ibid., 3–5; [Charles Knowlton], *Fruits of Philosophy: A Treatise on the Population Question* ([London?]: Charles Bradlaugh and Anne Besant [1877])—Bradlaugh and Besant are listed on the title page as authors, but Knowlton was the author, as their own "Publishers' Preface" makes clear; E. H. Heywood, *Cupid's Yokes; or, The Binding Forces of Conjugal Life: An Essay to Consider Some Moral and Physiological Phases of Love and Marriage, Wherein Is Asserted the Natural Right and Necessity of Sexual Self-Government* (Princeton, Mass.: Co-operative Publishing, n.d.)—the title page also announces "*The Book which the United States Government and Local Presumption have repeatedly sought to suppress, but which Still Lives, Challenging Attention*" (emphasis in original). I obtained photocopies of these pamphlets and those in the note below during a 1982 research visit to the Palmer College of Chiropractic in Davenport, Iowa, and I remain grateful to the then-librarian there.

26. Juliet H. Severance, *A Lecture on the Evolution of Life in Earth and Spirit Conditions* (Milwaukee: Godfrey and Crandall, 1882); Juliet H. Severance, *A Lecture on the Philosophy of Disease, and How to Cure the Sick without Drugs, with an Explanation of Magnetic Laws* (Milwaukee: Godfrey and Crandall, 1883); M[arcenus]. R. K. Wright, *The Moral Aphorisms and Terseological Teachings of Confucius, the Sapient Chinese Philosopher . . . To Which Is Added a Correct Likeness of the Great Philosopher, and a Short Sketch of His Life* (Battle Creek, Mich.: [Review and Herald Steam Press], 1870); William Denton, *The Deluge in the Light of Modern Science: A Discourse* (Boston: William Denton [George C. Rand and Avery], 1872), 3, 34–35.

27. D[aniel]. D[avid]. Palmer, *The Chiropractor's Adjuster: Text-book of the Science, Art, and Philosophy of Chiropractic for Students and Practitioners* (1920; rpt., [Portland, Oreg: Portland Printing], 1966), 319, 104–5; Moore, *Chiropractic in America*, 4, 100; Gielow, *Old Dad Chiro*, 82–83. My assessment of the familiarity of the term *chiromancy* in Palmer's discourse world is based on impressionistic evidence from the metaphysical periodical literature of the day.

28. Moore, *Chiropractic in America*, 18–23, 22; Palmer, *Chiropractor's Adjuster*, 493.

29. Palmer, *Chiropractor's Adjuster*, 19, 493–94, 8.

30. On the chiropractor as priest (his hands on the "Philosopher's Stone"), see Moore, *Chiropractic in America*, 21. On B. J. Palmer, see Moore, *Chiropractic in America*, 42–49; and Walter I. Wardwell, "Chiropractors: Evolution to Acceptance," in Gevitz, ed., *Other Healers*, 158–59.

31. Joy M. Lob[a]n, "The Completeness of Chiropractic Philosophy," *The Chiropractor: A Monthly Journal Devoted to the Interests of Chiropractic* 4, nos. 7 and 8 (1908): 31 (upper case in original).

32. Ibid., 32.

33. Ibid., 33–36 (upper case in original).

34. Ibid., 36; Moore, *Chiropractic in America*, 45, 47, 48. The case against B. J. Palmer was dismissed by a grand jury in 1914, with the jury warning that it might investigate the motives of the complainants. Moore says—surprisingly enough in light of the hyperbole of the Loban essay—that the suit was likely "a ploy on the part of Loban and the Universal College to discredit B. J. and to disrupt the operations of the Palmer School" (Moore, *Chiropractic in America*, 45). The textbook that inspired the younger Palmer was the first in the chiropractic profession: Solon Langworthy, Oakley Smith, and Minora Paxson, *Modernized Chiropractic* (Cedar Rapids, Iowa: S. M. Langworthy, 1906). According to Moore, the text was used by lawyer Tom Morris in a trial in 1907 to defend the Japanese chiropractor and Palmer graduate Shegataro Morikubo, charged with the illegal practice of medicine, surgery, and osteopathy, and it was in this context that B. J. Palmer became impressed with the role of the brain (Moore, *Chiropractic in America*, 48).

35. Moore, *Chiropractic in America*, 62–63, 66; Palmer, *Chiropractor's Adjuster*, 490; Edwin D. Babbitt, *The Principles of Light and Color: Including among Other Things the Harmonic Laws of the Universe, the Etherio-Atomic Philosophy of Force, Chromo Chemistry, Chromo Therapeutics, and the General Philosophy of the Fine Forces, Together with Numerous Discoveries and Practical Applications* (New York: Babbitt, 1878).

36. John F. Thie with Mary Marks, *Touch for Health: A Practical Guide to Natural Health Using Acupuncture Touch and Massage to Improve Postural Balance and Reduce Physical and Mental Pain and Tension* (Marina del Rey, Calif.: DeVorss, 1973), 6, 5, 7; Moore, *Chiropractic in America*, 140–41.

37. Charles Sanders Peirce, *Collected Papers of Charles Sanders Peirce*, vol. 7, *Science and Philosophy*, and vol. 8, *Reviews, Correspondence, and Bibliography*, ed. Arthur W. Burks (Cambridge, Mass.: Harvard University Press, 1966), 7: 194 n1; Louis Menand, *The Metaphysical Club: A Story of Ideas in America* (New York: Farrar, Straus, and Giroux, 2001), 201; Paul Jerome Croce, *Science and Religion in the Era of William James*, vol. 1, *Eclipse of Certainty, 1820–1880* (Chapel Hill: University of North Carolina Press, 1995), 151–55.

38. Menand, *Metaphysical Club*, 227; Charles Sanders Peirce, "The Logic of 1873," in Peirce, *Collected Papers*, 7: 218–19; Charles Sanders Peirce, "A Definition of Pragmatism" (c. 1904), in Louis Menand, ed., *Pragmatism: A Reader* (New York: Vintage, 1997), 56 (emphasis in original), 481. Peirce's manuscript remained unpublished in his lifetime (Menand, ed., *Pragmatism*, 481).

39. Menand, *Metaphysical Club*, 80–86.

40. Ibid., 92–93, 75, 93, 94.

41. William James, *The Principles of Psychology*, 2 vols. (New York: H. Holt, 1890); William James, *The Will to Believe, and Other Essays in Popular Philosophy* (New York: Longmans, Green, 1897); William James, *The Varieties of Religious Experience: A Study in Human Nature* (New York: Longmans, Green, 1902); William James, *Pragmatism: A New Name for Some Old Ways of Thinking* (New York: Longmans, Green,

1907); William James, *A Pluralistic Universe: Hibbert Lectures at Manchester College on the Present Situation in Philosophy* (New York: Longmans, Green, 1909); and William James, *The Meaning of Truth: A Sequel to "Pragmatism"* (New York: Longmans, Green, 1909).

42. Ann Taves, *Fits, Trances, and Visions: Experiencing Religion and Explaining Experience from Wesley to James* (Princeton: Princeton University Press, 1999), 272, 289; Henry Samuel Levinson, *The Religious Investigations of William James* (Chapel Hill: University of North Carolina Press, 1981), 9–10, 23.

43. William James, "The Energies of Men" (1907), in William James, *The Writings of William James*, ed. John J. McDermott (Chicago: University of Chicago Press, 1977), 679–80. McDermott printed the 1907 version from the *American Magazine* for October 1907, there titled "The Powers of Men," but he reverted to James's earlier (and preferred) title "The Energies of Men," as in the presidential address he delivered before the American Philosophical Association in 1906 and published in the *Philosophical Review* in January 1907.

44. Ibid., 682. "Fearthought" was a term coined by New Thought author Horace Fletcher, whose book *Happiness as Found in Forethought Minus Fearthought* (Chicago: H. S. Stone, 1897) James had read.

45. Taves, *Fits, Trances, and Visions*, 271.

46. Ibid., 280; William James, *The Varieties of Religious Experience: A Study in Human Nature*, intro. Reinhold Niebuhr (1961: rpt., London: Collier-Macmillan, 1969), 375–76, 58 (all subsequent quotations from *Varieties of Religious Experience* are from this edition).

47. James, *Varieties of Religious Experience*, 59, 62 (emphasis in original), 91 n14, 92–95, 100 n22, 105–7.

48. Francis William Newman, *The Soul, Her Sorrows and Her Aspirations: An Essay towards the Natural History of the Soul, as the True Basis of Theology* (London: J. Chapman, 1849). James cited a third edition of 1852, which had by then been retitled *The Soul, Its Sorrows and Its Aspirations: An Essay toward the Natural History of the Soul as the True Basis of Theology*.

49. James, *Varieties of Religious Experience*, 80, 81, 82, 87, 89–90, 99.

50. Ibid., 90–91, 94, 91.

51. Ibid., 99, 101–2 (emphasis in original), 103–4, 108.

52. William James, *Pragmatism and Four Essays from The Meaning of Truth* (1907 and 1909; rpt., Cleveland, Ohio: World Publishing, 1970), 42–43, 46 (all subsequent quotations from *Pragmatism* are from this edition).

53. Ibid., 46–47 (emphases in original).

54. Ibid., 47, 49, 57, 59 (emphases in original).

55. James, *Varieties of Religious Experience*, 400, 141.

56. Taves, *Fits, Trances, and Visions*, 207; William James, "Final Impressions of a Psychical Researcher" ["Confidences of a Psychical Researcher," *American Magazine*, October 1909], in James, *Writings of William James*, ed. McDermott, 793, 798–99 (emphases in original).

57. James, *Varieties of Religious Experience*, 396, 390, 393–94, 399–400, 401 (emphases and upper case in original).

58. Ibid., 110; James, *Pragmatism*, 133 (emphases in original), 142–43; William James, *A Pluralistic Universe*, in Louis Menand, ed., *Pragmatism*, 133.

59. James, *Pluralistic Universe*, 134–35.

60. Warren Meyer and Phoebe P. Knapp, "Confident Living," in Unity School of Christianity, *Wings of Song* (Unity Village, Mo.: Unity Books, 1984), no. 159. The hymn may be heard on a Unity CD: Carrie "Shanti" Norman, *Quiet Waters: Inspirational Songs from Unity's Wings of Song Hymnal* (Unity Village, Mo.: Unity, 1997), band 4; see Eileen W. Lindner, *Yearbook of American and Canadian Churches 2004* (Nashville: Abingdon Press, 2004), esp. 219–25, 366–77.

61. For Divine Science, see Judah, *History and Philosophy of the Metaphysical Movements*, 194–206; Braden, *Spirits in Rebellion*, 264–84; J. Gordon Melton, "Divine Science Federation International," in J. Gordon Melton, *Encyclopedia of American Religions*, 4th ed. (Detroit: Gale Research, 1993), 678–79.

62. On Emmet Fox, see Emmet Fox, *Power through Constructive Thinking* (1932; San Francisco: HarperSanFrancisco, 1989), esp. 133–36; and Emmet Fox, *The Sermon on the Mount: The Key to Success in Life* (1934; rpt., San Francisco: HarperSanFrancisco, 1989); Judah, *History and Philosophy of the Metaphysical Movements*, 198; Braden, *Spirits in Rebellion*, 273–74; Hazel Deane, *Powerful Is the Light: The Story of Nona Brooks* (Denver: Divine Science College, 1945).

63. See Judah, *History and Philosophy of the Metaphysical Movements*, 207–9; Braden, *Spirits in Rebellion*, 287–89.

64. On affective and noetic New Thought leaders, see Gary Ward Materra, "Women in Early New Thought," 507 (Materra did not list Ernest Holmes because his major work fell outside the period of the study); Richard Maurice Bucke, *Cosmic Consciousness: A Study in the Evolution of the Human Mind* (1901; rpt., New York: E. P. Dutton, 1969); Braden, *Spirits in Rebellion*, 291.

65. Ernest Holmes, *Science of Mind: A Complete Course of Lessons in the Science of Mind and Spirit* (New York: Robert M. McBride, 1926); and Ernest Holmes, *The Science of Mind*, rev. and enl. ed., ed. in collaboration with Maude Allison Lathem (New York: Dodd, Mead, 1938); Judah, *History and Philosophy of the Metaphysical Movements*, 208; Holmes, *Science of Mind* (1938), 27, 29 (emphases and upper case in original; all subsequent quotations are from this edition).

66. Holmes, *Science of Mind*, 31.

67. Ibid., 31–32, 35–37, 40–41 (upper case and emphasis in original).

68. Ibid., 58 (emphasis in original).

69. Ibid., 54–55.

70. Ibid., 327, 337 (emphasis in original).

71. See Melton, "Religious Science International" and "United Church of Religious Science," in Melton, *Encyclopedia of American Religions*, 4th ed., 685–86, 688–89, for the late-twentieth-century situation and a general historical overview.

72. Melton, "Unity School of Christianity," in Melton, *Encyclopedia of American Reli-*

gions, 4th ed., 691; on Unity as a movement, see, e.g., Juan Enrique Toro, "Unity for Humanity—Heart Deep and World Wide," *Contact* 38, no. 4 (August–September 2004): 4–5.

73. Myrtle Fillmore, as quoted in Thomas E. Witherspoon, *Myrtle Fillmore: Mother of Unity* (Unity Village, Mo.: Unity Books, 1977), 39; Myrtle Fillmore, "How I Found Health" (1899), in James A. Decker, ed., *Unity's Seventy Years of Faith and Works* (Lee's Summit, Mo.: Unity School of Christianity, 1959), 12; Neal Vahle, *The Unity Movement: Its Evolution and Spiritual Teachings* (Philadelphia: Templeton, 2002), 6–7; Myrtle Fillmore, as quoted ibid., 7.

74. For background on the early history of Unity, see Vahle, *Unity Movement*, esp. 5–70, 145–80; see, also, the chronology in Unity School of Christianity, *Unity: 100 Years of Faith and Vision* (Unity Village, Mo.: Unity Books, 1988), 163–68. Material in the following paragraphs may generally be found in both these sources and in Melton, "Unity School of Christianity," 689–91.

75. Russsell A. Kemp (1975), in H. Emilie Cady, *Complete Works of H. Emilie Cady*, ed. Michael A. Maday (1995; rpt., Unity Village, Mo.: Unity House, 2002), 16; Vahle, *Unity Movement*, 71; H[arriet]. Emilie Cady, *Lessons in Truth: A Course of Twelve Lessons in Practical Christianity* (Kansas City, Mo.: Unity Tract Society, 1901); for a politically correct and recent version, see Cady, *Complete Works*. Unity sources claim initial book publication in three paperback volumes in 1896–1897 and in a single volume in 1903. Vahle, however, cites a 1901 date for the first book version (Vahle, *Unity Movement*, 471), and the on-line World Catalog cites a 1901 edition.

76. H. Emilie Cady, *Lessons in Truth: A Course of Twelve Lessons in Practical Christianity* (Kansas City, Mo.: Unity School of Christianity, 1935), 134, 6, 9, 12, 23–24. All subsequent quotations are from this edition.

77. Ibid., 85, 120, 6, 153–72.

78. See Vahle, *Unity Movement*, 175–76, 252; *Daily Word*, 142, no. 8 (August 2004): 27 (13 August 2004). Rosemary Fillmore Rhea, in her memoirs published in 2003, claimed seven languages, 140 countries, and over a million readers (see Rosemary Fillmore Rhea, *That's Just How My Spirit Travels: A Memoir* [Unity Village, Mo.: Unity House, 2003], 164).

79. Charles Fillmore, *Atom-Smashing Power of Mind* (Unity Village, Mo.: Unity School of Christianity, 1949), 13 (the work appeared posthumously).

80. Charles Fillmore, *The Twelve Powers of Man* (1930), in Charles Fillmore and Cora Fillmore, *The Twelve Powers* (1999; rpt., Unity Village, Mo.: Unity House, 2003), 5, 8 (emphasis in original), 13, 15–16 (all subsequent quotations are from this edition). Charles Fillmore's *Twelve Powers of Man* has a complex publishing history, with the introduction published in 1912 in *Weekly Unity* and the chapters published serially in 1920, and again in 1925–26 and 1929–30 in *Unity Magazine* (see Fillmore and Fillmore, *Twelve Powers*, v).

81. Charles Fillmore, *Christian Healing: The Science of Being* (1909), reprinted as *Christian Healing* (Unity Village, Mo.: Unity School of Christianity, n.d.), 61, 62, 68, 69, 70; May Rowland, *Dare to Believe!* (Unity Village, Mo.: Unity School of Christianity,

1961), 18; Charles Fillmore, *Prosperity* (1936; rpt., Unity Village, Mo.: Unity Books, 1983), 37, 36.

82. James, *Varieties of Religious Experience*, 90; Fillmore, *Twelve Powers*, 6.

83. William Walker Atkinson, *Thought-Force in Business and Everyday Life; Being a Series of Lessons in Personal Magnetism, Psychic Influence, Thought-Force, Concentration, Will Power, and Practical Mental Science* (Chicago: Psychic Research, 1901; London: L. N. Fowler, 1901; Chicago: New Thought Publishing, 1903; New York: Sydney Flower, 1903; Chicago: A. C. McClure, 1911; Chicago: A. C. McClure, 1913). The 1903 Sydney Flower edition announced itself to be the 18th edition. The Russian edition was titled *Sila Mysli* (1910; rpt., Orel: Obshchestvo "Kniga," 1992).

84. William Walker Atkinson, *Thought Vibration; or, The Law of Attraction in the Thought World* (Chicago: New Thought Publishing, 1906; rpt., Whitefish, Mont.: Kessinger, 1997); see the on-line review by "F. UYS 'irridium'" at www.amazon.com/exec/obidos/tg/detail/-564596605/qid=1092618351/sr=1–7/ref=sr.

85. William Walker Atkinson, *The Secret of Mental Magic: A Course of Seven Lessons* (Chicago: W. W. Atkinson, 1907); William Walker Atkinson, *Mental Fascination: Being the First Manual in the Nature of a Supplement or Sequel to "The Secret of Mental Magic," and Designed as Special Instruction for the Students of That Work* (Chicago: William Walker Atkinson, 1907); William Walker Atkinson, *Mind-Power: The Secret of Mental Magic* (Chicago: Advanced Thought Publishing, 1912; Chicago: Yogi Publishing, 1912; Chicago: W. W. Atkinson, 1912; London: L. N. Fowler, 1912). Atkinson also published *Mind-Power* with, as an alternate subtitle, *The Law of Dynamic Mentation* the same year: William Walker Atkinson, *Mind-Power; or, The Law of Dynamic Mentation* (Chicago: Advanced Thought Publishing, 1912). For a contemporary reprint (on which this discussion is based), see William Walker Atkinson, *Mind Power* (1912; rpt., Whitefish, Mont.: Kessinger, 1997).

86. See Donald Meyer, *The Positive Thinkers: Religion as Pop Psychology from Mary Baker Eddy to Oral Roberts* (New York: Pantheon, 1980), 196–199 (this is a second edition of Meyer's 1965 *The Positive Thinkers: A Study of the American Quest for Health, Wealth, and Personal Power from Mary Baker Eddy to Norman Vincent Peale* [New York: Random]); and see Ralph Waldo Trine, *The Power That Wins* (Indianapolis: Bobbs-Merrill, 1928).

87. Charles Fillmore, *Prosperity* (Kansas City, Mo.: Unity School of Christianity, 1936); Napoleon Hill, *Think and Grow Rich: Teaching, for the First Time, the Famous Andrew Carnegie Formula for Money-Making* (Chicago: Combined Registry, 1937); see Decker, ed., *Unity's Seventy Years*, 162, where the Fillmores' covenant is photocopied; Charles Fillmore, *Prosperity* (1983), 4–5 (all subsequent quotations are from this edition).

88. Fillmore, *Prosperity*, 56, 121, 123, 125–26, 128–29, 141, 145, 155, 157, 164.

89. Meyer, *Positive Thinkers*, 170, 168, 170–71.

90. Napoleon Hill, *Think and Grow Rich*, rev. ed. (1960; rpt., New York: Fawcett Books, 1996), 13–15, 19, 33, 49, 50 (emphasis in original), 53.

91. Ibid., 71, 168–69, 176–77, 202–3, 205, 210–11, 213.

92. Ibid., 222–29, 18.

93. See Carol V. R. George, *God's Salesman: Norman Vincent Peale and the Power of Positive Thinking* (New York: Oxford University Press, 1993), esp. 221, 7, 69, 36–37, 50–51, 63, 134.

94. Braden, *Spirits in Rebellion*, 388–89; Norman Vincent Peale, *The Tough-Minded Optimist* (New York: Prentice-Hall, 1961).

95. George, *God's Salesman*, 105, 114–15, 119, 103, 6, 104, 115, 130. The phrase "motel theory of existence" comes from Jonathan Z. Smith, who employed it in classes at the University of Chicago in the late 1960s and early 1970s to refer to religionists in the ancient Mediterranean world.

96. George, *God's Salesman*, 136, 138 (George cites forty-three books, with the last published in 1991, but reprints of Peale's works by Simon and Schuster with a 2003 imprint, in blurbs on their back covers, have boasted of forty-six); Louis Schneider and Sanford M. Dornbusch, *Popular Religion: Inspirational Books in America* (1958; rpt., Chicago: University of Chicago Press, 1973), 162; Alice Payne Hackett, *Sixty Years of Best Sellers, 1895–1955* (New York: R. R. Bowker, 1956). The Schneider-Dornbusch study used a list of forty-six books in the Judeo-Christian tradition that inspired readers with the "hope of salvation" and offered them techniques to effect the same (see Schneider and Dornbusch, *Popular Religion*, 3–4).

97. Judah, *History and Philosophy of the Metaphysical Movements*, 192, Norman Vincent Peale, *The Power of Positive Thinking* (1952; rpt., New York: Simon and Schuster, 2003), viii–ix, xi–xiii (all subsequent quotations are from this edition).

98. Peale, *Power of Positive Thinking*, 12, 36.

99. Ibid., 18, 23, 56, 83, 101.

100. Ibid., 111, 217.

101. George, *God's Salesman*, 140, 145–46.

102. Ibid., 145.

103. On Phineas F. Bresee and the language of "Supply," see Sandra Sizer Frankiel, *California's Spiritual Frontiers: Religious Alternatives in Anglo-Protestantism, 1850–1910* (Berkeley: University of California Press, 1988), 103–19; on Robert H. Schuller, see Dennis Voskuil, *Mountains into Goldmines: Robert Schuller and the Gospel of Success* (Grand Rapids, Mich.: Eerdmans, 1983); on Oral Roberts, see David Edwin Harrell Jr., *Oral Roberts: An American Life* (Bloomington: Indiana University Press, 1985).

104. Deepak Chopra, *The Way of the Wizard: Twenty Spiritual Lessons in Creating the Life You Want* (New York: Harmony, 1995), 3, 116, 47 (emphases in original). Reference to Chopra's medical degree can nowhere be found on the book jacket or in its front matter.

105. W. Emmett Small, comp. and ed., *The Wisdom of the Heart: Katherine Tingley Speaks* (San Diego, Calif.: Point Loma, 1978), 25–26, 31–33; Emmett A. Greenwalt, *California Utopia: Point Loma, 1897–1942*, rev. ed. (San Diego: Point Loma, 1978), 12–16; Bruce F. Campbell, *Ancient Wisdom Revived: A History of the Theosophical Movement* (Berkeley: University of California Press, 1980), 131–33.

106. Edward Bellamy, *Looking Backward, 2000–1887* (Boston: Ticknor, 1888); Greenwalt,

California Utopia, 20; Katherine Tingley, *San Diego Union*, 24 February 1897, as quoted in Greenwalt, *California Utopia*, 34; Campbell, *Ancient Wisdom Revived*, 134–35.

107. Greenwalt, *California Utopia*, 35–36; W. Michael Ashcraft, *The Dawn of the New Cycle: Point Loma Theosophists and American Culture* (Knoxville: University of Tennessee Press, 2002), 41, 38.

108. See the account in Campbell, *Ancient Wisdom Revived*, 136–39; Small, ed., *Wisdom of the Heart*, 97.

109. See Ashcraft, *Dawn of the New Cycle*, 42–43.

110. Small, ed., *Wisdom of the Heart*, 14–16.

111. Ibid., 16.

112. Ibid., 72; Katherine Tingley, *The Gods Await* (1926), 2d rev. ed. (Pasadena: Theosophical University Press, 1992), 67, 78, 73, 33, 37, 39, 41.

113. Small, ed., *Wisdom of the Heart*, 105–6, 104, 113.

114. Ashcraft, *Dawn of the New Cycle*, 93; Campbell, *Ancient Wisdom Revived*, 140–42.

115. C[harles]. W. Leadbeater, *The Chakras* (Wheaton, Ill.: Theosophical Publishing, 1927).

116. I have compiled this data using WorldCat, essentially a subscription-based "Union Catalog" of the Internet that includes the holdings of approximately twelve thousand libraries worldwide. This is a conservative listing. The printing that I have used (from 1980—see next), e.g., is held by no library in WorldCat. For the numbers claim, see C[harles]. W. Leadbeater, *The Chakras* (Wheaton, Ill.: Theosophical Publishing, 1980), back cover. Subsequent quotations of the Leadbeater work are from this printing.

117. Leadbeater, *Chakras*, 1, 3–4; Arthur Edward Powell, *The Etheric Double: The Health Aura of Man* (Wheaton, Ill.: Theosophical Publishing, 1925). Significantly, WorldCat shows no reprint of the Powell work until 1969; there have been at least four reprintings, beginning with the 1969 one, the latest in 1996.

118. Leadbeater, *Chakras*, 9, 16, 95–121, 95, 104–5, 107–8, 109, 116, 18.

119. Ibid., 18, 18–21, 21, 21–22, plate VII ("The Chakras, according to Gichtel"); C[harles]. W. Leadbeater, *The Hidden Life in Freemasonry* (Madras: Theosophical Publishing, 1926).

120. Anodea Judith, *Wheels of Life* (St. Paul, Minn.: Llewellyn, 1987); Anodea Judith, *Wheels of Life*, 2d ed. (1999; rpt., St. Paul, Minn.: Llewellyn, 2001), back cover, xix–xx (subsequent quotations are from this edition).

121. Ram Dass, *The Only Dance There Is: Talks Given at the Menninger Foundation, Topeka Kansas, 1970, and at Spring Grove Hospital, Spring Grove, Maryland, 1972* (Garden City, N.Y.: Anchor, 1974); Judith, *Wheels of Life*, 428, xx–xxi, 4 (emphasis in original).

122. Judith, *Wheels of Life*, 4, 7, 176–83, 25–26, 369–77, 396–97.

123. Rosalyn Bruyere, *Wheels of Light: A Study of the Chakras* (Glendale, Calif.: Healing Light Center, 1987; Sierra Madre, Calif.: Bon, 1989); Rosalyn L. Bruyere, *Wheels of Light: Chakras, Auras, and the Healing Energy of the Body*, ed. Jeanne Farrens (1989;

rpt., New York: Simon and Schuster, 1994), 19–20 (subsequent quotations are from this edition); Diane Goldner, *Infinite Grace: Where the Worlds of Science and Spiritual Healing Meet* (Charlottesville, Va.: Hampton Roads, 1999), 112–13, 116.

124. Goldner, *Infinite Grace*, 124; Bruyere, *Wheels of Light*, 20, 22–27, 57, 29 (emphasis in original). For Valerie Hunt's autobiographical account of the aura experiments, see Valerie V. Hunt, *Infinite Mind: Science of the Human Vibrations of Consciousness*, 2d ed. (Malibu: Malibu Publishing, 1996), 9–36.

125. Goldner, *Infinite Grace*, 125–26, 131, 143; Barbara Ann Brennan, *Hands of Light: A Guide to Healing through the Human Energy Field* (1987; rpt., New York.: Bantam, 1988), 5.

126. Brennan, *Hands of Light*, 13, 54; Barbara Ann Brennan, *Light Emerging: The Journey of Personal Healing* (New York: Bantam, 1993); Catherine L. Albanese, "The Aura of Wellness: Subtle-Energy Healing and New Age Religion," *Religion and American Culture: A Journal of Interpretation* 10, no. 1 (Winter 2000): 32; www.barbarabrennan .com.

127. Brennan, *Hands of Light*, 43, 45.

128. Ibid., 284, 29–30 (emphasis in original), 74, 194.

129. Ibid., 42, 499–54, 63, 61, 68.

130. Ibid., 86, 131–32, 109–10.

131. Alice A. Bailey, *The Unfinished Autobiography of Alice A. Bailey* (1951; rpt., New York: Lucis, 1994), 20–37, 27, 35–37 (subsequent quotations are from this edition); see, also, Judah, *History and Philosophy of the Metaphysical Movements*, 119–20; Campbell, *Ancient Wisdom Revived*, 150.

132. Bailey, *Unfinished Autobiography*, 34, 41–42; Judah, *History and Philosophy of the Metaphysical Movements*, 120.

133. Bailey, *Unfinished Autobiography*, 39–40, 80–81.

134. Ibid., 96–193; Alice Bailey, *Initiation, Human and Solar* (New York: Lucifer Publishing, 1922); Judah, *History and Philosophy of the Metaphysical Movements*, 121–22.

135. Bailey, *Unfinished Autobiography*, 139–40.

136. Alice A. Bailey, *Initiation, Human and Solar* (1922; rpt., New York: Lucis, 1992), 30, 206, 138 (subsequent quotations are from this edition); Alice Bailey, *A Treatise on Cosmic Fire*, 2 vols. (New York: Lucis, 1925); Alice A. Bailey, *A Treatise on Cosmic Fire* (1925; rpt., New York: Lucis, 1995), 166 (subsequent quotations are from this edition); Alice Bailey, *A Treatise on White Magic; or, The Way of the Disciple* (New York: Lucis, 1934); see, e.g., her detailed descriptions in Alice A. Bailey, *A Treatise on White Magic; or, The Way of the Disciple* (1934; rpt., New York: Lucis, 1997), 87, 362 (subsequent quotations are from this edition).

137. Alice Bailey, *A Treatise on the Seven Rays*, vol. 1, *Esoteric Psychology*, 1; vol. 2, *Esoteric Psychology*, 2; vol. 3, *Esoteric Astrology*; vol. 4, *Esoteric Healing*; vol. 5, *The Rays and the Initiations*. All were published in New York City by Lucis.

138. Theosophy Company, *Index to The Secret Doctrine by H. P. Blavatsky* (Los Angeles: Theosophy Company, 1939), 129; Bailey, *Initiation, Human and Solar*, 223–24; Bailey, *Unfinished Autobiography*, 278; Bailey, *Treatise on Cosmic Fire*, 69; Bailey, *Treatise on White Magic*, 32.

139. See Campbell, *Ancient Wisdom Revived*, 119–22, 128–30; Bailey, *Unfinished Autobiography*, 170.

140. Alice Bailey, *The Reappearance of the Christ* (New York: Lucis, 1948).

141. Judah, *History and Philosophy of the Metaphysical Movements*, 127–29; Robert S. Ellwood Jr., *Religious and Spiritual Groups in Modern America* (Englewood Cliffs, N.J.: Prentice-Hall, 1973), 103–6.

142. See www.lucistrust.org.

143. Bailey, *Unfinished Autobiography*, 256; J. Gordon Melton, *Encyclopedia of American Religions*, 7th ed. (Detroit: Gale Research, 2003).

144. Godfré Ray King [Guy Warren Ballard], *Unveiled Mysteries* (Chicago: St. Germain, 1934); Charles Samuel Braden, *These Also Believe: A Study of Modern American Cults and Minority Religious Movements* (New York: Macmillan, 1949), 257–71, 269, 266, 294; J. Gordon Melton, "Soulcraft," in Melton, *Encyclopedia of American Religions*, 4th ed., 780.

145. Braden, *These Also Believe*, 257–58; J. Gordon Melton, "The 'I AM' Activity," in James R. Lewis, ed., *The Encyclopedic Sourcebook of New Age Religions* (Amherst, N.Y.: Prometheus, 2004), 275; J. Gordon Melton, *Encyclopedic Handbook of Cults in America* (New York: Garland Publishing, 1986), 45–46; Annie Rix Militz, "Translation Instead of Reincarnation," *Master Mind*, as reprinted in J. Gordon Melton, ed., *New Thought: A Reader* (Santa Barbara, Calif.: Institute for the Study of American Religion, 1990), 213–14.

146. Melton, "The 'I AM' Activity," 274; Braden, *These Also Believe*, 298–99, 263.

147. Braden, *These Also Believe*, 291; Melton, "The 'I AM' Activity," 274; Emma Curtis Hopkins, *The Radiant "I AM"* (Putnam, Conn.: Emma Curtis Hopkins, n.d.); Thomas J. Shelton, *I Am Sermons* (Denver, Colo.: Christian, 1900); Annie Rix Militz, *Primary Lessons in Christian Living and Healing: A Textbook of Healing by the Power of Truth as Taught and Demonstrated by the Master Lord Jesus Christ* (Los Angeles: Master Mind Publishing, 1904); Militz's book was likewise published in New York by the Absolute Press the same year.

148. Braden, *These Also Believe*, 303, 276; Melton, *Encyclopedic Handbook of Cults*, 48–50.

149. See *United States v. Ballard* 322 U.S. 78 (1944), in John T. Noonan Jr., *The Believers and the Powers That Are: Cases, History, and Other Data Bearing on the Relation of Religion and Government* (New York: Macmillan, 1987), 300–305; Melton, "The 'I AM' Activity," 279–80; J. Gordon Melton, "The Church Universal and Triumphant: Its Heritage and Thoughtworld," in James R. Lewis and J. Gordon Melton, eds., *Church Universal and Triumphant in Scholarly Perspective* (Stanford, Calif.: Center for Academic Publications, 1994), 13–16.

150. Clara H. Whitmore, *Jo, the Indian Friend* (Boston: Christopher Publishing, 1925), 19–20; Jerome Croce and Paul Jerome Croce, "Keepers of the Veil: Life Stories of Cassadaga's Senior Residents," in John J. Guthrie Jr., Phillip Charles Lucas, and Gary Monroe, eds., *Cassadaga: The South's Oldest Spiritualist Community* (Gainesville: University Press of Florida, 2000), 138, 147, 154, 165.

151. Goldner, *Infinite Grace*, 118, 128, 4; on Black Elk, see Clyde Holler, *Black Elk's Reli-*

gion: The Sun Dance and Lakota Catholicism (Syracuse, N.Y.: Syracuse University Press, 1995).

152. Yvonne P. Chireau, *Black Magic: Religion and the African American Conjuring Tradition* (Berkeley: University of California Press, 2003), 123; Hans A. Baer and Merrill Singer, *African American Religion in the Twentieth Century: Varieties of Protest and Accommodation* (Knoxville: University of Tennessee Press, 1992), 58, 62.

153. Gilbert E. Cooley, "Root Doctors and Psychics in the Region," *Indiana Folklore* 10, no. 2 (1977): 193, 196; Chireau, *Black Magic*, 139–44, 141.

154. Joyce Elaine Noll, *Company of Prophets: African American Psychics, Healers, and Visionaries* (St. Paul, Minn.: Llewellyn, 1991), vii, xi–xiv, 39, 43, 58–59; Master Yogi Thomas, *Divine Light Meditation* (Chicago: Divine Light Temple, 1986); Master Walter N. Thomas, *Spiritual Meditation* (Chicago: CFS Healing Temple, 1983).

155. Chireau, *Black Magic*, 113–14, 195 n47, 48, 49; Joseph R. Washington Jr., *Black Sects and Cults* (Garden City, N.Y.: Anchor/Doubleday, 1973), 112; Claude J. Jacobs and Andrew J. Kaslow, *The Spiritual Churches of New Orleans: Origins, Beliefs, and Rituals of an African-American Religion* (Knoxville: University of Tennessee Press, 1991), 38–43, 1.

156. Washington, *Black Sects and Cults*, 113; Chireau, *Black Magic*, 114–15; Zora Neale Hurston, "Hoodoo in America," *Journal of American Folklore* 44 (1931): 317–417; Jacobs and Kaslow, *Spiritual Churches*, 1, 8.

157. Jacobs and Kaslow, *Spiritual Churches*, 136–38.

158. Ibid., 138–47, 145.

159. Baer and Singer, *African-American Religion*, 215–19; Ronald Moran White, "New Thought Influences on Father Divine" (M.A. thesis, Miami University of Oxford, Ohio, 1980); Jill Watts, *God, Harlem U.S.A.: The Father Divine Story* (Berkeley: University of California Press, 1992), 26–29.

160. Watts, *God, Harlem U.S.A.*, 22–23, 25, 24.

161. Ibid., 58–59; Jiddu Krishnamurti, *The Kingdom of Happiness* (New York: Boni and Liveright, 1927); Baird T. Spalding, *The Life and Teaching of the Masters of the Far East*, vol. 1 (Los Angeles: DeVorss, 1924).

162. My summary here and in what follows is largely based on Catherine L. Albanese, *America: Religions and Religion*, 3d ed. (Belmont, Calif.: Wadsworth Publishing, 1999), 207–8.

163. Robert T. Trotter II and Juan Antonio Chavira, *Curanderismo: Mexican American Folk Healing* (Athens: University of Georgia Press, 1981), 25.

164. Bernard R. Ortiz de Montellano, "Mesoamerican Religious Tradition and Medicine," in Lawrence E. Sullivan, ed., *Healing and Restoring: Health and Medicine in the World's Religious Traditions* (New York: Macmillan, 1989), 360, 361, 363, 379–80, 387–88; Trotter and Chavira, *Curanderismo*, 30, 36–38, 80–82; on the poetry of curanderismo, see the reading by Luis D. León in *La Llorona's Children: Religion, Life, and Death in the U.S.-Mexican Borderlands* (Berkeley: University of California Press, 2004), 127–62, esp. 130–31, 158.

165. Rafaela G. Castro, *Chicano Folklore: A Guide to the Folktales, Traditions, Rituals, and*

Religious Practices of Mexican Americans (New York: Oxford University Press, 2001), 26; Trotter and Chavira, *Curanderismo*, 32–33, 66.

166. See the biographical sketch in June Macklin, "Belief, Ritual, and Healing: New England Spiritualism and Mexican-American Spiritism Compared," in Irving I. Zaretsky and Mark P. Leone, eds., *Religious Movements in Contemporary America* (Princeton: Princeton University Press, 1974), 388–89. Kardec's two most well-known spiritist books, in English translation, are Allan Kardec, *Spiritualist Philosophy: The Spirits' Book; Containing the Principles of Spiritist Doctrine . . . according to the Teachings of Spirits of High Degree, Transmitted through Various Mediums* (Boston: Colby and Rich, 1875); and Allan Kardec, *Experimental Spiritism: Book on Mediums; or, Guide for Mediums and Invocators; Containing the Special Instruction of the Spirits on the Theory of All Kinds of Manifestations, the Development of Mediumship, the Difficulties and the Dangers That Are to Be Encountered in the Practice of Spiritism* (Boston: Colby and Rich, 1874).

167. Frank Podmore, *Modern Spiritualism: A History and a Criticism*, 2 vols. (1902), reprinted as *Mediums of the Nineteenth Century* (New Hyde Park, N.Y.: University Books, 1963), 2: 161; Macklin, "Belief, Ritual, and Healing," 390, 388 n5.

168. León, *La Llorona's Children*, 167, 178–85, 179; Trotter and Chavira, *Curanderismo*, 34–35.

169. Macklin, "Belief, Ritual, and Healing," 383; León, *La Llorona's Children*, 137, 151–56 (emphasis in original; quotations are from El Niño Fidencio, as quoted by León from another source); Trotter and Chavira, *Curanderismo*, 35.

170. León, *La Llorona's Children*, 166–67 (emphasis in original); Trotter and Chavira, *Curanderismo*, 102, 175, 63, 85.

171. Trotter and Chavira, *Curanderismo*, 63–64 (emphasis in original).

172. León, *La Llorona's Children*, 142, For the Pennsylvania Germans and the Pennsylvania Dutch, see, e.g., Edwin Miller Fogel, *Beliefs and Superstitions of the Pennsylvania Germans* (Philadelphia: Americana Germanica, 1915); Ann Hark, *Hex Marks the Spot: In the Pennsylvania Dutch Country* (Philadelphia: Lippincott, 1938); and Richard E. Wentz, ed., *Pennsylvania Dutch Folk Spirituality* (New York: Paulist, 1993). For Italian American evil-eye beliefs, see Phyllis Williams, *South Italian Folkways in Europe and America* (New Haven: Yale University Press, 1938); and Richard Swiderski, "From Folk to Popular: Plastic Evil Eye Charms," in Clarence Maloney, ed., *The Evil Eye* (New York: Columbia University Press, 1976), 28–41.

173. Melton, *Encyclopedic Handbook*, 108.

174. Ronald E. Kotzsch, "Georges Ohsawa and the Japanese Religious Tradition" (Ph.D. diss., Harvard University, 1981), esp. 30–64, 62; see, also, Ronald E. Kotzsch, *Macrobiotics: Yesterday and Today* (New York: Japan Publications, 1985), 21–35, 33.

175. George Ohsawa, as quoted in Michio Kushi, with Alex Jack, *One Peaceful World* (New York: St. Martin's, 1987), 20; Kotzsch, *Macrobiotics*, 183.

176. Kotzsch, *Macrobiotics*, 47; Georges Ohsawa, *Zen Macrobiotics: The Art of Rejuvenation and Longevity*, ed. Lou Oles and Shayne Oles Suehle (Los Angeles: Ohsawa, 1965), 113–14, 37–44.

177. See Kotzsch, *Macrobiotics*, 172, 25–26, 238–39.

178. Ibid., 171, 235; see Michio Kushi, with Edward Esko and Wendy Esko, *The Gentle Art of Making Love* (Garden City Park, N.Y.: Avery Publishing, 1990).

179. See, e.g., Michio Kushi, with Alex Jack, *The Gospel of Peace: Jesus's Teachings of Eternal Truth* (New York: Japan Publications, 1992); Kushi, *Gentle Art of Making Love*, 100–101; see the Ohsawa chart in Kotzsch, *Georges Ohsawa*, 150, and Kotzsch, *Macrobiotics*, 155; Michio Kushi, with Alex Jack, *The Book of Macrobiotics: The Universal Way of Health, Happiness, and Peace*, rev. ed. (New York: Japan Publications, 1986), 29.

180. See the summary in Kotzsch, *Macrobiotics*, 244–45, 172; Kushi, *Book of Macrobiotics*, 253–55, 255 (emphasis in original; *ki* is the Japanese for the Chinese *qi* ["ch'i"]).

181. Kushi, *Book of Macrobiotics*, 266–67.

182. Elijah Siegler, "The Dao of America: The History and Practice of American Daoism" (Ph.D. diss., University of California, Santa Barbara, 2003), vi–vii, 117.

183. J. J. Clarke, *The Tao of the West: Western Transformations of Taoist Thought* (London: Routledge, 2000), 9; Siegler, "Dao of America," 10, 13, 35, 50, 17, 252ff.

184. See Siegler, "Dao of America," 159, 137, 332, 122–23, 161–62, 119, 186, 295, passim.

185. Ibid., 224–25, 227–28, 236, 19–35.

186. Mantak Chia, *Awaken Healing Energy through the Tao. Ancient Chi-Kung: Learn How to Circulate Energy through Acupuncture Channels by Yourself* ([New York?]: Taoist Esoteric Yoga Center and Foundation], 1981); Mantak Chia, *Awaken Healing Energy through the Tao: The Taoist Secret of Circulating Internal Power* (Santa Fe: Aurora Press, 1983), 1–3 (all subsequent quotations are from this edition).

187. Chia, *Awaken Healing Energy*, 4–8, viii.

188. Ibid., 17–28, 27.

189. Stuart Alve Olson, comp. and trans., *Cultivating the Ch'i*, 3d ed. (St. Paul: Dragon Door, 1993), 15, 17 (original edition, 1986); Y[earning]. K. Chen, *Tai-Chi Ch'uan: Its Effects and Practical Applications* (1947; rpt., North Hollywood, Calif.: Newcastle Publishing, 1979), 10, 1–3 (emphasis in original), 28.

190. Olson, comp. and trans., *Cultivating the Ch'i*, 16; Chen Kung [Chen Yen-lin/Yearning K. Chen], "Discourse on Mind-Intent and Ch'i," in Olson, comp. and trans., *Cultivating the Ch'i*, 38–39.

CODA: THE NEW NEW AGE

1. Doug Boyd, *Rolling Thunder* (New York: Dell, 1974), 112, 7–8.

2. Marilyn Ferguson, *The Aquarian Conspiracy: Personal and Social Transformation in the 1980s* (1980), 2d ed. (Los Angeles: J. P. Tarcher, 1987), 17–21, 19.

3. Ibid., 422 (emphasis in original), 423.

4. Shirley MacLaine, *Out on a Limb* (New York: Bantam, 1983); Robert Butler, Shirley MacLaine, et al., *Out on a Limb* (Video recording; Los Angeles: ABC Video, 1986); Robert Butler, Shirley MacLaine, et al., *Out on a Limb* (Video recording; Troy, Mich.: StarMaker, 1986).

5. J. Gordon Melton, "Whither the New Age?" in Timothy Miller, ed., *America's Alternative Religions* (Albany: State University of New York Press, 1995), 349; see, also, J. Gordon Melton, "An Overview of the New Age Movement," in J. Gordon Melton, Jerome Clark, and Aidan A. Kelly, *New Age Encyclopedia* (Detroit: Gale, 1990), xxv.

6. See Jerome Clark, "UFOs in the New Age," in Melton, Clark, and Kelly, eds., *New Age Encyclopedia*, 312–13; Carl G. Jung, *Flying Saucers: A Modern Myth of Things Seen in the Sky* (New York: Harcourt Brace Jovanovitch, 1969).

7. See Clark, "UFOs in the New Age," 313; George Adamski and Desmond Leslie, *Flying Saucers Have Landed* (New York: British Book Center, 1953); George Adamski, *Inside the Flying Saucers* (New York: Abelard-Schuman, 1955).

8. Robert S. Ellwood Jr., *Religious and Spiritual Groups in Modern America* (Englewood Cliffs, N.J.: Prentice-Hall, 1973), 150–51; George Hunt Williamson and Alfred C. Bailey, *The Saucers Speak! A Documentary Report of Interstellar Communication by Radiotelegraphy* (Los Angeles: New Age, 1954); F. P. B. [George Hunt Williamson], *The Brotherhood of the Seven Rays (Secret of the Andes)* (Clarksburg, W. Va.: Saucerian, 1961); J. Gordon Melton, "Brotherhood of the Seven Rays," in J. Gordon Melton, ed., *Encyclopedia of American Religions*, 4th ed. (Detroit: Gale, 1993), 729–30.

9. Ellwood, *Religious and Spiritual Groups*, 131; on channeling, see Michael F. Brown, *The Channeling Zone: American Spirituality in an Anxious Age* (Cambridge: Harvard University Press, 1997), esp. 51–53, where Brown compares channeling to old-style spiritualism; on JZ Knight, see J. Gordon Melton, *Finding Enlightenment: Ramtha's School of Ancient Wisdom* (Hillsboro, Oreg.: Beyond Words, 1998).

10. J. Gordon Melton, "Seth," in Melton, *New Age Encyclopedia*, 407–9; Roberts's novel —on overpopulation—was Jane Roberts, *The Rebellers* (New York: Ace, 1963); the first Seth book was Jane Roberts, *The Seth Material* (Englewood Cliffs, N.J.: Prentice-Hall, 1970).

11. Melton, "Seth," 407; Jane Roberts, *Seth Speaks: The Eternal Validity of the Soul* (1972), 2d ed., with notes by Robert F. Butts (San Rafael, Calif.: Amber-Allen, 1994), 3–4.

12. MacLaine, *Out on a Limb*, 142ff., 164–65, 181, 187.

13. Ibid., 298–99, 302, 305 (emphasis in original), 308, 309 (emphasis in original), 312–13.

14. See Brad Steiger, *Revelation: The Divine Fire* (Englewood Cliffs, N.J.: Prentice-Hall, 1973); Shirley MacLaine, *Going Within: A Guide for Inner Transformation* (New York: Bantam, 1989), 18, 25, 27 (emphasis in original), 29, 53–63, 68.

15. MacLaine, *Going Within*, 69, 95–96, 226–27.

16. Ibid., 232 (emphasis in original), 263.

17. For a discussion on which this one is in part dependent, see Catherine L. Albanese, *America: Religions and Religion*, 3d ed. (Belmont, Calif.: Wadsworth, 1999), 352–69.

18. Ken Wilbur, *The Spectrum of Consciousness* (1977; rpt., Wheaton, Ill.: Theosophical Publishing, 1993), 37, 326–27 (upper case in original).

19. Ken Wilber, *No Boundary: Eastern and Western Approaches to Personal Growth* (Boston: Shambhala, 1985), 158 (emphasis in original), 159–60.

20. David Toolan, *Facing West from California's Shores: A Jesuit's Journey into New Age*

Consciousness (New York: Crossroad, 1987), 3–25, 229, 238, 285, 291, 309, 311, 313; David Bohm, *Wholeness and the Implicate Order* (London: Routledge and Kegan Paul, 1980).

21. David Ray Griffin, "Introduction: The Reenchantment of Science," in David Ray Griffin, ed., *The Reenchantment of Science: Postmodern Proposals* (Albany: State University of New York Press, 1988), 2, 12–13, 13, 15.

22. On Reiki, see Catherine L. Albanese, *Nature Religion in America: From the Algonkian Indians to the New Age* (Chicago: University of Chicago Press, 1990), 186–89; and Barbara Weber Ray, *The Reiki Factor: A Guide to Natural Healing, Helping, and Wholeness* (Smithtown, N.Y.: Exposition, 1983). On Therapeutic Touch, see Dolores Krieger, *The Therapeutic Touch: How to Use Your Hands to Help or to Heal* (Englewood Cliffs, N.J.: Prentice-Hall, 1979), esp. 12–13.

23. For a discussion of levels of commitment and "membership" in the New Age movement, see Paul Heelas, *The New Age Movement: The Celebration of the Self and the Sacralization of Modernity* (Oxford, England: Blackwell, 1996), 117–20.

24. On New Age entrepreneurialism, see Kimberly J. Lau, *New Age Capitalism: Making Money East of Eden* (Philadelphia: University of Pennsylvania Press, 2000); Heelas, *New Age Movement*, 90–98; and Brown, *Channeling Zone*, 142–73. On Catholic New Age nuns, see the practices reported in Sarah McFarland Taylor, "Sisters of Earth: Catholic Nuns Reinhabiting Religion at Genesis Farm (Ph.D. diss., University of California, Santa Barbara, 1999), although the nuns themselves reject the New Age designation.

25. Barry Kosmin and Seymour Lachman, *One Nation under God: Religion in Contemporary American Society* (New York: Harmony, 1993), 17; Harold Bloom, *The American Religion: The Emergence of the Post-Christian Nation* (New York: Simon and Schuster, 1992); on survey data on reincarnation beliefs, see the survey conducted by sociologists of religion Wade Clark Roof and Phillip E. Hammond in the states of North Carolina, Ohio, Massachusetts, and California, which reported 19, 25, 28, and 30 percent of Catholics and Protestants believing in reincarnation in the respective states, in Phillip E. Hammond, *Religion and Personal Autonomy: The Third Disestablishment in America* (Columbia: University of South Carolina Press, 1992), 131; on the unchurched in America from the early 1970s to the mid-1980s, see Wade Clark Roof and William McKinney, *American Mainline Religion: Its Changing Shape and Future* (New Brunswick: Rutgers University Press, 1987), 255, 172–81, passim.

26. Heelas, *New Age Movement*, 120 (emphasis in original).

27. Wouter J. Hanegraaff, *New Age Religion and Western Culture: Esotericism in the Mirror of Secular Thought* (Leiden: E. J. Brill, 1996), 77–93, 84 (emphasis in original), 87–88; Margaret Murray, *The Witch-Cult in Western Europe* (1921; rpt., Oxford, England: Clarendon, 1967).

28. Sarah M. Pike, *Earthly Bodies, Magical Selves: Contemporary Pagans and the Search for Community* (Berkeley: University of California Press, 2001), 145 (boldface in original), 96.

29. For an optimistic reading of toleration, see, e.g., the theologically driven account by Diana L. Eck, *A New Religious America: How a "Christian Country" Has Now Become*

the World's Most Religiously Diverse Nation (San Francisco: HarperSanFrancisco, 2001); and, for a more conflictual reading of pluralism, see R. Laurence Moore, *Religious Outsiders and the Making of Americans* (New York: Oxford University Press, 1986).

30. See Jonathan Z. Smith, *Imagining Religion: From Babylon to Jonestown* (Chicago: University of Chicago Press, 1982), esp. 43, 57, 89. On "a magic dwells" (below), see ibid., 19–35.

INDEX

Abif, Hiram, 128–30
Adair, James, 148
Adams, Hannah, 349, 373
Adamski, George, 499
Aether, 308–9. *See also* ether
Aetherius Society, 500
affirmations, 167, 231; in Atkinson, 438, 439; in Divine Science, 425, 428, 431; in Warren Felt Evans, 304, 306; in Hill, 441; in Hopkins, 321–22, 402; in I AM, 468, 469; in New Thought, 406, 421, 445, 468–69, 508; in Peale, 445; in Religious Science, 428; in Unity, 431, 433, 434. *See also* affirmative prayer
affirmative prayer, 306, 313, 431, 434, 445. *See also* affirmations; prayer
African Americans, 13, 16, 21, 66, 85, 103, 113, 346, 472–78, 515; African Methodist Episcopal Church, 238; Leafy Anderson, 474–75; Asante (Akan), 90; Black Hawk, 476; conjuring (hoodoo), 92–96, 117, 242, 472–73; Cuddymonk, 92; Father Divine, 476–78; Jackson, 238–40; and magic, 117; National Colored Spiritualist Association, 242; obeahism, 93–94; Prince Hall Masonry, 127, 133; Pascal Beverly Randolph, 244–46; and revelation, 87–89, 96, 103, 112, 472–78; as spirits, 240–42, 501; Spiritual churches, 474–75; in spiritualism, 113, 238–46; Sojourner Truth, 243–44, 267, 385; and West Africa, 85–96; Wheatley, 117–18
Afro-Caribbeans, 66, 90–93; Cumina societies, 91; myalism, 90–91; obeahism, 90–92
Agrippa, Cornelius (Heinrich Cornelius Agrippa von Nettesheim), 31, 38; American uses of, 69, 76, 82, 122–23, 172, 198, 261; English uses of, 43–44, 47, 62; in Mormonism, 143, 146, 172, 198, 261; writings of, 33–35
Ahlstrom, Sydney, 3, 295, 396
akasa (akasha/akashic records), 280, 308, 502
alchemy, 3; in Alcott, 164, 172; in Chopra, 448; in colonial America, 69, 70, 71, 75; in Mormonism, 140; in the Renaissance, 31–40, 43, 46, 54; revelation in, 33
Alcott, Amos Bronson, 163–64, 179–80, 375, 413; Fruitlands, 171–72, 188
Algonquian religion, 97–99, 102–4, 107, 111; Green Corn Ceremony, 97–98. *See also* Native Americans
Allen, Ethan, 155
Allen, John, 173
almanacs, 64, 76, 78
American Indians. *See* Native Americans

DATE DUE

FEB 10 2009
